Central
Asia

Kyrgyzstan
p54

Uzbekistan
p197

Turkmenistan
p375

Tajikistan
p141

Stephen Lioy
Anna Kaminski, Bradley Mayhew, Jenny Walker

Contents

MANTY (STEAMED
DUMPLINGS) P462

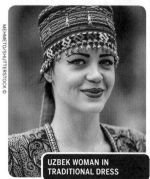

UZBEK WOMAN IN
TRADITIONAL DRESS

KALTA MINOR MINARET,
P264, KHIVA, UZBEKISTAN

Contents

Welcome to Central Asia

With its medieval blue-domed cities, kinetic bazaars and remote yurtstays, Central Asia encapsulates the romance of the Silk Road like nowhere else.

A Warm Welcome

Whether you want to explore the architectural gems of Bukhara or take a horse trek across the high Pamirs, everywhere in Central Asia you'll be greeted with instinctive local hospitality and offered a shared meal, a helping hand or a place to stay. Beyond Uzbekistan's Silk Road cities, mass tourism has yet to make any inroads in Central Asia, lending an authentic sense of discovery to each trip. Add to this the intrinsic fascination of a forgotten region slowly emerging as a geopolitical pivot point and you have one of Asia's most absorbing hidden corners.

Footprints of History

From Alexander the Great to Chinggis (Genghis) Khan to Timur (Tamerlane), Central Asia's page-turning history litters the land at every turn. From the right angle and with one eye closed, the storied oasis caravan stops of Samarkand and Bukhara, with their exotic skylines of minarets and medressas, really do seem to be lifted directly from the age of Marco Polo. Share a round of kebabs with an Uzbek trader or wander an ancient caravanserai and historical romantics will find the past and present begin to blur into one in Central Asia.

Mountains & Yurts

East of the desert and steppe settlements rise the snow-capped Pamir and Tian Shan ranges of Kyrgyzstan and Tajikistan, home to traditional herding communities and some truly epic mountain scenery. Here community-based tourism projects can bring you face to face with nomadic Kyrgyz herders, meeting them in their yurts and on their terms. Ride out to remote lakes on horseback, hike from one village homestay to another, or take a 4WD out to remote archaeological sites. The scope for adventure and exploration here is almost limitless.

Travel off the Map

For decades – centuries even – much of the world has regarded Central Asia as a blank on the map, synonymous with the middle of nowhere, rather than the heartland of Asia. For a certain type of wanderer, this is all part of the attraction of a land that has been largely off-limits to travellers for the last 2000 years. Head even a little bit off the beaten track and you'll likely have the place to yourself. The region's little-visited oddities, namely Turkmenistan and most of Kazakhstan, are even further removed from the modern world and offer an addictive interest all of their own.

Why I love Central Asia

By Bradley Mayhew, Writer

Each republic in Central Asia has its own attraction for me. In Tajikistan and Kyrgyzstan I love the unrivalled mountain scenery and the incredible tradition of hospitality among the local Wakhi and Kyrgyz. In Uzbekistan it's the glorious weight of history and the sense of travelling in the sand-prints of some of history's greatest travellers and invaders. There's also something unique and even slightly weird about Central Asia, as if the normal rules of tourist engagement don't quite apply. For me it's a completely addictive place; I freely admit to being a Stan-oholic.

For more about our writers, see p512

Above: Uzbek children, Bukhara (p247)

Central Asia

RUSSIA

Penza

Konye-Urgench
Tantalising architectural ruins
of a once great city (p393)

Saratov

Khiva
Fantastically preserved former
slave-trading outpost (p262)

Ufa

Turkestan
Timurid architecture
and Sufi centre (p322)

Kurgan

Chelyabinsk

Petropavlovsk

Kokshetau

Uralsk

Orenburg

Kostanay

Rudny

Orsk

Aktobe

Astrakhan

Atyrau

KAZAKHSTAN

Zhezkazgan

Ural

Lake
Tengiz

Arkalyk

Aralsk

Beyneu

Aral
Sea

Aktau

Ustyurt
Plateau

Zhanaozen

Moynaq

Kyzylorda

Turkesta

Caspian
Sea

Kyzylkum
Desert

Sy Darya

AZERBAIJAN

BAKU

Konye-Urgench

Nukus

Dashogus

Sarykamish
Lake

Khiva

UZBEKISTAN

Badai-Tugai
Nature Reserve

Urgench

Zeravshan

Turkmenbashi

Karakum
Desert

Amu-Darya

Navoi

Jizzakh

Bukhara

Samarkand

Balkanabat

TURKMENISTAN

Turkmenabat

Karshi

ASHGABAT

Mary

Merv

Termiz

Bukhara
Historic medieval old town
of Islamic monuments (p247)

TEHRĀN

Mashhad

IRAN

Samarkand
Audacious Islamic monuments in
Timur's (Tamerlane's) capital (p228)

AFGHANISTAN

0 — **800 km**
0 — **500 miles**

Astana
Surreal modern architecture
on the steppe (p333)

RUSSIA

Son-Köl
Horse treks and yurtstays
at this lovely lake (p102)

Omsk

Almaty
Central Asia's most
cosmopolitan city (p292)

Ulaangom

Burabay
National
Park

Pavlodar

Ust-
Kamenogorsk

Belukha
(4506m)

MONGOLIA

ASTANA

Kogalzhyn
Nature
Reserve

Semey

ALTAY
MOUNTAINS

Altay

Karaganda

Lake
Zaysan

Ayagoz

Tacheng

CHINA

Balkhash

Lake
Balkhash

Taldykorgan

Ürümqi

Yining

Karakol
Base for fabulous
Tian Shan trekking (p85)

Muyunkum
Desert

Almaty

Ile-Alatau
National Park

Altyn-Emel
National
Park

Khan
Tengri
(7010m)

BISHKEK

Taraz

Shymkent

Talas

Kochkor

Lake
Ysyk-Köl

Karakol

Pobedy
(7439m)

Fergana Valley
Join the locals for some
Silk Road haggling (p154)

Aksu-Zhabagyly
Nature Reserve

Son-Köl

Naryn

High Roads to China
Cross the Torugart or Irkeshtam
passes to Kashgar (p138)

Sayram Ugam
National Park

TASHKENT

Namangan

KYRGYZSTAN

Guliston

Kokand

Andijon

Osh

Torugart
Pass

Khojand

Fergana

Irkeshtam
Pass

Kashgar

CHINA

FAN
MOUNTAINS

DUSHANBE

Koh-i-
Somoni
(7495m)

Kongur
(7719m)

Fan Mountains
Turquoise lakes and great
trekking (p162)

Kulob

TAJIKISTAN

THE PAMIRS

Pyanj

Khorog

Pamir

Pamir Highway
One of the world's great
mountain road trips (p173)

ELEVATION

	5000m
	3000m
	1000m
	500m
	200m
	0
	dep

Wakhan Valley
Silk Road forts and views
of the Hindu Kush (p180)

PAKISTAN

KABUL

Irtysh

Yarkand

Central Asia's
Top 15

Almaty, Kazakhstan

1 Central Asia's most cosmopolitan and hedonistic city, Almaty (p234) is a leafy mix of Russian and Central Asian styles. In a couple of days you can visit the Tsarist-era Zenkov Cathedral (pictured below left, p293), view a replica of the famous Scythian-era Golden Man suit, soak in the Arasan Bathhouse and enjoy the region's best cafes, clubs and shops, all fuelled by the country's petrodollar boom. The city is also a gateway to mountain treks and winter sports just south of town and a springboard to Silk Road bus and train routes into China.

Astana's Architecture

2 Kazakhstan's custom-built capital (p333) rises from the steppe like a mirage to reveal some of Asia's most audacious and cutting-edge modern architecture, such as Bayterek Monument (pictured below right, p335). From the Norman Foster designs of the world's largest tent, and the glass-pyramid design of the Palace of Peace and Accord, Astana is the symbolic brainchild of President Nazarbayev and the face of post-*Borat* Kazakhstan. The constantly evolving city got a huge boost from the 2017 World Expo and an emerging restaurant scene makes visiting the city a pleasure, not just a curiosity.

G&M THERIN-WEISE/GETTY IMAGES ©

JANE SWEENEY/GETTY IMAGES ©

MARIUSZ PRUSACZYK/ALAMY STOCK PHOTO ©

AMOS CHAPPLE/GETTY IMAGES ©

Bazaars

3 Central Asia's bazaars have been fuelling Silk Road trade for two millennia. Shopping for melons, carpets and silly hats is the quintessential Central Asian activity and the local bazaars offer the most direct route to the region's soul. Every town has its own, lined with chaikhanas (teahouses), shashlyk, fruit stalls and even animals. Our favourite is possibly the Kumtepa Bazaar (p226) outside Margilon, in the Fergana Valley, though nearby Andijon's Jahon Bazaar (p226) and Osh's Bazaar (pictured top; p59) are also excellent.

Bukhara, Uzbekistan

4 Central Asia's most interesting town, Bukhara (p247) rewards exploring. Visit the medieval Ark, from where emirs ruled, sip green tea beside the Lyabi-Hauz pool and then head to the towering Kalon Minaret (pictured above; p252), where you can stroll through the surrounding network of bazaars, bathhouses and trade halls. Best are the labyrinthine backstreets, home to hidden synagogues, Sufi shrines and half-forgotten medressas. Bukhara also boasts the region's most stylish B&Bs, many in converted merchants' houses.

Community-Based Tourism

5 This network of homestays, guides, drivers and yurt owners spreads across Kyrgyzstan in an attempt to bring the financial benefits of tourism directly to local communities. For travellers it gives you a contact in every town and opens up a wealth of friendly, affordable homestays and potential excursions to remote sights, lakes and herding communities. Kochkor (p101) in Central Kyrgyzstan is the original and best place to start, but the idea has also taken firm hold in neighbouring Tajikistan. Arslanbob (p112), Kyrgyzstan

Fan Mountains

6 These mountains (p162) rank as one of Central Asia's premier trekking destinations. Dozens of turquoise lakes stud the high mountain valleys. Go on a multiday trek to meet local Tajik shepherds, or drive to the seven lakes (Haft Kul) of the Marguzor Valley and do some delightful day hikes from a chain of homestays. You can even visit the ruined old Sogdian city of Penjikent en route. Visit from the Tajik towns of Dushanbe or Khojand, as the international border between Samarkand and Penjikent remains closed. Iskander-Kul (p163)

Khiva, Uzbekistan

7 The former khanate of Khiva (p262) is an entire walled city of traditional mud-baked architecture, frozen in time in the desert wastes of Khorezm. It may lack the lived-in backstreet life of Bukhara, but in return you get the best preserved medieval city in Central Asia, if not the Islamic world. You can wander city walls, former slave markets and extensive royal palaces, where khaki walls burst with green and blue tilework and brick yurt bases hint at the formerly nomadic life of the region.
Bazaar, Ichon-Qala (p263)

Pamir Highway, Tajikistan

8 From the deep, rugged mountain valleys of beautiful Badakhshan, the Soviet-built Pamir Highway (p173) climbs up on to the treeless Pamir plateau to the 'wild east' town of Murgab and on past the dramatic azure lake of Kara-Köl in to Kyrgyzstan's stunning Alay Valley. En route you'll pass ancient tombs, hot springs, remote Kyrgyz yurt camps and some of the most spectacular mountain scenery in Asia. It's one of the world's great mountain road trips. Tackle it in a rented Soviet 4WD or as a challenging bicycle ride.

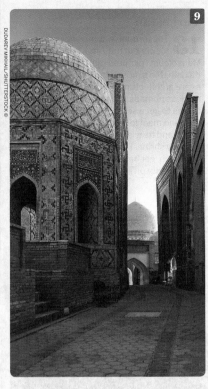

Samarkand

9 Already an important oasis town, it was Timur who turned Samarkand (p228) into one of the most beautiful cities in Asia. Visit Timur's mausoleum, the Gur-e-Amir, followed by the spectacular street of tombs of his Timurid relatives. For audacious architecture it's hard to beat the crumbling remains of the epic Bibi Khanum Mosque, built for Timur's wife. Then throw in the breathtaking Registan Square (one of Uzbekistan's, if not the Islamic world's, greatest architectural ensembles), fascinating bazaars and the 2000-year-old remains of Afrosiab, the original Silk Road trading town. Shah-i-Zinda (p231)

Konye-Urgench

10 Turkmenistan's premier historical site of Konye-Urgench (p393) is a Unesco World Heritage Site. Once the capital of the Khorezmshahs and a major intellectual centre of the Muslim world in the 12th century, the city was pulverised by both Chinggis (Genghis) Khan and Timur (Tamerlane). The enigmatic remains include royal mausolea, Sufi shrines and a 59m-tall 14th-century minaret. It's a short hop across the Uzbekistan border, but you'll need a guide in order to get a Turkmen tourist visa. Il-Arslan Mausoleum (p394)

Son-Köl

11 The jewel of central Kyrgyzstan is the high-alpine lake Son-Köl (p102), fringed with lush summer pastures and summer-only Kyrgyz yurt camps. You can trek or drive here, but the best option is a horse trek, overnighting in yurtstays along the way. June to August are the best months to visit Kyrgyzstan's idyllic *jailoo* (summer pastures), when you might even catch a horse-games festival or a performance by a Kyrgyz bard or eagle hunter. Bring a sleeping bag.

Hiking

12 Few people realise that Central Asia has some of the world's most beautiful mountain scenery. Karakol (p85) in Kyrgyzstan is the most popular base camp for treks into the alpine meadows of the Tian Shan, but the high-altitude Pamir valleys also offer top-notch trekking. Hike from homestay to homestay in places such as Tajikistan's Jizeu Valley (p176) or Kyrgyzstan's Alay region (p122), or go with an agency on a fully supported trek to the stunning amphitheatre of Khan Tengri (p313) and the Inylchek Glacier (p313).
Karakol Valley (p93)

Turkestan

13 The turquoise dome and ornate tilework of the Timurid-era Yasaui Mausoleum (pictured right; p322) is easily Kazakhstan's most beautiful building and a rare architectural gem in a land ruled by restless nomads. It's also one of the best places to get a sense of Central Asian Sufism and meet local pilgrims as they pray, picnic and tie wishes to trees surrounding the holy shrine. For the most atmospheric approach, get here on an overnight train from Almaty or Tashkent.

ANA FLASKER/SHUTTERSTOCK ©

The High Roads to China

14 The mountain border crossings (p139) of the Torugart and Irkeshtam passes are without doubt the most exciting and scenic ways to enter or leave Central Asia. The high valleys of the Tian Shan are splendid and there's a satisfying continuity in crossing from ex-Soviet Central Asia into Chinese Turkestan via the storied Uyghur city of Kashgar. The Irkeshtam Pass is logistically easier, but the Torugart Pass offers the chance to stop overnight at the atmospheric Tash Rabat caravanserai (pictured top right; p109) in Kyrgyzstan.

Wakhan Valley

15 The Tajik side of the Wakhan Valley (p180) feels like a hidden Shangri-La. Bordered by the Hindu Kush and a finger of remotest Afghanistan, the valley is dotted with Silk Road forts, Ismaili shrines and village homestays run by welcoming Wakhi Tajik families. It's an essential add-on to a Pamir Hwy trip and a potential springboard into northern Afghanistan. Even Marco Polo was impressed when he passed through. To get the most out of the valley, hire transport or hike the valley.

Milking a yak, near Murgab (p184)

Need to Know

For more information, see Survival Guide (p457)

Visas

Much easier to obtain than a few years ago. Kyrgyzstan and Kazakhstan are visa-free, Tajikistan has an easy online process, Uzbekistan is fairly easy and Turkmenistan is tricky.

Money

Bring a combination of cash US dollars (especially for Uzbekistan and Turkmenistan) or euros (especially for Kazakhstan), and a debit card for ATMs in the cities.

Mobile Phones

Local SIM cards are easy to get in Kazakhstan, Kyrgyzstan and Tajikistan, and only somewhat harder to get as a foreigner in Uzbekistan and Turkmenistan. Local calls and data are inexpensive.

Time

Uzbekistan, Tajikistan and Turkmenistan (GMT/UTC plus five hours)

Kyrgyzstan (GMT/UTC plus six hours)

Kazakhstan (straddles both time zones)

When to Go

- Astana **GO** May–Sep
- Kochkor **GO** May–Sep
- Samarkand **GO** mid-Mar–May, Sep–Oct
- Ashgabat **GO** Mar–Apr, Oct–Nov
- Murgab **GO** Jul–Sep

Desert, dry climate
Dry climate
Warm to hot summers, mild winters
Warm to hot summers, cold winters
Mild summers, cold winters

High Season
(Apr–Jun, Sep & Oct)

➡ Comfortable temperatures in the lowlands.

➡ Bazaars are overflowing with fruit in September.

Shoulder
(Jul & Aug)

➡ Hot in the lowlands, especially in Uzbekistan, Turkmenistan and western Tajikistan.

➡ Best time to visit mountainous areas.

➡ Prime time for trekking (July to September).

Low Season
(Nov–Mar)

➡ Cold in Uzbekistan, frozen in sub-Siberian Kazakhstan and snowy in the mountains.

➡ Many tourist hotels and B&Bs close in Uzbekistan; the rest offer big discounts.

➡ March is good for Turkmenistan.

Useful Websites

Lonely Planet (www.lonely planet.com) Destination information, hotel bookings, traveller forum and more. The Central Asia branch of the Thorn Tree forum has news on visas and border crossings.

Caravanistan (www.caravan istan.com) Peerless online travel guide to the region.

Oriental Express Central Asia (www.orexca.com) Virtual travel guide from a local travel agency.

EurasiaNet (www.eurasianet.org) News and cultural articles, with resource pages for each country.

Pamirs.org (www.pamirs.org) Definitive travel and historical guide to the Pamir region in Tajikistan from Robert Middleton.

Important Numbers

Fire	☑101
Police	☑102
Ambulance	☑103

Opening Hours

Banks and offices 9am to noon and 1 to 5pm Monday to Friday, possibly 9am to noon Saturday. Exchange offices keep longer hours, including weekends.

Museums Generally closed Monday.

Restaurants 11am to 9pm; longer opening hours in major cities.

Daily Costs

Budget: Less than US$45

➡ Homestay per person with two meals: US$10–20

➡ Chaikhana (teahouse) meal: US$3–5

➡ Horse hire in Kyrgyzstan per day: US$15

Midrange: US$25–80

➡ B&B in Bukhara or Samarkand: US$25–50

➡ Double room in a midrange hotel: US$30–80 (US$50–130 in Kazakhstan)

Top End: More than US$80

➡ Double room in a four-star hotel: US$110

➡ Tour in Turkmenistan per person per day in small group: US$150–200

Arriving in Central Asia

Almaty Airport, Kazakhstan Official taxis run to the centre for around 2500T and there are minibuses.

Dushanbe Airport, Tajikistan A taxi to the centre costs US$12 to US$15.

Manas International Airport, Kyrgyzstan (Bishkek) A taxi to central Bishkek costs 500som. Minibus 380 (40som) to the centre departs from just to the right of the arrivals exit.

Saparmurat Turkmenbashi Airport, Turkmenistan (Ashgabat) A taxi to the centre costs 10M.

Tashkent International Airport, Uzbekistan A taxi to the centre costs around US$5 in som. Guesthouses will pick you up for around US$10.

Getting Around

Transport in Central Asia is relatively convenient and abundant in the plains but much patchier in the mountains.

Train High-speed modern trains run to Samarkand, Bukhara and soon Khiva in Uzbekistan and between Almaty and Astana in Kazakhstan. Long-distance rail services are less comfortable but a common way to get around huge Kazakhstan.

Bus Fairly reliable and comfortable coaches run between major cities, but comfort, reliability and frequency plummet rapidly in rural areas.

Shared taxi The best way to get around Kyrgyzstan, Tajikistan and Uzbekistan. Pay by the seat or buy all four of them for cheap car hire on set routes.

Hire car Useful for the Pamirs and mountain areas of Kyrgyzstan and generally priced per kilometre, with a driver.

Travelling Safely

➡ Travel in Central Asia is generally trouble-free and certainly much easier than a decade ago.

➡ Watch for pickpockets in crowded bazaars or bus stations.

➡ Central Asian officials and police generally create more problems than they solve.

➡ Make sure your documents, permits and registration (if needed) are watertight at all times.

➡ At night don't get into a taxi with more than one person in it.

PLAN YOUR TRIP NEED TO KNOW

For much more on **getting around**, see p479

First Time Central Asia

For more information, see Survival Guide (p457)

Checklist

➡ Give yourself a couple of months to get a Turkmen visa and a couple of weeks to get an Uzbek visa (longer if you need a letter of invitation).

➡ If heading to Uzbekistan, amass all the crisp, clean US dollar bills you'll need.

➡ Inform your debit-/credit-card company that you'll be travelling abroad.

What to Pack

➡ Sleeping bag and water purification tablets for mountainous Kyrgyzstan and Tajikistan.

➡ A Russian phrasebook or translation app.

➡ Postcards and photos from home to break the ice in homestays.

➡ Floss – to get the mutton out from between your teeth.

➡ The latest government travel warnings and a small pinch of salt.

Top Tips for Your Trip

➡ Learn the Cyrillic alphabet and some basic Russian – it will really help.

➡ Bring a history book or good travelogue, as the more you know about Central Asia, the more rewarding it becomes.

➡ If you are a vegetarian stock up on fruit, nuts, Korean salads, bread and honey at the local bazaar, rather than rely on vegetarian options in restaurants or chaikhanas.

➡ Make use of homestays in Tajikistan and Kyrgyzstan; they are almost always more comfortable than budget hotels.

➡ Bring all your hiking and camping gear with you as equipment is very limited in Central Asia.

➡ Have a back-up travel plan if trying to get a visa for Turkmenistan.

Etiquette

Clothing Western-style clothes are acceptable in capital cities and large towns, but avoid wearing singlets, shorts or short skirts in rural areas or the conservative Fergana Valley.

Mosques Working mosques are generally closed to women, though men will likely be invited in outside prayer times. When visiting a mosque, always take your shoes off at the door.

Visiting someone's home Take your shoes off at the door. Avoid stepping on any carpet if you have your shoes on.

Blowing your nose Try not to in public; it's considered rude.

Respect for the elderly Central Asian society devotes much respect to its elderly, known as *aksakal* (white beards). Always make an effort to shake hands with an elder. Young men generally give up their bus seat to *aksakal* and foreigners should offer their place in a crowded chaikhana (teahouse).

What to Wear

Loose-fitting, light fabrics are best for lowland areas in summer as temperatures can be hot. Long trousers, skirts and shirts are useful for travelling in conservative areas such as the Fergana Valley or rural areas. Don't wear shorts.

A sun hat, sunglasses and sun cream are essential for the strong desert and mountain sun.

Bargaining

Shops have fixed prices, but in markets (food, art or souvenirs) bargaining is usually expected.

➡ Asking prices are usually in proportion to the expected outcome. Sellers will be genuinely surprised if you reply to their '5000' with '1000'; they're more likely expecting 3500, 4000 or 4500 in the end.

➡ Always negotiate when arranging transport hire.

➡ In Kyrgyzstan bargaining is usually reserved only for taxi drivers.

➡ The Russian word for 'discount' is *skidka*.

Tipping

Tipping is common in Central Asian cities. Most cafes and restaurants in the capitals add a 10% to 20% service charge to the bill, or expect you to round the total up.

Sleeping

Accommodation options are somewhat uneven across the region. The budget homestays of Kyrgyzstan are excellent and the B&Bs of Uzbekistan offer the most stylish and comfortable midrange options. Kazakhstan has a couple of backpacker hostels, some rural homestays, and good midrange and top-end choices. Tajikistan's Pamir region in particular has an informal network of homes and yurts that offer a fascinating and intimate look at the way local people live.

Budget travellers off the beaten track may still have to use the occasional fossilised Soviet-era hotel, but these are generally a last resort.

Budget accommodation can be considered anything under US$30 for a double room in high season.

Midrange hotels and B&Bs range from US$30 to US$70 per night (US$50 to US$100 in much of Kazakhstan). For this you can expect air-con, satellite TV, free wi-fi and a decent breakfast.

Many hotels also offer *lux* (luxury) and half *lux* suites, which normally have an extra room and can often sleep four or more; good for families. Homestays and yurtstays are priced per person and we use the term dm (dorm) in our reviews.

Eating

Food should not be the main reason you come to Central Asia. In the first years of independence most restaurants served only standard slop, which somehow seemed to taste (and smell) indelibly of the old USSR. The situation has improved in recent years, particularly in the cities, with a rush of pleasant open-air cafes, fast-food joints and Turkish restaurants. The best way to appreciate regional cuisines, and the region's extraordinary hospitality, is still a meal in a private home.

Solo Travellers

You'll meet other travellers in backpacker guesthouses or hostels in Bishkek and Osh (Kyrgyzstan), Almaty (Kazakhstan), Khorog (Tajikistan) and the main towns in Uzbekistan.

It's generally not too difficult to find travellers to share car-hire costs for the Torugart, Irkeshtam or Pamir Hwy trips. Local travel agents and community tourism providers can often help link you with other travellers, or try posting on Thorn Tree (www.thorntree.lonelyplanet.com).

Most hotels offer single rates, but these are often in tiny box-like rooms. Places that offer a single rate for a solo traveller in a double room are much better value.

Travelling alone in Turkmenistan can be expensive. Hotel rooms cost almost the same whether you have one or two people in your party, and if you are on a tourist visa you'll have to bear the burden of hiring a guide for yourself.

If You Like...

Silk Road Architecture

Nothing connects Central Asia to its storied past quite like its mosques, minarets and medressas. Uzbekistan is the place for some of the world's greatest Islamic architecture.

Registan, Samarkand This jaw-dropping ensemble is of not one but three medressas in a stunning public square in Uzbekistan. If possible climb the corkscrew minarets for views over Timur's showcase city. (p229)

Kalon Minaret, Bukhara This towering Uzbek minaret is so impressive that it stopped Chinggis (Genghis) Khan in his tracks 800 years ago. (p252)

Shah-i-Zinda, Samarkand Uzbekistan's head-spinning turquoise-blue Timurid tilework doesn't get any better than this sublime street of royal tombs. (p231)

Ichon-Qala, Khiva An entire walled city of royal palaces, blue-tiled tombs and mud-baked city walls, frozen in time in Uzbek's Khorezm oasis. (p263)

Tash Rabat Caravanserai Singularly romantic refuge for caravans and traders, hidden in a high mountain valley near the Chinese border, in Kyrgyzstan. (p109)

Hiking

Central Asia's best-kept secrets are its remote Tian Shan and Pamir ranges, hiding some of Asia's most sublime mountain trails.

Fan Mountains, Tajikistan Jewel-like azure-blue lakes, rugged peaks and homestays make this the region's most popular trekking spot. (p166)

Tian Shan, Kyrgyzstan Behind Karakol lies a network of lush forested alpine valleys, hidden lakes and snow-capped peaks, linked by treks of two to seven days. (p92)

Bartang Valley, Tajikistan Hike from homestays into one of the wildest and most memorable valleys in the Western Pamirs. (p175)

Zailiysky Alatau, Kazakhstan Hiking trails and short trek routes lead from the Almaty city limits through Ile-Alatau National Park to picturesque Bolshoe Almatinskoe Lake. (p305)

Alay Valley, Kyrgyzstan Wonderful day hikes beneath Peak Lenin to mountain lakes, or multiday treks over the Jiptik Pass. (p122)

Arslanbob, Kyrgyzstan Hike through walnut forests and past waterfalls to the Köl-Mazar lakes (four days). Book guides and horses through CBT. (p113)

Nomadic Life

Yurts Stay overnight in an authentic yurt in the high eastern Pamirs or the pastures of Kyrgyzstan, and visit the world's only three-storey yurt in Osh. (p132)

Manaschi There's something other-worldly about listening to a white-bearded bard reciting the Kyrgyz national epic, *Manas*. It's a direct link to the Kyrgyz nomadic past. (p130)

Horse games Summer brings the good life to the *jailoos* (summer pastures), along with horse races, horseback wrestling and Kyrgyz-style kiss-chase. (p129)

Eagle hunting Real hunts (*with* eagles, not *for* eagles) take place in winter but several spots in Kyrgyzstan offer summer displays from authentic *berkutchi* (eagle hunters; p98)

Son-Köl The best way to visit this lovely mountain lake is on a horse trek, stopping in herders' yurts en route. Allow four days. (p102)

Bazaars

Haggling for carpets, camels or car parts is perhaps the quintessential Central Asian activity.

Jayma Bazaar, Kyrgyzstan The riverside bazaar in Osh bustles every day but goes mad on

Top: Shah-i-Zinda (p231), Samarkand, Uzbekistan

Bottom: Yurt, Karakul (p186), Tajikistan

Sunday, and is a great place to pick up a white Kyrgyz *ak kalpak* (traditional felt hat; p115)

Kumtepa Bazaar, Uzbekistan Sunday offers the best selection of local *khanatlas* (tie-dyed silks) and Uzbek white-beards at this rollicking market 5km outside Margilon. (p226)

Siob Bazaar, Uzbekistan This Samarkand bazaar is the city's most photogenic place to stock up on fruit and hot bread in the shadows of the epic ruined Bibi-Khanym Mosque. (p238)

Carpet shopping Bukhara (p258) and Khiva (p269) in Uzbekistan, and Ashgabat (p384), Turkmenistan, are the best places to invest in this quintessential Silk Road souvenir, and don't forget Kyrgyz felt *shyrdaks* in Kochkor (p101).

Urgut Bazaar, Uzbekistan Sunday and Wednesday mornings are the best times to day trip from Samarkand to this village bazaar, strong on jewellery and *suzani* textiles. (p238)

Jahon Bazaar, Uzbekistan The bazaar in Andijon is the biggest in the Uzbek Fergana Valley, especially on Sunday and Thursday. (p226)

Community-Based Tourism

Kyrgyzstan Pioneering country-wide network of homestays and service providers that can arrange everything from feltmaking to horse trekking. (p132)

Pamirs Ecotourism Association Information Centre (PECTA) Yurtstays are the only way to really see the herding communities, mountain lakes and archaeological sites of the high Pamir mountain range. (p179)

Jizeu Valley, Western Pamirs This network of homestays allows hikers to trek to a scenic

TUUL AND BRUNO MORANDO/GETTY IMAGES ©

Chaikhana (teahouse), Fergana (p223), Uzbekistan

chain of mountain lakes without the need for bulky camping equipment or food. (p176)

Aksu-Zhabagyly Nature Reserve Kazakhstan's best ecotourism project is great for wildlife-watching and hiking. (p321)

Nuratau Mountains Uzbekistan's only real homestay organisation offers village walks, hiking and horse riding south of Aidarkul Lake. (p246)

Archaeological Sites

Come equipped with a history book and your imagination, for the following ruins rank as some of the pivotal historical sites in Asia.

Afrosiab, Uzbekistan Stand in the footprints of Alexander the Great and view Sogdian-era murals at the melted remains of this 2500-year-old city. (p234)

Penjikent, Tajikistan Wander among the crumbling mounds and eroded citadel of this once-cosmopolitan Sogdian city. (p159)

Merv, Turkmenistan The 'Queen of the World' boasts eight overlapping cities, including the capital of the Seljuq Turks. (p388)

Otrar, Kazakhstan This dusty hill changed the course of Central Asian history when Chinggis Khan's emissaries were murdered here, plus it's where Timur (Tamerlane) died. (p323)

Gonur Depe, Turkmenistan This active archaeological site in the Margiana Oasis dates from

the Bronze Age and may have been the birthplace of Zoroastrianism. (p386)

Termiz, Uzbekistan Visit Buddhist monasteries, Bactrian temples and Islamic shrines at Termiz, on the banks of the Oxus River. (p242)

Off the Beaten Track

Central Asia's remoter gems take a bit of getting to, but offer some of the region's most memorable experiences.

Savitsky Museum, Nukus Tick off the 'Stan within a Stan' with a visit to Karakalpakstan in Uzbekistan, home to some of the greatest avant-garde Soviet art of the 1930s. (p270)

Mangistau Underground mosques, necropoli and the enigmatically named 'Valley of Balls' await exploration in the deserts around Aktau in western Kazakhstan. (p330)

Desert Castles of Ancient Khorezm Hire a car and track down the dozen or more two-millennia-old fortresses known as Elliq-Qala that rise from the Karakum desert in Uzbekistan, like giant sandcastles. (p261)

Altay, Kazakhstan Gorgeous mountain valleys, snow-capped peaks and the myths of Shambhala are the drawcards, if you can get around the red tape. (p353)

Western Pamirs The wild and re-mote Tajik valleys around Khorog, especially Bartang Valley, boast incredible scenery, homestays and tough treks, making it great for mountain exploration. (p176)

The Weird & the Downright Odd

Central Asia supplies a daily dose of the unexpected, but for the really odd head to Turkmenistan and remoter Kazakhstan.

Baykonur Cosmodrome, Kazakhstan Book a tour months in advance to watch a rocket blast off from Soviet cosmonaut Yuri Gagarin's former launch site. (p325)

Aral Sea, Kazakhstan Drive across the former lake bed to the receding shores of the dying sea and ponder the nature of environmental folly. (p273)

Astana, Kazakhstan Lie on a beach beside palm trees inside the world's largest tent, Khan Shatyr, then gawp at 2000-year-old horse innards at the Presidential Cultural Centre. (p333)

Darvaza Gas Craters At night this burning pit in the Karakum desert resembles nothing less than the fiery gates of Hell. It's weird, even for Turkmenistan. (p392)

Ashgabat A mix between Las Vegas and Pyongyang, odd highlights include the Ministry of Fairness, the world's largest handwoven rug and a 12m golden statue of former dictator Turkmenbashi. (p377)

ALZhIR Museum This sober-ing museum outside Astana, Kazakstan, shows the horrors of Soviet labour camps. You can also visit a former KarLag camp outside Karaganda. (p335)

Semipalatinsk Polygon, Kazakhstan This post-apoca-lyptic wasteland comes com-plete with underground bunkers and the Atomic Lake. (p358)

Cultural Immersion

Arasan Baths, Kazakhstan Sweat the day away or indulge your inner kink with a birch-branch flogging at Almaty's favourite *banya* (public bath; p296)

Chaikhana culture Nothing beats the experience of join-ing the local *aksakals* (white beards) over a pot of green tea, a round of kebabs and a fresh watermelon. (p463)

Assumption Cathedral, Uzbekistan Babushkas, incense and sacred liturgies offer a different aspect of Central Asian religious life in this Orthodox centre in Tashkent. (p199)

Yasaui Mausoleum, Kazakh-stan If you visit this Sufi shrine in Turkestan on a weekend, you'll see families praying, feasting and making wishes by tying rags to sacred trees. (p322)

Alisher Navoi Opera & Ballet Theatre, Uzbekistan Shell out a couple of bucks for a classy performance of *Aida* or *Swan Lake* at this impressive Tashkent theatre (p212), or its equivalent in Almaty, Kazakhstan, the Abay State Opera & Ballet Theatre (p301).

Month by Month

March

Perfect weather in the deserts of Turkmenistan, southern Tajikistan and Uzbekistan (towards the end of the month). The Karakum desert blooms like a Jackson Pollock canvas.

☆ Nauroz

Central Asia's biggest festival around the equinox (21 March in most republics; 22 March in Kazakhstan) marks the beginning of spring and the Persian new year with games of *kokpar* (traditional polo-like game played with a headless goat), family feasts and funfairs.

April

Spring is kicking in, as blooms start to appear in mountain foothills. An excellent month to visit lowland areas.

☆ Bishkek Jazz Festival

Three evenings of jazz jams at venues across Bishkek, with a dozen international acts attending. One of Central Asia's better music festivals.

☆ Horse Day

Turkmenistan's Horse Day (the last Sunday in April) offers a chance for horse-lovers to see the country's famous Akhal-Teke horses in action at hippodromes across the country.

May

It's starting to get hot in the lowlands, but can still be chilly in the highlands. High season in Uzbekistan means you should make advance hotel bookings.

☆ Silk & Spices Festival

Four-day cultural festival in Bukhara, featuring music and dance, folk art, fashion, handicrafts, exhibitions and maybe even the odd tightrope walker. It can be held in June too.

🏃 Watching Wildlife

April and May are the best months to spot Kazakhstan's 36 species of tulip, while May and June are the time to spot hundreds of migratory bird species, especially at Korgalzhyn Nature Reserve. (p345)

July

High summer is the time to visit the mountains of Kyrgyzstan, Tajikistan and southeast Kazakhstan. Rich pastures bring herders to their summer camps.

☆ Astana Day

This festival on 6 July (which just happens to be President Nazarbayev's birthday) sees concerts, fireworks, fairs and parades in Kazakhstan's capital city.

☆ National Horse Games Festival

Kyzyl-Oi village in Kyrgyzstan's Suusamyr Valley celebrates the summer pastures with games of *ulak-tartysh (buzkashi;* polo with a dead goat),

Top: Eagle hunting, Kazakhstan

Bottom: *Shirinliklar* (sweets), Nauroz (p438)

August

Summer continues to sizzle in the lowlands as the mercury hits 40°C (104°F). The good life is up in the mountains, with August a great month for trekking at higher altitudes.

🎏 At Chabysh Horse Festival

This lively horse-games festival (www.atchabysh. org) on the second weekend in August takes place in Murgab in Tajikistan's eastern Pamirs and Peak Lenin in Kyrgyzstan. Count on horse races, equestrian games, handicrafts and *Manas* (Kyrgyz epic) recitals.

☆ Birds of Prey Festival

Visit Bokonbaevo, on the southern shores of Lake Issyk-Köl, to see hunting displays with golden eagles, folklore music and traditional ceremonies. Great for photos. Third Saturday of August. (p98)

🎏 FourE Festival

This alternative-lifestyle festival (www.foure.kz/en) brings together three days of yoga, art, workshops and ethnic and spiritual music in a different location outside Almaty each year.

🎏 Independence Day: Kyrgyzstan

There are parades, music concerts and traditional horseback games at Bishkek's hippodrome on 31 August to celebrate the anniversary of Kyrgyzstan's independence from the USSR in 1991.

☆ Sharq Taronalari Music Festival

The 'Melodies of the Orient' Festival (www.sharqtaronalari.uz) in Samarkand, Uzbekistan, hosts a collection of 50 concerts by Central Asian and world musicians, with fantastic locations such as the Registan as a backdrop. It's held every other year (the next ones are in 2019 and 2021).

September

A great month to visit almost anywhere. Temperatures are still pleasant in the highlands but the worst of the summer heat is over in the oases. Markets burst with fruit.

★ Independence Days: Uzbekistan & Tajikistan

There are nationwide celebrations on 1 September in the capital of each region of Uzbekistan, with the largest event in Tashkent's Mustaqillik maydoni (Independence Sq). Similar festivities are held in Tajikistan on 9 September.

☆ World Nomadic Games

The first week of September brings an epic week of spectacularly photogenic nomadic sports, such as horseback wrestling, eagle hunting, archery and horse racing, to the north shores of Issyk-Köl near Cholpon-Ata. It's held every two years, with the next events in 2018 and 2020 (www.worldnomadgames.com).

October

A great month in lowland areas, with cool air and sunny skies, though the mercury is starting to drop in the mountains and in northern Kazakhstan.

★ Independence Day: Turkmenistan

On 27 and 28 October there's a two-day public holiday in the desert republic, marked by military parades and much pageantry, with the biggest displays in Ashgabat.

December

As Central Asia shivers in sub-zero temperatures, the winter sports season kicks in at ski resorts, notably Chimbulak in Kazakhstan.

★ Independence Day: Kazakhstan

Concerts, parades, conferences and exhibitions mark the last of the year's Independence Day celebrations on 16 December.

Itineraries

 Silk Road Cities

This loop route through Uzbekistan takes in almost all of Central Asia's greatest historical and architectural sites. Fly into **Tashkent** and get a feel for the big city before taking a domestic flight to Urgench and then a short bus or taxi ride to **Khiva**, which is comfortably seen in a day. Then take a taxi for a day trip to the crumbing **Elliq-Qala** desert cities of neighbouring Karakalpakstan.

From Khiva see if the new express train is running to **Bukhara** (if not, take a shared taxi from Urgench). Bukhara deserves the most time of all the Silk Road cities so try to spend at least two full days to take in the sights, shop the bazaars and explore the backstreets.

If you want to get off the beaten track make a detour to **Nurata** and then overnight at either a yurt camp at Lake Aidarkul or a mountain village homestay at **Sentyab**.

From here take the golden (actually tarmac) road to **Samarkand** for a day or two. Soak in the glories of the Registan and Shah-i-Zinda and, if you have time, add on a day trip to **Shakhrisabz**, the birthplace of Timur (Tamerlane).

 Central Asia Overland – The Silk Road

Much of this itinerary follows ancient Silk Road paths and modern travellers will likely make the same route decisions as early traders, based on cost, ease of transport and the time of year.

Western roads into Central Asia lead from Mashhad in Iran to Ashgabat in Turkmenistan, or from Baku in Azerbaijan (by boat) to Turkmenbashi, also in Turkmenistan. If you only have a transit visa for Turkmenistan you can travel from Mashhad to Mary (to visit the Unesco World Heritage–listed ruins of Merv) in one long day via the crossing at Saraghs, giving you more time at Merv and bypassing Ashgabat.

From **Ashgabat** the overland route leads to **Merv** and the Silk Road cities of **Bukhara**, **Samarkand** and Tashkent. Figure on at least two full days in Bukhara and two full days each in Samarkand and Tashkent, preferably more. In **Tashkent** take a ride on the metro, shop at Chorsu Bazaar and visit the History Museum and Fine Arts Museum of Uzbekistan, two of Central Asia's best.

From Tashkent take the new morning train to **Kokand** in the Fergana Valley to see the khan's palace, then continue to **Margilon** to shop for silks. From here head to **Andijon** to catch the twice-weekly Jahon Bazaar and then cross the border to the bustling bazaar town of **Osh**, before swinging north along the mountain road to relaxed **Bishkek**. From Bishkek cross the border into Kazakhstan to cosmopolitan **Almaty**, visit the sights, attend the opera and make some excursions from the city before taking the train (or bus) to Ürümqi in China.

An alternative from Bishkek is to arrange transport through an agency to take you over the dramatic **Torugart Pass**, visiting the summer pastures around **Kochkor** and Son-Köl and the photogenic caravanserai at **Tash Rabat**, before crossing the pass to Kashgar. You can then continue along the northern or southern Silk Roads into China proper. A third alternative if you are in a hurry is to travel from **Osh** by shared taxi into the high and scenic Alay Valley, before finally crossing the remote **Irkeshtam Pass** to Kashgar.

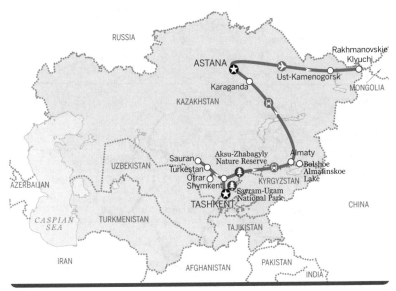

 Kazakhstan – South to North

This Kazakh taster takes you from Central Asia into sub-Siberian northern Kazakhstan. From **Tashkent** it's a half-day trip across the border to vibrant **Shymkent**, with its Central Asian–style bazaars and chaikhanas (teahouses).

From here detour west to **Turkestan** to soak up Kazakhstan's only architectural masterpiece, the blue-domed 14th-century Timurid tomb of Kozha Akhmed Yasaui. Keep the historical vibe going with a side trip to the nearby ruined Silk Road city of **Sauran** and a visit south to **Otrar**, the spot where Chinggis (Genghis) Khan's troops first attacked Central Asia and where Timur (Tamerlane) breathed his last.

Back in **Shymkent** stock up on supplies before heading out for some rural hiking, horse riding and tulip-spotting at **Aksu-Zhabagyly Nature Reserve** or **Sayram-Ugam National Park**, both of which have homestays and ecotourism programs.

An overnight 'Silk Road by rail' train trip will drop you in **Almaty**, Kazakhstan's largest city. There is plenty to do here, including visiting the iconic Scythian-era Golden Man, before hitting Central Asia's most active cultural and club scene. Walk off the next day's hangover on a hike to **Bolshoe Almatinskoe Lake**, set in the lovely spurs of the Tian Shan. From Almaty take the high-speed overnight train to the gritty coal city of **Karaganda**. Touch Soviet-era rocket parts at the excellent Ecological Museum and then take a sobering day trip to the former gulags at Dolinka and Spassk.

Just a few hours away across the steppe is the modern capital of **Astana**. After ogling the bizarre mix of architecture you can visit the Oceanarium and guess how far you are from the nearest sea (1700km).

Plenty of international flights serve Astana, but to continue exploring take a flight to **Ust-Kamenogorsk** and then a long drive to **Rakhmanovskie Klyuchi** to start some fabulous hikes or horse treks through the valleys of the Altay, with views of mystical Mt Belukha. You'll need to arrange a tour a month or more in advance to get required permits.

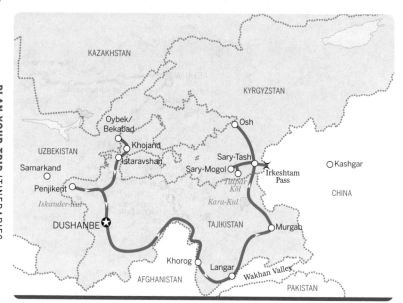

Osh via the Pamir Highway

This wild three-week jaunt ranks as one of the world's most beautiful and remote mountain-road trips and is not one to rush. Hire a vehicle for at least part of the way and do the drives in daylight.

There are several options to get to **Penjikent**. The border crossing between Samarkand and Penjikent remains frustratingly closed, so either fly from Dushanbe, or cross into Tajikistan from Uzbekistan at Oybek/Bekabad, transit through **Khojand** and continue through **Istaravshan** by shared taxi over the Shakhristan Pass.

In Penjikent you can check out the Sogdian-era archaeological site and then either hire a car for a day trip up to the Marguzor Lakes or arrange a taxi through the mountains to scenic lake **Iskander-Kul**.

Continue the taxi ride through stunning vertical scenery to Tajikistan's mellow capital **Dushanbe**, where you should budget a couple of days to arrange the flight, shared jeep or hired car for the long but impressive trip along the Afghan border to **Khorog** in Gorno-Badakhshan.

You can drive from Khorog to Murgab in a day, but there are lots of interesting detours here, so take a full day to take in the beautiful **Wakhan Valley** and its storybook Yamchun and Abrashim forts. With hired transport, you can cut from **Langar** to the Pamir Hwy and continue to Murgab.

There are loads of side trips to be made from **Murgab**, so try to spend a few days here and visit a local yurt camp in the surrounding high pastures. Heading north, **Kara Kul** is a scenic highlight and worth at least a lunch stop or picnic. Once over the border in Kyrgyzstan at Sary-Tash, it's worth detouring 40km to **Sary-Mogol** for its fine views of towering Peak Lenin. For the absolute best views, overnight at the stunning **Tulpar Köl** yurtstay at the base of the peak. There are some fine day hikes from the yurt camp.

From here you can continue over the mountains to the Silk Road bazaar town of **Osh** or better still exit Central Asia via the **Irkeshtam Pass** to Kashgar.

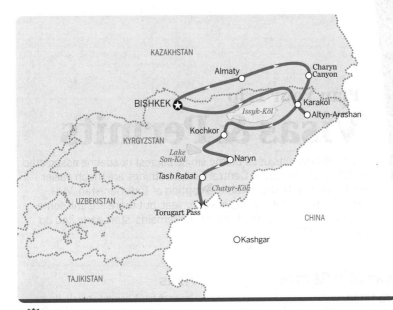

Over the Torugart – Lakes, Herders and Caravanserais

This trip takes in fabulous mountain scenery, a taste of traditional life in the pastures and the roller-coaster ride over the Torugart Pass to Kashgar. There are lots of opportunities for trekking or horse riding on this route.

Kick off with a couple of days in cosmopolitan **Almaty**, with visits to Panfilov Park and the Central State Museum and a soak in the Arasan Baths. It's an easy four-hour drive to Kyrgyzstan's capital **Bishkek**, from where you can head east to the blue waters and sandy beaches of Issyk-Köl, the world's second-largest alpine lake.

For an adventurous alternative between Almaty and Issyk-Köl, hire transport to take you to the colourful, eroded **Charyn Canyon** and on to the Kyrgyz border through the immense, silent Karkara Valley to Karakol.

Spend a couple of days trekking or instead visit the alpine valleys around **Karakol**. The idyllic valley of **Altyn-Arashan** offers great scope for horse riding or the short trek to alpine Ala-Köl and the glorious Karakol Valley. If you have time you can explore the little-visited southern shore and visit an eagle-hunter en route to Kochkor. If you are low on time head straight to Kochkor from Bishkek.

In small and sleepy **Kochkor** take advantage of the Community-Based Tourism (CBT) program and spend some time in a yurt or homestay on the surrounding *jailoos* (summer pastures). This is one of the best ways to glimpse traditional life in Kyrgyzstan. Try to allow three days to link a couple of yurtstays by horse, although most can be visited in an overnight trip. The most popular trip is to the herders' camps around peaceful **Lake Son-Köl**, either by car or on a two-day horseback trip. The pastures are popular with herders and their animals between June and August.

From here head to **Naryn** and then the Silk Road caravanserai of **Tash Rabat**, where you can stay overnight in yurts and even take an adventurous horse trip to a pass overlooking Chatyr-Köl. From Tash Rabat it's up over the **Torugart Pass** and into China to wonderful Kashgar for its epic Sunday Market.

Plan Your Trip

Visas & Permits

Visas and permits used be the single biggest headache associated with travel in ex-Soviet Central Asia, but things are much easier these years, with the notable exception of Turkmenistan. Visa regulations are getting easier every year, but there are still some potential pitfalls and our best advice remains 'start early and do your research'.

Visas at a Glance

Kyrgyzstan

The easiest: visa-free for most nationalities for stays of up to 60 days for both air and land entry; extensions are possible, or simply leave and reenter the country; no registration for tourists.

Tajikistan

Easily obtained online. Specify at time of application if the visit includes GBAO (ie Pamirs). Extensions are not possible. Registration is needed for tourist visas within 30 days in order to remain for the full 45 days.

Uzbekistan

No Letter of Invitation is needed for US citizens and most European nationalities for visas up to 30 days; visas are date-specific; extensions are impossible.

Kazakhstan

Most travellers do not need a visa for stays of up to 30 days; for another 30 days leave the country and reenter the next day; no extensions are possible; registration is not normally required but check.

Turkmenistan

The hardest: tourist visas are only possible with expensive prebooked tours and even then are unreliable; three- to five-day transit visas are possible with fixed dates and entry/exit points.

Visas

These are much easier to obtain than a few years ago. Kyrgyzstan and Kazakhstan are visa-free, Tajikistan has an easy online process, Uzbekistan is fairly easy and Turkmenistan is tricky. See the relevent visa section in the country chapters for more information.

Applying for a Visa

If you need a visa, applications can be made in person or via post at most of the republics' overseas embassies or consulates. If your country doesn't have Central Asian representation you'll have to courier your passport to the nearest embassy, arrange a visa on arrival, or arrange your itinerary to get the visa in another Central Asian republic or elsewhere en route. Embassies will want the following documents:

➡ A photocopy of the validity and personal information pages of your passport (some Uzbekistan embassies require a copy of all passport pages, even blank ones).

➡ Anywhere between one and three passport-size photos.

➡ A completed application form, which you can generally download from the embassy website.

In addition to these, you will also need the following:

➡ At least six months' validity in your passport and two clean pages.

➡ Proof of onward transport (for a transit visa).

MEIRAM NURTAZIN/SHUTTERSTOCK ©

Palace of Peace & Reconciliation (p339), Astana, Kazakhstan

With the exception of Turkmenistan, visas do not list the towns to be visited. The tourist-visa application for Turkmenistan requires you to list the name of every town you want to visit, and most of these places, excluding the capital, will be printed on your visa.

Bear in mind that most visas have either fixed-entry dates or fixed-validity dates, so you will have to carefully plan the dates of your itinerary in advance. If you are weaving in and out of republics, eg from Uzbekistan to Tajikistan's Pamir Hwy, Kyrgyzstan and then back to Uzbekistan, you'll need to ensure that the first visa is still valid when you return to that republic (and that it's a double- or multiple-entry visa).

Even the most helpful Central Asian embassies in the West normally take a week to issue a visa. Many embassies will speed the process up for an express fee (often double the normal fee). Central Asian embassies within the Commonwealth of Independent States (CIS) seem to be quicker.

Visa payment sometimes has to be in a neighbouring bank, not the embassy itself, and you'll need to bring back the receipt as proof of payment.

Visas can be quite expensive, especially for US citizens who routinely pay much more for their visas than other nationalities (retaliation for the fees the US government charges Central Asian visa applicants). Budget a couple of hundred dollars for a multi-'Stan trip.

Try to allow time for delays and screwups. Errors do happen – check the dates and other information on your visa carefully before you hit the road and try to find out what the Cyrillic or other writing says.

Letters of Invitation

The key to getting a tourist visa for Turkmenistan or a business, longer-duration or multiple-entry visa or a visa on arrival for other republics is 'visa support', which means a Letter of Invitation (LOI), approved by the Ministries of Foreign Affairs and/or Interior, from a private individual, company or state organisation in the country you want to visit. After obtaining ministry approval, your sponsor (normally a travel agent) sends the invitation to you, and when you apply at a consular office for your visa it is matched with a copy sent directly to them from the Ministry of Foreign Affairs.

The cheapest way to get a visa invitation is directly through a Central Asian travel agency, many of whom will sell you a letter of visa support for between US$40 and US$100. Stantours (www.stantours.com) is one agency that is frequently recommended. A few Western travel agencies can arrange visa invitations, but charge up to five times the local fee.

Try to apply for Letters of Invitation a month, or preferably two months, in advance. Individual sponsors may need months to get their invitations approved before they can even be sent to you.

Visas on Arrival

If there's no convenient embassy in your country, you can get a visa on arrival at Astana and Almaty (in Kazakhstan, for visa-required nationalities), at Tashkent (Uzbekistan) and Ashgabat (Turkmenistan) airports, but normally only if you have a LOI and have arranged this in advance with your agency. A visa on arrival at Tashkent (Uzbekistan) is possible (with an LOI), but only if you come from a country without an Uzbekistan embassy. Visa-free entry at airports in Kyrgyzstan and Kazakhstan make these the easiest fly-in options.

Responsible sponsors and agencies send representatives to meet their invitees at the airport and smooth their way through immigration. Even so, consular officials at the airport can be notoriously hard to find, especially if your flight arrives in the middle of the night, and they may not be able to find your records scribbled in their big black book.

CHINESE VISAS IN CENTRAL ASIA

Chinese visas are a real pain to organise in Central Asia, with most Chinese embassies now demanding a LOI, a letter from your employers, hotel bookings and even bank statements. The Chinese embassies in Almaty (Kazakhstan) and Dushanbe (Tajikistan) do not issue visas to nonresidents. Bishkek (Kyrgyzstan) and Tashkent (Uzbekistan) change like the wind, but often refuse visas to nonresidents. The best advice is to get a Chinese visa before you set off, though remember that you must normally enter China within 90 days of a tourist visa being issued.

You may also need to persuade the airline that you are guaranteed a visa as many are keen to avoid the costs and fines associated with bringing you back if your papers aren't in order. Bring a copy of your LOI and visa authorisation if you have one. Try to get a visa in advance if possible.

Getting Central Asian Visas in Central Asia

If you are on a long overland trip it's possible to get your Central Asia visas en route in Central Asia, as long as you don't mind hanging around the Central Asian capitals for a few days (or even weeks) and spending a lot of time in visa queues. Bishkek (Kyrgyzstan) is a good place to load up on Central Asian visas.

However, it's generally best to get a visa in your home country when possible.

Transit & Multiple-Entry Visas

You might need transit visas for some trips even if you're not stopping in the country. For example, if you don't have a passport allowing you a visa-free stay, you will need a Kazakh transit visa to take the bus or train from Tashkent in Uzbekistan to Bishkek in Kyrgyzstan, or to take the train from Moscow to Tashkent, as both routes pass through Kazakhstan.

You may also need a multiple-entry visa to get back into the first country if your bus or train dips temporarily into a neighbouring republic (most likely in remote parts of the Fergana Valley).

Visa Extensions

Extending an ordinary tourist visa after you arrive is relatively easy in Kyrgyzstan but almost impossible in all the other republics. If you want a longer stay you may find it easier to get a business visa, or just travel to a neighbouring republic and arrange another tourist visa.

Visa Registration

This relic of the Soviet era allows officials to keep tabs on you once you've arrived.

➡ In Uzbekistan the hotel in which you stay the night should register you and give you a flimsy chit of paper. It's important to keep these.

➡ Kyrgyzstan has ended the need to register.

GETTING CURRENT INFORMATION

Online

Central Asia visa rules change all the time. The following websites are a good option for up-to-date visa information.

Caravanistan (www.caravanistan.com)

Thorn Tree (www.lonelyplanet.com/thorntree)

Stantours (www.stantours.com)

Embassies

Central Asian embassies abroad offer comprehensive information on visas.

Kazakhstan www.kazakhembus.com, www.kazconsulny.org, www.kazembassy.org.uk; also www.mfa.gov.kz/en

Kyrgyzstan www.kgembassy.org, www.kyrgyz-embassy.org.uk, www.botschaft-kirgisien.de

Tajikistan www.tajemb.us, www.tajikembassy.be, www.tajembassy.org.uk, www.botschaft-tadschikistan.de

Turkmenistan www.turkmenistanembassy.org, www.turkmenembassy.org.uk

Uzbekistan www.uzbekconsulny.org, www.uzbekistan.org, www.uzbekistan.de, www.uzbekembassy.org, www.ouzbekistan.fr (in French)

➡ In Kazakhstan tourists who enter the country generally do not need to register. Other travellers will get a white registration card: two stamps indicates you are registered; one stamp indicates you still need to register.

➡ Tourist-visa holders in Tajikistan only need to register if staying for over 30 days.

If you do need to register, the place to go is OVIR (Migration Police). There's one in every town, sometimes in each city district, functioning as the eyes and ears of the Ministry of the Interior's administration for policing foreigners. Though it has a local name in each republic (eg Koshi-Kon Politsiyasi in Kazakhstan, OPVR in Tajikistan, IIB in Uzbekistan, UPVR in Kyrgyzstan), everybody still understands the word OVIR. In some remote areas where there is no OVIR office you may have to register at the *passportny stol* (passport office).

Travel Permits

Visiting some border or strategic areas requires additional permits. Some are easy to obtain, but others will require travel-agency support and several weeks of planning. The most common destinations requiring permits include the following.

➡ Areas in Kazakhstan near the Chinese border, including the Altay mountains in the northeast and areas close to Mt Khan Tengri in the southeast, require special permits that can take up to 45 days to procure.

➡ Baykonur Cosmodrome in Kazakhstan can only be visited on tours organised through agencies. You need to start the paperwork process at least one month before your visit.

➡ Visits to the Semipalatinsk Polygon nuclear testing site and its command town Kurchatov (both in Kazakhstan) need to be organised through tour agencies or Kazakhstan's National Nuclear Centre.

➡ In Kyrgyzstan any place within 50km of the Chinese border and not an open border crossing (such as the Inylchek Glacier, Alay Valley and Peak Lenin) requires a military border permit that is fairly easy to obtain through a trekking agency.

➡ The Gorno-Badakhshan (GBAO) region of Tajikistan needs a separate permit, which you can get online at the same time as applying for your e-visa.

Turkmenistan presents a more complicated picture, as much of the country outside the main cities (restricted border regions) has to be listed on your visa for you to be able to visit it. You'll need a travel agency to get the visa in the first place, so your visa acts as your permit.

Plan Your Trip

Border Crossings

Whether kicking back on a Silk Road train trip to China or opting for an adventurous mountain crossing to Kashgar, several of Central Asia's border crossings rank as regional highlights. Others, unfortunately, can be a chaotic, tiresome nightmare. Avoid the pitfalls with some preplanning.

Most Scenic Border Crossings

Ishkashim, Wakhan Valley (Afghanistan–Tajikistan)

Torugart Pass (Kyrgyzstan–China)

Irkeshtam Pass (Kyrgyzstan–China)

Most Remote Border

Temirbaba (Turkmenistan–Kazakhstan)

Biggest Border Headache

Torugart Pass (Kyrgyzstan–China)

Currently Closed

Penjikent (Uzbekistan–Tajikistan)

Karamyk/Jirgital (Kyrgyzstan–Tajikistan)

To & From Central Asia

Central Asia is like a giant colander, pierced by a huge range of border crossings, from snowy mountain passes to desert crossings, and ferries across the Caspian Sea to bridges over the Syr-Darya (Oxus River).

When crossing international borders to or from Central Asia, you essentially have the choice of using international through transport or using separate local transport on either side of the border. Through services such as the train or bus service between Almaty (Kazakhstan) and Ürümqi (China) are convenient. The main downside is that you often have to wait for hours at the border as a whole bus or trainload of passengers go through immigration and customs. Most passengers are local traders and so have giant bags that customs officers root around in until they find a bribe.

At most other borders you'll likely arrange a taxi or shared taxi to the border, go through border formalities on both sides and then arrange onward transport on the other side. It's only tricky if there's a gap of no man's land that you have to cross, such as at Uzbekistan–Turkmenistan crossings, or the Irkeshtam Pass in Kyrgyzstan.

Within Central Asia

Central Asian republics share some extremely convoluted borders. During the Soviet era most of these existed on paper only, but since independence they have solidified into full international crossings so make sure you have the necessary visas.

Except for a few transborder connections between Kazakhstan and Kyrgyzstan, there's little through transport between republics these days, so at most crossings you'll have to take a bus, taxi or shared taxi to/from the border, walk across the border and arrange onward transport on the other side. Shared taxis run to and from most borders from the nearest town, but only in daylight and with most traffic before lunch. Transport is generally only a problem at the most remote crossings.

Borders between the Central Asia republics are subject to political tensions and can close suddenly in the event of demonstrations or violence. The Uzbekistan–Tajikistan border is particularly susceptible to closure so check beforehand.

General Tips

➡ You'll likely have to change money at the borders. Most don't have formal exchange booths so you may have to use money changers. Check rates online or at banks in the nearest towns before making a crossing.

➡ Bring small, clean bills to change money at the border and if you are unsure of the rate only change as much as you need to get you to the nearest town, as rates are often lower at the border. Most taxi drivers at the border will take US dollar bills.

➡ It's a good idea to isolate the $50 bill you want to change before arriving at the border, so you don't have to dig around in your money belt and see all your $100 bills spill on to the floor.

BORDER CROSSINGS TO/FROM CENTRAL ASIA

BORDER (SEE MAP P38)	CROSSING	TYPE	COMMENTS
1 Iran–Turkmenistan	Gaudan/Bajgiran	car	From Mashhad to Ashgabat; change transport at the border. (p403)
2 Iran–Turkmenistan	Saraghs	car/rail	The best bet if you want to head straight for Mary/Merv. (p403)
3 Azerbaijan–Turkmenistan	Turkmenbashi	boat	12 to 18 hours on an unreliable cargo boat. Try to upgrade to a cabin when on board. (p404)
4 China–Tajikistan	Qolma Pass	taxi	Normally closed to foreigners but a few travellers reported crossing in 2017, so check. (p196)
5 China–Kazakhstan	Khorgos	bus	Direct sleeper buses run from Ürümqi (24 hours) to Almaty, or take the train to the border and then a bus on to Yining in China. (p370)
6 China–Kazakhstan	Dostyk/Alashankou	rail	Twice-weekly direct trains between Almaty and Ürümqi. (p371)
7 China–Kazakhstan	Maykapshagay/Jeminay (Jimunai)	bus	Little-used crossing but direct buses between Ürümqi and Ust-Kamenogorsk. (p371)
8 China–Kyrgyzstan	Torugart Pass	car	Tricky to arrange and relatively expensive as you must hire your own transport in advance on both sides. Closed weekends. (p138)
9 China–Kyrgyzstan	Irkeshtam Pass	taxi/bus	Twice-weekly bus between Kashgar and Osh (US$40) or take a taxi. Closed weekends. (p138)
10 Uzbekistan–Afghanistan	Friendship Bridge Termiz/Hayratan	taxi	Security is a major concern on the Afghan side. One hour from Mazar-e-Sharif. (p285)
11 Tajikistan–Afghanistan	Ishkashim	taxi	Incredibly scenic; for access to Afghanistan's Wakhan Valley. (p196)
12 Azerbaijan–Kazakhstan	Aktau	boat	Passenger-carrying cargo boat with no fixed schedule goes roughly once a week in summer, once every two weeks in winter; takes 18 hours or more. (p372)

Border Crossings

OYBEK

(Uzbekistan–Tajikistan) The best option from Tashkent to northern Tajikistan. The nearby Bekabad crossing is not open to foreigners. (p196, p286)

CHERNYAEVKA

(Uzbekistan–Kazakhstan) No through transport, onward shared taxi or marshrutka to Shymkent and Tashkent. (p285, p371)

TAZHEN

(Kazakhstan–Uzbekistan) Remote desert road and rail crossing between Beyneu and Kungrad, used by trains to Aktau and from Russia to Tashkent. (p285, p371)

RUSSIA

SHAVAT/DASHOGUZ

(Turkmenistan–Uzbekistan) The best option between Khiva and Dashoguz/Konye-Urgench. From Nukus take the less-used alternative further west via Khojeli. (p286, p404)

KAZAKHSTAN

TEMIRBABA/GARABOGAZ

(Turkmenistan–Kazakhstan) Extremely remote, partially dirt track between Zhanaozen and Turkmen-bashi, with 4WDs making the 10-hour trip. (p371, p404)

12 ⊗

⊗

Khojeli

3 ⊗

UZBEKISTAN

TURKMENISTAN

ASHGABAT

★

⊗1

Gudurolom

⊗
10

FARAB/ALAT

(Turkmenistan–Uzbekistan) Turkmenabat to Bukhara, requires a 10-minute walk across no-man's land. US$12–14 entry tax into Turkmeni-stan must be paid in US dollars. (p286, p404)

IRAN

⊗2

Serkhetabat

AFGHANISTAN

PENJIKENT

(Uzbekistan–Tajikistan) Currently closed due to political tensions. Check in advance.

DENAU/TURSUNZADE

(Uzbekistan–Tajikistan) Useful crossing at Sariosiyo if headed from southern Uzbekistan to Dushanbe. (p196, p286)

⊕ N 0 ▬▬▬▬▬ 800 km
       0 ▬▬▬▬▬ 500 miles

KANIBODOM

(Tajikistan–Uzbekistan) Quiet crossing between Khojand and Kokand in the Fergana Valley. (p196, p286)

KORDAY

(Kyrgyzstan–Kazakhstan) The main crossing between Bishkek and Almaty, so can be busy with traders. Plenty of public transport, including direct through transport. (p139, p371)

Border Crossings to/from Central Asia (See table p37)

1 Gaudan/Bajgiran
2 Saraghs
3 Turkmenbashi
4 Qolma Pass
5 Khorgos
6 Dostyk/Alashankou
7 Maykapshagay/Jeminay (Jimunai)
8 Torugart Pass
9 Irkeshtam Pass
10 Friendship Bridge Termiz/Hayratan
11 Ishkashim
12 Aktau

★ ASTANA

MONGOLIA

KARKARA

(Kazakhstan–Kyrgyzstan) Scenic summer-only option between Kegen and Tüp reopened in 2013. Hire a car or makes for a good bike ride. (p84, p139)

7 ⊗
⊗ Tacheng
6 ⊗
5 ⊗

UCHKURGAN

(Uzbekistan–Kyrgyzstan) Minor crossing that offers a shortcut to Namangan if you're not visiting Osh. Little public transport here. (p285)

Chaldybar
Taraz ⊗ ★ BISHKEK
TASHKENT KYRGYZSTAN
★
8 ⊗
⊗ 9 Heiziwei Customs & Immigration Post
★ TAJIKISTAN Wuqia (Uluk Chat) Customs & Immigration Post
DUSHANBE ⊗ 4

DOSTYK/DUSTLYK

(Uzbekistan–Kyrgyzstan) The most reliable crossing between Andijon and Osh, with plenty of local transport but subject to political tensions. The nearby Khanabad crossing to Jalal-Abad is less reliable. (p140, p285, p371)

⊗ 11
Panj-e-Payon/
Shir Khan Bandar

CHINA

INDIA

External boundaries shown reflect the requirements of the Government of India. Some boundaries may not be those recognised by neighbouring countries. Lonely Planet always tries to show on maps where travellers may need to cross a boundary (and present documentation) irrespective of any dispute.

PAKISTAN

KYZYL-ART

(Tajikistan–Kyrgyzstan) Scenic high pass on the Pamir Hwy, freezing in winter with snow possible even in June. Need a GBAO permit to enter Tajikistan. Little public transport. (p139, p196)

BATKEN/ISFARA

(Tajikistan–Kyrgyzstan) Relaxed crossing for Kyrgyzstan's southern arm. (p196)

JIGSAW BORDERS

When Stalin drew the borders between the different republics in 1924 no one really expected them to become international boundaries. Areas were portioned off on the map according to the whims and horse-trading of Party leaders, without much regard to the reality on the ground. As these crazy jigsaw borders solidified in the early years of post-Soviet Central Asia, many towns and enclaves found themselves isolated, as the once-complex web of regional ties shrank behind new borderlines.

The Fergana Valley has been particularly affected. Vehicles and trains no longer run from central Uzbekistan into the Fergana Valley along the natural route via Khojand (in Tajikistan) but rather take the mountain road from Tashkent over the Kamchik Pass. Shakhimardan is an enclave of Uzbekistan that lies entirely in Kyrgyzstan, as does the tiny Tajik enclave of Vorukh, creating all kinds of headaches and tensions for local people. Some of the best trekking in Central Asia lies effectively off limits behind these crazy border lines.

Trains between Dushanbe and Khojand (both in Tajikistan) route via Uzbekistan (twice) and Turkmenistan, making the line impractical for foreign travellers. Trains running from Aktobe to Uralsk, and Semey to Ust-Kamenogorsk (all in Kazakhstan), pass through Russian territory and foreigners are either not allowed on these trains or may be asked for a Russian visa.

Some problems are short-lived as new transport connections spring up across the region. Uzbekistan built a railway line to Urgench and Nukus bypassing Turkmenistan and roads have sprung up in Kyrgyz parts of the Fergana Valley to avoid Uzbek border guards. But these are just a few of the thousands of ties that bind the ex-Soviet republics to one another and to Russia, and disentangling them will take decades.

➡ Make sure you go through customs and get a customs form on arrival. This is especially important when entering Uzbekistan, where you should declare all money and fill out two customs forms to avoid trouble later.

➡ Some borders are open 24 hours, and most close at dusk. Aim to cross before midafternoon to ensure onward transport.

➡ If crossing to China, avoid crossing on the public holidays of either country (or even Russia for the Torugart).

➡ Chinese national holidays fall on 1 January, 8 March, 1 July, 1 August, the spring festival (some time in February) and the days following the major holidays of 1 May and 1 October.

➡ Russian national holidays fall on 1 and 7 January, 8 March, 1 and 9 May, 12 June and 7 November.

➡ Be aware that the Torugart and Irkeshtam border crossings with China are closed at the weekend.

➡ If crossing a border on a train, bus or, especially, boat bring enough food and water for potential delays at the border.

➡ In general always be patient, friendly and calm at borders.

Plan Your Trip
Activities

The soaring peaks, rolling pasturelands and desert tracts of Central Asia offer some of Asia's finest active adventures. Make like the Kazakh hordes on a horse trek across the Tian Shan, explore the Pamirs on foot like the first Russian explorers, or cycle the Silk Road along some of the world's most scenic roads.

Hiking

Central Asia is not only one of the world's great trekking destinations but also one of its best-kept secrets. Kyrgyzstan, Tajikistan and southeastern Kazakhstan hold the cream of the mountain scenery, thanks to the outrageously scenic spurs of the Tian Shan and Pamir ranges.

With many established routes and excellent trekking companies to offer support, Kyrgyzstan is probably the best republic for budget trekking. Treks here have the added bonus of adding on a visit to an eagle hunter or a night or two in a yurt en route. You can even use yurts as a base for day hikes in many regions, notably the Alay region of southern Kyrgyzstan.

Tajikistan packs a double whammy, with the Fan Mountains in the west and high Pamirs in the east. The former offers a wide range of route options and difficulties, passing dozens of turquoise lakes. Treks in the Pamirs are more hard core and anyone but the most experienced trekkers will really need some kind of professional support for these remote, demanding routes.

In Kazakhstan, the mountains south of Almaty conceal some great mountain scenery just an hour's drive from the city, though sadly the transborder treks to Lake Issyk-Köl in Kyrgyzstan are now off limits due to border restrictions. Other less-visited regions in Kazakhstan include the Altay Mountains in the far northeast.

Best Places for...

Hiking
Tian Shan, Kyrgyzstan

Pamirs, Tajikistan

Fan Mountains, Tajikistan

Horse Trekking
Kochkor, Kyrgyzstan

Turkmenistan

Biking
Pamir Hwy, Tajikistan

Camel Riding
Uzbekistan

Birdwatching
Korgalzhyn Nature Reserve, Kazakhstan

Winter Sports
Chimbulak and Medeo, Kazakhstan

Mountaineering
Ala-Archa National Park, Kyrgyzstan

Peak Lenin, Kyrgyzstan

USEFUL WEBSITES

www.trekkinginthepamirs.com
Trekking in the Pamirs and
Zerafshan regions.

www.pamirs.org/trekking.htm
There's a great trekking section on
this excellent website, with other
sections on cycling and rafting.

www.kac.centralasia.kg Kyrgyz
Alpine Club for climbing and
expeditions.

www.pamirs.wordpress.com Dated
but still useful blog on kayaking Tajikistan's rivers.

For more off-the-beaten-track treks in
Kyrgyzstan, try the three-day trek from
Sokuluk Canyon to Suusamyr Valley; from
the Shamsy Valley south of Tokmok to
yurtstays at Sarala-Saz; or from Kyzyl-Oi
to Köl-Tör lake. Another option is the trek
from Chon-Kemin Valley to Grigorievka
or to Jasy-Köl and back; arrange horses in
Kaindy.

In Tajikistan there are several interesting
short trekking routes in the western Pamirs
that combine trekking with rural homestays, including at Bodomdara and Rivak.

What Kind of Trek?

Self-supported trekking is possible but not
always easy in Central Asia. There are no
trekking lodges and few porters, so you
will have to carry all your own food for
the trek. Public transport to the trailheads
can be patchy, slow and uncomfortable,
so it's generally worth shelling out the
extra money for a taxi. It's possible to hire
donkeys at some trailheads (eg in the Fan
Mountains) and hire horses in Kyrgyzstan
(for around US$15 per day) and the Tajik-
istan Pamirs (US$20 per day). Organisa-
tions such as CBT (p69) in Kyrgyzstan and
PECTA (p179) in Tajikistan can often offer
logistical support.

There is some outdoor gear for sale in
Bishkek and Almaty. You can also hire
simple tents, sleeping bags and stoves
from Karakol, Arslanbob and Bishkek in
Kyrgyzstan and in Penjikent and Khorog
in Tajikistan, but in general you are always
much better off bringing your own gear.
A multifuel (petrol) stove is most useful,
though you will need to clean the burners
regularly as local fuel is of extremely poor
quality. Camping gas canisters are generally available in Karakol, and sometimes
in Osh.

Karakol is the main trekking centre.
The tourist information centre here sells
1:100,000 topo maps and has a folder de-
tailing trekking routes. Several companies
offer a range of logistical support.

Trustworthy local knowledge and
preferably a local guide are essential for
trekking in Central Asia. The various
branches of CBT in Kyrgyzstan can put you
in touch with a general guide, though for
someone with a guaranteed knowledge of
mountain routes you are better off arranging this with a trekking agency. Trekking
and horse guides are available for around
US$20 to US$35 through community-tourism programs in the Fan Mountains.

There are lots of competent trekking
agencies in Central Asia that can arrange a
full-service trek. Treks organised through
local trekking agencies cost from US$50
per person per day, which is far cheaper
than international companies.

When to Go

The best walking season is June to September, but be ready for bad weather
at any time. Most high-altitude treks or
climbs take place in July or August; lower
areas and approaches can be scorching hot
during these months.

Trekking Permits
& Problems

Permits are needed for some border areas
of Kazakhstan, including the central Tian
Shan and the Altay region. These take up
to 45 days to procure so apply ahead of
time if you plan to trek in these regions.

In Kyrgyzstan any place within 50km of
the Chinese border (such as the Inylchek
Glacier or Achik Tash Base Camp at Peak
Lenin) requires a military border permit,
which takes a couple of weeks to arrange
through a trekking agency.

While most commonly used trekking
routes are quite safe, get travel-agency
advice before heading into remote areas
on the borders of southwestern Kyrgyzstan
and Tajikistan, especially as the border
areas themselves might be mined. Always
take an experienced local guide in border
areas.

Maps

The major trekking/climbing maps for Central Asia are published and available abroad.

Central Tian Shan (EWP; www.ewpnet.com) 1:150,000; Inylchek Glacier and surroundings.

Fan Mountains (EWP; www.ewpnet.com) 1:100,000; Fan Mountains in Tajikistan.

Khan Tengri, Tian Shan and **Inylchek** (Alpenvereinskarte) 1:100,000; two detailed climbing maps of the central Tian Shan.

Lenin Peak (Gecko Maps; www.geckomaps.com) 1:100,000; topographical map of the mountain.

Pamir Trans Alai Mountains (EWP; www.ewpnet.com) 1:200,000; Peak Lenin and the Fedchenko Glacier.

TUK (p59) and NoviNomad (p70) in Bishkek sell useful maps of major trekking regions. You can buy 1:100,000 topographical maps of the trek routes around southeast Issyk-Köl at the tourist information centre at Karakol.

Note that on Russian maps, passes marked Unclassified (N/K) or 1A are simple, with slopes no steeper than 30°; glaciers, where they exist, are flat and without open crevasses. Grade 1B passes may have ice patches or glaciers with hidden crevasses and may require ropes. Passes of grade 2A and above may require special equipment and technical climbing skills.

Hiking

Day hiking is a major outdoor pursuit for Almaty residents and there are fine hikes from Chimbulak, among others. The Sayram-Ugam National Park and Asku-Dzhabagly Nature Reserve are two beautiful areas of hiking country on the fringes of the Tian Shan between the southern Kazakhstan cities of Shymkent and Taraz. Rakhmanovskie Klyuchi, in far east Kazakhstan, is the starting point for hikes up the sublimely beautiful Altay valleys that fall off the slopes of Mt Belukha. Zapadno-Altaysky (Western Altay) Nature Reserve near Ust-Kamenogorsk is also good for hiking.

You can make nice day hikes from bases in Ala-Archa National Park, near Bishkek, and Altyn Arashan, near Karakol, both in Kyrgyzstan. The Wakhan and Pshart valleys in the Pamirs of Tajikistan offer superb valley walks, as does the Geisev Valley, where you can leave the tent behind and overnight in village homestays. Tulpar Köl in the Alay Valley offers great scope for dramatic day hikes from a cosy yurt base.

Local hiking clubs are an excellent way to get out of the cities for the weekend, get some mountain air and meet up with local expats. If you're in Dushanbe for the weekend in summer tag along with one of the day hikes led by Hike Tajikistan (p143).

Horse Trekking

Kyrgyzstan is the perfect place to saddle up and explore the high pastures. CBT and Shepherd's Life coordinators throughout the country arrange overnight horse treks to *jailoos* (summer pastures) around central Kyrgyzstan, or longer expeditions on horseback lasting up to two weeks. Horse hire costs the equivalent of US$10 to US$15 per day, or around US$50 per person per day with a guide, yurtstay and food.

Horseback is the perfect way to arrive at Son-Köl. Trips can depart from either Jangy Talap, Chaek, Jumgal or Chekildek and take around three days, staying in yurts en route. The six-day horse trek from Son-Köl to Tash Rabat via the Mazar Valley is an adventurous choice.

There are also good horse treks from Karakol (Altyn Arashan offers some lovely day trips) and Tamga (on the southern shores of Lake Issyk-Köl), as well as Naryn, Arslanbob, Kazarman and Ak-Terek north of Uzgen (Özgön). Kegeti Canyon, east of Bishkek, is another popular place for horse riding.

For organised trips in Kyrgyzstan, Asiarando (www.asiarando.com), Pegasus

---

TRADITIONAL TURKMEN HORSES

Horse-lovers from around the world flock to Turkmenistan to ride the unique Akhal-Teke thoroughbreds. Many travel agencies offer specialist horse-trekking tours with these beautiful creatures.

Horse Trekking (p82) and Shepherds Way (p70) have all been recommended.

The Pamirs of Tajikistan and Kyrgyzstan are also sublime places for a horse trek. The Pamir Trek Association (www.pamirtrek.com) is an association of horse guides from the Tajikistan Pamirs and Kyrgyzstan Pamir Alay Valley that offers horse treks in these regions.

For a classy ride, you can't do better than astride a thoroughbred Akhal-Teke in Turkmenistan. Tour agencies can arrange rides at stables near Ashgabat, including at Geok-Dere, or multiday horse treks.

Kan Tengri (p313), in Almaty, offers horse treks through the desert landscapes of Altyn-Emel National Park and also in the central Tian Shan. There are further horseback options in the ecotourism centres of Aksu-Zhabagyly Nature Reserve and Sayram-Ugam National Park (ride between them in three days), at the Kolsai Lakes in southeast Kazakhstan and at Zapadno-Altaysky (Western Altay) Nature Reserve near Ust-Kamenogorsk. These are generally more expensive than in neighbouring Kyrgyzstan.

Camel Trekking

If you still have Silk Road fever and imagine a multiday caravan across the wastes of Central Asia, you could be in for a disappointment. Bukhara travel agencies arrange camel treks north of Nurata around Lake Aidarkul and there are also possibilities at Ayaz-Qala in northwest Uzbekistan, but these are mostly short jaunts from comfortable tourist yurts (with electricity, plumbing and three-course meals). The best time for low-altitude desert camel trekking is from March to May, when the spring rains turn the floor of the Kyzylkum desert into a Jackson Pollock canvas.

Mountain Biking & Cycling

Several tour companies offer supported biking trips over the Torugart Pass, although diehard do-it-yourselfers will find the Irkeshtam Pass logistically easier.

The Kegeti Canyon and pass in northern Kyrgyzstan is another biking location favoured by adventure-travel companies.

In Kyrgyzstan, the Karkara Valley offers quiet country back roads. From here you can cycle around the southern shore of Issyk-Köl and then up into central Kyrgyzstan. Karakol's IGPA (p90) is a cooperative of guides that can take you on five-day mountain-bike trips from Karakol if you bring your own bike. Mountain bikes can be rented in Karakol and Arslanbob for local rides, though most travellers on multiday trips bring their own bikes.

A growing number of diehards organise their own long-distance mountain-bike trips across Central Asia. The most popular route is probably the Pamir Hwy in Tajikistan, which is a spectacular but hard trip. Cyclists who have done the route recommend transporting your bike to Khorog and starting from there. The highway is paved, but winds can make pedalling hard work. Several cyclists have reported being harassed and extorted in border areas, including by border guards. Still, it's one of the world's great bike trips. For tips and

Top: 4WD in the Pamirs (p167), Tajikistan

Bottom: Skiing (p133), Kyrgyzstan

TAJIKISTAN'S OUTDOOR ACTIVITIES

With some of the wildest landscape in the world, Tajikistan is a paradise for outdoor activities.

Alaudin Lakes (p163) This beautiful Fan Mountains region offers some challenging high-altitude treks.

Haft-Kul (p164) The hike up to the seventh of this heavenly chain of lakes is a must.

Jizeu Valley (p176) This vehicle-free valley offers gentle hiking – for those who can master the suspension bridge.

Roof of the World Regatta (p186) Once a year kite-surfers, kayakers and swimmers converge on the high-altitude lake of Karakul.

Ski Complex Safed-Dara (p143) An opportunity to ski is offered at Takob, an hour from the capital.

bike travelogues around Central Asia see the following websites:

➡ www.carryoncycling.com

➡ www.crazyguyonabike.com/doc/standiet

➡ www.travellingtwo.com/resources/kyrgyzstan

You can rent mountain bikes for local trips in Karakol, Arslanbob and Murgab. You can get repairs and some bike parts in Bishkek.

MuzToo (p481) in Osh, Kyrgyzstan, arranges motorbike tours of Central Asia and rents out trail bikes.

Rafting

Intrepid rafters and kayakers have started to explore Central Asia's remote white water, but commercial operations are still limited. Hamsafar Travel (p153) in Tajikistan can help with information on kayaking and rafting in Tajikistan.

Tashkent operators run fairly tame rafting trips in September and October on the Syr-Darya river. There's plenty of exciting white water nearby on the Ugam, Chatkal and Pskem Rivers: talk to Asia Raft (p216) in Tashkent.

Mountaineering & Rock Climbing

Central Asian 'alpinism' was very popular during the Soviet era, when climbers dragged their crampons from all over the communist bloc to tackle the region's five impressive 'Snow Leopards' (peaks over 7000m).

Top of the line for altitude junkies are Khan Tengri, Pik Pobedy and other peaks of the central Tian Shan in eastern Kyrgyzstan and southeast Kazakhstan. Khan Tengri is a stunningly beautiful peak. Massive Pobedy is the world's most northern 7000m-plus peak and the hardest of Central Asia's 7000m-plus summits.

Several Almaty and Bishkek tour agents can arrange trips to this region, including helicopter flights to the base camps during the climbing season from the end of July to early September. Even if you're not a climber, these are fine treks that lead into a breathtaking mountain amphitheatre. You will need a border zone permit for either side and a mountaineering permit (US$105) on the Kyrgyz side to climb here.

The other prime high-altitude playground is the Pamir in southern Kyrgyzstan and eastern Tajikistan, especially Pik Lenin (Ibn Sina), accessed from the north side at Achik Tash base camp. Lenin is a nontechnical climb and is considered one of the easiest 7000m summits, yet it has claimed the most lives. The season is July and August. Bishkek-based companies (p69) such as Ak-Sai, Tien Shan Travel and Asia Mountains operate commercial expeditions from base camps at Achik Tash.

The most accessible climbing is in Ala-Archa National Park, just outside Bishkek, where popular routes from the Ak-Say Canyon require just a couple of days. Mt Korona, Mt Uchityel and Mt Free Korea are the most popular peaks here.

Other 4000m-plus peaks include Pik Sayram in the Aksu-Zhabagyly Nature Reserve and Mt Belukha in east Kazakhstan's northern Altay Mountains. Experienced climbers will find that plenty of unclimbed summits await, especially in the Kokshal-Tau range near the border with China.

Kyrgyzstan: A Climber's Map & Guide by Garth Willis and Martin Gamache, published by the American Alpine Club, is a map and miniguide that covers Ala-Archa, the western Kokshal-Tau and regions.

Two of the most exciting and least-known rock-climbing destinations in Asia are Ak-Suu peak in southwestern Kyrgyzstan (known as 'Central Asia's Patagonia') and the Zamin-Karkor tower at Margeb in northern Tajikistan. For something a lot less technical try the four-day ascent of Babash-Ata from Arslanbob in southern Kyrgyzstan.

Mountaineering and climbing equipment is hard to find in the region so you should bring your own gear.

International School of Mountaineering (www.alpin-ism.com/courses/expeditions/virgin-peaks-expedition) runs interesting exploratory annual climbing trips in Kyrgyzstan and Tajikistan. Contact Adrian Nelhams.

Winter Sports

Central Asia's ski season is approximately November to April, with local variations. The region's best-known and most modern downhill resort is Chimbulak (p306), a day trip from Almaty in Kazakhstan. Other options are available in the vicinity of the city, but none compare. For something less extreme, the Medeo Ice Rink (p306) just below Chimbulak is one of the largest speed-skating rinks in the world (larger than a football pitch). It's open to the public daily from November to March. Kazakhstan's pristine Altay Mountains are renowned for cross-country skiing; the best place to do this is Rakhmanovskie Klyuchi.

Skiing is growing quickly in Kyrgyzstan, with several small ski bases in the valleys south of Bishkek, particularly local favourites Chunkurchak (p74) and ZiL (p74). And the relatively modern Karakol Ski Resort (p93) has three new chairlifts and equipment rental running roughly from mid-November to mid-March. Where the country really shines, though, is in freeride potential. Ecotourism village Jyrgalan (p95) is an up-and-coming base for the sport with snowcat and skidoo rental and warm guesthouses to crash in, while 40 Tribes Backcountry (http://40tribesbackcountry.com) offers the upmarket experience with catered yurts deep in the hills of Ak-Suu valley near Karakol. Freeride and cross-country opportunities are starting to pop up in other corners of the country, from the Alay and Arslanbob to deep-freeze Naryn, so connect with the local community and start asking around if you want to really explore. It's possible to rent skis and boards in Bishkek through TUK (p59), as well as from a number of operators in Karakol.

Less of a major destination than a 'while you're there', Chimgan (p217) outside Tashkent is Uzbekistan's most reliable and worth a day or two of freeride.

Nearly every adventure-sports-related agency in Central Asia offers heli-skiing, in which old Aeroflot MI-8 helicopters drop you off on remote high peaks and you ski down. Most guarantee from 3000 to 4000 vertical metres per day for descents of up to 5km, but require a group of 12 to 15 people – or at least payment for that many seats. The Kyrgyz Alatau range behind Bishkek is one of the best-value places in the world to try out heli-skiing – contact **HeliPro** (0)555-966775; http://helipro.kg) or try the Chimgan and Chatkal ranges behind Tashkent, through Asia Adventures (p214).

KAZAKHSTAN'S MOUNTAINS

Kolsai Lakes (p311) Three gorgeous lakes surrounded by dense spruce forest, ideal for day hikes.

Central Tian Shan (p313) Kazakhstan's most challenging trekking in a high-altitude mountain range.

Kaiyndy Lake (p311) Earthquake-formed glacial lake with crystal-clear water and drowned trees.

Altay Mountains (p353) Remote hiking on the border between Kazakhstan and Russia.

Aksu-Zhabagyly Nature Reserve (p320) Wild tulips in spring and horse riding amid mountain scenery.

Four-Wheel Drive Trips

The back roads of Kyrgyzstan, and particularly Tajikistan's Badakhshan region, offer great scope for adventure travel in an indestructible Russian UAZ 4WD. Four-wheel drives can be hired from around US$0.50 to US$0.80 per kilometre.

In Kyrgyzstan, one possible 4WD itinerary leads from Talas over the Kara Bura Pass into the Chatkal river valley and then around to Lake Sary-Chelek. Other tracks lead from Naryn to Barskoön, and Barskoön to Inylchek, through the high Tian Shan. It's well worth hiring a 4WD in the Pamirs for trips out to such gorgeously remote places as the Bartang, Shokh Dara and Pshart Valleys.

More 4WD fun, of a slightly sandier nature, is possible in Turkmenistan. One exciting itinerary is the trip from Yangykala Canyon across the Karakum desert to the Darvaza Gas Craters. Expect plenty of dune bashing, sleeping under starry skies and stops for tea in remote Turkmen villages.

Other Activities

Several companies organise caving trips, especially around Osh, in Kyrgyzstan, and Chimgan, north of Tashkent in Uzbekistan. Spelunkers will get a kick from exploring the miles of twisting tunnels that make up the Karlyuk Caves (Central Asia's largest), deep underneath Turkmenistan's Kugitang Nature Reserve. Dark Star Cave, north of Boysun in Uzbekistan, is thought to be one of the deepest caves in the world, and is only one of several huge cave complexes in the remote Hissar Mountains.

OFF THE BEATEN TRACK IN UZBEKISTAN

Aral Sea (p273) Getting to the Aral Sea is a major expedition these days, so figure on a two-day 4WD trip from Nukus.

Chimgan (p216) Uzbekistan may be light on mountains but you can still stretch your legs in the western reaches of the Tian Shan, near Tashkent.

KOK JAYIK (p246) Avoid architecture overload and get a taste of village life in this network of mountain homestays.

It's even possible to scuba dive in Lake Issyk-Köl, though some of the equipment used looks like props from a 1960s Jacques Cousteau documentary.

There are some fine opportunities for nature spotting. The wetlands of Kazakhstan's Korgalzhyn Nature Reserve (p345) lie at the crossroads of two major bird migration routes, attracting 300 species including the world's most northerly flamingo habitat (April to September). The tulips of Aksu-Zhabagyly Nature Reserve (p320) are world famous and several local and foreign companies run tours to this area in spring. The following tour-operator websites are a great resource for birdwatching in Kazakhstan:

➡ www.kazakhstanbirdtours.com

➡ www.naturetrek.co.uk

➡ www.wingsbirds.com

Sport fishing is an option in the Ili delta in Kazakhstan.

Plan Your Trip

Community-Based Tourism

Central Asia's community-based tourism organisations offer some of the region's best and most exciting experiences, at fantastic value. Enjoy an incredible grass-roots experience and sleep better in your yurtstay at night knowing your money is going directly to the family you're staying with.

The Idea

At the end of the 1990s, with few economic options left to Kyrgyzstan, development organisations started to look to new sources of income to support remote communities, starting with tourism. The idea was to help connect intrepid tourists to a series of local service providers, from drivers to herders, in a fair and mutually beneficial way, while supporting local craft production and sustainable tourism practices.

The phenomenon started in central Kyrgyzstan with Swiss help (Helvetas) and has since rapidly spread throughout the region. Today these organisations offer everything from homestays and vehicle hire to horse treks and adventures across the country. They are your keys to an authentic budget adventure.

In addition to gung-ho adventures, most community-tourism organisations offer a range of cultural activities. CBT (p69) in Kyrgyzstan can organise displays of feltmaking or eagle hunting. EIRC (p302) in Kazakhstan arranges fun workshops making *kumys* (fermented mare's milk) and concerts of traditional Kazakh music.

Program coordinators sustain themselves through a 15% commission or a

Community-Tourism Contacts

Kyrgyzstan
CBT (p69)

CBT plus Eco (p102)

Tajikistan
PECTA (Pamir Eco-Cultural Tourism Association; p179)

ZTDA (Zerafshan Tourism Development Association; p161)

META (Murgab Ecotourism Association; p487)

Uzbekistan
Responsible Travel (p246)

Kazakhstan
EIRC (Ecotourism Information Resource Centre; p302)

Wild Nature (p321)

small coordinator's fee. A few teething problems remain to be addressed: issues with nepotism and reliability, the tendency for service providers to break away and start their own rival businesses, and that most of the organisations are not yet financially self-supporting. Remember also that these are not professional tourism companies, so be sure to pack a sense of humour and expect some delays and schedule changes during your trip.

Country Programs

The regional leader is CBT (p69) in Kyrgyzstan, with a network of a dozen locations across the country, sometimes overlapping with original organisation Shepherd's Life (p103). Most towns in Kyrgyzstan have CBT-inspired homestays and CBT now offers everything from homestays and horse treks to folk-music concerts and horse-racing festivals.

In Tajikistan, META (p487) can put you in touch with remote yurtstays, fixed-price 4WD hire and English-speaking guides in a region devoid of any formal tourist infrastructure. Mountain Societies Development & Support Project (MSDSP) in Khorog has helped establish homestays in the western Pamir, including the popular homestay and hiking program in the Geisev Valley. For information on these and

local drivers and guides visit the nonprofit PECTA (p179) office in Khorog.

Further east in Penjikent, the ZTDA (p161) is the key to linking homestays to make a 4WD trip in the remote Haft-Kul, Zerafshan and Yagnob valleys, or hiring guides, donkeys and equipment for a trek in the dramatic Fan Mountains.

The hub for ecotourism in Kazakhstan is the Ecotourism Information Resource Centre (p302), which offers similar grassroots adventures and homestays, from flamingo-watching at Korgalzhyn Nature Reserve to horse riding in Sayram-Ugam National Park, though at higher prices than elsewhere in the region. Wild Nature (p321) also offers homestays, horse treks and nature trips. The best destinations are probably Aksu-Zhabagyly Nature Reserve and nearby Sayram-Ugam National Park (www.ugam.kz).

The idea has made limited inroads in Uzbekistan, but a series of homestays in the mountain villages of the Nurata-Kyzylkum Biosphere Reserve offer the chance to get off the well-beaten Silk Road trail.

Central Asia's community-based tourism projects are a fantastic resource for independent travellers and deserve your support. Our advice is to try to pack some flexibility and extra time into your trip to take advantage of what a particular branch offers. You can expect the experience to rank among the highlights of your travels.

TOP COMMUNITY-BASED ADVENTURES

The following adventurous trips can be arranged by community-tourism programs in Kyrgyzstan and offer exciting ways to get off the beaten track without blowing your budget.

➡ Two- or three-day horse trips across the *jailoo* (summer pasture) from Kyzart, Jumgal or Kurtka (Jangy Talap) to Son-Köl (p104), Kyrgyzstan.

➡ Hikes from your guesthouse in ecotourism-base Jyrgalan (p96) for a day or a week or more into the Central Tien Shan.

➡ Excursions to Chatyr-Köl from Tash Rabat (p109) – day hike/horse trip or overnight at the lake, Kyrgyzstan.

➡ Day hikes to the glaciers tumbling off Pik Lenin (p125) from CBT yurt camps at Tulpar Köl or Tuiuk.

➡ Horse rides between yurt camps in the Sary-Oi Valley or continue over the Ak-Tör Pass on a four-day trek arranged through CBT Alay (p120) in Osh.

➡ Two- or three-day horse treks with CBT that lead to expansive Sary-Chelek (p110) lake – one of Kyrgyzstan's best.

Countries at a Glance

The vowel-challenged mountain republic of Kyrgyzstan is the place for outdoorsy types to find a grass-roots adventure on the cheap. Plus it'll give you a gazillion points at Scrabble.

Tajikistan offers the region's most outlandish high-altitude scenery and its most stunning road trips. Fabulous trekking and humbling hospitality make this the cutting edge of adventure travel.

Tops for cultural travellers is Uzbekistan, home to historic Silk Road cities, epic architecture and the region's most stylish private guesthouses. Don't miss it.

Kazakhstan is one of the last great blanks on the travel map, with interesting and quirky sights separated by vast amounts of nothing.

Turkmenistan is the 'North Korea of Central Asia' – it's hard to get a visa but is fascinating and a real curiosity once you are there.

Kyrgyzstan

Activities
Culture
Road Trips

Alpine Splendour

Forests, valleys and summer pastures beg to be explored. The Tian Shan mountains are a highlight, but don't forget about the stunning Alay region in the far south.

Nomadic Life

Community-based homestays and yurts offer the keys to unlock rural Kyrgyzstan. Use them as a base to learn how to make a *shyrdak* (felt carpet), hear a performance of the epic *Manas,* take in some traditional horse games or watch an eagle hunter in action.

Silk Routes

Ancient trading routes criss-cross Kyrgyzstan. From the 2000-year-old bazaar town of Osh take the high roads to the pitch-perfect caravanserai of Tash Rabat, before crossing the high passes to Kashgar.

p54

Tajikistan

Road Trips
Scenery
Culture

Mountain Drives

Central Asia's most spectacular drive is from Khorog to Osh along the Pamir Hwy, but the taxi rides from Penjikent to Dushanbe and around Khorog are also stunning. Hire a vehicle for a multi-day adventure.

The Pamirs

Mountains are the big draw here, from the Fan Mountains in the west to the huge Pamir peaks in the east and the views of the Hindu Kush from the Wakhan Valley. Trek, drive, ride or climb; the landscapes are stunning.

Valley Homestays

The many homestays in the spectacular valleys of the western Pamirs or Fan Mountains offer humbling hospitality. Alternatively, experience the semi-nomadic life at a herder's yurt in the eastern Pamirs.

p141

Uzbekistan

Culture
History
Architecture

Chaikhana Culture

After a visit to photogenic bazaars in Andijon, Margilon and Samarkand, join white-bearded *aksakals* (revered elders) for a pot of tea at the region's most atmospheric teahouses.

Empires & Emirs

The centre of the Silk Road is the heartland of Timur (Tamerlane), from his birthplace in Shakhrisabz to his mausoleum in Samarkand. It's a land of despotic emirs, desert castles and the footprints of Alexander the Great and Chinggis (Genghis) Khan.

Mosques & Minarets

Uzbekistan boasts some of the Islamic world's greatest architecture. Samarkand, Bukhara and Khiva are the unmissable standouts, all offering epic ensembles and backstreet gems.

p197

Kazakhstan

Scenery
Surreal Sights
Steppe

Mountains & Valleys

For mountains, hike the Tian Shan valleys around Almaty; for valleys, try the ecotourism project at Aksu-Zhabagyly Nature Reserve; and for remote splendour, visit the Altay.

Offbeat Kazakhstan

For moments of weird, nothing beats Kazakhstan; our favourites are the Aral Sea at Aralsk and the underground mosques in the deserts of Mangistau. For cutting-edge architecture in the middle of nowhere, Astana is unrivalled.

The Kazakh Heartland

The centre and north are the Kazakh heartland, where Eurasian steppe meets Russian sub-Siberia. Labour camps, nature reserves, ecotourism projects and literary icons are the attractions.

p288

Turkmenistan

History
Desert
Offbeat Travel

Lost Empires

Turkmenistan's deserts are littered with the bones of the past. Five different cities make up Merv, once one of Asia's great cities, while the ruins of the Khorezmshah empire lie among the mausolea and minarets of Konye-Urgench.

The Karakum

Cross the Karakum desert on the overland routes to Uzbekistan, stopping at the burning crater pit at Darvaza. Come early in March for cooler temperatures and desert blooms.

Weird & Wonderful

Ashgabat is full of oddly grandiose buildings and surreal monuments to the cult of personality. From underground lakes to dinosaur footprints, almost everything in Turkmenistan is unexpected.

p375

On the
Road

Kazakhstan
p288

Kyrgyzstan
p54

Uzbekistan
p197

Turkmenistan
p375

Tajikistan
p141

Kyrgyzstan

🎵996 / POP 5.76 MILLION

Best Places to Eat

➡ Chaikana Navat (p64)

➡ Pur-Pur (p64)

➡ Shashlyk No. 1 (p64)

➡ Supara Ethno-Complex (p64)

➡ Tsarskii Dvor (p119)

Best Places to Stay

➡ Southside B&B (p62)

➡ Supara Chunkurchak (p75)

➡ Kara-Kyz Yurt-Camp (p95)

➡ Sary-Oi Yurt-Camp (p122)

➡ BUGU Hotel (p60)

➡ Bel-Tam Yurt-Camp (p98)

Why Go?

Officially the Kyrgyz Republic (Кыргызская Республика), Kyrgyzstan (Кыргызстан) is a nation defined by its natural beauty. Joyously unspoilt mountainscapes, stark craggy ridges and rolling *jailoos* (summer pastures) are brought to life by seminomadic, yurt-dwelling shepherds. Add to this a well-developed network of homestays and visa-free travel, and it's easy to see why Kyrgyzstan is the gateway of choice for many travellers in Central Asia.

As can be expected in a country where the vast majority of attractions are rural and high altitude, the timing of your visit is crucial. Summer is ideal with hikes and roads generally accessible. Midsummer also sees Kazakh and Russian tourists converge on the beaches of never-freezing Lake Issyk-Köl. From October to May, much rural accommodation closes down and the yurts that add such character to the Alpine vistas are stashed away – think twice about a winter visit unless you've come to ski or snowboard.

When to Go
Bishkek

May–Jun Flowers bloom and tourist numbers are low; higher mountains may be snowbound.

Jul–Sep Ideal for treks; many festivals; accommodation heavily booked; cities stiflingly hot.

Dec–Mar Rural accommodation closed; trekking areas inaccessible; great for skiing and winter sports.

Visas & Permits

At least 60 nationalities can visit Kyrgyzstan without visas, including citizens of Korea, Japan, most major Western countries and former Soviet countries. Many visitors who do need a visa can arrange for one online (www.evisa.e-gov.kg).

COSTS

Relative Cost
Marginally the cheapest state in Central Asia.

Daily Expenses

➡ Hostel dorm (Bishkek) or rural homestay: 400–700som

➡ Midrange hotel: US$30–50

➡ Street snack: 40–60som

➡ Self-service cafeteria meal: 60–150som

➡ Good restaurant meal in Bishkek: 400–1200som

➡ Full day horse riding with guide: 1800–3000som

➡ Long-distance share-taxi seat: 300–1000som

➡ Long-distance car with driver per day: 3000som

Price Ranges

Sleeping (double room with bath): **$** >1750som, **$$** 1750–4800som, **$$$** >4800som

Eating (main course): **$** <250som, **$$** 250–700som, **$$$** >700som

Itineraries

➡ **One Week** Head for Lake Issyk-Köl, where Karakol makes an ideal base for exploring the diversity of Kyrgyzstan's culture and heading out for a few days' skiing or hiking in the mountains (depending on the season).

➡ **Two Weeks** Visit Issyk-Köl and Son-Köl, then head through the mountains via the Kazarman route or back to Bishkek on public transport. Either way, your destination is the Fergana Valley via Osh, stopping in pretty Arslanbob en route or continuing south all the way to the spectacular Alay mountains.

➡ **One Month** With more time you can add a two-week pre-arranged horse trek, mountaineering or trekking expedition to the two-week itinerary, or plan trips to remote corners of the country like Köl-Suu lake or Inilchek glacier.

TOP TIP

➡ The real draw is exploring the countryside, and our suggestions are just initial pointers. The best way to explore is to simply head out into *jailoos* and hills and find your own way. But remember that everything is seasonal.

KYRGYZSTAN

Fast Facts

➡ **Area** 199,990 sq km

➡ **Capital** Bishkek

➡ **Currency** som

➡ **Languages** Kyrgyz, Russian

Exchange Rates

Australia	A$1	54.18som
Canada	C$1	54.06som
China	¥1	10.90som
Euro zone	€1	84.74som
Japan	¥100	63.44som
NZ	NZ$1	50.13som
Russia	R10	11.90som
UK	UK£1	95.40som
USA	US$1	68.85som

For current exchange rates, see www.xe.com.

Resources

➡ **CBT** (www.cbtkyrgyzstan.kg)

➡ **GoKG** (http://gokg.asia)

➡ **Tenti** (http://tenti.kg)

➡ **Trip to Kyrgyzstan** (https://triptokyrgyzstan.com/en/map)

Kyrgyzstan Highlights

1 **Lake Son-Köl** (p102) Stargazing and experiencing life in a summer herder's yurt at this high-altitude lake.

2 **Alay Valley** (p122) Trekking amid the Alay's snowy peaks en route to China or Tajikistan, or scaling 7134m Peak Lenin.

3 **Jyrgalan** (p95) Exploring the surrounding mountains by foot, bike or horseback, from right outside your guesthouse door.

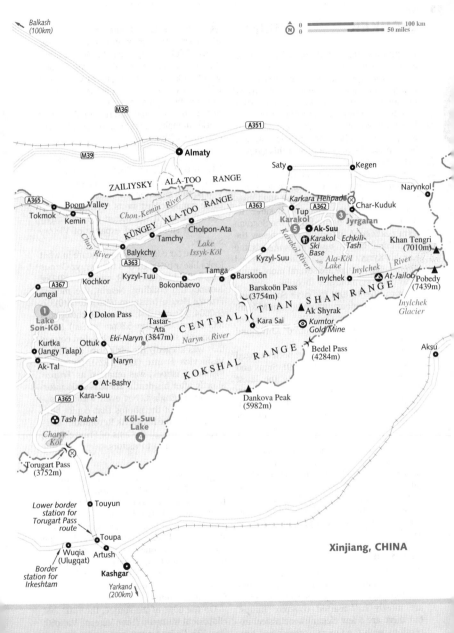

④ Köl-Suu Lake (p107)

Winding past steep rock walls into a remote corner of Naryn *oblast* to experience the magnificent colours and dramatic setting of this unforgettable lake.

⑤ Karakol (p85)

Experiencing Karakol's cultural, accommodation and dining offerings between hikes.

BISHKEK БИШКЕК

(0)312 / POP 988,300 / ELEV 800M

Delightfully green and full of post-Soviet anachronisms, Bishkek doesn't get anywhere the appreciation it deserves as a cultural hub. Many travellers stick around just long enough to pick up visas for further travels in Central Asia, but dig into the culinary diversions, arts scene or nightlife of Kyrgyzstan's capital city and you may well be surprised by the vibrancy of this gateway to the Tien Shan.

Modern Bishkek was founded in 1878 on the site of a Russian garrison. Before that, all that was here was the small 1825 Pishpek fortress of the Khan of Kokand. Its name is probably derived from the Sogdian term *peshagakh*, meaning 'place below the mountains', but as *pishkek/bishkek* is the Kazakh/Kyrgyz term for a plunger-equipped *kymys*-churn, there are several more amusingly crude etymological theories.

From 1926 to 1991 the city's Soviet name was Frunze, honouring locally born Mikhail Frunze, a Russian Civil War commander whose Bolshevik forces seized Khiva and Bukhara in 1920.

Most city street names have been changed at least once or twice since 1991. Signs and business cards usually indicate the latest Kyrgyz names; however, in speech many locals use the old Soviet-era names. Also note that Russian grammar gives different forms to names according to usage. Thus, for example, major east–west roads Kiev and Moskva will often be pronounced as Kievskaya and Moskovskaya. Be aware that Soviet (aka Sovietskaya) is now officially known as Abdrakhmanov north of the railway but as Baytik-Baatyr to the south, while Soviet-era Mira is now Manas north of the railway and either Chingiz Aitmatov or Tynchtyk to the south.

◉ Sights

Bishkek's main central attractions are the parks and museums north of Chuy around Ala-Too Square. Bigger Soviet buildings are mostly half-hearted concrete lumps, but there are a few elegant neoclassical exceptions such as the Opera, some spired university buildings and a sculpture complex around the boxy Philharmonia, and a delightful collection of Soviet-era murals and modern street art hidden among the city's buildings.

★ **State Museum of Fine Arts** GALLERY
(Gapar Aitiev Museum of Applied Art; Map p60; (0)312-661544; http://knmii.kg; Abdrakhmanov (Soviet) 196; adult/student 100/40som; ◉10am-6pm Tue-Thu & Sat-Sun, 10-5pm Fri) Collections of Kyrgyz embroidery and felt rugs, a splendid variety of paintings, and rotating exhibitions of local and international touring works all make a visit here worthwhile. Last entrance 5.30pm.

Victory Square MONUMENT
(Map p60; Frunze, cnr Shopokov) Commemorating the 40th anniversary of the end of WWII, this monument is designed to evoke three symbolic yurt struts curving above an eternal flame. It sits within the dauntingly oversized sun-bleached expanse of Victory Square.

On the far edge of Victory Square in what looks like a 1950s UFO is the Kyrgyz **Circus** (Map p60; (0)312-681808; http://circus.312.kg; Jumabek 119) building. Nearby, the modest **Frunze House-Museum** (Map p60; (0)312-660604; Frunze 364; admission/photography 100/110som; ◉9.30am-5.30pm Tue-Sun) forms a concrete shell around the thatched cottage that was allegedly the birthplace of Mikhail Vasilievich Frunze (1885–1925), for whom Bishkek (Pishpek) was renamed as 'Frunze' shortly after his death. There is little information in English, but even without captions many of the photos that depict both Bishkek and the Bolshevik Revolution (as interpreted through the lens of Frunze's role) will be of interest to visitors.

Ala-Too Square SQUARE
(Map p60; Chuy) Surveyed by a triumphant statue of Айкол Манас (Mighty Manas), Bishkek's nominal centre is architecturally neobrutalist in style but has a photogenic quality – especially when slowly goosestepping soldiers change the guard beside the soaring national flagpole. In summer, the concrete of the square's northern half is relieved by attractive floral displays and fountains that double as swimming pools for local children.

On the edge of the square, the **National Historical Museum** (Lenin Museum; Map p60; Chuy 122, Ala-Too Square) was under renovation at the time of research, but is slated to reopen in early 2018. Behind it is Bishkek's **Lenin Statue** (Map p60; Abdumomunov), moved from a central Ala-Too location in 2013 to the less-prominent Old Square.

To the west of Ala-Too is a monument to the 2002 and 2010 revolutions and the Stalinist Modern **White House** (Map p60; Chuy 205), Kyrgyzstan's seat of government.

East of Ala-Too Square, pleasant **Dubovy (Oak) Park** (Map p60) has a small open-air sculpture garden amid the oaks behind the statue of **Kurmanjan Datka** (Map p60; Erkendik, cnr Pushkin). The park has officially been renamed for local author Chingiz Aitmatov, but nobody seems to refer to it as anything other than Oak Park. Worth a stop is the **Nissa Art Salon** (Map p60; ☑(0)312-662343; Pushkin 78A, Dubovy (Oak) Park; ⊙11am-5pm Tue-Sun) [FREE], originally built as the St Nicholas Cathedral but converted to an art museum during the Soviet period, which still hosts rotating exhibits of local artists that change every .six to eight weeks.

Osh Bazaar BAZAAR
(Map p60; Chuy 202; ⊙9am-7pm) Bishkek's most central bazaar has a certain compulsive interest and is an important city landmark. For traditional Kyrgyz clothes, including white imitation-felt *ak kalpak* hats (80som) and colourful shepherds' chests, find the stalls (p59) outside the south tip of the bazaar's Khial building. Mondays are quiet, but on any other day it bustles.

For traditional Kyrgyz goods, including white imitation-felt ak kalpak hats (80som) and colourful shepherds' chests, there a series of **clothing stalls** (Map p60) at the south tip of the Khial building in Osh Bazaar (limited activity on Mondays).

🏃 Activities & Tours

A free self-guided walking tour of the city is available online via the izi.Travel mobile app (https://izi.travel/en/188d-bishkek-city-walking-tour/en).

★ **Zhirgal Banya** SPA
(Map p60; ☑(0)312-486031; Toktogul 53, cnr Sultan Ibraimov (Pravda); incl locker & towel adult/child 300/150som; ⊙9am-11pm Mon-Tue & Fri, noon-11pm Wed, 8am-11pm Thu & Sat-Sun) This large, sex-segregated bathhouse has a twin-cupped facade that looks like a bad architectural joke. However, the low-lit, artistic interior is well maintained and makes a great place to unwind...unless you're uncomfortable with wide-spread nakedness. Manicures (350som) and massages (500som) cost extra, but there's no charge for flogging yourself with *venik* (birch twigs) in traditional Russian style.

★ **TUK** TREKKING
(Trekking Union of Kyrgyzstan; Map p60; ☑(0)556 101933, (0)312-909115; www.tuk.kg; Kiev 168, enter from Turusbekov 51; ⊙9am-5pm Mon-Fri) A Bishkek-based association organising walking and hiking trips to a variety of regional beauty spots, mostly one-day excursions at weekends. Joining one of these is a great way to save money on transport but, more importantly, can be a wonderful way to meet a cross-section of expats and locals. TUK members get discounts. Trekking maps and good-value ski rental are available.

B'Art Contemporary VOLUNTEERING
(Map p66; ☑(0)312-530092; www.bishkekart.kg; Karasaev 3) This local nonprofit runs art and social projects several times a year, and accepts the help of volunteers with skills in the arts. With notice, they can arrange tours of the art-studio spaces in the same building. Some English spoken.

🛏 Sleeping

Backpacker accommodation is spread throughout the city centre and beyond in residential neighbourhoods to the north and west. In the centre and south, prices tend to be higher but so do services and standards. Rates for midrange hotels generally include breakfast, as do some budget guesthouses and hostels.

Apple Hostel HOSTEL $
(☑(0)553-280881; http://applehostel.kg; Shymkent 1B; dm/d incl breakfast US$8/25; P⊖❋🛜) The large common space and guest-accessible kitchen, and the attached cafeteria serves up cheap and tasty local dishes (and can organise cooking classes). The location just beside the main bus station is convenient for overnights between trips, while ever-affable proprietor Aigul provides plenty of tips on what to do for longer stays in Bishkek.

Capsule Hotel HOTEL $
(Map p60; ☑(0)776-227789, (0)556-227789; http://hotelinkg.com; Razzakov 2; dm 500som; ❋🛜) Billing itself as the first capsule hotel in Central Asia, 20 individually lockable sleeping spaces all with locker and power plugs are cramped but comfortable and include towels and toiletries. Breakfast is 200som extra. Enter via Linenaya, across from the gas station.

Bishkek

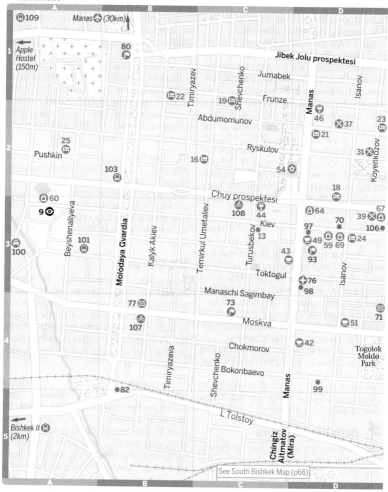

See South Bishkek Map (p66)

Lotus Guesthouse GUESTHOUSE $
(Map p60; ☑(0)772-163240; Frunze 454; r incl breakfast US$17; ❄ 🛜) The extremely friendly family that runs this cosy two-storey guest-house make stays a delight, and tasty break-fasts are a welcome start to each day. Not much English spoken, but that never seems to be a problem here.

Viva Hostel HOSTEL $
(Map p60; ☑(0)708-060500; vivahostelkg@gmail. com; Pushkin 203; r 800-1000som; ❄ 🛜) Just between Osh bazaar and the Western Bus Station, these simple but clean rooms are perfect for late-night arrivals or early morn-ing departures. Second-floor rooms, 200som more expensive, include access to a commu-nal kitchen.

★BUGU Hotel DESIGN HOTEL $$
(Map p60; ☑(0)312-892050; http://buguhotel.kg; Umetaliev 98; s/d/ste incl breakfast US$60/70/120; ❄) From the rustic log-cabin style common space to the airy rooms, this boutique hotel gives off a vibe somewhere between 'modern nomad' and 'Scandinavian chic'.

★Asia Mountains HOTEL $$
(Map p60; ☑(0)312-690235; www.asiamountains-hotels.com; Lineynaya 1A; s/d incl breakfast

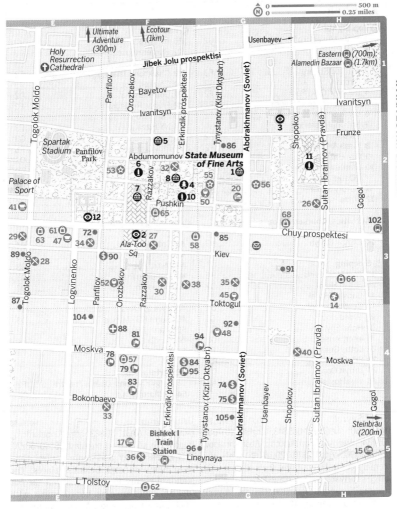

US$40/60; P✲@🛜🏊) Hidden between rail tracks and apartment blocks, this delightful 19-room getaway is striking for its gardens and birdsong. Sun-drenched communal spaces include an open kitchen/sitting room with help-yourself hot drinks and a splendid central fireplace.

Spacious rooms at the co-owned, similarly priced **Asia Mountains-2** (Map p66; ☑(0)312-540206; http://asiamountains-hotels. com; Gorky 156, (Shoorukov 32); s/d US$60/80; ✲🛜) might be more comfortable, but the second campus doesn't quite have the atmosphere of the original.

Central Hostel   HOSTEL **$$**
(Map p60; ☑(0)312-611911; http://hostelkg.com; Chuy 227; dm/d US$12/30; ✲@🛜) The 10-bed dorms can feel a little busy, but private rooms are great and the location can't be beaten; plus there's a small outdoor space out the front that's great for a quiet evening.

InterHouse   HOSTEL **$$**
(Map p60; ☑(0)312-323075; www.interhouse.kg; Manas 91/1; dm/d incl breakfast US$22/35; ✲🛜) An upmarket hostel in the heart of the city, this is a great place for meeting other travellers. There's a second, slightly cheaper, branch at Toktogul 170A.

Bishkek

Hotel Sayrake
BOUTIQUE HOTEL **$$**

(Map p60; ☑(0)312-665843, English (0)708-705434; www.hotel-sayrake.com; Abdrakhmanov (Soviet) 190; r/ste US$70/120; ❄🛜) This extremely central villa-hotel feels like an oligarch's private lodge, ringed by wrought-iron railings and guarded (in the foyer) by a suit of armour. Most of the 13 super-comfortable rooms are oversized with claw-foot baths, modernist Kyrgyz art, large rugs on parquet floors and heavy new wooden fittings. Top (3rd) floor rooms are timber-clad, some leading off a communal, foliage decked balcony-verandah.

Grand Hotel
HOTEL **$$**

(Map p60; ☑(0)312-340000; www.grandhotel.kg/en; Frunze 428; s/d incl breakfast US$50/60; ❄🛜) The overload of sparkling glitz and kitschy nouveau-riche decor is almost comical in this quiet yet reasonably central hotel for business travellers. Rooms feel a bit dated, but comfortable.

Urmat Ordo
HOTEL **$$**

(Map p60; ☑(0)312-311883; http://urmatordo.kg; Isanova 85; s/d/ste incl breakfast US$50/60/70; ❄🛜) Less glitzy and more central than most new midrange business places. The standard rooms are functional but the *lux* (deluxe) suites are a big improvement, with thick pile carpets and pleasant, almost cohesive, beige-brown decor. For longer stays, there are apartment rentals available off-site at the intersection of Manas and Kiev.

★ Southside B&B
B&B **$$$**

(Map p66; ☑(0)555-800278; http://southside.kg/; Suhomlin 6; B&B shared/private bath 3000/3500som; P❄🛜) Run by the American couple behind Iron Horse Nomads (p72), this comfy B&B's Central Asian styling and on-site sauna are an oasis from the hectic centre of Bishkek.

Bishkek Boutique Hotel
HOTEL **$$$**

(Map p66; ☑(0)312-593312; www.bishkek-hotel.com; Baytik Baatyr (Sovietskaya) 67/1, cnr Kulatov;

s/d/lux US$60/100/110; ❄ 🛜) Smart if compact, chocolate-and-cream rooms aimed at business clients on a (relative) budget. Vibrant location near Vefa Center restaurants, and coffee shops.

Silk Road Lodge HOTEL $$$
(Map p60; 🕿 (0)312-324889; www.silkroad.com. kg; Abdumomunov 229; s/tw/d/ste incl breakfast 4000/5000/5500/6000som; ❄ 🛜 ☒) Spread over five floors, the 28 spacious rooms each have safe, kitchenette and superclean bathrooms. The basement hides a 3m by 6m swimming pool. Credit cards accepted, 20% off-season discounts are possible, and rates include breakfast plus airport transfers. The entrance is off Koyenkovoz, a small street one block west of the stadium. In-house tour agents are extremely helpful.

🍴 Eating

Bishkek's food scene runs the gamut of options. *Samsas* (samosas) sold from street stands make a great snack-meal. **Narodnyy** (Map p60; Chuy 162; ⊙24hr) and 7-Day supermarkets (24hr) are found all over town for basic prepared foods.

If stocking up for trips to the mountains, **Frunze Hypermarket** (Map p60; 🕿 (0)312-986100; www.gipermarket.kg; Tolstoy 24; ⊙8am-midnight) is the best of the city-centre self-catering options. Cheap cafeteria-style food is available at many an *askhana* (restaurant) and *stolovaya* (canteen). Restaurants and cafes are not necessarily any more expensive, though many add service charges between 8% and 15%.

Vkys Vostoka CENTRAL ASIAN $
(Map p60; 🕿 (0)312-436483; Moskva 51; mains 150-240som; ⊙24hr) A quick and cheap 'taste of the east' is available 24 hours a day at this casual national cuisine restaurant – the *laghman* with black mushrooms (Гуйру лагман с грибами муэр) is particularly good.

Ordo
CAFETERIA **$**

(Map p60; [☎](0)707-999966; Abdrakhmanov (Soviet) 170/1; mains 60-140som; ⊗8am-8pm Mon-Sat; 🔊🥢) Among the tastiest and nicest of Bishkek's ubiquitous столовая (cafeterias). Walk through the glassed-in *à la carte* dining room for the cafeteria, through the double doors.

Chaikhana Jalal-Abad
CENTRAL ASIAN **$**

(Map p60; [☎](0)312-610083; Togolok Moldo 30; mains 80-160som, tea per pot 20som; ⊗9am-11pm; 🍴) The faceted facade evokes an archetypal Central Asian teahouse with carved wooden columns, *tapchan* (bedlike platform) and octagonal lattice-work pavilions. The main restaurant interior has far less character, but produces a fine selection of well-priced local, Kazakh and southern Kyrgyz dishes. Outside of meal times, which get busy, it's also a relaxing place to sit around and drink tea.

Chicken Star
KOREAN **$**

(Map p60; [☎](0)558-041111; www.chickenstar.com; Erkendik 36A; mains 190-275som; ⊗11am-midnight Mon & Fri-Sat, 11am-11pm Tue-Wed & Sun; 🔊🥢🍴) The chicken, *kimbob* and *bingsoo* are authentic tastes straight out of proprietor Chihoon's native Korea, and when he's in there's top-quality coffee as well. As much a centre for local art shows and music performances as a restaurant, check their social media for weekly events like jazz performances, tango night and open mic.

Burger House
BURGERS **$**

(Map p60; [☎](0)776-287437; http://burgerhouse.kg; Kiev 71; mains 120-250som; ⊗10am-11pm; 🍴) Fast-casual has come to Bishkek with this American-style burger joint, and the combination of fresh ingredients and a diverse menu put it well ahead of competitor 'Gamburger' stalls around town.

Ak-Bata
CHINESE **$**

(Map p60; [☎](0)312-681412; Sultan Ibraimov (Pravda) 108, Victory Sq; mains 150-480som; ⊗10am-11pm; ❄) Authentic Chinese cuisine and cheap cold beer, especially nice on a warm evening from the plastic patio furniture that overlooks Victory Square.

★Supara Ethno-Complex
KYRGYZ, INTERNATIONAL **$$**

([☎](0)312-465051; www.supara.kg; Karagul Akmata 1, Kok-Jar village; mains 240-850som; ⊗11am-midnight; 🅿🔊🍴🚻; 🚌318, 373) This delightful though somewhat contrived 'eth-

no' complex is a rapid-fire presentation of all things traditionally Kyrgyz, attracting mainly well-heeled urban locals. Costumed waiters serve a full range of authentic and original Kyrgyz meals, in comfortably furnished yurts and wooden patio seating. Beware that extras are unexpectedly pricey (tea 150som, bread 120som).

Supara makes a good stop if you're en route to/from the Alamedin Valley. Marshrutka 318 and 373 take roughly 45 minutes to get here from Alameddin Bazaar.

★Shashlyk No. 1
GRILL **$$**

([☎](0)551-706080; www.shashlyk.kg; Karalaev 15; shashlyk 150-300som; ⊗noon-2am; 🔊) It claims to be the best shashlyk in town...and may actually be right. Aside from the obvious meaty treats, the mushroom (шампиньон) kebabs are a real delight, and all of it goes down well with a cold beer on the screened-in patio during warm summer evenings.

★Chaikana Navat
TEAHOUSE **$$**

(Map p60; [☎](0)551-531111; www.navat.kg; Kiev 141/1; mains 170-350som; ⊗10am-midnight; 🍴) The city-centre outpost of this expanding local chain is among the most atmospheric, with Central Asian handicrafts decorating the space and *tapchan* (bedlike platforms) booths lining the upstairs dining room. The menu runs clear across Central Asia, and it's all reliably good.

★Pur-Pur
GEORGIAN **$$**

(Map p60; [☎](0)312-323053; Abdymomunov 259A; mains 180-590som; ⊗11am-2am; 🔊🥢) Perhaps the best Georgian food this side of the Caspian, gigantic *khachipuri* (Georgian cheesy bread) and flowing decanters of house wine keep this cosy dining room full. Very little English spoken.

★Vinoteka
EUROPEAN **$$**

(Map p60; [☎](0)707-330105; http://vinoteka.kg; Chuy 140A; mains 250-600som; ⊗noon-midnight) Classy ambience and well-executed European dishes are a hit with local expats, as is the wine list that for Bishkek approaches encyclopaedic.

Frunze Restaurant
CENTRAL ASIAN, EUROPEAN **$$**

(Map p60; [☎](0)312-664466; Abdymomunov 220A, Dubovy (Oak) Park; mains 380-750som; ⊗11am-midnight; 🔊🥢🍴) A classy addition to the Bishkek dining scene, local favourites plus European and pan-Asian food is served in an elegant outdoor garden with fountains or in an indoor space decorated with local art. Come early to grab one of the two coveted bar tables on the 2nd-floor balcony, but don't even try looking like you just came back from the mountains.

Plov Center   CENTRAL ASIAN **$$**
(Map p60; ✆ (0)777-977779; Tygolbai-Ata (Linenaya) 1/1; mains 170-250som; ⊗ 10am-midnight) Despite the large menu of Central Asian and international favourites, there's little reason to stray too far from the namesake *plov* (pilaf). The smaller portions will be enough for most, but spice things up with a side of quail eggs (Перепелиные яйца) or horse sausage (Чучук).

Dolce Vita   ITALIAN **$$**
(Map p66; ✆ (0)312-543984; Akhunbayev 116A; mains 170-560som; ⊗ 11am-midnight; ☎🅿🗐) Authentic Italian pizza, pasta and cappuccino in the south of town.

Derevyashka   RUSSIAN, CENTRAL ASIAN **$$**
(Map p60; ✆ (0)312-323574; Ryskulov 3; mains 110-280som, beer 60-120som; ⊗ 24hr) Airy if bare, this pine-and-glass beer hall has large indoor spaces with low couches plus ample outdoor space that can get rollicking late at night. Fine pub food includes excellent 'snow chicken' (fried with onions, mushrooms and cheese) and shashlyk. Big TVs screen pop-vids or sports matches.

SlimFit   HEALTH FOOD **$$**
(Map p60; ✆ (0)550-114115; Erkindik 37; mains 180-420; ⊗ 9am-9pm; ☎🅿🗐) Soups, salads and sandwiches make up the bulk of this fitness-conscious menu, though you certainly won't go wrong with the steaks or duck fillets either. Decent coffee and a nice selection of herbal and Chinese teas.

NY Pizza   PIZZA **$$**
(Map p60; ✆ (0)312-909909; http://nypizza.kg; Kiev 89; pizza 520-660som; ⊗ 11am-midnight) We won't go quite so far as to say it's as good as the New York namesake, but it's certainly tasty pizza. They'll even deliver it to your hotel after a long day in the mountains if you can't be bothered to make it into the dining room on Kiev.

Furusato   JAPANESE **$$**
(Map p60; ✆ (0)554-400633; Bokonbaevo 132; mains 250-550som; ⊗ 11.30am-3pm & 5-10pm Mon-Fri, 5-10pm Sat; ☎🅿🗐) Authentic Japanese noodles and sushi by an expat Japanese chef, though the service can be a little over

the top. Reservations are a good idea, especially on weekends.

Saad's Kitchen   INDIAN **$$**
(Map p60; ✆ (0)700-125111; www.thesaadskitchen. com; Manas 91; mains 180-350som; ⊗ 11am-11pm; 🗐) Catering to the large South Asian student populations that attend Bishkek's universities, drop in for authentic curries and delicious paratha and roti.

🍷 **Drinking & Nightlife**

There's a fine line between restaurant and bar in Bishkek, with many serving as dinner destinations in the early evening before transitioning to serve more raucous crowds.

⭐ **Q Coffee**   CAFE
(Map p60; ✆ (0)776-778558; www.facebook.com/ qcoffee.kg; Logvinenko 26A; ⊗ 7am-10pm Mon-Fri, from 9am Sat, from 11am Sun; ☎) Hands-down the best coffee in Bishkek, the Aussie-style flat whites may well be the best in all of Central Asia. It's small and can get quite crowded, but seating spills out to tables on the street built from repurposed pallets.

There's a larger **partner location** (Map p60; ✆ (0)779-695579; ⊗ 7am-9pm Mon-Sat; ☎) at Manas 30.

Vanilla Sky   COFFEE
(Map p60; ✆ (0)550-529911; Moskva 147; ⊗ 8am-1am) Excellent coffee and comparable cakes and ice cream are a hit, and if you're searching for coffee beans this is one of the surest bets in Bishkek.

Sierra KG – Manas   CAFE
(Map p60; ✆ (0)312-0311248; www.sierra.kg; 57/1 Manas; ⊗ 7.30am-11pm; ☎) This buzzing international-style coffeehouse roasts its own beans and whips up soups, sandwiches and even Tex-Mex. There's outside seating in summer and a small library of English books.

There's a second large branch at **Tash Rabat mall** (Map p66; ✆ (0)312-903849; Gorky 1; ⊗ 7.30am-11pm; ☎).

Coffeé   CAFE
(Map p60; ✆ (0)312-626125; http://coffee.kg; Togolok Moldo 40/1; ⊗ 8am-midnight; ☎) Quite good coffee amid dangling espresso cups, modern vases and 1890s fashion prints, or a medieval city-mural at the **Manas 9 branch** (Map p60; ✆ (0)312-312892; Manas 9; ⊗ 8am-midnight; ☎). Verandah seating available.

South Bishkek

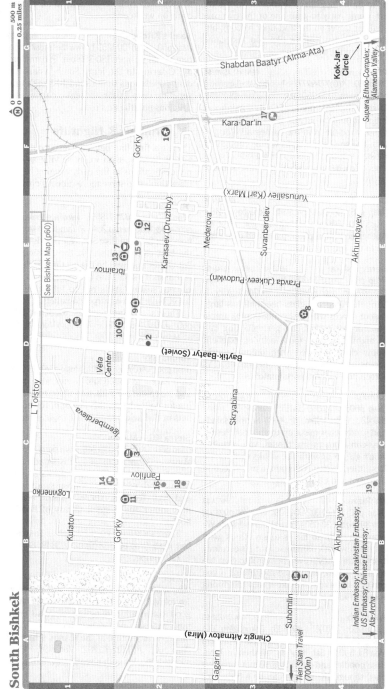

Chingíz Aitmatov (Mira)

Gagarin

Tien Shan Travel
(700m)

Suhomlin

Indian Embassy; Kazakhstan Embassy;
US Embassy; Chinese Embassy;
Ala-Archa

Akhunbayev

Kulatov

Gorky

Logvinenko

Vefa
Center

Igemberdieva

Panfilov

Skryabina

Baytik-Baatyr (Soviet)

Pravda (Jukeev-Pudovkin)

Suvanberdiev

Akhunbayev

Mederova

Karasaev (Druzhby)

Yunusaliev (Karl Marx)

Ibraimov

Kara-Dar'in

Shabdan Baatyr (Alma-Ata)

Kok-Jar
Circle

Supara Ethno-Complex;
Alamedin Valley

Gorky

L Tolstoy

See Bishkek Map (p60)

0   500 m
0   0.25 miles

★ **Save the Ales**   CRAFT BEER
(Map p60; ☑(0)555-241811; Tynstanov 193a;
🕑5pm-midnight Tue-Sun) Bishkek's favourite
craft-beer bar, where drinking the best beer
in town straight from the taps more than
makes up for the higher than average prices.
On warm evenings, tables spill out from the
small indoor seating area and into the yard
out the front.

★ **Staryy Edgar**   PUB
(Map p60; ☑(0)312-664408; Tynstanov 122,
Dubovy (Oak) Park; 🕑noon-midnight) Bishkek's
most loveable old pub is hidden in a basement beneath the west side of the Russian
Drama Theatre (p68). The walls are festooned with old tape-recorders, typewrit-
ers, bottles and 20th-century 'antiques', and
from around 7pm there's usually a low-key
live band playing blues or soft-rock covers.
Decent food, too. Gets pretty full but there's
summer seating outside in the park.

München Pub   PUB
(Map p60; ☑(0)555-103017; Toktogul 87, Moto
Center, 5th fl; 🕑5pm-6am) Hidden away on
the top floor of a business centre, this Ger-
man-themed pub's beer (brewed in-house)
and burgers make for a good start to a night
out, and the 6am closing time makes it a
good place for a nightcap as well.

Zolden Beer Pub   PUB
(Map p60; ☑(0)559-979222; Orozbekov 62;
🕑noon-midnight Mon-Thu, to 2am Fri-Sun; 🛜)
The 'it' place in Bishkek at time of research,
a cavernous dance hall and surprisingly
good pub grub might keep this new spot
around for the long haul. Their beer, brewed
in-house, isn't half bad either.

Steinbräu   BEER HALL
(☑(0)555-787025; www.steinbrau.com; Gerzen
5; 🕑11am-midnight) The setting sun pouring
through an upper window illuminates a
Kyrgyz yurt-crown draped in hops in this
spacious two-level beer hall. The bar is
built around a gleaming copper brew-ves-
sel whose micro-brewed beers are the main
draw. There's a full menu of German and European meals, or seven types of sausages to
snack on. It's hidden amid apartments at the
east end of Bokonbaevo.

Pinta Pub   PUB
(Map p60; ☑(0)312-323099; Frunze 418; 🕑10am-
2am) Locally brewed draught beers and
chechyl (smoked cheese) make for a classic

chilled night out in Bishkek, though for big
sporting events you'll need to make a reservation for the patio tables near the big pro-
jector screens.

Metro Pub   BAR
(Map p60; ☑(0)312-310711; Chuy 168A; 🕑24hr)
Shoehorned into the column-filled foyer of a
once-grand Soviet-era theatre, this popular
boozer has a regular rotation of live-music
acts (some of which charge a cover).

Promzona   CLUB
(☑(0)312-900244; www.promzona.kg; Cholpon-
Atinskaya 16; cover 200-450som; 🕑8pm-5am Tue-
Sun) High-quality live bands and dancing
without the strict dress codes of the more
central clubs. A taxi from town costs around
200som.

🛍 Shopping

Bishkek has the country's best collection
of souvenirs and handicrafts, though you

might find individual items cheaper at their source (notably *shyrdak* – felt carpets with appliquéd coloured panels – in Kochkor and Issyk-Köl's South Shore).

The city's major markets are Osh Bazaar (p59); and **Dordoi Bazaar** (Kodjevennaya 16; ⊙9am-4pm; 🚌4, minibus 191, 230, 233, 234).

Shopping centres include the Soviet-era TsUM (p68), the big, glitzy **Bishkek Park** (Map p60; ☑(0)312-691111; http://bishkekpark.kg; Kiev 148; ⊙10am-10pm) and **Tash Rabat** (Map p66; ☑(0)772-022293; www.tashrabat.kg; Gorky 1; ⊙10am-10pm).

Outdoor Equipment

Alpinist Gear (Map p66; ☑(0)555-311882; Gorky 86; ⊙9am-6pm Mon-Sat) For outfitting climbing parties.

Gergert Sport (Map p66; ☑(0)772-921002; http://gergert.kg; Gorky 182; ⊙10am-9pm) For purchase and repair of mountain bikes, ski equipment and other types of outdoors gear.

Marco Polo (Map p66; ☑(0)312-443407; http://markopolo.kg; Gorky 48/1; ⊙9am-6pm Mon-Fri, to 2pm Sat) To buy a wide range of camping and outdoors equipment.

Red Fox (Map p60; ☑(0)312-909359; www.redfox.kg; Sultan Ibraimov (Pravda) 113/2; ⊙9am-8pm Mon-Fri, to 7pm Sat & Sun) To find camping supplies, mountaineering equipment and brand-name hiking boots.

Books

Book'Ingem (Map p66; ☑(0)550-475588; bookingem.shop@gmail.com; Gorky 19; ⊙9am-9pm) It can also order from abroad with advance notice.

Raritet (Map p60; ☑(0)312-665037; Pushkin 78, basement, Dom Druzhby; ⊙9am-6pm Mon-Fri, 10am-6pm Sat, 10am-5pm Sun) Carries postcards, basic maps and a handful of English-language books plus a museum section.

Crafts & Souvenirs

Akbara Design Studio (Map p60; www.lamaisonduvoyageur.com; Moskva 122; ⊙10am-7pm Mon-Sat)

Asia Gallery (Map p60; ☑(0)312-624505; Chuy 108; ⊙10am-1pm & 2-5pm Mon-Sat)

Epos (Map p60; ☑(0)312-919191; https://epos.kg; Chuy 128/22; ⊙9am-8pm)

Kyrgyz Oyu (Map p60; ☑(0)708-777410; Chuy 134; ⊙9am-8pm)

Saima (Map p60; ☑(0)312-613392; Chuy 140; ⊙10am-7pm Mon-Sat)

TsUM (Map p60; ☑(0)312-909808; Chuy 155; ⊙10am-8pm Sun-Fri, to 7pm Sat)

Tumar Art Salon (Map p60; ☑(0)312-311323; www.tumar.com; Isanov 80; ⊙10am-8pm) Particularly worth visiting, with stylishly presented high-quality embroidery and pottery both modern and traditional. Credit cards are accepted.

☆ Entertainment

In addition to the venues listed here, the **Kyrgyz National Conservatory** (Map p66; Jantoshev 115) hosts occasional musical performances open to the public. Plays can be seen at the **Kyrgyz Drama Theatre** (Map p60; ☑(0)312-665717; Abdumomunov 222) and **Russian Drama Theatre** (Map p60; ☑(0)312-662032; Tynystanov 122, Dubovy (Oak) Park), with shows divided between the two according to language.

On national holidays head out to the **Ak-Kula Hippodrome** (Termechikova 1, Pishpek) for competitions of national horse games.

State Opera & Ballet Theatre THEATRE (Map p60; ☑(0)312-661841; Abdrakhmanov (Soviet) 167) Classical and local productions are staged in this elegant building, usually starting at 5pm Friday to Sunday, autumn to spring. Check the billboards outside for upcoming shows. Tickets are often available up until performance start times.

Philharmonia CONCERT VENUE (Map p60; ☑(0)312-614015; Chuy 251; ⊙ticket office 10am-3pm & 4-6pm) Features Western and Kyrgyz orchestral works and the occasional Kyrgyz song-and-dance performance. The *kassa* (ticket office) is on the west side.

ℹ Information

DANGERS & ANNOYANCES

Bishkek smiles during the day, but many streets are unlit after dark and all the normal Central Asian security rules apply: stick to main streets, avoid the parks, and steer clear of the area around the train station. In all reality, however, travellers are far more likely to fall victim to stumbles on rough pavement in poorly lit areas than to run foul of local hooligans.

If you're drinking late, and especially leaving alone, for safety's sake it's wise to call a cab even if you're only planning to stagger on to the next den of iniquity. Revellers who walk off into the dark streets are occasionally targetted by rascals.

Osh Bazaar Police Scam

Crooked plain-clothed 'policemen' are a problem in Bishkek, particularly at Osh Bazaar. Some demand your passport and want to rifle through your bag and wallet with unfortunately predictable results. Legally you are required to carry your passport at all times, but it's always worth trying to give them only a copy, at least until you reach a genuine police station. Try not to be cajoled into an unmarked car or other hidden corner.

If you have to leave your passport at an embassy for visa purposes, ask the embassy to stamp an explanation on a photocopy in case you're questioned by 'real' police.

The best advice for travellers who encounter these issues is to contact their embassy (p134) and the local police hotline at ☏ (0)312-266027.

LANGUAGE COURSES

Ease of obtaining student visas, relatively low living expenses and the use of Russian as a virtual *lingua franca* in the city make Bishkek an appealing destination to study Russian. **London School** (Map p66; ☏ (0)312-545262; www.londonschool.kg; Baytik Baatyr (Soviet) 39; per hour 250som, registration basic/intensive 300/1200som) is the gold standard, but look for signs advertising private schools and individual tutors around town.

MEDICAL SERVICES

Ubiquitous pharmacies are marked *darykhana* (Kyrgyz) or *apteka* (Russian), and many open 24 hours, including the large **Diplomat Pharmacy** (Map p60; ☏ (0)312-901122; Manas 41A; ☺24hr) at Manas/Toktogul. For medical attention by English-speaking physicians, **NeoMed** (Map p60; ☏ (0)312-906090; www.neomed.kg; Orozbekova 46; ☺8am-6pm Mon-Fri, to 4pm Sat) is the institution preferred by most local expatriates.

MONEY

Exchange desks (Map p60; Abdrakhmanov (Soviet), between Moskva & Bokonbaevo) and banks offering change are widespread, especially on the central section of Soviet between Moskva & Bokonbaevo. **Demir** (Map p60; ☏ (0)312-610610; www.demirbank.kg; Bokonbaevo 104A, entrance via Soviet; ☺9am-noon & 1-5.45pm), **KICB** (Map p60; ☏ (0)312-620101; www.kicb.net; Erkendik 21; ☺9am-noon & 1-5pm Mon-Fri) and **Optima Bank** (Map p60; ☏ (0)312-905959; www.optimabank.kg; Kiev 207; ☺9am-5pm Mon-Fri, 9am-noon & 12.30-4pm Sat) can handle international transactions – exchange rates are lower, but there's less risk of scams than private exchange booths.

ATMs dispensing Kyrgyz som and US dollars are widespread, but most accept only Visa. One of the only banks to take MasterCard or Maestro is Demir bank, which has a number of branches through town.

POST

Bishkek's **Main Post Office** (Map p60; ☏ (0)312-662461; Chuy 96A; ☺7am-7pm Mon-Fri, 8am-6pm Sat & Sun) can handle sending postcards or packages, but service can be slow.

For faster and surer service at a higher price check with **DHL** (Map p60; ☏ (0)312-611111; www.dhl.kg; Kiev 107; ☺9am-7pm Mon-Fri) or **FedEx** (Map p60; ☏ (0)312-353111; www.fedex.com; Moskva 217; ☺9am-6pm Mon-Fri, to 4pm Sat), or for larger shipments **ARI Cargo** (Map p60; ☏ (0)312-660077; http://aricargo.com/; Manaschi Sagunbya 77; ☺9am-6pm Mon-Fri).

TOURIST INFORMATION & TRAVEL AGENCIES

There is no government tourist office in Bishkek. For activities and meet-ups, Bishkek has a reasonably active Couchsurfing group and the TUK excursion program (p59) might give you ideas for your own adventures. Tour and trekking agencies are often helpful with travel-planning enquiries.

Myriad tour operators can whisk you out of the capital and into Kyrgyzstan's glorious hinterlands. Many specialise in trekking and mountaineering. Most will also book flights, arrange transport and help with other travel logistics.

Advantour (Map p60; ☏ (0)312-900592; www.advantour.com/kyrgyzstan/index.htm; Kiev 131; ☺9am-noon & 1-6pm Mon-Fri, 10am-2pm Sat)

Ak-Sai Travel (Map p60; ☏ (0)312-544278; www.ak-sai.com; Sultan Ibraimov (Pravda) 113/2; ☺9am-6pm Mon-Fri, 10am-4pm Sat)

Asia Mountains (Map p60; ☏ (0)312-690235; www.asiamountains-hotels.com; Lineynaya 1A)

C.A.T. (Central Asia Tourism Company; Map p60; ☏ (0)312-663664; www.cat.kg; Chuy 124; ☺10am-7pm Mon-Fri, 11am-4pm Sat)

CBT (Map p66; ☏ (0)312-540069, (0)770-443311; www.cbtkyrgyzstan.org; Gorky 58; ☺9am-5pm Mon-Fri, to 2pm Sat)

Ecotour (☏ (0)557-802805, (0)772-802805; www.ecotour.kg; Donskoy pereulok 46A, Umai Hotel)

Edelweiss (Map p66; ☏ (0)312-542045; http://edelweisstravel.org; Gastello 19; ☺10am-6pm Mon-Fri)

ITMC Tien Shan (Map p60; ☏ (0)312-651404; www.itmc.centralasia.kg; Molodaya Gvardia 1A; ☺8am-7pm Mon-Sat, 9am-4pm Sun)

Kyrgyz Concept (Map p60; ☑ (0)312-900883; www.concept.kg; Tynystanov 231; ⊙ 8.30am-7pm Mon-Fri, 10am-5pm Sat & Sun)

NoviNomad (Map p60; ☑ (0)312-622381; novinomad@elcat.kg; Togolok Moldo 28; ⊙ 9am-noon & 1-5pm Mon-Sat)

Persia Agency (Map p60; ☑ (0)312-663701; Abdrakhmanov (Soviet) 166b; ⊙ 8am-7pm Mon-Fri, 10am-4pm Sun)

Shepherds Way (☑ (0)772-518315, (0)312-661392; www.kyrgyztrek.com)

Tien Shan Travel (☑ (0)312-466034; www.tien-shan.com; Bakinsky 3/1; ⊙ 10am-6pm Mon-Fri)

Ultimate Adventure (☑ (0)312-671183, (0)779-112211; www.kirghizie.fr; Kurenkeeva 185)

VISAS & REGISTRATION

The **Ministry of Foreign Affairs** (Consular Section; Map p60; ☑ (0)312-663270, ext 122; www.mfa.gov.kg; Togolok Moldo 10A; ⊙ 9.30am-12.30pm & 5-6pm Mon-Tue & Thu-Fri) and **Visa Registration Office** (Visa Registration Office; Map p60; ☑ 662329; Kiev 58; ⊙ 9.30am-12.30pm & 1.30-5pm Mon-Fri) handle questions related to visa registration and extensions.

ⓘ Getting There & Away

AIR

Manas International Airport (FRU; ☑ (0)312-693109; www.airport.kg; Manas Airport Rd; 🕱) is a 30km drive north of central Bishkek.

From Manas airport there are between two to five daily connections to Osh (1700som to 4000som), plus several weekly services to Jalal-Abad (from 2500som), Batken (3200som) and Isfana (3500som). Each route crosses high mountains and can be glorious on a clear day. Fierce competition on the Osh route means that fares can sometimes be discounted as low as 1400som even a day or two before departure.

BUS & SHARED TAXI

There are two main bus stations, with the Western Bus Station servicing most long-distance routes (including international) and the Eastern Bus Station covering primarily the eastern half of the Chuy Valley.

Two other places to look for a ride are:

Osh Bazaar (Map p60; cnr Pavlov and Kuliev) Informal taxi drivers typically lurk towards the southern corner, across the canal at the intersection of Pavlov and Kuliev; there is no organised system, but the standard prices are around 1200som in a minivan or 1500som in a sedan.

Dordoi Motors (Osh shared taxis; Deng Xiao Ping 302; 🚌 9, 14, 42, minibus 148, 220,) Official shared taxis to Fergana Valley towns often start in front of the Dordoi Motors company, 3km from Osh Bazaar on the western extension of Chuy. Signs help you find the destinations for which cars are bound. Consider arriving the afternoon before departure to find a driver and phone number rather than waiting around – potentially for hours. And don't confuse Dordoi Motors with Dordoi Bazaar or Dordoi Plaza, which are each in entirely different parts of town.

Eastern Bus Station

The **Eastern Bus Station** (Vastotshny Avto-voksal; ☑ (0)312-482004; Jibek Jolu 263; ⊙ 7.30am-6pm) is much smaller and better organised than the western one. Services are mostly to the eastern Chuy Valley including Tokmok (slow/express 40/60som, around one hour, several per hour), Kemin (120som, around two hours, hourly from 9am to 6pm), Kegeti (50som, two hours, 9.30am and 3.30pm) and Issyk-Ata Sanatorium (60som, 2½ hours, 8.30am, 10am, 11.30am, 1pm, 5pm and 6pm). For the mountain valleys nearest to Bishkek, most marshrutkas start from a variety of points around Osh Bazaar.

Western Bus Station

The sprawling **Western Bus Station** (Zapadny Avtovozkal, Avtobeket; Map p60; ☑ (0)312-656575, (0)312-344696; Shymkent 1, on Jibek-Jolu prospektesi; 🚌 7, 113, 114) handles most long-distance services, notably Karakol and the Issyk-Köl towns, Naryn via Kochkor, Jumgal, Talas, and Almaty. Take a deep breath – this place is thoroughly confusing even for locals. The main Soviet-era building in the middle is almost entirely redundant, except for a few windows pre-selling tickets for night buses and international routes. Then there are three essentially separate minibus areas, each tending to duplicate each other's routes. Minibuses depart from the east and west areas once they're full, while the north area has approximately time-tabled services, though departure times rarely seem to fit with those posted. The result is considerable uncertainty, making the whole process much more stressful that it needs to be. Out the front the same destinations are served by a mass of shared taxis. Prices fluctuate with petrol costs and seasonal demand variations. The per seat fares for minibuses/shared taxis include the following:

Karakol (347som, six to seven hours) minibuses leave between 7am and 11pm via the north shore and Cholpon-Ata (270som, five to six hours). Karakol by the longer south route runs between 2pm and 6pm via Barsköön (240som, four to five hours) and Jeti-Ögüz (320som, five to six hours).

Buses to Naryn (300som, five to six hours, 8pm) or Chaek (252, five hours, 7pm) both run via Kochkor, as do frequent minibuses (150som, three hours). Talas buses (360som, five to six hours) via Suusamyr (240som, two to three hours) depart at 8pm, 9pm and 11pm.

If you visit the main bus station, you're unlikely to see any vehicles bound for Osh or the south. Yet tucked away on the outer west side of the main building is a small office from which shared taxis are coordinated. Find a Russian or Kyrgyz speaker and call Shermamat Majunusov ☑ (0)772-429426) for rides across Kyrgyzstan, Bilal Tochtonazarov ☑ (0)773-623640) to arrange rides to Osh *oblast*, or Kebekbai Begimkulov ☑ (0)772-902470) for Jalal-Abad *oblast*. Rides to anywhere in Osh and Jalal-Abad *oblast* are generally 1000som to 1200som.

There are no minibuses or buses for Osh, Jalal-Abad and Southern Kyrgyzstan. But there is a plethora of shared taxis plus commercial vehicles offering spaces in their cabs or even among the cargo. As such, rides can take all day (around 11 hours to Osh is common); it's best to start early and better still to pre-book a place with a driver.

International Routes

Buses drive to various international cities:

Almaty, Kazakhstan Use direct minivans (400som, five to six hours) or shared taxis, or travel in stages taking marshrutka 285 or 333 (20som, marked Tamozhna) to the Kazakh Border via Leninskoe and Lugovoe villages.

Astana, Kazakhstan (1500som, around 20 hours) Departs Tuesdays and Fridays at 12.30pm.

Moscow, Russia (4500som, 48 hours) Departs Tuesday at 9pm and Friday at 1pm.

Shymkent, Kazakhstan Overnight bus (376som, around eight hours) departs at 9.30pm. Handy if you're heading towards Tashkent.

Minibus Stands

Tiny **Alamedin Bazaar Bus Station** (Jibek Jolu prospektesi, at Kurmanjan Datka (Almatinskaya); ◫ 7, 8, 9, 11) has regular service to Koi-Tash village (25som, around one hour, half-hourly 7.15am to 8pm) or occasional service all the way to Tyoplye Klyuchi (50som, around two hours, 8am, 1pm and 4pm).

Marshrutka 265 (Map p60; Tokgotul 247, cnr Beyshenaliyeva; ◷7.15am-5.30pm) heads towards Ala-Archa from the stand at Beyzhenaliyeva/Toktogul (40som, around one hour, 7.15am to 5.30pm), but at best they'll only go as far as the park gate.

Marshrutkas 285 & 333 (Map p60; Chuy 127; 20som, 30 minutes) run near the 'tysach melochey' shopping centre to the Kazakh border at Korday. Ask for tamozhna marshrutki.

TRAIN

A handful of Russia-bound trains depart from **Bishkek I train station** (Lev Tolstoy 65B; ◫ 8, 9, 139, 204, 227), all of which pass through Kazakhstan (so transit visas are required for those that don't get visa-free entry).

Moscow Train 17 runs Monday and Wednesday (*platskartny/kupeyny* 14,100/21,000som), arriving three days later via Kyzyl-Orda, Aktobe and Samara.

Novokuznetsk Train 358 (*platskartny/kupeyny* 7200/9650som) departs every four days in summer via Almaty.

Yekaterinburg Train 305 departs Tuesday and Thursday (*platskartny/kupeyny* 7350/9825som) via Karaganda, Astana (3600/4400som) and Kurgan, arriving in Yekaterinburg two days later.

Trains depart from **Bishkek II station** (☑ (0)312-656932; www.kjd.kg; Erkendik 1/a) in the city centre for Kyrgyzstan's sole domestic train route:

Balykchy (70som, five hours) This snail-paced, summer-only curiosity departs at 6.40am Friday and Saturday from mid-June through August, departing the same afternoon from Balykchy at 5pm.

ⓘ Getting Around

ARRIVING IN BISHKEK

For Manas International Airport, **Marshrutka 380** (Map p60; ◷7am-7.30pm) picks up and drops off passengers on Molodaya Gvardiya just 20m north of Chuy. From the airport, the first departure is at 6.30am, the last is at 7.30pm; to the airport, the first departure leaves at 7am, with the last at 7.30pm. At the airport the marshrutka parks just to the right as you exit Arrivals.

Manas Taxi is the only official taxi outfit from the terminal car park. The fee (450som) should be per car, but some drivers will try to wait for extra passengers to double up fares. If you walk through the barrier out of the car park you'll likely find cheaper cars that don't want to drive back empty, but there can be safety issues with using such random drivers. From town to the airport it can be hard to find a ride for under 600som, but **Namba Taxi** (☑ (0)312-976000, 9797) offers a 500som flat-rate at all hours.

BICYCLE

Navigating Bishkek's centre by bicycle can be a bit treacherous, with heavy traffic and lots of potholes, but in the calmer outskirts and the hills south of the city it's a nice way to get around. Bike purchase, rental and repair is available at **Velo Leader** (Map p60; ☑ (0)555-451265; Moskva 226; ◷10am-6pm Mon-Fri) and

ATA-BEYIT MEMORIAL COMPLEX

The **Ata-Beyit Memorial Complex** (Chon-Tash village; 20som; ☺8am-7pm Tue-Sun), meaning 'Grave of Our Fathers' in Kyrgyz, commemorates a mass grave in which the bodies of 137 local intelligentsia were dumped on a single night of murders in 1938 during Stalin-era purges. The secret location of the site is said to have been passed down in a deathbed confession by a guard who witnessed the events of that night, and whose daughter kept the dark secret herself until the country gained independence in 1991.

The small on-site museum offers insight into the people who are buried here, while beyond the main memorial is a large plinth commemorating those who died in the *Urkun* flight from Imperial Russian troops in 1916 towards the Chinese border, as well as a small white grave of national man of words Chingiz Aitmatov. The site is 25km south of Bishkek, off the road towards Ala-Archa.

Velopro (Map p60; ☑(0)555-991137; Chuy 176; per day/week US$15/70; ☺9am-7pm).

BUS & MINIBUS

Municipal buses and trolleybuses (8som, pay on exit) run a fair network of routes, but stops can be a little far apart. Marshrutkas (10som, or 12som after 9pm; pay on entry) are faster and somewhat more frequent but they can be uncomfortably overfull, and with claustrophobically low ceilings it can be hard to see where you are. There are hundreds of routes. The superb www.2gis.kg website and app allows you to find the most appropriate service based on your start and end points, and shows each route on a map. However, it's still worth learning major routes and the major signboard shorthand.

Key city-centre junctions:

f-nya Philharmonia, ie Manas-Chuy junction

goin Soviet–Jibek Jolu juction

mossovet Soviet–Moskva junction

osh r/k Osh Bazaar

ploshad Ala-Too Square (usually on Kiev)

tserkov Jibek Jolu–Togolok Moldo junction

yug2 [OR] **Vefa** Soviet–Gorky junction

Areas generally indicating out-of-centre directions (working anticlockwise from north):

Dordoi R/k Far north usually via Soviet

Jal Inner southwest suburb at west end of Akhunbaev

Pishpek West, just south of rail tracks at west end of Tolstoy

Vostok 5 East via Chuy

Some useful routes:

4 Up Manas from Gorky, east along Kiev, left on Soviet and then north to Dordoi Bazaar.

7 Handy for getting from Philarmonia to the Western Bus Station.

110 From/to Osh Bazaar, along Moskva/Toktogul (east/westbound) then all the way along Soviet to the south and the **American University of Central Asia** (www.auca.kg; Aaly Tokombaeva 7/6).

113 Eastern Bus Station to Western Bus Station, then circling back via Osh Bazaar to Moskva then Chuy (east of Pravda) and loop back via Vostok-5 and Alamedin Bazaar.

114 Essentially the 113 loop in reverse but mostly via Toktogul (westbound).

175 Jibek Julo to Goin (Soviet/Jibek Jolu) and the Eastern Bus Station, down Shabdan Baatyr and Gorky to the Yusunaliev/Suvanberdiev junction (for the Tajik Embassy).

200 Moskva, Manas/Mira, Akhunbaev and Supara Ethno-Complex.

212 A long run down Chuy/Kiev through the centre, south past Vefa down Soviet and Yusunaliev to the Suvanberdiev junction (for the Tajik embassy).

213 Anticlockwise loop around the central area heading westbound on Jibek-Jolu, shimmying along Manas, Frunze, Turusbekov, Chuy, Jash Gvardinya (airport bus stop) and Osh Bazaar's Beishenaliyev before returning mostly via Moskva, Vostok 5 and Almatinskaya.

265, 266 Osh Bazaar along Moskva then south down Manas/Mira all the way to Kashka-Suu village (for Ala-Archa).

286 Jibek-Jolu, Jash Gvardia (airport bus stand), Chuy and west past Dordoi Motors.

CAR & MOTORCYCLE

Generally car rental in Central Asia assumes that you engage a vehicle with driver. In Bishkek this is quite easily organised through **CBT** (p69) for 14som to 18som per kilometre, or tour agencies, who can find a decent 4WD for around US$0.35 per kilometre. Drivers' meals and overnight expenses usually add US$20 per day, and if you're doing a one-way journey you'll have to pay the return.

Iron Horse Nomads (☑(0)555-800278; http://ihn.kg; Tynalieva St; ☺9am-5pm Mon-Fri) and **Kyrgyz Rent-Car** (☑(0)777-509253; http://carforrent.kg; Tokombaev 52/2; ☺9am-8pm) have a growing selection of self-drive vehicles, but although they offer a selection of prices and styles, if you don't book well ahead you might find that choice is limited or non-existent. Plumping for a 4WD vehicle is wise if you're going off the main highways, and doesn't necessarily cost more than a city car. Be aware that there is no roadside assistance so if you have a breakdown and are not mechanically adept or fluent in local languages, things can prove awkward. Dealing with occasional police stops will also be a linguistic challenge, and it is often expected that palms will be greased even when the driver is not at fault.

Generally you'll require a passport, driving licence and security deposit in cash (typically between US$300 and US$1000 depending on the vehicle). Insurance should be included but, as ever, you'll need to check the small print carefully.

TAXI
Reliable taxi companies using meters in Bishkek include **Namba Taxi** (✆ (0)312-976000, 9797) and **Tez Taxi** (✆ (0)708-001535, 1535). A short ride in the city centre costs less than 100som, though prices increase at night.

CHUY OBLAST

For a break from Bishkek head out towards one of the mountain valleys along the south of Chuy for trekkers' lodges, homestays and full-service resorts; or just pack up a tent

and a few days' food and head into the hills to live with the shepherds.

Ala-Archa Canyon
Ущелье Ала-Арча
ELEV 2100M

In the grand Ala-Archa Canyon, an accessible Y-shaped valley south of Bishkek, you can sit by a waterfall, hike to a glacier or mountaineer up the region's highest peaks. Around 30km from Bishkek is the *vorota zapovednika* (park gate) where entry fees for the **Ala Archa National Park** (✆ (0)701-551693; http://ala-archa.kg; Kashka-Suu village; foreigner/motorist 80/120som) are payable. Another 12km beyond, the sealed road ends at the main trailhead known as the *alplager*.

The state cartography agency's 1:50,000 topographic map *Prirodnyy Park Ala-Archa*, purchasable at TUK (p59), covers the area should you wish to go off-trail.

Hiking

Ala-Archa's trailhead is a seasonal gaggle of yurts selling *kymys* (fermented mare's milk), plus a pair of small hotels. The river divides 300m north of here where two idyllic alpine valleys converge. Relatively well-marked trails lead walkers up both branches

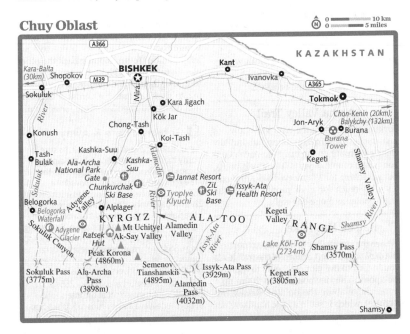

Chuy Oblast

0 ——— 10 km
0 ——— 5 miles

WINTER SPORTS AROUND BISHKEK

At least 12 ski resorts are dotted around the Chuy Valley, catering mostly to beginner and intermediate skiers, with facilities range from a single T-bar to modern lifts and services. The two best, also among the closest to Bishkek, are **ZiL** (ЗиЛ; ☑(0)773-515050; http://zil. kg; Issyk-Ata region; lift pass adult/child 1000/600som, ski & snowboard rental adult/child 600/400som) and **Chunkur- chak** (☑(0)558-586898; www.chunkur chak.kg; Chunkurchak Valley, Alamedin region; lift pass 1100som). Equipment rental is available on-site from 700som to 1200som per day. For backcountry skiiers, almost every valley to the south of Bishkek has something interesting to offer, and Ala-Archa was once a training ground for the USSR's Olympic ski team.

– left to the initially steep Ratsek hike; right through the main Ala-Archa Canyon. The area gets relatively busy with picnicking locals on summer weekends but can be altogether deserted from October to May.

At the **Alplager Hostel** (☑(0)700-929366; Alplager; d with/without bathroom 2000/500som) are musty old Soviet-era rooms with clean sheets. 'Toilet' outside. More upmarket is the **Ala-Archa Lodge** (☑(0)312-507944, (0)700-929366; Alplager; d/ste 2500/5500som), a recently renovated A-frame building.

🚶 Ala-Archa Valley Trail

Forking right where the river valley divides just above the *alplager* offers an initially clear, easy route up the main Ala-Archa Canyon past a couple of yurts. The way is pretty, but stretching for 15km beyond the *alplager* it's a bit much for most people to trek the entire valley as a one-day walk.

🚶 Ratsek Hut Hike

Where the river valley divides 300m north of the *alplager*, the left branch of the trail leads you in four to five glorious hours to a glacier viewpoint. The viewpoint is just 200m up a minor ridge above the isolated 'Ratsek' hut (3370m), which is set in a little handkerchief

of meadow surrounded by rocky spires with Patagonian ambitions. For mountaineers, Ratsek is used as the base camp for a series of acclimatisation peaks, notably Korona (4860m) and Uchityel (4572m).

In dry summer conditions it's a strenuous but straightforward day hike to Ratsek. However, snow can fall in almost any month, wet conditions can leave a few steep sections seriously muddy, and high water can make the two stream crossings virtually impassable. Even if you don't make it all the way to Ratsek hut, there are marvellous alpine views from the 'split-rock' viewpoint just 40 minutes' climb from *alplager* (well before the first stream crossing), and there's a waterfall (frozen November to May) to admire at around the half-way point to Ratsek.

Ratsek Hut (Ak-Sai Mountain Lodge; ☑(0)312-657011, (0)312-651404; itmc@elcat.kg; Ala-Archa; dm/camping 500/150som) has accommodation in two 14-space bunk rooms and a six-space 'private' room, plus there are tent sites outside.

🚶 Adygene Valley

From the *alplager*, backtrack around 300m down the road and cross a footbridge, and you should find yourself heading southwest up the steep Adygene Valley trail. Along this way is a poignant climbers' cemetery in a larch grove. The track continues for about 7km to 3300m, below Adygene Glacier. Where the track divides it's better to keep left – you can return looping back the other way, but if you fork right, the way is harder to find outbound and involves a river crossing to avoid a scramble across a landslide that destroyed a section of the former trail.

ℹ Getting There & Away

If you're taking a taxi from Bishkek, be sure to clarify that the agreed price is to the *alplager* (typically 500som one way) rather than the Ala-Archa park gate (*vorota zapovednika*, 250som). Otherwise you'll need to hitch the last 12km or pay a very considerable supplement. Especially off-season, it might be worth arranging a pick-up to take you back again. Bargaining might be necessary as some drivers ask a whopping US$40 return, especially when ordered through hotels. You can usually agree on around half that through drivers around Osh Bazaar.

By public transport marshrutka 265 (p71) from Bishkek's Toktogul street at the intersection of Beyshenaliyeva usually runs to Kashka-Suu village, terminating 7km short of the park gate, while for a consideration some drivers will continue to the end of the public road. Traffic is sparse out of season.

Chunkurchak Valley
Ущелье Чункурчак
ELEV 1810M

Chunkurchak Valley is a nice destination for day hikes in summer, especially for overnight guests of the **Supara Chunkurchak resort** (📞(0)554-961414; https://supara.kg; Alamedin region; rm 7000som, yurt 11000som; 🛜), but really comes into its own as a quick and easy ski trip from Bishkek during the winter months. In winter, cafes operate at the ski complex for hungry skiers.

ℹ Getting There & Away

Minibuses from Bishkek's Alamedin Bazaar (p71) go as far as Koi-Tash village (25som, one hour), beyond which is the turn-off for Chunkurchak, but this is still 13km short of the ski complex and 16km short of Supara. A hired taxi from the city should run 500som to 800som each way, depending on the season. On winter weekends the ski complex organises transfer shuttles to/from Bishkek – call for details and reservations.

Alamedin Valley
Ущелье Аламедин
📞3139 / ELEV 1615M

The beautiful alpine Alamedin Valley is among the most accessible options for those wanting to savour Bishkek's fabulous mountain backdrop with a picnic rather than a serious trek. The valley has a relatively open aspect with curtains of spiky white peaks rising from a grassy meadowland valley. Views begin along the road from Bishkek, well before the trailhead 1km beyond the Soviet-era mineral-water swimming pool, **Tyoplye Klyuchi** (📞0701-485880; per hr 200som; ⏰8am-8pm Wed-Sat, 8am-6pm Sun).

Almost as soon as you leave the final little car park at the end of the valley there's a choice of walking routes: you can descend, cross the river and follow the left bank pastures towards a waterfall that's tucked away in the third side valley (around 1½ hours' walk one way). Alternatively, stay on the right bank for somewhat finer views. However, after around an hour's walk, when your reach a large grassy area, the right-bank

path peters out amid thorn bushes and crossing the river there is not recommended unless the water level is very low.

Twelve Fireplaces Tavern is a popular day trip for Bishkek residents year-round; during summer small cafes set up along the highway into the valley selling national cuisine and *kymys*. There are cabins at **Twelve Fireplaces** (📞0312-690690; www.12kaminov.kg/en; mains 250-700som; ⏰10am-midnight; 📞🍴), but hikers who push further into the valley's trails can camp at any number of informal sites.

Buses depart throughout the day from Bishkek's Alamedin Bazaar (p71) to Koy-Tash village, at the head of the valley. From here, it is necessary to hire a car (from 750som) to continue the last 12km to the trailhead.

Kegeti Valley
Ущелье Кегети

Unassuming at first glance, a drive up the Kegeti Valley reveals a succession of increasingly impressive vistas that would alone justify the trip. Whether for an easy waterfall jaunt, a steep lake walk, or an ambitious itinerary that takes it all in, this valley will become a quick favourite.

The 20m Kegeti Waterfall is a popular picnic destination for locals in the warmer months, situated just off the road in *Chon-* (Big-)Kegeti Valley.

Trekkers would be better advised to head left at the bridge to *Kichi-*(Small-) Kegeti Valley for turquoise-hued glacial lake Köl-Tör, one of the most beautiful in Chuy *oblast*, and the surrounding peaks and verdant pastures. It's two to three hours of often-steep hiking beyond the Kegeti Tour Guesthouse, but the return trip should only take about half that. Continue beyond the lake to a glaciated bowl at the top of the valley, from which it's possible to pass west into Shamsy Valley or east into Chon-Kegeti.

Self-sufficient travellers have the run of the upper reaches of Kegeti – it'll likely just be you, a few shepherds and their hundred-odd sheep and horses. For a little more comfort, track down to the **Kegeti Tour Guesthouse** (📞(0)555-614416; http://kegety.inspiro.kg; Panfilov 188/1, Köl-Tör Valley; incl breakfast dm/r 1300/1100som) below Köl-Tör Lake or all the way back to Rotfront village's The Farm Guesthouse (p76).

HIKING AROUND BISHKEK

Small mountain valleys branch south off the main Chuy Valley, each more spectacular than the last, but most travellers overlook these in favour of points further afield. Any given valley has something to offer, but the most reliable include the following:

➡ Ala-Archa National Park (p73) with its three main routes, which graduate from an easy walk up the main valley to the steep climb up the Adygene Valley.

➡ Kichi-Kegeti Valley's Köl-Tör Lake (p75) as a one-day or overnight or continuing over a pass into Chon-Kegeti before circling back to the highway via Kegeti village. Either way, don't miss the spectacular panorama of peaks at the top of Kichi-Kegeti.

➡ Hiking up the Issyk-Ata Valley (p76), camping at the valley junction for day hikes or continuing on a multiday route through to Suusamyr or back down Alamedin Valley (p75) to Bishkek.

➡ The red-rock canyon at Suluu-Terek (p78) is an unusual landscape compared to generally lush Chuy, good for either a day trip or a loop through to Kok Moiniok to the south.

TUK (p59) organises inexpensive day trips around the region, the best option for many visitors, but experienced trekkers will want to push deeper than a single day allows.

Marshrutka 303 (55som, 1½ hours) departs twice per day from Bishkek's Eastern Bus Station (p70) to the village of Kegeti, at the foot of the valley. From there it's about 10km up the valley to a T-junction – left to Kichi-Kegeti and Köl-Tör Lake, or right to Chon-Kegeti and the Kegeti waterfall.

Issyk-Ata Valley Ысык-Ата

ELEV 1778M

Widely known throughout the former Soviet Union for its curative waters, Issyk-Ata has served as a health centre for those suffering bone and muscle ailments for centuries and was a rehabilitation centre for wounded soldiers during WWII. For independent travellers, the Issyk-Ata Health Resort is more often an interesting Soviet-era throwback admired en route to a walk in the Issyk-Ata Valley just beyond.

While the health resort does keep rooms for guests, they're generally overpriced and dismal. Ask about homestays in the handful of apartment blocks across a small bridge from the sanatorium entrance (300som to 500som per person).

From the top of the health resort, a trailhead on the east bank of the river leads towards the pyramid-shaped 3950m peak at the end of the valley. One to two hours in, a tall waterfall up a side valley is as far as most local visitors will go. Continuing to the foot of the valley's dominant peak, a nice

camping spot makes a good first night from which to explore the glacial moraine down an alternative valley to the south.

From the campsite, the main valley curves southwest past small Ortoköl lake to a 3900m pass, from which it's possible to descend towards a remote road out of Suusamyr or angle west over another 4010m pass and return towards Bishkek via the Alamedin Valley (p75).

Marshrutkas leave from Bishkek's Eastern Bus Station (p70) to the Issyk-Ata Sanatorium (60som, 2½ hours) six times a day, returning to the city shortly after arrival at Issyk-Ata. The last departure is around 4pm, though shared taxis to Tokmok are sometimes available beyond that time.

Tokmok Токмок

📞 3138 / POP 60,300 / ELEV 816M

The town of Tokmok, a little over 70km east of Bishkek, is of interest primarily for the Kharakanid-era Burana Tower (p77) and Sunday animal bazaar. Combine the two on a day trip from Bishkek, or stop through en route to Issyk-Köl if you've got your own transportation.

The friendly **Farm Guesthouse** (📞 (0)555-922933; Podgornaya 27, Rotfront village; incl meals dm 1000som; ❄ 🎧), in Rotfront village south of the Burana Tower, makes a nice escape from the city bustle. Aside from this, options are generally better back in Bishkek.

Minibuses to Bishkek's Eastern Bus Station (p70) – slow/express 40/60som, around one hour – depart several times per hour from Tokmok's bus station before the main roundabout. Taxis to Burana Tower charge 500som to 600som round-trip, including time waiting at the site.

◉ Sights

Tokmok Animal Bazaar   MARKET
(Мал Базар; ☺to 10am Sun) `FREE` Herders from the Chuy Valley and beyond gather early on Sunday to sell livestock at this weekly market. Come early, as it's mostly wrapped up by 10am. From the bus station, turn left onto Sultan Ibraimova (Gorky) and just keep heading north – you'll probably be able to follow a trail of sheep the whole way.

Burana Tower   HISTORIC BUILDING
(Башня Бурана; admission 60som, guided tour 10som; ☺9am-6pm summer, to 5pm in winter) Burana is a popular side-trip when driving between Issyk-Köl and Bishkek. In the fields south of Tokmok, the Burana Tower is the 24m-high stump of a huge brick minaret, supposedly 11th-century though what you see dates predominantly from a 1950s Soviet restoration. You can climb it from 9am to 5pm (6pm in summer), or admire the slightly leaning structure with its distant mountain backdrop from a grassy mound to the northwest. This is all that's left of the ancient citadel of Balasagun, founded by the Sogdians and later a capital of the Karakhanids, excavated in the 1970s by Russian archaeologists.

Suusamyr Valley
село Суусамыр

Suusamyr village is equidistant (13km by gravel road) from both Kojomkul and the Bishkek–Osh road. The river to the south and the foothills to the north both make for nice wandering, and in winter residents of the valley are renowned for local teams' prowess at national game *kok boru* (a traditional polo-like game played with a headless goat/sheep/calf carcass).

There's a **homestay** (☏(0)773-415003; Nazirjan 7; incl breakfast & dinner dm 800) in the village, marked 'tourist info' just south of the main road, which is a better option than the several unlovable hotels along the highway. For a rather more immersive experience, join locals looking to boost their immune systems

with daily *kymys* treatment at the **Baytur resort** (☏(0)777-900874, (0)770-900713; www.baytur.kg; dm/half lux/lux 1500/4000/6000som incl meals; ☏).

There are no restaurants in the village itself. Back along the highway, the **Lepota Cafe** (mains 120-300som; ☺10am-8pm) is the best of several similar options. In a pinch, stock up on snacks at the small village shops along the main road.

Cut by the main Bishkek–Osh highway, all major north–south transport runs through the Suusamyr Valley. Getting off the highway and into the three villages to the east is a different story – look for shared taxis from Bishkek's Western Bus Station (p70) or try your luck at hiring a car from the junction. With your own wheels or a hired car, it's also possible to continue past Kyzyl-Oi on the back road into Jumgal and on to Son-Köl.

En route to Kyzyl-Oi it's worth a brief stop in the village of Kojomkul (Кожомкул), named after a local hero who stood 2.3m tall and weighed 165 kilos. Kaba-uulu Kojomkul (1889–1955) remains a legend in these parts, and all the sites of interest in town are centred on his memory. On a hilltop behind the village school is the final resting place of the legend himself, Kojomkul's Mausoleum, while at the foot of the hill is a large silver Soviet-era plinth that was constructed as a memorial. Further down the road is the two-room **Kojomkul Museum** (50som; ☺10am-4pm Mon-Fri), with a collection of Kojomkul's clothing and tools, and a number of media clippings. On the way out of town look for the 1924 Yurt-Shaped Mausoleum, the large inscribed stone (said to weigh 690kg) outside of which was reputedly placed there by Kojomkul single-handedly.

Kyzyl-Oi   Кызыл-Ой
POP 822 / ELEV 1757M

The name Kyzyl-Oi means 'red bowl', though the majestic wide dell it occupies is beautifully burnished in fresh green should you visit in early summer. Idyllically quiet but for birdsong, sighing poplars and rushing river rapids, access from either direction is through a curtain of steep mountain peaks and ridges along the Kökömeren Valley.

CBT Kyzyl-Oi (☏(0)555-417847, English (0)312-464785; Jibek Jolu 20; ☺hours vary), beside the main road in the village centre, can suggest hikes and horse treks such as the six-hour ride up the Char Valley and over the Kumbel Pass to Balik Köl, where

HIKING THE RED ROCKS OF SULUU-TEREK

A small red bridge towards the end of Boom Canyon (en route to Issyk-Köl) leads to the impressive desert landscapes and red-rock cliffs of Suluu-Terek Canyon (Красный мост). Pack lots of water in summer, as it gets quite hot and there's very little shade, but in winter the generally snow-free canyon makes an excellent alternative to a ski day.

Any transportation between Chuy and Issyk-Köl can drop you off here, though it may be slightly harder to find a ride back if minibuses are full.

shepherds graze their flocks in summer, or to the parallel Chon-Tash Valley. Yurtstays might be possible en route, including for the three-day circle route linking the two. Closer to town, cross the bridge beside the road towards Suusamyr for a half-day hike to a nearby waterfall.

There are 12 homestays in Kyzyl-Oi marked with 'Hospitality Kyrgyzstan' signs, including the home of helpful CBT (p77) coordinator Artyk Kulubaev.

Katya's Guesthouse (☑(0)554-771786; Jibek Jolu 4; dm 800som incl breakfast & dinner) has warm pallet beds off a central dining room at the southern end of town, with a nice *tapchan* out back overlooking the river.

The homestay of **Elvira Mamytbekova** (☑(0)553-818807; Jibek Jolu 7; dm 800som incl breakfast), who unusually among rural homestays speaks a fair bit of English, has a decent-sized dining room with helpful maps and info sheets on the wall.

Transport is very thin, with shared taxis leaving a few times weekly to Bishkek via Suusamyr. Hitching or private hire (20som per kilometre through CBT) is the only realistic option for the 45km stretch through attractive canyonlands to Jumgal (p104), but for a hired car you'll probably need to pay for the empty return journey as well.

NORTHERN KYRGYZSTAN: TALAS OBLAST
ТАЛАССКАЯ ОБЛАСТЬ

☑ 3422 / POP 219,615 / ELEV 1364M

Kyrgyzstan's north, more Russified than the south, still shows the benefits of the greater Soviet presence. Infrastructure is better, economic prospects more promising, and links with the rest of the world stronger. Tourists traditionally spend most of their time in the north, where relaxing on the beaches of Issyk-Köl's north shore or trekking the mountains of southern Issyk-Köl and Naryn.

Talas *oblast* may be most famous locally for the monument to Kyrgyz hero Manas and the white beans that are exported en masse to Turkey, but visiting travellers come for national parks and remote petroglyphs that are still far off the beaten tourist trail. For visitors headed to or from Kazakhstan, it also makes an excellent crossing point that obviates the need for doubling back to Bishkek.

The major draw of Talas, at least for domestic tourists, is the **Manas Ordo Cultural Complex** (Manas, Tash Aryk village; adult/child 200/100som; ⊙9am-8pm), 12km east of Talas city. Built in 1995, heralded as the 1000-year anniversary of the Manas epic, it celebrates the life and death of the great leader. A visit is equally worthwhile for a look at the Karakhanid-era mausoleum (reputedly that of the hero himself) or a walk up the hill behind the museum for views over the complex and valley.

CBT Talas (☑(0)772-643466, (0)342-252919; cbt_talas@list.ru; Kaimov 76) can coordinate horses (800som per day) and guides (1200som per day including horse) for trips to petroglyphs, lakes and national parks across Talas *oblast*. Perhaps the most interesting is a visit to the **Tuyuk-Tör Petroglyphs** (Köpurö-bazar) and Köl-Tör lake before continuing across the mountains to the Kara-Balta valley in Chuy. Another popular option is the hike into **Besh-Tash National Park** (Kozuchak village; 220som), staying in yurts en route (850som including breakfast) with the option to continue across the mountains to Chuchkan or Toktogul.

CBT Talas works with four homestays (800som with breakfast) in Talas city, including that of coordinator Turdubek Ayilchiev, though the basic **Hotel Erlan** (Sarygulov; r 1600som; ☎) is a more central option. There's also a very simple hotel on the ground of Manas Ordo). Enquire at the gate.

Even in Talas city, dining options are quite limited. If you're heading out into the region's villages or rural areas, be sure to stock up in the city's bazaar and markets before leaving. Good options in town are **Cafe Aider** (☑(0)703-965462; Sarygulov; ☺8am-midnight), in an unassuming 2nd-floor cafe a block south of Berdik Baatyr at the corner of Turdalieva, or **Coffee** (☑(0)703-231414; ☺8.30am-midnight; 🛜) for coffee (respectable) and cakes (somewhat lacklustre) with fast wi-fi. It's on Sarygulov between Berdike Baatyr and the bazaar. To stock up on supplies for camping or self-catering, look for **Iziom Market** (Myrzalieva 44; ☺24hr) one block west of Coffee.

Several banks clustered around the intersection of Berdike Baatyr and Sarygulov have 24-hour ATMs, including **RSK** (Berdike Baatyr 198; ☺8am-noon & 1-8.30pm Mon-Fri, 9am-1pm & 2-7.30pm Sat-Sun).

ⓘ Getting There & Away

Marshrutkas and shared taxis depart from Talas' **bus station** (Chingiz Aitmatov) to the west of the centre.

Some prices and travel options include the following:

Besh-Tash National Park Hire taxi (2500som return, two hours)

Bishkek Marshrutka/shared taxi (500/600som, six hours)

Köpürö-bazar Shared taxi (100som, 1½ hours)

Osh Shared taxi (1500som, 10 hours)

Taraz, Kazakhstan Shared taxi (300som, 2½ hours)

Toktogul Shared taxi (500som, three hours)

NORTHERN KYRGYZSTAN: ISSYK-KÖL OBLAST
ОЗЕРО ИССЫК-КУЛЬ

Over 170km long and 70km across, Lake Issyk-Köl (Ysyk-Köl, Issyk-Kul) is the world's second-largest alpine lake. The name, meaning 'hot lake', comes from a combination of extreme depth, thermal activity and mild salinity, which ensure the lake never freezes even in the fierce Central Asian winters – despite lying at an altitude of over 1600m. Visitors who swim in the vivid blue waters find views framed not by palms but by the remarkable backdrop of the snow-dappled Ala-Too mountains.

Indeed, while beach 'resorts' attract Kazakh visitors and can make for amusingly discordant photos, the main attraction for Western travellers tends to be the accessible mountain hiking. The central Tian Shan range accessible from the lake settlements comprises some of the finest trekking in Central Asia, with the best routes hopping between the spectacular valleys stretching from the Kazakh border near Jyrgalan past Karakol and on along the southern shore.

The lake level has periodically risen and fallen over the centuries, inundating ancient shoreline settlements. Artefacts have been recovered from what is now known as the submerged city of Chigu at the lake's eastern end, dating from the 2nd century BC. The Mikhaylovka inlet near Karakol also reveals the remains of a partly submerged village, though in the last 500 years geological evidence suggests that water levels have been dropping, albeit only around 2m overall.

Before the Kyrgyz people arrived in the 10th to 15th centuries, this area appears to have been a centre of Saka (Scythian) civilisation. Legend has it that Timur

---

CYCLING BISHKEK TO ISSYK-KÖL

The new Bishkek–Balykchy highway bypasses Kant, Tokmok and Kemin. Cyclists are advised to take the old road, but will still face the heavy traffic and headwinds of the eroded Boom Valley (Boömskoe Ushile, Shoestring Gorge). Leading away from the main road in the Boom Valley is a series of wind-eroded sandstone towers and pillars in Suluu-Terek Canyon (p78), sometimes known misleadingly as the Aeolian 'Castles'.

Of several other minor attractions that warrant a short detour, the best known is the Burana Tower (p77). Further south are several attractive canyon-valleys, most notably the Kegeti Valley (p75) and the 20m Kegeti Waterfall and turquoise Köl-Tör Lake within, and the beautiful Issyk-Ata Valley's sanatorium (p76) and hiking opportunities.

Lake Issyk-Köl

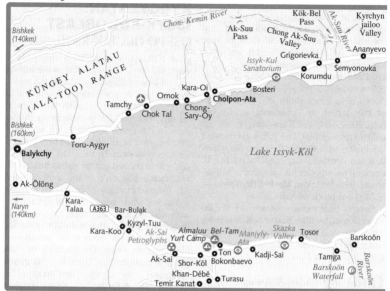

(Tamerlane) later used it as a summer headquarters. There are at least 10 documented settlements currently under the waters of the lake, and treasure hunters have long scoured the lakebed for trinkets, attributing finds to everyone from Christian monks to Chinggis (Genghis) Khan.

In the 1860s and 1870s, after tsarist military officers and explorers had put the lake on Russian maps, immigrants flooded in to found low-rise, laid-back, rough-and-ready towns – the establishment of Karakol in 1869 was followed in the 1870s by Tüp, Teploklyuchenka (now Ak-Suu), Ananyevo, Pokrovka (now Kyzyl-Suu) and a string of others, many of whose Cossack names have stuck. Large numbers of Dungans and Uyghurs arrived in the 1870s and '80s following the suppression of Muslim uprisings in China's Shaanxi, Gansu and Xinjiang provinces. At that time local Kyrgyz and Kazakhs were still mostly nomadic.

In the USSR era health spas were dotted along the lake's shores, but the Issyk-Köl region (along with much of Kyrgyzstan beyond Bishkek), was off limits to foreigners. Locals mention vast, officially sanctioned plantations of opium poppies and cannabis around the lake, though most of these had disappeared under international pressure

by the early 1970s. More importantly, Issyk-Köl was used by the Soviet navy to test high-precision torpedoes, far from prying Western eyes. An entire military-research complex grew around Koy-Sary, on the Mikhaylovka inlet near Karakol. After independence in 1991, Russia's new president, Boris Yeltsin, asked that it be continued but Kyrgyz President Askar Akaev shut down the whole thing.

These days the most secretive thing in the lake is the mysterious *jekai,* a Kyrgyz version of the Loch Ness monster. Jokes about the 'Kyrgyz navy' refer to a fleet of some 40 ageing naval cutters, now mothballed at Koy-Sary (which remains out of bounds to visitors) or decommissioned and hauling goods and tourists up and down the lake. Tourism, which initially crashed along with the Soviet Union, has revived in the last decade thanks to an influx of moneyed Kazakh tourists and Russian athletes, who favour the area's mild climate and high altitude as a winter-training zone.

Issyk-Köl Northern Shore
Северный берег

Midsummer weekends on Lake Issyk-Köl's Northern Shore see the main road trans-

formed into a veritable tourist conveyor belt, but out of season it remains a quiet, mostly charming drive with mountainscapes rising directly to the north and like apparitions across the lake away to the south. The main tourist centre is Cholpan-Ata (and Bosteri), but laid-back Tamchy is a quieter alternative for those not interested in the party scene.

Well over a hundred hotel complexes are dotted along the northern coast of Issyk-Köl, but that doesn't mean the whole area is one long resort. Indeed, hotels are well spread out, most are rather discreet and visitors are often surprised by the extent to which many of the agricultural villages in between seem to have changed little in recent decades.

Tamchy   Тамчы

3943 / POP 1427

This small lakeside village 35km west of Cholpon-Ata has a pretty beach, which is much quieter than the main tourist centres. Tamchy's appeal to tourists is mostly as a laid-back alternative to Cholpon-Ata, especially handy for a lazy day before or after a flight at the international airport on the outskirts of town. Outside the summer season the whole village is virtually dormant.

The easy-to-spot branch of **CBT** ((0)554-331428; Manas 49; 9am-noon & 1-5pm) on the main road through town has 10 homestays (two of which are within a block of the beach) and can organise hikes and horse treks to Chok-Tal Peak and Köl-Tör lake, and *jailoos* (summer pastures) in the mountains to the north.

Signs all over Tamchy offer rooms for rent (Сдаю комнату) and prices are eminently negotiable, but it's hard to find a cosier atmosphere than the Med-themed vibes at **Caravan Guesthouse** ((0)555-444435; Akeeva 8; r 2400som;).

A string of nearly-identical national cuisine restaurants run the length of the developed beach area.

Getting There & Away

Around 3km east of Tamchy is the **Issyk-Köl International Airport** (IKU; (0)555-939555; Tamchy), which hosts seasonal summer flights. At the time of research flights departed at least weekly for Osh, Almaty, Tashkent, and Novosibirsk, with occasional charters from elsewhere.

By road, Bishkek (250som, 3 hours) to Cholpon-Ata (50som, 30 minutes) marshrutkas will drop off or pick up along the highway in Tamchy.

Cholpon-Ata   Чолпон-Ата

3943 / POP 12,200 / ELEV 1608M

In midsummer Cholpon-Ata awakens from its long off-season slumber to become the epicentre of an improbable northern Issyk-Köl beach scene: by day there are tanning bods, zipping jet skis and ice-cream-licking tots; by night it's open-air cafes, thumping discos and young lovers breaking social mores. Most of the visitors are wealthy Kazakhs and Russians, joined by members of the Bishkek glitterati. That doesn't mean that Cholpon-Ata itself is particularly sophisticated. Most of the swankier resorts are hidden away on exclusive beaches a considerable distance from Cholpon-Ata, with a major cluster 10km east at Bosteri where you'll also find a roller coaster and Kyrgyzstan's biggest **Ferris wheel** (Bosteri; 200som; 9am-midnight). As well as the main beach, a smaller but pleasant public beach lies directly north of the yacht club inlet, behind Hotel Ai-Petri.

For most Westerners the beach scene is of minor interest and travellers generally stop here to glimpse the petroglyphs and organise short-notice horse treks.

The main commercial strip around the post office on Soviet has several exchange booths and Visa ATMs. A MasterCard ATM

Cholpon-Ata

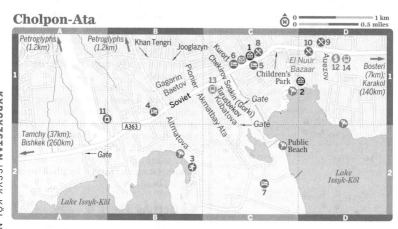

is at **Ayyal Bank** (Soviet; ⊘9am-6pm Mon-Fri) near the Karakol bus stand.

◉ Sights & Activities

North of the centre is an extensive field of glacial boulders, many with pictures scratched or picked into their surfaces. Some of these **petroglyphs** (Saimaluu Tash; Almakuchkov; 80som; ⊘9am-7pm) date from the Bronze Age (about 1500 BC), but most are Saka-Usun (8th century BC to 1st century AD), predating the arrival of Kyrgyz in the area. Saka priests used this sacred site for sacrifices and other rites to the sun god and they lived in the settlements that are currently underwater in the Cholpon-Ata bay.

In town, the **Regional Museum** (Soviet 69; admission/camera 80/50som; ⊘9am-6pm) **FREE** includes copies of locally found Scythian (Saka) gold jewellery and has displays on ethnography, Kyrgyz bards, textiles and underwater archaeology. Minimal English, but plenty of photos.

In a large and somewhat surreal beach-front complex, the curious museum-cum-theme-park **Rukh Ordo** (650som; ⊘9am-8pm) depicts Kyrgyz legends, historical characters, and the interplay of five religions. The setting is quite attractive, though without a guide visitors may be a bit lost as to the significance of it all.

This surprisingly well-curated **Nomad Museum** (www.thenomadmuseum.org; Chon-Sary-Oi village; ⊘10am-5pm Tue-Sun) **FREE** displays artefacts and exhibits on traditional Kyrgyz culture, clothing and history in an airy space that draws inspiration from the yurt. The location is outside of Chon-Sary-Oi

village, 17km west from the Cholpon-Ata bus station, and all west-bound transport can stop here.

In spring, the setting at the **Kruiz Yacht Club** (☑(0)555-271366, (0)3943-43373; boat trip adult/child 300/150som, boat rental per hr 7000-12000som; ⊘boat trips 12.30pm, 3pm, & 5pm Jul-Sep), of moored boats against the snow-capped mountains, makes for a very photogenic scene. In summer, several boats offer 90-minute cruises into the middle of the lake, allowing a 15-minute swim stop in the deepest section. The club also hosts a free, two-cabinet 'museum' and a scuba-diving centre.

Pegasus Horse Trekking, run by the same family who operates the **Pegasus Guest House** (☑(0)772-459901, (0)3943-42450; pegaso @mail.ru; Soviet 81; dm 550som incl breakfast; 🛜), organises horse treks to Ornok Valley and along the lake shore, offers expert instruction for less-confident riders and can arrange multiday excursions to Grigorievka, Kyrchyn and beyond.

🛏 Sleeping & Eating

There are over 100 hotels, resorts and *sanatoria* in Cholpan-Ata and neighbouring settlements, and probably as many local homes rent out rooms. However, if you come outside of the summer season, almost all will be closed. Contrastingly at weekends in July and August virtually everything will be full and you might need to rely on elderly women who appear at the bus station offering *komnaty* (homestay rooms). From Thursday to Saturday in summer, virtually all prices – from taxis to hotels – double. But

Cholpon-Ata

on weekdays outside high season (mid-July to August) you may have the whole place to yourself.

Tourism centres Cholpon-Ata and Bosteri have the widest range of restaurants, and the **bazaar** (Airport 7; ⊙9am-6pm) is a good place to stock up on fruit and veg. Cholpon-Ata is nightlife central for Issyk-Köl's northern-shore summer scene, though the 'in' spots change regularly. Out of season, a bottle from **Supermarket Narodnyy** (Soviet 57; ⊙24hr) or cold beer from U Rybaka may be your only option.

Albatross Hotel   HOTEL $
(☑(0)555-790979, (0)708-790979; Soviet 196; r US$17-25) This laid-back hotel's vibe is just as relaxed as the service, but the rooms are nice and comfy and the larger top-floor rooms are worth paying extra for. The on-site restaurant serves reliably good local and European dishes – but the shashlyk is best avoided.

Apple Hostel   HOSTEL $
(☑(0)553-280881; www.applehostel.kg; Soviet 66; dm US$10; @ 🛜) Directly across from the museum, this dorm-only hostel is a simple but friendly family-run affair associated with the establishment of the same name in Bishkek.

Tri Korony   RESORT $$
(☑(0)555-908643; www.3korony.com; s/d/ste 3200/4600/6300som) Handily central yet away from the main concentration of developments and traffic, this modern 60-room resort has its own stretch of beach and comparatively new facilities. Quoted rates are without board – full board is an additional US$20 per room.

Ak-Jol   CENTRAL ASIAN $
(☑(0)703-190456; Turusbekov; mains 60-200som; ⊙8am-9pm; 🛜) Behind the bus station, this semi-smart if hardly glorious place serves tasty, rapidly prepared local meals plus more exotic *zharovnya* (sizzler) plates.

Barashek   CENTRAL ASIAN $$
(☑(0)3943-42185; barashek_ik@mail.ru; Soviet 57; mains 180-540som; ⊙10am-midnight) The Cholpon-Ata branch of this popular Bishkek restaurant serves up reliable local dishes and hit-or-miss European favourites. It's also one of the few in this summer city that stays open year-round.

U Rybaka   SEAFOOD $$
(☑(0)550-314111; Soviet 20; mains 300-500som; ⊙8.30am-11.30pm Wed-Mon, from 10am Tue; 🛜) As one might expect from a place called 'the fisherman', seafood is the highlight of the menu as this local favourite. Both the ground floor tables and the 2nd-floor terrace get boisterous on summer evenings, but drop by in winter and you may be the only customer around.

Green Pub   RUSSIAN, BBQ $$
(☑(0)555-767373, (0)555-812177; Soviet 112; mains 160-490som; ⊙8.30am-midnight; 🛜) With more atmosphere than most and open year-round, this low-lit, green-decor pub-restaurant with heavy wooden tables and a partially covered summer terrace offers excellent if pricey Russian bar meals including barbecued fish (350som).

ℹ Getting There & Around

Cholpon-Ata, being the premier resort town for comparatively wealthy Kazakhs, is particularly

DON'T MISS

WORLD NOMAD GAMES

Held every two years in even-numbered years, the **World Nomad Games** (http://worldnomadgames.com), and a gathering of global sportsmen competing in traditional nomadic sports is a highlight of the entire region.

Sports competitions are held at the Hippodrome just east of Cholpon-Ata, while cultural events take place at the Kyrchyn *jailoo* in the mountains above the village of Semenovka.

prone to fluctuating transport costs. During summer, shared-taxi prices double for tourists and locals alike. Prices here are low-season rates.

Westbound transport starts from the **Avto-vokzal** (bus station; ☎ (0)3943-43326; Soviet 96; ☉ 24hr) or from the corner of Kubatova at Soviet directly north.

Eastbound transport uses the Karakol bus stand (Soviet).

Frequency and price can vary radically with day and season. In season, buses or minibuses run at least hourly from 6am to 9pm to Bishkek (300som, four hours) and Karakol (150som, three hours). Off-season the choice will be largely limited to Bishkek–Karakol through transport or shared taxis (200som to Karakol; 600som to Bishkek), which you may have to charter outright from mid-afternoon.

Heading further afield, buses leave thrice daily for Almaty (670som) from 7am to 8pm, and head to Omsk (3570som) on Tuesday and Thursday at noon. Tickets can be purchased around the back of the main station.

Marshrutka 304 links Cholpan-Ata to Bosteri (20som), but is also the local bus within town, starting in the MPK estate southwest of the petroglyphs then trundling all the way along Soviet (10som).

Local taxis rarely charge less than 150som.

Kyrchyn Valley   Кырчын

A wide mountain pasture at the conflux of three valleys 15km north of Semenovka village, Kyrchyn *jailoo* (summer pasture) is an excellent base for day hikes or horse treks into the surrounding mountains. There's a 100som fee to enter the valley, which in theory goes towards conservation activities.

During the biennial World Nomad Games, the otherwise quiet pasture comes alive as a massive ethno-village of over one hundred yurts pops up here for a week to provide cultural attractions and touristic services to visitors.

Several small yurt-camps provide accommodation for visitors, with **Hamlet** (Kyrchyn jailoo; dm 300som incl breakfast) the notable standout.

Public transportation only goes as far as the town of Semenovka (Семёновка), from which a taxi may be possible to arrange for around 700som. More reliably, cars from the nearby village of Ananyevo (Ананьево) or Cholpon-Ata will take visitors from 1000/1200som per vehicle.

Karkyra Valley   Ущелье Каркыра

Rich pastures fill the immense, silent Karkyra ('black crane') Valley that straddles the Kyrgyzstan–Kazakhstan border. Attractions include the eponymous migratory birds that stop here in June and again from August to September, as well as a large stone monument known as San-Tash. As the story goes, en route to an invasion of China the conqueror Timur (Tamerlane) instructed his soldiers to each place one stone from Issyk-Köl into the mound. Upon returning victorious from the battle, each soldier again removed one stone; and by this device Timur estimated his battle losses.

There are no formal accommodation options in the Karkyra Valley, but in a pinch it may be possible to arrange a homestay or set up a tent.

The Karkyra Valley stretches about 60km east of Tüp or is accessible via 80km of much prettier (but rougher) road from Karakol via Novovoznesenovka just before the turn to Jyrgalan. On the Tüp route a round trip by taxi from Karakol is about 1800som return. Ask for *pamyatnik San-Tash* (San-Tash Monument), located 20km from the **Karkara border crossing** (☉ 8am-6pm) into Kazakhstan.

A derelict marshrutka (100som, 1.15pm) runs from Karakol's Ak-Tilek Bazaar (p92) to Sary-Mogol village (15km short of the Kazakh border) via Tüp and the San-Tash stones. It returns the following morning. If you're driving or biking, the signed turn-off to Karkyra from the Issyk-Köl road is beside the Gazprom petrol station 2km northwest of Tüp. The attractive A363 heads northwest to the border with Kazakhstan around 60km further on. A car from Karakol to the border (or vice versa) is possible to negotiate from 2000som to 3000som, and more from travel agencies.

Karakol   Каракол

🚩 3922 / POP 71,500 / ELEV 1745M

A shady grid of tree-lined streets, Karakol has limited sights but lots of activities, and is a good base from which to access some of Central Asia's best skiing and most gloriously accessible alpine trekking. The town offers clear-day backdrops of snowy peaks contrasted against the old blue shutters and whitewashed walls of some remnant antique colonial-period houses. These recall the town's Russian-era heyday.

History

After a military garrison was established at nearby Teploklyuchenka (Ak-Suu) in 1864, the garrison commander was told to scout out a place for a full-sized town. Karakol was founded on 1 July 1869, with streets laid out in a European-style chequerboard, and the garrison was relocated here. The town's early population had a high proportion of military officers, merchants, professionals and explorers.

The Bolsheviks trashed the town's religious buildings, destroying eight of its nine mosques and turning the Orthodox cathedral into a club, but remnants of this history remain for those who care to search.

Great Gamer

Karakol was called Przhevalsk in Soviet times, after the explorer Nikolai Przhevalsky, whose last expedition ended here, and who is buried on the lakeshore at nearby Pristan. Born in Smolensk on 12 April 1839, Przhevalsky joined the Imperial army but was reputedly unhappy as a young officer. However, he persuaded them that he'd make a better explorer and set off to explore the Ussuri River region in the Russian Far East from 1867 to 1869. Funding proved insufficient but, undeterred, Przhevalsky managed to cover the costs by raising 12,000 roubles in a poker match. The results of the expedition impressed everyone. The Russian Geographical Society agreed to help finance future trips, and the army gave him the time he needed in return for debriefing him on his return from each trip making him, in effect, an army agent.

He never married, going on instead to become a major general and the most honoured of all the tsarist explorers. He focused on Central Asia, launching four major expeditions in 15 years, mainly to Mongolia, Xin-jiang and Tibet. On one of his journeys, he discovered the tiny steppe-land horse that now bears his name (in the original Polish) – Przewalski's horse.

During 1888, while preparing for the last of these trips, Przhevalsky unwisely drank the Chuy River water while hunting tigers near Bishkek (then Pishpek). The result was a bout of typhus. He was bundled off to Lake Issyk-Köl for rest and treatment, but realising his imminent demise he wrote to the tsar asking to be buried beside the lake, clothed in full explorer's dress. His gravesite at Pristan is now home to a Przhevalsky Memorial Museum (p89).

KYRGYZSTAN KARAKOL

⊙ Sights & Activities

Karakol's nicest green spaces are great places to while away low-intensity days between treks, with the brand-new **Karakol River Park** (Karakol River; ⊙24hr; minibus 110, 111) FREE among the most pleasant.

Also attactive is the city's **Victory Park** (Karasayeva St, cnr Abdrakhmanova; ⊙24hr), which in addition to the standard Victory statue memorialising the end of WWII also includes an interesting monument to the victims of Stalinist repression (to the right upon entering the park) and one of the most poignant memorials to the Great *Urkun* (exodus; see p127) anywhere in the country (further in behind Victory).

For a more active approach to exploring the city, several initiatives run by the Destination Karakol (p90) information office offer excellent insight into local culture. The easy standout is the Dungan Family Dinner (p87), but the tip-based **Free City Walking Tour** (⊙9.30-11am Tue, Thu & Sat) and relaxing **Sunset Yacht Cruise** (1200som; ⊙6.30-8.30pm Wed, Fri & Sat) are worthwhile options to consider as well. Drop by their office next to Fat Cat Cafe (p89) to discuss options and tour timings.

Early on Sunday mornings one of Kyrgyzstan's biggest **animal markets** (Mal Bazaar, Skotski Bazaar; Udilova; ⊙3am-10am Sun) takes place around 2km north of central Karakol. Typical of such markets, you'll observe locals bargaining over thoroughbred horses or improbably bundling voluptuous fat-tailed sheep into the back seats of Lada cars. On clear days the backdrop of white-topped mountains is more striking from here than from the town centre. Across the street, a car market keeps similar hours.

Karakol

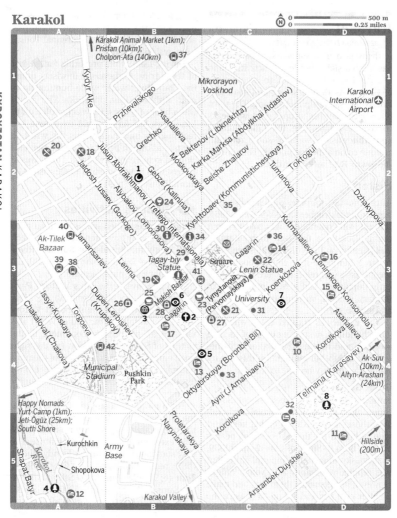

Dungan Mosque
MOSQUE

(cnr Bektenov & Jusup Abdrakhmanov; 20som; ⊙8am-6pm) A tip-tilted triple roof, carved-layered eaves and wooden exterior pillars give this colourful 1910 mosque the look of a Chinese Buddhist temple. Remarkably it survived the early Bolshevik era, which saw the town's other eight mosques destroyed, though it was closed for worship between 1933 and 1943.

Holy Trinity Cathedral
CATHEDRAL

(Gagarin 16; ⊙8am-5pm) Set peacefully amid trees, this hefty wooden structure is topped with green-roofed towers and almost-golden onion domes. The 1872 stone original was destroyed by an 1890 earthquake. Built on the same foundations a new wooden version, finished in 1895, was turned into a club by the Bolsheviks who also removed its five onion domes in the 1930s. Serious reconstruction began in 1961, but church services only recommenced after 1991. Women need to wear a headscarf to enter.

Karakol History Museum
MUSEUM

(☏(0)3922-53268, (0)552-669623; Jamansariev 164; admission/camera 70/30som; ⊙9am-5pm Mon-Fri, 10am-4pm Sat & Sun) Occupying an

Karakol

archetypal 1887 Russian house, this museum has a few Scythian bronze artefacts, local tools and musical instruments. Taxidermists' victims share a room with exhibits celebrating the Kumtor Gold Mine. Little is in English except for the remarkable section exhibiting the photography of Swiss explorer Ella Maillart, who came this way in 1932.

★ **Dungan Family Dinner** FOOD
(☑ (0)558-508808; bookingdmo1@gmail.com; Yrdyk village; 1400som; ⊗ 5.30-8.30pm) Join Destination Karakol (p90) to experience the culture of Kyrgyzstan's Dungan community, Chinese Muslims who fled to Kyrgyzstan in 1877 to escape oppression, in the minority village of Yrdyk (15 minutes from Karakol). Visit the local mosque and museum before trying your hand at making *ashlyanfu*, the Dungan's most famous dish, and feasting on a table of traditional local foods.

SkyTrial Paragliding PARAGLIDING
(☑ (0)555-434753; troffs@mail.ru) Soar above the Ak-Suu Valley with reputable paragliding operator Sergey, who launches near the

village of Ak-Suu in summer (1200som) and from the Karakol Ski Resort on longer winter flights (3000som plus ski lift tickets).

⌂ Sleeping

Karakol has exploded with new accommodation, from honest-to-goodness hostels and backpacker digs to midrange boutique hotels and even a touch of luxury. Between them Destination Karakol (p90), CBT (p90) and TIC (p90) can suggest around 50 homestays, guesthouses and hotels. Most homestays start from 600som per person including breakfast.

★ **Teskey Guesthouse** HOMESTAY $
(☑ (0)772-801411, (0)3922-57726; http://teskeytravel.com/; Asanalieva 44; s/d 1000/1600 with shared bath; ❄ ☎) On a quiet, unpaved backstreet, Teskey's great plus is its knowledgeable, ever-obliging, English-speaking host Talaai. The brand-new guesthouse has super views from the top floor over the large garden, though note that all rooms here have shared baths. A 'family horse tour' day trip is offered to a panorama over the lake

shore west of Karakol, using Talaai's family's horses.

Laundry service is available and they rent out two Giant-brand mountain bikes (US$10 per day, no lock).

Duet Hostel HOSTEL $
(☑(0)707-703828; https://duetkarakol.wordpress.com; Karasayev 150; dm 400som; ✴☎) Though it's tiny – just one 12-bed dorm – this modern hostel space could just as easily be in Krakow or Kiev as Karakol. Lockers, bed curtains, plenty of plugs, and a coffee shop just next door. Book online for a 5% discount.

Tulpar Guesthouse GUESTHOUSE $
(☑(0)559-065510, (0)709-398141; Kutmanalieva 114; s/d 700/1400som; ☎) It's certainly simple, but for some of the cheapest private rooms in town it's hard to beat the value of this clean new guesthouse.

Jamilya's B&B HOMESTAY $
(☑(0)3922-41718, English (0)554-980980, French (0)555-208282; http://hotelkarakol.kg; Shopokova 34B; r with shared bath 800som, en suite 1000som; ☎) The mother-and-son team here both speak excellent English, the daughter French; and they offer 10 rooms with spotless bathrooms, hot showers and sit-down toilets. Public spaces include a lounge, dining room, lovely garden and shared balcony looking towards the Karakol River Park (p85) just steps away.

Yak Tours Hostel HOSTEL $
(☑(0)3922-56901; yaktours@mail.ru; Gagarin 10; s/d 350/700som; ℗) Like stepping into your great-aunt's summer house, rooms here are old-world creations that ramble on for days.

COLONIAL BUILDINGS IN KARAKOL

The older part of town sprawls southwest from the cathedral with numerous simple but archetypal 'gingerbread' timber houses. A few are comparatively grand former homes of Russian merchants and industrialists, including what's now the **Pedagogical College** (Gagarin 15) on Gagarin, opposite the cathedral, the **Radio & TV Office** (Gebze 114) on Gebze (Kalinina) and another old merchant's home at the corner of Koenközova and Lenina.

Decoration with framed embroidery and painted trunks adds to the joy. The solitary bathroom suffers from an ever-running toilet and a water heater that's rarely turned on, but rooms remain a great deal and this is a good place to meet other travellers.

So-named because they once ran yak-riding tours into the mountains, more mainstream options can still be arranged on request by the in-house tour agency.

Happy Nomads Yurt-Camp YURT $$
(☑(0)556-521138, (0)770-521138; www.happynomads.info; Elebaev, cnr Toktogul; dm 1000som; ☉Mar-Nov) These yurts, with heated floors electricity in the middle of a manicured garden, are some of the most comfortable around. The English-speaking family that runs the place is great, though the 2.5km distance from the centre will be off-putting for some.

Hillside BOUTIQUE HOTEL $$
(☑(0)3922-50286, (0)555-201332; www.hillside.kg; Salieva 152; d/tr/ste US$52/66/87) Wood-panelled hallways and bright modern rooms make this family property hidden in the southern residential area of Karakol a hit, especially the large family suite with a balcony overlooking the mountains to the southeast of town. English-speaking owner Ahmet is full of energy and enthusiasm.

KBH HOSTEL $$
(☑(0)3922-51985, (0)550-998801; karakolbasedhostel@gmail.com; Koenkozova 24; dm/r 450/1100som; ✴☎) Spacious dorms, a large well-stocked kitchen, bright and spotless bathrooms, and a large outdoor common area all point to this as one of the best hostels around.

Interhouse Hostel HOSTEL $$
(☑(0)700-446176; www.interhouse.life; Salieva 119; dm/d incl breakfast US$8/27) A branch of the popular Bishkek-based chain, expect the same high standards and clean rooms here. Dorms and private rooms are bright and comfortable, the kitchen is open to guests, and best of all there's a sauna on-site for those post-hike aches and pains.

Hotel Amir HOTEL $$
(☑(0)3922-51315; www.hotelamir.kg; Ayni 78; s/d US$50/63, basement US$45/58; ℗✴@☎) Cheerful rooms have a 1970s retro vibe and there are brilliant *ala-kiyiz* wall hangings throughout, including a Picasso-like masterpiece behind reception. Downstairs rooms

OFF THE BEATEN TRACK

PRISTAN PRZHEVALSK

Karakol's port and beach is around 12km north at Pristan, a long stretch of sand backed by *datchas* (weekend cottages) above which rise a couple of Soviet-era cranes. The sand is decent, but the water not especially clear.

The main attraction of the shrine-like Przhevalsky memorial garden is the small, well-presented **Przhevalsky Memorial Museum** (Pristan; admission 70som, guided tour 70som; ⊙ 9am-5pm), dedicated to Nikolai Przhevalsky, the Russian explorer who died here in 1888 and for whom Karakol was previously named. Entered through a Neo-Grec portal, there's a giant map of his Tibet and Central Asia travels behind a big globe. Many exhibits have English captions, but for an over-arching explanation of his life you'll really need the guide (who speaks good German but no English).

have less light but are discounted. There's a power generator for electricity blackouts.

Tagaytay HOTEL **$$**
(📞(0)3922-52161; Tynystanov 29A; s/d 2200/3500som; 🍴🛜) New and central, the Tagaytay's finest feature is the ceiling-less communal lounge with attractive artwork, saddle-display and real fire. However, noise from here can reverberate, disturbing light-sleeping guests. Rooms could be a little larger but are brought to life with vivid traditionally patterned duvets. Free wi-fi.

🍴 Eating & Drinking

Karakol's food scene is defined by the many ethnic communities that call the Ak-Suu region home, from Dungan and Tatar to Kyrgyz and Russian. Eat well yourself, or even take a **Karakol Food Crawl** (500som per person) with Destination Karakol (p90) to learn these communities' histories first-hand. The Dungan snack-meal *ashlyanfu* (cold, gelatine noodles in a spicy-vinegary sauce) is a local favourite, sold for a few som at the Ak-Tilek Bazaar and at many local dives for 30som a bowl.

★**Ashlyan-Fuu** CENTRAL ASIAN **$**
(Jusaev; mains 50som; ⊙ 8am-4pm) When the people of Karakol go for *ashlyanfu*, this tin-roofed shack off Jusaev is where they go. It's the best in the city, therefore perhaps the best in the whole world. There's no menu, just bowls of *ashlyanfu* and fried *pirozhki* bread, and one of each is 50som.

Expect lines, and don't show up too late as they close when the day's ingredients run out.

Zarina CENTRAL ASIAN **$**
(📞(0)778-877777, (0)3922-59939; Lenina, cnr Toktogul; mains 110-350som; ⊙ 9am-11pm; 🛜📶)

A wood-panelled dining room and log-cabin feel sit just fine with the particularly good *laghman* and shashlyk. Beer lovers should order the salted fish, an excellent accompaniment.

Caravan Cafe CENTRAL ASIAN, CHINESE **$**
(📞(0)553-775112, (0)3922-50737; Toktogul; mains 85-350som; ⊙ 9am-11pm; 🛜📶) A wide menu of Kyrgyz, Russian and Chinese dishes in an arabesque-styled dining room overlooking the main drag. Food is of a reliably high quality, and there's more atmosphere here than most places.

Kochevnik Cafe CENTRAL ASIAN **$**
(📞(0)3922-51905; Alybakova; mains 130-270som; ⊙ 10am-midnight) As you might expect from a name like 'Nomad', it's heavy on Kyrgyz cuisine and the *kuurdak* (fried meat, onion and potato) is particularly good.

Dastorkon CENTRAL ASIAN **$$**
(📞(0)555-400270,(0)3922-31120;www.dastorkon-cafe.kg; Przhevalsk 107; mains 160-370som; ⊙ 11am-midnight; 🛜📶📶) Local and western dishes, including hard-to-find meats like horse and yak. Service is quite good and excellent English is spoken, making it a popular stop for travellers and locals alike.

Lovely Pizza PIZZA **$$**
(📞(0)3922-57640, (0)553-597555; Tynystanov 125; mains 130-430som; ⊙ 10am-midnight; 🛜📶) Karakol's best pan-pizza is served in a slightly scrappy summer yard or in the small, oh-so-pink cocktail bar area with its pearl-effect settee seating. *Kalyan* (water-pipes) to smoke from 250som.

★**Fat Cat Cafe** CAFE
(📞(0)777-066603; www.facebook.com/Fat-CatKarakol; Gagarin 22; ⊙ 8am-midnight Mon-Sat, from 9am Sun; 🛜) Quality coffee and

desserts, a menu of Western dishes, speciality beers and even cocktails here are the stuff of whispered longings for travellers in the rural regions of Kyrgyzstan. What they don't always mention is that owner Jamiliya also dedicates part of the cafe's profits to social enterprises around Karakol. They can get busy, but it's worth the wait.

Karakol Coffee   COFFEE
(☑ (0)552-876321; www.facebook.com/karakol coffee; Toktogul 112a; ☺ 9am-10pm; 🛜) Karakol's first barista-savvy venue still makes well-brewed coffee and a range of sweets, breakfast and sandwiches while serving as an informal traveller hub. English spoken.

Green Club   PUB
(☑ (0)559-909988; Abdrakhmanova, cnr Karl Marx; ☺ 3pm-3am) Have a beer downstairs or rent a private billiards room (200som per hour) upstairs at one of the few places that passes for a nightlife spot in Karakol.

🛍 Shopping

Pick up souvenirs at the **Kork Art Gallery** (☑ (0)555-150761, (0)707-464623; Lenina 152, Makish Bazaar; ☺ 9am-8pm) womens' collective or the NGO-supported **One Village One Product** (OVOP; ☑ (0)3922-54357; ovop. kyrgyzstan@gmail.com; Toktogul St; ☺ 9am-7pm) initiative, which also carries delicious jam and apricot juices from Jeti-Ögüz.

More offbeat, the Soviet-era products for sale at the small corner **Antique Shop** (☑ (0)772-102727; Toktogul 249; ☺ 10am-5pm) come with a history that far outweighs their size or price and owner Alexander seems to know the stories of absolutely everything in the store.

ℹ Information

There are several money changers and banks along Toktogul, especially surrounding the intersection with Gebze, including banks with ATMs.

Mail home postcards from the main **post office** (☑ (0)3922-722200; Gebze 124; ☺ 8am-noon & 1-5pm Mon-Fri, 9am-1pm Sat) on Gebze.

A string of clinics along Abdrakhmonov past CBT attends to various ailments, but take a Russian-speaker.

TOURIST INFORMATION & TRAVEL AGENCIES
Destination Karakol (☑ (0)558-508808; www. destinationkarakol.com; Gagarin 22; ☺ 9am-8pm Mon-Fri & weekends in summer) offers

unbiased advice on where to stay, what to do, and who to work with in Karakol; as does **TIC** (Tourist Information Centre; ☑ (0)3922-52341; tourinfocentre@gmail.com; Abdrakhmanov 130; ☺ 9am-5pm Mon-Fri, 9am-2pm Sat).

Karakol's many travel and tour agencies organise a wide range of outdoor activities including trekking, horse riding, skiing, mountaineering and mountain biking.

For extensive outdoor activities contact the following:

Arashan (☑ (0)551-136040; Jusaev 148; ☺ 9am-6pm) Sells outdoor equipment and rents winter-sports gear, though no guiding services are on offer.

Bulak-Say (☑ (0)555-264166, (0)3922-60195; apievalmaz@rambler.ru; Toktogul, cnr Abdrakhmanova; ☺ 9am-6pm Mon-Fri) Organises some of the most reliable horse trekking in the Ak-Suu region. Be sure to confirm all details in writing, however, as price breakdowns don't include line-by-line info.

CBT Karakol (☑ (0)3922-55000, (0)555-150795; cbtkarakol@gmail.com; Abdrakhmanov 123; ☺ 9am-5pm Mon-Fri, to 3pm Sat) A relaxed attitude to customer service but knowlegeable when answering questions on activity, accommodation or trekking options. As well as homestays in town, CBT can organise seasonal yurtstays (from mid-June) along with excursions, guides, equipment and permits.

EcoTrek (Trekking Workers Association; ☑ (0)709-511155, (0)3922-51115; www.ecotrek. kg; Abdrakhmanova 116; ☺ 9am-12.30pm & 1.30pm-5pm Mon-Sat) Guided treks, horse trips, biking and skiing. Equipment rental available.

Extreme Tour (☑ (0)772-517364, (0)3922-59486; khanin2003@mail.ru; Karasayeva 154; ☺ 8am-8pm) In Karakol's best-equipped mountaineering-equipment shop, this professional company offers a range of treks, serious climbs and transfers. Contact Igor.

Kyrgyz Tour (Issyk-Köl Guides & Porters Association; ☑ (0)3922-52929, Aigul 0552-552529; www.kyrgyz-tours.info; Lenina 130/1; ☺ 8am-8pm) A cooperative of young guides can arrange treks with English, French or German interpreters and five-day mountain-biking trips to Barskoön (bring your own bike).

Turkestan Tours (☑ (0)543-911451; www. turkestan.biz; Toktogul 273; ☺ 8am-6pm) Specialises in group trekking, has an 'indestructible' Ural 6WD truck-bus and is the local agent for helicopter flights (US$400) to the Inylchek base camps.

Visit Karakol (☑ (0)772-150951, (0)551-451515; www.visitkarakol.com; Gagarin 28; ☺ 9am-5pm Mon-Sat) Offers a range of trekking and outdoor programs.

TREKKING AROUND KARAKOL

For a half-day or full-day trek out of Karakol the Jolgolot Viewpoint is comparatively high payoff with comparatively little effort. Hike the hour or two up from the village of Jolgolot (a suburb of Karakol) to take in stunning views of the city and Issyk-Köl to the north and the Karakol Valley to the south. Return the same way, or loop through the lush Ak-Suu Arboretum to catch a marshrutka back from Ak-Suu village.

For more extensive hikes, get out into Ak-Suu region (p92). Karakol has no shortage of tour operators that can arrange guides, horses, porters, equipment or anything else you need.

🛈 Getting There & Away

AIR

Though **Karakol International Airport** (🖉 (0)3922-51359; Tokgotul 305a) was out of operation at the time of writing, rumours say it may reopen to domestic and international flights as early as 2019.

BUS

Use the Main Bus Station for Bishkek or Almaty, the Southern Bus Stand for towns along the south side of Issyk-Köl. Marshrutka services from either station run to Balykchy, where passengers for Naryn and Kochkor usually need to change. For destinations in the Ak-Suu region surrounding Karakol, services leave from various points around Ak-Tilek bazaar.

Main Bus Station

In addition to the scheduled services from the **main bus station** (🖉 (0)3922-22911; Przhevalsk; 🚌 110, 111), untimetabled minibuses and shared taxis leave from outside the station when full to Bishkek (shared taxi 600som) and Cholpon-Ata (shared taxi 200som).

DESTINATION	FARE (SOM)	FREQUENCY	DURATION (HR)
Almaty, Kazakhstan (via Bishkek)	750	4pm	11
Balykchy (via North Shore)	178	16 daily (7am-2pm)	3
Bishkek (via North Shore)	322	11 daily (8am-6pm)	5
Bishkek (via South Shore)	322	11 daily (7am-6pm)	6
Bokonbaevo	107	2.20pm, 3.10pm	2
Cholpon-Ata	111	12 daily (7.30am-6pm)	2½
Naryn	450	8.30am	6

Southern Bus Stand

Buses for the southern shore of Issyk-Köl depart from the **Southern Bus Stand** (🖉 (0)3922-51353; Toktogul), as do shared taxis for the same destinations.

DESTINATION	FARE (SOM)	DEPARTURE	DURATION (HR)
Balykchy (via South Shore)	178	7.50am, 8.50am, 9.50am, 10.50am	4
Barskoön	67	9.50am, noon, 2pm, 3pm, 5pm	1¼
Bishkek (via South Shore)	322	7.50am, 8.50am, 9.50am, 10am	6
Bokonbaevo	107	1.10pm, 3.10pm, 4.10pm, 5.10pm	2
Tamga	68	1pm, 3pm	1½

Ak-Tilek Bazaar Area

Most regional buses leave from one of three points around Ak-Tilek Bazaar. Shared taxis use the same points.

Ak-Suu Region For villages along the Ak-Suu highway, many of which are trailheads for local hikes, marshrutka 383 stops on the highway near Jergez (30som, 30 minutes) and Boz-Uchuk (40som, 45 minutes) from Ak-Tilek bazaar's Ak-Suu bus stand.

Ak-Suu Village Marshrutka 350 (30som plus 20som per piece of luggage, several per hour) from the southeast side's Ak-Suu stand.

Jeti-Ögüz Marshrutka 371 to Jeti-Ögüz village runs roughly hourly when full (60som, 30 minutes) but rarely before 10am. Marshrutka 355 to Jeti-Ögüz Korort (100som, 45 minutes) departs several times weekly on an unscheduled service, typically late morning and possibly mid-afternoon. A shared taxi from the village to the resort should charge 60som.

Jyrgalan Minibus 331 (80som, 1¾ hours) departs thrice daily (8.30am, 11.30am and 4.30pm). They're generally labeled *Shakta*, by which the village is often still known, departing from the Ak-Suu stand.

Karkara and Tüp area Rickety marshrutkas leave once daily (200som, two hours) at 1pm for the Karkara Valley via Tüp and the San-Tash stones. They're generally signed as 'Sary-Tologoy', where the service terminates about 35km before the Kazakh border. Some marshrutka drivers can be convinced to continue to the border for an additional 250som per person. A taxi to the border should be between 2000som and 3000som. It's also possible to head to Tüp on the 120 (30som, one hour) and try to transfer to a taxi there.

Pristan Minibuses marked Plazh or Dachy (which has the longer stretch of beach) leave roughly half-hourly from near the corner of Gagarin and Alybakova from 6am to 6pm, and pass within 200m of the Przhevalsky Garden (p89).

❶ Getting Around

BICYCLE

Teskey Guesthouse (p87) and Ecotrek (p90) both have a couple of mountain bikes for rent (US$10 per day), and Destination Karakol (p90) can advise on the best routes both within the city and in the foothills beyond.

MINIBUS

Almost all of the dozen lines pass Ak-Tilek Bazaar on Torgoeva. Useful routes (10som, from 7am to dusk) include:

101 Torgoeva–Toktogul–Jaldosh Jusaev (Gorkogo) then southwest on Karasayev and down Fuchika almost to the gates of the national park. Same in reverse.

102 Northwest down Gebze, Toktogul, Torgoeva then a one-way loop passing the animal market northbound.

105 Starts from Ak-Tilek Bazaar and down Toktogul to the suburb of Jolgolot (for the walk up to Jolgolot Viewpoint).

111 Loops from the Main Bus Station via Ak-Tilek Bazaar, the Southern Bus Stand, Madanur Hotel and the Karakol River Park then round the south edge of town and back via Kutmanalieva.

110 Route 111 in reverse.

TAXI

For trips within town, taxis including Alfa Taxi charge 70som (but add extra for stops). Going further afield, be sure to fix the fare and waiting time (100som per hour is normal). It's best to call for a taxi. There are several taxi stations dotted about town, or wave one down on Toktogul near Makish Bazaar. Ak-Tilek Bazaar tends to be better for longer-distance shared taxis.

Ak-Suu Region
Район Ак-Суу

The Ak-Suu region is one of the best places in the country to launch yourself into the

---

HIKING IN AK-SUU

The Terskey Ala-Too range that rises behind Karakol offers a fine taste of the Tian Shan. Of the numerous possible routes that climb to passes below 4000m, the most popular is the two-day route to alpine lake Ala-Köl.

Stretching from Jyrgalan in the east to Jeti-Ögüz in the west (and onwards to the southern shore), the most impressive valleys include the following:

Tyup Directly parallel to the east of Jyrgalan Valley, this wide valley leads south to the Kara-Kyya Pass and on to the settlement of Echkili-Tash 58km away, or beyond to the beautiful Sary-Jaz valley (the latter both require border permits).

Jyrgalan Circle from the village and back along the 65km Kesenkija Loop Trail, past Eki-Chat yurt-camp and the Ailampa lakes, or south at Eki-Chat up the Terim-Tör Bulak valley for several small lakes and a two-pass day through Tiorgei Ak-Suu and on to Boz-Uchuk.

Boz-Uchuk Two small but astounding lakes crown a plateau at the south of the valley, with a pass connecting to Jyrgalan in the east and Jergez in the west.

Jergez Visit Köl-Tör Lake (p95) as a long day trip, or push all the way to the south of the valley for a smattering of small lakes as the path climbs west to the Aylanysh Pass and on to Ak-Suu.

Ak-Suu Though short, the Ak-Suu valley makes an attractive alternative route to or from Altyn-Arashan or as a connection to Jergez.

hills and mountains of the Tian Shan. With so many trekking opportunities and a concentration of well-informed travel agencies, there is no good reason not to. Using Karakol as a base, hike up to remote mountain lakes or down red-rock valleys with views out over Issyk-Köl far below.

The trekking season around Karakol normally runs from late June to early October. August is a popular time for picking mushrooms; blackcurrants are in season in September. For Altyn-Arashan, you could go as early as May or as late as the end of October, but nights drop below freezing then and the surrounding mountain passes are snowed over.

Weather is the region's biggest danger, with unexpected chilling storms, especially in May, June, September and October. Streams are in flood in late May and early June; plan crossings for early morning when levels are lowest.

Karakol Valley   Ущелье Каракол

Due south of Karakol lies the beautiful Karakol Valley, a national park for which a 250som entry fee per person and 50som per vehicle is collected from foreigners at the gate. The valley offers some fine hikes, although you really need to invest in a tent, stove and a day or more of hiking before the area reveals its charm. Push in far enough, though, and there's fantastic trekking or

challenging climbing – and plenty of peaks left unconquered.

Traditionally viewed as a summer playground, the Ak-Suu region has become popular in recent years for winter sports as well. **Karakol Ski Resort** (☑(0)392-251494, (0)772-534081; www.karakol-ski.kg; lift pass adult/ child 1100/700som, ski & snowboard rental 400-1200som) is without argument the best in the country. It Operates three chairlifts, ending at the 3040m Panorama viewpoint. Together they access over 20km of trails, most of which run through fir woodlands. The ski rental equipment is priced by its age, ranging from 2006 to 2015 gear, but make sure you get any gear back before the 4pm closing time. In summer, it's possible to book a ride on the Panorama lift (for any number of people) for 5000som round-trip.

For many, however, the real draw is getting off-piste and into the backcountry in areas like Jergez Valley and Jyrgalan, both of which have some limited infrastructure to cater to adventure-seeking winter visitors.

Up the main valley at the junction of several valleys and trekking routes is the Ai Tör camp, run by ExtremeTour (p90), with shower, *banya* (€5), tent sites (€1), yurts (350som), mountain rescue, radio service and park permit check.

From May to mid-October you can make a strenuous day hike (or better yet, an overnight-camping trip) to a crystal-clear lake called **Ala-Köl** (3530m).

Altyn-Arashan The popular hot springs make it the most-visited of any valley near Karakol, but the joy of a long soak after trekking can't be denied. Visit as a radial hike from Ak-Suu village or connect to the Karakol Valley on a two-day hike via Ala-Köl.

Karakol Using this valley as a conduit to Ala-Köl or Jeti-Ögüz is most common, but look a little further for a number of challenging walks that tackle the glaciers at the end of the valley. Take care and, for all but the most experienced of trekkers, a guide.

Jeti-Ögüz Starting from the Jeti-Ögüz sanatorium, set aside a minimum of four or five nights to hike from Jeti-Ögüz to Altyn-Arashan (via the Karakol Valley). The trail heads up the Jeti-Ögüz river valley (there are spots to camp along the way), crossing east over the 3800m Teleti Pass into the Karakol Valley.

You can combine any number of these parallel valleys to make as long a trek as you like. You can also add on wonderful radial hikes up the valleys, eg from Altyn-Arashan to Pik Palatka. There are also longer technical variations of many of these routes that should not be attempted without a knowledgeable guide and experience with glacier walking.

Maps of the region are available from TUK (p59) in Bishkek, Destination Karakol (p90) and Destination Jyrgalan (p95), as well as many tour and trekking agencies. Most routes are only faintly marked, if at all, and should not be attempted without a quality map or a trekking guide.

Ak-Suu Region

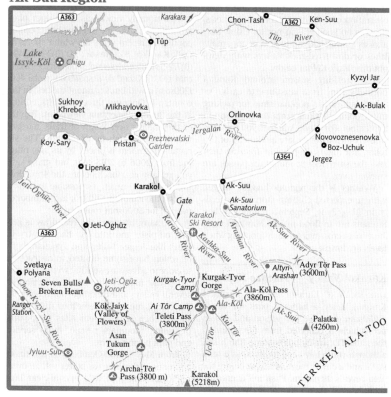

In winter, of the two hotel complexes located at the ski base the nicer option is **Kapriz** (☑(0)312-905170; www.kapriz. kg/karakol.html; Karakol Ski Base; d/ste from 10650/17040som; ☺Dec-Mar). It has unexpectedly stylish rooms in a 21st-century pyramid building accessed through a tunnel beneath the main piste-end quite a bit classier (and more expensive) than the **Ski Lodge** (☑(0)772-534081; Karakol Ski Base; d from 2000-4000som, chalet 8000-10000som; ☎) opposite the lift. One cheaper guesthouse, **Tumar Guesthouse** (☑(0)703-222576, (0)555-222576; Karakol Ski Base; tw/tr from 2000/3000som incl breakfast; ☺Dec-Mar), is around 1km back down towards Karakol at the first hairpin.

ⓘ Getting There & Away

Public transport (marshrutka 101) only runs as far as the Karakol Valley gate. For the 'second bridge', generally the starting point for hikes to Ala-Köl Lake, taxis in summer charge 600som. In winter, for the ski base, expect 700som each way.

Altyn-Arashan   Алтын-Арашан

Probably the most popular destination from Karakol is the spartan hot-spring development of Altyn-Arashan (Golden Spa), set in a postcard-perfect alpine valley at 3000m, with 4260m Palatka Peak looming at its southern end.

Much of the area is a botanical research area called the Arashan State Nature Reserve, which is home to snow leopards and a handful of bears, although the only animals you're likely to see are the horses and sheep belonging to local families.

During Soviet times it is rumoured that 25 snow leopards were trapped here and shipped to zoos around the world until Moscow cancelled all collecting and hunting permits in 1975.

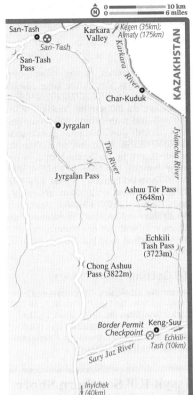

Char-Kuduk

San-Tash

Karkara Valley

Kégen (35km); Almaty (175km)

KAZAKHSTAN

San-Tash Pass

San-Tash

Karkara River

Jyrgalan

Tüp River

Jylancha River

Jyrgalan Pass

Ashuu Tör Pass (3648m)

Echkili Tash Pass (3723m)

Chong Ashuu Pass (3822m)

Border Permit Checkpoint

Keng-Suu

Echkili-Tash (10km)

Sary Jaz River

Inylchek (40km)

10 km
6 miles

From the **hot springs** (200som), it's about a five-hour walk on foot to the snout of the Palatka Glacier, wrapped around Pik Palatka.

Altyn-Arashan is not a village and its half-dozen houses are not permanently inhabited, though **Yak Tours** (☑(0)3922-60298; r ste/lux 400/650som, tent 50som) and sometimes others have a caretaker in residence year-round – at least in theory. In summer **Elza** (☑(0)3948-60293, (0)702-929324; ⊘ dm 400som) has a handful of small rooms near the bridge that leads onwards to Ala-Köl. The *banya* (200som per person), on the large side, is well placed for mid-soak dips in the river.

Pitching your tent near one of the lodges usually carries a 100som charge.

Lodges serve meals for pre-booked guests (at additional payment to listed rates) and in midsummer either place might be able to sell nonguests a few food items, but it's wise to carry your own food (and water-purifying tablets).

From Karakol, agencies and some independent drivers offer 4WD transport for 6000som per vehicle (less if a pre-arranged vehicle be going up empty). But before booking a transfer, read on.

ℹ Getting There & Away

Around 12km east of central Karakol by good, asphalt road is the Ak-Suu Sanatorium ('*kurort*'), terminus of frequent Ak-Suu marshrutka 350 (p92; last return 6pm winter, 8pm summer). From here, Altyn-Arashan is 14km away, using the lane that branches south some 200m before the main sanatorium entrance. This lane soon degrades into a contender for the world's worst motorable road. The track is easy to follow. Cross the river after 3km then ignore all further bridges; at 12km from the kurort keep left (up, away from the river). You'll follow the jeep tracks all the way.

Jergez Valley   Ущелье Жергез

Just 25km from Karakol, the mouth of Jergez Valley beckons enticingly from the highway. Visit as a day trip to the Köl-Tör Lake, overnight at the lovely Kara-Kyz Yurt-Camp, or head all the way up and over passes for Boz-Uchuk to the east or Ak-Suu and Altyn Arashan to the west.

Though a day trip from nearby Karakol is eminently practical, the beautiful location of **Kara-Kyz Yurt-Camp** (☑(0)707-044144, (0)557-044144; karakyzyc@gmail.com; Pioneer village; dm €15) makes an overnight visit appealing as well.

ℹ Getting There & Away

Marshrutki (30som) and shared taxis (50som) run to and from the Ak-Suu bus stand (p92) in Karakol throughout the day, dropping passengers at the turn-off to Pioneer village upon request.

Jyrgalan   Жыргалан
POP 1014

Founded as a coal-mining village but finding new life as an ecotourism base, welcoming little Jyrgalan is equally attractive for insight into Kyrgyz village life or as a launching point into the mountains that start just outside your guesthouse door. Come for a few days, linger for a week, and before you know it you're basically a local.

The **Destination Jyrgalan** (www.facebook.com/destinationjyrgalan/) public association manages tourism in the village, and ensures that income from the tourism sector benefits the entire community. To make reservations for guides, guesthouses or other services in advance, contact them. Though prices may be higher than elsewhere in the country, fees go towards improving village life and ensuring tourism activities are conducted in a sustainable manner.

Destination Jyrgalan can arrange hikes and horse treks, generally on short notice, for numerous routes in and around the Jyrgalan Valley or beyond.

Day trips head up to pretty Tulpar-Köl lake or the Kök-Bel waterfall (though this one dries up in summer), but the village also makes an excellent base for circle routes or longer trekking routes in Ak-Suu (p92).

All services are charged at standard set rates per day, regardless of route:

Guide (Kyrgyz/Russian-speaking; on foot, bike, or horseback)	2500som
Guide/Cook (for groups up to two)	3000som
Assistant guide (for groups larger than three)	2200som
Cook (per group per day)	2500som
Assistant cook (for groups larger than three)	2200som
Porter (including horse)	2000som
Horse rental	1200som
Horseman (per group)	2200som
Food for tourists (per person 3 meals)	750som
Mountain bike rental	1000som

Additionally, camping gear can be rented directly from Destination Jyrgalan:

Kitchen equipment	300som
Tent	250som
Sleeping bag	170som
Sleeping mat	70som

Before it became a hiking hub, Jyrgalan was popular as a centre for winter sports and especially freeride skiing with the season running roughly mid-November to mid-April, the village now hosts ski-touring and snowshoe treks in addition to more extreme sports, and locally based snowmobiles and a snowcat keep powderhounds happy all winter long. Equipment rental from Destination Jyrgalan (p95) is available.

Skis, boots and poles	1500som
Airbags and shovels	1500som
Splitboards	1500som
Snowshoes	500som

Five guesthouses in the village offer beds to tourists, though the large **Ala-köl Guesthouse** (☑(0)557-207777, (0)551-916924; Asanbayeva; dm 1500som incl breakfast; ☎) is the only one with private bathrooms and wi-fi (though slow). **Salamat guesthouse** (☑(0)777-085296; Asanbayeva; dm 1000som incl breakfast), run by the lovely Nazira, is our other favorite; but **Ulan** (☑(0)778-406888; dm 1000som incl breakfast), **Rahat** (☑(0)772-857920; Asanbayeva; dm 1000som incl breakfast), and **Baitor** (☑(0)778-992486; Asanbayeva; dm 1000som incl breakfast) guesthouses are all cosy as well. All can arrange meals – 350som each at most but 500som per meal at Ala-köl.

ⓘ Getting There & Away

Marshrutka 331 (80som, 1½ hours) leaves from the Ak-Suu bus stand (p92) at Karakol's Ak-Tilek bazaar three times per day (8.30am, 11.30am, 4.30pm) for Jyrgalan (labeled шахта), returning shortly after arriving in the village. Private taxis will make the trip for 1300som.

Issyk-Köl Southern Shore
Южный берег

There's much dispute as to whether the Northern or Southern Shore of Issyk-Köl is the more scenic. Traditionally Western visitors have tended to err in favour of the quieter southern road, especially in summer when it is spared the heaviest tourist traffic en route to the Cholpan-Ata resorts. This is even though only relatively limited sections of the route have any real lake view – notably between Tamga and Tosor and between Km102 and Km95 (east of Ton). What isn't up for debate, though, is that the southern shore is by far the better place to learn about local culture – eagle hunters, religious sites, yurt-building villages and more await.

Jeti-Ögüz   Джеты-Огуз
☑ 3946 / POP 3428 / ELEV 2031M

Counterpointing striking red-rock bluffs, pine forests, upland *jailoo* meadows and a soaring Alpine backdrop, the Jeti-Ögüz area makes a charming day trip from Karakol or a good starting point for summer-only hikes, including taxing multiday treks to Altyn-Arashan and Ala-Köl.

For a quick, easy excursion, come and point your camera at the Seven Bulls for which the whole area is named. To make the experience last a day or two, head up to Kök-Jaiyk *jailoo* and beyond by 4WD or on foot.

Just before you arrive at the Jeti-Ögüz resort from the north, the partly wooded back side of the Seven Bulls ridge appears to be a single splintered hill. Its heart-shaped form has led to many a tragic legend. Most common is that where two suitors both spilled their blood fighting for the affections of a beautiful woman: both died and this rock is her Broken Heart (Razbitoye Sertse).

Head to **Jeti-Ögüz Sanatorium** (☑ (0)394-697711; Jeti-Ögüz Korort; d/tr 2000/3000som, lux d 2800som) for various spa 'treatments' including paraffin-wax compresses, mud-electrocutions, sulphur baths and a kind of blanket mummification procedure (all cost from 100som). It retains a distinctly Soviet atmosphere. All rates are full-board, and include some treatments and access to all the facilities of the resort.

ⓘ Getting There & Away

Public transport is very limited and not timetabled. Marshrutka 355 (100som, one hour) runs from Jeti-Ögüz Korort to Karakol several times per week.

Marshrutka 371 runs from Jeti-Ögüz village to Karakol several times daily (60som), though the first service rarely travels *from* Karakol before 11am. Be aware that Jeti-Ögüz village, while pleasant and with a fine mountain backdrop, has no sights per se and is 12km north of the Korort, ie 5km south of the Karakol–Tamga main road. Shared taxis between the village and Korort cost 60/240som per person/car. Out of season these only run a few times daily. The village's minibus/shared-taxi stops are easy to spot, within 50m of the new silver-domed mosque.

Barskoön   Барскоон

☑ 3946 / POP 6912 / ELEV 1753M

Barskoön (Barskaun in Russian) is a useful starting point for southern Issyk-Köl's best horse treks. If you're driving past, it's also worth the minor detour from the main road into Barskoön town to visit the

TOP OF THE TIAN SHAN

Tian Shan means 'Celestial Mountains' in Chinese and the range does indeed achieve a most heavenly majesty at Kyrgyzstan's easternmost tip. Here in the Central Tian Shan (Центральный Тянь-Шань), a knot of immense summits culminates in 7439m Jengish Chokusu (Pik Pobedy/Victory Peak in Russian), the second-highest peak in the former USSR. But though it's slightly shorter, the gracious pyramidal form of 7010m Khan Tengri (Sky Ruler) makes it possibly the most stunningly beautiful of all the region's peaks. Locals call it 'Blood Mountain' due to a crimson hue it often adopts at sunset. Though reported by 7th-century Chinese explorer Xuan Zang, Khan Tengri was not climbed until 1931 (by a Ukrainian team).

Ak Örgö yurt workshop (☑ (0)779-308491; mekenbek_1958@mail.ru; Lenin 97; 1hr tour 200som). The workshop became famous after one of its products won the 'most beautiful yurt' competition at the 1997 'Manas 1000' festival and had its work exhibited six times in the USA at several museums and cultural centres across the country. However, it was almost bankrupted when a luxurious US$50,000 yurt ordered for President Bakiev was never paid for, following the president's sudden ousting in the 2010 revolution. If you speak Russian, it's fascinating to hear more of these stories.

The lovely former shepherding family at **Shepherds Way Trekking** (☑ Barskoön (Gulmira) (0)550-124144, Bishkek (Ishen) (0)772-518315; www.kyrgyztrek.com; Podgornaya 35) run a homestay (full board 1600som) for travellers, most of whom visit Barskoön to take advantage of their horse-trekking services to get deep into the Tien Shan mountains that rise just beyond the village.

Marshrutkas and shared taxis run towards Karakol (70/120som, 1½ hours) and Bokonbaevo (80/100som, one hour) and drop passengers en route. Barskoön village is around 3km off the highway, so coming the other direction you'll have to walk in if you don't find a direct marshrutka into the village.

Barskoön Valley Ущелье Барскоон

By far the easiest way to get deep into the appealing alpine landscapes behind southern Issyk-Köl is driving up Barskoön Valley along the wide, well-maintained, unpaved truck road that leads all the way to the controversial Kumtor Gold Mine, turning south off the coast road at Km140/80. If you go too far you'll need permits and invitations, but an uncontroversial compromise is stopping after 21km for the Barskoön Waterfall, 2km beyond a curious truck-on-a-plinth monument. The smaller, more accessible waterfall is reached within 20 minutes' walk, above two busts of cosmonaut Yuri Gagarin. The upper falls are distantly visible through the pine trees nearby, but getting there takes a couple of hours' scramble.

In summer, *kymys* and simple meals are sold from yurts at the base of the waterfall.

No public transit runs up here, but taxis can be arranged from any of the major settlements along the South Shore.

Bokonbaevo Боконбаево

📞 3947 / POP 10,648 / ELEV 1809M

Bokonbaevo is the Southern Shore's largest town and central trekking hub, as well as home to two tourist yurt-camps and a mid-August **Birds of Prey Festival** (600som) when falconers from around Issyk-Köl compete here with their eagles, hawks and falcons.

Any time of year the **Salburuun Federation** (📞(0)707-395094; Jolchoro@mail.ru; demonstration US$20-500) is a fascinating

piece of ancient Kyrgyz culture kept alive into the modern day. Falconry demonstrations are most popular, though the use of a sacrificial rabbit trapped for the purpose will seem cruel to some; but it depicts authentic hunting traditions: this is often how young eagles are trained.

The **Destination South Shore public association** (southshoreik@gmail.com) or Bokonbaevo's **CBT** (📞(0)779-455045, (0)705-001723; cbtbokonbaevo@gmail.com; Mambetov 16; ⊙9am-5pm) can provide details of local treks, homestays and yurtstays, and other cultural activities in the region. Various offerings include:

Tour/Trekking guides (per day)	1400som
Golden eagle hunting show	5000som
Folklore show	5000som
Shyrdak show	2000som

CBT is affiliated with six guesthouses in the village proper (750som with breakfast), though some are far from the centre. The unaffiliated **Emily Guesthouse** (📞(0)708-313076, (0)778-310946; tilebaldievagulmira@gmail.com; Toigonova 83; dm 800som incl breakfast; @🔊) is more central than most of CBT's, with a friendly family and great food.

For a little luxury (though quite removed from town) head out to **Almaluu's** (📞(0)556-856799; www.jurtendorf.com; Ton region; dm US$17 incl breakfast) upmarket yurt-camp or the more basic **Bel-Tam** (📞(0)773-881129, (0)709-881129; Ton area; dm 800som incl breakfast) right on the lake shore. For a more authentic yurt experience, CBT (p98) and

---

KUMTOR GOLD MINE

Amid eternal snows at a phenomenal 4200m altitude, Kumtor is the world's eighth-largest gold field and produces an estimated 12% of Kyrgyzstan's GDP. Throughout the summer of 2013 protestors clashed with police while barricading the access road and attempting to cut power supplies to the mine. Local people seemed divided as to which story they believe about the motivations of the protesters. Were they genuinely concerned for better environmental conditions? Was it part of a political move agitating for the mine's nationalisation? Or was this simply an attempt to persuade the mine's owners to spend more money in local communities as retribution for the mine not paying its dues to a major protection racket?

Disputes and nationalisation threats continued for several years, until a 2017 agreement that saw the company agreeing to make massive investments in cancer-support and environment-protection funds administered by the Kyrgyz government. Whatever the changing situation, there are no tours of the mine operations and even getting up onto the higher sections of the access road requires a permit to get past the various checkpoints.

TREKKING & HORSE RIDING ON THE SOUTH SHORE

A network of trekking and horse riding routes extends across the mountains of the Southern Shore, linking up in an almost unbroken chain of valleys and passes all the way from Jeti-Ögüz to Kochkor (in Naryn). Maps of the region are available from TUK (p59) in Bishkek, Destination Karakol (p90) and CBT offices, as well as many tour and trekking agencies. Most routes are only faintly marked, if at all, and should not be attempted without a quality map or a trekking guide.

CBT Bokonbaevo (p98) can arrange guides and horses (as well as equipment rental) for a number of excellent trekking routes across the Southern Shore, the best of which include:

Panorama Four days on a circle route south of Bokonbaevo, peaking at a 3300m pass with fantastic Issyk-Köl views.

Teshik-Köl Four days riding up an old jeep road over the 4023m Ton pass and into the hills to a small mountain lake, returning to Bokonbaevo along the same route.

Boz-Salkyn–Barskoön Four days connecting Bokonbaevo to the Barskoön Valley via Boz-Salkyn *jailoo*, and the Shatyly Viewpoint (p99) via the Tosor Pass, Kokui-Köl lake and the Kerege-Tash gorge.

Juku–Barskoön Four days from high up the Barskoön valley to the shore of Issyk-Köl at Saruu village via the Düngürömö and Juku valleys, with a side-trip up the 3672m Juku pass.

Ak-Sai Petroglyphs A small collection of Tibetan-script **petroglyphs** (Ak-Suu village) and accompanying Soviet-era graffiti make for a nice 3km walk (one way) from the nearby highway, but the extended 8.3km that loops back towards Ak-Sai village (14km west of Bokonbaevo) takes in some extraordinary views of red-rock hills with the deep blue of Issyk-Köl beyond.

Shatyly Viewpoint At the beginning of the attractive Boz-Salkyn Valley an easy 1.75km walk leads to a viewpoint with extraordinary panoramas over Issyk-Kül, especially at sunrise.

Destination South Shore can arrange transfers and overnights at the Jaichy yurt-camp, a one-day horse trek away from the Kök-Sai Glacier.

If spending an extended time in town, **Cafe Ylazyk** (Lenina, cnr Mambetov; 100-200som; ⊙10am-6pm) and **Argymak** (☑(0)707-903050; Mambetov 16; mains 100-200som; ⊙8am-8pm; ☎) (both near the intersection of Lenina and Mambetov) can make a good change from homstay fare.

Souvenir hunters should head to **Altyn Oimok** (☑(0)778-846731, (0)3947-91590; Karymshakov 69; ⊙8am-7pm), a craftsworkers' collective that also arranges demonstrations of the felt-making process from 2500som per group. It's exactly two blocks due north of the CBT office – look for signs on the road in from Karakol.

Minibuses leave from in from of the CBT office for Bishkek (250som, four hours) and Karakol (200som, two hours), stopping at points in between to pick up and drop off passengers.

AROUND BOKONBAEVO

East of Bokonbaevo on the road to Karakol are two sights of note.

The Skazka Valley is an area of bare red earth eroded into photogenic corridors and spires of rosy rock. It's hardly Bryce Canyon but it makes a colourful curiosity.

Rumoured to cure everything from upset stomach to infertility, the many springs that dot the **Manjyly-Ata** (⊙24hr) site have been the focus of pilgrimage since at least the region's animist Tengrism tradition. A visit is particularly nice at sunrise, when early-morning light brings out the colour in the otherwise dull rocky hillsides of the site. Look for the signed turn-off around 10km east of Bokonbaevo onto a dirt road that dead ends at the entrance. This is still an active religious site, so tread with respect.

In the small village of Kyzyl-Tuu, 30km west of Bokonbaevo, is a centre of yurt-making in Kyrgyzstan. Whole families devote themselves to the craft, and can arrange an introduction to yurt building and the traditions the underlie the process (from 3500som per group including transport from Bokonbaevo). Call ☎(0)700-411011 or contact tolosunb@gmail.com to arrange a demonstration.

NORTHERN KYRGYZSTAN: NARYN OBLAST
НАРЫНСКАЯ ОБЛАСТЬ

The mountainous centre of Kyrgyzstan – Naryn *oblast* – offers travellers unrivalled opportunities to explore *jailoos* (summer pastures) on foot, horseback or by 4WD. The central gem around which the region's

tourism revolves is mesmerising Son-Köl (p102). It's a very special place, but don't overlook the crucial fact that the lake is frozen until late spring. Snow is possible year-round and the signature yurts don't appear until June, so timing is everything.

Plenty of other options abound, from light day hikes near Naryn and Kochkor to long-distance hikes or horse treks to remote nature preserves and on to the south shore of Issyk-Köl. A real highlight – though access is tough – is lake Köl-Suu (p107) in a remote valley just before the Chinese border.

En route to China along the highway through the scenic but bureaucratically frustrating Torugart Pass, stop by Tash-Rabat caravanserai or make a quick hike or horse trip along the wide expanse of Chatyr-Köl lake.

Be aware that if you plan to cross Torugart to/from China you'll need to arrange things in advance through a tour agency. Remember that the border closes at week-

Naryn Oblast

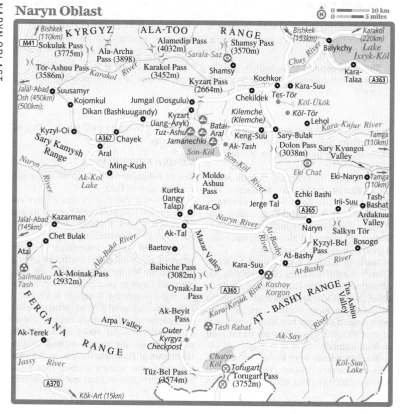

ends and on holidays. To explore Chatyr-Köl you'll need a border-zone permit, though this might not be checked if you hike there and back from Tash Rabat.

Kochkor   Кочкорка

✈ 3535 / POP 9863 / ELEV 1767M

Multiple competing community-tourism outfits make Kochkor an eminently practical base from which to visit Son-Köl and other Kyrgyz *jailoos* (summer pastures) nearby. Do be aware that such activities are generally only practicable in summer and part of the shoulder season, as shepherds move their herds back to the villages during cooler months. The town is not an attraction in its own right, despite a distant backdrop of mountain peaks, but is at its most interesting on Saturday mornings for the **animal bazaar** (Mal Bazaar; ⊙7am-11am Sat). On weekdays the **Regional Museum** (Sapar Alieva 8; 50som; ⊙9am-noon & 1-6pm Mon-Fri) is worth a brief stop.

There are more than two dozen homestays in Kochkor, costing 500som to 700som with breakfast. Each is affiliated with at least one of the four community-tourism agencies so it's worth comparing availability and prices at each. If the agencies are closed, most taxi drivers will know a few B&Bs, many of which are 1km south down Shamen and Shopokova or in a southwestern suburb near the stadium.

Aliman (☑(0)777-385798, (0)773-606117; Shamen 14, off Ömurov, first alley; dm 700som; 🛜), which is friendly family and in a central location, and **Tulekeev** (☑(0)559-27 2788; Soltonkulova 19; dm 550som incl breakfast), with a great family and a nice balcony, are particularly worth asking for, and the location of basic **Jailoo Tourism Hostel** (☑(0)555-494203, (0)771-008482; www.jailoo.com.kg; Orozbakov 125-3; dm 350som; 🛜) is unbeatable.

Restaurants along Orozbakov serve the national cuisine, but the food is just as good at many of the community-tourism-affiliated guesthouses that travellers generally book at. Self-cater and prep for treks at the **bazaar** (Orozbakov).

Of note is **Shashlyk Nur** (mains 90-120som; ⊙11am-midnight) on the bypass road that swings around town. The grounds are run-down, the music's too loud and it's too far from the centre – but taste a bit of the delicious shashlyk and you'll agree it's worth the trip. Puzzlingly, shashlyk is listed on the

---

OFF THE BEATEN TRACK

HIKING TO KÖL-ÜKÖK

The beautiful 'Treasure Chest' mountain lake above Tes-Tör *jailoo* (summer pasture) usually has a couple of yurtstays in July and August – bed/breakfast/dinner 400/100/300som, booked through Jailoo (p102) – from which another couple of hours' hike brings you to Köl-Tör glacial lake.

The trip to Köl-Ükök (3042m) is often sold as a horse trek but, if you can handle the 1km gain in altitude, the route is relatively straightforward to follow as an unguided hike. The starting point is Isakaev (formerly Bolshevik) village, turning right after the bridge.

To Isakaev from Kochkor private/shared taxis cost 60/20som; they leave from beside the traffic lights in Kochkor (at the intersection of Ömurov and Orozbakova). If you pay 150som the taxi should continue 5km further to Küpke, the 'winter barns' where the road peters out. Simply continue up the valley along the obvious trail from there.

Allow around six hours for the 17km hike up to the lake; somewhat less for the return.

---

menu in Kyrgyz only. It's lamb (кой), beef (уй), chicken (тоок) and duck (өрдөк).

For national foods and hot drinks – most notably a proper coffee – **Retro Cafe** (☑(0)770-389938; Orozbakov 114; ⊙8.30am-11pm; 🛜) is a bit of a traveller hang-out in Kochkor. Just inside the entrance, the Nomad Travel tour agency arranges the standard range of horse and hiking tours.

Kochkor is one of the best places in Kyrgyzstan to buy *shyrdak* rugs. Both Jailoo Tourism (p102) and CBT's **Altyn Kol** (☑(0)3535-22534, (0)502-136590; www.altyn-kol.com; Pioneerskaya 22A; ⊙9am-7pm) showrooms have selections of naturally dyed felt products.

☞ Tours & Activities

What makes Kochkor such an central stop for travellers is that numerous community-tourism organisations each offer advice, information and a range of services in English. All can arrange homestays (both in town and in the surrounding countryside), yurtstays, guides, horses, luggage storage

Kochkor

Kochkor

◉ Sights
1 Lenin Statue A2
2 Regional Museum B2

🛏 Sleeping
3 Aliman Homestay A1
4 Jailoo Tourism Hostel........................ A1
5 Tulekeev B&B.................................... B1

🍷 Drinking & Nightlife
6 Retro Cafe A1

🛍 Shopping
7 Altyn Kol Handicraft Coop B1
8 Bazaar... A1

ℹ Information
CBT Kochkor.................................... (see 7)
9 CBT Plus Eco...................................... B1
Jailoo Tourism Community........ (see 4)

ℹ Transport
10 Marshrutka for Bishkek...................... B1
Shared Taxis for Bishkek &
Balykchy .... (see 8)
11 Shared Taxis for Chaek (via
Jumgal)... A1
12 Shared Taxis to Naryn........................ A1

and transport. **CBT Kochkor** (☏(0)777-265559, (0)3535-51114; www.cbtkochkor.com; Pioneerskaya 22A; ⊙9am-noon & 1-7pm) is the biggest and generally most professional, but **Jailoo Tourism** (☏(0)771-008482, (0)555-494203; www.jailoo.com.kg; Orozbakova 125/3; ⊙9am-8pm) and **Plus Eco** (☏(0)3535-50299, (0)772-510628; www.cbtpluseco.kg; Pioneerskaya 20; ⊙9am-6pm) are often slightly cheaper.

In addition to Son-Köl, the major attraction that brings travellers through Kochkor, hikes and horse rides can be organised to a handful of other destinations nearby. Peaceful Köl-Ükök lake is one of the easiest to arrange, doable as a one-day trip or with an overnight in a yurt on the lake shore. Continuing on, self-sufficient hikers can continue for another day over a splendid 4040m pass to the village of Ak-Kiya or for an additional five days in a loop hike via the Ulaxol and Semiz-Bel valleys to Kara-Kungoy on the outskirts of Kochkor. Enquire at any of the community-tourism organisations for maps, guides and more details.

ℹ Getting There & Around

Many a marshrutka passes through Kochkor, mostly Bishkek–Naryn and Bishkek–Chaek services. So it's easy to arrive from Bishkek but, as many tend to be full on arrival, it can be relatively tough to board here. The only Kochkor-specific services leave the bus station for Bishkek a few times daily. Buy tickets (150som) one day ahead if possible.

Shared taxis leave from various points near the bazaar:

Balykchy (150som, 40 minutes)
Bishkek (250som, 3½ hours)
Chaek (250som, two hours)
Naryn (250som, 2½ hours)

Once the new national highway is completed in 2018, Kochkor will lie along the main route between Bishkek and Osh, and transportation options should expand considerably.

Jailoo and CBT can help organise rides to Son-Köl, Köl-Ükök or other trailheads.

Rides generally cost 60som within city limits with **Kochkor Taxi** (☏0772-31 1511, 0705-311511) and other firms.

Son-Köl   Сон-Куль
ELEV 3016M

Distantly ringed by a saw-toothed horizon of peaks, the wide open landscapes of Son-Köl create a giant stage for constant performances of symphonic cloudscapes. Almost 18km across and 29km wide, and fronted by lush summer pastures, the lake's water colour changes magically from tropical turquoise to brooding indigo in seconds as the sun flashes or the storms scud by in a vast meteorological theatre. It's a sublime place to watch the sun come up or to gaze into a cold, crystal-clear night sky heavy with countless stars. At 3016m it's too cold for permanent habitation, but between June and September herders' yurts dot the shoreside meadows every few kilometres. Since many are part of the community tourism schemes, the area offers an unparalleled opportunity for yurtstay visits or multi-yurt hikes and horse treks – which can generally be organised at very short notice.

Typical activities are hiking and horse riding (300/1000som per hour/day, for guide/horse-guide 1000/1400som per day), which is easiest to arrange at the tourist-focused camps at Batai-Aral and Jamanechki (p104) though also possible at most yurts with negotiation if you speak some Russian/Kyrgyz. Birdlife includes vultures, numerous raptors and waterfowl, including the Indian mountain goose.

Unpaved tracks, often little more than tyre tracks in the turf, loop around the lake linking the main concentrations of summer yurts. Each grouping is typically known by the name of the valley/stream that runs through it or at larger camps by the name of the owner. The road along the northwest side of the lake grows much rougher, and should only be attempted in 4WDs or with knowledgeable drivers.

Be aware that weather is highly unpredictable. Snow can fall at any time so plan accordingly; mid-June to mid-September is essentially the only season to come.

🛏 Sleeping & Eating

A great part of the delight of visiting Lake Son-Köl and its environs is staying in a yurt. For travellers arriving by car from Kochkor, the easiest drop-in yurtstays to access are **CBT Naryn's** (☑(0)559-567685, (0)3522-50865; www.cbt-naryn.com; Lenina 8/33; ⊙8am-8pm; ☎) south-coast yurts or the 10 yurtstays at Batai-Aral.

Some yurtstays can whip up a 300som *tushku tamak* (lunch) for passing hikers if you're not in a hurry. All yurtstays offer *kechki tamak* (dinner) to their guests for a similar price. There are absolutely no shops nor anywhere else to purchase food supplies. When trekking to the lake there are some drinkable streams but few springs, so bring water-purifying gear.

Groups of yurts, often forming trios, are affiliated with the community tourism agencies in Kochkor and offer either beds or a floor space with padded bed mat, blankets and sheets for around 600som to 800som (including breakfast) and 300som each for

lunch/dinner. Such places are usually run by genuine herders, but the guest yurt is often a little fancier than a regular shepherd yurt and is shared with other travellers but not the family. Booking many such places is impossible due to the lack of telephone signal at Son-Köl, and typically it's fine to simply turn up and request a bed. If you want an advance reservation, try an SMS a day or two before in case the family rides up a nearby mountain to connect to mobile networks.

When things get very busy in mid-August, those arriving independently might lose out to a guided group. Choosing where to sleep is more often a matter of location, and is determined by how you are travelling rather than the price or quality, which tends to be relatively uniform.

Travellers looking to linger for a few days to explore the mountains near the lakeside would be well advised to stay at CBT-affiliated **Ainura Yurt-Camp** (☑(0)701-450073; Northwest Shore, Lake Son-Köl; dm 800som incl breakfast) on the northwest shore.

🏠 Northern Shore

The biggest concentration of yurtstays is at Batai-Aral, very close to the water's edge starting around 5km off the Sary-Bulak–Ak-Tala road. Turn off at Ak-Tash Jailoo at km47/43 and cross the muddy ford. The first cluster of yurts is Shepherd's Life-affiliated, then come two trios working with Plus Eco, then a kilometre further seven families each with three or four yurts comprise the relatively tight-packed CBT-Kochkor group, before the final Shepherd's Life yurts at **Gulnaz yurt-camp** (Northeast Shore; dm 700som incl breakfast). Altogether there are more than 70 yurts in this area, though even these high numbers seem somehow inconsequential next to the wide and beautiful stretch of the lake just nearby.

Steep-sided green *jailoos* fill the Kilemche (Klemche) Valley, which runs parallel to the north shore of Lake Son-Köl. There are three small family yurtstays well up on the south side of the valley, each about 25 minutes' walk from the 'road' from Kyzart, but up separate side valleys.

Although not on the lake itself, sleeping or arranging lunch at Kilemche makes an excellent addition to the Son-Köl experience. To walk to the lake from here, take the side valley that leads south around 10 minutes' walk east of the farthest yurts. The path seems to fade at first but becomes clearer up higher as you approach the impressive Jalgis-Karagai Pass. The lake is visible from the top. Continue straight ahead into the gulley for Tuz-Ashu, or contour diagonally left on the bigger horse-trail for Jamanechki (around four hours' walk from Kilemche).

To reach Kilemche from Kyzart or Jumgal takes between four and five hours on foot or horseback along a well-worn motor-track, or is an 800som taxi ride.

🛏 Jamancheki

After two hours' dawdling anticlockwise along the lakeside from Batai-Aral you'll spy the **Andash Kumbez** (Jamanechki, Northern Shore, Lake Son-Köl) across a meandering stream. Following that stream for around a kilometre up into the Jamanechki valley you'll discover many yurts. The first is CBT affiliated. It's just across an ankle-deep ford on the west side of the stream, and belongs to Birdbek Karayev.

🛏 Southern Shore

Directly accessible from the southern Ak-Tala road is the large **Baiysh yurt-camp** (☑ (0)779-580202, (0)770-616215; Southern Shore, Lake Son-Köl; dm 1500som incl meals), an insider's favourite – in no small part because of the Russian-style *banya* cabin set a few hundred metres from the lake shore. Horses are available by the hour (200som) or day (1000som), but it's also well positioned for day hikes up into the hills that ring the southern shore.

Affiliated with CBT Naryn (p103), the three yurts at **Raxhat Yurt-Camp** (☑ (0)773-337509, (0)705-337509; Northwest Shore; dm 600som incl breakfast), set along the southern road as it approaches the shore, are also a good choice here.

Before the southern Moldo-Bel Pass access route to Son-Köl rejoins the main highway at Ak-Tala en route to Naryn, stop by **Nomad's Valley** (☑ (0)773-581368; Kurtka village; ⊙ 8am-7pm) for a chat with affable owner Marsbek and try his international quality espresso and quite respectable ashlyanfu just off the road in the village of Kurtka.

ⓘ Getting There & Away

Getting to Lake Son-Köl is a large part of the experience, especially if hiking or riding in. But even when driving, the unpaved road between Sary-Bulak and Ak-Tala crosses a spectacular pass on either side of the lake, the southern road

being marginally better surfaced. The lake is huge, so before heading out consider which is the most appropriate area for your desires.

There is no public transport to Son-Köl, traffic is very thin and access routes are generally impassable from November to early May. Kochkor agencies want around 3000som for a vehicle to the largest yurt cluster at Batai-Aral or to the south-coast yurts (around three hours), a price that would be the same one way or return. Private drivers might charge less and you'll pay less than half if you wait at the lake for a car that's going back empty. But that can sometimes take a day or two even in midsummer.

The cheapest way to reach the lake is to walk in from the north. A taxi from Kyzart to Kilemche costs around 700som if you want to skip part of the hike.

Lake access is also possible via the unpaved Kara-Keche mining road that branches off the Suusamyr road opposite the copper-roofed new mosque in Dikan (aka Bashkuugandy at Km123/99), 14km east of Chaek. This is currently only accessible by horse or 4WD only (best arranged through EcoTour Travel in Chaek), and is in a ragged state with several bridges washed out, though self-sufficient cyclists have managed to pedal this way.

If trekking without a guide, the Kyzart–Tuz-Ashu route is the easiest one-day option while the Kilemche–Jamanechki–Batai-Aral route makes a good two-day alternative. With a guide, starting from Kyzart or Jumgal then looping around via Tuz-Ashu and Uzbek-Ashu makes a fine two-night out-and-back option. Horses can be hired for any of the above hikes, but aren't strictly needed if you've left your main luggage in Kochkor or Naryn and are travelling light between yurtstays. These areas are criss-crossed by shepherds' trails, however, so a map of the area is handy for route-finding.

Jumgal   Жумгал

☑ 353 / POP 43,000

The Jumgal region provides a logical starting point for those wanting to reach Lake Son-Köl on foot with minimum expense. Trekking over the Tuz-Ashu Pass, it is quite feasible to reach Son-Köl's north shore in one day from either village. Alternatively, you could walk (for four hours or so) to Kilemche, stay there in a family yurt and continue the next day to the lake. For either, it's also possible to hire horses from **Shepherd's Life** (☑ (0)773-098018; Jetigenov Akun 16; dm 350som incl breakfast) in Jumgal village.

Community tourism representatives run homestays in Jumgal and Kyzart villages – **Zamir Guesthouse** (☑ (0)772-606292, (0)705-

782873; Kyzart; dm 700som incl breakfast; 🛜) is among the nicest.

Jumgal region is located on the newly opened Kochkor–Kazarman road between the Kyzart pass and Kazarman. From the west, Jumgal village is the first travellers encounter after Kyzart pass, while Kyzart village is off the main road just beyond: turn south on an unpaved road beside the graveyard at Km71.3, then turn east by the mosque and continue 1km to find the homestays. Continue across the valley to the regional seat, Chaek, which offers more services for exploring Jumgal region but is further away from the passes to Son-Köl.

Most visitors will arrive via Kochkor, though with a private car it's possible to continue along the very rough road to Kyzyl-Oi or the newly opened highway to Kazarman.

Chaek   Чаек

☑ 3536 / POP 7009 / ELEV 1742M

Jumgal administrative centre Chaek, on the western side of the valley, is the area's best base for exploring the small mountain villages and lakes that make up the most impressive attractions in Jumgal.

In town, the **Regional Museum** (☑ (0)700-616021; Matiev 108; 50som; ⏱ 9am-noon & 1-6pm Mon-Fri) may be of minor interest. The rough road past the Tagai Guesthouse makes an easy 30-minute walk past the local *kok boru* field and then up a Panorama Hill with views out over Chaek village and the Jumgal Valley. The metal building to the northeast is a run-down sauna complex where locals soak in water from the radon hot spring just beyond (9am to 6pm, 50som).

Tagai Guesthouse (☑ (0)773-141315, (0)701-015201; dm 600som incl breakfast; 🛜), across from the museum, and **Geniy Guesthouse** (☑ (0)709-918542, (0)353-623879; Moldaliev 4; dm 450som incl breakfast), just west of the hospital, both make excellent homestay overnights.

EcoTour Travel & Hostel (☑ (0)551-795151; Matiev 129; dm 500som) has seven beds across three rooms, and the travel agency can also organise trips around Jumgal and beyond – Ak-Köl Lake (p105) is a true treat, they run a yurt camp near the Kyzart Pass, and the Arab Mausoleums north of town will be of interest to some.

This is the best bet for a sit-down meal between Kochkor and Kazarman, with several small cafes and canteens that prepare the usual range of Kyrgyz and Russian

AK-KÖL LAKE

Winding 10km up a dirt road off the Kazarman–Chaek highway, brilliant Ak-Köl lake, reflecting the surrounding peaks and the village beyond, are a real delight. Originally established as a psychiatric ward (the runs of which can be seen on the far lake shore) and later converted to a lead mine (sealed after WWII), the small Russian-style log cabins here are still home to around 15 villagers who use the area as a base from which to graze livestock in the surrounding valleys.

It's possible to use the village as a base for horse rides or trekking, if arrangements are made in Chaek. From here it's one hour to a small waterfall to the east, two/four hours on horse/foot to a larger waterfall to the south, and another four/eight hours over the ridge to Kazarman.

favourites. **Cafe Aika** (Matiev 113; mains 100-180som) above the bus station is the pick, though **Cafe Daam** (☑ (0)708-911440; Matieva 84; mains 80-110som; ⏱ 9am-7pm Mon-Sat) is also reliable.

ℹ Getting There & Away

Chaek is the main regional transport terminus, with several daily minibuses and an overnight bus service to Bishkek (shared taxi/bus 500/300som, eight hours) via Jumgal village (50/30som, one hour) and Kochkor (300/250som, two hours).

Naryn   Нарын

☑ 3522 / POP 38,200 / ELEV 2040M

Wedged into a striking canyon, Naryn is an excellent place to hook up with other summer travellers to ride-share (and thus save money) on crossing the Torugart Pass to China, visiting Tash Rabat Caravanserai, heading up either of two more-adventurous routes to Son-Köl, or heading across the very rough road to Kazarman (for Osh). It's also the access point for adventures across the region – horse riding, hiking or bike trips galore.

Naryn is pleasant, though there aren't major sights in town. On the main square is a large **Freedom Statue** (Main Square) –

Naryn

Naryn

Sights
1 Art Gallery B1
2 Freedom Statue B1
3 Regional Museum D2

Sleeping
4 Beyshegul's Homestay..........................D2
5 Celestial Mountains Guest House D1
6 Datka's Guesthouse C1
  Dushegul's Homestay ....(see 4)
7 Hotel Ala-Too C1
8 Khan Tengri Hotel..................................D2

Eating
9 Anarkul Apa Café B1
10 Kafe Ademi A1
11 Zubr Cafe..C2

Drinking & Nightlife
12 Nomad Cafe C1

Shopping
13 Kyrgyz Uz C2
14 Naryn City Supermarket......................C1

Information
15 Aiyl Bank C1
16 CBT Naryn C2
17 Kubat Tour C2
18 OVIR C1

Transport
19 Bus Station C2
20 Taxi Stand A1

the go-to photo spot for newly-weds - and just off the square is the local **Art Gallery** (☑(0)550-207786, (0)770-207788; Jakypov 5; 50som; ☺8am-8pm) museum space. On the road towards Bishkek is the **Regional Museum** (Razzakov 4; 60som; ☺9am-noon & 1-6pm Mon-Fri) – interesting for the 1960s photos of Naryn in its Soviet heyday...and for Kojum-kul's giant pyjamas – and they run *Beshbarmak* cooking classes through CBT.

Marshrutkas towards Baetov can drop travellers at the Naryn Panorama off a dirt road turn-off as the highway towards tops a small pass. It's popular with locals.

Known as *shyrdak*-central in the country, it's no surprise that Naryn is home to an annual Kyrgyz Shyrdak Festival. A combination exhibition and handicrafts fair, it's

generally held sometime around late June. Contact CBT (p103) for details.

Locally produced *shyrdak* and souvenirs can be purchased from **Kubat Tour** (☑(0)772-689262; www.kubat-tour.from.kg; Lenina 6/51; ☺9am-6pm), CBT (p103) or next door at a shop called **Kyrgyz Uz** (☑(0)700-548254, (0)777-419051; skst_beka@mail.ru; Lenina 8; ☺8am-7pm). The Art Gallery (p106) exhibition space on the square also has a gift shop.

🛏 Sleeping

CBT (p103) and Kubat Tour together coordinate around 20 homestays in the city (400som to 600som per person, including breakfast). Most are in suburban houses and apartment blocks, often in the eastern Moscovskaya suburb. When the community tourism offices are closed for the winter, try **Dushagul** (☑(0)701-326019, (0)773-326019; Razzakov 3, apt 3; dm 700som incl breakfast) or **Beyshagul** (☑(0)704-500010; Razzakov 7, apt 2; dm 600som incl breakfast), who both have comfortable, fairly standard homestays in apartment blocks near the main bridge.

Affiliated with CBT, the small but excellent **Datka's Guesthouse** (☑(0)553-155792, (0)708-228830; datkasguesthouse@gmail.com; Lenina 54/2; s/d 1000/2000som incl breakfast; ☎) is probably the best in town. For a standard hotel experience reserve ahead at the popular **Khan Tengri Hotel** (☑(0)3522-54946, Nazgul (0)556-035063; Jusepov 2; s/d 1800/2400som incl breakfast; @) or **Celestial Mountains Guesthouse** (☑(0)3522-50412, (0)700-412925; www.celestial.com.kg; Razzakov 42; r without bathroom 1000som, lux 1300som, dm in yurt 500som; @), though both are a bit out of the centre. If you're really slumming it, the Soviet-era **Hotel Ala-Too** (☑(0)707-343188, (0)3522-52189; Chanachov 19; s/d without bathroom 400/800som, with bathroom 700/1400som) has a photogenically abandoned restaurant with smashed windows and trees growing out the roof.

Be aware that occasionally on Thursday and Monday nights in midsummer accommodation can be overloaded with groups heading to/from Torugart, aiming to arrive for the Sunday market in Kashgar and avoid the border closures on weekends.

🍴 Eating & Drinking

Naryn region's lamb meat is considered the best in the country, and any of the cafes and restaurants in the city are happy to prove that adage true. To stock up on packaged good for trekking, **Naryn City Supermarket** (Lenina; ⊙8am-2am) is the biggest around.

Zubr Cafe (Lenina; mains 120-200som; ⊙11am-mid) – the obvious grouping of green tent roofs just before the stream on the CBT end of town – serves excellent shashlyk and slightly chilled beer.

Small but relatively upmarket by Naryn standards, **Anarkul Apa** (☑(0)550-075907; Orozbak 23; mains 110-250som; ⊙9am-11pm Mon-Sat; 🍴) is remarkable for an English-language menu and for serving meat-free dishes (roast vegetables, cheese spaghetti), but only the brave will try the sushi in remote Naryn.

KÖL-SUU LAKE

Remote even by Kyrgyzstan standards, magnificent Köl-Suu lake stretches over 10km through a sheer mountain gorge that reaches nearly to the Chinese border. It's hard to grasp the true scale until locally run boat trips (from $200 per person) strike out for the centre of the lake, where they seemed dwarfed by rock walls on every side. At 3500m the weather here can change rapidly so be sure to pack warm clothes and carry extra provisions.

It's over 150km from Naryn through increasingly bad roads and two border checkpoints, but the final 7km from Jyrgal jailoo into the Kurumduk Valley's dramatic panorama of craggy peaks would be worth the trip even without the lake to cap it off. Horses are available to rent for the river crossing beyond Jyrgal or for the full trip up to the lake, but a determined driver in a reliable 4WD can sometimes make it all the way to the lake's shore.

Of several eateries facing the east side of the bazaar, the standard local menu at **Kafe Ademi** (Bazaar Area; mains 70-150som; ⊙8am-8pm Mon-Sat, from 9.30am Sun) is a good value.

Nomad Cafe (☑(0)704-580302; Lenina 70; ⊙9am-11pm; ☎) serves up coffee and cakes along with a menu of pizza and local classics, and the location is convenient just off the main square.

ℹ Information

Naryn is the first/last place to change money after/before the Chinese border. Several banks east of the main square along Lenin, including **Aiyl** (Lenina 72; ⊙8.30am-5.30pm Mon-Fri), change US dollars and euros and have Visa ATMs.

If you find yourself stuck on the wrong side of a Chinese holiday and need to extend your visa, count on several visits to the **OVIR** (☑(0)312-624140; Lenina; ⊙9am-12.30pm & 1.30-6pm Mon-Fri) and **Police Station** (☑(0)3522-50921; Lenina; ⊙9am-12.30pm & 1.30-6pm Mon-Fri) offices. CBT (p103) has contacts that can help.

At CBT Naryn (p103), energetic Gulira speaks excellent English and is tirelessly keen to help visitors. She can arrange guides, horses,

GUIDED TOURS AROUND NARYN

CBT (p103) and Kubat Tour (p106) can give you the low down on a range of trips around Naryn, including yurtstays in the Ardaktuu Valley, and Tyor Jailoo in the Eki-Naryn Valley. With a day or two of notice, it can organise multiday horse treks. Most horse trips start from Kurtka (Jangy Talap) or Eki-Naryn. Ask about visits to the Tian Shan deer nursery at Irii-Suu (great for kids) and day trips up the Ak-Tam Valley to see petroglyphs.

Trip costs are generally set, and calculated by trip length per person:

Yurtstay 600som (includes breakfast) per person, per day

Horse rental 800som per person, per day

Horse guide 1500som per day

Lunch/dinner 400som per person, per meal

Transportation costs vary somewhat by season, but will generally be charged per car at the following round-trip rates departing from Naryn city:

Chatyr-Köl (via Tash-Rabat)	5000som
Eki-Naryn	1200som
Köl-Suu	US$200
Son-Köl	4000som
Tash-Rabat	3000som
Torugart Pass (via Tash-Rabat and Chatyr-Köl)	US$120
Torugart Pass to Kashgar, China (charge is per person)	US$120
Waiting fee for drivers (if extending trips beyond required driving days)	500som per day

Possible excursions include:

Eki-Naryn to Bokonbaevo Six days by horse or foot, via Jiluu Suu.

Kurtka to Son-Köl Two days by horse, or three days by foot. Starting from Kurtka village, west of Naryn to Son-Köl's southern shore, overnighting in yurts (July and August) or tents.

Naryn State Reserve Two and a half days by horse or 4½ days by foot. Transport by car to the state reserve then you follow the Big Naryn River to Karakalka village, overnighting with the ranger or staying in tents. It is also possible to arrange transport or trek to Barskoön from Karakalka.

Tash-Rabat to Chatyr-Köl Five hours each way hiking or horseback riding, or four hours by car (which necessitates a border permit).

Köl-Suu Five hours by car, depending on road conditions.

---

yurtstays, homestays, transport, eagle shows, cooking classes...and basically anything else you can dream up. Helpfully the office tries to pair up visitors to save costs on shared rides or programs.

Within a day, border permits (US$25) and rides can be organised to get you across the Torugart Pass to Kashgar. They even serve espresso on the patio out front of the office.

Kubat Tours offers competitive prices on tours and Torugart transfers, with some homestay options available.

Naryn's **post office** (Toktosunov; ⊗9am-5pm Mon-Fri) offers the standard range of services.

ⓘ Getting There & Around

Long-distance buses, minibuses and shared taxis leave from the **bus station** (Lenina). Those for regional villages leave from the bazaar.

Bishkek Minibuses (275som, seven hours) depart between all day, with a night bus (275som) at 9pm. Shared-taxi drivers linger all day (450som). Any Bishkek service will drop you at Kochkor.

Issyk-Köl Buses leave at 8am and 10am for Karakol (450som, six to seven hours).

Kazarman In summer shared taxis (1500som, six to eight hours) leave from the bazaar taxi stand at around 8am once or twice a week. Hiring a full taxi costs around 7000som.

Tash Rabat/Son-Köl Only possible by charter taxi from the bus station or through CBT (p103) and Kubat Tour (p106).

Two minibus lines run along Lenina, both originating in the west of town at the University of Central Asia campus. At the roundabout on the east end of Lenin, bus 1 turns left towards Bishkek while bus 2 heads right towards the Khan Tengri hotel and Eki-Naryn. Hold out the appropriate number of fingers to flag down passing buses.

Eki-Naryn Эки-Нарын
POP 759

At the intersection of the Naryn river and the other Naryn river, little Eki-Naryn, literally 'two Naryns' – we'll let you figure out where they got the name) draws visitors with its red cliffs and plentiful hiking opportunities around the surrounding mountainsides, and serves as the starting point for several intrepid horse treks organised by CBT Naryn (p103). There's not much in the way of organised tourism, but visitors with a thirst for wandering may well stay twice as long as expected to explore the area.

The friendly matriarch at **Mira Guesthouse** (🖉 (0)708-643259; Orozaliev Abdyzhaper; dm 500som incl breakfast) has the only show in town, though outside of the village there's plenty of scope for camping.

Eki-Naryn is located 42km outside of Naryn. A taxi here costs around 2000som, but with luck you may find a shared taxi leaving from Naryn's bazaar. With your own transport it's possible to continue northeast and then swing west to follow the Kara-Kujur Valley back to Sary-Bulak and the main Naryn–Kochkor road.

Tash Rabat Таш Рабат

Tash Rabat Valley's main draw is the historic caravanserai of the same name, but what makes it especially worth the detour from the main Torugart route is the peaceful valley setting where the only habitation is a series of seasonal yurt-camps (mostly for tourists) offering interesting walking or riding options and overnight accommodation.

The small stone **Tash Rabat Caravanserai** (100som) is sunk into the hillside of a photogenic narrow shepherds' valley that's given definition by occasional rocky outcrops. Local sources say it dates from the 15th century, although some sources trace the origins to a 10th-century Christian mon-

---

LOCAL KNOWLEDGE

SALKYN-TÖR NATIONAL PARK

Naryn locals love to picnic at the foot of this **national park** (20/50som per person/car) just outside of the city, but head up the valley past the small collection of cabins and you may have lush forests all to yourself. Be prepared to cross the river several times as the valley rises gently uphill, and push past the last steep section of the 10km trail from the cabins to a small lake.

It's around 17km east of Naryn, off the highway at a large gateway. CBT (p103) can organise cars, guides or horses; if you're hiking solo, cross two bridges to start the hike up the valley – it begins on the west bank of the river.

---

astery. Either way, historians agree that at one time Tash Rabat (Kyrgyz for 'stone fortress') must have had significant political and trade importance on the Silk Road to justify the investment in labour required for its construction. Enquire at the yurts across the road if it's locked when you try to enter.

From Tash Rabat, roughly six hours on foot or by plodding horse should get you to a broad ridge overlooking massive lake **Chatyr-Köl** (Чатыр-көл) – 23km long and 11km at the widest, but only around 20m deep. Continue for a couple of hours and you can stay the night in a yurt on the shore at just over 3500m, but note that after rains the area is often a boggy mess. Tash Rabat yurt owners arrange horses and guides.

Visiting the area requires a border-zone permit, though yurt owners report that these are rarely checked for hikers approaching over the mountains. However, you'll need to return the same way as these are certain to be checked at a police post on the road route, and ideally all visitors would prepare one before visiting.

If you've got the time and freedom, a stop en route at the **Koshoy Korgon Ruins** (🖉 (0)703-734340; Kara-Suu village; 50som; ⊙9am-6pm) is well worthwhile. Koshoy's fortress is a 250m square of muddy wall remnants from what is thought to have been a powerful 12th-century Karakhanid citadel, constructed on a site inhabited since at least the 8th century. Walk the path that follows the tops of the old ramparts, past the western-wall remains of a minaret and the southern-edge excavations of what is claimed to be Koshoy's home. Just before the entrance is a museum – rarely open, so call ahead – which has a striking design and an attractive art collection alongside artefacts from historic sites across Naryn *oblast*. It's 3km off the main road from Naryn to Torugart at Km409: head 800m down Köchör, the easternmost street in Kara-Suu village, then left on Abit (at Köchör 44/Abit 33), which curves around to the site.

There are several yurt-camps in the valleys around Tash Rabat. At the two biggest, **Omurbek** (☑(0)707-821139; dm 600som incl breakfast) and **Sabyrbek** (☑(0)772-221252, (0)772-471020; a.tursun23@mail.ru; dm 600som incl breakfast; ☺ Jun–mid-Oct), it's usually possible to drop in without reservations. Anyway calling is useless as there's no reception in the valley – try an SMS for when the owners next drive up to the main highway to catch a signal.

Yurt-camps include breakfast in the price and can generally arrange lunches and dinner for around 300som per meal.

ⓘ Getting There & Away

Tash Rabat is located 117km from Naryn. There's no public transport here. A CBT (p103) taxi return (day trip or overnight return) costs 3000som including a side trip to Koshoy Korgon. For US$120 you can continue the next day to Torugart.

SOUTHERN KYRGYZSTAN: JALAL-ABAD OBLAST
ДЖАЛАЛ-АБАДСКАЯ ОБЛАСТЬ

Osh and the surrounding lowland areas of the Fergana Valley feel sometimes like a different country from the north of Kyrgyzstan. Southern Kyrgyzstan (Южный Кыргызстан) is hotter in terms of climate and of human temperament, the nation's modern bread basket, and a historic Silk Road centre. Osh and Jalal-Abad in some ways have more in common with the more-conservative portions of the Fergana Valley just over the border than with industrialised, Russified Bishkek and the north. Throughout, the people are unfailingly hospitable and the region has far more of a classic 'Central Asian' feel than you'll find in the north.

Yet, leave Fergana for the climb to the Pamirs and it's mountains once more. Here lies the Alay: a wide open valley topped by the dramatic 7134m Peak Lenin. This is every part the modern Silk Road, and busy borders with China and Tajikistan still serve as a backbone for the region's commerce.

Jalal-Abad *oblast* gets less attention from tourists than most, but a comfortably modern city, enormous mountain lakes, and remote mountains stretching to the Uzbek border combine to make this a playground for the adventurous.

Sary-Chelek   Сары-Челек
ELEV 1878M

The largest of seven lakes in the Unesco-recognised Sary-Chelek Biosphere Reserve is widely considered among Kyrgyzstanis as one of the most beautiful places in the country, but a remote location and poor public transit connections see most international visitors giving it a pass. Spend an hour on the shore of the country's third-largest lake, a day in the surrounding mountains, or a week overlanding the backcountry route to Talas and it will quite likely be the highlight of a trip to the country.

Though the full Unesco **Sary-Chelek Biosphere Reserve** (Arkyt; per person/vehicle 400/100som; ☺ gate admission 8am-3pm) includes seven mountain lakes and numerous rare flora and fauna, the star attraction for most visitors is the massive Sary-Chelek lake itself. Over 2km at its widest and over 7.5km long, the lush shoreline vegetation and dramatic crags facing the lake's accessible south shore make it a favourite local travel destination and it isn't hard to understand why. From the car park, follow a path uphill beyond the few small buildings to loop around several of the small lakes and several breathtaking high-perspective views of Sary-Chelek lake itself.

Numerous guesthouses line the final few kilometres leading up to the park entrance in the village of Arkyt, with **Rysbek B&B** (☑(0)777-253915, (0)777-615944; Arkyt; dm 700som incl breakfast) across the small bridge a clear favourite. It's also possible to camp in the reserve upon payment of 500som per person at the park entrance, but make sure you pay before you go in or the rangers at the lake will send you on your way come nightfall.

The CBT guesthouse is the only show in town for trekkers planning trips out of Kyzyl-Köl village.

CBT Sary-Chelek (☑(0)559-254959, (0)374-260414; cbt_sary-chelek@mail.ru), based in the tiny village of Kyzyl-Köl (which many locals know by its former name, Kuzgun-Tas) up the parallel Karasuu valley, organises horse and hiking tours. Their most popular program is a two- to three-day route looping around one easy pass and six smaller lakes before descending to the main Sary-Chelek lake, but they also organise trips as ambitious as an eight-day horse trek to the Talas valley through some quite wild backcountry.

With advance notice they can arrange guides (English/non-English speaking 1500/1200som), horses (900som) and gear rental (500som) at daily rates.

ⓘ Getting There & Away

The park entrance is 100km off the Bishkek–Osh highway, travelling 50km from the coal-mining town of Tash-Komur on a road that's more good than bad before turning onto a smaller road at the bazaar town of Altykaragai (Алтыкарагай) for a considerably slower journey the remaining 50km. From the park entrance in the village of Arkyt, it's a windy 11km up to to the lake itself.

With a private car, the trip takes about two hours total without stops. On public transport, it takes a little longer. One direct marshrutka departs **Osh** (400som, six to nine hours) at 7.40am each morning, returning at 6am the next day. If that's sold out, Kerben-bound minibuses from Osh via Jalal-Abad and Tash-Komur pass by the Altykaragai junction, where it's possible to transfer to once-daily afternoon marshrutkas to Arkyt that return to Kerben early the next morning.

For the CBT (p111) office, up the parallel Kara-Suu Valley in Kyzyl-Köl, transfer in Altykaragai to one of several daily minibuses departing from Kerben (80som), Kara-Jyrgach (80som) or Tash-Komur (100som).

Jalal-Abad   Джалал-Абад

☑3722 / POP 106,000

If you're transiting between Osh and Kazarman or Arslanbob, you'll probably need to change vehicles in the leafy, laid-back spa-town of Jalal-Abad. Although it's Kyrgyzstan's third-largest city, there are no real sights in the city itself; CBT can offer details on villages nearby. Almost everything of use to travellers is within 10 minutes' walk of the central bazaar.

CBT (☑(0)772-376602, (0)3722-25643; cbt_ja@rambler.ru; Toktogul 20; ⊙9am-5pm Mon-Fri) can arrange trips to Saimaluu-Tash and Kazarman or to a handful of valleys closer to the city. Enquire for details.

MOUNTAINEERING IN BATKEN OBLAST

Tucked in between Osh and the Uzbek–Tajik borders, the need for border permits and the smattering of Tajik and Uzbek enclaves along the main highway makes travel in Batken more difficult for independent travellers than most of the country. It's an old favourite for rock climbers and mountaineers though, and with the right contacts it's possible to find some proper adventure in Kyrgyzstan's least-visited *oblast*.

The beautiful pyramid-shaped Ak-Suu peak (5359m), with its sheer 2km-high wall, is one of the world's extreme rock-climbing destinations. The region is totally lacking in infrastructure, or even roads, so you'll have to trek in from Ozgorush, where esteemed local guide Nuruddin runs a small homestay. Another superlative area for climbers is the trio of valleys lined with granite spires that lead south from Karavshin. Ak-Sai Travel (p69) operates four fixed-tent **summer camps** (dm/breakfast/lunch/dinner €10/10/20/20) at Ak-Tash Valley, Orto-Chashma Valley, Kara-Suu Gorge (Karavshin) and Ak-Suu Valley (Lyalak). These are open to independent travellers. Several Bishkek mountaineering companies offer treks and climbs in these areas including Tien Shan Travel (p70), whose 21-day climbing tours for groups of at least four experienced mountaineers from €1056 per person (excluding flights). Or you can arrange a tailor-made program via local specialist **Batken Travel Service** (☑(0)772-776691; batkentravelservice@gmail.com; Batken town; ⊙8am-7pm Mon-Sat). Plan ahead as the higher mountain areas typically require permits.

Aside from the city's hotels, CBT (p111) offers eight comfortable **homestays** (350som to 450som), all of which are good, although a little way from the centre. For something entirely different, try the Soviet-era **Jalal-Abad Health Resort** (Курорт; ✉(0)3722-60471, (0)3722-23055; szhalalabad@mail.ru; Kurortnyi Klioch 4; s/d 1720/2900som) on the hill above town.

Hotel Mölmöl's (✉(0)550-112575, (0)3722-55059; Lenina 17; s/d/ste 750/1200/2000som; 🖥) central location is appealing, though the musty foyer and temperamental showers are not. On the northern outskirts, **Roza Park** (✉(0)3722-73090; www.facebook.com/rozaparkhotel; Baltagula 183; s/d/tw 2000/2500/3000som; 🅿🌀@🖥; minibus 102,112,113) is the favoured Jalal-Abad address for visiting expats.

The largest concentration of cafes and restaurants is near the bazaar along Lenina. Appealingly tree-shaded **Kafe Elnura** (Lenina; mains 90-260som; ⊙ 7am-midnight), diagonally across Lenin from the southeast corner of the bazaar, makes an ideal place to linger over shashlyk and local favourites.

ℹ Getting There & Around

Minibuses use the main **bus station** (Lenina) 3km west of the bazaar (by marshrutka 110). Shared taxis departing from various points around the bazaar charge up to double.

For **Osh** (120som, 1¾ hours) a twice-hourly minibus departs until 7pm via **Uzgen** (60som, 50 minutes).

For Arslanbob transfer in Bazaar Korgon (30som, 40 minutes) on Maci- or Kochkor Ata–bound minibuses (three per hour).

The direct minibus from Osh to Sary-Chelek (260som, four hours) passes through Jalalabad around 9am. If you miss it, it's also possible to take Kerben-bound minibuses (185som, three hours) to the turn-off for the lakes at Altykaragai and transfer to a local minibus.

Shared taxis for Bishkek (typically 1100som, nine hours) depart from the bus station.

In summer, when the road is open, cars to Kazarman depart from the northeastern corner of the yard behind the Manas Avtobeket. To find it from the bazaar, walk up Chekhov one block, turn right on Babkina then right again through the covered toll gateway. The Kazarman cars lurk immediately to the left but hidden behind a pile of wrecked old kiosks.

Minibus 110 runs along Lenina from the bazaar to the bus station and beyond (10som). For Roza Park hotel, switch at the bazaar for minibus 102, 112 or 113.

Arslanbob   Арсланбоб

✉3736 / POP 11,291 / ELEV 1481M

The Babash-Ata Mountains form an impressive wall of snow-sprinkled crags behind the elevated 'oasis' of Arslanbob. Ethnically Uzbek and religiously conservative, the very large village sprawls almost invisibly along a network of tree-shaded lanes, and is surrounded by a vast tract of blossoming woodland that constitutes the world's largest walnut grove. According to local legend, the grove's seed-nuts were a miraculous gift from the Prophet Mohammed to a modest gardener who he had charged with finding paradise on earth, and it was from here that Alexander the Great was said to have brought seeds back to Europe.

The real attractions around Arslanbob are hikes, horse treks, cycle-rides or ski adventures in the surrounding mountains and forests. But Arslanbob's glorious garden-homestays are also a great place to unwind.

If you're just here to relax, it's worth sampling the village's schizophrenic atmosphere at Arslanbob's signature waterfalls. Neither is especially memorable per se, but the excitable local tourists buying candy-floss, yoghurt-balls and dodgy ice creams are fun to observe. And just walking there you'll get a better sense of the village's layout, impressive setting and part-timbered older mud-brick architecture. Just beyond the top of the smaller, more accessible **Twin Waterfall** (Vodapad; 10som), a footpath leaves behind the melee of souvenir stalls and crosses the stream. It zigzags up for 15 minutes cutting through a brief taster of the walnut grove then emerging onto an upper bank with glorious views over the Babash-Ata peaks. You can distantly make out the narrow 80m ribbon of the **Long Waterfall** (Bolshoy Vodapad; 10som), which is probably more satisfying than the two-hour walk to get there (locals go by 4WD) and 15-minute scree scramble to the base.

🎊 Festivals & Events

CBT hosts two one-day festivals each year, which are geared towards encouraging local participation in the village's most popular tourism offerings but also accepting traveller participation.

CBT Ski Challenge (1000som; ⊙ Jan)
CBT Bike Challenge (1000som; ⊙ May)

🛏 Sleeping & Eating

There are 18 **CBT-affiliated homestays** (📞(0)773-342476; cbtarslanbob@gmail.com; Rahim Palvan 6; incl breakfast family 350-550som; lunch or dinner 200som) scattered very widely around the village. These are hard to find without help and some are as much as 5km from the central square/bazaar. The best tactic is generally to visit CBT, which numbers each guesthouse and displays basic descriptions and photos on the wall. They'll find out which places have space and call someone to show you the way.

There are simple cafe-chaikhanas (meals 80som) in the main square/bazaar area, of which three are perched over the river (none with great views) and one (meals 80som; ⊙8am-8pm) attractively shaded beneath an ancient Chinor (plane) tree. There are even less sophisticated drink-stands and shashlyk burners at the Twin Waterfall (p112) and beside the **turbaza** (📞(0)3736-52840; Rahim Palvan 83; ⊙24hr) **FREE**.

By arrangement any homestay offers a choice of dinner (200som), but all guests should agree to take the same option for the family's convenience.

ℹ Information

A very well-organised branch of **CBT** (📞0773-342476; cbtarslanbob@gmail.com; Rahim Palvan 6; ⊙9am-1pm & 2-6pm Mon-Fri) can help organise virtually anything you're likely to need. Their office is 200m uphill from the shop-ringed main square/minibus stand. When the door is locked, phone.

CBT can arrange a wide variety of activities: mountaineering, skiing, mountain biking, fishing, birdwatching and cooking classes, as well as joining the walnut harvest; all often at very short notice. Tents/sleeping bags/mats (400/300/100som per night) are available for hire, but it's best to bring your own gear as CBT runs a bit short on stock.

The agency has six English-speaking guides (1200som per day), and can provide horses (1000som per day) and horse guides (2000som per day) on request as well. Note, though, that the CBT director has a reputation for stonewalling tourists who try to plan or organise activities outside of the CBT framework, so advanced or independent-minded hikers and mountaineers may be well advised to head elsewhere.

There are no internet cafes in Arslanbob, but mobile phone access is good. There are three exchange offices around the central square and one Visa ATM.

THE ARSLANBOB WALNUT HARVEST

From mid-September the town undergoes a mass exodus as locals move into the forest and go nuts. Each year 1500 tonnes of walnuts (and 5000 tonnes of apples, pistachios and cherry plums) are harvested in the Arslanbob Valley, and by all accounts gathering nuts is fun. Tradition dictates that during the harvest each family kills a sheep and shares the meat with their neighbours, so the fire-lit autumn nights are a time to sing songs, retell stories and eat way too much greasy mutton. CBT can arrange for travellers to camp on the territory of local families, whether to help in the harvest or use it as a base for wandering further into the forest.

ℹ Getting There & Around

Arslanbob is 3½ hours' drive from Osh. Twice a day, direct buses (200som) run between here and Arslanbob.

By marshrutka you'll need to change in both Jalal-Abad and Bazar Kurgan. Although the latter is 3km west of the Osh–Bishkek highway, Jalal-Abad–Masy and Jalal-Abad–Kockor Ata minibuses divert here (30som, 40 minutes from Jalal-Abad). Bazar-Kurgan–Arslanbob marshrutkas (marked Arstanbap) run roughly three times an hour until 6pm or later (60som, one hour). If arriving from the north, jump off at Sovetskoye (Km543/121) where there's a well-signed junction. Direct shared taxis leave from Arslanbob to Bishkek some mornings – CBT can book a space if you ask the day before.

In summer, shared bench-seat pickups with stripey canopies gather in the main square to shuttle visitors to the turbaza (25som per person) or Twin Waterfall (20som per person). To the access path for the Long Waterfall, 4WDs ask 700som per vehicle.

Kazarman   Казарман

📞3738 / POP 9486 / ELEV 1310M

The primary jumping-off point for a visit to the Saimaluu-Tash petroglyph site, sleepy Kazarman's setting is an attractive, wide, mountain-edged valley. Around 20 minutes' walk north of the Soviet-era culture centre, Dom Kulturi, a series of sandy riverside cliffs, is best appreciated from the

SAIMALUU TASH PETROGLYPHS

The several thousand 'embroidered stones' of **Saimaluu Tash** (300som) are Central Asia's most celebrated collection of petroglyphs. Over the millennia Aryan, Scythian and Turkic peoples have added to the earliest Bronze Age carvings. The carvings are spread over two slopes and depict hunting, shamanistic rites and battle scenes, some dating back more than 4000 years.

Kazarman is the obvious jumping-off point for a visit, which can be arranged by CBT Kazarman as one very long 14-hour day on horse and foot from 5200som (all-inclusive for up to four people) or as a multiday itinerary for slightly more. You start with a two-hour 4WD ride, then a steep five- to six-hour hike in places through shoulder-high grass, in others across a snow/ice field. It's worth overnighting near the valley to really have time to explore – the one-day trip only allows for around three hours at the site.

If you're planning to visit on your own, visit the **Saimaluu Tash Park Office** (Mon-pekettik zharalypish parky; ☑ (0)378-50284; Jeenaliev 64; ☺ 9am-1pm & 2-6pm Mon-Fri) a day or two beforehand to purchase the necessary permits.

CBT can't provide much information about other valleys near Kazarman, but these beautiful mountains are prime territory for exploration by independent and self-supported hikers.

Kara-Suu bridge. For a brilliant overview of the poplar-punctuated townscape and soaring backdrop, head in the opposite direction and climb the low, flat cemetery hill at the southern end of Mambetjanov.

CBT (☑ (0)777-688803; cbtkazarman@gmail.com; Kadyrkulova 35) works with three local homestays, all of which charge 700som including breakfast. Of these, the home of **Gulsaira Toktosunova** (☑ (0)773-340557; Kadyrkulova 25; dm 700som incl breakfast) is by far the most comfortable.

Of a handful of cafes on Jeenaliev, our favourite for food quality and variety is **Kafe Dostuk** (mains 60-90som; ☺ 24hr) beside Dom Kulturi, though the well-executed menu is often quite limited. Homestays can generally also prepare meals.

Just east of the Saimaluu-Tash park office, the 24hr ATM at **Bai Tushum Bank** (☑ (0)773-477222; Jeenalieva St; ☺ 8.30am-noon & 1-5.30pm Mon-Fri) is the most reliable in town.

ⓘ Getting There & Away

Historically one of the most poorly connected areas of Kyrgyzstan, completion of the new Bishkek–Osh highway will put Kazarman squarely back on the map and right along major transport routes.

At the time of research all access to the town was often impossible in the winter months, when snow blocks the passes from both Jalal-Abad and Naryn. At any time, double-check the road situation before setting off.

Road conditions permitting, one or two shared taxis can usually be found for Jalal-Abad (700som, four hours) departing from Jeenaliev in front of the bazaar some mornings. Cars for Bishkek (1400som to 1700som, 12 hours) start from across the road. Bishkek cars could drop you in Naryn or Kochkor, but the price will still be 1200som to 1500som. Naryn-specific cars (900som, five hours) only leave a couple of times a week. If you're in a hurry it's worth budgeting for the worst-case scenario of having to fork out for all four seats, which can always be arranged independently or through CBT (p114).

SOUTHERN KYRGYZSTAN: OSH OBLAST
ОШСКАЯ ОБЛАСТЬ

Most famous as a Silk Road centre, Osh *oblast* lives up to its cultural heritage but also throws in a bit of adventure for nature-loving visitors who head out into the high mountains of the Alay Valley on the southern border with Tajikistan.

Osh   Ош

☑ 3222 / POP 260,800 / ELEV 948M

With a remarkable five-headed crag leaping out of the very town centre, Kyrgyzstan's second city certainly has a highly distinctive visual focus. While there's little of architectural note to show for 3000 years of history,

Osh's sprawling bazaar and hospitable citizens provide an atmosphere that is far more archetypically Central Asian than you will find in Bishkek.

Aside from the city itself and the interesting outdoor opportunities nearby, Osh is also a launch or arrival point for travellers to/from China, for transiting from Uzbekistan's Fergana Valley, or for accessing Tajikistan's memorable Pamir Highway. Inexpensive international flights can also make it a savvy gateway to Central Asia.

Locals maintain that 'Osh is older than Rome'. Legends credit all sorts of people with its founding, from King Solomon (Suleyman) to Alexander the Great. Certainly it must have been a major hub on the Silk Road from its earliest days. The Mongols smashed it in the 13th century, but in the following centuries it bounced back, more prosperous than ever. In 1496, Babur, later the founder of the Mughal-Indian dynasty, passed through as a teenager from his native Fergana and commissioned the modest prayer-room on top of Suleiman Too. Osh was absorbed into the Kokand Khanate in 1762 and later fell to Russian forces.

Osh has a distinct demographic mix, being a major centre of Kyrgyzstan but with a strong (44%) Uzbek population more in tune with Uzbekistan and the rest of the Fergana Valley.

◉ Sights

Osh's sights centre on the massive Suleiman Too mountain, and many are of a religious nature that have origins early in Osh's long history. If you're in Osh on a Sunday morning, hundreds of sheep, donkeys, horses and cattle go on sale at the traditional **Malbazaar** (Animal Market; M41 road, Km4; ⊗ 7am-noon Sun). To get there, hop on marshrutka 105 or bus 5 to the routes' eastern terminus.

Jayma Bazaar   MARKET
Osh Bazaar is one of Central Asia's biggest markets dealing in everything from traditional hats and knives to seasonal fruit to horseshoes forged at the smithies in the bazaar. Many stalls are crafted from old container boxes and banal warehouse architecture, but there's a fascinating bustle nonetheless, stretching for about 1km astride the river. Most dynamic on Sunday mornings; partly closed on Monday.

The eastern entrance section is the point most minibuses mean when stating simply 'bazaar' on their signs.

Navoi Park   PARK
Stretching south along the river from where the bazaar ends, leafy Navoi Park is a favourite local hang-out. Highlights inside include a gaming area where *ak-sakal* (white-beard) elders play chess, and a Yak 40 airplane decommissioned during Soviet times to serve as an oddball theatre and now as shade for a terrace cafe. The entire park is one of the pleasantest parts of the city.

It's named after poet and writer Alisher Navoi (1441–1501), a point of pride for local Uzbeks who claim him as their own.

Suleiman Too   MOUNTAIN
(Solomon's Throne; 20som; ⊗ 9am-8pm) This five-peaked rocky crag seems to loom above the city wherever you go. It has been a Muslim place of pilgrimage for centuries, supposedly because the Prophet Mohammed once prayed here. Its slopes are indented with many a cave and crevice each reputed to have different curative or spiritual properties; many are detailed on photo-boards in the **Cave Museum** (150som; ⊗ 9am–noon & 1–6pm). One such is fertility mini-cave Ene-Beshik, its rocks worn smooth by young women slithering in to aid their motherly aspirations.

You'll see it right beside the path to the Cave Museum as you descend westward from Suleiman Too's main viewpoint. On that crag lies the one-room **Dom Babura** (Babur's House), the reconstruction of an historic prayer-room whose tradition dates back to 1497. In that year the 14-year-old Zahiruddin Babur of Fergana built himself a little prayer-retreat here. Later famed as progenitor of the Mogul Dynasty, Babur's place of private worship became highly revered but various incarnations have been destroyed notably by earthquake (1853) and, in the 1960s, by mysterious explosion. This version dates from 1989.

Allow around 20 minutes of sweaty climbing on the hairpin stairway to Dom Babura from Suleiman Too's main entrance, which is beside the strange silver-domed building that looks like an alien fairy cake, but actually formerly contained a photography salon popular with newly-weds.

Osh Regional Museum   MUSEUM
(✆ (0)3122-27132; Alymbek Datka Park; 50som, photos each 10som; ⊗ 9am-noon & 1-6pm) Built during the Osh 3000 celebrations, this museum has some imaginative displays like a case of weapons apparently caught up in a

Osh

KYRGYZSTAN OSH

N 0 — 500 m
0 — 0.25 miles

Bazaar

Osh

Lenin

Zaina Betinova
(Jodoshbek Ramizbekov)

18

20

3
35

39
34

Masalieva

Bazaar

38

Navoi (Alayskaya)

Malbazar
(Animal Market);
Alay Baza (Shared
Taxis to Murgab);
Sary-Tash

6
Navoi (Alayskaya)

32

11

37

Kelechek
Bazaar

Lenin

Ak-Buura River

Navoi
Park
7

Masalieva

10
2

Israil
Sulaimanov

26

13
Muslim
Cemetery

1

8 21
25

14

12

5
Gapar Aytiev
33

30

24

Aravan (25km)

28

Mominova

31

17

Abdykadyrov

Bridge

Lenin

Inset

4
15

Ak-Buura River

City
Central
Hospital

Footbridge

9

23

Aliev

19

36

Golubev

Bayalinov

Stadium

27

Lenin

Kurmanjan Datka

Soviet

Kurmanjan Datka

Silk Factory
(1km)

29

Frunze

Lomonsov

Kurmanjan Datka

Inset

N 0 — 200 m
0 — 0.1 miles

Michurin

22

16

Osh

mad whirlwind. The great archaeological finds, historical documents and moving photos of the 1916 uprising would be so much more interesting were there more English explanations.

Just outside the museum is a **Three-Storey Yurt** (Alymbek Datka Park; 80som, photos 10som each; ☉8am-10pm). Athough interesting for its mere existence, the colourful interior is little more than a gift shop with a skippable museum.

Behind the museum is the ornate **Mausoleum of Asaf ibn Burhiya** (Alymbek Datka Park), fenced off from visitors but worth a peek for intricate carvings on the front facade. A Suleiman Too ticket is required.

Fine Arts Museum MUSEUM
(Köl-Onorculor; 25som; ☉9am-5pm) A surprisingly well-curated collection of art ranges from socialist realism to Central Asia modern museum staff are passionate art lovers and happy to share their knowledge with visitors who can speak Russian or Kyrgyz.

Don't miss the 11th- to 12th-century Karakhanid hamman on the hill just to the left of the museum, fenced off but still worth a look.

Directly beside the museum is the 16th-century **Rabat Abdullakhan Mosque** (☉9am-6pm), believed to be one of the oldest structures in the city, and though the ornate wooden doors to the 'Old Mosque' compound are considerably newer they certainly add to the aesthetic appeal of the place.

Petrovsky Park PARK
(Lenin) Centred on the 1909 St Michael's Cathedral, this large park off the central square is worth a wander to see monuments dedicated to WWII soldiers, Chernobyl victims, and the 2010 events in Osh. Visit during the Destination Osh City Walking Tour (p118) for a full background of each.

On the square behind the park is one of the most impressive **Lenin statues** (Central Square; ☉2) still standing in all of Central Asia; he appears to be objecting to the massive Kyrgyz flag flapping in front of him as he faces down the modern city hall.

Mosque of Mohammed Yusuf Bai Haji Ogli MOSQUE
(Novoi) Founded in the 16th to 17th centuries, the main prayer hall is around 170 years old. Visit outside of prayer times, and ask the imam before taking a peek inside

🏃 Activities

The Destination Osh public association (p120) organises a collection of interesting tours that open the city's history and culture to visitors. In addition to those listed here they can arrange private options, including guided visits to Suleiman Too.

Free City Walking Tour
WALKING TOUR
(☑(0)571-190190; ⊙9am-noon Tue & Thu) **FREE** Tip-based 2½-hour group walking tour to introduce visitors to the city, meeting at the main square and following Lenin and Navoi Park all the way up to the bazaar. The informative tour explores the city's traditional and Soviet past via the main sites and several offbeat highlights.

Osh Foodie Tour
TOUR
(⊙noon-3pm; Mon, Wed & Fri) Sample four of Osh's most iconic foods on this 2½-hour tour. The price includes all food, an English-speaking guide, and transportation between restaurants and back to the city centre.

Osh Plov Journey
COURSE
(⊙3-7pm Tue & Thu) Join English-speaking guide Atabek in his family's home to learn the secrets of making *plov* (pilaf), one of the Fergana Valley's most iconic dishes. Vegetarian groups can be accommodated with advanced notice.

🛏 Sleeping

In addition to the full range of hotels and hostels, some of them quite excellent, CBT Osh/Alay (p120) works with a number of homestays in the city (700som to 1000som per person, per night).

★ Biy Ordo
HOSTEL **$**
(☑(0)556-008989, (0)773-018900; www.biyordo. com; Saliyeva 39; dm/s/d 500/1000/1500som; P꙱@☎; minibus 122) Biy Ordo is worth the 10-minute marshrutka ride (122 from Kelechek Bazaar) for the great-value dorms and perfect hostel vibe. Dorms have lockers, and all rooms come with new air-con and en suite bathrooms.Owner Munar and his staff speak fluent English and understand backpacker needs, and at the time of research were planning to launch a second location in the centre.

From the airport a booked pick-up costs 200som, or get off marshrutka 107 outside BTA Bank on Razzakov, then walk one block west to Saliyeva street.

Maatova Guesthouse
GUESTHOUSE **$**
(☑(0)3222-55936, (0)773-041002; Mominova 7A; dm incl breakfast 850som; ☎) Incredibly central and run by a friendly family, this is a great choice for guesthouse enthusiasts, though on the downside all rooms share just two bathrooms. Look for the sign off Mominova, just across from Brio cafe (p120).

Osh Guesthouse
HOSTEL **$**
(☑(0)772-37 2311, (0)5530372311; http://osh guesthouse.ucoz.com; Masalieva 8/48; dm/d/apt US$6/12/25; ☎) Osh's unlikely traveller hub has expanded into a collection of apartments, and signage off Masalieva now points travellers straight in. English-speaking fixer-owner Daniyar uses a big whiteboard to match travellers seeking to share rides to Mughab (US$180 per car), the Afghan Wakhan, Sarez Lake and much more. Tajikistan GBAO permits can also be arranged.

The owners are opening a second campus, more akin to a modern hostel, and can also put travellers in touch with a partner guesthouse in Bishkek.

Orto Asia
HOTEL **$$**
(☑(0)775-583222, (0)3222-83222; Razzakov 23; s/d/tr US$70/70/80 incl breakfast; ꙱☎; minibus 128) For a little bit of luxury after a long hike or horse trek, this marble-studded hotel north of town is easily the best choice in Osh. Though it's a bit out of the centre, rooms are spacious and comfortable enough that you won't want to leave anyway. Turn off Razzakov onto small Avicenna – it's right at the end.

Silk Way Boutique Hotel
HOTEL **$$**
(☑(0)557-901555, (0)322-82527; silkway hotel@gmail.com; Avicenna 10; s/d incl breakfast US$35/42; minibus 128) The midrange rooms here are good value for the price, and though the northern location isn't terribly convenient, the 128 marshrutka route terminates just a few minutes' walk away.

Eco House
HOTEL **$$**
(☑(0)553-411800, (0)3222-20945; guesthouse_osh@mail.ru; Lomonsov 25; s/d/tr 1600/2400/3000som; ꙱☎; ☐2) Popular with short-term business visitors, this cosy, superclean guesthouse has a small verandah–breakfast room and garden. The guest rooms are unusually well appointed with great hot showers, satellite TV, free wi-fi and some modest attempts to add decorative touches (artificial flowers, leaf paintings, wall hangings).

TES Guesthouse GUESTHOUSE **$$**
(☑(0)3222-21548, (0)779-630603; http://osh
testravel.com/; Say Boyu 5; dm/s/d incl breakfast
800/1800/2500som; P❋❁) TES is notable
for its peaceful garden setting where there
are two bedded yurts rented out dorm-style
(no lockers) in summer. Rooms are fault-
lessly clean if staid. Help yourself to coffee
or tea in the pine-floored lounge. Laundry
costs 150som per load. Camping (400som
per person) includes breakfast, shower and
internet. English spoken.

✖ Eating & Drinking

Osh has an excellent food scene that's often
much cheaper than the rest of the country.
Shashlyk is of a generally high standard,
plov (pilaf) is some of the best in the country
(chalk it up to Uzbek influence), and humon-
gous *osh samsa* are a meal and a half. Food
lovers would be well advised to ask about the
Osh Foodie Tour, which samples some of the
city's best dishes in optimal form.

Not surprisingly, in the more conserv-
ative south, Osh's nightlife scene doesn't
match up to those in Bishkek or even Chol-
pon-Ata. **Aztec** (Atstek; ☑(0)557-500100;
Kurmanjan Datka 94; ⊘10am-midnight; ❁) and
Izyum (p119) are usually reliable for some
music, at least, or there's always a warm
drink to curl up over at Brio (p120).

Islambek Cafe BBQ **$**
(☑(0)3222-72077; Lenin 243; shashlyk 70-
260som; ⊘9am-11pm) This is where locals
head for shashlyk, and even at odd hours it's
usually busy. Try the *oromo kebab* – tender
meat wrapped in a thin layer of fat and then
grilled...it's better than it sounds.

Alymbek Datka Village CENTRAL ASIAN **$**
(Alymbek Datka Park; mains 40-220som; ⊘9am-
8pm) At this handful of *tapchans* and yurts
off the centre of Alymbek Datka Park, the
menu at first glance looks like the standard
array of Central Asian fare. Look again for
the эт боорсок, meat-stuffed layers of fried
dough that are tempting (if heavy) when
fresh in the mid-afternoon.

Ala-Too TEAHOUSE **$**
(Masaliev 16A; mains 100-250som; ⊘8am-9pm)
Airy modern chaikhana-restaurant with ret-
ro diner seating and excellent homemade
laghman noodles.

Osh Ordo CENTRAL ASIAN **$**
(Gapar Aytiev 11; mains 170-280som; ⊘9am-11pm)
Above the over-glitzy main restaurant is a

KYRGYZ-ATA NATIONAL PARK

Long a favourite of local day trippers,
Kyrgyz-Ata National Park (Nookat
region; 150som) is slowly becoming pop-
ular with international travellers as well.
Though just under 12 sq km, it packs in
a diverse arrange of scenery along the
valleys of the Mazar and Kara-Koi rivers
and at only 40km from Osh makes an
easy single-day or weekend visit.

Public transport runs from Osh to
the village of Nookat, past the turn-off
to Kyrgyz-Ata in the village of Chapaeva,
but from there you'll have to find trans-
port the last 28km to the park gate and
beyond. Kyrgyz Pamir Tours (p120) runs
an interesting day-trip option (1750som
per person) that includes transport,
lunch, a cultural show and demonstra-
tions of national horse games.

summer rooftop with great views of Sulei-
man Too from stylish new tea pavilions,
some set on rocker-wheels. The view is more
of a draw than the food, but it's not bad.

Oasis FAST FOOD **$**
(☑(0)555-935593; Kurmanjan Datka; snacks 15-
100som; ⊘9am-midnight) This tiny fast-food
joint on the corner of Kurmanjan Datka and
Gapar Aytiev has a surprisingly large menu
but, trust us on this one, go for the late-night
shwarmas.

★ Tsarskii Dvor INTERNATIONAL, PUB **$$**
(☑(0)559-858527; Lenin; mains 180-350som;
⊘11am-4am, kitchen to 11pm; ❁▢) This big
ski-lodge–style log chalet has heavy wooden
throne seats, a rear beer terrace and a range
of barbecues, fish dishes and sausages. The
shashlyk is excellent, but really everything
on the menu seems reliable. There's a 20som
cover when musicians play (soft sax). Nightclub behind.

Izyum INTERNATIONAL, BAR **$$**
(☑(0)556-777795, (0)551-119119; Lenin 214; mains
300-460som; ⊘8am-midnight, kitchen to 11pm;
❋▢) Osh's most complete drinking/dining
experience is a hit in summer for its river-
side and woodland tea/dining platforms, but
it also has a stylishly angular cafe with am-
ply piled cushions on wide sofa seats. Steaks
and local food choices are good; pizza and

sushi less so. Dancing is a possibility as the evening wears on.

Brio CAFE

(☑ (0)550-832595; http://brio.kg; Kurmanjan Datka; ⊘ 8.30am-10pm Mon-Sat; 🛜) Sip on the best (only?) espresso drinks this side of Bishkek, dig into a sandwich or salad of the healthy-living menu, and watch out the large bar windows as happy couples tie the knot at the wedding-registry service next door.

🛍 Shopping

The southwest entrance to the main bazaar has several stalls selling cheap *ak kalpak* hats (from 80som), embroidered gowns, satin tunics and musical instruments.

Osh Market MARKET

(☑ (0)3222-25423; Gapar Aytiev 11; ⊘ 24hr) Nope, you're not at the bazaar. This local supermarket carries the normal range of local products, plus a surprisingly large selection of imported goods and craft beers – music to the ears of travellers who have been too long in the mountains.

Saimalu Tash ART, GIFTS & SOUVENIRS

(☑ (0)3222-29595, (0)554-068068; saimaluu.t@ gmail.com; Kurmanjan Datka 244; ⊘ 9am-noon & 1-7pm) A small but attractive art and textiles showroom featuring hand-embroidered carpets, patchwork panels, framed art and a variety of handmade souvenirs.

Kyrgyz Konyagy DRINKS

(☑ (0)551-047116, (0)3222-23381; www.cognac. kg; Lenin 233/9; ⊘ 9.30am-7pm) Sells a full range of Kyrgyz brandies from 200som to 7000som per half-litre according to quality and ageing (various sizes of bottles available). Flavoured brandies make great gifts and there are also herb-honey liqueurs infused with barberry, walnut, buckthorn or pomegranate. A stand-bar allows you to taste your purchases – once you've paid.

ℹ Information

For banks with good dollar, euro and rouble exchange rates look on Lenin, south of the post office, and along Navoi. A few money-changers' kiosks hidden deep within the bazaar will change Uzbek sum, Tajik somoni and Chinese CNY at miserly rates. Visa ATMs are widespread and there are multicard ATMs at the airport.

The **main post office** (Lenin 320; ⊘ 9am-noon & 1-5pm Mon-Fri, 9am-2pm Sat) handles mail services in the city.

Osh's **City Central Hospital** (☑ 103; Kurmanjan Datka; ⊘ 24hr) is one of the largest in the country's south, though standards are still not always at an international level.

TOURIST INFORMATION & TRAVEL AGENCIES

CBT Osh/Alay (☑ (0)555-077621; www.visit alay.kg; Kurmanjan Datka 280, Hotel Alay, 2nd fl, room 3; ⊘ 9am-6pm Mon-Sat, to 4pm Sun) At one of the best CBT offices in the country, coordinator Talant works with a handful of Osh homestays and organises a range of tours and treks, most notably from Sary-Mogol and Gulcha but even as far as Dushanbe via the Pamirs. It's one of the best sources for information in the entire region, hands down. The office also sells gas canisters for camping stoves and a range of maps, including the Tajik Pamirs.

Destination Osh (☑ (0)571-190190; www. facebook.com/destination.osh; Gapar Aytiev 15; ⊘ 9am-6pm) The Destination Osh public association organises a collection of interesting tours including a *plov* cooking class, city food tour, tip-based city tour, bread-baking classes and visits to Suleiman Too.

Kyrgyz Pamir Tours (☑ (0)772-826661; kg. pamir777@gmail.com; Masalieva 30; ⊘ 9am-6pm Mon-Fri) This friendly office arranges tours throughout Southern Kyrgyzstan and the Tajik Pamirs, and organises an interesting full-day trip to Kyrgyz-Ata National Park (p119) around 40km away from Osh.

Munduz Travel (☑ (0)3222-55500, (0)772-947475, (0)552-947475; munduz_tourist@ hotmail.com; Kurmanjan Datka 124A, enter from Asrankulov; ⊘ 9am-6pm Mon-Sat) This reliable, long-standing commercial agency can arrange transport to Irkeshtam (US$200 per vehicle) and Murgab (Tajikistan; US$450 jeep), get Peak Lenin permits relatively rapidly (US$35 in three working days) and GBAO permits for Tajikistan (US$85/50 same day/ two working days) and much more.

ℹ Getting There & Away

AIR

Up to five flights daily link with Bishkek on a variety of carriers (discount/standard/business 1300/2200/4000som), and in summer several weekly flights head to **T**amchy (p81) airport on the northern shore of Issyk-Köl (2850som).

There's one weekly flight to Ürümqi (Xinjiang, China) on both **Air Kyrgyzstan** (http://air. kg/) and China Southern (p138). There are also direct flights to nearly a dozen Russian cities on Aeroflot (p138), S7 (p138) and **Ural Airlines** (☑ (0)550-086677; www.uralairlines.ru; Masalieva 28; ⊘ 9am-6pm); Moscow starts around 12,000som.

Facilities at **Osh Airport** (⌨ (0)3222-90101; www.airport.kg/osh; off Joldasheva St; ⊙24hr) are basic. There's a trio of ATMs, but minimal shopping facilities.

BUS, MINIBUS & SHARED TAXI

Minibuses to the following destinations leave from the new bus station north of Osh's centre:

Batken (for Khojand, Tajikistan) Minibus 537 (290som, 4½ hours) and regular shared taxis (400som) leave throughout the day.

Jalal-Abad (120som, 1¾ hours) Every 30 minutes, via **Uzgen** (60som, one hour)

Sary-Chelek (400som, six to seven hours, 7.40am)

Sary-Tash (300som, four hours, 2pm) Continues via Sary-Mogol (400som, five hours) to Daroot-Korgon (500som, five to six hours). Shared taxis/informal minibuses charge similar fares, but are generally faster.

Toktogul (500som, seven hours, 7.15am) As well as shared taxis (600som, six hours)

From near the **old bus station** (Stary Avto-vokzal; Navoi) under the Dostyk Bridge:

Bishkek There are no buses. Shared-taxi fares fluctuate according to demand and vehicle type but 1200som to 1500som is common. Typically takes 10 hours. Cars lurk in a **parking area** (Navoi) hidden away just off Navoi in front of the Deluxe Hotel.

Dostyk (border with Uzbekistan) Marshrutka 107 and 113 (10som) leave across the street from the station.

TO & FROM CHINA

Murgab (Tajikistan)

Tajik 4WDs charge 2000som per person in a crushed-full jeep (typically six people in four seats) taking around 12 hours. You might find such a jeep at the Old Bus Station, but more likely you'll need to head out to the **Alay-Baza** (off M41; ☐105), some 4km east of the Masalieva junction. Take marshrutka 105, get off 300m before the Animal Market (Malbazaar) turning and walk three minutes up the dead-end lane directly east of Aida timber shop.

Departures could be at any time, but are most typically around 3am. If so it usually makes sense to sleep the night before at the Alay-Baza's very rough-and-ready crash-pad.

To see the scenic route more comfortably (and by day) consider sharing a charter vehicle. Note that such 4WDs will need special drivers' papers for the border zone and preferably an oversized fuel tank. Osh Guesthouse (p118) can often find vehicles at short notice (US$180) and can sort out GBAO permits (essential) should you have forgotten to get one with your Tajik visa.

Kashgar (Xinjiang, China)

Shared taxis depart between infrequently from the Old Bus Station for 6500som to 7000som per vehicle in summer, and nearly double in winter. Making the trip in hops via Sary-Tash to Irkeshtam (3000som) and on to the Chinese border (¥533) to connect to a bus to Kashgar (¥33) is more complicated but cheaper and generally more interesting.

ⓘ Getting Around

Marshrutka 107 takes 25 minutes from Jayma Bazaar to the airport (10som) via Masalieva, but be aware that some 107 buses go instead to Dostyk, the Uzbekistan border post, so check the destination panel. Routes 113, 136 and 137 also head to the border post for the same cost.

Bus 2 and numerous marshrutka routes drive along Navoi, past the minibus station, then head southbound on Kurmanjan Datka, returning northbound on Lenin (at least north of Lomonsov).

Marshrutka 105 comes up Temur, turns east on Gapar Aytiev near the Suleiman Too Mosque, uses Lenin/Kurmanjan Datka north/south to Navoi, then sidesteps heading east to the Animal Market on Furkat.

A taxi costs from 50som within the centre or 200som to the airport. If you arrive at the airport after 8pm, taxis will rarely accept less than 400som to take you into town.

Uzgen   Узген

⌨ 3233 / POP 51,000 / ELEV 1085M

While its sights don't add up to much, the predominantly Uzbek town of Uzgen makes a good brief stop if you're driving the main road to/from Osh. The busy bazaar has an untouristed charm and is fronted by a pair of majolica-pattern tiled towers, which might be mid-20th-century but still dream Silk Road dreams. Citadels on this raised riverbank site reputedly date back 2000 years and the town was a Karakhanid capital a millennium ago.

The only genuinely historic buildings today are an 11th-century brick minaret and a neighbouring three-in-one 12th-century **mausoleum complex** (Lenina; 40som; ⊙8am-8pm) in shades of red-brown clay. The monuments, 600m east of the bazaar, are worth a brief look, and climbing the dark and winding stairway inside the large minaret nearby and nice views from the top look out over panoramas of the mausoleum complex and the town's most famous modern export: fields of Uzgen rice.

Excellent tours of Uzgen's historical and cultural sites in English are provided by local guide Husniddin Sharipov, who can generally be found at the mausoleum complex or contacted directly at (0)556-868756. Half-day tours including lunch start at US$50 per person.

Fast food and shashlyk stalls are dotted in the area around the bazaar, but if you're with a group order up the fantastic *plov* (pilaf) at **Ash Borboru** (☑(0)770240284; Amir Timur; mains 140-250; ⊗8am-midnight) on the south edge of town.

ℹ Getting There & Away

Marshrutkas between Osh (60som, one hour) and Jalal-Abad (60som, 50 minutes) pick up and drop off passengers near the bazaar along the main highway. For services to both that originate or terminate in Uzgen there's a minibus station tucked away one block further east, then north.

Alay Valley   Долина Алай

Platoons of vast, ever-snowy mountains march along the southern flank of the Alay Valley, whose considerable width (up to 30km) makes the scene especially memorable – at least when the clouds lift off the peaks that surround the valley.

Visitors en route to China via Irkeshtam or to Tajikistan via Bordöbo get a taste of the scenery from Sary-Tash. However, it's well worth continuing to Sary-Mogol (p124) and Daroot-Korgon (p126) for trailheads to gentle lake hikes, week-long traverses of the Alay range, or the expedition to the top of Peak Lenin. Heading back towards Osh, look for CBT-posted hikes (p120) off the highway that vary from several hours to several days.

ℹ Getting There & Away

One daily bus departs each day to and from Osh and Daroot-Korgon, stopping at all settlements en route. Buses depart Osh around 2pm to arrive in Daroot-Korgon by roughly 7pm, returning in the morning at 6am to arrive in Osh around 11am. An excellent new road follows from the Alay Valley southwest from Sary-Tash to Garm (Tajikistan), but for now the Tajik–Kyrgyz border at Karamyk is closed to foreigners.

Leaving the Alay over international borders, it's possible to cross into the Tajik Pamirs or China's region of Xinjiang. Both routes cross high-altitude passes, but only the Chinese route over the Irkeshtam pass is fairly easy to do in DIY hops. Hitching the road to the Tajikistan town of Murgab (via Bordöbo border) can be frustratingly slow with no regular transport: bring a tent in case you're stranded in the (potentially frigid) wilderness.

Sary-Oi & the Ak-Tör Pass

CBT (p120) in Osh can arrange a fantastic three-or four-day walk through the alpine valleys of the Alay mountains an hour's drive south of Osh. The trek takes you past herding camps selling fresh mare's milk, up a gentle ridge to the 3086m Kum Bel pass and then down to a **CBT yurtstay** (☑(0)556-562678; Sary-Oi jailoo; dm 1000som incl meals; ⊗mid-May–September) in the Sary-Oi Valley. From here it's a day's walk up the wild valley to a lovely campsite nestled at the base of granite peaks. The next day takes you up into the stunning mountain amphitheatre around the 3540m Ak-Tör Pass, before descending to a final night's yurt-camp just above the Murdash Valley. The scenery ranges from lush corduroy green valleys dotted with white yurts and horseback Kyrgyz herders to high alpine vistas of rock and ice. CBT can arrange yurtstays in Chyrchik, Sary-Oi and Murdash and offers horse-trek itineraries that stay only in yurts, though you'll need a tent and food for a night if you want to cross the Ak-Tör Pass.

Between Gulcha & Sary-Tash

Along the highway between Osh and Sary-Tash are signed turn-offs for a series of trails ranging from a few hours (such as the Kolduk Lakes, Uch-Tobo Lake and Chon Bulolu forest reserve). A full-day walk from the Taldyk Pass (3614m) descends into the town of Sary-Tash.

Above a hilly *jailoo* (summer pasture) ringed by yurts, the larger **Kolduk Lake** (Kolduk jailoo) is backed by a craggy mountain gorge. Families that take residence here from May to September are insistent in their offers of fresh dairy products from the livestock that roam these hills – it's impolite to not at least take a small piece of bread dipped in kaimak (sweet cream).

Jiptik Pass

The most interesting way to access the Alay Valley is on foot, crossing the Alay range over the 4180m Jiptik Pass. It's a relatively easy three-day trek and in July and August CBT (p120) runs yurtstays on either side of the pass, which means you technically don't

HIKING IN THE ALAY

With the help of CBT Osh/Alay (p120) or CBT Sary-Mogol (p124) you can hike several routes in the Alay with little more than a day pack, offering all the convenience of Nepali-style teahouse trekking without the crowds. It's that rarest of travel alignments: world-class mountain scenery, easy accessibility and low cost.

There are some fabulous day trips that can take you up to the high mountain lakes of the Alay range. The Besh Köl lakes just north of Sary-Mogol are a beautiful chain of five tarns and can also be accessed as part of a four-day trek back to Osh over the Sary-Mogol Pass, but both the pass and lakes are often snowed in until mid-June. A taxi here costs 2000som with CBT.

Another option is the Dam jailoo valley hike, which winds up through lush pastures for three hours to a pair of high-altitude lakes known as the Kosh Köl (Double Lakes), at 4130m. The treeless, rolling valley feels like it could be lifted from Iceland or Greenland and offers great camping spots if you want to go exploring. CBT can arrange a day's jeep hire to the start of the trek for US$45 to US$55.

Pushing far into the Alay, two- and three-day loops ring Daroot-Korgon and Kashka-Suu, while an immense nine-day route tracks past high-mountain lakes and the furthest reaches of Kyrgyz-Ata National Park (p119) to connect Daroot-Korgon to Kojo-Kelen and potentially Sary-Mogol.

The trekking season here is short – the mountains are high and the winters cold. However, in recent years the region has become an offbeat but growing destination for off-piste ski tours. Pamir Extreme (p124) is one of the only operators with a wide experience in the region, and their product list makes an appealing alternative for experienced skiers looking for untouched powder.

need to drag a tent or stove over the pass. The trek starts in Kojo-Kelen (where there's a homestay) and follows an old Soviet-era road, now little more than a faded track, up into the high valleys. From the pass there are epic views south to a 100km wide swath of muscular 7000m Pamir peaks. This can be extended with four additional days of camping to loop back around to where it began, in which case Sary-Tash is the more convenient trailhead.

From the pass it's a two-hour descent to first of several campsites. A further 90 minutes away is the Tash Darwaza yurt-camp (late June to September), through the first of two rock gorges (*tash darwaza* means 'stone gates'). You can get picked up here and avoid the flat three-hour valley walk past two coal mines to Sary-Mogol.

Peak Lenin Base Camp

An hour-long (1500som) jeep ride from the town of Sary-Mogol (p124) drops you at a CBT yurt-camp at Tulpar Köl (p124), a 3500m high lake at the base of the mountains. A 90-minute walk from the camp takes you to the foot of glaciers tumbling off the massive peak. At the beginning and end of the season you can cross the stream near Tulpar Köl and hike past the climbers' base camp at Achik Tash up to astonishing views at Wild Onion Meadow (Lukovaya Polyana), though you need to double-check with CBT whether permits are needed. There are also lovely walks around Tulpar Köl.

For a quieter experience make the 90-minute horse ride east to the Tuiuk yurt-stay in the neighbouring valley, where more fabulous day hikes await. Both sets of yurts provide dinner, breakfast, tea and a cosy bed of duvets for just US$15 per person.

Gulcha   Гульча

☎ 3234 / POP 11,691 / ELEV 1553M

Gulcha is the true gateway to the Alay and home to the region's best museum, even though most travellers zip right by on the highway between Osh and the border. It's also the gateway to three of CBT Osh/Alay's (p120) most underappreciated hikes, and a possible transfer point for the spectacularly located Sary-Oi yurt-camp (p122).

The **Kurmanjan Datka Museum** (☎ (0)779-163754; 50som; ☺ 9am-8pm) is worth a stop. Dedicated to Kyrgyzstan's very own 'Queen of the Alay', Gulcha's ethnography and history museum is most notable for exhibits on the local female chieftain who

DON'T MISS

YAK AND HORSE GAMES FESTIVAL

The Yak and Horse Games Festival, a gathering of horse games and a somnolent rendition of *kok boru* on yaks held by the shores of Tulpar Köl (p120), is worth planning around if you'll be in the area in late July. Contact CBT in Sary-Mogol, for exact dates.

resisted and eventually acquiesced to the hegemony of Imperial Russia in the region. It's beyond a signed turn off the town's main road, at the intersection before **Kairat Cafe** (Lenina; mains 80-120som; ⊙8am-5pm). Further on the main road, just before the **RSK Bank ATM** (Lenina 115; ⊙9.30am-5.30pm Mon-Fri, 24hr ATM), Gulcha's small **Victory Park** (⊙daylight hours) is a somber reminder of the toll Soviet wars took on even rural Central Asian communites.

CBT Osh/Alay (p120) has four affiliated guesthouses in Gulcha, with **Klara's place** (☑(0)777-086327; Toktogul; dm 1200som incl breakfast & dinner; 🛜) generally the most comfortable. Alternatively, the small **Yurt-Camp Alay** (☑(0)559-280582, (0)777-019724; http://campalay.com; Kyrkool village; dm 1100som incl breakfast & dinner) 2km east of town makes a relaxing base away from even the little bustle of central Gulcha.

Small cafes surround Lenina and the bazaar, though generally guesthouses offer meals as well.

ⓘ Getting There & Away

Shared taxis congregate around the bazaar for Sary-Tash (200som, two hours), Osh (150som, 1½ hours) and Bishkek (1100som, 14+ hours). For points elsewhere, you'll need to hire a private ride or arrange a car through CBT.

Sary-Tash   Сары-Таш

☑3243 / POP 1427 / ELEV 3167M

Conveniently situated at the convergence of the roads to Osh, Murgab (Tajikistan) and Kashgar (China) via Irkeshtam, Sary-Tash is a small triangle of a village with superb mid-distance views over a southern horizon of dazzling mountains. There are minimal facilities (two small shops, no regular taxis), but there are a few homestays and it

makes a great base to start exploring the beautiful Alay Valley or the mountains en route to Osh.

There are nine homestays in town, four of which are associated with CBT (p120) and the remainder independent. Look for the map of Sary-Tash at the main junction/petrol stand for guesthouse locations. Spotless **Muras Guesthouse** (☑(0)554-067279; moonbeam.ainuea@gmail.com; M41 Hwy; dm US$10) is among the best, though lack of wi-fi here means some travellers will stop at **Eliza Guesthouse** (☑(0)773-848811; dm 700som incl breakfast & dinner) instead just off the main junction.

Local adventure-sports junkie Shamurat Matiev organises a range of summer hiking or horseback tours and winter freeride ski trips throughout the Alay region and into the Tajik Pamir through his **Pamir Extreme** (☑(0)772-227794; shamu6164@gmail.com) travel agency.

ⓘ Getting There & Away

In summer, the Daroot-Korgon–Osh minibus passes through Sary-Tash at around 8am (300som, four hours) returning around 5pm. Shared taxis to Osh cost 350som.

Sharing a ride up the well-paved 74km to the Irkeshtam border (one hour) is fairly easy from around 7am (expect to pay around 300som per person) or leave the evening before and sleep in one of several basic cafe-wagons at the Kyrgyz border post to ensure an early start for Kashgar.

Sary-Mogol   Сары-Могол

☑3243 / POP 3391 / ELEV 3067M

The highway village of Sary-Mogol offers the valley's best views of Peak Lenin. Homestays and horse treks to Tulpar Köl and Peak Lenin Base Camp in the south, or Jiptik Pass and beyond to the north, make this a popular choice for mountain delights.

The **CBT** (☑(0)773-505939, (0)556-092627; ⊙9am-11pm) office is the centre of all things tourism in Sary-Mogol. Turn off the highway at the signed road on the west edge of town, and look for CBT off a small road to the east past the bazaar.

They can arrange guides/horse treks including a seven-hour hike across the valley towards the mountains ending up at a yurtstay near **Tulpar Köl**. The largest of a string of 42 small lakes, Tulpar Köl stretches for nearly a kilometre in between the final small foothills and the first major ridge of the Trans-Alay range. Strolling the quiet lake shore or searching out the other 41 lakes nearby offers ever-changing angles on the peaks and glaciers leading towards Peak Lenin far above. At 3500m, though, you may well run out of breath before you run out of lakes.

Near here there are views across the river to the Peak Lenin Base Camp at Achik Tash, but as long as you stay on the Lake Tulpar side CBT claims you don't need the border-zone pass. It's also possible to hike for around four hours up the river to a viewpoint overlooking the surrounding glaciers.

In the mountains to the north of town, a three-day hike or horse trek over the **Jiptik Pass** (4186m) with yurtstay overnights leads to the village of Kojo-Kelen, from which an additional four days of tent camping circles back towards Sary-Mogol.

CBT has three homestays in town, the best of which is the one they run themselves just next door to the office. They also run three yurt-camps along the foot of the mountains south of town, catering to horse treks and hiking up the nearby valleys.

Several small cafes off the bazaar prepare a limited range of dishes for lunch or dinner.

🛈 Getting There & Around

Sary-Mogol is located 30km west of Sary-Tash. The afternoon bus from Osh to Daroot-Korgon drives through to Sary-Mogol and on via Kashka-Suu, and shared taxis (400som) depart for the three to four hour trip throughout the day. A 4WD to Achik Tash costs 3000som from CBT in Sary-Mogol, but you might get a cheaper ride from Kashka-Suu. The 4WD track is painfully degraded. To other points CBT keeps a standard rate sheet in their office, or it may sometimes be possible to hire a ride from the bazaar.

Peak Lenin & Achik Tash Peak

The highest summit of the Pamir Alay, 7134m Peak Lenin (Пик Ленин) straddles the border between Kyrgyzstan (where it's officially called Koh-i-Garmo) and Tajikistan (which renamed it Mt Abuali Ibn Sino). For climbers, access is almost always from the Kyrgyz side where the lack of any peak fees and the unusually straightforward approach from Achik Tash (Ачык-Таш) make Peak Lenin one of the world's most popular and accessible 7000ers. But although the snow-covered ridges and slopes are not technically difficult for most experienced mountaineers, the altitude and infamously changeable weather can be. And the mountain holds the sad record for the world's worst mountaineering disaster when, in 1990, an earthquake-triggered avalanche obliterated Camp II on the Razdelnaya approach, killing 43 climbers in the process.

Base camp at Achik Tash meadows (3600m), 30km south of Sary-Mogol, is usually comfortable for a mountain of this height, with a series of agencies operating a veritable tent city in summer. Amenities are largely the same throughout, and with any it's ideal to book in advance to make sure there's space. Some agencies also open space to travellers in advance camps some way up the mountain.

Central Asia Travel (📞(0)555-146998; www.centralasia-travel.com; Achik Tash; tent US$35) provides tented accommodation at Base Camp and Camp 1, and it's possible to arrange meals for US$29 per day.

ITMC (📞(0)312-651404; https://itmc.central-asia.kg; Achik Tash; tent US$8) is very easy to work with for border permits or arranging services, and they run one of the most comfortable base camps in Achik Tash. It's also possible to arrange daily meals from US$25.

Tien-Shan Travel (📞(0)312-466034; www.tien-shan.com; Achik Tash; tent US$5) offers accommodation in their tents or your own, plus it's also to possible to arrange daily meals at Achik Tash/Base Camp 1 from US$30/40.

Tour-agency base camps can organise meals for independent travellers, though large groups would do well to give advance notice to make sure there's enough food to go around.

Hikers will want to head up the Peak Lenin trail past 'Traveller's Pass' and 'Onion Glade' towards Base Camp 1. Only experienced mountaineers with proper equipment should head out onto the glacier, but land-based trekking routes are quite safe at

> ## 🛈 BORDER ZONE: PEAK LENIN BASE CAMP
>
> You'll need a border-area permit (US$20 to US$50) organised through a trekking agency. Some agents take a month to get this, but Munduz Travel (p120) and CBT (p120) can usually organise things in a few days, as can all the agencies that operate base camps in the area.

lower elevations. It's also possible to cross the river to Tulpar Köl (p124) and the four-hour ascent to a fantastic viewpoint of the surrounding glaciers and peaks.

❶ Getting There & Away

You should be able to hire a 4WD from Sary-Mogol to Achik Tash (17km) for the cost of 6000som return. A hired 4WD from Osh to Achik Tash can be negotiated down to US$150 if you ask around the Argomak 4WD stand. Trekking-agency vehicles come at about US$160 to US$200 one way. Tour agencies that operate camps on the mountain and many other Bishkek- and Osh-based agencies all organise transport to Achik Tash; you may be able to work in with one of their trips to Irkeshtam Pass to help reduce the cost.

Daroot-Korgon   Дароот-Коргон

☑ 3234 / POP 4726 / ELEV 2465M

At the far end of the wide-open Alay valley, quiet Daroot-Korgon might seem like a dead end if it weren't for the excellent trekking opportunities that radiate from here. From a two-day loop in the mountains north of the city to a fantastic nine-day traverse that heads through Kyrgyz-Ata National Park and back down to Sary-Mogol, there are plenty of rewarding walks for travellers that make the effort to get here.

Four CBT-affiliated guesthouses are available in the village, with **Ak-Bata** (☑ (0)779-445857; Sulaimanov Cholponbai 29; dm 700som incl breakfast & dinner; 🛜) and **Zalkar** (☑ (0)772-152991, (0)776-303048; ular_2304@ mail.ru; Koilybaev Abyt 7; s/d 750/1000som incl breakfast) on the west edge of the village the most comfortable and easiest to find.

Though it may be possible to find a simple meal near the bazaar, generally guesthouses provide a higher standard of quality.

A single daily bus departs around 6am for Osh (500som, five to six hours) and points between, and shared taxis leave throughout the day along the same route.

UNDERSTAND KYRGYZSTAN

Kyrgyzstan Today

For years Kyrgyz politicians have been navigating a geopolitical tightrope between China, Russia and the USA over the Manas Air Base. From 2001 it was used by the US to conduct cargo and fuel sorties to Afghanistan and later was the main gateway from which US troops were being withdrawn from that war. However, true to Almazbek Atambayev's presidential pledge, the base closed in June 2014. Meanwhile Russia's air base at Kant, 20km east of Bishkek, will continue to function and has even expanded in recent years. Some analysts see this as a major geopolitical victory for Moscow.

Kyrgyzstan maintains good relations with its eastern neighbour and biggest trading partner, China. Seemingly endless trucks bring goods across the Torugart and Irkeshtam Passes but, worryingly for the Kyrgyz economy, almost all return empty.

Kazakhstan is both the figurative and literal big brother to Kyrgyzstan, with Kazakhstan owning 40% of the nation's banks. Relations with Uzbekistan are contrastingly tense, with an ongoing war of words over water and energy usage exacerbated by ethnic tensions, notably the fallout of the June 2010 Osh riots but also the 2013 skirmishes around the Uzbek enclave of Sokh.

The national economy is disproportionately reliant on the Canadian-owned Kumtor mine, which accounts for up to 12% of GDP annually. During 2013 there were major disturbances on the south coast of Issyk-Köl as demonstrators cut roads and power supplies to the high-altitude mine, perhaps to persuade the company to renegotiate a joint-venture agreement giving the state a substantial stake in the business.

In August 2015 Kyrgyzstan became a full member of the Moscow-led Eurasian Customs Union, which experts say hurt the country's re-export trade of Chinese goods into former Soviet states, but also allowed Kyrgyz economic migrants continued access to employment in Russia and beyond.

In the same period Chinese investment in Kyrgyzstan has risen significantly, with the country eyeing entry into China's 'One Belt, One Road' economic initiative as the country's direct investment into the local economy has risen from US$45 million in 2005 to nearly US$1 billion in recent years.

As ever, Kyrgyzstan's position at the heart of the Silk Road remains both one of its greatest assets and most difficult hurdles to overcome.

History

The earliest recorded residents of what is now Kyrgyzstan were Saka warrior clans (aka Scythians). Rich bronze and gold relics have been recovered from Scythian burial mounds dating between the 6th century BC and the 5th century AD. Thereafter the region came under the control of various Turkic alliances with a sizeable population living on the shores of Lake Issyk-Köl. The Talas Valley was the scene of a pivotal battle in 751, when the Turks, along with their Arab and Tibetan allies, drove a large Tang Chinese army out of Central Asia.

The cultured Turkic Karakhanids ruled from the 9th to 11th centuries, instilling Islam as a generalised creed from multiple city-centres including Balasagun (the site of the now-lonely Burana Tower) and Uzgen (Özgön), at the edge of the Fergana Valley.

Ancestors of today's Kyrgyz people probably lived in Siberia's upper Yenisey Basin until at least the 10th century, when, under the influence of Mongol incursions, they began migrating south into the Tian Shan – more urgently following the rise of Chinggis (Genghis) Khan in the 13th century. Present-day Kyrgyzstan was part of the inheritance of Chinggis' second son, Chaghatai.

In 1685 the arrival of the ruthless Mongol Oyrats of the Zhungarian (Dzungarian) empire drove vast numbers of Kyrgyz south into the Fergana and Pamir Alay regions, and on into present-day Tajikistan. The Manchu (Qing) defeat of the Oyrats in 1758 left the Kyrgyz as de facto subjects of the Chinese, who mainly left the locals to their nomadic ways.

The Russian Occupation

As the Russians moved closer during the 19th century, various Kyrgyz clan leaders made their own peace with either Russia or the neighbouring khanate of Kokand. Bishkek – then comprising only the Pishpek fort – fell in 1862 to a combined Russian–Kyrgyz force. The Kyrgyz were gradually eased into the tsar's provinces of Fergana and Semireche while Russian settlers arrived steadily over subsequent decades. In 1916 the Russian Imperial army attempted to 'requisition' Kyrgyz men for noncombatant labour battalions as part of WWI mobilisation. The result was a revolt that was put down so brutally that over 120,000 died – nearly a sixth of all Kyrgyz in the empire.

A similar number fled to China in what became known as the Great *Urkun* (exodus). Played down by Russian authorities through the fall of the USSR, the events have never been fully acknowledged by Russian authorities. This is even despite a 2016 visit by President Vladimir Putin to Kyrgyzstan's Ata-Beyit Memorial Complex to present wreaths marking the 100th anniversary of the exodus.

After the Russian revolutions, Kyrgyz lands became part of the Turkestan ASSR (within the Russian Federation, 1918), a separate Kara-Kyrgyz Autonomous province (*oblast*) in 1924, then a Kyrgyz ASSR from February 1926, which became a full Soviet Socialist Republic (SSR) in December 1936, when the region was known as Soviet Kirghizia.

Many nomads were settled in the course of land reforms in the 1920s, and more were forcibly settled during the cruel collectivisation campaign during the 1930s, giving rise to a reinvigorated rebellion by the *basmachi*, Muslim guerrilla fighters. Vast swaths of the new Kyrgyz elite died in the course of Stalin's purges.

Remote Kyrgyzstan was a perfect place for secret Soviet uranium mining (at Mayluu-Suu above the Fergana Valley, Ming-Kush in the interior and Kadji-Sai at Lake Issyk-Köl) and naval weapons development (at the eastern end of Issyk-Köl). Kyrgyzstan is still dealing with the environmental problems created during this time.

Soviet Secrets

The town of Chon-Tash, 10km from Kashka-Suu village, holds a dark secret. On one night in 1937, the entire Soviet Kyrgyz government – nearly 140 people in all – were rounded up, brought here and shot dead; their bodies dumped in a disued brick kiln on the site. By the 1980s almost no one alive knew of this, by which time the site had been converted to a ski resort. But a watchman at the time of the murders, sworn to secrecy, told his daughter on his deathbed, and she waited until *perestroika* to tell police.

In 1991 the bodies were moved to a mass grave across the road at what is now known as the Ata-Beyit Memorial Complex (p72), with a simple memorial, apparently paid for by the Kyrgyz author Chinghiz Aitmatov (whose father may have been one of the victims). The remains of the kiln are inside a fence nearby.

Kyrgyz Independence

Elections for the Kyrgyz Supreme Soviet (legislature) were held in traditional Soviet rubber-stamp style in February 1990, with the Kyrgyz Communist Party (KCP) walking away with nearly all of the seats. After multiple ballots a compromise candidate, Askar Akaev, a physicist and president of the Kyrgyz Academy of Sciences, was elected as leader. On 31 August 1991, the Kyrgyz Supreme Soviet reluctantly voted to declare Kyrgyzstan's independence, the first Central Asian republic to do so. Six weeks later Akaev was re-elected as president, running unopposed.

Land and housing were at the root of Central Asia's most infamous 'ethnic' violence, during which at least 300 people were killed in 1990, when violence broke out between Kyrgyz and Uzbeks around Osh and Uzgen, a majority-Uzbek area stuck onto Kyrgyzstan in the 1930s.

Akaev initially established himself as a persistent reformer, restructuring the executive apparatus to suit his liberal political and economic attitudes, and instituting reforms considered to be the most radical in the Central Asian republics.

In the late 1990s the country faced a new threat – Islamic radicals and terrorism. In 1999 and 2000, militants from the Islamic Movement of Uzbekistan (IMU; based in Tajikistan) staged a series of brazen kidnappings of foreign workers and climbers in the province of Batken. Kyrgyz security forces largely contained the threat, while IMU leadership fell to US bombs in Afghanistan.

The Tulip Revolution

By the early 2000s, Kyrgyzstan's democratic credentials were once again backsliding in the face of growing corruption, nepotism and civil unrest. The 2005 parliamentary elections were plagued by accusations of harassment and government censure. Demonstrators stormed government buildings in Jalal-Abad and civil unrest soon spread to Osh and Bishkek. On 24 March the relatively peaceful Tulip Revolution effectively overthrew the government amid bouts of looting and vandalism. President Akaev fled by helicopter to Kazakhstan and on to Moscow – subsequently resigning and becoming a university lecturer. New presidential elections were held in July 2005; the opposition leader and former prime minister, Kurmanbek Bakiev, swept to victory.

The Bakiev Era

Bakiev's first term in office was hardly a bed of tulips. The one-time opposition leader soon faced the same criticisms levelled at his predecessor – corruption and abuse of power. Wide-scale street demonstrations in 2006 and 2007 forced him into concessions that curbed his presidential power. Bakiev's promises of peace and security were also derailed by a spate of high-profile political assassinations – three members of parliament were murdered in the late 2000s.

Bakiev was re-elected in July 2009 amid widespread accusations of ballot rigging and media censure. Voters, unable to unseat Bakiev with the ballot, reverted to a tried and true method of overthrowing Kyrgyz leaders – revolution. On 6 and 7 April 2010, opposition crowds massed in Talas and Bishkek. What was intended to be a demonstration against the government turned into a riot in both cities. Security forces were overwhelmed and the protestors stormed the halls of government. By the end of the day some 88 people had been killed and more than 500 injured in the fighting.

Bakiev fled, first to southern Kyrgyzstan, then to Kazakhstan and finally to Belarus. The Kyrgyz opposition set up an interim government with Roza Otombayeva as its new leader. While many in Bishkek saw Bakiev's overthrow as positive in the fight against corruption, his removal caused serious ripples in southern Kyrgyzstan, where local politicians saw the changes as an attempt to weaken their position. When a 'power grab' by Bakiev loyalists in Jalal-Abad was countered by a local militia consisting partly of ethnic Uzbeks, the result was an explosion of politicised riots that culminated in the June 2010 Osh riots. While the exact circumstances remain highly controversial, the result was over 400 deaths (74% of these Uzbeks) and more than 100,000 ethnic Uzbeks fleeing, at least temporarily, to Uzbekistan.

People & Culture

The term Kyrgyz derives from *kyrk* (40) for the 40 Kyrgyz tribes of the *Manas* epic, each of which is represented by a 'flame' on the sun-circle of the national flag. Confusingly, Russians colonising the region originally used the term Kyrgyz more generally for both Kyrgyz and Kazakhs, the former being initially specified as 'Kara-Kyrgyz' (Black Kyrgyz).

Of approximately 80 ethnic groups in Kyrgyzstan, the main trio are Kyrgyz 72%, Uzbek 14% and Russian 6%

Other notable minorities include Ukrainians, Uyghurs, Kalmyks, Tatars and Dungans (Hui Muslims originally from China).

Since 1989 there has been a major exodus of Slavs and Germans, but the Kyrgyz (along with Kazakhs) remain probably the most Russified group in Central Asia. Russian remains the *lingua franca* in Bishkek and northern Kyrgyzstan, but is less commonly spoken in the south. About one fifth of working adults are overseas and send home remittances, most notably from Russia.

About two-thirds of the population lives in rural areas. Regional clan identities are relatively strong with a north–south cultural division that's a potentially destabilising factor within society, along with the tensions between ethnic Kyrgyz and Uzbek groups. Although generally invisible to visitors, such tensions have occasionally boiled over very violently, notably in 1990 at Uzgen, in Bishkek in March 2005, and in Osh and Jalal-Abad in June 2010.

Horsing Around

Horse sports are very popular in Kyrgyzstan and have seen a revival in recent years. The most unforgettable of these is an all-out mounted brawl over a headless goat whose body must be thrown into a circular 'goal'. Known as *kok boru* (grey wolf), *ulaktartysh* or *buzkashi,* the Kyrgyz term reveals its origins as a hunting exercise. The form played in Kyrgyzstan is essentially a team sport, in contrast to the free-for-all version of Tajikistan, but either way it's a remarkably full-on event at which riders and horses can take an incredible battering. A national competition comes to a climax in Bishkek during Nooruz on 21 March. Games are also often incorporated into Independence Day celebrations and other festivals.

Other classic equestrian games include *at chabysh,* a horse race over a distance of 20km to 30km; *jumby atmai,* horseback archery; *tiyin enmei,* where contestants pick up coins off the ground while galloping past; and *udarysh,* horseback wrestling. Then there's *kyz-kumay* (kiss the girl) in which a male rider furiously chases a woman on horseback in an attempt to kiss her. Then in the return leg, the woman gets to chase and whip her pretend 'suitor'. Ah, young love.

Community tourism outfits can often arrange demonstrations of any of these traditional sports upon request if you give several days' notice.

THE KIDNAPPED BRIDE

Kyrgyz men have a way of sweeping a woman off her feet – off her feet and into a waiting car. *Ala kachuu* (bride kidnapping) is a very hands-on way to find a wife. There is some dispute as to how 'traditional' the practice is and it's officially illegal, but it also seems to be on the upswing, with some reports putting around one-third of the country's marriages as a result of bride kidnapping. Many locals say the practice is a reassertion of national identity, while others point to the rising cost of wedding celebrations and the expense of the traditional 'bride price'. If both sides tacitly agree, a well-executed abduction can in fact prove a clever way to dramatically slash wedding costs.

But not all *ala kachuu* grabs are quaint money-saving devices. In the case of a genuine kidnap, the woman does still have the right to refuse if she can weather hours of haranguing by the groom-thief's female family members, who attempt to make her wear a symbolic bridal headscarf. But often she'll succumb, fearing an implied shame or worse if she refuses; and the girl's family, once contacted, often pressure her to agree to the marriage.

The issue of *ala kachuu* came to the fore in local conversation with the 2007 Kyrgyz movie *Boz Salkyn* (Pure Coolness).

Religion

The population is overwhelmingly Muslim. Northern Kyrgyz are more Russified and less likely to follow strict Muslim doctrine than their cousins in the south. Nonetheless, Islamic observance is growing rapidly, partially as a reaction against perceived corruption in the secular sphere. Dwindling communities of Russian Orthodox Christians are still visible, particularly in Bishkek and Karakol, both of which have active Orthodox cathedrals.

Arts

Kyrgyz traditional music is played on a mixture of two-stringed *komuz* lutes, a vertical violin known as a *kyl kyayk,* flutes, drums, long horns and mouth harps (*temir komuz, or jygach ooz* with a string).

Crafty Carpets

Quintessential Kyrgyz felt rugs or decorative pieces called *shyrdak*s are pieced together by female artisans from cut pieces of sheep's wool after weeks of washing, drying, dyeing and treatment against pests. The appliqué patterns are usually of a *kochkor mujuz* (plant motif), *teke mujuz* (ibex-horn motif) or *kyal* (fancy scrollwork) bordered in a style particular to the region of production. Designs became strikingly colourful after synthetic dye became readily available in the 1960s, but natural dyes are making a comeback, notably using pear and raspberry leaves, dahlia and birch root. A handmade *shyrdak* tends to have irregular stitching on the back and tight, even stitching around the panels. More pictorial *ala-kiyiz* (rugs or hangings with 'blurred' coloured panels pressed on) are made by laying out the wool in the desired pattern on a *chiy* (reed) mat, sprinkling hot water, then rolling and pressing until the wool strands compact.

There are felt-making cooperatives in Bishkek, Karakol, Bokonbaevo and Kochkor that offer demonstrations of the craft, with pieces often sold through CBT and other community tourism offices.

Film

Kyrgyzstan's Aktan Abdykalykov is one of Central Asia's most accomplished filmmakers. His 1998 bittersweet coming-of-age *Beshkempir* (The Adopted Son) was released to critical acclaim, and *Maimil* (The Chimp) received an honourable mention at Cannes in 2001.

Tengri: Blue Heavens (2008) is a French-made film that follows the romantic pairing of a down-on-his-luck Kazakh fisherman with a Kyrgyz widow, set and shot in Kyrgyzstan.

Kurmanjan Datka: Queen of the Mountains (2014), by local director Sadyk Sher-Niyaz, was released to international popular acclaim and nominated for a Best Foreign Language Film Oscar award.

Literature

Central Asian literature has traditionally been popularised in the form of songs, poems and stories by itinerant minstrels or bards, called *akyn* in Kyrgyz. Among the better-known 20th-century Kyrgyz *akyns* are Togolok Moldo (aka Bayymbet Abdyrakhmanov), Sayakbay Karalaev and Sagymbay Orozbakov.

Kyrgyzstan's best-known author is Chinghiz Aitmatov (1928–2008), whose works have been translated into English, German and French. Among his novels, which are also revealing looks at Kyrgyz life and culture, are *Jamilia* (1967), *The White Steamship* (1970), *Early Cranes* (1975), *Piebald Dog Running Along the Shore* (1978) and *The Day Lasts More Than 100 Years* (1980); *Piebald Dog* was made into a prize-winning Russian film in 1990.

THE MANAS EPIC

The *Manas* epic is a cycle of oral legends, 20 times longer than Homer's *Odyssey*. It tells of the formation of the Kyrgyz people with the original narrative revolving around the exploits of *batyr* (heroic warrior) Manas as he carves out a homeland for his people in the face of hostile hordes. Subsequent stories feature his son Semetei, grandson Seitek and widow Kanykei.

The epic was only first written down in the mid-19th century (by Kazakh ethnographer Chokan Valikhanov) and even today it remains very much part of oral tradition. *Akyn* who can recite or improvise from the epics are considered in a class by themselves and are known as *manaschi*. According to tradition, bona fide *manaschi* find their role in life after a long illness or life-changing dream in which the warrior of legend calls them to the task.

Since independence, the *Manas* epic has become a cultural rallying point for the Kyrgyz. Manas statues grace virtually every city. Although there's much dispute as to the age of the epics, Kyrgyzstan celebrated what was purported to be the 1000th anniversary of Manas' birth in 1995. There's also a tomb near Talas touted as being the hero's final resting place, a legend that certainly encourages local pilgrims.

Environment

Wildlife

Kyrgyzstan offers an annual refuge for thousands of migrating birds, including rare cranes and geese that stop over in the Unesco-affiliated biosphere reserves of Issyk-Köl and Sary-Chelek lakes. The country is believed to have a population of a few hundred snow leopards, and is also home to populations of brown bears, Marco Polo sheep, ibex and wolves. The large Sarychat-Ertash area in the Central Tien Shan a closed reserve, which partially intended to preserve wild animals, particularly imperilled snow leopards.

Environmental Issues

Fresh water locked up in the form of glaciers is one of Kyrgyzstan's greatest natural resources, but the glaciers have been shrinking alarmingly – albeit not perhaps as catastrophically as a 2008 UN report feared.

Despite a well-established seasonal rotation, there are problems with overgrazing of meadows near villages. And contrastingly there's a simultaneous under-grazing of more distant *jailoos* made inaccessible by the increasing costs of transport or lack of infrastructure.

In Soviet days, the Kyrgyz SSR's uranium-mining sector earned the sobriquet 'Atomic Fortress of the Tian Shan'. A number of former mine sites still threaten to leak their radioactive contents into rivers and groundwater. Meanwhile there remain major controversies over the ownership and operation of active mines, notably the massive Canadian-run Kumtor Gold Mine. According to the BBC, this operation reportedly produces around 12% of Kyrgyzstan's GDP, but its high mountain location at the source of many river systems makes its environmental credentials particularly sensitive. In 1998 a Kumtor truck carrying almost 2 tonnes of cyanide and sodium hydrochloride fell into the Barskoön River, leading to a widespread evacuation, though the exact number of casualties remains a source of considerable dispute.

Food & Drink

Tea is liquid hospitality and cups should only be half-filled, as adding more suggests that one's in a hurry to get away. In homes, but not restaurants, tea is traditionally made very strong in a pot then diluted when served. Nightlife is limited mostly to vodka and cheap beer in the regions of the country, but look for more options and better service in Bishkek.

A great resource on Kyrgyz cuisine is http://tastes.kg. Typical Kyrgyzstani dishes include:

➡ *Laghman*: Mildly spicy, fat noodles generally served in soup, though *bozo laghman* is fried. There are numerous other variants.

➡ *Beshbarmak*: Literally 'five fingers', since it is traditionally eaten by hand. The usual recipe sees large flat noodles topped with lamb and/or horsemeat cooked in vegetable broth.

➡ *Kesme*: Thick noodle soup with small bits of potato, vegetable and meat.

➡ *Mampar*: Tomato-based meat stew with gnocchi-like pasta pieces.

➡ *Shorpa*: Mutton soup.

➡ *Jurkop*: Braised meat and vegetable dish with noodles.

➡ *Hoshan*: Fried and steamed dumplings, similar to *manty* (stuffed dumplings); best right off the fire from markets.

➡ *Ashlyanfu*: Cold rice-noodles, jelly, vinegar and eggs; a Dungan favourite.

➡ *Azu*: Tatar dish of meat fried with pickles and vegetables, often served atop french fries.

➡ *Fynchozi*: Spicy, cold rice noodles.

➡ *Ganfan*: Rice with a meat and vegetable sauce.

➡ *Manty*: Steamed dumplings made with meat or vegetables; particularly delicious with *jusai*, a mountain grass of the onion family.

➡ *Boorsok*: Empty ravioli-sized fried dough-parcels to dunk in drinks or cream.

➡ *Kurut*: Small, very hard balls of tart, dried yoghurt; a favourite snack.

➡ *Kazy, karta* or *chuchuk*: Horsemeat sausages; a popular vodka chaser or addition to *plov* (Central Asian pilaf consisting of rice and fried vegetables).

Local drinks to look out for:

➡ *Kymys*: Fermented mare's milk, mostly available in spring and early summer; the national drink.

➡ *Bozo*: Thick, fizzy drink made from boiled fermented millet or other grains.

➡ *Jarma* and *maksym:* Fermented barley drinks, made with yeast and yoghurt. 'Shoro' is the best-known brand name with vendors serving from chilled barrels at most street corners in Bishkek and Osh.

SURVIVAL GUIDE

❶ Directory A–Z

ACCOMMODATION

Homestays are the bedrock of accommodation in rural Kyrgyzstan, with bed and breakfast (B&B) rarely costing more than 700som. There's an approximate rating system of one, two or three edelweiss, but even some of the best options are likely to have an outside toilet. The lowliest will have a long drop and bucket-water bathing.

Yurtstays – easiest to arrange for tourists around Son-Köl and Tash Rabat but increasingly prevalent elsewhere – work on a homestay basis, with mats on the floor and shared long drop somewhere nearby. There are also private tourist yurt-camps where you might get a bed and some privacy, and even a sit-down (but still outside) toilet. The latter cater mostly to groups on pre-arranged tours, but are open to anyone if there's space.

Bishkek, Osh and Karakol now have a range of backpacker-style hostels that are a huge step above the makeshift apartment-hostels of the last decade. Surviving Soviet-era hotels can often prove horribly decrepit or only half-heartedly reconstructed. Such places are sometimes useful as crash-pad options and have an atmosphere of accidental nostalgia, but with midrange and high-end hotel options increasingly more available in the main cities (Bishkek, Osh, Jalal-Abad and Karakol), these have become increasingly less relevant. When staying at cheaper local hotels, double-check whether a price quoted is per room or per person. If the latter, it may mean a random stranger plonking his backpack on the bed beside you, dormitory style.

Home Sweet Yurt

Nothing gets the nomadic blood racing through your veins like lying awake in a yurt at night under a heavy pile of blankets wondering if wolves will come and eat your horse.

Yurts (*boz-uy* in Kyrgyz) are the archetypal shepherd shelters – circular homes made of *kiyiz* (multilayered felt) stretched around a *kerege* (collapsible wooden frame). The outer felt layer is coated in waterproof sheep fat, the innermost lined with woven grass matting to block the wind. Long woollen strips secure the walls and poles. The interior is richly decorated with textiles, wall coverings, quilts, cushions, camel and horse bags, and ornately worked chests. Floors are lined with *oro kiyiz* (thick felt) and covered with bright carpets (*shyrdaks* or *ala-kiyiz*).

Look up: the central wheel-like *tunduk* that supports the roof is none other than the design depicted in the middle of Kyrgyzstan's national flag, with the four main sections representing the four seasons of the year.

Learn more with Celestial Mountains' online yurt website: www.yurts.kg.

In authentic *jailoos* (summer pastures) very few people speak even a word of English, and they may be limited in Russian, so two useful phrases to learn in Kyrgyz are:

➡ **** boz ui kaisy jerde?* (Where is *** yurt?)

➡ *Men ushul jirge jatsam bolobu?* (May I stay here tonight?)

Adventure-minded travellers with a bit of Russian or Kyrgyz might find a more authentic (but also more basic) experience off the tourist trail. When you see just a single yurt the chances are that it doesn't generally accept tourist stays, though if you say hello you might find yourself invited for tea, *kymys* or sheep's-head snacks. Larger encampments will more often be willing to accept guests for overnight stays, where you can expect true hospitality but not exactly customer service. Having goodies to share (chocolates, biscuits, sausage etc) is useful for any such occasions.

COMMUNITY-BASED TOURISM

One of the great appeals of Kyrgyzstan is the relative ease with which one can organise homestays, yurtstays, local guides and horses thanks to several Kyrgyz grass-roots organisations. The most widespread network is CBT (p69) whose most active sub-branches effectively double as tourist offices – notably in Arslanbob (p113), Karakol (p90) and Naryn (p103). You can often approach CBT providers independently, but typically this won't get you a discount. That's arguably a good thing as the

CBT network is a valuable resource and is worth funding. Nonetheless, several smaller CBT-like outfits do compete in some towns, especially in Kochkor for trips to Son-Köl.

Homestay prices vary slightly between regions and according to the 'edelweiss' ranking (the CBT version of a star rating), but the typical range is 450som to 700som per day for bed and breakfast, plus 250som to 350som per additional meal. Depending on the quality and availability of local restaurants, it is often cheaper to eat out. Horse hire is usually around 700som per day and guides range from 600som to 1400som per day – sometimes you'll need to pay for the guide's food and lodging on top of their daily rate, and occasionally even for their horse. Be sure to clarify all costs and services provided before departing.

ACTIVITIES
Hiking

Covered in mountains and lakes, Kyrgyzstan offers unrivalled opportunities to take to the hills. The areas around Bishkek, Karakol, Kochkor, Naryn and Sary-Chelek are the major trekking regions, although most CBT offices can suggest countless alternatives.

Border-area permits are required to access some of the most important mountaineering and trekking areas areas, notably the central Tian Shan (Khan Tengri), Chatyr Köl/Köl-Suu, and Peak Lenin regions. Agencies can organise these as part of a package, but many are increasingly reticent to do so for nonguests.The cost is typically around US$30 and agents advise leaving a month for the processing, but some agents can speed things up and have the documents within a couple of days at extra cost.

Horse Riding

Kyrgyzstan is the best place in Central Asia to saddle up and join the seasonal nomads on the high pastures. **CBT offices** (www.cbt-kyrgyzstan.kg) throughout the country can organise horse hire for around 700som per day on short notice. Several agencies advertise organised horse treks, though most simply sub-contract. For a well-organised tour with decent horses it's worth approaching reputable providers directly, including Shepherds Way Trekking (p97) and CBT, or through yurt-camps.

Some self-sufficient travellers have occasionally purchased their own horses/donkeys for around US$1000/300 at animal markets in Osh or Karakol (where prices are relatively reasonable) and after a month or two riding or cajoling them across the mountains, sell them again in Bishkek, conceivably for a modest profit. In reality such an idea requires considerable experience and relies on finding a well-trained animal, not the cheapest one around.

A good source of equestrian insight, notably about the sturdy Kyrgyz breed, is Kyrgyz Ate, coordinators of the At-Chabysh Festival (p186).

Mountaineering

For those seeking real expeditions, Kyrgyzstan offers the allure of three 7000m+ peaks, notably the majestic Khan Tengri and relatively 'easy' Peak Lenin (partly in Tajikistan but accessed from Kyrgyzstan). The latter is also probably the world's most accessible and inexpensive 7000m to climb, but don't let those relative terms fool you into complacency. It can still be a killer. There are many unclimbed peaks, notably in the Kokshal range bordering China, and a remarkable series of cliffs and ridges in southwestern Kyrgyzstan. The granite walls of the Karavshin area are world class, but their popularity has yet to fully recover from an infamous episode in 2000 when four rash American climbers were kidnapped by IMU militants on the 750m-tall Yellow Wall. The tale, thought by some to be highly overdramatised, was the subject of Greg Child's 2002 book *Over the Edge*.

For climbers and mountaineers wanting less full-on challenges, there are lots of options in the valleys south of Bishkek.

Kyrgyz Alpine Club's useful website (www.kac.centralasia.kg) is blocked by some servers as a security threat.

Rafting

Silk Road Water Centre (☑ (0)773-772994; www.rafting.kg) organises rafting on the Kökömeren (Grade IV), Chuy (Grade III), Naryn (Grade IV) and Chon-Kemin Rivers (Grades II to III). The season runs from 25 June until mid-September. Wetsuits are essential in the glacial meltwater.

Skiing

Despite the fact that 94% of the country averages over 2700m, skiing in Kyrgyzstan is still not well known. Currently the only developed ski bases are around Bishkek and Karakol, but freeride skiing is increasingly popular near Jyrgalan, Arslanbob and the Alay. The season runs from mid-November until mid-March. With the advent of heli-skiing, Russian-built MI-8 helicopters are ferrying adrenaline junkies to altitudes of over 4500m for descents of up to 5km.

CUSTOMS REGULATIONS

Exporting antiques is heavily restricted. If you've bought anything that looks remotely old and didn't get a certificate saying it's not, you can get one from the 1st floor of the Foreign Department of the **Ministry of Education, Science & Culture** (Map p60; ☑ (0)312-626817; Room 210, cnr Tynystanov & Frunze, Bishkek).

Taxes & Refunds

Taxes are included in stated prices, and no tax refund allowances are available for visitors.

DANGERS & ANNOYANCES

According to Kyrgyz law, international visitors should keep their passports on hand at all times. In practice, most make do with a photocopy. Bribery is relatively common for locals in many instances, but is something travellers should stay away from. If detained or arrested, contact your embassy or consular representative immediately.

Whatever news reports might imply during the country's very occasional riots and revolutions, Kyrgyzstan is a pretty safe place to travel. For those planning adventure activities in wild, open mountainous spaces, precautions should be obvious: before setting off, be aware of rapidly changeable weather patterns, extreme mountain terrain and the easily underestimated effects of altitude sickness. Always let someone know where you are going and when you expect to be back.

Driving If possible before engaging a ride, double-check the road-readiness of the vehicle and the sobriety of your driver. Reputable tour operators might charge slightly more but have an image to maintain.

Theft Kyrgyz cities are generally safe but theft can happen, especially at night in Bishkek. Keep valuables locked in your hotel and consider taking taxis if venturing out late.

Police trouble Although generally limited to a few annoying hotspots (Osh Bazaar in Bishkek is the major one), travellers continue to report shake-downs from corrupt cops wanting an excuse to fine you or simply rifle through your cash and appropriate some of it. The best approach is generally not to hand over your passport to plain-clothes officers until you have reached an official station, though in reality this isn't always as easy as it sounds, especially as legally you are supposed to carry your passport at all times.

Flowers In rural areas don't pick flowers, especially not the pale-blue bell-shaped ones known as Issykulskiy Koren. Though attractive, this is in fact *aconitum soongaricum*, a highly toxic variant of wolfsbane that can cause fatal heart attacks if the sap is ingested.

Ticks Recent research suggests that life-threatening strains of tick-borne encephalitis, already present in Kazakhstan, have recently become a potential danger in Kyrgyzstan. The first recorded human fatality was a person bitten at Ala-Archa in 2009. Tick-repellant and suitable protective clothing are thus recommended if walking and camping especially during June/July, in long grass at around 2000m.

EMBASSIES & CONSULATES

For a full list of embassies, see the website of the **Ministry of Foreign Affairs** (www.mfa.gov.kg).

The following embassies and consulates are all in Bishkek.

Afghan Embassy (Map p66; ☑ 0312-543802; Chekov 28; ☺ 9.30am-noon & 2-4pm Mon-Fri) Can issue visas for onward travel.

Canadian Consulate (Map p60; ☑ (0)312-650506; www.canadainternational.gc.ca; Moskva 189; ☺ 9am-1pm & 2-5pm Mon-Fri) Limited services for nationals.

Chinese Embassy (☑ (0)312-597483; http://kg.chineseembassy.org; Chingiz Aitmatov (Mira) 299/7; ☺ 9am-noon Mon, Wed & Fri; ▣ 8, 265, 295, 307) At the time of research, only issuing visas to residents of Kyrgyzstan.

French Embassy (Map p60; ☑ (0)312-979714, emergency (0)555-783803; https://kg.amba-france.org; Orozbekov 32; ☺ 8.30am-noon & 1-5pm Mon-Sat) No consular section; for citizen services contact the German embassy.

German Embassy (Map p60; ☑ (0)312-905000; www.bischkek.diplo.de; Razzakov 28; ☺ consular section 2-3pm Mon-Thu) Handles consular affairs for most EU citizens.

Indian Embassy (Map p60; ☑ (0)312-979256; http://embassyofindia.kg; Jash Gvardia (Molodaya Gvardia) 100a; ☺ 9am-1pm & 2-5.30pm Mon-Fri) Issues visas for those that still need them.

Iranian Embassy (Map p60; ☑ 0312-621281; Razzakov 36; ☺ 9am-1pm & 3-5pm Mon-Fri) Issues visas, but not directly. Contact Persia Agency (p70) for help in applying.

Japanese Embassy (Map p60; ☑ 0312-325387; www.kg.emb-japan.go.jp; Razzakov 16; ☺ 9am-12.30pm & 1.30-5.45pm Mon-Fri) Handles consular matters for citizens.

Kazakhstan Embassy (☑ (0)312-565376; www.kaz-emb.kg; Chingiz Aitmatov (Mira) 95A; ☺ 9am-1pm & 3-7pm Mon-Fri; ▣ 8, 265, 266, 295) Issues visas for those passports that do not have visa-free travel to the country.

Russian Embassy (Map p60; ☑ (0)312-612615; www.kyrgyz.mid.ru; Manas 55, consular entrance off Kiev) At the time of research, only issuing visas to residents of Kyrgyzstan.

Tajikistan Embassy (Map p66; ☑ 0312-511464; www.tajikemb.kg; Kara-Dar'in 36; ☺ 9am-1pm & 2-5pm Mon-Fri; ▣ 17 (12), marshrutka 122, 175, 212) Issues visas in as little as one day when the consul is in town.

Turkish Embassy (Map p60; ☑ (0)312-905900; http://bishkek.emb.mfa.gov.tr; Moskva 89; ☺ 9am-12.30pm Mon-Fri) Addresses consular requests.

UK Embassy (Map p60; ☑ (0)312-303637; www.gov.uk/world/kyrgyzstan; Erkindik 21, 4th fl, Orion Business Center; ☺ 9am-noon

& 2-5pm Mon-Fri) Friendly staff provide the normal range of consular services.

US Embassy (☑ (0)312-597000; http:// bishkek.usembassy.gov; Chingiz Aitmatov (Mira) 171; ☺1.30-5.30pm Mon, Wed, Fri; ☐8, 265, 295, 307) Nonemergency services by appointment only.

Uzbekistan Embassy (☑ (0)312-986296; www. uzbekistan.kg; Chingiz Aitmatov (Mira) 177; ☺10am-1pm Tue-Fri, phone for appointment 2pm-4pm Mon-Fri) Visas by appointment only.

ETIQUETTE

Bread Considered holy; never waste bread, throw it away or place it upside down on the table.

Greetings Men will always shake hands upon meeting, though very rarely will women be expected to do so with men.

Toasts When drinking alcohol, most often members of a group will take turns making short speeches before drinking as a group.

FESTIVALS & EVENTS

Kyrgyzstan offers a number of festivals in summer, though many of them are put on primarily for tourists. The best and most authentic events are the horse games at the end of July and August (notably Independence Day, 31 August) at Bishkek, Cholpon-Ata and Karakol, and the *jailoos* (summer pastures) around Son-Köl and Kochkor.

During Navrus (Nooruz; 21 March) celebrations there are numerous sporting events, traditional games and music festivals, especially in larger cities.

The World Nomad Games (p84) brings together sportsmen from across the globe to compete in traditional nomadic sports, with a strong focus on horse sports and wrestling. The event is held in even-numbered years, with sports competitions at the Cholpon-Ata Hippodrome (p84) and cultural events at the Kyrchyn (p84) *jailoo*.

The Birds of Prey Festival (p98), held early August in Bokonbaevo, offers an excellent opportunity to see eagle hunters and falconers compete.

The Yak and Horse Games Festival (p124) in Sary-Mogol is worth stopping by if only for the sheer oddness of yak-back *kok boru*, and the location alongside Tulpar Köl certainly doesn't hurt either.

FOOD

Food offerings vary across the country from multitudinous cultural restaurants in Bishkek to a single cafeteria in smaller towns and villages. Expect a standard menu of Kyrgyz favorites in rural areas, primarily mutton-based and heavy on carbs. As everywhere in Central Asia, finding meat-free meals is a tall order. In big cities your best hope will be Chinese or Italian restaurants.

In smaller areas, some homestays can prepare vegetarian options.

INTERNET ACCESS

Wi-fi is now easy to find in hotels and smarter city cafes, but speeds can be variable. Mobile 3G and 4G internet is also variable but increasingly widespread; if you have a laptop it's well worth investing in a dongle to allow you mobile wi-fi almost anywhere there's a phone signal. Dongles (around 1000som plus SIM card) tend to be company-specific. Beeline's work consistently well, and flat-rate plans are available, but in many rural regions only one carrier has a data network so verify beforehand if internet access is essential to you.

LGBTIQ TRAVELLERS

Local LGBTIQ organisation **Labrys** (☑ (0)312-902963; www.labrys.kg) provides support and services for LGBTIQ locals and travellers, and can provide information on local LGBT-friendly events. Though there is no law in Kyrgyzstan making homosexuality or homosexual acts illegal, in general Labrys' recommendation is to avoid dating services (often targeted by local police looking for extortion opportunities) and to remain discreet when in public (to avoid provoking negative reactions); social norms generally take a negative view of LGBTIQ relationships.

MAPS

TUK (p59) in Bishkek is usually the most reliable source of trekking maps, though numerous tour agencies through the country have begun to carry the same products. TUK's topographic maps include:

Ala-Archa (1:50,000) In English.

Around Karakol and Enylchek Glacier (1:100,000) Schematic map of Inylchek Glacier and the area southwest of Karakol.

Kyrgyz Range/Kungey Ala-Too (1:100,000) Topographical map covering the mountains south of Bishkek on one side, and the trekking area south of Tamga (Issyk-Köl) on the other.

Northern Issyk-Kul (1:100,000) Topographical map covering trekking routes between Grigorievka and the Chon-Kemin Valley.

OruxMaps (www.oruxmaps.com) is a very powerful map source and viewer for Android smartphones.

MEDICAL SERVICES

Insurance

Health insurance is recommend, particularly policies that cover mountain rescue and repatriation in the event of serious injury.

Health care in Kyrgyzstan

International-standard care is available in Bishkek, where Neomed (p69) is an expat favourite, but limited in the rest of the country. However, pharmacies across the country carry a wide variety of medicines and rarely or never require a prescription.

Tap Water

Tap water is safe to drink across Kyrgyzstan, though for taste many travellers prefer bottled water in smaller towns and villages.

MONEY

Banks and licensed money-changer booths (marked *obmen valyot*) exchange US dollars and other major currencies. Trying to get change for a 5000som note will likely be met with a look of horror, even in cities.

There is no black market for currency transactions and changing money back out of som is not problematic. We quote prices in the currency that the businesses themselves use. That's normally som, but can be US dollars or euros for some hotels and tour companies.

If you need to wire money, MoneyGram has services at main post offices and Western Union works through many banks.

ATMs are increasingly common in all major towns. Many dispense both US dollars and som and work with Visa, but for Mastercard and Maestro look primarily for Demir banks across the country.

Tips of 10% to 20% will be included in restaurant and bar bills when appropriate.

Bargaining

Bargaining is extremely common, from bazaar stalls to CBT offices and more.

OPENING HOURS

Official offices and many business open from 9am to 6pm Monday to Friday, often with a one-hour break for lunch. Official offices remain closed on weekends, though service-sector business will generally remain open.

POST

Airmail postcards cost 31som to any country from Bishkek's main post office (p69) or regional branches. Courier agents DHL (p69) and FedEx (p69) are represented in Bishkek.

EMERGENCY & IMPORTANT NUMBERS

Ambulance	☑103
Fire	☑101
Mountain search and rescue	☑161
Police	☑102

PUBLIC HOLIDAYS

Muslim festivals change dates annually. The most important, Orozo Ait (Eid al-Fitr, the end of Ramazan) and Kurban Ait (Eid al-Azha, Feast of Sacrifice), are national holidays. Other dates are fixed, but might actually be celebrated on the nearest Monday or Friday:

1 January New Year's Day
7 January Russian Orthodox Christmas
23 February Defenders of the Fatherland Day
8 March International Women's Day
21 March Navrus (Nooruz)
1 May International Labour Day
5 May Constitution Day
9 May WWII Victory Day
31 August Independence Day
7 November Anniversary of the October Revolution

SHOPPING

The classic souvenir is a traditional *(ak) kalpak* hat, available in a range of qualities from as little as 80som from bazaars, and much more from souvenir shops. Classic feltwork including colourful *shyrdak* (felt carpet with appliquéd coloured panels) make great presents and are available in most towns through community tourist offices and souvenir shops; One Village One Product (p90) and Tumar Art Salon (p68) have particularly fine collections, and Naryn is known as a hotspot for their production.

Other typical mementos include pottery figurines, miniature yurts, embroidered bags, horse whips, *kymys* shakers, leather boxes, felt slippers, Kyrgyz musical instruments and chess sets featuring Manas and his entourage. For some Soviet-era throwback souvenirs, stop by the small antique shop (p90) in central Karakol.

TELEPHONE

Mobile numbers are 10 digits; landlines have five or six digits. Central telecom offices usually offer booths with Skype-enabled computers for cheaper international calls, but the prevalence of wi-fi across the country means most travellers will never need to visit.

Mobile Phones

SIM cards are very inexpensive and are often given away to arriving passengers at Manas International Airport. No registration is required. Calls are only a few som per minute and a mobile phone can prove highly useful when hoteliers aren't home when you arrive.

TOILETS

➸ Sit-down toilets are common in major cities and at many tourist-focused hotels across the country.

➨ Squatters are the norm in rural regions and conditions may be distressing.

➨ Paper is often not provided.

TOURIST INFORMATION

Discover Kyrgyzstan (www.discover kyrgyzstan.org) National tourism website.

Trip to Kyrgyzstan (https://triptokyrgyz stan.com/en/map) Useful interactive map of tourism destinations.

VISAS

Some visa applications require a letter of Invitation (LOI), usually an expensive formality organised through a travel agency or online fixer.

Registration & Permits

If you're one of the unlucky nationalities to need a visa you might also need to register within three days of arriving in Kyrgyzstan. Ask your hotel or at OVIR (p70).

Many frontier areas and virtually any place within 50km of the Chinese border require military border permits. Peak Lenin base camp and the whole Khan Tengri area fall into such zones, as do large parts of Naryn *oblast*. For around US$30, CBT (p69) or trekking agencies can usually get one for you. Applications can take anywhere from two days to a month depending on the agent. If you're travelling to/from an open border crossing with a valid onward visa, you are generally exempt from the permit requirement, but special (easy to get, if pricey) permission is required for the Torugart Pass crossing.

Afghanistan

Visa costs vary by nationality, starting from US$30/60 transit/tourist and going to US$160 or more. Issuance takes only a day or two, but seems to depend on your discussion with the consul (p134) about your ability to demonstrate you understand the security situation where you're planning to head, and sometimes requires a letter of invitation or a statement from your country's embassy indicating that they give permission for your travel to Afghanistan. Travellers planning to visit the Afghan Wakhan may have better luck applying in Khorog, Tajikistan.

China

Until late 2013 it was possible to get a Chinese visa through agents in Kyrgyzstan. However, for several years now China has been increasingly less willing to issue visas to any non-resident foreigners. Get this one from your home country.

Iran

Once you have a visa clearance code from Tehran the visa application takes two days and costs €50 for most nationals. Americans and Brits can only visit by organised tour. The sensible way to be sure of getting visa clearance is by applying online through a reputable travel agency like www.key2persia.com or www.persianvoyages. com, ideally allowing several weeks for the procedure; you can start from anywhere – you simply need to know which embassy you plan to collect it from. In principle such clearance can be arranged much more cheaply (US$10) in Bishkek through Persia Agency (p70), but we have not tested the theory ourselves. Some nationalities report getting a five-day transit visa without supporting documents in around one week.

Kazakhstan

Kazakhstan is visa-free for a growing number of passports, including all EU countries, USA, UK, New Zealand, Australia, Japan and many more.

For those that do require a visa, one-month tourist visas are available from the Kazakhstan embassy (p134), usually ready in five working days. Single/double transit visas cost US$20/40 and are generally available the next working day.

Tajikistan

Providing that the consul (p134) is in town, 30-day visas (or 45-day visas on request) are painlessly available for US$55 to US$75, plus a 100som processing fee. A full GBAO permit is stamped in on request at no extra cost. One photograph; no need for a LOI. The process usually takes one day, but can last only 15 minutes if there's no queue. If the consul's away there's no visa issuance at all.

Uzbekistan

Call for an appointment before visiting – though at the time of research all appointments seem to be scheduled for 10am on the next working day. Fill in the online application form at http://evisa.mfa.uz, then turn up at the appointed hour with a 3 x 4cm photo and a copy of your passport including every page with any kind of stamp. Most nationalities pay US$90/100 to receive a single-/double-entry visa, but Americans and Japanese pay more and things can take considerably longer if the embassy is busy. Fortunately they usually allow you to keep your passport during processing so you can apply then head off to the hills. Alternatively, visas can be issued the same day if you have a pre-arranged agency LOI, but that requires advanced planning and more money.

WORK

Multi-entry business visas of up to 90 days are available online (www.evisa.e-gov.kg), though full work visas generally require a sponsoring organisation. Most short-term employment for foreigners is with language schools, though candidates with relevant experience have been known to find work consulting for international organisations based in Bishkek.

ⓘ Getting There & Away

Most visitors will arrive by air at Bishkek's Manas International Airport (p70), though many still travel overland as part of larger Silk Road itineraries.

AIR

Bishkek (p70) and Osh (p121) international airports host regularly scheduled international flights year-round, while Tamchy's Issyk-Köl International Airport (p81) sees summer service only. Rumour has it that Karakol International Airport (p91) may reopen as soon as 2019, but for now no concrete details are available.

Departure tax is included in the price of a ticket.

Airports & Airlines

Bishkek's Manas International Airport (p70) is the main hub with relatively inexpensive international connections:

Turkish (Map p60; ☑ (0)312-301600; www.turkishairlines.com; Abdrahmanov (Soviet) 136; ⊗ 9am-12.30pm & 1.30-6pm Mon-Fri) and **Pegasus** (Map p66; www.flypgs.com; Maldybaeva 35; ⊗ 9am-6pm Mon-Fri). Via Istanbul

FlyDubai (Map p60; ☑ (0)312-319000; www.flydubai.com; Kerimbekov 13, entry via Bokonbaevo; ⊗ 9am-7pm Mon-Fri, 10am-4pm Sat & Sun). Via Dubai

S7 (Map p60; ☑ (0)312-910460; www.s7.ru; Panfilov 164/1; ⊗ 9am-6pm Mon-Fri, 10am-5pm Sat-Sun). Via Novosibirsk

China Southern (Map p60; ☑ (0)708-548082; www.csair.com; Manas 41/A; ⊗ 9am-noon & 2-5pm Mon-Fri). Via Urumqi

Air Astana (☑ airport desk 906906; www.airastana.com). Via Almaty or Astana

Uzbekistan Airways (Map p60; ☑ (0)312-610364; www.uzairways.com; Kiev 107; ⊗ 9am-7pm). Via Tashkent

Aeroflot (Map p60; ☑ (0)312-301689; http://aviatravel.kg; Tynystanov 62/19; ⊗ 9am-6pm Mon-Thu, to 5pm Fri). Via Moscow

Osh International Airport (p121) is also increasingly well linked via Istanbul, Dubai and various Russian cities.

On the lake's Northern Shore near Tamchy, Issyk-Köl International Airport's (p81) schedule seems to change by year, but often includes some combination of Uzbekistan Airways (via Tashkent), S7 (via Novosibirsk) and Qazaq Air (www.flyqazaq.com/en) via Almaty.

Tickets can be booked online or at helpful ticket agents in Bishkek and elsewhere such as **Avia Traffic** (Map p66; ☑ (0)312-544788; www.aero.kg; Panfilov 26; ⊗ 8am-7pm Mon-Fri, to 5pm Sat, to 2pm Sun), **Avia Travel Club** (Map p60; ☑ (0)312-301689; http://aviatravel.kg; Tynystanov 62/19; ⊗ 9am-6pm Mon-Thu, to

5pm Fri), **C.A.T.** (Central Asia Tourism Company; Map p60; ☑ (0)312-896339; www.cat.kg; Manas 57; ⊗ 10am-7pm Mon-Fri, 11am-4pm Sat) and many others.

LAND

To & From China

There are two land routes to Kashgar in Xinjiang, China, where the official time zone ('Beijing Time') is GMT plus eight hours, though unofficial 'Xinjiang Time' is GMT plus six hours, ie the same as Kyrgyzstan in summer.

Both routes are fiddly and essentially take a very long day, sometimes two, so start early and bring food and drink. Both are scenically inspiring (the Torugart route more consistently so) and cross high mountain passes. Beware of intense cold and potential road closures when snowbound in winter.

Both borders close at weekends and public holidays. Be careful if travelling on Fridays in case there's a delay or road closure (landslide, unexpected holiday) meaning you're stuck until Monday.

On the Chinese side, both routes involve crossing well over 100km between inner and outer frontier posts through a restricted border zone within which bicycles must be put on a vehicle. Hitching through Irkeshtam is officially no longer allowed, so expect to pay a Chinese taxi to cover the distance if you haven't hired a vehicle for the whole trip.

Irkeshtam Route

At the easier of Kyrgyzstan's two borders with China (no border permit required), shared taxis from Osh to Irkeshtam (2000som, four to five hours) can be arranged near the new bridge taxi stand. These will leave you on the Kyrgyz side of the border. Expected numerous checkpoints, baggage checks and long waits...one of which will inevitably be when one side or the other of the border checks closes for a three-hour lunch break. Arrange a seat a day or two in advance.

Doing the trip in sections works out much cheaper – typically under US$35, albeit highly variable depending on how many other travellers cross that day and share the taxi or van cost between Chinese border posts. Crossing independently you get the added bonus of a night in Sary-Tash, with its beautiful clear-weather views of Alay Valley mountainscapes, plus the views between there and Osh which the through-bus typically passes at night.

From Sary-Tash hitch or share a taxi (300/1500som per person/car) for 73km to the main Kyrgyz border post. Either leave around 7am to reach the border just after 8am, or start the afternoon before and sleep at one of the basic cafe-wagons (bed 100som to 200som) right beside the border compound, though the CBT

Alay (p120) guesthouse in the village of Nura (5km back) is much better value. Note that the border closes on weekends as well as Kyrgyz and Chinese holidays, some of which are announced with very little notice, so always keep a back-up plan in mind if you're headed this way with your visa running down.

Either way walk past the queue of trucks and get your passport stamped, then after that's checked, arrange a ride with the next passing truck for the following 7km. Leave your bags in the truck for the first two passport checks, but say goodbye at the upper Chinese customs station. Here your passport is checked but not stamped while your bags, camera, computer, iPad, books etc are very extensively searched for anything suspicious (films watched, photos checked, files opened).

Once a decent number of travellers have been thus checked, their passports are collected and given to an approved taxi driver who will drive you the whopping 140km to the main Chinese border station. This costs 550 Chinese yuan or more per car, and if you're alone you might have to pay for the whole vehicle. Hitching is no longer allowed.

You get stamped into China at a big, airport-style complex. There's no bank but there is usually a money changer lurking just after customs offering a not unreasonable six yuan for one US dollar. A taxi to Wuqia minibus/shared taxi station costs 5 Chinese yuan. Or walk 3km – down a long grand avenue then right on Yingbin Lu. Minibuses to Kashgar (23 to 33 yuan) take 1½ hours.

Torugart Route

The Torugart Pass to Naryn is used by Bishkek–Kashgar and Bishkek–Artush sleeper buses, but foreigners are not allowed to take those services and can only use this border by using agency transfers on both sides. Your name needs to be on a stamped passenger manifest (Chinese side) and a passport copy must be sent to the Kyrgyz agent. Such bureaucracy makes this route disproportionately expensive – the cheapest offers we found for groups were around US$120 per head. Alone you'd be asked nearly US$500.

There are several ways to find other travellers or pre-arranged groups to join:

➜ In Bishkek, consult the notice board at NoviNomad (p70).
➜ In Naryn, ask CBT (p103) or Kubat Tour (p106).
➜ In Kashgar, seek out fellow travellers at the **Pamir Youth Hostel** (喀什帕米尔青年旅舍; Kāshí Pàmǐ'ěr Qīngnián Lǚshè; ☑ 180 9985 1967, 0998 282 3376; www.pamirhostel.com; 3f Id Kah Bazaar District 7, Section A; dm ¥40-50, d ¥140; ❀ ⚥) or **Kashgar Old Town Youth Hostel** (喀什老城青年旅舍; Kāshí Lǎochéng

Qīngnián Lǚshè; ☑ 0998 282 3262, 152 7610 6605; www.kashgaroldcity.hostel.com; 233 Ostangboyi Lu, 吾斯塘博依路233号; dm ¥45-60, d ¥130-165; @ ⚥) and/or ask agencies **Silk Road Tours** (☑ +86 180 9377 1979; www.uighurtour.com; Chini Bagh Royal Hotel) or **Old Road Tours** (☑ +86 1389 9132 103; www.oldroadtours.com; Sèmǎn Hotel) whether they have groups you can join.

Cyclists need to have agency-arranged vehicles organised on the Chinese side (where riding is not allowed) and a border permit allowing them to ride under their own steam on the Kyrgyz side: this is subject to some strict rules about not deviating from the main road before the inner frontier post.

The whole Kashgar–Naryn route (typically nine to 12 hours) is scenically delightful, if weather conditions oblige, though the mesmerising views of high-altitude lake Chatyr-Köl tend to be slightly marred by power lines.

To & From Kazakhstan

Aisha Bibi

Regular minibuses run from Talas city across the Aisha Bibi border to Taraz, Kazakhstan.

Karkara

The back-door route into Kazakhstan via the Karkara Valley is open in summer, but there's no cross-border public transport. Coming from the Kazakhstan side, take a Kegen-bound marshrutka, then a taxi for the last 28km to the border. Pre-arranged with CBT Karakol (p90), a pick-up from the border costs US$60 per car to Issyk-Köl. Hitchhiking is possible if you have tents and are prepared to wait a day or two.

Korday

Minibuses depart from Bishkek's 'tysyach melochey' shopping centre (p71) for the busiest border crossing into Kazakhstan, which is popular with merchants moving between the two countries. Alternatively, minibuses from the Western Bus Station (p70) in Bishkek run all the way to Almaty's Sayran bus station.

To & From Tajikistan

Kyzyl-Art is the main border crossing for travellers, into the Tajik Pamir, but there's no public transport and you'll need a GBAO (Gorno-Badakhshan Autonomous Oblast) permit along with your Tajik visa.

Other borders into Tajikistan's Fergana Valley towns at Kulundu and Batken are reportedly open to third-country nationals, but very few visitors make it as far as Kyrgyzstan's Batken *oblast* to try.

To & From Uzbekistan

Most travellers will cross at Kyrgyzstan's Fergana Valley town of Dostyk, headed for Andijan in

ℹ NORTH–SOUTH HIGHWAY

At the time of research, work was being done on a new north–south highway that would radically alter the country's tourism infrastructure sometime in 2018. The new road, connecting Jalalabad, Kazarman, Jumgal, Kochkor and Balykchy, is expected to cut transport times from Bishkek to Osh nearly in half and will drastically reshape public transport connections. Ask for updated schedules before planning journeys across the country.

Uzbekistan. A shared taxi from Osh to the border is around 200som. All other crossings are generally only open to Uzbek and Kyrgyz nationals.

ℹ Getting Around

ARRIVING IN KYRGYZSTAN

Manas International Airport (Bishkek) Minibus 380 (40som) departs just to the right of the arrivals exit, or taxis to anywhere in central Bishkek are 500som.

Osh International Airport Minibus 107 and 142 connect the airport to the city centre, or a taxi should cost 200som.

Korday border crossing (Kazakhstan) Regular minibuses (20som) depart for central Bishkek from just beyond the border control station for travellers who haven't booked through-transport from Almaty.

AIR

Air Kyrgyzstan (AC Kyrgyzstan; (0)312-316600; www.air.kg; Manas International Airport; ⊙8.30am-5.30pm Mon-Fri) and AirManas (p138) connect Kyrgyzstan's major cities, with regular service between Bishkek and Osh as well as several weekly connections Osh–Tamchy (summer only), Bishkek–Batken and Bishkek–Jalal-Abad. Rumour has it that Karakol airport will recommence operation in 2018.

BICYCLE

Kyrgyzstan is a popular country for long-distance cyclists, and many of the routes that are most difficult by car are perfect for intrepid bikers. Keep in mind that there are very few repair facilities outside of Bishkek that are familiar with upmarket cycles, so you'd do best to remain self-sufficient as much as possible.

BUS, MINIBUS & SHARED TAXI

Only a handful of routes employ full-size buses, but shared taxis and minibuses – some timetabled but more often departing when full – wait for passengers at most bus stations. If you pay all four seats the latter will also act as private one-way taxis. Agency or CBT-arranged drivers generally cost around double since they must cover the probability of returning empty, but such options are still worth considering for complex routes with multiple or overnight stops, and you'll often get a better vehicle (not necessarily English-speaking drivers, though). Typical rates are between 14som and 18som per kilometre, plus an overnight fee between 500som to 1000som to cover the driver's expenses.

CAR & MOTORCYCLE

Self-drive car rental is a new concept, but there are two local agencies in Bishkek: Iron Horse Nomads (p72) and Kyrgyz Rent-Car (p72). Swiss-run **MuzToo** (http://muztoo.ch; 101 St; ⊙9am-5pm Mon-Fri) in Osh rents Yamaha-600 trail motorbikes, but they don't come cheap.

When stopped by traffic police, standard regulations involve a driver surrendering their licence until a fine is paid in the nearest regional centre. In practice local drivers often negotiate an informal bribe of 200som to 500som on the spot, and while from foreigners more would be expected, Lonely Planet does not recommend engaging in illegal activities.

HITCHING

Catching a ride along roadsides is common practice in Kyrgyzstan, but note that most drivers will expect payment of some sort. Always ascertain whether car (and driver!) are in roadworthy shape before accepting a ride.

Hitching is never entirely safe, and we don't recommend it. Travellers who hitch should understand that they are taking a small but potentially serious risk.

TRAIN

The only train route of note to travellers is the five-hour link between Bishkek and Balykchy, but most travellers will prefer the two-hour bus ride joining the towns (or bypassing the town completely for other points in Issyk-Köl).

Tajikistan

☎992 / POP 8.7 MILLION

Best Places to Eat

➜ Chaykhona Rokhat (p151)

➜ Davlatkhon Homestay (p183)

➜ Dilovar's Villa (p163)

➜ Delhi Darbar (p178)

➜ Darvaz Sangakov Bahrom (p174)

➜ Sayokhat (p161)

Best Places to Stay

➜ Marian's Guesthouse (p147)

➜ Serena Hotel (p150)

➜ Karon Palace (p174)

➜ Guesthouse Shahboz (p163)

➜ Lal Hotel (p178)

➜ Erali Guesthouse (p184)

Why Go?

The term 'predominantly mountainous' doesn't do justice to a country where over 90% of the land is upland. This fact of nature has given Tajikistan a precious advantage over its neighbours, namely some of the most inspiring, high-altitude landscape in the world. Within an hour of Dushanbe lie multi-hued lakes, peaks that beg to be climbed and high passes that thrill even reluctant travellers. In among this natural splendour are scattered villages and towns that survive cheek-by-jowl through each extreme season. It hasn't been easy for these traditional communities to adapt to the changing world beyond their mountain strongholds, but despite this they are unfailingly welcoming of outsiders and cheerfully excuse cultural faux-pas as part and parcel of their proud democracy. For visitors tolerant of a few travelling hardships (outdoor loos, cold water, potholed roads), the country more than compensates with a rare glimpse into life lived on 'The Roof of the World'.

When to Go
Dushanbe

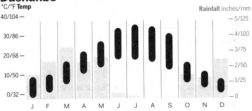

Mid-Jun–Sep The cities sizzle, but this is the only viable time for High Pamir treks.

Apr–May Mild in the lowlands; heavy showers cause landslides blocking mountain roads.

Nov–Feb Temperatures in the Pamirs drop to between -20°C and -45°C (-4°F to -49°F).

TOP TIP

➡ Hire a 4WD. With public transport minimal to non-existent in much of the country, a car and driver transforms a visit to Tajikistan, especially in the Pamirs.

Fast Facts

➡ **Area** 143,100 sq km

➡ **Capital** Dushanbe

➡ **Currency** US dollar, Tajik somoni (TJS)

➡ **Languages** Tajik, Russian, Uzbek, Sogdian, several Pamiri languages, Kyrgyz

Exchange Rates

Australia	A$1	6.93TJS
Canada	C$1	7.13TJS
China	¥10	13.90TJS
Euro zone	€1	10.84TJS
Japan	¥100	8.11TJS
NZ	NZ$1	6.40TJS
Russia	R100	15.11TJS
UK	UK£1	12.20TJS
USA	US$1	8.82TJS

For current exchange rates, see www.xe.com.

Resources

➡ **Asia Plus** (www.asiaplus.tj/en)

➡ **Pamirs** (www.pamirs.org)

➡ **PECTA** (www.visitpamirs.com)

➡ **Tajik Tourism** (http://tajiktourism.com)

➡ **Trekking in the Pamirs** (www.trekkinginthepamirs.com)

Visas & Permits

For most nationalities e-visas (US$50) are available online at www.evisas.tj. These e-visas are valid for 45 days and include the permit for GBAO (eastern Tajikistan).

COSTS

Relative Cost
More expensive than Kyrgyzstan, but cheaper than Uzbekistan (unless you're renting a 4WD).

Daily Expenses
➡ Floor space in homestay: US$10
➡ Double room with bathroom: US$50–100
➡ Self-catering: US$5
➡ Three meals in homestays: US$15
➡ Overnight guided trek: US$100–150
➡ Seat in shared taxi: US$45
➡ Charter of small 4WD with driver: US$80

Price Ranges

Sleeping (double room with bath, including breakfast): **$** <US$40, **$$** US$40–150, **$$$** >US$150

Eating (main course): **$** <US$5, **$$** US$5–30, **$$$** >US$30

Itineraries

➡ **One week** After two nights in Dushanbe travel north to Khojand. On the outward journey spend two nights at Iskander-Kul and Sarytag to allow a day's trekking in the Fan Mountains. Overnight in Khojand and spend the morning enjoying the citadel and bazaar and either return to the capital or travel on to the Uzbekistan or Kyrgyzstan borders.

➡ **Two weeks** Allow five days to travel from Dushanbe to Osh along the Pamir Hwy. Break the journey in the friendly towns of Kalai-Kum and Khorog and allow a day to absorb the windswept isolation of Murgab. In 10 days, add in the southern route between Khorog and Murgab, through the timeless Wakhan Valley with its ancient shrines and traditional culture.

➡ **Three weeks** Combine the one- and two-week itineraries (with the relevant multiple entry visa) to make a circuit through Tajikistan either starting in Dushanbe or in Osh. Travelling anticlockwise has a slight edge on the journey in reverse.

DUSHANBE ДУШАНБЕ

🗹 372 / POP 679,400 / ELEV 800M

With a rural hinterland of grassy pastures and snow-capped mountains visible from down town, Dushanbe is a delightful city built around parks, lakes and fountains. With the frenetic building project of the past decade mostly complete, there is a palpable air of satisfaction about the city centre. Its grand plane tree boulevard, Rudaki, threads past pastel-hued remnants of the Soviet era and just as proudly past the modern icons of statehood. Chief of these is the golden statue of 10th-century Ismoil Somoni presiding over Friendship Square, representative of the sense of renaissance that marks the current era, both in Dushanbe and Tajikistan as a whole.

During warmer months, it is easy to while away a few days in Dushanbe, strolling the parks, visiting museums and relaxing into the city's tranquil atmosphere. As such, it makes for an island of comfort and convenience in a country of exciting but tough travel.

History

Strolling along the grand boulevards of modern Dushanbe (meaning Monday), it is hard to imagine that less than 100 years ago there was little here but a village named after its weekly bazaar.

Despite hints of settlement dating back to the 5th century BC, the city only began to evolve after the establishment of the railway in 1929 when, under the name Stalinabad, it was made the capital of the new Soviet Tajik republic. Reverting to its former name in the 1950s, it was populated by Tajik émigrés from Bukhara and Samarkand and included 50,000 Germans, both POWs and Soviet-German exiles from Russia, and functioned as an industrial and administrative centre for the country's cotton and silk industries.

During the last decade of the 20th century, as the Soviet Union fell, Dushanbe became marred in the violent struggles of civil war. By 2002, however, peace prevailed and the city has subsequently been transformed into a quietly prosperous commercial hub, matched by a growing number of cultural icons and institutions.

⊙ Sights

★**Ethnography Museum**   MUSEUM
(Inside National Museum of Antiquities of Tajikistan; 🗹 372 27 1350; Ak Rajabov 7; admission 10TJS; ⊙10am-5pm Tue-Sun) Sharing the same complex as the National Museum of Antiquities, this small museum houses an exquisite

---

ACTIVITIES AROUND DUSHANBE

Dushanbe is one of the few capital cities where the rural hinterland can be spotted from the centre of downtown. Within half an hour it is possible to escape the urban heat of summer and be in glorious countryside. Nearby attractions invite participation in a number of activities, from a gentle stroll to jet-skiing, and some of the attractions offer accommodation for anyone wanting to make a weekend of it.

North of Dushanbe, the Varzob River flows beside the main M34, dotted along much of its length by villas, *dachas* and chaikhanas and offering some gentle hiking. In particular, there are two pleasant short walks, circumnavigating the **Varzob Reservoir** (M34, Varzob) and following the footpath to the 30m-high **Gusgarf Waterfall** (Varzob Valley). At Takob, just a little further up the Varzob Valley, winter sports are offered at **Ski Complex Safed-Dara** (🗹935 71 0114; Takob; admission 120TJS, ski rental 90TJS, full kit rental 150TJS; 🛏).

South of Dushanbe, just a 30-minute drive from the city, **Hissar Fort** (Hisor; fort & medrassa 5TJS, guide 20TJS; ⊙8am-5pm) is mostly a cultural destination but it also offers horse riding for children. A little further afield and towards the southeast, a range of water sports including boating, waterskiing and jet skiing, are available at Nurek Reservoir through the **AquaClub** (🗹937 32 7777; http://aquaclub.tj/en; Nurek Reservoir; full board per person Mon-Thu 360TJS, Fri-Sun 410TJS).

International running group **Hash House Harriers** (🗹939 99 9160) does its thing at 5pm on Saturday, and **Hike Tajikistan** (www.facebook.com/hike.tajikistan; ⊙Sun) organises Sunday hiking or skiing day trips when weather permits. Check the Facebook pages for details.

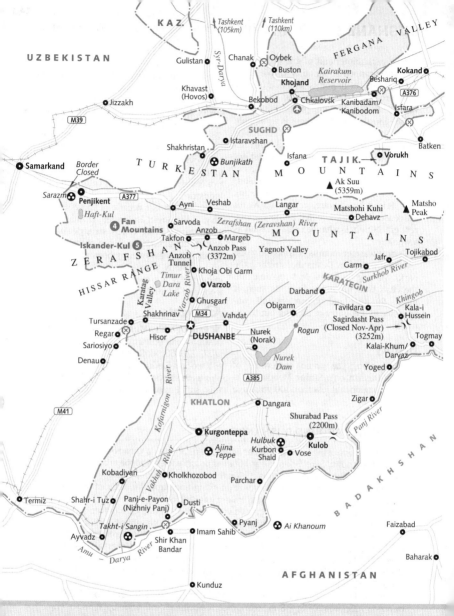

Tajikistan Highlights

1 Pamir Highway (p168)
Travelling along one of the world's most famous roads, offering high-altitude vistas and fine community-based homestays.

2 Wakhan Valley (p180)
Observing rural life along the narrow Pyanj River corridor, bordering Afghanistan, with Silk Road forts and spectacular views of the snowbound Hindu Kush.

3 Jizeu (p176) Bouncing over angry waters on a suspension bridge as a prelude to hiking to this carless Pamir valley.

collection of traditional Tajikistan clothing (including a great set of woollen socks and gloves that seem disproportionately large for the average wearer) and some fine enamel jewellery in the form of amulets and earrings. The real gems of the collection, though, are the samples of vertically striped silk cloth known as 'atlas' – a fabric still worn by Tajikistani women on special occasions.

National Museum of Antiquities of Tajikistan   MUSEUM
(☑ 372 27 1350; www.afc.ryukoku.ac.jp/tj; Ak Rajabov 7; admission 50TJS; ⊘ 9am-5pm Tue-Sat, to 1pm Sun) Looking almost as aged as some of the exhibits it houses, this dusty old museum, with its threadbare carpets and uneven floors, has a certain charm about it, not least for the quality of the collection therein and the enthusiasm of its friendly caretakers. Many of the exhibits, which focus largely on archaeological finds, represent key pieces of Central Asian history and trump the copies in the National Museum.

★ Rudaki Park   PARK
(Rudaki; ⊘ 24hr) Extensive Rudaki Park, with its beautiful canopy of mature trees, offers a series of pathways through flower gardens and alongside lakes and fountains. Home to the giant flagpole and a much-photographed statue of Rudaki, and with glorious views of the city's iconic new buildings and monuments, it makes for a great location for a picnic in summer or snowy vistas in winter.

Throughout the park are a number of notable buildings. The grand modern **Palace of Nations** (Kohi millat; btwn Shotemur & Tehran) in the south, dubbed locally as the White House, is the official seat of the president of Tajikistan. Beyond are the Parchan national monument, a slender white-marble pillar featuring a gilded version of the national emblem of Tajikistan, and the **Statue of Ismoil Somoni** (Ismail Samani; Maydoni Dusti/ Friendship Sq) built to celebrate the 10th-century founder of the Samanid dynasty. On the southern edge of the park is the **National Library** (☑ 929 35 5554; Tehran; ⊘ 8am-5pm), a US$40 million archive constructed to resemble an open book and reputed to be Central Asia's biggest library.

To the west of the central park section is the **World's Biggest Teahouse** (Navruz Palace, Kohi Navruz; Somoni; admission TJS25), based on traditional architectural design and encompassing some exquisite national motifs but now used as a conference centre and banqueting hall. Tours of the interior, with its inlaid marble, carved wood work and tiling produced by local craftsmen, are occasionally available – it's best to call in on the off-chance. Just across Lake Komsomol is the **Borbat Concert Hall** (Somoni 26), which hosts occasional Tajik music concerts.

Just north of the park, across Ismoili Somoni diagonally from the National Museum, the facade of the **Writers' Union Building** (Somoni) gives an indication of the esteem in which Tajikistan's Persian past is still held, adorned as it is with sculpted-stone figures of Sadruddin Ayni, Omar Khayam, Firdausi and other writers from the Persian pantheon. Nearby, at the intersection with Rudaki, the attractive Soviet-style Palace of the President makes a useful reference point for navigating in the centre of the city. Built originally as the headquarters of the Tajik Communist Party, the palace and the adjacent square (Shahidan Sq) are now railed off from the road – a reminder that this was the site of mass protest in the 1990s and one of many preludes to the civil war that followed.

National Museum   MUSEUM
(Osorkhonai Milli; ☑ 372 27 8561; www.newnmt. tj; Ismoil Somoni; admission/camera 25/10TJS; ⊘ 10am-5pm Tue-Sat, 11am-4pm Sun, ticket office closes 1hr earlier) Tajikistan's national museum is housed in an impressive modern building with an elliptical roof and giant atrium. The collection encompasses three main sections – natural history, archaeology and contemporary fine arts – and displays include minerals (including a giant mineral tree), dioramas of snow leopards and Marco Polo sheep, suits of armour and musical instruments. Among the most important exhibits are the murals from ancient Penjikent and an exquisite 10th-century wooden *mehrab* (mosque prayer niche) found near Ayni.

Gurminj Museum   MUSEUM
(☑ 935 731 076; www.gurminj.tj; Bokhtar 23; |admission/concert 10/20TJS; ⊘ 8am-5pm) Hidden within a private family compound behind unmarked green gates is a precious collection of antique musical instruments originating from across Central Asia. The collection took over 20 years to assemble and was housed with support from the Ministry of Heritage and Culture. While the original owner (a renowned musician) died in 2003, the family has continued a tradi-

tion of music-making within the museum's three darkened rooms.

Victory Park PARK

(Park Pobedy; Anzobskya; ⊙24hr) With the best views over the city, this hilltop park makes a tranquil spot in which to enjoy a shaded stroll. The park encompasses a well-kept WWII monument and there's a teahouse selling brews of all sorts (including beer). Sitting in one of the leafy bowers watching the sun set is a classic capital pastime. The cable car is still awaiting an overhaul, making a taxi ride (20TJS from the centre of town) the most convenient way of getting there.

Shah Mansur Bazaar MARKET

(Green Bazaar; cnr Lokhuti & Nissor Muhammed; ⊙6am-9pm, closed 1st Mon of each month) The Shah Mansur Bazaar, known in English as the 'Green Bazaar', is the heartbeat of Dushanbe trade and a great place to gain a sense of local life in the city. Carts of golden-coloured bread, trolleys of locally grown melons, apricots and peaches, and giant aluminium dishes of yoghurt being stirred with wooden spoons contribute to the colourful and mobile chaos of this central meeting point.

Botanical Gardens PARK

(Samadi Gani; admission 5TJS; ⊙7am-7.30pm) The extensive Botanical Gardens, with its Persepolis-inspired gateway, is home to a fine collection of mature deciduous trees (labelled in Latin) and offers a shady retreat in the heat of the summer. A favourite with courting couples and strolling families, it also features a series of fitness stations, many designed for children. The park comes alive on Saturday afternoons when one of the many elaborate wooden pavilions becomes a showcase for local musical talent. On the way from the centre look out for the pale blue neoclassical facade of the **Tajik State Pedagogical University** (Rudaki 121), one of Tajikistan's top higher education institutions.

🛏 Sleeping

Dushanbe has one or two international five-star hotels and some new business-oriented accommodation, but by far the most characterful options come in the form of modern, midrange mansion hotels, many of which are hidden along suburban lanes. Often family-run, these hotels are usually set in gardens, include slippers to replace shoes at the front

KURUTOB

Tajikistan's contribution to vegetarian cuisine is the *kurutob*, pieces of flat bread replacing meat in a warm yoghurt-based sauce topped with a salad of tomatoes, onions, fresh herbs and perhaps a hot pepper. In Dushanbe, the best *kurutob* is often found in small, barely marked cafes like the family yard of **Oshi Abdurahman** (Loik Sherali 25; kurutob/sambusa/tea 15/6/3TJS; ⊙10am-7pm). More central is **Puppet Kurutob** (off Shotemur; kurutob 12TJS; ⊙8am-10pm), around the side of the mosaic-covered *kukli teatr* (puppet theatre).

door and serve home-cooked dishes for breakfast. Budget accommodation is more elusive and represents less value for money.

Zebo's Homestay HOMESTAY $

(☑372 24 5781, Nidora 934 803300; Mirzo Tursunzoda 178; r per person US$20, breakfast US$5) 🖉 This simple, very friendly single-storey private home is surrounded by a garden of fruit trees. Three guest beds are available in two small (and somewhat airless) rooms and there's access to a hot shower, Western-style loo and modern kitchen with washing machine. If full, guests may be offered the lounge floor. Discounts are possible. No wi-fi.

Makhbuba Mansurova's Homestay HOMESTAY $

(☑378 56 9166, 372 21 2083; Zekhni 1st side lane, 11; dm incl breakfast US$20; ❄) Offering clean mattresses in newly decorated rooms in the upstairs storey of the family house, this homestay is set within a lovely garden with a spreading grape vine. There is a hot-water bathroom with Western-style loo and guests can use the tea-bed to relax in the garden. It's southeast of the obvious TV transmitter.

★ Marian's Guesthouse GUESTHOUSE $$

(☑372 23 0191; www.mariansguesthouse.com; Shotemur 67/1; s/d US$85/95; P❄@🛜🏊) 🖉 This 70-year old Australian-owned mansion with Moroccan-style swimming pool offers six characterful rooms with tasteful decor and antique furnishings. The large, beautiful garden, with its lily pond and lion fountain, willows and poplars, hollyhocks and rose arbours, makes this a top choice for those

Dushanbe

Samadi Gani

54

6
State Medical
University

23

67

Tsementzavod
(Cement
Factory) 2km;
Varzob (30km)

Omar Khayam

See Inset

Park
Khayyam

Karamov

Big
Wheel

Tolstoy
(Gafir Gulom)

Rudaki
Plaza

Gani Abdullo

Said Nosirbov

61

Shahobob

Nizomi Ganjavi

Pedagogical
University

16

Rudaki

37 Loik
Sherali

29

40
36

Badakhshan

30

Ozodi Zanon

31

Gogol
(Mahmadi
Kholov)

Sharq

Hofiz Sherozi

Mir Said Mirsakar

Gogol

Turdiev

Bokhtar

Mirzo Tursunzoda

Hisor (30km);
Hissar Fort
(37km)

Mahmudov

66

Rakhimzade

57

Hyatt
Hotel

47

18

50

Ismoili Somoni

19

49

32

Kurbon

35

Rakhimov

38

9

52

12 34

Sheroz

53

43

Foteh Niyezi

69

Children's
Park

39

5

71 41

51

Shotemur

27

Shotemur

11

Rudaki 2
Park

14

7

Shota Rustaveli

Azizbekov

Statue of
Ismoil Somoni

59

63

Tehran

13

Maydoni
Dusti

Bokhtar

Pushkin

Mirzo Tursunzoda

T Pulodi

8

3

56

74

62

Sheroz

Gorky

45

4

70

Asian Express
(700m)

Hippodrome

44

Bukhoro

42

Ayni
Park

46

Husseinzoda

60

48

Nizomi Ganjavi

Hofiz Sherozi

Shevchenko

Narzikulov

Istaravshan

73

10

Ethnography
Museum

1

64

28

Rudaki

Ak Rajabov

20

Maydani
Sipar

Ayni

Saadi Sherozi

Circus
(Tsirk)

Karaboev

M Nazarshoev

seeking some peace and tranquillity in the heart of the city. Airport transfer is included.

Lotte Palace Dushanbe
BOUTIQUE HOTEL **$$**

(☎ 372 24 3030; www.lottepalace.tj; Gagrin 19A; r from US$100; ⊖ ❈ @ 🛜) Around 8km north of central Dushanbe, this modern mansion with its manicured garden, sweeping double staircases, marble floors and gilded flowers manages to retain a sense of private house while providing a full hotel service. Slippers are provided at the entrance and a home-cooked breakfast is available in the basement. Rooms and modern bathrooms are huge and the friendly service excellent.

Hotel Lotus
HOTEL **$$**

(☎ 918 84 7777, 487 01 8800; www.hotel-lotustj. com; Pervii proezd Lohuti 5; s/d from US$80/100; P ⊖ ❈ 🛜 ≋) This smart business hotel feels more like a mountain resort than a city hotel with its mansion-style building set in a large plot with panoramic views of the hills. The modern, comfortable rooms, gym, pool, airport pick-up, free bikes and helpful staff are all big ticks, but it's lacking a bar.

Hotel Twins
BOUTIQUE HOTEL **$$**

(☎ 908 99 9998, 372 21 4414; www.hoteltwins. tj; Adkhamova 21; s/d from US$80/90; ❈ 🛜 ≋) This friendly family-run hotel has two 'twin' properties on-site, joined by an Escheresque staircase. Each wing has its own character; the west wing is decorated with chandeliers, potted plants, painted rondellas and Persian carpets. There's a fire in winter, pool and sauna (US$30 per hour). The clearly beloved garden, complete with pavilions, is a sociable hang-out for visitors. Airport transfer (US$10) available.

Hotel Meridian
GUESTHOUSE **$$**

(☎ 550 45 0145, 446 20 3399; www.hotel-meridian. tj; Khayrullo Mirzoev; s/d/ste US$80/100/120; ❈ @ 🛜 ≋) Hidden in a backstreet walled garden with two tea pavilions, this modern mansion hotel offers great value with fully equipped rooms with computer, fridge and lots of space. There's a pool, sauna (extra charge) and fitness centre in the basement and the guesthouse offers free airport pick-up and laundry.

Hotel Tajikmatlubot
HOTEL **$$**

(☎ 372 24 6487; Rudaki 137; s/d US$30/50; ❈ 🛜) This good-value hotel has 11 rooms that are each veritable suites. The parquet floor and flock wallpaper lend the rooms something of an antique character – a theme continued

Dushanbe

in the shared dining space. Despite being in the southern wing of a rather unattractive block, the hotel manages to feel more like a guesthouse with a pretty garden attached.

★ **Serena Hotel** HOTEL **$$$**
(☑487 01 4000; www.serenahotels.com; Rudaki 14; r from US$120; ❈ ❋ ⚐) Not the newest but arguably Dushanbe's top address weaves traditional colours, fabrics and woodwork into a bright 21st-century tower topped by a rooftop swimming pool. The spacious rooms with mountain views sport tribal rugs and local ceramics and there's an excellent shop selling similar crafts. With a garden and extensive nightly buffet, this good-value central hotel is a winner. And the **Suzani Lobby Bar** (beer 22TJS, cocktails from 35TJS; ⊙7am-1am) here is also stylish venue for a pre-dinner drink or a post-supper rendezvous.

Eating

Dushanbe is relatively small and this is reflected in the style and range of restaurants available. Representing the best local dining experience are the unpretentious *laghman* and kurutob (p147) diners; for the best value, brunch and evening buffets in the five-star hotels serve local favourites with the best ingredients, adding a 10% service charge. To eat at mansion hotels, advance notice is generally required. Self-caters will appreciate the well-stocked **Poitakht Supermarket** (Mirzo Tursunzoda 45; ☺8am-midnight).

★**Ghalaba** CENTRAL ASIAN $
(Victory Park, Park Pobedy; mains 25-70TJS; beer 18TJS; ☺4pm-2am) For sweeping views over the city it's hard to beat the rustic, vine-draped open-air booths and thatch-covered *chorpoy* (bed-like platform) at Ghalaba. Serving tea, beer and cocktails, it's the perfect place to unwind at sunset. Access is easiest by 10-minute taxi ride (20TJS) from the city centre; the adjacent cable car is not functioning.

★**Chaykhona Rokhat** CENTRAL ASIAN $
(Rudaki 84; mains 15-25TJS, herb salad/lagman/beer 12/15/16TJS; ☺6am-11pm; 🖷) This grand Soviet-era, Persian-style, open-sided chaikhana (teahouse) is *the* Dushanbe classic – a great place to sip tea, slurp a bowl of noodles or enjoy a Simsim beer while joining locals in watching the world go by. Kitchens work all day, even in Ramadan. The wedding hall, with its magnificent, painted wooden ceiling, is worth a peep on the way in.

Sary Osyo UZBEK $
(Mirzo Tursunzoda 129; plov 21TJS; ☺11am-5pm) This simple family-run restaurant in a vine-covered yard attracts a local crowd at lunchtime hoping to dine on Dushanbe's best *plov* (pilaf).

Café Merve TURKISH $
(www.merve.tj; Rudaki 92; mains 20-40TJS; ☺8am-11pm; 🖉🖷) This hugely popular bustling cafeteria makes a lively spot for Turkish breakfasts, kebabs, pizza, salads, cakes and instant coffee (but no alcohol).

★**Traktir Konservator** UKRAINIAN $$
(☏446 00 8888, 987 960505; mains 25-70TJS; ☺11am-11pm; ✻🖨🖷) In an unprepossessing alley near the Opera House, this surprisingly atmospheric restaurant is a treat both in terms of its rural Russian decor (think theatre posters, heavy beams and samovars) and extensive Ukrainian menu (pot roasted pork,

cutlets with buckwheat, sweet and sour pikeperch, and compote). A cosy outdoor terrace attracts a lively crowd in summer.

Taj Mahal INDIAN $$
(☏931 06 0708; Rudaki 81; curries from 25TJS; ☺11am-11pm; ✻🖨🖉🖷) A range of well-prepared Indian dishes, cooked by an Indian chef, is served at brightly clothed tables in this ever-popular central favourite.

Marco Polo EUROPEAN, AFGHAN $$
(☏372 27 0073, 904 304114; marcopolo.tj@gmail.com; Mirzo Tursunzoda 80; mains 45-100TJS; ☺10am-11pm; ✻🖨🖷) This fun little venue, designed as an odd combination of stalactite-filled cavern with covered tables and cloth serviettes, provides a cool spot on a hot day. The menu offers a hotchpotch of dishes, but the night-time ambience compensates for the lack of culinary focus.

Morning Star Café INTERNATIONAL $$
(☏918 55 3857; www.morningstarcafe.net; Mirzo Tursunzoda 187; sandwiches from 10TJS, coffee 10-20TJS; ☺8am-6pm Mon-Sat, to 11am Sat brunch; 🖉🖷) With a menu of choices popular among homesick travellers and resident expats, this welcoming cafe serves good locally roasted coffee, cakes, wraps and sandwiches. It's a friendly place to come for a relaxed Saturday brunch.

Izum INTERNATIONAL $$
(☏908 66 6666; Foteh Niyezi 44; mains 50-120TJS, beer 25TJS; ☺10am-11.30pm; ✻🖨🖉🖷) Local fabrics and piled cushions lend an exotic aura to this trend-setting restaurant, with its intimate booths and hubble-bubble bar. The tablet menus feature an extensive range of vegetarian dishes including baked pumpkin, lentil burgers and cauliflower cheese.

Arirang KOREAN $$
(☏372 24 4343; Rudaki 96; mains 50-100TJS; ☺11.30am-10pm Mon-Sat) The smell of garlic hints at the authentic Korean food offered behind the misleadingly dreary facade of Arirang. Ropes, manuscript panelling and bundles of twigs give character to this popular restaurant where dining is at heavy wooden tables or on raised floor mats.

★**Rudaki Restaurant** INTERNATIONAL $$$
(☏487 01 4000; www.serenahotels.com; Rudaki 14, Serena Hotel; breakfast/lunch/dinner buffet 140/185/220TJS; ☺6.30-10.30am, noon-3.30pm & 8-11.30pm) Offering a full à la carte menu in addition to an excellent buffet selection, the Rudaki Restaurant at the Serena Hotel is a

popular choice for a celebration. When it's not too windy, tables are set under the trees in the garden making for a romantic night out. Reservations recommended.

Drinking & Nightlife

★Café Segafredo
ITALIAN, CAFE

(☑487 01 5777; Rudaki 70; mains from 25TJS; ☺8am-11pm; 🖝) The large terrace of this central cafe makes the perfect spot to pause on a stroll along leafy Rudaki. With excellent service, good coffee and reliable ice cream, Segafredo deserves its reputation as a fashionable and popular rendezvous, and the pasta and pizza tempt a longer stay.

★Dushanbe Plaza
Restaurant Club
ROOFTOP BAR

(☑915 497777, 931 06 0708; Rudaki 19, 19th fl, Dushanbe Plaza; ☺10am-1am) With a 360-degree view of Dushanbe, the top floor of this building offers the perfect place for sundowners. A DJ ensures that the dance floors of the adjoining club are kept pulsing with the latest house music and a few limited dining options mean party types can make a night of it.

Public
PUB

(☑987 97 8080; www.facebook.com/irish. publicpub; Bokhtar 2; beer/Guinness/cocktails from 13/65/25TJS; ☺11am-11pm) This convivial Irish pub is standing room only with expats after work on Friday evening. At other times it offers a breezy, street-side venue in which to enjoy a beer and a plate of homemade sausages (179TJS), although the cramped table space and 'pack 'em in' approach won't please everyone.

Entertainment

★Ayni Opera & Ballet Theatre
THEATRE

(☑372 21 3494; www.operabalet.tj; Rudaki 28; ☺Oct-Jun) Built in 1942, this fine Opera House was completely refitted in 2009 and the gardens re-landscaped in 2013. It attracts quality international and local productions. There's no English website but it's easy enough to book in person at the front desk. A smart dress code is observed.

Every evening the small square opposite the theatre comes alive with a throng of Dushanbe citizens and visitors, drawn by the square's musical fountains. After dark, the fountains are transformed into a fun music and light show that rival the theatre in terms of drawing the crowds.

Shopping

Barzish Sport (Rudaki 91; ☺8am-6pm Mon-Sat) is handy for basic outdoor equipment. For souvenirs try the following:

Noor Art Gallery
ARTS & CRAFTS

(☑487 02 1234; www.facebook.com/NOORART SHOP; Ismoili Somoni 26/1, Hyatt Hotel; ☺8am-8pm Mon-Fri, 10am-8pm Sat & Sun) This attractive gallery is stocked with tasteful modern crafts, including hand-painted ceramic plates, wooden boxes and woollen items.

Asia Gallery
ARTS & CRAFTS

(☑937 30 4248; Rudaki 14, Serena Hotel; ☺8am-8pm) Adbul Ahmad, the owner of this small arts and crafts shop, is very knowledgeable about regional carpets, including the lost art of hand looming in Tajikistan. His son speaks some English, but most of the crafts (including some exquisite Tajiki embroidery, lapis lazuli bowls and Afghan shawls) speak for themselves.

Silk Road
GIFTS & SOUVENIRS

(Shotemur 32; ☺9am-6pm Mon-Fri) A selection of local crafts and souvenirs are offered here including mineral trees, embroidery and scarves in among the fridge magnets.

Tajik Painters Union
Exhibition Hall
ART

(cnr Rudaki & Somoni; ☺10am-5pm Mon-Fri, to 3pm Sat) Comprises of three floors of modern Tajik art, with most pieces for sale. The opening hours here are somewhat erratic.

TsUM
GIFTS & SOUVENIRS

(Rudaki 83; ☺9am-6pm Mon-Sat) Largely providing outlets for mobile-phone sellers and pharmacists, the city's original department store has a small selection of souvenirs on the ground and top floors. Water pipes, traditional musical instruments and local and Turkish ceramics compete with Soviet-era medals and Tajik robes for the shopper's eye in a rather grand, pillared interior.

Information

What's On In Dushanbe (WOID) is an expat-oriented email newsletter with a wealth of classifieds, jobs, events, restaurant ads and so forth. Email marians@tajnet.tj to get on the mailing list or access it via the Marian's Guesthouse (p147) website.

East Vision (☑938 58 5555; www.travel tajikistan.net; Rudaki 40A; ☺9am-6pm Mon-Sat, 10am-5pm Sun) Sells maps, gives travel advice, and organises tours, rural homestays and air tickets. Mirzo speaks English well.

Hamsafar Travel (☑ 935 014593, 372 26 7030; www.hamsafar-travel.com; Pulod Tolis 5/11, A Savdo 27; ☺ noon-6pm Mon-Sat) This backpacker-oriented agency can arrange 4WD, trekking and tailor-made tours on short notice.

CULTURAL CENTRES

At cultural centre **Bactria Centre** (☑ 372 21 2558; www.bactriacc.org; Tursunzoda 12A; ☺ 9am-5pm Mon-Fri) language classes are available in Russian and Persian, together with concerts, art exhibitions and a showroom of Tajikistan artisan crafts. Check the Facebook page (www.facebook.com/bactriacc) for events. The building is hidden down a short lane behind 10 Tursunzoda opposite a new 10-storey apartment building.

MONEY

ATMs and licensed money changers are widespread across the city, most centrally on Rudaki around the Shotemur junction.

POST

DHL Office (☑ 372 22 1999; Druzhba Narodov 62, Dushanbe; ☺ 9am-6pm Mon-Fri, to noon Sat)

ⓘ Getting There & Away

MINIBUS

Departures on Asian Express and other bus services leave from Dushanbe's efficient modern **bus station** (☑ call centre 1616; www.asiangroup.tj; Sino 110) to destinations in southwestern Tajikistan. The terminal is 3km west of Dushanbe's centre, a two-minute walk north (across rail tracks and through a market) from marshrutka 16, or slightly further, but more obviously, just west of the road running south from the Russian Embassy (marshrutka 25).

Destinations leaving from here include services to Kurgonteppa (20TJS, two hours, at least hourly), Kulob (Kulyab; 35TJS, two hours, four daily) and Shahr-i Tuz (25TJS, 8am and 2.30pm).

SHARED TAXI

Shared taxis are the main form of transport from Dushanbe to all parts of the country other than the southwest.

Services North

For Varzob (3TJS) and Takob (5TJS) shared taxis leave from outside Vadonasos Bazaar.

For Ayni (four hours) and onwards to Khojand (six hours), Istaravshan (five hours) or Penjikent (seven hours), shared taxis depart from the Tsementzavod (Cement Factory; Rudaki; 🚌 3) stand in the north of town. Prices range from 100TJS to 120TJS according to vehicle and demand. The stand can be reached on bus/trolleybus 3 along Rudaki.

Services Southeast

For Khorog, shared 4WDs/minivans (300/270TJS) take anything from 14 to 20 hours, departing mostly between 6am and 8am from the **Badakhshan auto-stand** (Badakshanskaya avtostansiya; M Nazarshoev 149). This stand is behind a blue gated footpath behind Donish 15 (marshrutka 8 from Green Bazaar) or through the bazaar at Nazarshoev 149 (marshrutka 33 from the train station, or route 1 from Maydani Ayni). For Kalai-Khum drivers at the same auto-stand charge around 170TJS per person (nine to 12 hours).

Services East

For Garm (60TJS to 70TJS, four hours), Tojikabod (five hours) and Jirgatol, shared taxis leave from **Garm Dok** (Ayni 82), accessible by marshrutka 4 or 18 from Green Bazaar.

TRAIN

The train to Moscow (US$210, four days) leaves at 3.10am on Saturday and Tuesday routed via Termez, Karshi and Uchkuduk (Uzbekistan), Makat (Kazakhstan) and Volgograd. The **ticket office** (Rudaki 2; ☺ 8am-noon & 1-5pm) is diagonally across the square in front of the train station. It is something of a challenge to gain transit visas in advance for each of the countries en route.

ⓘ Getting Around

Most taxis charge 25TJS to 30TJS for a ride almost anywhere in town. Agree the fare in advance or choose a metered taxi.

Trolleybuses/buses cost 1TJS per hop. Marshrutkas cost 1TJS for a short ride and 2TJS for a long ride. Useful routes include the following:

Bus/trolleybus routes 1 and 3 (but not minibus 1) Traverses Rudaki.

Trolleybus 12 Somoni and Sino past the main bus station.

Marshrutka 8 Somoni and connects the giant flag (westbound only), OVIR, Green Bazaar, the Badakhshan taxi stand and passes the airport on Titov.

Marshrutka 16 Much the same as route 8 but at the western end it passes south of the bus station and joins Somoni east of the Hyatt Hotel.

Marshrutka 25 Southwest from Bekhzod via Bukhoro, Sherozi, Sino (past the bus station), then west at the Russian embassy.

TO/FROM THE AIRPORT

Arriving at **Dushanbe Airport** (☑ 474 49 4233; www.airport.tj/; Titov 32/2) is straightforward and taxis are readily available outside the arrivals hall. It costs around US$12 to US$15 to the city centre. The airport services international flights and local flights to Khojand (twice weekly with Somon Air (p195; US$60).

FERGANA VALLEY

Settled for over 2000 years, this green and gentle land is one of the most densely populated parts of the whole of Central Asia. Ringed by semi-arid mountains whose topography largely forbids large-scale, mechanised agriculture, it's unsurprising that this fertile belt that stretches across three countries (Uzbekistan, Tajikistan and Kyrgyzstan) has been prized and fought over for centuries. The land is watered by the Syr-Darya (once known as the Oxus River) and its numerous tributaries support the growing of rice (visible on the outskirts of Isfara), cotton, wheat and vegetables. One of the joys of travelling from town to town is stopping to sample peaches, apricots, cherries and melons sold along the roadside.

Part of the Russian Empire in the 19th century, the Fergana Valley was incorporated into the Soviet Union in the 1920s and was divided between the three Central Asian republics when they gained independence in 1991.

Isfara   Исфара

📞 3462 / POP 37,738 / ELEV 830M

Mentioned in 10th-century chronicles as an important watering hole on the Silk Road, the small provincial town of Isfara continues its role as a transit point today. Although lacking any major sights that may suggest its illustrious past, it is a pleasant enough place to overnight while travelling to or from Kyrgyzstan.

The town is renowned in the Fergana Valley for the cultivation of apricots, a fact commemorated by a giant fibreglass **Apricot Monument** (Rudaki-Dzhami Roundabout) in one of the main roundabouts. Just along from the roundabout, the **Isfara Bazaar** (Dzhami; ⊙ 8am-8pm) makes a good landmark as shared taxis pull up outside. It also offers an opportunity to buy supplies before a long haul to Dushanbe or Osh. Nearer the centre of town, a large and impressive Statue of Lenin presides over Rudaki.

If lingering in town, two small sites make interesting historic diversions.

A portion of the 16th-century **Abdullo Khan Mosque** (Dzhami, Navigilem suburb) was destroyed in a flood in 1836; another portion has been restored while part remains in its original condition. The minaret was added to the site in the 19th century.

The small brick-fronted **Isfara Museum** (Dzhami 7; admission 3TJS; ⊙ nominally 9am-4pm, or find the caretaker) has a modest natural history collection and some ancient artefacts from Silk Road days. Most of the exhibits relate to the Soviet era, including a gramophone used to announce victory after WWII.

At the time of writing, the main road into town from Konibodom (on A376), across a semi-arid desert, was being upgraded into a major road and construction looked likely to last for some years to come. As such, the alternative orchard route along the Isfara River is a better option. Passing wheat fields and apricot orchards and lined with pink hollyhocks, it makes for an altogether prettier route.

Only the **Meros hotel** (📞 9295 1 1200; Markezi; r from 100TJS; ❋) is to be relied upon in Isfara, so if staying the night is an important part of your itinerary, ring ahead to book a room. No English is spoken and breakfast is not included.

Lots of inexpensive eateries selling soup and kebabs are dotted in and around the bazaar. If pushing on to Khojand, it may be tempting to buy a rotisserie chicken from the entrance of the bazaar and some regional apricots, peaches or cherries for an en route picnic. There's an excellent local tandor for fresh bread just as the road leaves town. Two local teahouses, the **Oriyol** (cnr Rudaki & Dzhami; mains 20TJS; ⊙ 9am-6pm) with carved wooden stylings and the **Lola** (Tulip Teahouse; Dzhami; plov 15TJS; ⊙ 9am-6pm) opposite the bazaar with good *plov*, are worth seeking out.

The main east–west street, Markazi, has banks including Amonat Bank and Eskhata Bank with ATMs.

❶ Getting There & Away

Isfara bus station has shared taxis that travel direct to Dushanbe (150TJS), but they fill very slowly. It's often cheaper and just as quick to change in Khojand (shared/chartered taxi 30/210TJS) even though it requires a change of bus stations.

Minibuses (25TJS, 40 minutes) bound for Batken (Kyrgyzstan) leave when full between 8am and 9pm. Only early departures arrive in time to connect with the last Batken–Osh marshrutka (70TJS). It's more convenient to take a shared taxi from Isfara to Osh (150TJS, six hours); these leave from the bazaar area by the Lola Teahouse when full.

To get to Markazi, the main street in the centre of town, from the bus station take marshrutka 1 or 9 or walk a block north past the bazaar, then for 10 minutes, crossing the bridge.

Khojand   Худжанд

📷 3422 / POP 144,865 / ELEV 360M

The attractive northern city of Khojand (Khojent/Khujand, formerly Leninabad) is Tajikistan's second-largest. Commanding (and taxing) the entrance to the Fergana Valley, the founding father, Komil Khojandi, built palaces, grand mosques and a huge citadel here before the Mongols destroyed most traces of it in the early 13th century. Famed as the point where Alexander the Great once founded his northernmost Central Asian outpost, Alexandria-Eskhate, the city today is an outward-looking commercial hub whose museums, bazaars and parks offer much to keep a visitor engaged for a day or two.

Despite Khojand's strong Uzbek contingent, the city is proud of its links to Tajikistan's ruling elite. When President Nabiev, a Khojand man, was unseated in 1992 and Tajikistan appeared to be evolving into an Islamic republic, Khojand province threatened to secede. Secure behind the Fan Mountains, it escaped the ravages of civil war and remains the wealthiest part of the country.

◎ Sights

Layers of history – from Alexander the Great and the Mongol invasion to the Soviet era and WWII – are in evidence throughout the city of Khojand and easily experienced through the citadel's museums and the Islamic complex of Sheikh Massal ad-Din. Just as captivating is the Panchshanbe Bazaar, one of the best in the region.

In an obscure retirement spot surrounded by roses in the Victory Park of the 18th-microrayon suburb is the city's 22m-tall Lenin Statue, moved here from Moscow in 1974 when Khojand was called Leninabad. A taxi here costs 20TJS return.

★ Citadel   FORTRESS

(cnr Rajabov & Tanbyri; admission 10TJS; ⊘ 8am-9pm Tue-Fri, 9am-9pm Sat & Sun) The city's top sight is the citadel, the reconstructed corner of which is open to visitors. From the top of the 10th-century ramparts, the disintegrating baked-earth walls suggest hints of the seven gates and 6km of fortifications that were rebuilt in the 13th century and which mark the site of Alexander the Great's original settlement. The citadel's military history

continued into recent times when, in 1997, 300 people died in battles between Uzbek warlords and government troops.

The reconstructed eastern gate houses the Museum of Archaeology & Fortifications (Tanbyri 4; admission 5TJS; ⊘ 9am-9pm Tue-Sun), which has some interesting 19th-century photos and plans of the original citadel.

Historical Museum of Sughd Province   MUSEUM

(cnr Rajabov & Tanbyri, Citadel; admission 5TJS; ⊘ 8am-9pm Tue-Fri, 9am-9pm Sat & Sun) Built within the reconstructed southeastern bastion of the city wall, this museum houses a fascinating set of modern marble mosaics depicting the life of Alexander the Great – the war scenes with their multiple horses are particularly finely crafted. The great warrior's funeral procession shows his hand dangling empty as he had reputedly requested, showing he had conquered half the world but went to his grave with nothing. With its basement dioramas of prehistoric life, this is Khojand's best museum.

★ Panchshanbe Bazaar   MARKET

(Sharq; ⊘ 5am-7pm summer, 6am-5.30pm winter) The core of this great bazaar, reputedly the largest in Central Asia, is an unusually elegant, purpose-built hall (1964) with arched entrance portals and a pink-and-lime-green neoclassical facade. If not the largest it's certainly one of the best-stocked markets in Central Asia, especially on Thursday (*panchshanbe* in Tajik) when people and produce flood into the main hall.

Sheikh Massal ad-Din complex   MOSQUE

(Ploshchad Pobedy) This religious complex comprises the 1394 brick mausoleum of Sheikh Massal ad-Din (1133–1223), covered porticoes with carved wooden pillars, a 20th-century mosque with attractive whitestone facade and a 21m-high brick minaret dating from 1865. A newly built matching second minaret is attached to a new, traditionally designed brick mosque with a reflective emerald-green dome. Visitors are welcome to wander around the outside of the buildings, but the complex is perhaps best appreciated from across the Panchshanbe Bazaar square.

🛏 Sleeping & Eating

Most hotels and sights are close to Lenin, which snakes north–south-southeast for almost 10km, crossing the Syr-Darya. There

Khojand

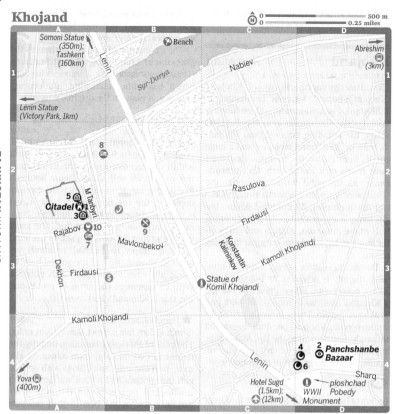

are no truly top-end hotels in town, but the midrange options represent good value for money. Khojand acts as a hub of social activity for the region. There are lots of incidental cafes for tea, particularly around the bazaar. None of these warrant a special mention but are fun to drift in and out of when visiting the centre of town. For a chat over something stronger, the Grand Hotel Khujand and Hotel Sugd both have pleasant bars.

Hotel Leninobod HOTEL **$**
(☎ 3422 6 5535; Nabiev 51; s/d 100/140TJS; **P**) Well placed on the corniche with views across the Syr-Darya to northern Khojand's stark rocky backdrop, this patched-up Soviet tower operates only two floors and decor has evolved little since 1990, with dim lighting and a broken lift. While some rooms have been repainted, others still have damp patches. The *dezhurnaya* (floor-lady) will fix a pot of tea for 2TJS.

★ **Grand Hotel Khujand** BOUTIQUE HOTEL **$$**
(☎ 3422 4 2936, 3422 6 0599; www.grand-hotel. tj; Tamburi 20; s/d from 550/650TJS; ❄ 🛜) This attractive hotel, ideally located opposite the citadel, is Khojand's best luxury choice. Rooms are large and more businesslike than boutique, but the communal part of the hotel, including the excellent restaurant, has lots of character thanks to the friendly staff. A tab of 100TJS can be used against breakfast, lunch or dinner.

Hotel Sugd HOTEL **$$**
(☎ 3422 4 1616, 3422 4 1188; sogdhotel@mail. ru; Lenin 179A; incl breakfast s/d 180/290TJS, lux 370-400TJS; ❄ 🛜) The carpeted rooms of this friendly hotel make it feel more like a guesthouse than a hotel. The attractive traditional-style suite on the top floor (no lift) is decorated with fine plaster work and ceramics. Some English is spoken and the bar in the bright, open-plan lobby is a sociable

Khojand

◎ Top Sights
1 Citadel...A2
2 Panchshanbe Bazaar D4

◎ Sights
3 Historical Museum of Sughd
   Province...A2
4 Mausoleum of Sheikh Massal ad-Din...D4
5 Museum of Archaeology &
   Fortifications A2
6 Sheikh Massal ad-Din complex D4

◎ Sleeping
7 Grand Hotel Khujand...........................A3
8 Hotel Leninobod A2

◎ Eating
9 Café Ravshan.......................................B3
   Omar Khayan................................(see 7)

◎ Drinking & Nightlife
10 Marifat Restaurant A3

meeting place. It's around a five-minute taxi drive to the citadel.

Marifat Restaurant CAFE $
(Tamburi; karaoke 5TJS; ⊙10am-11pm) A bit of fun in a city without too much of a nightlife culture, this cafe transforms into a karaoke bar from 9pm.

Omar Khayan GEORGIAN $$
(☑3422 6 0599; Tanburi 20, Grand Hotel Khujand; mains from 25TJS; ⊙7am-11pm) Delicious Georgian cuisine is served from the decorated interior of this upmarket restaurant, and the bar in the corner offers a pre-dinner rendezvous point. Georgian favourites *khachapuri* (flaky pastry filled with cream cheese with a fried egg on top) and *khinkali* (chewy dumplings) are among the dishes on offer.

Café Ravshan CENTRAL ASIAN $$
(Rajabov 102; mains from 12TJS; beer 10TJS; ⊙6am-11pm; ❄) This central semi-smart cafe features mirror-facet flowers and chequerboard couch seats. The kitchen serves great barbecues, particularly *okaroshka* (chicken kebabs).

⊙ Getting There & Around

The Khojand airport is located 16km southeast of the city at Chkalovsk. There are flights three times per week to Dushanbe on Somon Air (from US$60) and to numerous Russian cities including Moscow (from US$570). Ural Airlines and China Southern both have flights from Khojand to many international destinations, including Urumqi (US$380).

There are three main 'bus' stations.

Minibuses and shared taxis to Kanibadam/ Kanibodom (minibus 328; 15TJS, 1½ hours) for Kokand, Uzbekistan, and to Isfara (minibus 301; 15TJS, two hours, 10am only) for Osh, Kyrgyzstan, leave from the inconspicuous little **Isfara Avtostanitsa** (Lenin), opposite some metal silos 5km southeast of Panchshanbe Bazaar.

Shared taxis to Penjikent (120 to 150TJS, seven hours) and Dushanbe (120TJS to 150TJS, six hours) and regular minibus 314 to Istaravshan (4TJS, 1½ hours) all leave from the **Yova (Ёва) bus station** (Kamoli Khojandi).

Other Dushanbe shared taxis, plus transport to Oybek (for Tashkent, Uzbekistan) via Buston (45 to 50TJS) use the big Abreshim bus station in the distant northeastern suburbs.

Marshrutka 55 (2TJS) links Abreshim bus station to Isfara Avtostanisa, passing Khojand's two main attractions. For the citadel get off opposite the Hotel/Trade Centre Kheson and walk two blocks west of Lenin down Rajabov. Marshrutka 29 and 33 link the Yova and Abreshim bus stations. The airport is accessible by minibus 80 (2TJS). All these routes and many more pass along Lenin near the central Rajabov junction. Route 3A links Yova to the Isfara Avtostanisa via Panchshanbe Bazaar.

Istaravshan
ИСТАРАВШАН

☑3454 / POP 52,851 / ELEV 1088M

Called Kir by the Parthians, Cyropol by Alexander the Great and Ura-Tyube by the Russians and Soviets, Istaravshan has a small historical core that is one of the best preserved in Tajikistan. Established over 2500 years ago and once encircled by a 6km wall, this former staging post on the Silk Road has had its share of ill fortunes from the execution of male citizens at the hands of Alexander the Great, the slaughter of innocents by Genghis Khan's marauding armies and shelling by Russian forces in the 19th century. It still carries something of the spirit of endurance in the present day, with a re-creation of the citadel's main gate symbolic of the town's defiance over the odds. With poor accommodation options, the town is ideally best visited as a day trip from Khojand or in transit between the north and Dushanbe or Penjikent.

⊙ Sights

The vast and colourful central **bazaar** (Lenin; ⊙7am-7pm) is a town unto itself. A three-storey, triple-arched building indicates the main hub, but stalls have flooded out into the surrounding apron of land.

In an arcade opposite the gateway of the main bazaar, artisans at the **Blacksmiths Arcade** (Lenin; ⊙7am-4pm) whet the edges of top-quality knives using traditional tools that uphold a tradition dating back 2000 years. Buy a knife (from US$10) and the handmade scabbard is free.

Sary Mazar   ISLAMIC SITE
(Yellow Tomb) Shaded by ancient *chinar* (plane) trees, a pair of small but ornately stucco-fronted 17th-century tombs are set beside a fine old mosque with tapering wooden columns. A set of 18 tiny windowless cells known as *chehlkhona* here would have been used for meditation by those studying the Koran in order to become religious leaders. Generally the sequestration would last 40 days, during which time the pilgrim would leave the cell only briefly at night to attend to bodily functions.

From the bazaar take marshrutka 3A, get off 300m beyond the cross-sabres gateway, walk along Ehsan (15 minutes), then ask!

Mug Teppe   FORTRESS
In the northeast of the city, rising above low-level housing, this grassy, flat-topped hill once boasted a fine citadel. Stormed by Alexander the Great in 329 BC and Arabs in AD 772, only minimal mud-wall traces of the original remain. These, however, have been grandly augmented since 2002 by a blue-domed gateway, built for Istaravshan's 2500th anniversary celebrations. Weathering nicely, it looks impressive from afar and provides a good vantage point from which to survey the city's mountain horizon. Access is from the first traffic lights north of Sadbargi hotel. From the bazaar take marshrutka 5A.

Shahr-e-kuhna   OLD TOWN
(Old Town) The old town is an intriguing maze of mudbrick lanes with water channels running along the centre of the thoroughfare. Houses are tantalisingly hidden from view behind straw-and-wattle plastered walls, but occasionally an open doorway allows for a glimpse into the central courtyard decorated inevitably with roses. Access is via Krupskoe or Tursunzoda streets heading west from 102 or 98 Lenin respectively, either side of the Hazrat-i-Shah Mosque.

Marshrutka 3A links the old town with the bazaar near one-room **Chor Gumbaz** (Said Nizomaddin Hoja Mazor; Old Town; ⊙8am-4pm, or ask locally for the caretaker) **FREE**, whose four tin cupolas conceal some of Tajikistan's most impressive old painted ceilings.

Abdullatif Sultan Medresse   ISLAMIC SITE
(Kök Gumbaz, Blue Dome; Tursunzoda; ⊙8am-5pm) **FREE** The 15th-century Abdullatif Sultan Medressa is also known as the Kök Gumbaz (Blue Dome) after its turquoise Timurid dome. Closed in Soviet times, the religious school now gives a broad tuition, including English, to around a hundred boys – some of whom are sure to offer a welcome at the main gate.

Hauz-i-Sangin   MOSQUE
(Menzhinski 9, at Krupskoe) Tucked behind the site of a giant new mosque, the 1910 Hauz-i-Sangin Mosque has fine ceiling paintings and a dry octagonal *hauz* (pool) flanked by hollyhocks in the yard. The tiny renovated shrine room is the tomb of Shah Fuzail ibn-Abbas.

🛏 Sleeping & Eating

The **Sadbargi** (☑9187 3 7788; www.sadbarg.tj; Lenin 101B; s without bathroom 100TJS, tw 190TJS) hotel is the only one worth recommending in Istaravshan, and this is only worthwhile if transport options leave no other alternative. From the bazaar take marshrutka 6 to get to the hotel.

Istaravshan is famed for its pears (ripe towards the end of summer) and sweet *kishmish* grapes. There are lots of kebab stands in front of and at the back of the bazaar.

Taking tea on the daybeds at **Restaurant Murodi** (Lazzati shom; Bitonka, Markazi Farogatti; half/full plov incl bread & salad 12/18TJS; ⊙10am-8pm), the chaikhana near the new mosque, makes a pleasant way to while away a summer's evening.

ⓘ Getting There & Away

Shared taxis to Dushanbe (100TJS per seat, four hours, 276km) leave from the southern end of the bazaar. To charter a taxi with an overnight in Iskander-Kul starts at around US$150.

Taxis to Penjikent (100/120TJS in winter/summer, five hours) leave from 100m further south than the Dushanbe taxis, beyond the terminus of marshrutkas 4 and 5.

Although minibus 314 (10TJS to 15TJS, 1½ hours) for Khojand should start 3km north of town from the Avtovokzal, some fill up at the same place as the shared taxis (20TJS to 25TJS, 50 minutes), near the blacksmiths workshops opposite the central bazaar. From the bazaar take marshrutka 6 for Avtovokzal.

ZERAFSHAN VALLEY
ДОЛИНА ЗЕРАВШАН

The glorious Zerafshan Valley has two distinct characters: its deep river gorge in the east remains pretty much an undiscovered wilderness dotted with remote villages and hamlets, while the flatter, fertile agricultural plain around Penjikent in the west is home to one of the most populous parts of the country. The area attracts visitors for good reason.

Edged to the south by the Fan Mountains, an easy two-hour drive from Dushanbe or a one-hour drive from Penjikent, this is an easily accessible trekking, climbing and 4WD destination, offering not just an inspiring snow-capped landscape of colourful alpine lakes and flower-strewn meadows, but also a fascinating cultural experience among communities who live life on the edge.

Penjikent   Пенжикент
☑ 3475 / POP 35,085 / ELEV 1000M

Located in the middle of the western arm of the Zerafshan Valley, the rural city of Penjikent sits on a rare piece of flat ground in the middle of high mountains. With an ancient history extending back to Silk Road days, and famed for its connection with beloved poet Rudaki, the city boasts an archaeological site, a worthwhile regional museum and a lively bazaar. In the days when the border with Uzbekistan was open to foreigners, Penjikent attracted many tourists from Samarkand, but there is little sign of this reopening any time soon. In the meantime, those visitors who do venture out this way from Dushanbe or Khojand are assured of a warm welcome.

◉ Sights & Activities

Ancient Penjikent   ARCHAEOLOGICAL SITE
(www.orientarch.uni-halle.de/ca/pandzh.htm; admission 5TJS, with camera permit 10TJS; ☺8am-6pm) On a terrace above the banks of River Zerafshan, 1.5km southeast of today's Penjikent, the ruins of a major Sogdian town slow-

ly bake to dust. Looking across the minimal ruins, dubbed the 'Pompeii of Central Asia', it's hard to imagine that from the 5th to 8th centuries this was the site of one of the most cosmopolitan cities on the Silk Road. Thankfully a museum, in a traditional single-room building, brings the former settlement to life with copies of the best finds.

The site has been extensively excavated over the years and has yielded several important finds, including the so-called 'Penjikent frescoes'. Depicting hunting scenes, these frescoes would once have adorned a palace with pillars carved in the shape of dancing girls. Part of the original fresco sequence is now on display in the museum in Penjikent, part is exhibited in the National Museum (p146) in Dushanbe, while the best portion is in the Hermitage in St Petersburg. A site map outside the museum helps to explain the ruins, or just to wander at random among the sun-baked ridges.

To reach the site, drivers of marshrutka 5 will stop about five minutes' walk from 'Stary Penjikent'. On a clear day the mountain panoramas are splendid and from this raised position it's easy to plot a course back to town, descending between the main ruins and the distinct citadel site further west. The route leads down to Beruni, a 15-minute stroll from the bazaar.

Rudaki Museum   MUSEUM
(Rudaki 67; admission 15TJS, with camera permit 25TJS; ☺9am-5pm) This elegant single-storey museum, with its white Doric columns

ACTIVITIES IN PENJIKENT

With over 20 years of experience in the tourist industry and 10 years spent running the successful **Hasrasho Homestay** (☑ 9351 2 9003; akhurikshoh@mail.ru; mattress per person incl breakfast US$10, lunch/dinner US$4), the owner, Mr Hasrasho, knows exactly what kind of adventure visitors to the Fan Mountains are looking for. He can arrange a guide, cook, donkey and 'donkey-driver' for around US$100 per day and has a tent (US$5 per person per day) and sleeping bags (US$3) for rent. Activities include a short amble along the Urech River to major multiday hikes to the Kulikalon lakes and over the Alaudin Pass (3860m), or the Laudon Pass (3630m) to Alaudin Lake.

Penjikent

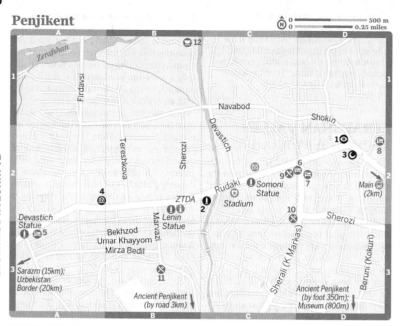

Penjikent

and fine floral display, assigns a room to its namesake, Abu Abdullah Rudaki (858–941), the 'father of Persian poetry'. The museum is of more interest, however, for its display of textiles and costumes, the frescoes found at Ancient Penjikent and the Neolithic tools from nearby Sarazm.

Olim Dodkhokh Complex　　　MOSQUE
(Rudaki 164) On cold Friday lunchtimes, dozens of older men with flowing white beards, turbans, upturned boots and swishing purple/green iridescent *joma* robes make their way to prayers at this mosque-madrassa complex opposite the bazaar. Though mostly a contemporary rebuild, its origins are from the 14th century.

Loik Sherali Statue　　　STATUE
(Rudaki) Modern-day poet Loik Sherali was born in Mazari Sharif near Penjikent in 1941. He earned the title 'People's Poet of Tajikistan' and when he died in 2000 was buried alongside other notables in Dushanbe. His statue shows him in a suit standing between what could be interpreted as the symbolic leaves of a book.

🛏 Sleeping & Eating

More town than city, Penjikent, with its small range of reasonable hotels, makes a relaxing staging or supply post for hiking trips in the Fan Mountains. Beware, though, that from November through April some hotels close and in the height of summer it's important to book. Opening up behind a fanciful traditional archway at the corner of the bend in Rudaki, the local **bazaar** (Rudaki; ⊙ 7am-7pm, closed 1st Mon of each month) is a perfect place to buy fruit (cherries, mulberries, melons) for the onward journey.

★ Zurmich Homestay ⠀⠀⠀⠀⠀ HOMESTAY $

(☑9292 6 7100, 9275 9 9123; zurnach@mail.ru; Bakoli 1st lane, 24; r per person US$10, breakfast, lunch or dinner US$5) This charming homestay is tucked down a leafy lane behind the bazaar. With a kitchen, dining room, billiard room and sitting area shared by three pleasant, simple rooms above the central iris garden, it feels like home. From the bazaar, walk down the steps beside Bashani Hamam (201 Rudaki), then right for 50m along a small footpath that crosses a stream.

Hotel Zarafshan ⠀⠀⠀⠀⠀⠀⠀⠀ HOTEL $

(☑9049 9 5999, 9290 2 5999; hotelzarafshon@mail. ru; Loiq Sheraly 24; s/d incl breakfast 200/240TJS) Occupying the top two storeys (no lift) above tailoring workshops, this simple establishment has clean en suite rooms and a shared space with a balcony overlooking the street. Ideally central and with a lively restaurant for a beer and kebab next door, this a good choice.

Elina Guest House ⠀⠀⠀⠀⠀ GUESTHOUSE $

(Sogdiana Hotel; ☑Tatiana 935 663737; www.travel-pamir.com; Rudaki 24/16; s/d budget without bathroom US$16/26, standard US$20/30, superior US$35/50; ⊛) The Sogdiana Hotel refers to the five quality rooms occupying the upper floor of this friendly establishment. The Elina Guesthouse refers to the rest! The budget rooms are well maintained and arranged around a small courtyard with modern shared bathrooms. It's recessed back from the road but is well signed, with an enormous mosaic mural depicting the arts on the adjacent building.

Maqsud Guesthouse ⠀⠀⠀⠀⠀ HOMESTAY $

(Hotel Suqd; ☑927 711210; kumaj-1959@mail.ru; Loiq Sherali 2; guesthouse per person 80TJS, hotel s/d 120/200TJS; ⊛@⊙) Building on the success of the original homestay, the owner has invested in a two-storey modern hotel block with big en suite rooms, shared lounge and a breakfast area overlooking what remains of the central garden. A limited amount of English is spoken.

Café Safina ⠀⠀⠀⠀⠀⠀ CENTRAL ASIAN $

(Loiq Sherali, cnr Rudaki; mains from 10TJS; ⊙8am-10.30pm) This popular meeting point has menus (unlike most chaikhanas), curtained booth seats for private soirées and a large outdoor terrace on the street made cheerful with fresh flowers and fairy lights. With a tasty range of kebabs showcased at the counter and excellent soups, this is a good place to relax with a beer in the company of Penjikent locals.

Obod ⠀⠀⠀⠀⠀⠀ CENTRAL ASIAN $

(Loiq Sherali 42; kebabs from 5TJS; mains 10-15TJS; ⊙8am-10pm) Behind a vine-fronted facade, eight tables are arranged around a central fountain pool in a shaded courtyard, making this a lovely choice for lunch or tea on a tranquil summer evening.

Dilkusho ⠀⠀⠀⠀⠀⠀ TEAHOUSE $

(Obody Poyon; mains 10-25TJS, beer 7TJS; ⊙11am-10pm) A smart chaikhana with traditional pillars and painted ceilings. The riverside tea-beds offer a delightful perch for lazy afternoons, but on summer evenings the mosquitoes are fearsome. It's a 1.5km dogleg walk, downhill from the Somoni Statue.

★ Sayokhat ⠀⠀⠀⠀⠀⠀ CENTRAL ASIAN $$

(☑9277 4 0737; Marvazi; mains 15-25TJS; ⊙6am-11pm Mar-Oct; ⊛🍴) Penjikent's most imaginative eatery, this eccentric wooden structure with its timber stairways and cosy booths is festooned with traditional artefacts and beautiful Tajiki textiles. The delightful owner, Sharif Badalov, goes out of his way to make guests feel welcome and is justly proud of the establishment's 'high-level' *plov* (pilaf). The *gharmij* (wheat drink) is worth trying and the *osh* is a must.

ⓘ Information

Several ATMs can be found along Rudaki, but it may take a bit or trial and error to find one with money to dispense.

Police Station (Rudaki) Next to the post office, near the Somoni Statue.

Post Office (Rudaki; ⊙8am-5pm Mon-Sat)

ZTDA (Zerafshan Tourism Development Association; www.ztda-tourism.tj; Rudaki 108) Promotes community tourism and organises tours across the region, often revolving around rural homestays. See p168 for more. It produces an excellent catalogue (available online in English) of all homestays in the Zerafshan region with photographs of the houses and a juniper branch rating system. The catalogue indicates the activities (eg hiking, horse riding) available from each. The Land of Lakes Trek (six days, five nights, 582km) costs US$499 (including transport/guide/full board). The information

WORTH A TRIP

THE SHRINE CIRCUIT

As an excursion from Penjikent, a visit to two shrines that lie just south of the Zerafshan Valley gives an interesting insight into Tajiki culture. Both sites are revered by locals, who regard the mausoleums as a place of pilgrimage. The shrine of Mohammad Bashoro at **Mazor-i Sharif** (donation appreciated; ☉ daylight hours, closed during Fri prayers) FREE , the nearer of the two shrines to Penjikent, is an easy day trip from the city, while the **Rudaki Cultural Complex** (☉ 8am-5pm) FREE in Panjrud may more easily be visited en route to or from Ayni. Alternatively, it's possible to make an overnight trip of the two shrines from Penjikent by staying at the well-recommended Hasrasho Homestay (p160) at Artush, 9km further up the Urech Valley from Panjrud. Beyond Artush, there are some fine hikes (p160) with overnight camping possible, such as in the mountain hut at Alplager.

The circuit is most easily covered with private 4WD transport, but there is some public transport too. Three daily buses from Penjikent pass the junction for Mazor-i Sharif and continue along to the Rudaki mausoleum at Panjrud before lumbering over the rough road to Artush.

centre in Penjikent is not currently functioning, but it is possible to make reservations through the website and book trekking tours.

ℹ Getting There & Around

The scenic Penjikent–Ayni road (A377) is currently in reasonable condition, particularly nearing Penjikent as the road follows along the broad, mostly flat valley. The most reliable public transport services from Penjikent are shared taxis. For time-saving convenience, however, chartering a private 4WD is well worth considering. A saloon/4WD vehicle can be hired (around US$70/100 per day) at short notice through the Zurmich Homestay (p161). Beware that many of the mountain roads in the region are prone to mudslides that can block a route for days, especially in spring.

The bus station is 2km east of the central bazaar. It's best to pre-book tickets and for shared taxis request to be collected from your hotel where possible.

The following sample of public transport services leave from different locations around Penjikent. Ask locally to be sure of the latest departure points.

Artush Three buses leave from the bus station at 9.30am, noon and 2.15pm (50TJS, 1½ hours).

Dushanbe Shared taxis (100TJS tp 120TJS per seat, five hours) leave from the bus station.

Haft-Kul 4WD shared taxis (50TJS, three hours) leave from the Takhta bazaar around noon, returning the next morning at 6am.

Istaravshan Shared taxis (100/120TJS summer/winter, five hours) leave from beside Rudaki 206, opposite the Guliston clothes bazaar. Departures are most plentiful Monday and Friday morning before 10am.

Khojand Shared taxis (120TJS to 150TJS per seat, seven hours) leave from the bus station.

Marguzor Crammed 4WDs (40TJS to 50TJS) depart once or twice daily around noon from a building supplies yard, 200m downhill (along Shokin) from the Penjikent bazaar. They return the next morning at around 6am.

Shing Minibuses (15TJS, two hours) leave at 2pm from the same building supplies yard as the Marguzor 4WDs.

Minibuses 1 and 4 run along Rudaki from Elina Guest House, past the museum to the bazaar and on to the bus station. Taxis around town cost 20TJS to 25TJS.

Fan Mountains

With tiny hamlets occupying slivers of green, terraced slopes, silt-laden waters crashing through the valleys, emerald green lakes and even the mausoleums of a poet and a missionary, this majestic mountain range could keep a visitor occupied for days. Ideally suited to hiking, the area attracts all levels of enthusiasm, skill and fitness, from a gentle walk through pastures of flowers to serious alpine rock climbing. Guides can usually be summoned at short notice from the many homestays dotted through this beautiful region or, for more serious hikes, they can organise multiday expeditions with some notice. For those who prefer four wheels to two legs, the region offers some of the most exciting off-road driving in the country.

One of the joys of travelling in the entire Zerafshan Valley is the network of excellent homestays set up by the ZTDA (p161). Charging more or less a fixed price of around US$10 per person, these simple lodgings offer home-cooked meals (typically US$5 for breakfast, lunch or dinner), a mattress in a communal room, separate from the family area, and clean shared bathrooms generally with squat toilets.

Minibuses, shared taxis and shared 4WDs serve some but not all of the small villages in the region and they do not necessarily travel every day. As and when transport turns up, it is often full to the brim with people returning home with goods from the market. While generally tolerant and good natured about it, locals often wonder why visitors try to pile in too when chartered taxis are available to them. Those with a fear of heights or uncomfortable with apparently reckless off-road driving may find chartering much easier on the nerves!

Iskander-Kul & Sarytag
Искандеркуль, Сарытаг

☑ 3479 / POP 500 / ELEV 2214M

Between Sarvoda and Ayni, the main Dushanbe road hints at the magnificent landscape hidden beyond the canyon walls. The easiest way to access the beauty beyond is driving to Iskander-Kul, an opal-blue mountain lake that looks almost tropical in strong sunlight. It isn't. At 2195m, it invites a distinctly chilly swim even in summer. The approach to the lake is made particularly interesting by the streaks of copper and iron oxide that striate the barren mountains, contrasting with pockets of virulent green vegetation along the river's edge. The canyon scenery is especially dramatic around 1.5km before arriving at the lake, but breathtaking views continue along the 6km of coast road.

From the president's lakeside *dacha* (holiday bungalow), a 5km road zigzags up to the highlands beneath majestic snow-capped peaks. The tiny village of Sarytag here makes a great walking base and supports longer treks into the Fan Mountains.

Guesthouse Shahboz (☑ 9076 0 8300, 9043 9 4510; guest.hous-tjk@mail.ru; Sarytag; full board per person incl sauna US$20; **P**), at the entrance to Sarytag, is arguably the village's most attractive option.

The eight rooms in the grand two-storey **Dilovar's Villa** (☑ Dilovar 901 107340, Kareem 9070 9 5544; Upper Sarytag; per person incl breakfast US$12; **P**) have beds and boast spectacular views in all directions, with generous meals (lunch/dinner US$5) shared round a communal table. There's no missing the villa as it sits on top of a small knoll in the middle of the landscape at the confluence of two rivers. The family also runs a small **homestay** (☑ 9011 0 7340; Sarytag; per person incl breakfast US$12, lunch/dinner US$5) at the same rates.

The former Soviet **Turbaza** (☑ 9333 9 9595; Iskander-Kul; cabin dm 50TJS, lux chalet d with bathroom 250TJS, breakfast/lunch/dinner US$3/5/5; **P** ❉) holiday camp comprises a collection of four-room cabins and more modern en suite chalets dotted around a mature woodland on the edge of the lake. The shared institutional bathroom blocks spare no blushes in terms of privacy, but they're basically clean. It's possible to pitch a tent here for 20TJS including hot-water showers. A sauna costs 300TJS per person per hour, or 50TJS per person for a group of six people. From the camp a short **boat trip** (☑ 9333 9 9595; Turbaza, Iskander-Kul; 30/45min boat ride 125/250TJS, up to 5 people) draws close to the president's dacha on the far shore, while a longer option circumnavigates the whole lake.

Shared taxis for Iskander-Kul and Sarytag depart from Sarvoda market (38km, one hour, 50/350TJS per seat/chartered). During peak season weekends, it may be possible to cadge a ride from the M34 junction with party-goers heading to the lakeside Turbaza resort; it is customary to contribute to the cost of the fuel – around 50TJS would be fair. Guesthouse Shahboz can arrange a taxi (saloon/4WD 400/700TJS) to Dushanbe most days in summer.

Alaudin Lakes

Beautiful Alaudin Lake (2780m) is a glorious place for camping and a possible base for walking into the heart of the Fan Mountains. Surrounded by an array of mountains over 5000m, Mutnye ('Muddy') Lake (3510m) is a popular day hike.

Alaudin is helpfully accessible, just 3km on foot (45 minutes) from a trail-head camp where three valleys meet. The western valley eventually leads (after around eight hours of hiking) over the breathtaking Laudan Pass (3630m) to Kulikalon lakes, from where it is possible to reach Artush. There is a trail of sorts to Iskander-Kul, but it crosses the seriously challenging Kaznok Pass (4040m) and ice axe and crampons are required.

The only way to reach Alaudin is by chartered taxi from Sarvoda (180TJS). The

Fan Mountains

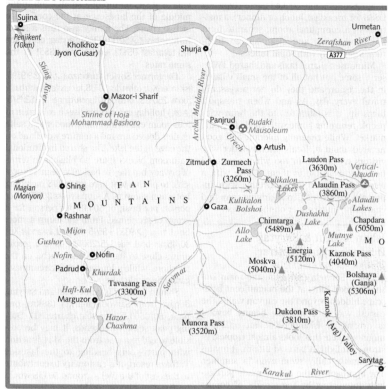

unpaved road is generally reasonable to Pasrud and even Marguzor, but after this, rock falls sometimes make the route impassible and the track is very rough.

Haft-Kul

Haft-Kul (Seven Lakes, Marguzor Lakes) refers to a spectacular 20km chain of pools strung along the western edge of the Fan Mountains. Just 63km from Penjikent, it makes for one of the most easily accessible and satisfying excursions from the city. With a couple of nights spent in nearby homestays, they could easily become the focus of much longer trekking routes.

The first lake is an astonishing azure blue, the next four are aquamarine and the sixth is a pale turquoise. And the final lake needs to be seen to be believed. Six of the lakes are just about accessible (albeit along minimal tracks) by 4WD, but the final

lake (Hazor Chashma) is most enjoyable reached on two legs, despite a vague track that suggests that locals manage to coax four wheels up to the water's edge.

The walk to Hazor Chashma is one of the most lovely walks in the region. It's an easy 2km ascent through beautiful wild flower meadows, above Marguzor village, following a racing river whose waters rush down the hillside to the six lakes below. There's a satisfyingly broad shore at the mouth of Hazor Chashma offering a perfect opportunity to picnic by the water's edge. For those with restless legs, a narrow footpath continues on around the lake.

Longer hikes are possible from trails (p166) that lead between the sixth and seventh lakes.

The area around the seven lakes of Haft-Kul is served by a number of delightful homestays, most notably at Shing, Nofin and

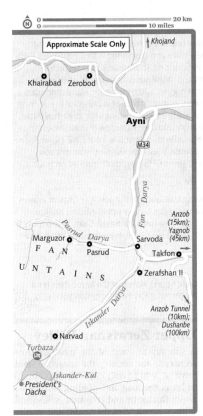

The easiest way to explore the area is to rent a private 4WD with a driver. From Penjikent a return trip costs around US$100 or an overnight trip US$150; book through **Nematov Niyozkul** (📞 9358 8 9668; niyozkul@mail.ru; Rudaki 20/16). Failing that, 4WDs to Marguzor (40TJS to 50TJS, two to three hours depending on the condition of the track) depart once or twice around noon from a building supplies yard around 200m downhill from the main Penjikent bazaar. They return the next morning at around 6am.

Sarvoda Сарвода

📞 3479 / POP LESS THAN 5000 / ELEV 1643M

Sarvoda, on the main road (M34) between the Anzob Tunnel and Ayni, is almost at the confluence of three rivers, the Fan Darya, Pasrud Darya and Iskander Darya, but is known chiefly as a junction of mountain roads. As such it makes a good place to break a journey and buy petrol, or some supplies for the surrounding beauty spots of Margeb, Iskander-Kul or the Alaudin Lakes. It's fair to say that Sarvoda is not the most attractive of towns, with its old Soviet apartment blocks and factory ruins, but it nevertheless has a buzz about it – as befitting perhaps of a major transport hub between challenging stretches of high-altitude road. A grand bridge straddles the fast-flowing river, dividing the town from its roadside, back-of-the-truck bazaar.

Towards the northern end of town is the **Mehmonkhona Yazdon** (📞 9281 1 1398; M34; dm 20TJS), useful for those who find onward transport elusive. The guesthouse is the last house on the left, 1km north of the Sarvoda bazaar.

There are taxi stands along the M34 at either end of the Savoda bazaar but only local transport is feasible from here. Shared taxis ply the 38km route to Iskander-Kul (50/350TJS per seat/charter) and to Margeb in the Anzob Valley (25TJS).

Margeb

📞 3479 / POP LESS THAN 1000 / ELEV 2190M

The timeless old village of Margeb (Margeb Bolo), with its high-altitude orchards of apricot, cherries and peaches, sits at the end of the dramatic Yagnob Valley. The village, which means 'green blossoming place' in the local language, spills over the steep hillsides,

Padrud, all of which can be booked through the **ZTDA** (www.ztda-tourism.tj) website.

Beautiful **Najmuddin Guesthouse** (📞 9263 6 6748; Nofin; r per person incl breakfast US$12, lunch & dinner US$5; 🅿) 🍴 unusually sports beds in traditionally decorated rooms and daybeds set beside the river. The hospitable landlord, Mr Najmuddin, can organise three-day treks (US$100 per person per day).

The owner of lovely **Guldara Homestay** (📞 9281 2 7602; Shing; mattress incl breakfast US$10, lunch & dinner US$5) 🍴 in Shing is Mr Khodjamov Sarvar, the village chemist, beekeeper and herbalist. His engineer son speaks some English and the family have been in the homestay business for more than a decade. A 5km walk from the homestay in and around the Rudaki Gorge is recommended. Children under 10 years stay and eat for free.

HIKING IN THE FAN MOUNTAINS

The rugged, glaciated Fan Mountains (p162) are one of Central Asia's premier trekking destinations. Studded with dozens of turquoise lakes and burnished with wind-blown, high-altitude vistas, they beg to be walked, hiked and climbed. It is feasible to drive up to any of the hamlets that cling to the mountainsides and strike out unaccompanied along the shepherd and goatherd tracks that lead into the rugged wilds; for longer, more ambitious treks, however, a guide is strongly recommended. With a lifetime of experience in surviving in these mountains, guides not only help negotiate the terrain, aiding with stream and ice crossings, but they also introduce the human story into the landscape of their ancestors.

Detailed maps of the Fann Mountains are available for sale online from EWP (www.ewpnet.com/fannmap.htm). Another good resource is www.trekkinginthepamirs.com, which includes photos, timings, route notes and some GPS waypoints marked on trails.

Routes from Artush

Kulikalon Lakes A two-hour (7km) uphill walking trail leads to the *alplager* (mountaineers camp; 2200m). From here, a tough three-hour trail leads further uphill into the Kulikalon bowl with a dozen deep-blue lakes. Camping is possible near Dushakha Lake, at the foot of Chimtarga (5489m), the region's highest peak. There are two high-pass routes from here to the beautiful Alaudin Lakes.

making cultivation in the surrounding terraces something of an extreme sport.

In and around Margeb many community elders speak Sogd[ian], a language largely unchanged since the time of Alexander the Great. Some 500 Sogd-speaking families were forcibly relocated to Zafarobad in 1970, partly as a modernisation initiative, but the language has survived.

An annual international rock-climbing championship takes place on the 'Yagnob Wall', the 1200m vertical face of Zaminkaror (2250m), which rears up magnificently behind Upper Margeb. Visitors can enquire about finding a rock-climbing guide at **Veterok homestay** (☑ 9345 5 0577, 9273 3 2801; Margeb Bolo; mattress incl hot shower & breakfast US$10), but ideally guides are better sourced through the climbing fraternity in advance of a visit.

ℹ Getting There & Away

Margeb lies at the end of the Anzob Valley along a road that's barely more than a goat track. The route is not for the faint-hearted with narrow ribbons of track clinging perilously to the cliff edge and dramatic drops to a fast and angry river below. At one point, the road traverses a perennial tongue of ice with a layer of hay preventing a fatal skid.

The valley is accessed from Sarvoda (25TJS in a shared taxi, two hours) via the small step-layered villages of Takfon on the M34 and the market town of Anzob.

Cars leave Margeb every Monday morning for Dushanbe (70/700TJS per seat/charter, around

eight hours). Note that the Anzob Pass is no longer navigable even for motorcyclists.

Upper Zerafshan Valley

A gateway to some of the most gorgeous scenery in the country, the attractive small town of Ayni (Айнй) offers an opportunity to break the long and winding journey between Dushanbe and Penjikent or Khojand. With a small area of traditional garden homesteads hidden along footpaths to the north of the main road, and a few gracious municipal buildings, it invites an hour or two of ambling.

The town currently only has one **hotel** (☑ 9274 3 8880; r 170-400TJS), but it may make a change from the traditional homestays that are the more common form of accommodation in the area. Some 3km south, just across the M34 bridge, *krug* refers to the main taxi stand for Dushanbe (70TJS per seat, 2½ hours) and Sarvoda (20TJS per car). Near to Ayni Hospital is where the 4WD stand for Veshab (15TJS, 20 minutes) and points further east is located.

From Ayni, the Upper Zerafshan Valley is around 200km in length and it takes some determination and a whole day's 4WD travel to reach the end of it. The painfully slow, rough road puts most travellers off the effort and it has to be said that there are few obvious attractions (other than the starkly striking landscape) and virtually no tourist infrastructure. Veshab, just 30km from

Iskander-Kul A three-day trek from the Zitmud village homestay southwest of Artush that crosses the Dukdon Pass (3810m) to Sarytag and Iskander-Kul.

Routes from Shing & Marzugor

Archa Maidan Valley Trails of between two to four days thread between the sixth and seventh lake of Haft-Kul (Seven Lakes) to the Tavasang Pass (3300m). This is a gateway to the Archa Maidan Valley, which descends to Zitmud.

Iskander-Kul A tough hike cuts across the Munora Pass (3520m) and Dukdon Pass (3810m) to Sarytag and Iskander-Kul, taking between three to five days.

Routes from Veshab

Yagnob Valley A series of little-promoted trails links the parallel valleys of Zerafshan and Yagnob. These are rough trails in a particularly remote region and each take around a week of wilderness trekking and camping in the territory of bears and elusive snow leopards. One trail leads from Veshab via Shamtuj-Bedev to Hishortob. Guides or considerable experience and self-reliance are required for hikes in this area.

Ayni but a two-hour drive, gives a good indication of the valley's distinctive character and **Homestay Umar** (☑ 9356 0 4921; Veshab; mattress incl breakfast US$10) offers one of the few places to stay. The village is claimed to be home to the tomb of **Shams-i-Tabrizi** (Vershab), the muse of Sufi poet Rumi. In fact almost all the villages of the valley harbour a shrine, including the neighbouring village of Zosun with its fine modern monument to the Tajik writer, Naqibhon Tugral (1865–1919). A satisfying two-hour hike from Vershab leads to the summer pastures at Tagob. Or, if properly equipped, there is a steep two- to three-day trek to Hishortob in the Yagnob Valley.

For the very few who make it beyond Veshab, there are a couple of noteworthy villages in the upper reaches of the valley, including Oburdon with its small renovated fortress, Hatishahr, a village of stone-and-wattle walled homesteads, and the district capital Mehergun, on a barren hillside isolated from any sign of habitation. Above Hairobod, a 10km gold-mining road presents a head start for a weeklong adventure trek into the Yagnob Valley via the snowbound Tabaspin Pass (4040m). Langar offers a accommodation in the characterful **Kholov Homestay** (Habib Homestay; ☑ 927 746202, 9276 1 1521; ztda_zarafshon@yahoo.com; Langar, Mastchoh; r incl breakfast US$12) and a base for valley adventures.

The 'road' more or less peters out at 175km in the tiny shrine village of Dehavz.

With 5000m peaks in sight, this is the starting point for visiting the Zerafshan Glacier, a whole day's drive and trek from Dehavz and back. The 4WD track ends 7km from the village from where it's a 15km hike to the glacier, whose loss of 2.5km in 90 years has been attributed to climate change. Anyone attempting a visit to the hinterland, beyond the rural belt of the valley and home to snow leopard and bear, needs a guide and a measure of self-reliance.

A variety of shared 4WDs depart from Ayni's hospital 4WD stand, mostly in the afternoon, returning the next morning. Seats in shared vehicles (around 60TJS per seat) can take hours (or even days if heading beyond Langar) for the vehicle to fill up. It's less frustrating to charter the whole vehicle, but this costs around 900TJS to Langar (five to six hours) along a miserably rough road.

THE PAMIRS

Eastern Tajikistan has an almost entirely different character from the rest of the country. Mountainous, remote and difficult to access, the land is incised by deep river canyons along the edges of which cling rural hamlets, decorated by ribbons of cultivation in an otherwise barren landscape. High above these river valleys lie the Pamirs, a series of level pastures where herders lead their yaks, sheep and goats across the wilds in a semi-nomadic life, battling the ravages of

MOUNTAIN VILLAGE HOMESTAYS

ZTDA (Zerafshan Tourism Development Association; www.ztda-tourism.tj; Rudaki 108, Penjikent) was set up with German assistance in 2008 to bring economic benefit to remote villages overlooked by conventional tourism. Over the years it has benefited an estimated 12,000 people through the 20 participant homestays and 200 service providers. While the association itself has somewhat declined as an organisation in the last few years, its initiatives continue to thrive in many parts of the Fan Mountains and beyond. Staying at any of the homestays that continue to be promoted on the association website is not only worthwhile in terms of sustainable tourism but also offers visitors a unique perspective on the intimate workings of remote mountain villages and the tough, enduring nature of the communities therein.

Participant homestays are listed with photographs on the ZTDA website. Each homestay offers traditional-style accommodation on a mattress (or occasionally a bed) in a simple, usually shared and carpeted room, separate from the owner's family sleeping room. Most charge US$10 to US$15 per person including breakfast, with lunch and dinner possible for an extra US$5 per meal; there is almost always some form of vegetables, honey or fruit from their own gardens in the Tajiki dishes they prepare. Some form of hot water for washing is usually provided in a shared 'bathroom' outside the house. Toilets are generally of the squat type, but many homestays are beginning to introduce Western-style loos in the hope of attracting more visitors.

Overnighting in a homestay makes it possible to access some of the most beautiful and remote parts of the Sughd region. ZTDA recommends guides (around US$30 per day) and flags the languages they speak. Any of the guides can organise pack donkeys (US$20 for two donkeys with driver per day), tents (US$5), mats and sleeping bags (US$3). The website also suggests all-inclusive hiking packages.

Getting to some of the homestays presents a challenge as most of them are in small villages that are ill-served by public transport and have only limited infrastructure. A 4WD is often necessary to negotiate the rough roads and sometimes these are impassable for much of the year when heavy snow or flooding cut some villages off for months at a time. By and large, the easiest way of moving from one homestay to the next is with a driver-guide in a 4WD.

winter for eight months of the year and relaxing into the brief respite of spring.

Officially called Kohistani Badakhshan (GBAO or Gorno-Badakhshan Autonomous Oblast), the region accounts for 45% of Tajikistan's territory but only 3% of its population. The famous Pamir Hwy, the second highest international highway, traverses this sparsely populated 'Roof of the World'. Mostly unpaved, potholed, often flooded and one car wide, it's an experience not to be missed.

Technically the M41 and the **Pamir Hwy** (Памирское шоссе) are not identical thoroughfares: the M41 starts from Dushanbe and extends to the Kyrgyzstan border. The Pamir Hwy, by contrast, refers to a section of the M41 that runs only between Khorog and Osh. But who cares about the technicalities! The route, by whatever name it's given, is famous for a reason.

Under the Soviet Union, with no arable land suitable to large-scale agriculture and no industry to speak of, virtually all processed goods and fuel came from outside the region. As such, the collapse of the USSR, which left mines, research stations and observatories abandoned across the Pamirs, was a particularly hard blow for local communities.

Frustrated by its marginal position and seeing no future in a collapsing Tajikistan, Badakhshan nominally declared its independence in 1992 and chose the rebel side in the civil war. After the war, little was forthcoming in the way of aid or reconstruction except through humanitarian aid. Indeed, throughout the 1990s, convoys kept the region from starvation and helped in the establishment of agricultural and hydroelectric programs to promote a degree of self-sufficiency. In 1993 the region grew just 16% of its basic food needs; currently that figure has risen to over 80%. Despite this success, 80% of the local population still earns less than US$200 per year and over 15,000 Badakhshanis have left their homes in search of work outside the region. Recent projects are helping to address this exodus by creating local employment opportunities through improved education and tourism. The latter, promoted through homestays, guiding and chartered taxi services, is anticipated as a sector of ever-growing promise.

Encouragingly, farmers and herders have begun to relearn the traditional farming techniques and skills that had been suppressed for decades. Today one of the striking features of travelling through the Pamirs is witnessing these skills in action – every village is a veritable garden of Eden with a rich variety of largely organically grown crops and healthy herds of livestock in the meadows beyond. So naturally has the land returned to its pre-Soviet incarnation that it's hard to imagine the hiatus lasted for nearly a century.

Pamiri People

Centuries of isolation in high-altitude valleys has resulted in many cultural differences between the peoples of the Pamirs. This is particularly evident in the number of different languages in the region. Each mountain community speaks its own dialect of Pamiri, a language that, although sharing the same Persian roots as Tajik, is as different as English is from German. Shugnani (named after the emirate of Shugnan once based in the Gunt Valley) is one of the most predominant dialects, spoken in Khorog, the Gunt Valley and among Badakhshani Tajiks in Murgab. Other languages in the mosaic include Wakhi, Ishkashimi and Rushani.

While separated by linguistic differences, the peoples of the Pamirs are at least united in faith, with Islam prevailing as the common religion. In the eastern Pamirs people observe the tenets of Ismailism, a breakaway sect of Shiite Islam, introduced into Badakhshan in the 11th-century by Nasir Khusraw. Ismailism has no formal clerical structure, no weekly holy day and no mosques (rather multipurpose meeting halls called *jamoat khana,* which also double as meeting halls and community guesthouses). Ismailis greet each other with *yo-ali madat* (may Ali bless you), rather than the standard Islamic *asalam aleykum.* Each village has a religious leader known as a *khalifa,* who leads prayers and dispenses advice, assisted by a *rais* (community leader).

One of the few visible manifestations of the religion are the small roadside *oston* (shrines), covered in ibex horns, burnt offerings and round stones, at which passers-by stop to ask for a blessing. The horns are often the remnants of hunting trips and ensuing community meals known as *khudoi.* The shrines also act as charity stations; in return for a blessing, the Ismailis customarily leave some money or bread for anyone in need.

The spiritual leader of the Ismailis is the Swiss-born Aga Khan, revered by Pamiris as the 49th imam. He's no remote, abstract figure – it's the Aga Khan Foundation that has kept almost certain starvation at bay since the 1990s, while latterly providing healt care and educational opportunities. The foundation has an outward-looking mandate and many Pamiris receive scholarships to Western universities, and several bridges have been rebuilt across the Pyanj River, reuniting communities severed by the formation of the USSR.

Pamiri hospitality is legendary and visitors to this harsh land unfailingly receive a warm welcome. Those travelling alone are often offered a place to stay in villages along the route without any hidden agenda. This tradition of hospitality has become formalised into a highly successful homestay system where, for the minimal standard charge of U$15 to $25 per person (depending on the number of meals), visitors receive not just a cosy place to sleep and home-cooked meals, but also a rich insight into local life.

The homestay system contributes greatly to the survival of communities with few other opportunities for income and helps to ensure that visitors can continue to travel widely across the Pamirs on limited budgets. It is customary to respect this aspect of regional development by leaving the standard sums of money (discreetly in an envelope or tucked under a dish) if invited in to stay (US$10) or eat (US$5), however insistently the host refuses.

Pamiri Houses

From outside, a traditional *huneuni chid* (Pamiri house) looks like a simple construction. Inside the design is anything but, with each element of the interior rich in cultural and religious allusion that dates back over 2000 years.

The most distinctive feature of a house is the wooden ceiling built in four concentric squares, each rotated 45 degrees then crowned with a skylight that provides most of the illumination. Each square represents

The Pamirs

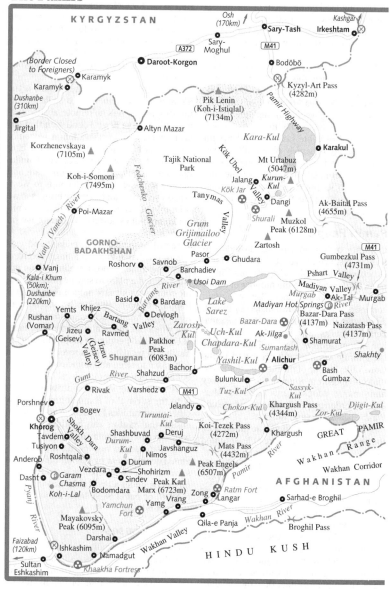

one of the Zoroastrian elements of earth, fire, air and water. Guests are received in the large, five-pillared room with raised platforms on three sides. Each of five vertical pillars symbolises Imam Ali, his wife Fatima, the prophet Mohammed and brothers Hassan and Hussein. The place of honour, next to the Hassan pillar (one of two pillars joined together), is reserved for the *khalifa* (village religious leader): visitors should avoid sitting there.

Shoes are always removed before entering a house and visitors to Tajikistan will inevitably become adept at shuffling them on and off in record time.

A good place to spot some of the sophistications of Pamiri architecture is at a homestay, many of which to this day are modelled on traditional designs.

🛏 Sleeping & Eating

There are hotels in Kala-i Khum, Khorog and Murgab. Outside these towns accommodation in rural Badakhshan is in simple homestays (half board per person Western Pamirs US$15 to US$18, Eastern Pamirs US$20 to US$22, reflecting the cost of supplies in the remoter Eastern region). Homestays generally offer mattresses in a shared room (separate from the family) in a typical Pamiri home with outdoor bathrooms and long-drop toilets. PECTA (p179) in Khorog has an extensive homestay list.

The best food is offered in homestays (around US$5 per person per meal), but the main towns all have cafes with a choice of regional and popular travellers' dishes. Bazaars are well stocked with bread, fruit, vegetables and bottled water for most of the year, while basic supplies are available in all but the high-altitude villages around Murgab where many villages are cut off for much of the year.

ⓘ Getting There & Around

Traffic throughout the Pamirs is sparse to non-existent and there is virtually no scheduled public transport. For most travellers, planning how to travel in the region is the main pre-departure task, and for those with a limited time frame, this generally means hiring a 4WD. The Pamir Hwy (1250km from Khorog to Osh) and the Wakhan Valley attract a few cyclists and motorcyclists, despite the many challenges of the almost entirely off-road (or at least broken road) route.

Shared 4WDs run at least daily from Khorog to Murgab, Murgab to Osh and from Khorog to local destinations within an hour or two's drive. Frequency is so low, however, that it is a far better option to rent a 4WD with a group of fellow travellers.

The 1106km M41 connects Dushanbe with its eastern territories, crossing some of the most dramatic scenery in Central Asia. For part of its length, from Khorog to the border, it is referred to as the Pamir Hwy (Памирское шоссе), a highway that continues to Osh in Kyrgyzstan. It was built by Soviet military engineers between

Carpets usually line the walls and floors, and mattresses take the place of furniture. Amid panels of photographs, pride of place almost invariably goes to a portrait of the Aga Khan.

1931 and 1934 to facilitate troop transport and provisioning and has become one of the world's classic high-altitude journeys.

Blue kilometre posts are used to mark distances, initially from Dushanbe with distance to the Kyrgyz border marked on the opposite side. Khorog at Km641 is more or less halfway. At Murgab, marker Km930, the system changes showing distances from Osh with distances to Khorog on the reverse.

Apart from the painful Jelandy–Bulunkul section, the road is vaguely asphalted, although the winter takes its toll each year leaving parts of the surface in ruins. Potholes and corrugated surfaces are the norm for much of the way.

At the time of writing the route between Dushanbe and Khorog, at the start of the Pamir Hwy, was via Kulob and the A385, as the road beyond Tavildara on the M41 was impassable and likely to remain that way for the foreseeable future. From Khorog, the Pamir Hwy crosses a bleak plateau through the Gunt Valley to Murgab; many travellers, however, prefer to opt for the off-road route to Murgab along the Pyanj River, through the picturesque Tajik Wakhan Corridor.

4WD HIRE

If there is one route that rewards the extra cost of hiring private transport, the Pamir Hwy is surely it. A 4WD is necessary to negotiate the generally appallingly poor quality of the off-road route, and in Tajikistan this means hiring a driver as well. Many drivers also act as English-speaking guides – helpful if travelling without knowledge of Russian. The joy of being able to stop on request quickly compensates for the added expense as this is a route, with its spectacular landscape, that demands to be photographed.

Anticipating costs Typical per kilometre rates range from US$1 to US$1.5, plus US$20 per day to cover the driver's living expenses on overnight or longer trips.

Selecting a vehicle It's best to see the intended vehicle in advance of the journey to check the 4WD works. It can also be disappointing if the windows are blacked out obscuring the view for the passengers in the rear.

Meeting the driver Meeting the driver the day before can be revealing: the journeys are long and a sullen or reckless driver can ruin the experience. Drivers should have a passport and GBAO permit – and ideally be mechanically minded!

Agreeing terms It's important to be clear about what is included in the cost. Most prices quoted include the driver's board and lodge and his return journey. Many drivers are not prepared to venture out after dark (often for good reason as the roads are universally rough) and expect to drive for only a certain number of hours per day with a break for lunch. Exchang-

TOP TIPS FOR TRAVELLING IN THE PAMIRS

What to Pack

➡ cash in both US dollars and Tajik somoni (TJS)

➡ sunglasses and sunscreen

➡ warm clothing (a fleece and windproof shell in summer)

➡ sleeping bag and tent (if going it alone)

➡ mosquito repellent in summer

➡ spare batteries and torch (electricity supply is unreliable)

➡ water purification tablets (if hiking)

➡ pillow (the journeys are *long*)

Maps

The Marcus Hauser 1:500,000 *Pamirs* map is packed with icon-based information including sights and homestays. It's sold at Dushanbe's East Vision (p152), Yak Tours (p88) in Karakol, Kyrgyzstan or via www.geckomaps.com. A similar Pamir Tourist Map costs 60TJS from PECTA (p179).

Money

The only ATMs are in Khorog. None accept Maestro and increasingly are failing to work with international cards. For this reason, it's best not to rely on this service and bring cash instead. Banks in Khorog and Murgab can change US dollars, but not always euros. Homestays accept US dollars as well as somani. Kyrgyz som are accepted in Karakul. Any left over somani can be spent or changed in Sary Tash in Kyrgyzstan.

ⓘ PAMIR HIGHWAY IN FIVE DAYS

Regardless of how much pre-trip planning made before reaching Tajikistan, the reality of a trip through the Pamirs is that the limited availability and cost of transport, the lack of petrol and spare parts, and the relative scarcity of accommodation and supplies inevitably affects how you form an itinerary. Most trips end up following a reversible five-day route between Dushanbe and the Kyrgyzstan border.

Day 1 Dushanbe to Kalai-Khum (285km, six hours). Follow the main southern route via Kulob – the northern route via Tavildara is not well maintained and often impassable.

Day 2 Kalai-Khum to Khorog (250km, 5½ hours) The M41 passes Rushan and the western end of the Bartang Valley. The interesting town of Khorog makes a good rest day if time allows.

Day 3 Khorog to Langar (150km, 3½ hours) Journey along the Wakhan Valley passing through many interesting villages, including Ishakashim and Zong.

Day 4 Langar to Murgab (320km, seven hours) Ascend from the Pyanj River, leaving the Afghan border behind, and cross the high mountain plateau via Alichur.

Day 5 Murgab to the Kyrgyzstan Border (130km, two hours) Spend the morning comparing notes with fellow travellers in the frontier town of Murgab before heading to the border via Lake Karakul. The border to Osh is 228km and takes four hours.

ing expectations about the length of the driving day and attitudes towards unplanned diversions and excursions before the trip can help immensely in maintaining good relations over multiple days, especially if language is an issue.

Finding a ride Most agencies in Murgab and Khorog plus many in Osh, Bishkek and Dushanbe can help in sourcing a reliable vehicle. For a vehicle at short notice, Hamsafar Travel (p153) in Dushanbe and PECTA (p179) in Khorog are helpful.

Filling up Finding petrol can be a problem in the Pamirs. A trip into the more remote corners of the region generally involves at least one dash around town to find a obliging local with a jerry can of diluted fuel and a bucket.

HITCHING

Hitching in the Pamirs is possible, but getting a ride can take hours or days and should be paid for. Fellow travellers are the most likely source of a ride, but bear in mind that they will have spent a large sum of money in hiring transport and offering a contribution towards costs is likely to improve the atmosphere on long, cramped journeys. On the Pamir Hwy between Khorog and Murgab there is a chance of a ride with Chinese truckers, but as they often travel at night, the chief attraction of the journey (namely, the scenery) is missed. Hitching between Sary Tash to Murgab is virtually impossible.

Western Pamir Highway

Threading through spectacular canyon scenery, with Afghanistan an arm's stretch away, the western section of the Pamir Hwy (from Dushanbe to Khorog) is the more gentle, and relatively low-altitude twin of this characterful road. That's not to say it is without its excitements. Running so close to the roaring Pyanj River that in parts the water snaps at the wheels of passing vehicles, the weather-battered road clings tightly to the cliff's edge and falling rocks can delay progress for hours. But dotted along the length of this remarkable outpost of engineering are oases of civilisation – little villages whose neat and orderly market gardens could lie along any B-road in rural Central Asia, mindless of their apparent isolation. These villages, together with the amiable hub of Kalai-Kum, offer an intimate introduction to the Pamirs and to the Pamir Hwy proper that runs east from Khorog.

Kulob

📞 3322 / POP 78,786 / ELEV 627M

The third largest city in Tajikistan, Kulob (sometimes transliterated as Kulyab) nonetheless feels more like a provincial town with wide open streets lined with hollyhocks and punctuated with polished civic statues. First referred to by historians in AD 737, the city celebrated a special milestone in 2006 – namely, its 2700th birthday – and several reminders of that proud occasion still decorate the town. There are a couple of sights in and around town that make for a worthwhile break on the long drive from Dushanbe towards the Pamirs, including nearby **Hulbuk Fortress** (Kurbon Shahid; 📞 9080 0 1708, 9066 6 7766; admission 15TJS; ⊙ 8am-5pm Mon-Sat).

Destroyed by the Mongols, the sparse remnants of this fortified palace have been undergoing excavation since 1951 and now a fine reconstruction of the palace walls, complete with minaret and battlements, has been completed. Seen from the main road driving east, it seems to loom out of nowhere (8km west of Vose) and is an impressive sight. It's not possible to enter the ruins, but a small museum opposite offers some helpful interpretation including a large model of the site.

Shomi Khulob (Shamsiddin Shohein; lunch around 20TJS; ☉9am-9pm; ✳), by the statue of Shamsiddin Shohein and unpromisingly sited in the forecourt of an NFC petrol station, offers delicious local and national dishes served at smart new tables with plush sofa seats. There's also a big bazaar selling watermelons and fruit; together with some supermarkets there's plenty of chances in town to stock up on water and snacks for the journey.

Kalai-Khum

☑3552 / POP LESS THAN 5000 / ELEV 1287M

With a river raging through the centre, channelled between houses with terraces overhanging the impatient water, and with an attractive mosque and civic buildings, Kulai-Khum (Darvoz) is one of the Pamir's most attractive towns. It is the first community of any significant size between Kulob and Khorog, and is one that most driver-guides

attempt to reach as an overnight stop from Dushanbe. This piece of geography, together with the fact that it sits at the junction of the A385 with the legendary Pamir Hwy (M41) on a particularly fertile snippet of land, lends a sense of welcome oasis to the town.

The journey between Dushanbe and Khorog can take anywhere between 14 and 20 hours, making it pretty much essential to stop somewhere en route. The town of choice for a night's stay is Kalai-Khum, boasting the improbable luxury **Karon Palace** (☑8811 0 7772, 9370 7 0246; www.karon-palace.com; M41; r from $200; ☻✳☎) hotel among characterful and simple homestays like the one run by **Darvaz Sangakov Bahrom** (☑9810 3 8046, 9341 0 2750; M41; half board per person US$20) in a lane immediately after the bridge.

Most people eat at their hotel, but there are several options dotted around the bazaar, including the verandah of the **Oriyona** (☑9354 6 9695; mains 13-17TJS; ☉10am-10pm Mon-Sat) overlooking the river. The Karon Palace also offers an international choice of cuisine for hotel guests (or non-guests who book in advance) and a smart bar. Stock up on supplies for the onward journey at the **Europa Supermarket** (M41; ☉8am-10pm).

Rushan   Рушан

☑3556 / POP LESS THAN 5000 / ELEV 2000M

Rushan is quintessential Pamir – little more than a sliver of houses amid cultivated fields that seem impossibly wedged be-

---

LAKE SAREZ: A LOOMING DISASTER

Geologists warn that Tajikistan faces a potential natural disaster of Biblical proportions in the shape of stark 3239m Lake Sarez, a disarmingly placid-looking body of turquoise water formed in 1911 when an earthquake dislodged an entire mountain side into the path of the Murgab River, obliterating the villages of Usoi and Sarez. A deep lake, now 60km-long and half the size of Lake Geneva, gradually formed behind the 770m-high natural dam of rocks and mud known as the Usoi Dam. This 'dam' is currently considered stable. However, if an earthquake broke or breached it, a huge wall of water could come sweeping down the mountain valleys, washing out roads and villages as far away as Uzbekistan and beyond. Experts warn that it would be the largest flood ever witnessed by human eyes. Villagers in the Bartang Valley (who would be most affected) have been drilled on escape procedures. These are pretty simple – head for the hills when the doomsday alert arrives.

Visiting Lake Sarez requires advance planning as permits (US$50) are required from Dushanbe. These can take a month to issue, and even then they are usually only available as part of a tour: contact PECTA (p179) in Khorog for the latest advice. The Sarez trail head is at Barchadiev which, along with nearby Savnob, has homestays; otherwise there is no tourist infrastructure here. If the difficulties involved in getting there aren't off-putting, **Sarez Travel** (☑934 072546; http://sarez.travel/en) can help facilitate trips to the lake.

ROGUN HYDROPOWER PROJECT: HIGHEST DAM IN THE WORLD

Drive along the somewhat perilous road from Dushanbe to Garm, high above the Vakhsh River, and a surprise awaits at the point where the river canyon narrows. Perched above the cliffs on the other side of the valley, in the middle of an otherwise pastoral idyll of high-altitude meadows and wilderness peaks, lies a half-hidden city of high-rise buildings. Below this new metropolis, off the map in terms of tourism, the open jaws of an enormous building site yawn between the canyon walls as diggers gnash their way day and night in the building of the Rogun Hydropower Project. Billed as the tallest in the world at 335m, the dam is expected to run six large turbines when it reaches its full height in 2025.

Naturally it is being hailed within Tajikistan as an engineering miracle, predicted to bring about an economic boon in an otherwise underdeveloped country. Providing much-needed electricity for home consumption, the project is also expected to generate export revenue with surpluses bound for Afghanistan and Pakistan. Beyond Tajikistan, however, the project is receiving less of a welcome as anxious downstream neighbours fear the effect that the taming of the mighty Vakhsh River may have on agriculture (cotton and grains are major crops in Uzbekistan and Kazakhstan). Despite the blessing of the World Bank, sporadic attacks on the dam have led to heightened security in the area and explains something of the sequestered nature of Rogun city. With nearly US$4 billion invested in the project, it's little wonder that the authorities chose to release doves at the project launching ceremony.

tween roaring river and vertical cliff. Edged with poplars and tinged with springtime green, it shouts out to be visited. The simple **Mubarak Homestay** (☑ 9340 5 2304; per person incl breakfast US$15) offers four beds and some floor mats, and some small teashops double as restaurants in the bazaar area.

Shared minivans from central Rushan to Khorog (15TJS to 20TJS) take around one hour on something of an asphalt road and depart before 10am, returning in the evening. Every morning there's a Rushan–Dushanbe shared 4WD (250TJS to 300TJS per seat), which leaves only if full.

Rushan makes a potential base for visiting the Bartang and Jizeu Valleys; transport is available through the Mubarak Homestay (p175). Little if any English is spoken in town so most travellers opt to head to Khorog first (65km south), where there's a much wider choice of transport available.

Bartang Valley
Долина реки Бартанг

Stark and elemental, the Bartang Valley is one of the wildest and most memorable valleys in the western Pamirs. Only the occasional fertile alluvial plain brings a flash of green to the barren rock walls. At times the fragile road inches perilously between the raging river below and sheer cliffs above. Indeed it's not rare for sections to become impossibly rough or require knee-deep fords. Still, strong 4WDs and even some adventurous motorcyclists (carrying enough fuel for 400km) have managed to traverse the whole valley in a few days.

The western reach of the Bartang Valley cuts through a high-walled canyon, not much wider than the river bed and punctuated only occasionally by isolated villages. At 42km off the Pamir Hwy (one hour's drive), Khigez is one of the most delightful of these, 13km east of the Jizeu Valley bridge. Home to one of the best homestays in the area, it is also the access point to the Ravmedara Gorge. The lovely village of **Basid** (Басид), 85km off the highway (2½ hour's drive), boasts shrines, scenic forests, good hiking, two homestays and the possibility of joining **PamirLink** (www.pamirlink.org) ✎, a three-week live-in-Basid working holiday experience. Nearby, **Bardara** (Бардара) also boasts shrines, a village ice-house (*khalodelnik*) and trails that lead up to summer pastures and beyond.

In Khigez the **Dishodar Homestay** (☑ 9370 1 9169; Khigez; half board US$18, lunch US$4; P) run by experienced and super-hospitable hosts, gives an opportunity to explore the Bartang Valley and remote village life in the Western Pamirs without having to commit to travelling too far off the Pamir Hwy. It's located on the river's edge in a beautiful, productive garden guarded by a stroppy goat and has hot water and electricity. It makes a great base for visiting the Jizeu Valley or breaking the arduous journey onwards to Karakul (250km).

HIKING THE JIZEU VALLEY

One of the best short-hike destinations in the region, the Jizeu (Jisev, Geisev) Valley offers idyllic landscape around a series of seasonally overflowing, tree-lined lakes. The prettiest lakes are bracketed by two halves of the tiny traditional hamlet of Jizeu (pronounced Jee-sao), which has a wonderful, timeless atmosphere. An added thrill of a visit, albeit a potential logistical problem, is that there's no road, and access to the village footpath starts by bouncing over the gnashing river on a swaying suspension bridge. For those wondering about the wooden contraption that looks like a sentry box, marooned on the shore, this was the former way of crossing, thankfully now retired.

The suspension bridge is 23km east of KM553 on the Pamir Hwy, around 6km beyond Bargu. The bridge is easily confused with a similar one 4km further west. From the bridge, the start of the village is a largely unshaded, two-hour walk up a steep scree-sided valley. Another half-hour leads through glorious scenery to the upper village. Beyond this, there are two more lakes and a horizon of high peaks that beckon ever further towards distant summer pastures. Guides (US$20 per day) can lead hikers over the Ravmed Pass to Ravmed village and Khijez, 18km upstream (two tough days, camping en route).

Many of the dozen or so homes along the Jizeu Valley offer bed spaces and some can arrange vehicles for the return to Rushan or Khorog. It's hard to recommend one homestay over another, but all offer a friendly welcome, a mattress in traditional fashion, shared outdoor bathroom and a good supper, and cost around US$18 per person for half board. Bookings are best made through PECTA (p179).

Chartered 4WD to the suspension bridge on the Pamir Hwy leave from Rushan (around 200TJS) and from Khorog (250TJS), where vehicles are easier to find. Although there is a minibus service in the Bartang Valley, it leaves early in the morning making it hard to reach the roadside from Jizeu in time. For those who miss the bus, it's a punishing 26km, unshaded hike to Rushan. It's safer to arrange return transport in advance or through a Jizeu homestay.

Basid is located 85km off the Pamir Hwy. There are two UAZ minibus services to Basid that operate most days; one leaves Rushan at around 3pm (20TJS, 2½ hours) and the other leaves Khorog at 5pm (30TJS, 3½ hours). Both services return in the morning leaving Basid at around 7am, passing the Khigez bridge on request at around 8am.

It's around 40km from Khigez to Basid (10TJS, one hour) and the bus reaches the Khigez bridge heading in that direction at about 4.30pm each day.

Khorog   Хорог

3522 / POP 30,000 / ELEV 2145M

When it comes to travelling in the Pamirs, all roads lead to Khorog. The administrative centre of Gorno Badakhshan and the Pamirs' largest town, it has the air and confidence of a capital, attracting people from far and wide to its well-stocked bazaars, supermarkets and teahouses. One of the best parts of a visit is sitting in the beautiful, tree-filled **Central Park** (⊙6am-midnight) and being part of the general sense of well-being occasioned by reaching this oasis of plenty in a land of limited resources.

Near Central Park is the fascinating Soviet-style **Regional Museum** (Lenin 105; admission 5TJS; ⊙8am-5pm Tue-Sun), which exhibits crampons and the first Russian piano to arrive in Badakhshan (10 Russian soldiers spent two months carrying it over the mountains from Osh in 1913) along with portraits of Stalin and the basket of a collective farm's star potato-picker.

Don't miss the **Saturday Market** (⊙9am-1pm Sat) some 5km west of Khorog across a bridge linking Afghanistan with Tajikistan at the point where the Gunt merges with the Pyanj, which offers an interesting way to observe Afghan traders at work, though the market is often suspended if security tensions in the region escalate. Back in town, the teeming **Khorog Bazaar** (Lenin; ⊙8am-5pm) overflows into stalls shaded by colourful umbrellas around the main building. Several stands sell woollen crafts, including traditional socks, and the attractive red or green velvet Pamir hats are also on sale.

Khorog

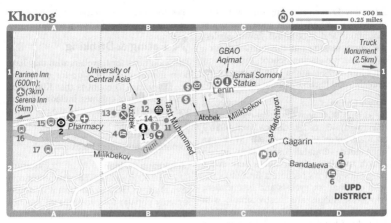

Khorog

At the eastern end of Lenin, a **truck on a plinth** (Khorog GES) just below the hydro-electric dam commemorates the opening of the Pamir Hwy to Osh in 1928 after over 20 years of effort.

There are nice views from the **Pamir Botanical Gardens** (Botanicheskii Sad; ☑ 5011 1 8056; ⊙ 8am-6pm) 5km to the east of town, claimed to be the world's second-highest botanical garden. Most three-route minivans go as far as the lower gate, from which it's a half-hour climb to the garden's second gate. It's better to go by taxi (12TJS) and conserve energies for wandering through the gardens instead.

🛏 Sleeping

Khorog has an ever-expanding selection of accommodation including midrange hotels and numerous homestays (typically US$15 to US$18), which offer simple rooms with shared toilet and bathroom facilities; almost all include breakfast in the room rates. PECTA (p179) maintains an updated list available online.

Umriniso Homestay HOMESTAY **$**
(☑ 9350 0 6942; Dubronov 14; r incl breakfast US$15) A location doesn't get more central than this. Wedged into the Central Park between PECTA and the riverside teahouse, this lovable Pamiri home has the further luxury of a small yard of flowerbeds, a low-powered hot shower, washing machine and Western-style loo. Litvia speaks English.

Lalmo Homestay HOMESTAY **$**
(☑ 9350 8 6999; mizhgona92@mail.ru; Gagarin (Bandalieva) 2; bed incl breakfast US$15; 🛜) With

a friendly English-speaking owner (helpful in giving travel advice), a good view of the mountains and a beautiful flower garden, it's worth seeking out this homestay up a small stairway facing School 7, some way out of town. Beer and a laundry service are available and luggage storage is offered free.

Pamir Lodge GUESTHOUSE $
(☑ 9359 2 1004; www.pamirlodge.com; Gagarin (Bandalieva) 46; bed in old/new room US$7/9, breakfast/dinner US$3/4; P 🖥) With an open-sided verandah overlooking an orchard, travellers sit for hours here swapping tales and it's become a firm favourite with overlanders, cyclists and independent travellers. Rooms are mostly simple with mattresses on raised platforms except for three *lux* (deluxe) rooms (US$40 including breakfast and wi-fi), which have en suite toilets. It's a 25-minute walk to town (20TJS by taxi).

★**Lal Hotel** BOUTIQUE HOTEL $$
(☑ 3522 2 6688, 3522 2 3230; www.lalhotel.tj; Azizbek 5/1; s & tw/d incl breakfast US$50/65; ❄ 🖥) Central and cosy, and tasteful in design, this hotel is wrapped around a garden with an apricot tree shading a sitting pavilion. There are a choice of stylish rooms, most with air-conditioning, and a laundry service (25TJS) is available. At night the flower garden is changed into a magical little space, highly popular as a meeting point for travellers.

Parinen Inn B&B $$
(☑ 9350 2 3750, 7770 0 9000; www.parinen.com; Lenin 193; s/d US$25/30; P ❄) This three-storey villa offers standards well above most typical homestays, but without doubt, its biggest draw is the gorgeous garden, which is clearly someone's pride and joy. A dovecote, rose arbours and displays of bright annuals make this garden an oasis a few minutes' walk from the bazaar. The hotel is next to a bakery, and close to an Oriyon petrol station.

Serena Inn BOUTIQUE HOTEL $$$
(☑ 9357 8 0095, 3522 2 3228; www.serena hotels.com; Safarmamad St; s/d incl breakfast US$161/186; P ❄ @ 🖥) Khorog's most luxurious hotel has just six bedrooms with Western-style bathrooms, mini-fridge and fine linens, arranged around a comfortable lounge-lobby built with Pamiri timbers and design elements. Built for the visits of the Aga Khan, a big attraction is the terraced riverside garden, with lawns, roses and wil-

lows framing views across to Afghanistan. It's 5km northwest of Khorog Bazaar.

🍴 Eating & Drinking

The good news for travellers who may have been living on *osh* or *plov* for more days than they care to count is that Khorog offers a selection of cuisines, including Indian and Italian. In common with the rest of the region, most homestays and guesthouses organise dinner with some notice, and all accommodation offers breakfast.

Chaykhana Parinen CENTRAL ASIAN $
(☑ 7770 0 9000, 9359 2 6768; www.parinen.com; Lenin 191; mains 15TJS; ⊙ 7am-11pm Mon-Sat) Deservedly popular for pre-prepared lunches, *manty* (steamed meat dumplings), shashlyk and chilled flagons of *kompot* (fruit cordial), this extensive, easily missed chaikhana (chaykhana) is pleasantly situated at the riverside within the large and beautiful gardens of the Parinen Inn.

Barmasar Cafe FAST FOOD $
(Lenin 179; breakfast pizza 6TJS, lunch burger 18TJS; ⊙ 8am-9pm) A tidy little cafe by the bazaar and opposite Pamir Plaza, this is a handy place for a fast-food snack after shopping for supplies in the large supermarket opposite.

★**Delhi Darbar** INDIAN $$
(☑ 3522 2 1299; ashok@delhidarbar.in; Azizbek 2; curries 25-30TJS, beer 15TJS; ⊙ 11am-10pm Mon-Sat; ❄ 🖊 📶) This is the most popular meeting place in Khorog, largely perhaps because it's exciting to find anyone even attempting to offer Indian cuisine in such a remote corner of Central Asia – and Delhi Darbar does a particularly good job of it. The vegetarian options include dhal (16TJS) and vegie curries.

The owners run a small hotel on-site too, above the Aga Khan Foundation office.

Lal Cafe PIZZA $$
(☑ 3522 2 6688; Azizbek 5/1, Lal Hotel; pizza 35-65TJS, beer 15TJS; ⊙ 10am-8pm) Attached to Lal Hotel and with access to the seating pavilion in the hotel garden, this fun, bright cafe is decorated with traditional patterns, and musical instruments are hung from the ceiling. Vegetarians may be pleased to find non-meat burgers on the menu and few can resist pizza fresh from a proper pizza oven.

Serena Inn Restaurant TAJIK $$
(Serena Hotel; mains from US$7; ⊙ 10am-10pm; P ❄ 📶) This small upmarket restaurant

sports tables with white linen and side plates, and the outdoor tables on the terrace overlook an attractive riverside garden. It makes a tranquil spot for a beer (21TJS) on the *topchan* (dining pavilion) in the summer and a cosy place to retreat from the winter snow.

Chor Bagh INTERNATIONAL
(☑ 3522 2 9057; Central Park; mains 20-40TJS; ⊙ 10am-10pm) Right in Central Park, Chor Bagh is the most attractive place to enjoy a drink in town with a great open-air pavilion perched above the river for those balmy summer evenings. Good for a cold beer and pancakes.

ℹ Information

MEDICAL SERVICES
Pharmacy (Lenin; ⊙ 8am-10pm) Stocks all the basics including high-altitude medication (although this is better brought with medical advice from home).

MONEY
Several banks along Lenin change US dollars and euros, at least on weekdays. At the time of writing none of the several ATMs were accepting international cards and it is advisable to bring enough cash for the whole journey.

Agroinvestbank ATM (Lenin 85)
Tojik Sodirot Bank (Lenin)

PERMITS & REGISTRATION
PECTA can organise permits for Zor-Kul (20TJS per person per day), the ruby mines south of Anderob (50TJS), the Tajik National Park (20TJS per day plus 20TJS per car required for visits to Yashil-Kul, for example) and for the gold mines near Rang-Kul. These require simply a passport photocopy and are instantly issued. Lake Sarez (p174) is the only permit to take a month or more.

Registration or enquiries concerning visa extensions are handled through **OVIR** (Lenin 117; ⊙ 8am-noon & 1-5pm Mon-Fri).

POLICE
Khorog is a peaceful town in a generally safe region, but the **police** (Lenin) can help with general mishaps.

POST
Post Office (Lenin 44; ⊙ 9am-4pm) Sending extra kit home may make for more room in a cramped shared 4WD, although the postal service from Tajikistan is not very reliable.

ON TOP OF THE WORLD

The **Roof of the World Festival** (☑ 9360 0 6813; www.pamirtours.tj/the_roof_of_the_world_festival; ⊙ July/Aug) is an annual celebration of culture, initiated as a small-scale festival in Khorog in 2008, and since expanded to become a regional expression of traditional Pamir customs and values. Dancers, artists, craftspeople and poets from Tajikistan's Gorno Badakhshan region and from neighbouring Pamiri nations come together in a gathering that attracts thousands of visitors each summer. Tickets can be booked online.

TOURIST INFORMATION & TRAVEL AGENCIES
Badakhshan Travel (www.visitbadakhshan. com; Central Park access lane; ⊙ 7.30am-7pm) Arranges tickets and trips to Afghanistan.
De Pamiri (☑ 9350 0 4803, 9352 0 2901; www.depamiri.org; Central Park; ⊙ 9am-5pm May-Nov) Sharing the same building as PECTA. De Pamiri showcases work by dozens of Pamiri artisans, including felt rugs and bags, musical instruments, *palas* (woven goat-hair carpets) and embroidered skullcaps.
Pamir Silk Tour (☑ 9350 5 2361; www.pamir silk.travel; 1 Azizbek St) Operating out of Dushanbe, highly experienced Mullo Abdo Shagarf can arrange mountaineering guides, horse treks and other tailor-made Wakhan adventures according to interest.
PamirMount (☑ 9193 6 6772; www.pamir mount-tour.com; Mirsaid Mirshakar 11; ⊙ 10am-5pm) Tour and trekking agent specialising in the Bartang Valley.
PECTA (Pamirs Ecotourism Association Information Centre; ☑ 9344 2 5555; www.visitpamirs. com; Central Park; ⊙ 8am-6pm May-early Sep; 🗍) An essential resource for any traveller in the Pamirs, this excellent information office has lists of guides, drivers and homestays, rents simple trekking gear (tents and sleeping bags) and can help organise transport, hikes and excursions. Zhandiya is a veritable fount of knowledge and extremely generous with her time. The office itself makes a pleasant place to sit with a coffee, read the travel brochures and plan the onward journey. It also makes a pleasant place to relax and check email (half-/full day 5/10TJS) if the hotel wi-fi is playing up.
Tour De Pamir (☑ 9350 0 7557; www.tourde pamir.com) Provide various tours and offers competitive rates for taxi hire. Contact Ergash.

OFF THE BEATEN TRACK

GARAM CHASHMA HOT SPRINGS

For locals, **Garam Chashma** (soak 10TJS; ☺ men 4.30am-7.30am & 3.30pm-4.30pm, women 8am-noon, 1.30pm-3.30pm & 4.30-5.30pm) is the Pamirs' most popular open-air hot spring. A single pool surrounded by a cascade of calcified deposits is a little reminiscent of Turkey's Pamukkale, albeit in very miniature form. The pool is exactly the right temperature and discreetly cordoned off for (same-sex) naked bathing. The spring is a 20-minute drive southeast of the highway.

The best way to reach Anderob and the hot springs, other than en route to Ishkashim, is as part of a day trip in a private vehicle, chartered from Khorog (around 150TJS). It's not possible to pick up public transport from Anderob south, but hitching with bathing locals may be possible.

ⓘ Getting There & Around

The legendary scheduled flights (the only route on which Aeroflot paid its pilots danger money) to Khorog were suspended in 2017 with no sign of being revived. An occasional helicopter makes the journey over the mountain tops to Dushanbe, but this shouldn't be relied upon whatever promises made at the airport.

As elsewhere, minibuses leave 'when full' (which may take several hours) and prices fluctuate with demand. Very few cars depart on Sunday.

Shared 4WDs for Dushanbe (around 300TJS, 14 to 20 hours) leave several times each morning from a parking area near the riverside. By lunchtime there's little hope of finding a seat.

Shared 4WDs (150TJS, seven hours) and minivans (10JS, 1½ hours) to Rushan, Roshtqala and Shahzud (for Bachor) depart from the main taxi stand in the bazaar area.

Hitching to Murgab is not recommended as it's easy to get stranded for days before a vehicle with available space turns up. If you do hitch it's customary to offer to contribute to the cost, even in a 4WD chartered by fellow travellers. Chinese trucks travel mostly at night, making this rather a pointless exercise.

If headed for the Wakhan Valley, shared 4WDs to Ishkashim (45TJS, three to four hours) and Langar (120TJS, seven to eight hours) wait in yards directly across the footbridge from the bazaar.

The most convenient form of transport is to charter a 4WD and pay for all the seven seats plus food and accommodation for the driver. This can be organised through PECTA (p179) or any of the travel agencies in Khorog. It doesn't take long to collect six fellow travellers to share the cost and this can save considerable time and anguish on lonely Pamir roads.

Marshrutkas 1 and 3 start beyond the Serena Inn and pass the airport, bazaar and Central Park. Route 1 continues along Lenin out past the First Truck monument, while route 3 travels along Gagarin and the foot of the Botanical Gardens. Fares are 1.5/2TJS for short/long rides.

Tajik Wakhan Valley Ваханская долина

The Wakhan corridor follows the Pyanj River south from Khorog along a narrow canyon to Ishkashim. Here the corridor rounds the bend and follows the Pyanj River through a wider valley towards Langar. The entire corridor on either side of the river is dotted with picturesque villages, nestled in fertile plots of intensively cultivated land and half-buried under fruit-laden orchards. Beyond these slivers of green, the towering valley walls give way to glimpses of the Hindu Kush ('killer of Hindus'), the mountains that mark the Afghanistan–Pakistan border. Apart from the beauty of the journey and the interest arising from travelling within view of Afghan communities across the river, there are several sites of interest along the way, including castle ruins, ancient shrines decorated with ibex horns and sets of petroglyphs. It's even possible to cross into Afghanistan and visit the Wakhan from the other side.

Renting a 4WD in either Khorog or Murgab for a four-day trip through the Wakhan costs from around US$400. Without your own wheels, transport is pitifully infrequent and hitching is pretty much a non-starter without a lot of time and patience.

Ishkashim Ишкашим

☑ 3553 / POP 26,000 / ELEV 2490M

Ishkashim is the Wakhan's regional centre and largest community of any size. After hours spent travelling the lonely highway either side of this bustling town, it's quite a novelty to see people again. There are no specific sights at such, but it does make a place to stock up on water and other supplies. This is also the main border crossing used by most visitors heading for the Afghanistan Wakhan. It's worth checking the status of the Langar and Shaimak borders because if these reopen they will prove altogether more useful for reaching the Little Pamir.

The scenery here is quite distinct from the northern part of the Pyanj valley; from around 90km south of Khorog (15km north of Ishkashim) the narrow canyon widens out into ribbons of flat plains along the river's edge, so green that they almost resemble golf fairways.

Currently there is only one homestay in town, the **Hanis Guesthouse** (☑ 9358 2 5820; vai4hope@gmail.com; Miyona 2; bed incl breakfast & laundry US$12, full board US$20), and it's become one of the key meeting places for travellers in the Wakhan.

On Saturday morning a **trans-border market** (Ishkashim; ⊙ 8am-noon Sat, intermittently closed due to political sensitivities) takes place on a no man's land island in the middle of the Pyanj River 3km west of town. It attracts Afghan traders in turbans and pakol (flat caps) and Tajiks who enjoy the opportunity to consort with the neighbours. A passport but no Afghan visa is required.

ⓘ Getting There & Away

Shared taxis from Ishkashim head north to Khorog (60TJS, three hours) and east to Langar (60TJS, three hours). They leave mostly in the mornings. Taxis also deliver travellers to the **border** (Km102, Ishkashim-Khorog Hwy; ⊙ 9-11.30am & 2-4pm Mon-Fri, 8am-2pm Sat) with Afghanistan (3km, 5TJS).

A permit is needed to cross into the Afghan Wakhan, known as the 'Little Pamir'. This can be organised through a tour operator such as Tajikistan Travel (www.traveltajikistan.net) or through a similar agency in Afghanistan. PECTA (p179) in Khorog also gives reliable advice on border crossing and tours.

OFF THE BEATEN TRACK

THE AFGHAN WAKHAN VALLEY

Unlike the beleaguered south, Afghan's portion of the Wakhan Corridor, on the opposite side of the Pyanj River to the Tajik Wakhan, is both peaceful and open to casual visitors. Arising out of the machinations of the Great Game, the Wakhan Corridor was established as a buffer zone between the Russian and British empires during the 19th and early 20th centuries. Looking across at the tranquil strip of rural life that characterises the Afghan Wakhan today, it's hard to imagine its former strategic importance. Indeed, so remote is this region that residents of part of this corridor must cross into Tajikistan if they want to travel to Kabul. The occasional truck inches along the river's edge on vertiginous paths, but mostly transport in this highly traditional and conservative part of the country is by donkey or mule.

For visitors it's easy enough to cross the border at Ishkashim, although it has to be said that the idea of independent travel here may be more appealing than the reality, given the lack of infrastructure involved in travelling on the Afghan side. A better option is to take a four-day escorted trip from Ishkashim through a tour company such as Tajikistan Travel (www.traveltajikistan.net). PECTA (p179) in Khorog can also give advice on extended trips into Afghanistan, including hikes into the remote Little Pamir.

Afghan visas are usually available within 48 hours in Khorog (a double-entry Tajik visa is required). Crossing the border at Ishkashim is simply a matter of walking across the bridge.

Trying to go it alone is an expensive exercise with visa charges in excess of US$100 for many nationalities (US$200 for US citizens), US$40 return for a taxi for the 6km between the border post and Sultan Eshkashim village in Afghanistan, and US$900 or more per car to proceed to the Little Pamir and back. Given that the track parallels the better road on the Tajiki side for most of the route, sharing similar views but lacking the network of homestays, many travellers may feel content just to observe the Afghan Wakhan from across the Pyanj River.

Tajikistan Travel (www.traveltajikistan.net) offers three-night stays in the Afghan Wakhan, as a round-trip from Ishkashim.

Darshai

🚩 3553 / POP LESS THAN 500 / ELEV 2713M

Darshai is the trail head for a couple of wild routes into the mountains. It's possible to hike along the gorge unaccompanied, but guides are needed to go beyond the owring, or ledge, at the path's narrowest point.

The trek up the Darshai Gorge starts near the bridge and continues around a knoll topped with some minimal fortress ruins. It then follows a clear path up the eastern bank of the side river. In under two hours it's easy enough to reach the trail's star attraction, a photogenic owring, or short section of footpath where the trail becomes so perilously narrow that it has been built out on branches and rocks 'sewn' onto the rock face using wire ropes.

With a guide, a yurt camp can be reached much further up the valley (a five- to eight-hour walk); it is used exclusively by hunting groups in winter but is available to walkers in summer. From there it's a very testing day hike past Mayakovsky Peak (6095m) and across a snowy 4941m pass to reach the signed homestay at Bodomdara in the Shokh Dara Valley.

A local **guide** (US$20/30 per half-/full day) can be tracked down through the **Gulmammad Matrobov Homestay** (📞 5011 6 0822, 9389 2 4013; Darshai Villlage; mattress with half board US$15), although Gulmammad Matrobov himself has hung up his boots. For wildlife photography 'safaris' see www.wildlife-tajikistan.org/tourism-in-darshay.

Yamchun

🚩 3553 / POP LESS THAN 1000 / ELEV 2743M

Two of the Tajik Wakhan's foremost attractions are high above a valley at Yamchun: the 12th-century Yamchun Fort and Bibi Fatima hot springs. Yamchun consists of a number of scattered homesteads at Tughoz and Vichkut strung together by the hairpins that wind up to **Yamchun Fort** (Zulkhomar Fort, Ямчун).

This 12th-century fort is the most impressive of the Wakhan Valley's many tumbledown castle ruins, complete with multiple walls and round watchtowers. The site is reached via a 6km zigzag drive from the main road (towards Bibi Fatima Springs) and sits about 500m above the valley.

The **Bibi Fatima Springs** (admission 10TJS; ⏰ 5am-9pm), probably the nicest in the region, are named after the Prophet Mohammed's daughter. Local women believe they can boost their fertility by visiting the womb-like calcite formations. There are no towels or lockers. Men's and women's bath times alternate throughout the day. The springs are located about 1km uphill from Yamchun Fort.

The valley has several homestay options and there are four simple hotels (or at least larger buildings with beds rather than mattresses), all within 300m of the Bibi Fatima Springs. The best of the lot is the **Bomi Johani Hotel** (📞 9005 6 9955; Bibi Fatima; half board per person US$15), but if you're not dead-set on proximity to the fortress and springs, head back about halfway down to the **Charshanbe Homestay** (📞 938 305239;

HISTORICAL SIGHTS BEYOND YAMCHUN

Some 500m off the main road in Yamg (Ямг) is the reconstructed **Wakhan House Museum** (📞 9345 6 5519; Yamg; admission 10TJS; ⏰ by arrangement) of Sufi mystic, astronomer and musician Mubarak Kadam Wakhani (1843–1903). One room in this brilliant little museum contains ethnographic artefacts and 27 books and 17 poems of the master. The other room is designed as a classic 19th-century Pamiri home with some traditional instruments on display.

On an obvious salt-bleached patch of mountainside directly behind the hamlet of Vrang (Вранг) is a five-level stone monument claimed to be an ancient **Buddhist stupa** (Vrang). Far harder to reach are the dozens of hermit caves in the crumbling cliff-face across the chasm from the stupa.

The ruined Afghan citadel of Qala-e Panja, once the largest settlement in the Wakhan, is visible across the Pyanj River from near Zugband, some 10km west of Langar.

At Zong, 5km west of Langar, the **Abrashim Qala** (Silk Fortress, Vishim Qala; Zong) fortress was built to guard a branch of the Silk Road from Chinese and Afghan invaders. The fortress ruins, while not much in themselves, offer perhaps the most scenic views of the whole Wakhan Valley. From **Mauluda Barieva's Homestay** (📞 9335 0 8083; www.pecta.tj; Zong; half board US$15), signed near Zong's western edge, the ruins are a steep one-hour hike straight up (half an hour back).

Vichkut; half board per person US$15), one of the best in the Wakhan.

The fort and springs are accessed via 6km of hairpin bends winding up from Tughoz (look for Chashmai signs, 3km east of central Ptup). There's no public transport of any description in the area, hence the columns of ladies marching up and down the hillside en route to the bathhouse at the hot springs.

Langar   Лангар

☑ 3553 / POP LESS THAN 2000 / ELEV 2740M

A glorious knot of jagged peaks rise above Langar where the Pamir and Wakhan Rivers join to form the Pyanj River. The village comprises a collection of homesteads scattered through the valley, and the broad open vistas this sudden piece of level, fertile land offers comes as something of a relief after hours of travel through the narrow Wakhan Corridor or across the semi-arid Pamirs.

Langar is more than just a pretty village: it is famous for the inscriptions that mark the steep rock face that rises above the fields nearby. Over 6000 ancient petroglyphs (Langar) have been found here, although sadly many have been spoiled by more modern graffiti. Guides offer to take visitors to a larger, more pristine group of petroglyphs higher up the cliff, but without specialist knowledge this doesn't offer much advantage for the considerable extra effort. An eroded trail leads further up beyond the rock face (around four hours) to a fine camping spot in Engels Meadows with a rare view of Engels Peak (6510m).

By the bridge across the main road from the village *jamoat khana* (prayer house; easily recognisable by its colourful murals decorating the window frames), the meticulously maintained **Shoh Kambari Oftab Mazar** (Langar) is decorated with collections of ram horns and shaded by ancient trees. Commemorating the man credited with bringing Ismailism to Langar, this site is walled and clearly revered lending a strong sense of presence to the place.

Around 10km from Langar, on a promontory fortified for at least 2300 years, the minimal Ratm castle ruins are signposted off the main Wakhan road. A path of sorts leads through fields and across streams towards this panoramic viewpoint. As one of the last (or first) views of the mighty Pyanj River, the constant companion during a journey through the Wakhan Valley, it is worth the 20-minute walk from the road to reach here.

With views from the raised Upper Langar garden and solar-heated showers, **Nigina Homestay** (☑ 9384 8 3720; Upper Langar; half board US$15) is the most appealing, if hardest to find, of official homestays in Langar. The other homestays, including **Davlatkhon Homestay** (☑ 9351 4 8819; Hisor; r incl half board per person US$20; [P]) in Hisor, are signposted along the main road, albeit spread out over a considerable distance. There are further options at nearby Hisor.

There is very little transport originating in Langar. Shared taxis from Langar make the journey to and from Khorog a couple of times a week (check locally as the day changes). The journey takes around eight to 10 hours and much longer when a flood or a rockfall (frequent occurrences) block the road. An occasional taxi goes on through to Dushanbe.

Eastern Pamir Highway

While much of the Western Pamir Hwy is characterised by deeply recessed canyon valleys, alive with full-spate rivers, the Eastern Pamir Hwy is a very different beast. The lonely, high-altitude *pamir* (pastures) of this remarkable landscape are still and almost silent in the thin air. There are few settlements here so inevitably attention is turned from the human story to the natural world, with yaks grazing mid-meadow and marmots standing on sentry duty. Tiny hardy shrubs bristle the high passes, while fields of sun-loving annuals decorate the lakes.

Alichur

☑ 3554 / POP LESS THAN 2000 / ELEV 3942M

Alichur (Km828) is situated in the middle of spectacular high-altitude scenery. In fact the only way to reach it is via three passes, each of which is over 4200m. The vegetation (or relative lack thereof) reflects this above-the-treeline location. On closer inspection the landscape is not as barren as it seems, however, with carpets of low-lying Alpine flowers hunkered down against the bitter winds and thick-furred marmots and yaks grazing on tentative grass shoots. The gateway to two famously beautiful lakes, Bulun-Kul and Yasil-Kul, Alichur itself is a wide scattering of low, whitewashed homesteads.

Mirrorlike lake **Balun-Kul** (3737m) looks magnificent in the morning light, reflecting the mineral streaks of a multicoloured ridge opposite. Close by, the end-of-the-world

EAST OF LANGAR

For those travelling the Wakhan Valley from west to east, Langar marks the point at which the road finally departs from the Pyanj River after days of intimate travel along its canyon banks. Afghanistan and its snowy peaks recedes into the distance and the road begins the long climb up to the highland plateaus of the Pamir proper. With no villages, and just two lonely houses along the 70km between Ratm and the Khargush military checkpoint, driving this lonely, traffic-less track east from Langar feels like entering a different world.

To appreciate the majesty of the stark mountain scenery, it's worth clambering up Panorama Ridge, marked very accurately as a 360-degree viewpoint on Marcus Hauser's *Pamir* map. The steep climb takes 1½ hours (30 minutes back) from a roadside cairn, 7km from Khargush, where the road levels out and the first of two smallish lakes come into view.

With prior permission (via PECTA, p179, in Khorog), it is possible to continue east along the Pamir River from the Khargush checkpoint. The track ambles past protected Zor-Kul. Once christened Lake Victoria, it was considered to be the source of the Oxus River by the 1842 British expedition of Lieutenant Wood. Most travellers, however, head north, rejoining the main Pamir Hwy (M41) near Bulunkul.

---

settlement of Bulunkul (Булункӯл) – reportedly the coldest place in Tajikistan – offers ways in which to connect with the lakes through horse riding and hikes – enquire at **Monira Homestay** (☑ 9005 2 7762; half board per person US$15).

From Bulunkul village, it's a 4km drive or uphill walk to Yashil-Kul, much bigger but arguably less photogenic than neighbouring Balun-Kul. With patience, hikers can find lukewarm springs on the southern side and stone circles at the mouth of the Bolshoi Marjonai River. Technically this requires a Tajik National Park permit (40TJS per day), obtained from PECTA (p179) in Khorog or META (p185) in Murgab.

Murgab   Мурга6

☑ 3554 / POP 10,815 / ELEV 3600M

Utterly isolated in the middle of the high Pamir plateau, the desolate town of Murgab fascinates as an example of life lived in extremis. The people here are used to a hard life; mostly Tajik and Pamiri, they share with surrounding Kyrgyz communities the knowledge of how to survive with very little means at their disposal. Freezing cold in winter and furnace hot in summer, the town has an air of gritty determination about it, from the siphoning of petrol if the tanker doesn't arrive to the make-do-and-mend attitude of a bazaar inside makeshift containers. On exceptionally clear days, the snowy hulk of Muztagh Ata (7546m) hangs like a cloud upon the eastern horizon, above the

dust storms that whirl around the dedicated plain below. It seems to draw visitors deeper into the high Pamirs, and Murgab is historically the base from which to do this.

On Friday the menfolk of the town walk down to the attractive old Jameh Mosque, on the edge of the flood plain below town. It makes for a pleasant stroll and the gold-toothed elders in the vicinity are ever welcoming to those showing an interest.

🛏 Sleeping & Eating

The **Pamir Hotel** (☑ 9192 6 1289, 9005 0 5863; dm/s/tw with shared bathroom US$10/20/30, r with bathroom US$40, lunch/dinner 15-18TJS) attracts large groups of hikers, motorcyclists and the odd hardy cyclist. For a quieter night's stay, there are a number of typical Pamiri homesteads offering mattresses in shared rooms with outside bathrooms and long-drop toilets. The **Sary Köl Lodge** (☑ 935 473391, 935 697101; Sorok Let Pobieda; d/r incl breakfast per person US$10/13; @) (1.5km northeast of the centre), **Erali Guesthouse** (☑ 919 260943; mattress/B&B/half board US$10/12/15) (on the slope northeast of Agroinvest Bank) and Suhrob Guesthouse (behind the apartment block at Somoni 33, around 200m northwest of Pamir Hotel) are among the best. All homestays offer half board if given some notice. A list and directions is supplied by META (p185).

Most travellers dine at their accommodation. For longer stays and different company, **Aida** (mains/sambusa 10/7TJS; ⊙8am-5pm, or on a whim) is marginally the best of the handful of basic cafes backing onto the container-box bazaar, though **Hojion Cafe** (Osh; mains 20TJS; ⊙9am-6pm) gives it some competition. Without doubt, though, the most obvious place to head for supper is the Pamir Hotel. It serves up huge, wholesome meals and has a shop for beer and snacks. Basic groceries and a small choice of vegetables and fruit are available from the bazaar.

ℹ Information

Murgab district (as far west as Bulunkul) operates on Kyrgyzstan time, ie one hour ahead of Dushanbe and Khorog.

TCell has the best mobile signal in town, but Megafon also works here and covers the outlying valleys too.

Electricity supply is irregular, and often very weak; Pamir Hotel has a more regular supply than most. Bring a safety plug to protect electrical gadgets from power surge.

Local women at **Yak House** (☑919 481774, Salamat 919 482685; Murgab House; ⊙9am-5pm Mon-Fri or by arrangement) are encouraged to supplement their income through learning old skills. Woollen shoulder-bags, socks and felt *shyrdak* squares are on sale in a building that incorporates architectural elements from both Kyrgyz yurts and Pamiri houses. It's 1.8km northeast along the M41 from Pamir Hotel.

TOURIST INFORMATION & TRAVEL AGENCIES

META (Murgab Ecotourism Association; ☑Gulnara (Director) 935 181808, Januzak (President) 934 652005; www.meta.tj; M41, Osh 102; ⊙call ahead) was the original driving force for community tourism in Murgab and its website remains an ever-evolving treasure trove of resources. The office, intermittently open, offers helpful advice and some brochures. It can theoretically organise permits for the Tajik National Park, but this is more easily managed through PECTA (p179) in Khorog.

Local tour agencies include **Pamir Highway Adventure** (☑904 091752; www.pamirhighway adventure.com), **Pamir Offroad Adventure Guide** (☑900 503076; www.pamirorat.com; Ayni 57) and **Pamir Guides** (☑917 328228, 9353 8 2545; www.pamirguides.org).

Kyrgyzstan-based **Pamir Trek** (☑+996 772 376036; www.pamirtrek.com; horse trekking per person per day from US$82) is a useful agency if travelling from Osh.

ℹ Getting There & Away

From the bazaar, vehicles (4WDs or minivans) head to a limited number of destinations. Ideally a place should be arranged one day ahead to

---

SIGHTS AROUND MURGHAB

Soviet archaeologists apparently took shelter in the caves at **Shakty** (Шахты; 4200m) during a storm one night in 1958, only to awake the next morning to the perfectly preserved red-ink paintings of a boar hunt (and strange bird man). Visitors are asked to keep a distance from these Neolithic paintings to avoid damaging them. The cave, a five-minute scramble uphill, is impossible to find without a knowledgeable driver-guide. The site is 50km southwest of Murgab (25km off the Pamir Hwy) in the dramatic Kurteskei Valley.

At the head of the Ak-Suu Valley, **Konye-Kurgan** (Old Tomb) is a collection of interesting beehive-shaped tombs. Just 7km east of Murgab, they make an diverting excursion from town or a drive by on the way to Shaimak, deep in the heart of this remote valley.

---

avoid waiting several hours while vehicles fill up. Frequency reduces in cold months. Murgab can be cut off entirely for a day or two after heavy winter snows or summer flash floods.

Two or three vehicles leave most mornings (120TJS, seven to nine hours, 320km) for Khorog. One or two vehicles head each morning for Osh (150TJS, around 12 hours, 420km).

Shared taxis for Rang-Kul (20TJS) leave in the late afternoon from behind Aida Kafe in the bazaar, returning the next morning.

There's no formal transport along the Wakhan Corridor, but 4WDs are available for multiday charter through travel agencies or from the taxi stand at the bazaar.

Pshart & Madiyan Valleys
Долины Пшарт и Мадиян

Two photogenic valleys strike west from either end of Murgab. Pshart, the more northerly valley, is initially arid and colourful with mineral layers. In contrast, the Madiyan Valley's rugged rock walls are set against lush green riverside pastures and even copses of small trees. This makes for an especially lovely sight before sunset around the tiny hamlet of Ak-Tal (Km32), whose tiny whitewashed mosque adds foreground to the rugged scene. From Ak-Tal, a corrugated 4WD track crosses the river and winds through the landscape towards isolated and barely accessible hot springs.

TAJIKISTAN TAJIKISTAN TODAY

AT-CHABYSH FESTIVAL

Organised by a French NGO concerned with the promotion of traditional horsemanship and the maintenance of genuine Kyrgyz horse breeds, the annual **At-Chabysh festival** (www.atchabysh. org) rotates each year between countries in Central Asia. See its website for more information.

There is a long and strenuous day hike between the Pshart and Madiyan valleys that requires a guide for navigation. The trail starts from the Gumbezkul side valley near a horse-breeding centre and yurtstay at the point where the Pshart Valley divides. After some steep scrambles and stunning views from Gumbezkul Pass (4731m), the path emerges on the Madiyan Valley road around Km18 from Murgab.

A couple of yurtstays provide the only accommodation in these remote valleys, but these should not be relied upon if hiking independently. Tour companies generally bring hikers back to Murgab. Tour companies operating out of Murgab can organise a guide plus 4WD drop-off or pick-up at either end of a Madiyan Valley trek for around US$150. A minivan taxi to Pshart yurt camp costs 95TJS.

Karakul & Ysil-Art Pass

Hunkered down at the edge of the eastern shore of the eponymous lake, Karakul has an embattled quality to it as if it has had to weather one too many storms but has survived regardless. The village sits within the Unesco-listed **Tajik National Park** (☑ 935 81 3390, 3522 2 9123; tnpgbao@mail.ru; per person per day 15TJS, plus for each vehicle 20TJS), but park tickets (available from PECTA in Khorog) are not needed for transitting or sleeping overnight in Karakul village.

Although salty, lake Kara-Kul is frozen and snow-covered until May, but throughout the summer this huge lake is transformed into a beautiful, sky-blue lozenge that changes colour with depth. An attempt by META to declare it the world's highest navigable lake, beating Lake Titicaca, is not likely to succeed, but a jetty erected a few years ago has enabled summer boat trips to the island and is the launching point for the **Roof of the World Regatta** (www.visitpamirs.com/roof-of-the-world-regatta; Karakul; ☉ July).

Several families offer simple accommodation in very well-signed homestays, all walking distance from the lakeshore. There is no accommodation at either the Tajik or Kyrgyz border posts, and due to the sensitivities of the area, this is not an advisable place to camp.

ⓘ Getting There & Away

North of Murgab, this high-altitude section of the Pamir Hwy follows a fenced area of 'neutral zone' between Tajikistan and China and crosses the Ak-Baital Pass (4655m). The **Tajik border post** (☉ 24hr) is 63km north of Karakul, just before the crest of the Kyzyl-Art Pass (4282m), from which there are briefly spectacular views of colourful mountain spires. The Kyrgyz post is 20km further on at Bordöbö, 24km south of Sary Tash. The 20km in between the two posts represents a no man's land. Taxis can cross this no man's land, but this has to be organised in advance to avoid getting stranded at either border post. The crossing is simple enough but can be bitterly cold even in midsummer and a warm layer is highly recommended while waiting at the immigration and customs points.

UNDERSTAND TAJIKISTAN

Tajikistan Today

Travelling through the rural hinterland of Tajikistan's tranquil countryside today, it's difficult to imagine that the evident peace is not intrinsic to the landscape but has been hard won through political strife, economic challenge and cultural upheaval. The civil war of the 1990s has quietly receded into history and despite the occasional ethnic and regional tension, modern Tajiki society is embracing of a new spirit of unity that is helping put the past behind while grasping the new opportunities ahead.

While nominally a democracy, it's fair to say that Tajikistan's interpretation of the concept is constrained by the role of the current president. Self-styled 'Leader of the Nation', President Emomali Rahmon came to power during the civil war and used the last challenge to his regime in September 2015 (which resulted in a number of armed conflicts close to Dushanbe) to strengthen his tenure and remove opposition.

Despite this, a referendum supported Rahmon's bid for unlimited terms of office and lifelong immunity from prosecution, suggesting he has the backing of many of Tajik's citizens. By and large he is credited with having ended the civil war and, in a country with little appetite among the general public for returning to civil strife, for maintaining law and order.

Under Rahmon's tenure (his fourth term in office), Tajikistan's economy has improved and the country became a member of the World Trade Organization in March 2013. New infrastructure (resurfaced roads, mobile phone networks, the building of the world's tallest dam in Roghun in the Garm Valley) are helping to secure the future and a general sense of optimism is reflected in the erection of fine civic monuments, particularly in the capital.

Economic challenges remain, however – inevitable perhaps given the country's extreme geography. In the summer of 2015 many roads in the Gorno Badakhshan Autonomous Oblast (GBAO) were severely damaged by flooding and are still far from repaired, and every spring brings new demands on limited resources as rock falls damage roads and power lines, and cut off remote communities. The country remains largely unattractive to foreign investors, resulting in few employment opportunities. Indeed many (more than one million by some accounts) Tajik citizens continue to work as expatriates, mainly in Russia; their remittances, despite the fluctuations in international currency, contribute to nearly half of Tajikistan's GDP.

While aluminium and cotton together constitute around 80% of Tajikistan's official exports, unofficially it is estimated that as much as 50% of Tajikistan's economic activity in the last decade has been linked to Afghanistan's narcotics trade. Inevitably, then, there is a need to find alternative revenue streams and much hope is being pinned on Tajikistan's main resource, namely water. With 40% of Central Asia's water supply, Tajikistan is defying the wrath of thirsty neighbours and harnessing some of this potential through the new Roghun Dam project. Work has begun in earnest on this major enterprise with the commissioning of Italian contractors, Salini Impregilo, in 2016. The much anticipated hydroelectricity plant that forms part of the project will generate a major new source of revenue; at full power it would supply 80% of Tajikistan's electricity requirements and provide much-needed export revenues.

Tajikistan is still in the process of formalising the exact delimitation of its borders with Kyrgyzstan and Uzbekistan, while the Chinese border was only settled in 2011. The Tajik government agreed to give Beijing 1142 sq km of territory (around Rangkul), much to the dismay of the people of Badakhshan who felt betrayed by their fellow citizens.

The Afghanistan border remains the most sensitive issue of foreign diplomacy, however. In the spring of 2017 there were clashes between the Taliban and Afghan government forces close to the border with Tajikistan, with conflict threatening to spill over. Fortunately this did not materialise, but the GBAO remains on alert. The Afghan markets hosted along the Wakhan Corridor in Tajikistan act as bellwether of regional tension; these were closed at the time of writing and visitors were being reminded to keep an eye on consular advisories and remain flexible in case of regional closure.

History

Tajikistan, always something of a poor relation given the challenges posed by its geography and topography, shares much of the history of neighbouring Central Asian nations. With a related language, the country maintains close cultural ties with its westward neighbour, Iran, while the Russian mantle of much of the 20th century continues to lend a Soviet character to Tajikistan's modern identity. Over the past two decades, however, the country has begun to emerge as a distinctive nation proud of its own regional traditions.

TAJIKISTAN TODAY FOR VISITORS

Despite the occasional threats from across the border, overall Tajikistan remains a peaceful country to visit. With much hope vested in the growing tourist trade, there is a concerted effort from the government official to the homestay host to ensure that visitors are kept safe and experience nothing other than a traditional Sogdian or Pamiri welcome. Nonetheless, casting an eye over the destination today, as reflected in consular advisories, is a sensible precaution before travelling.

DIGGING UP THE PAST

Visiting Tajikistan's best museums you'll often see finds from and references to a whole series of ancient temple and city sites. Although today most are little more than undulations in the earth, each has a glorious history. Discoveries from these sites are showcased at Dushanbe's National Museum (p146). The website www.afc.ryukoku.ac.jp/tj has more.

Tajik Ancestry

Tajik ancestry is a murky area, with roots reaching back to the Bactrians and Sogdians. Tombs from the eastern Pamir show that Saka-Usun tribes were grazing their flocks here from the 5th century BC, when the climate was considerably more lush than today.

In the 1st century BC the Bactrian empire covered most of what is now northern Afghanistan. Their contemporaries, the Sogdians, inhabited the Zerafshan (Zeravshan) Valley in present-day western Tajikistan, where a few traces of this civilisation remain near Penjikent. Alexander the Great battled the Sogdians and besieged Cyropol (Istaravshan), before founding modern-day Khojand. The Sogdians were displaced in the Arab conquest of Central Asia during the 7th century AD. The Sogdian hero Devastich made a last stand against the Arabs at Mount Mug in the Zerafshan (Zeravshan) Mountains, before he was finally beheaded by the Muslim vanquishers.

Modern Tajikistan extends back to the glory days of the Persian Samanid dynasty (AD 819–992), a period of frenzied creative activity that reached its peak during the rule of Ismail Samani (AD 849–907), transliterated in modern Tajik as Ismoil Somoni. Bukhara, the dynastic capital, became the Islamic world's centre of learning, nurturing great talents such as the philosopher-scientist Abu Ali ibn-Sina (known in the West as Avicenna) and the poet Rudaki. Both are now competitively claimed as native sons by Iran, Afghanistan and Tajikistan.

A Blurring of Identity

Under the Samanids, the great towns of Central Asia were Persian, which is one reason Tajikistan still claims Samarkand and Bukhara as its own. However, at the end of the 10th century a succession of Turkic invaders followed up their battlefield successes with cultural conquest. Despite contrasting cultures, the two peoples cohabited peacefully, unified by religion. The Persian-speaking Tajiks adopted Turkic culture and the numerically superior Turks absorbed the Tajik people. Both weathered conquests by the Mongols and Timur (Tamerlane), though most of the territory of modern Tajikistan remained on the fringes of the Timurid empire.

From the 15th century onwards, the Tajiks were subjects of the emirate of Bukhara, which received 50% of Badakhshan's ruby production as a tax. In the mid-18th century the Afghans moved up to engulf all lands south of the Amu-Darya (Oxus River), along with their resident Tajik population, and later seized parts of Badakhshan including, temporarily, the Rushan and Shughnan regions.

The Great Game & the Basmachi

As part of the Russian Empire's thrust southwards, St Petersburg made the emirate of Bukhara a vassal state in 1868, which gave Russia effective control over what now passes for northern and western Tajikistan. But the Pamirs (today's eastern Tajikistan) remained a no man's land, an anomaly that led to a strategic duel between Russia and British India that author Rudyard Kipling was to immortalise as the 'Great Game'. After visiting Murgab, Alichur and Rang-Kul, the famed explorer Francis Younghusband was thrown out of the upper Wakhan by his tsarist counterpart, sparking an international crisis. Russia built a string of forts, including at Murgab, across the Pamirs to reinforce Russian claims to the territory. Border treaties of 1893 and 1895 finally defined Tajikistan's current borders, leaving the Wakhan Corridor as Afghanistan's eccentric cartographical buffer between the two empires.

Following the Russian Revolution of 1917, new provisional governments were established in Central Asia and the Tajiks found themselves first part of the Turkestan (1918–24) and then the Uzbekistan (1924–29) Soviet Socialist Republics (SSRs), despite pushing for an autonomous Islamic-oriented republic. In 1930 Muslim *basmachi* guerrillas (literally 'rebels') under the leadership of Enver Pasha began a campaign to free the region from Bolshevik rule. It took four years for the Bolsheviks to crush this resistance, and in the process entire villages were razed. The surviving guerrillas melted away into Afghanistan, from where they continued to make sporadic raids over the border. Much of the population also fled south during the decade that followed to avoid a series of reprisals, repressions and, later, forced movements that saw whole villages removed from the mountains (notably around Garm) and moved to the Vakhsh Valley to cultivate cotton plantations.

Soviet Statehood

In 1924, when the Soviet Border Commission set about redefining Central Asia, the Tajiks were granted their own autonomous republic (ASSR). Although initially only a satellite of Soviet Uzbekistan, this represented the first official Tajik state. In 1929 the ASSR was upgraded to a full union republic (SSR), although, possibly in reprisal for the *basmachi* revolt, Samarkand and Bukhara – where over 700,000 Tajiks still lived – remained in Uzbekistan. As recently as 1989 the government of Soviet Tajikistan was demanding the 'return' of areas lost in this cultural amputation. Today tensions with the modern government of Uzbekistan over these cultural centres remain.

The Bolsheviks never fully trusted the Tajikistan SSR and during the 1930s almost all Tajiks in positions of influence within the government were replaced by representatives from Moscow. Some industrialisation of Tajikistan was undertaken following

WWII, but the republic remained heavily reliant on imports from the rest of the Soviet Union for food and standard commodities, as become painfully apparent after the 1991 collapse of the Soviet trading system.

In the mid-1970s, an underground Islamic Renaissance Party started gathering popular support, especially in the south around Kurgan-Tyube (Kurgonteppa). This region had been neglected by Dushanbe's ruling communist elite, who were mainly drawn from the prosperous northern city of Leninabad (now Khojand). Two 1979 events sent serious ripples through Tajik society. In Iran, the Shah was toppled by an Islamic revolution, and the same year the Soviets began an invasion of Afghanistan, launched largely through Tajikistan. The disparity between truth and propaganda became apparent as aid flowed to Afghanistan while Tajikistan suffered with the USSR's worst levels of education, poverty and infant mortality.

From Civil Unrest...

Moscow managed to hold the lid on the pressure-cooker of resentment, suppressed religious sentiments and clan-based tensions that had existed in the region for centuries until the Soviet Union began to collapse. The first serious disturbances in Tajikistan occurred on 12 February 1990 when it was rumoured that Armenian refugees were to be resettled in Dushanbe, a city already short on housing. Riots, deaths and the imposition of a state of emergency followed. Several opposition parties emerged as a result of the ensuing crackdown.

TAJIKISTAN HISTORY

THE OPIUM HIGHWAY

Although beyond the observable experience of most visitors, Tajikistan has developed an unfortunate reputation as the heroin highway of Central Asia. Worldwide, the country ranks third in seizures of opiates after Iran and Pakistan. Not so surprisingly, perhaps, as it shares well over 1000km of porous border with the world's largest opium producer (Afghanistan), much more than this gets through with estimates of around 200 tonnes of heroin passing unimpeded through Tajikistan each year.

Warlords and criminal gangs control most of the business, although a few members of the army, police, Afghan Taliban and border guards are also alleged to be implicated in the trade. In 2005 a homemade aircraft (a parachute with a motor attached) was shot down flying above the border with Tajikistan with 18kg of heroin. In 2009 Russian police seized 80kg of heroin from smugglers on the Dushanbe–Moscow train, a line known to anti-narcotic police as the 'Heroin Express'.

Over the years drug money has financed everything in Tajikistan from weapons for the civil war to the poppy palaces that line the Varzob Valley north of Dushanbe. Without more integrated support from international agencies, it's hard to see how this modern use of the Silk Road will be brought under control.

On 9 September 1991, following a failed Moscow coup, Tajikistan followed other Soviet SSRs by declaring independence. Less than two weeks later Dushanbe's central Lenin statue was toppled, watched by a large demonstration of rural Muslims bussed into the capital by Hezb-e Nahzat-e Islami. In November of 1991 elections appeared to favour Rakhmon Nabiev, a former Tajik Communist Party chief (1982–85) who riled the opposition by consolidating an old-guard, Leninabad-oriented power base rather than accommodating the various clan-factions that make up the nation. Sit-in demonstrations on Dushanbe's central square escalated to violent clashes. In August 1992 anti-government demonstrators stormed the presidential palace and took hostages. A coalition government was formed, but sharing power between regional clans, religious leaders and former communists proved impossible. As a way out of the internecine conflict, Emomali Rakhmonov (now known as Rahmon), the former communist boss of Kulob district, was chosen to front the government. Frustrated by its marginal position and seeing no future in a collapsing Tajikistan, GBAO (Eastern Tajikistan) nominally declared its independence in 1992.

Tajikistan descended into a brutal civil war that claimed over 60,000 lives. Kulyabi forces, led by Sanjak Safarov (who had previously spent 23 years in prison for murder), embarked on a campaign of ethnic cleansing. Anyone found in Dushanbe with a Badakhshan or Khatlon ID card was shot on the spot. November 1992 elections did nothing to resolve the conflict (the opposition in exile refused to take part in the vote) and the Islamic opposition continued the war from bases in the Karategin region and Afghanistan, echoing the *basmachi* campaigns of 70 years earlier. An economic blockade of Badakhshan led to severe famine in the Pamirs, whose people were kept alive by aid from the Aga Khan Foundation.

In late 1994 a second presidential election was held, won unsurprisingly by Rakhmonov – he was the only candidate as opposition parties had been outlawed.

Precarious Peace

Pressure from Russia (which retained forces at some 50 former Soviet military posts along the Afghan border), along with the faltering loyalty of military commanders, forced the government to negotiate with the opposition-in-exile. A December 1996 ceasefire was followed by a peace agreement on 27 June 1997 creating a power-sharing organisation. This guaranteed the United Tajik Opposition (UTO) 30% of the seats in a coalition government in return for an end to the fighting.

The civil war proved catastrophic, economically as well as physically. Always the poorest of the Soviet republics, Tajikistan's GDP per capita plunged a further 70% since independence. Although some fighting rattled on until 2001, overall peace prevailed and the reconstruction of the country has since been impressively rapid.

People

With their predominantly Persian ancestry and language, Tajiks constitute about 85% of the population, 14% of which are ethnic Uzbeks. Although 'Tajik' only came to denote a distinct nationality during the 20th century, there is a strong national identification, signified by men through the wearing of a black silk hat with white arabesque decoration. Women, on national occasions, wear a tunic of striped cloth made from a traditional textile known as 'Atlas'. In Badakhshan, Pamiris speak related local languages and follow Ismaili Islam, in contrast to their northern-western neighbours who are mostly Sunni. In the far northeast of the country, especially around Murgab district east of Alichur, most people are Kyrgyz. Average family sizes are high and over 30% of Tajikistan's population is under the age of 14.

Arts

When Tajikistan was split from Uzbekistan in 1929, the new nation state was obliged to leave behind much of its cultural baggage. The new Soviet order set about providing a replacement pantheon of arts, introducing modern drama, opera and ballet, and sending Tajik aspirants to study in Moscow and Leningrad. The policy paid early dividends and the 1940s produced a golden era of Tajik theatre. A kind of Soviet fame came to some Tajik novelists and poets, such as Mirzo Tursunzade, Loic Sherali and Sadruddin Ayni, the last now remembered for his campaign to eliminate all Arabic expressions and references to Islam from the Tajik tongue.

Since independence, ancient figures from the region's Persian past have been revived in an attempt to foster a sense of national identity. The most famous of these figures is Ismail Samani (Ismoil Somoni), but also revered is the 10th-century philosopher-scientist Abu Ali ibn-Sina (Avecinna, 980–1037), author of two of the most important books in the history of medicine. He was born in Bukhara when it was the seat of the Persian Samanids. Rudaki (888–941), now celebrated as the father of Persian verse and commemorated at a museum complex near his birthplace in Penjikent, served as court poet at the same court. Tajiks also venerate Firdausi (940–1020), a poet and composer of the *Shah Nama* (*Book of Kings*), the Persian national epic, and Omar Khayam (1048–1131), of *Rubaiyat* fame. Both were born in present-day Iran at a time when it was part of an empire that also included the territory now known as Tajikistan. Kamalddin Bekzod (1455–1535), a brilliant miniaturist painter from Herat, is similarly revered for his contribution to the arts.

Pamiris have a particular veneration for Nasir Khusraw (1004–1088), an Ismaili philosopher, poet and preacher who worked in Merv and was exiled to Badakhshan. Here he wrote his *Safarname,* the account of his extensive seven-year travels throughout the Muslim world.

Tajik Persian poetry is fused with music by *hafiz* (bard musicians). *Falak* is a popular form of melancholic folk music, often sung a cappella. Music and dance are particularly popular among the Pamiri and Kulyabi.

Environment

The Land

Landlocked Tajikistan is Central Asia's smallest republic. Although the western third comprises some scattered lowland plains (particularly around the rice- and fruit-growing Fergana Valley), 93% of the country is mountainous and more than half lies above 3000m. The high-altitude Pamir Plateau in the east is a mostly semi-arid region in contrast to the towering mountain ranges in the central and northwestern regions, which are spliced by fertile valleys full of terraced orchards and wheat fields.

At 7495m, Koh-i-Somoni (formerly Pik Kommunizma) is the highest peak in the former Soviet Union and its tributary Fedchenko Glacier, at 72km, is one of the

> ### RECOMMENDED READING
>
> Essential reading is *Land Beyond the River: The Untold Story of Central Asia* (2003) by former BBC Central Asia correspondent Monica Whitlock, who brilliantly pieces together the 20th-century history of Tajikistan through the life stories of local individuals who witnessed and shaped it. That's usefully supplemented by Paul Bergne's 2007 *The Birth of Tajikistan: National Identity and the Origins of the Republic* (2007). Middleton's more portable *The Pamirs – History, Archaeology and Culture* is sold at PECTA (p179) in Khorog for 60TJS.

world's longest. However, for pure spectacle, the most beautiful formations are arguably those in the spiky Fan Mountains, along with the distinctive Peak Engels (6510m), one of the world's toughest climbs.

Tajikistan's most significant rivers include Pyanj, which forms the Afghanistan border, and the Surkhob/Vakhsh whose potential for hydroelectric power generation holds both opportunity and threat.

The mountainous eastern border with China was redrawn in 2011, ceding around 1% of Tajikistan's territory to its powerful neighbour. To the north, Tajikistan's Stalin-drawn jigsaw of borders with Kyrgyzstan and Uzbekistan include the disconnected Vorukh enclave of Tajik territory stranded completely inside Kyrgyzstan's Fergana Valley region.

For administrative purposes the country has three *viloyat* (provinces): Sughd (Khojand), Khatlon (Kurgonteppa) and the 60,000-sq-km autonomous GBAO/Kohistani Badakhshan (Khorog). That leaves much of the central region (including the Garm Valley) ruled directly from Dushanbe.

Wildlife

Tajikistan is renowned in zoological circles as having one of the largest number of wild sheep in the world. In 2010 and 2012 surveys of Tajikistan's High Pamir area found around 2400 ibex (*echki* or *kyzyl kyik*) and 23,700 Marco Polo sheep living in the region (*arkhar* in Kyrgyz). Carefully controlled trophy-hunting of these iconic animals is practised in certain areas. Some argue that this has helped to secure numbers, as foreign hunters pay substantial tour fees (typically US$30,000 to US$60,000), which partly fund animal protection programs. They also say it has helped to limit instances of poaching. Animal rights groups argue that the killing of animals in the name of conservation is never an acceptable approach.

The Pamirs also support a tiny number of snow leopards. Around the Kayrakkum Reservoir (east of Khojand in Northern Tajikistan) there's a critically threatened population of goitered gazelles (*jeyran*).

Of the country's many attractive bird species, one of the most eye-catching is the bright turquoise European roller, often seen around Garm. Some unique butterfly species exist around Lake Sarez.

Environmental Issues

The 26,000-sq-km Tajik (Pamir) National Park was founded in 1992 as the largest in Central Asia, covering a significant 18% of Tajikistan. The park's recognition as a Unesco World Heritage Site in 2013 has helped consolidate the park's status.

The lack of burnable fuel in the eastern Pamir has led to the disappearance of the slow-growing (and fast-burning) *tersken* bush within a radius of 100km from Murgab, adding to desertification in the treeless region. This has contributed to the view that the growing population of Murgab is environmentally unsustainable despite the increasing use of solar and wind power, with wind turbines now providing electricity to run the new mobile phone transmitters.

While a very severe winter in 2017 has put discussion on global warming somewhat in the shade, there's no denying that Tajikistan's glaciers have been retreating. The cause remains to be fully proven.

Food & Drink

Despite sharing a similar cuisine with the neighbours, Tajikistan does have a few local specialities. A popular lunch dish is kurutob (p147): that's fatir bread morsels layered with onion, tomato, parsley and coriander and doused in a yoghurt-based sauce. Tasty *chakka* (known as *yakka* to Tajik speakers around Samarkand and Bukhara) is curd mixed with herbs, typically served with flat bread. Less commonly available Tajik dishes include *nahud sambusa* (chickpea samosas), *nahud shavla* (chickpea porridge)

and *oshi siyo halav,* a unique herb soup. It's worth looking out for *tuhum barak,* a tasty egg-filled ravioli coated with sesame-seed oil.

In Badakhshan *borj* – a meat and grain mix that resembles savoury porridge – is something of an acquired taste and even less instantly embraced is *shir chai,* somewhere between milk tea and Tibetan butter tea. Once the palate is initiated, however, it makes for a good breakfast in the Pamirs, along with rice pudding or *shir gurch (shir brench* in Tajik).

Many of these specialities turn up at lunchtime. Lunch is the main meal for many Tajiks, followed by a short nap. For travellers, unmarked lunch stops (often in pretty gardens overlooking a river) seem to be rooted out by local drivers as if by magic. These teahouses always have a brew on the go and in the absence of specialities, they always offer generally delicious, simple dishes such as meat or vegetable soups or small plates of fried, marinated meat eaten often with yoghurt. The turnover at these places is generally high and trustworthy and they offer a wonderful glimpse of life revolving around Tajikistan's highways – the lifelines of local communities.

Tea is the chief drink of choice in Tajikistan, and chaikhanas (chaykhana locally), some housed in traditional wooden-timbered buildings, are common all over the country, catering to this national drink. In urban centres, the Russian heritage has given rise to some lively bars and these offer a modest nightlife, especially in Dushanbe. Both Hissar and Dushanbe brew their own beer, though bottled Russian imports like the Baltika range are the most common.

SURVIVAL GUIDE

ⓘ Directory A–Z

ACCOMMODATION

Tajik cities offer respectable midrange and some international hotels. Good budget accommodation is supplied through the wide network of homestays across most of rural Tajikistan. These simple lodgings (US$10 to US$15) offer excellent value for money with meals by request (US$5 per meal). While external toilets, shared showers and mattresses rather than beds are the norm, they offer incomparable access to prime beauty spots. Community tourism organisations supply helpful lists; try PECTA (p179), META (p185) or ZTDA (p161).

ACTIVITIES

Trekking is the main outdoor activity in Tajikistan with extensive guided options ($20 to $40 per day) in the Fan Mountains around Artush and Alaudin Lakes. Rock climbers head for Margeb where Zamin-Karor is a near-vertical 1km rock wall, while acclimatised DIY mountaineers set up camp in Bachor in the central Pamirs.

CUSTOMS REGULATIONS

Money Less than US$5000 does not need to be declared.

Goods 'Reasonable quantities' of licit goods for personal use can be imported without charge for those over 18 years of age.

Antiques and cultural valuables All items of antique or cultural value require special permission from Customs to be exported.

DANGERS & ANNOYANCES

Generally Tajikistan is a safe travel destination.
➡ Around 7.5 sq km of landmines and UXO (unexploded ordnance) remain from the civil war in remote border zones; this is scheduled for clearance by 2020.

➡ Altitude sickness is a serious risk when hiking above 3500m without acclimatisation or driving the Pamir Hwy in a single day from Osh to Karakul or Murgab. Sufferers should retreat to lower ground if symptoms persist.

➡ Malaria is present in southwestern Tajikistan along the Afghan border and lower Vakhsh Valley as far north as Kurgonteppa.

➡ Bedbugs can be annoying in rural accommodation.

EMBASSIES & CONSULATES

Most embassies are located in Dushanbe.

Afghan Embassy (☑ 372 36 9902; www.afghanembassy.tj; Makhsum; ☺ 9am–noon & 2-4pm Mon-Fri)

Chinese Embassy (☑ 372 24 2007; www.tj.china-embassy.org; Rudaki 143; ☺ 9am–noon Mon, Wed & Fri)

French Embassy (☑ 372 21 5037; www.tjambafrance.org; Rakhimzade 17, proezd No 2; ☺ 9am-5pm Mon-Thu)

German Embassy (☑ 372 21 2189; www.duschanbe.diplo.de; Somoni 59/1; ☺ 8.30am-12.30pm Mon-Fri)

Iranian Embassy (☑ 372 21 0072; iranembassy.tj@gmail.com; Tehran 18; ☺ 8.30am-12.30pm)

Kazakhstan Embassy (☑ 372 21 8940; www.kazakhembassy.tj; Husseinzoda 31/1; ☺ 9.30am-noon Mon, Tue, Thu & Fri)

Kyrgyz Embassy (☑ 372 24 2611; www.kgembassy.tj; Said Nosirov 50)

Pakistan Embassy (☑ 372 21 1729, 372 27 6255; www.mofa.gov.pk/tajikistan; Azizbekov 20a, enter via Kurbonov; ☺ 10am-1pm Mon-Fri)

Russian Embassy (☑ 372 36 2441; www.rusemb.tj; Sino 29/31; ☺ 10am-12.30pm & 3-5.30pm Mon, 9am-12.30pm & 3-5.30pm Wed-Fri)

Turkish Embassy (☑ 487 02 4108; www.dushanbe.emb.mfa.gov.tr; Rudaki 15; ☺ 9am–1pm & 2-5pm Mon-Fri, visa application 10am–noon)

Turkmen Embassy (☑ 372 24 2640; www.tajikistan.tmembassy.gov.tm/en; Akhunbabaev 10; ☺ application 9.30am-12.30pm Mon-Fri, document collection 3-4pm)

UK Embassy (☑ 372 24 2221; www.gov.uk/world/organisations/british-embassy-dushanbe; Mirzo Tursunzoda 65; ☺ 9am-5pm Mon-Fri)

US Embassy (☑ 372 29 2000; www.tj.usembassy.gov; Somoni 109)

Uzbek Embassy (☑ 372 24 7539; www.uzbekistan.tj; Sanoi 32; ☺ 9am–noon Mon-Fri)

ETIQUETTE

➡ Shoes should be removed before entering all houses, homestays and museums. Slippers are often provided even in hotels.

➡ Public displays of affection and impinging on personal space should be avoided.

➡ Public gender roles are clearly defined and offence may be given if appearing to question this.

LGBTIQ TRAVELLERS

Male gay sex is illegal in Tajikistan. Affection shown between members of the same sex in public is generally considered a sign of friendship not of intimate relationship. In common with other parts of Central Asia, there is no obvious signposting of the LGBTIQ community.

MAPS

➡ Marcus Hauser's 1:500,000 maps cover Tajikistan in three very accurate, detailed sheets: *The Pamirs, Northern Tajikistan* and *Southern Tajikistan*. Each is available at www.geckomaps.com.

➡ A series of detailed maps is downloadable as an offline Android smart-phone app through www.oruxmaps.com.

MEDICAL SERVICES

Clinics are available in main towns but overall the country's medical facilities are underfunded and ill-equipped. Non-prescription medicines (mostly Russian brands) are available in pharmacies in Dushanbe, Khujand, Penjikent and Khorog at reasonable cost, but availability is not guaranteed outside the capital. There are very few opticians even in Dushanbe.

The most important health condition to be aware of in Tajikistan, other than the effects of increased radiation from the sun at high altitude, is altitude sickness. This can be avoided by taking time to aclimatise by overnighting at slowly increasing altitudes before attempting treks at 3000m or over. Some medication can alleviate the symptoms, but the only cure for accute mountain sickness is to descend to lower altitudes. Untreated, it can be fatal.

Health Insurance

Given the nature of the roads and the remoteness of the area, comprehensive cover is required for off-road driving, trekking and medical evacuation.

Tap Water

It is not safe to drink tap water in Tajikistan, due to *Giardia lamblia* which causes diarrhoea and other intestinal infection. Bottled water is widely available.

MONEY

Bargaining is expected in the bazaars but not in shops where fixed prices are the norm.

ATMs are available in Dushanbe and northern cities but are not reliable in the Pamirs. Cash is more useful than credit cards everywhere except Dushanbe.

Value-added tax (VAT) is added to all goods, but no refunds are available to foreigners on departure.

Exchanging Money

US dollars, euros and Russian roubles are easily changed at city exchange booths and at least one bank in any regional centre. Carrying some cash (preferably in US dollars) is advised as not all ATMs accept international cards (particularly in the Pamirs). Both Uzbek and Kyrgyz som are accepted in relevant border areas.

The Tajik somani (TJS) is divided into 100 dirham. Somani notes come in one, five, 10, 20, 50 and 100 denominations. Dirham coins are rarely used.

Tipping

Top-end hotels Around 10TJS or US$1 per bag is standard. Gratuity for cleaning staff is not the norm but is appreciated.

Top-end and midrange restaurants 10% is often added to the bill in Dushanbe; where this is not the case, and outside the capital, up to 10% is appropriate for good service.

Taxis Drivers don't expect a tip.

OPENING HOURS

Opening hours for bazaars, shops and restaurants vary considerably from town to town. Typically, shopping takes place mid-morning, followed by lunch around noon and a quiet period in the afternoon. A few city bars stay open until 1am or 2am in the morning. Some traditional restaurants close during Ramadan or open after sunset.

Bazaars 8am to 4pm (closed first Monday of each month)
Cafes 8am to 11pm
Offices 8am to 5pm Monday to Saturday
Restaurants 10am to 11pm
Shops 9am to 8pm

PUBLIC HOLIDAYS

1 January New Year's Day
8 March International Women's Day
21–23 March Nawroz, or Navrus (Persian New Year), called Ba'at in Badakhshan
1 May International Labour Day
9 May Victory Day (a commemoration of WWII)
27 June Day of National Unity and Accord (for reconciliation after the 1990s civil war)
9 September Independence Day
6 November Constitution Day

Major Islamic hoildays are also celebrated including Idi Kurbon (Eid al-Adha, Feast of Sacrifice) and Idi Fitr (Eid al-Fitr; the end of Ramadan).

As well as national holidays, Ismaili communities in Badakhshan and beyond celebrate **Imamat Day** (July 11, the anniversary of the current Aga Khan taking over the Ismaili Imamat), **Ruz-i-Nour** (Day of Lights; May 25, commemorating the first visit of the current Imam to Gorno Badakhshan 1995) and **Ruz-i-Mavlud** (December 13, the Aga Khan's birthday). On all three days concerts, folklore shows and/or sports events take place in Khorog City Park, Dushanbe's Ismaili Centre and almost any Ismaili village.

TELEPHONE

Area codes are assigned to each part of the country but few landlines exist. Mobiles are more commonly used, especially outside towns.

The widest coverage for mobile networks is on TCell (www.tcell.tj/en), which reportedly covers 99% of the country. Megafon (www.megafon.tj) is the only carrier in parts of the Zerafshan Valley and Alichur; Beeline (www.beeline.tj) and Babilon-M (www.babilon-m.tj/en) also provide targeted coverage.

Mobile internet coverage is reasonably widespread. Megafon and TCell are the best choices,

EMERGENCY & IMPORTANT NUMBERS

Ambulance	103
Emergency	112
Fire	101
Gas leaks	104
Police	102

though each has 'holes' in its coverage. Most hotels in cities and major towns offer free wi-fi.

TOILETS

Western-style toilets are available in most parts of Tajikistan in public areas. Squat and long-drop toilets are more common in homestays and rural areas.

TOURIST INFORMATION

A number of local tourist associations have been established in Tajikistan. PECTA and META were founded as nonprofit organisations, with international help, to enhance the potential of tourism in the Eastern Pamirs.

PECTA (p179) Has a very helpful centre in Kurog. Lists homestays and tour operators.

META (p185) Operates out of Murgab.

ZTDA (p161) Lists homestays in the Fan Mountains area.

VISAS & TRAVEL PERMITS

Travellers with tourist visas are required to register with **OVIR** (☑ 372 27 6711; www.tdc.tj; Mirzo Tursunzoda 5; ⊘ 8am-noon & 1-5pm Mon-Fri, 8am-noon Sat) if they are intending to stay for more than 30 days. Registration must take place before the 30 days expire and this can be done in Dushanbe or at the OVIR (p179) in Khorog.

Several specific destinations, including Zor-Kul and the Tajik National Park, require permits, but these are easily organised in a matter of minutes by PECTA (p179) in Khorog. Only permits for Lake Sarez take time; these can also be arranged through PECTA.

E-visas for tourists cannot be extended beyond 45 days.

Visas for Onward Travel

Afghanistan

A 30-day visa (from US$100 depending on nationality) requires a self-penned letter explaining motivation and route for travel, one photo and a copy of your passport. They are usually available the same or next day from either Dushanbe (p193) or **Khorog** (☑ 9354 5 6248; Gagarin, Khorog; ⊘ 9am-noon Mon-Fri).

Uzbekistan

Many travellers continue to report long delays in applying for Uzbek visas from the Uzbek Embassy (p193) in Dushanbe, with or without a Letter of Invitation (LOI). Applying from Bishkek (Kyrgyzstan) with a downloaded visa form (www.evisa.mfa.uz/evisa_en) is a better option.

ℹ Getting There & Away

Arriving by air in Dushanbe is easy and immigration is efficient. Arriving by road can take time if there are queues. It's important to plan how

to cross the neutral zone between countries before reaching the border post as there is often no onward transport. Most tour companies can advise on hiring a taxi – particularly important at Kyzil-Art at the Pamir border between Tajikistan and Kyrgyzstan.

Uzbek–Tajik border crossings are prone to sudden unannounced closure and it's best to check the status of crossings immediately before departure. Caravanistan (www.caravan istan.com) is a good resource for this. At the time of writing, the Penjikent–Samarkand and Karamyk borders remained resolutely closed but borders at Kyzyl-Art, Oybek and Isfara were functioning.

AIR

Tajik Air (www.tajikair.tj) and Somon Air (www.somonair.com) are the main national carriers. The latter has direct Dushanbe–Frankfurt flights. There are flights to various Russian cities from Dushanbe and Khojand. Regional connections include four weekly flights from Dushanbe to both Bishkek (Kyrgyzstan) and Almaty (Kazakhstan). There is no departure tax.

In addition to the airlines listed here, there are several other airlines flying to numerous cities in Russia.

China Southern (www.csair.com; Tursunzoda 45, Paitakht Business Centre; ⊘ 9am-5pm Mon-Fri)

FlyDubai (☑ 446 10 0123; www.flydubai.com; Bekhzod 1)

Iran Aseman (☑ 372 21 9703; Shotemur 22, Hotel Tojikiston; ⊘ 8am-5pm Mon-Fri, to 2pm Sat) Flights to Tehran on Monday and to Mashhad (Iran) on Thursday.

Kam Air (www.kamair.com) Flights to Kabul on Thursday.

Somon Air (☑ call centre 446 40 4040; www.somonair.com; Nissor Muhammed 3; ⊘ 8am-6pm)

Tajik Air (☑ 487 01 5042; www.tajikair.tj/en; Titov 32/1; ⊘ 7am-11am & noon-7pm)

Turkish Airlines (☑ 487 01 7571; www.turkishairlines.com; Istaravshan 13; ⊘ 9am-5pm Mon-Fri, to 2pm Sat)

Ural Airlines (☑ 372 21 4520; www.ural airlines.com/en; Bukhoro 78, Gulistan Tur Hotel; ⊘ 8am-5pm)

LAND

Import tax (US$40 to US$70) and other fees are levied on cars entering Tajikistan at land borders. Car insurance validity for off-road driving should be checked before departure.

To & From Afghanistan

Ishkashim (for Tajik Wakhan–Little Pamir) This border is open to foreigners (⊘ 8am to noon and 1pm to 4pm, Monday to Saturday) and gives access to the peaceful Afghan Wakhan. A double-entry Tajik visa (with GBAO permit) is required as returning to Tajikistan is the only safe onward option. A taxi to Afghan's Sultan Eshkashim village (6km from Ishakashim) costs US$20 from the border bridge.

Panj-e-Payon (for Dushanbe–Kunduz) This southwest border is technically open to foreigners but visiting the Kunduz area is highly dangerous for security reasons and should be avoided.

Sheghnan (for Khorog–Lake Shiva) A bridge over the Pyanj River at Khorog marks this crossing (⊙9am to noon and 1pm to 4pm, Monday to Friday), offering 4WD access to remote Lake Shiva. Pre-arranged transport on the Afghan side is necessary for this. The region is snowbound from October to June and the roads are often washed out in early summer.

To & From China

Qolma Pass (for Murgab–Kashgar) At the time of research, the 4762m Qolma Pass linking Murgab to the Karakoram Hwy in Xinjiang, north of Tashkurgan, had just opened to all foreigners and timings were being established. It should be open from 11am to 5pm, Monday to Friday, closing for an hour around lunchtime.

To & From Kyrgyzstan

Isfana (near Khojand) Officially open but of little practical use to most travellers.

Isfara (for Khojand–Osh) Taxis and three daily marshrutka link Isfara with Batken. From Batken to Osh there's a new road avoiding the Uzbek enclaves.

Karamyk (for Garm–Sary Tash) Closed to foreigners.

Kyzl-Art (for Murgab–Osh) This remote border crossing on the Pamir Hwy requires pre-arranged onward transport. This can be organised through drivers in Osh and Murgab, or better still through a tour operator – such as **Orient Adventure** (☑ Adib Hamrohzoda 9350 0 2232; orient50@mail.ru) or **Afreddun Travel** (☑ 9021 2 4800, 9343 8 4800; afredjon@mail. run) – in advance. Either way, it's important to establish which transport will be crossing the 20km of neutral zone to avoid getting stranded.

To & From Uzbekistan

Bekobod (Khojand–Tashkent) Closed to foreigners.

Kanibodom (Khojand–Kokand) Linking parts of the Fergana Valley; a minibus from Isfara travels the 9km to the border. Taxis to Kokand are available or marshrutkas leave for Besh Aryk (Beshariq). **Oybek** (Khojand–Tashkent) Usually open to foreigners. Shared taxis run direct from Khojand's Abreshim terminal to Oybek. Once across the border there's a short walk to the main crossroads for a marshrutka to Tashkent. Bekobod-bound buses from Tashkent's Kuyluk Bazaar go via Oybek.

Penjikent (for Dushanbe–Samarkand) This crossing is still closed to foreigners.

Tursanzade (for Dushanbe–Samarkand) Shared taxis from Dushanbe's Zarnisar Bazaar to the border take 1½ hours. At the border, minibuses run to Denau, from where shared taxis continue to Samarkand.

ⓘ Getting Around

AIR

Domestic flights are currently limited to Dushanbe–Khojand.

BICYCLE

Many cyclists test their stamina on a multiday, multi-country trip through Tajikistan and Central Asia. This requires not just fitness but also basic mechanical knowledge and skills and some spare parts (not readily available in country) as remote sections of the Pamir Hwy take their toll on both bike and rider.

BUS

The bus/minibus network is limited, though the new Asia Express bus company is slowly expanding. For now shared taxis are the only public transport between Dushanbe and Penjikent or Khojand, while shared 4WDs are the main link to Khorog and Murgab.

CAR & MOTORCYCLE

Travellers commonly organise themselves into groups to rent chauffeured 4WD vehicles in the Pamirs or for chartering a whole shared taxi/ vehicle to enable more frequent stops en route. Motorcylists struggle to negotiate the rough terrain along the Pamir Hwy, but this is becoming an increasingly popular form of transport that requires carefully planning from home.

Uzbekistan

☎ 998 / POP 32.1 MILLION

Why Go?

The region's cradle of culture for more than two millennia, Uzbekistan is the proud home to a spellbinding arsenal of architecture and ancient cities, all deeply infused with the bloody, fascinating history of the Silk Road. In terms of sights alone, Uzbekistan is Central Asia's biggest draw and most impressive showstopper.

Samarkand, Bukhara and Khiva never fail to impress visitors with their fabulous mosques, medressas and mausoleums, while its more eccentric attractions, such as the fast disappearing Aral Sea, the fortresses of desperately remote Karakalpakstan, its boom town capital Tashkent and the ecotourism opportunities of the Nuratau Mountains, mean that even the most diverse tastes can be catered for.

Despite being a harshly governed police state, Uzbekistan remains an extremely friendly country where hospitality remains an essential element of daily life and you'll be made to feel genuinely welcome by the people you meet.

Best Places to Eat

➡ Afsona (p211)
➡ National Food (p210)
➡ Platan (p237)
➡ Minzifa (p257)
➡ Terasse Cafe (p268)

Best Places to Stay

➡ Jahongir B&B (p235)
➡ Amelia Boutique Hotel (p255)
➡ Emir B&B (p256)
➡ Antica (p236)
➡ Meros B&B (p268)

When to Go

Tashkent

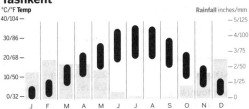

°C/°F Temp
Rainfall inches/mm

Apr–Jun Clear skies, sunshine and cool air combine to create perfect travel conditions.

July & Aug The extreme heat of the summer means bargains can be had at many hotels.

Sep & Oct Days remain warm despite the summer having passed and it's yet to get cold.

TOP TIP

⇒ Uzbekistan has charming accommodation (especially B&Bs), but book well in advance during high season, especially in Bukhara, Khiva and Samarkand, where all the best places will normally be full. Lesser options are unfortunately a big step down in comfort and atmosphere. Home- and yurtstays are possible.

Fast Facts

⇒ **Area** 447,400 sq km

⇒ **Capital** Tashkent

⇒ **Currency** som (S)

⇒ **Languages** Uzbek, Russian, Tajik, Karakalpak

Exchange Rates

Australia	A$1	6400S
Canada	C$1	6500S
China	¥10	12,940S
Euro zone	€1	10,100S
Japan	¥100	7600S
NZ	NZ$1	5800S
Russia	R100	14,300S
UK	£1	11,400S
USA	US$1	8200S

For current exchange rates, see www.xe.com.

Resources

⇒ **Advantour** (www.advantour.com)

⇒ **Karakalpakstan** (www.karakalpak.com)

⇒ **Orexca** (www.orexca.com)

⇒ **Lonely Planet** (www.lonelyplanet.com/uzbekistan)

Visas & Permits

Uzbek visas are needed by almost all nationalities. They are relatively painless to obtain, and most nationalities no longer require a letter of invitation.

COSTS

Relative Cost
Cheaper than Kazakhstan, but more expensive than Tajikistan.

Daily Expenses
Budget: Less than US$40

⇒ Hostel dorm: US$10–12

⇒ Bukhara B&B double: US$45–70

⇒ Shashlyk: US$1

⇒ Good restaurant meal: US$4

⇒ Shared taxi Bukhara to Khiva: US$10 per person

⇒ Tashkent fast train to Samarkand: economy class US$8

⇒ Flight from Tashkent to Urgench: US$102

Price Ranges

Sleeping (double room with bath, including breakfast)
$ <US$30, **$$** US$30–70, **$$$** >US$70

Eating (main course) **$** <10,00S, **$$** 10,000–20,000S, **$$$** >20,000S

Itineraries

⇒ **One Week** In one week you can cover 'the big three' in a trans-steppe dash. Start in impressive Samarkand to explore the pearls of Timurid-era architecture, zip to enchanting Bukhara to see the Lyabi-Hauz, tour the Ark and gape at the 47m Kalon Minaret and its stunning mosque, before continuing to perfectly preserved Khiva. Fly back from Urgench.

⇒ **Two weeks** In two weeks you can do the five major places of interest in Uzbekistan at an unhurried pace. Fly west to Nukus and spend a half-day appreciating Central Asia's greatest art collection before heading to Khiva via the ancient ruined fortresses of Elliq-Qala. Spend a few days in both Bukhara and Samarkand before ending up in Tashkent for some museum hopping, good food and a night or two on the town.

⇒ **One month** All of the above sights can be seen in a month at a more relaxed pace. You can also visit both Termiz and the Fergana Valley and devote more time to exploring Uzbekistan's natural wonders, including hiking in the Chimgan region and homestay tourism in the Nuratau Mountains.

TASHKENT (TOSHKENT)

📞 71 / POP 2.2 MILLION / ELEV 480M

Sprawling Tashkent (Toshkent) is Central Asia's hub and the place where everything in Uzbekistan happens. It's one part newly built national capital, thick with the institutions of power, and one part leafy Soviet city, and yet another part sleepy Uzbek town, where traditionally clad farmers cart their wares through a maze of mud-walled houses to the grinding crowds of the bazaar. Tashkent is a fascinating jumble of contradictions that's well worth exploring over several days.

Like most places that travellers use mainly to get somewhere else, Tashkent doesn't always immediately charm visitors, but it's a surprisingly fun and interesting place, with the best restaurants, museums and nightlife in the country. There's also plenty of opportunity to escape the metropolis for great hiking, rafting and skiing in Ugam-Chatkal National Park, just a 1½-hour drive away.

History

Tashkent's earliest incarnation might have been as the settlement of Ming-Uruk (Thousand Apricot Trees) in the 2nd or 1st century BC. By the time the Arabs took it in AD 751 it was a major caravan crossroads. It was given the name Toshkent (Tashkent, 'City of Stone' in Turkic) in about the 11th century.

The Khorezmshahs, one of the ruling dynasties of Central Asia and Persia from the late 11th to the early 13th centuries, and Chinggis (Genghis) Khan stubbed out Tashkent in the early 13th century, although it slowly recovered under the Mongols and then under Timur (Tamerlane). The city grew more prosperous under the Shaybanids, the founding dynasty of what effectively became modern Uzbekistan, ruling from the mid-15th until the start of the 17th century.

The khan of Kokand annexed Tashkent in 1809. In 1865, as the Emir of Bukhara was preparing to snatch it away, the Russians under General Mikhail Grigorevich Chernyaev beat him to it, against the orders of the tsar and despite being outnumbered 15 to one. They found a proud town, enclosed by a 25km-long wall with 11 gates (of which not a trace remains today).

The newly installed Governor General Konstantin Kaufman gradually widened the imperial net around the other Central Asian khanates. Tashkent also became the tsarists' (and later the Soviets') main centre for espionage in Asia, during the protracted imperial rivalry with Britain known as the Great Game.

Tashkent became the capital of the Turkestan Autonomous SSR, declared in 1918. When this was further split, the capital of the new Uzbek Autonomous SSR became Samarkand. In 1930 this status was restored to Tashkent.

Physically, Tashkent was changed forever on 25 April 1966, when a massive earthquake levelled vast areas of the town and left 300,000 people homeless. The city's current look dates from rebuilding efforts in the late '60s and '70s, though a slew of post-independence structures and statues have also graced the city.

Security in the city, particularly in the metro stations, has been high since February 1999, when six car bombs killed 16 and injured more than 120. The blasts were attributed by the government to Islamic extremists, but it will probably never be known who was responsible.

🅞 Sights

Modern Tashkent is a big, sprawling city that's best appreciated for its whole rather than its parts. If you're short on time, pick your spots and home in on them by taxi. At minimum check out Khast Imom, Chorsu Bazaar and a few museums.

Sheikhantaur
Mausoleum Complex   MAUSOLEUM

(Navoi; Ⓜ Alisher Navoi) Just north of Navoi boulevard are three 15th-century mausoleums. The biggest, on the grounds of the Tashkent Islamic University, bears the name of Yunus Khan, grandfather of the Mughal emperor and Andijon native Babur. The mausoleum itself sits locked and idle, but you can check out its attractive Timurid-style *pishtak* (entrance portal). Access is from Abdulla Kodiri.

Two smaller mausoleums are east of the university grounds, accessible via a small side street running north from Navoi – the pyramid-roofed Kaldirgochbiy and the silver-domed **Sheikh Hovendi Tahur** (Ⓜ Alisher Navoi). Next to the latter is a mosque with beautifully carved wooden doors and attractive tilework.

Assumption Cathedral   CHURCH
(Uspensky Sobor; Nukus) It's impossible to miss the handsome gold onion domes,

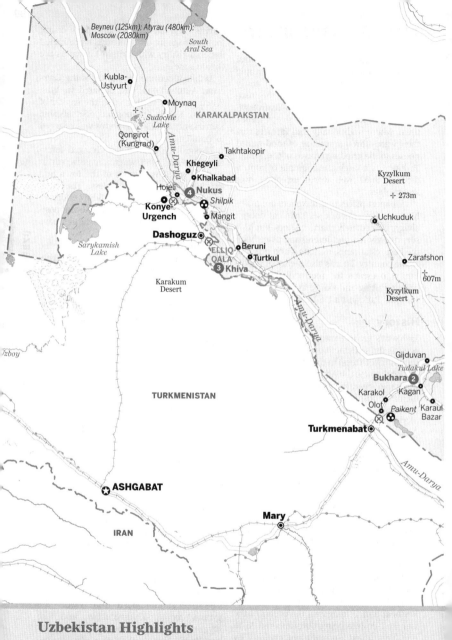

Uzbekistan Highlights

1 **Registan** (p229)
Marvelling at Central Asia's most stunning ensemble of larger-than-life Timurid architectural gems, in Samarkand.

2 **Bukhara** (p247)
Wandering the exquisitely preserved holy city, boasting stunning 15th-century medressas, stylish B&Bs and fascinating history.

3 **Khiva** (p262) Looking for the ghosts of the last independent Central Asian khanate, frozen in time behind mud walls in the middle of the Kyzylkum desert.

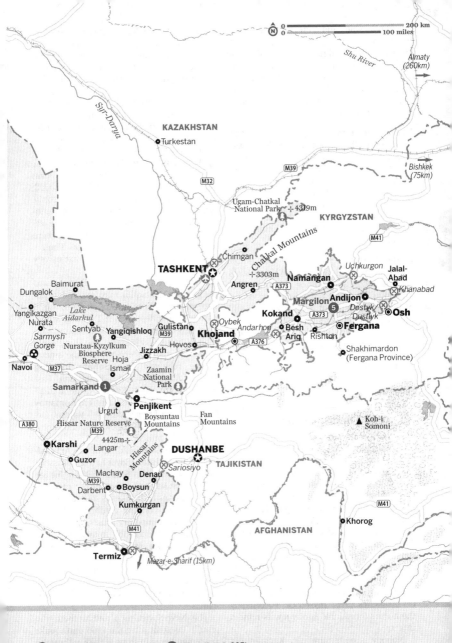

4 Savitsky Museum
(p270) Soaking in Central
Asia's greatest art collection
in Nukus, one of the country's
most remote corners.

5 Margilon (p225)
Watching silk worms and silk
weavers work their magic at
the Yodgorlik Silk Factory and
then shopping for the finished
ikat silks.

pastel blue walls and 50m bell tower of the impressive Assumption Cathedral. Built in 1958 and renovated in the 1990s, this is the biggest of the four Orthodox churches in Tashkent. It's particularly worth visiting on Sunday when Tashkent's Russian *babushkas* (old women) flock here to make devotions in a sea of incense.

Railway Museum
MUSEUM

(☑ 71-299 70 40; Amir Timur 1; admission/Russian guided tour 10,500S/15,000S; ☺ 9am-6pm; Ⓜ Toshkent) The magnificent collection of 1930s to 1950s Soviet locomotives at the open-air Railway Museum will thrill train buffs, though it's worth visiting even if you aren't one. You have licence to clamber all over any train with an open door. Kids will love the mini-railway.

Minor Mosque
MOSQUE

(Kichik Halqa Yuli; ☺ dawn-dusk; Ⓜ Minor) **FREE**
The striking new Minor Mosque, also known as the white mosque for the colour of its marble, is proof that Uzbekistan still knows how to create sublime Islamic architecture. The lovely circular prayer hall has a beautifully ornate mihrab (a niche indicating the direction of Mecca) and ceiling. Walk south back to Minor metro through the nearby Minor Cemetery or the pleasant canal-side path.

◉ Amir Timur maydoni

Tashkent's main streets radiate from Amir Timur maydoni, desecrated by ex-President Karimov without warning in 2010 as part of his grand plan to 'beautify' the city. The dozens of century-old chinar (plane) trees that provided shade for the legions of chess players and strollers who once populated the park were all cut down. With the chess players now gone, the **statue of Timur** (Ⓜ Amir Timur Hiyoboni/Yunus Rajab) on horseback in the middle of the square cuts a lonely figure. A glance under the statue reveals that the stallion has been divested of a certain reproductive appendage. Just who stole it is one of Tashkent's great mysteries. Fortunately the horse's formidable family jewels remain intact.

Nobody is quite sure why Karimov cut down the chinar trees, but conventional wisdom holds that he wanted to allow unobstructed views of the new, preposterously large Dom Forum (p212). It's usually closed, but occasionally hosts state-sponsored events for honoured guests. You may recognise the tigers on the facade from the Sher Dor Medressa at the Registan in Samarkand. Beyond the building is the **House of Photography** (Istikbol 4; ☺ 10am-5pm Tue-Sun; Ⓜ Amir Timur Hiyoboni/Yunus Rajabiy) **FREE**, which hosts rotating exhibits of Uzbekistan's top contemporary photographers as well as shows by international names in the field. It's one of Tashkent's artier, edgier spots.

Just off the square, the **State History Museum of the Timurids** (☑ 71-133 62 28; www.temurid.uz/en; cnr Istiklol & Amir Timur; admission/camera/guide 6000/10,000/5000S; ☺ 10am-5pm Tue-Sun; Ⓜ Amir Timur Hiyoboni/Yunus Rajab) museum was built to commemorate the 600th birthday of Timur. There are almost no genuine artefacts here, but there are some interesting displays on Timur's descendants and their almost exclusively violent deaths.

Further west, good-luck pelicans guard the gates to Mustaqillik maydoni (Independence square), where crowds gather to watch parades on Independence Day and whenever else the government wants to stir up a bit of nationalistic spirit. The shiny white edifice on the western side of the square is the relatively new **Senate building** (Paradlar Alleyasi; Ⓜ Mustaqillik Maydoni). East of the square across Rashidov, the animal-festooned facade of the tsarist-era **Romanov Palace** (Buyuk Turon; Ⓜ Mustaqillik Maydoni) faces the Art Gallery of Uzbekistan, and is now closed to the public.

The impressive building of the **Art Gallery of Uzbekistan** (Buyuk Turon 2; admission/camera 500/3000S; ☺ 10am-5.30pm Tue-Sat; Ⓜ Mustaqillik Maydoni) is one of the more recent additions to Tashkent's museum scene, and presents rotating exhibits of Uzbekistan's top contemporary artists.

North of Mustaqillik maydoni is the **Crying Mother Monument** (Ⓜ Mustaqillik Maydoni). Fronted by an eternal flame, it was constructed in 1999 to honour the 400,000 Uzbek soldiers who died in WWII. The niches along its two corridors enshrine their names.

The New Soviet men and women who rebuilt Tashkent after the 1966 earthquake are remembered in stone at the **Earthquake Memorial** (Ⓜ Mustaqillik Maydoni). Soviet propagandists made much of the battalions of these 'fraternal peoples' and eager urban planners who came from around the Soviet Union to help with reconstruction. But when Moscow later announced it would give 20% of the newly built apartments to these (mainly Russian) volunteers and invite them to stay, local resentment boiled over in street brawls between Uzbeks and Russians in the so-called Pakhtakor Incident of May 1969.

The 375m-tall, three-legged monster **TV Tower** (☑71-150 90 24; Amir Timur 109; admission US$15; ☉10am-8pm, restaurant 10am-11pm Tue-Sun; ⓜBodomzor), the epitome of Soviet design, stands around 4km north of the city centre but can be seen from all over town. The price of admission gets you up to the 100m viewing platform, but photos are technically forbidden. To go up to the next level (about 220m) you'll have to grease the guard's palm – US$5 in som should do the trick. You'll need your passport to buy a ticket.

★**History Museum of the People of Uzbekistan**　　MUSEUM
(☑71-239　17　79; www.history-museum.uz; Rashidov 30; admission/camera/English guided tour 10,000/25,000/8000S; ☉9.30am-6pm Tue-Sun; ⓜMustaqillik Maydoni) The History Museum is a must-visit for anyone looking for a primer on the history of Turkestan from its earliest settlements 5000 years ago to the present. The 2nd floor has some fine Zoroastrian and Buddhist artefacts, including several 1st- to 3rd-century Buddhas and Buddha fragments from Fayoz-Tepe area near Termiz.

★**State Fine Arts Museum**　　MUSEUM
(☑71-236 74 36; www.stateartmuseum.uz; Amir Timur 16; admission 10,000S, camera 50,000S, guide 40,000S; ☉10am-5pm; ⓜMing Oriq/Oybek) The four floors of this excellent museum walk you through 1500 years of art in Uzbekistan, from 7th-century Buddhist relics from Kuva and the Greek-inspired head of Hercules from Khalchayan near Termiz, to the art of Soviet Uzbekistan. There are even a few 19th-century paintings of second-tier Russian and European artists hanging about. There's an impressive section on Uzbek applied art – notably some lovely *ghanch* (plaster carvings) from Bukhara, carved wooden doors from Khiva and the silk-on-cotton embroidered hangings called *suzani*.

◎ **Old Town**

The Old Town (Uzbek: *eski shahar*; Russian: *stary gorod*) starts beside the Chorsu Bazaar. A maze of narrow dirt streets is lined with low mudbrick houses and dotted with mosques and old medressas.

Taxi drivers get lost easily here. On foot, you could easily get lost too, but that's part of the fun. Wandering around you may be invited into someone's home, where you'll discover that the blank outer walls of traditional homes conceal cool, peaceful garden courtyards.

On a hill overlooking Chorsu Bazaar, look for Tashkent's silver-domed **Juma (Friday) Mosque** (Beruni) and the working 16th-century **Kulkedash Medressa** (Beruni; admission 4000S; ☉10am-6pm) next door with an unusual garden courtyard.

★**Chorsu Bazaar**　　MARKET
(☉6am-7pm; ⓜChorsu) Tashkent's most famous farmers market, topped by a giant green dome, is a delightful slice of city life spilling into the streets off the Old Town's southern edge. There are acres of spices arranged in brightly coloured mountains, Volkswagen-sized sacks of grain, entire warehouses dedicated to sweets, and the freshest bread and fruits around. Souvenir hunters will find *kurpacha* (colourful sitting mattresses), skullcaps, *chapan* (traditional heavy quilted cloaks), ceramics and knives here.

◎ **Khast Imom**

The official religious centre of the republic, located 2km north of the Circus, is also definitely one of the best places to see 'old Tashkent'. A big renovation in recent years has left the complex looking better than ever. The Leviathan **Hazroti Imom Friday mosque** (Karasaray; ⓜGofur Gulom), flanked by two 54m minarets, is a recent construction, having been ordered by former President Karimov in 2007. Behind it is the

LOCAL KNOWLEDGE

RIDING THE TASHKENT METRO

It's worth taking the metro to reach Tashkent's sites, if only to visit some of the lavishly decorated stations. A must is the Kosmonavtlar station, with its unearthly images of Amir Timur's astronomer grandson, Ulugbek, and Soviet cosmonaut Yuri Gagarin, among others. Remember that photography is forbidden.

UZBEKISTAN TASHKENT (TOSHKENT)

Tashkent

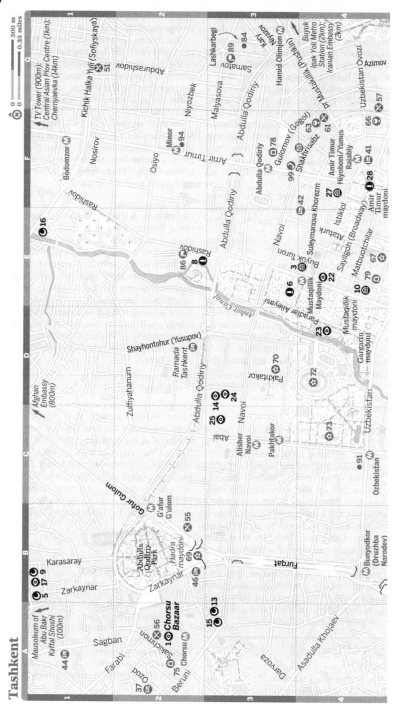

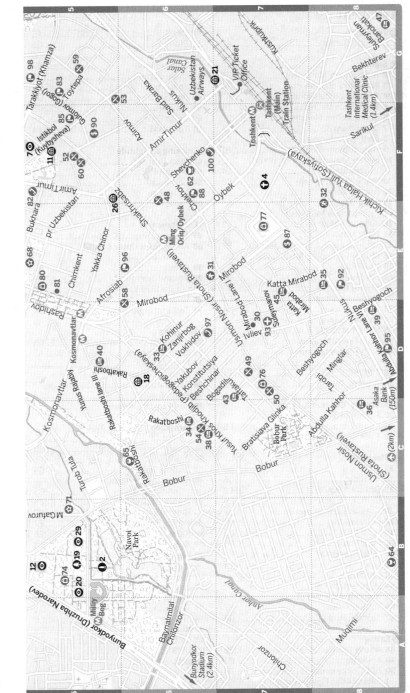

Tashkent

◎ Top Sights
1 Chorsu Bazaar A2

◎ Sights
2 Alisher Navoi Monument...................... B5
3 Art Gallery of Uzbekistan E4
4 Assumption Cathedral F7
5 Barak Khan Medressa B1
6 Crying Mother Monument E3
7 Dom Forum F5
8 Earthquake Memorial E2
9 Hazroti Imom Friday Mosque B1
10 History Museum of the People of Uzbekistan... E4
11 House of Photography F5
12 Istiklol Palace B5
13 Juma Mosque... A3
14 Kaldirgochbiy Mausoleum D3
15 Kulkedash Medressa A3
16 Minor Mosque E1
17 Moyie Mubarek Library Museum B1
18 Museum of Applied Arts....................... D6
19 Navoi Park B5
20 Oliy Majlis B5
21 Railway Museum.................................... G7
22 Romanov Palace E4
23 Senate Building..................................... D4
24 Sheikh Hovendi Tahur Mausoleum D3
25 Sheikhantaur Mausoleum Complex..... C3
26 State Fine Arts Museum F5
27 State History Museum of the Timurids F4
28 Statue of Timur F4
29 Wedding Palace B5

◎ Activities, Courses & Tours
30 Advantour D7
31 Asia Adventures.................................... E6
32 Asian Special Tourism.......................... E8

◎ Sleeping
33 Art Hostel D6
34 Art Hotel C6
35 Grand Art Hotel.................................... E8
36 Grand Orzu Hotel.................................. C8
37 Gulnara Guesthouse............................. A2
38 Hotel Bek C6
39 Hotel Ideal D8
40 Hotel Sharq D5
41 Hotel Uzbekistan F4
42 Hyatt Regency E4
43 Ichan Qala.. D7
44 Mirzo Guesthouse..................................A1
45 Rovshan Hotel..E7
46 Tojihon Serai B2
47 Topchan Hostel......................................G8

◎ Eating
48 Afsona.. F6
49 Amaretto D7
50 B&B Coffee House................................. D7
51 Central Asian Plov Centre G1

52 City Grill...F5
53 Efendi G5
54 Jumanji C6
55 National Food B2
56 Ovqat Bozari A2
57 Shalimar Restaurant G4
58 Stuzzico..D6
59 Sunduk G5
60 Urban Food F5
61 Yolki Palki F4

◎ Drinking & Nightlife
62 Black Bear Kofi F6
63 Brauhaus...F4
64 Cafe Dudek B8
65 La Terasse... C6
66 Tapas Bar F4

◎ Entertainment
67 Academic Russian Drama Theatre E4
68 Alisher Navoi Opera & Ballet Theatre...E5
69 Circus B2
70 Ilkhom Theatre D3
71 Muqimi Musical Theatre B5
72 Pakhtakor Stadium D4
73 Tashkent State Conservatory C4

◎ Shopping
74 Abulkasim Medressa............................. B5
75 Chorsu Antiques.................................... A2
76 Human House D7
77 Mirobod Bazaar E7
78 Oloy Bazaar F3
79 Sharq Ziyokori E4
80 Toshkent Univermagi............................E5

◎ Information
Advantour ....(see 30)
81 Arostr Tourism E5
82 Beeline..F5
83 Chinese Embassy G5
84 Culture Ministry Antiques Certification Office G3
85 French Embassy.....................................F5
86 German Embassy....................................E2
87 Kapital Bank...E7
88 Kazakhstan Embassy............................F6
89 Kyrgyzstan Embassy G3
90 National Bank of Uzbekistan F5
91 OVIR Central Office C4
92 Russian Embassy E8
93 Safo Tibbiyot Clinic D7
94 Steppe Journeys F2
95 Tajikistan Embassy...............................D8
96 Turkmenistan Embassy.........................E6
97 UCell D6
98 UK Embassy... G5
99 UMS F3
100 UzMobile F6

sprawling Khast Imom Square. The Muslim Board of Uzbekistan, whose grand mufti is roughly the Islamic equivalent of an arch-bishop, occupies a new building to the north of the mosque.

Beyond the major draw of the Moyie Mubarek Library Museum (p207), two other mausoleums of note in the area are worth a visit. Northwest of the square is the little 16th-century **Mausoleum of Abu Bakr Kaf-fal Shoshi** (Khast Imom Sq; Ⓜ Gofur Gulom), an Islamic scholar and poet of the Shaybanid period. The front room contains his large tomb and five smaller ones. Larger tombs of three more sheikhs are at the back. To the west of the square is the 16th-century **Bar-ak Khan Medressa** (Ⓜ Gofur Gulom) FREE, where the souvenir shops now occupying the student rooms make this one of the best places to pick up a last-minute souvenir. Crafts include textiles, miniatures, scarves, embroidered bags, ceramics and even mo-bile phone cases.

Moyie Mubarek Library Museum LIBRARY
(Khast Imom Sq; admission 10,000S; ☺ 9am-noon & 2-5pm Mon-Fri, 10am-3pm Sat; Ⓜ Gofur Gulom) The primary attraction of Khast Imom square is this library museum, which hous-es the 7th-century Osman Quran (Uthman Quran), said to be the world's oldest. This enormous deerskin tome was brought to Samarkand by Timur, then taken to Mos-cow by the Russians in 1868 before being returned to Tashkent by Lenin in 1924 as an act of goodwill towards Turkestan's Mus-lims. It is Tashkent's most important sight.

The museum also contains 30 or 40 rare 14th- to 17th-century books among its col-lection, including one thumb-sized koran in an amulet case. Photos are not allowed. The library is in the southeast of the square, next to the spartan 1856 Telyashayakh Mosque.

◉ Navoi Park

Downtown Tashkent's largest park will ap-peal to anyone with a taste for eccentricity. Soviet architects had a field day here, erect-ing a pod of spectacularly brutal concrete monstrosities, such as the **Istiklol Palace** (Navoi Park; Ⓜ Bunyodkur or Milliy Bog), formerly the People's Friendship Palace, which appears like a moon-landing station from a 1950s film set; and the chunky **Wedding Palace** (Bobur, Navoi Park; Ⓜ Bunyodkur or Milliy Bog).

The tightly guarded building southwest of Istiklol Palace is the **Oliy Majlis** (Parlia-ment; Ⓜ Bunyodkur or Milliy Bog), the lower house of parliament, which functions as a giant rubber stamp in its infrequent ses-sions. Nearby are a vast promenade and a post-Soviet **Alisher Navoi monument** (Ⓜ Bunyodkur or Milliy Bog).

★ **Museum of Applied Arts** MUSEUM
(☏ 71-256 39 43; www.muzeyart.uz; Rakatboshi 15; admission/camera/tour 10,000/6000/15,000S; ☺ 9am-6pm; Ⓜ Kosmonavtlar) The Museum of Applied Arts occupies an exquisite house full of bright *ghanch* (carved and painted plaster) and carved wood. It was built in the 1930s, at the height of the Soviet period, but nonetheless serves as a sneak preview of the older architectural highlights lurking in Bukhara and Samarkand. The ceramic and textile exhibits here, with English de-scriptions, are a fine way to bone up on the regional decorative styles of Uzbekistan. There's a small cafe and pricey gift shop here too.

🛌 Sleeping

Tashkent's accommodation remains under-whelming and quite overpriced, so book ahead during the peak months to ensure you can stay where you want.

Registration is taken far more seriously here than elsewhere in the country. You're won't be accepted in many places if you don't have all your registration stamps ready for inspection, so be sure your paperwork is in order!

★ **Topchan Hostel** HOSTEL $
(☏ +998 90 355 2949; www.topchan-hostel.com; 104 Vosmoye Marta; dm/s/d US$10/18/28; ✳ 🛜) This well-run hostel south of the railway tracks has a good mix of dorm and private rooms, all of which share the clean bath-room blocks. The friendly owners are a fount of local information and are flexible with prices, though they run things by the book when it comes to registration slips.

Dorms are either mixed or female-only. Economy twins are a bit cheaper but have no windows. Guests can use the kitchen, with its free tea and coffee, as well as the washing machine (US$2 per load). The lo-cation isn't great but marshrutka 22 runs from near the hostel to the train station and Tsum store.

★**Gulnara Guesthouse** GUESTHOUSE $
(☑71-240 63 36, +998 98 360 0774; gulnara
hotel@gmail.com; Ozod 40; dm US$11-13, s/d with
shared bathroom US$18/30, s/d US$23/40; ✳🛜;
Ⓜ Chorsu) Gulnara's has long been Tashkent's
budget favourite, though it's lost ground to
the new hostels in recent years. There's a
friendly-family atmosphere in the lovely
courtyard and manager Rovshan is very
helpful. The shared bathrooms are clean
and extras such as a laundry service, luggage
storage, vegetarian dinners, airport pick-up
and help obtaining a SIM card make this an
understandably popular choice.

Chorsu Bazaar is a convenient 10-minute
walk away, but the bazaar is dark and empty at night so women in particular should
consider using the better-lit Tinchlik metro
station after dark. Visa cards are accepted.

Art Hostel HOSTEL $
(☑+998 91 133 1015, +998 90 167 8337; www.art
hostel.uz; Zanjirbog 3; dm/s US$12/18, d US$32-34;
✳🛜; Ⓜ Kosmonavtlar) This sociable hostel
sets the bar high for Tashkent's budget accommodation. The pine fresh rooms and
shared bathrooms are spotlessly clean and
the clued-in owners understand backpacker needs, from individual bed lights and
lockers to cheap laundry, luggage storage,
female-only dorms and a shared kitchen.
There are *tapchans* (bedlike platforms) and
hammocks for socialising and even a plunge
pool to beat the summer heat.

The same folks run the slightly more upmarket **Art Hotel** (☑+998 93 573 0500; art
hoteltas@gmail.com; Rakatboshi 86; s US$20-25,
d/tr US$40/50; ✳🛜) and decidedly more
stylish Grand Art Hotel as well.

Mirzo Guesthouse GUESTHOUSE $
(☑+998 93 379 6668; www.turkturizm.uz; Sagbon
95; dm/s US$11/20, d US$30-35, tr US$40; ✳🛜;
Ⓜ Chorsu) This budget place has five modern
rooms set around a small courtyard, with
shared bathrooms, new mattresses and constant hot water. The two 'national rooms'
feature finely carved wooden ceilings and
serve as dorms or family rooms. It's not stylish but it works. Loquacious owner Mirzo,
an eccentric historian, likes to play the *dutar* (two-stringed guitar) and his son Oybek
speaks excellent English.

Tojihon Serai HOTEL $$
(Mannon Uygur, Shahriston 2-tor; d US$50-60;
✳🛜; Ⓜ Chorsu) This 20-room, three-star

place by the Circus is run by the people
behind Mirzo Guesthouse. Rooms are ar-
ranged medressa-style around a central
courtyard and there is even some luxury
yurt accommodation. Airport pick-up is free
if you stay three nights or more.

In-house travel agency Turktourism can
help with letters of invitation (US$35 to
US$50) and arrange cars with drivers. Con-
tact English-speaking Oybek.

Grand Art Hotel HOTEL $$
(☑71-147 12 22; grandarthotel@gmail.com; Ki-
chik Mirabod Street 11, 2nd proezd/alley; s/d from
US$25/40; ✳🛜🛁) Bigger, better value and
more of a proper hotel than its affiliate Art
Hotel, the Grand Art has 29 rooms, some
modern stylish touches, a small pool and a
pleasant terrace sitting area, with a proper
restaurant for dinner and a decent breakfast
buffet. All in all, a good upper budget bet,
and close to the train station in the south
of town.

Hotel Ideal HOTEL $$
(☑71-254 17 29, 71-254 70 77; www.hotel-ideal.uz;
Kichik Beshyogoch 96; s/d from US$50/60; ✳🛜;
Ⓜ Toshkent) This offbeat choice is a little out
of the way, but offers clean, cosy and pleas-
ant rooms and has friendly English-speaking
staff. The cheapest standards are warm attic
rooms with sloping ceilings (not great for
tall people), while the pricier ones are more
spacious. The attached Korean restaurant is
excellent and there's a small bazaar nearby.
There's room for negotiation here.

Rovshan Hotel HOTEL $$
(☑71-120 77 47; www.rovshanhotel.com; Katta
Mirobod 118; s/d from US$35/45; ✳🛜; Ⓜ Oybek)
This is a solid midrange option in the quiet
Mirobod District despite being rather char-
acterless. The standard rooms are small,
particularly the singles, so it's well worth
splashing out US$5 more for the half *lux*
(semi-deluxe) with a fridge and king-sized
bed.

Grand Orzu Hotel HOTEL $$
(☑71-120 88 77; www.grandorzu.com; Tarobi 27;
s/d from US$35/45; 🅿✳🛜🛁) This modest
but comfortable place within a green res-
idential neighbourhood boasts a pool and
pleasant restaurant out the back. Rooms are
forgettable but decent value, and the wood-
en ceilings add a vaguely Alpine chalet air.
The *lux* (deluxe) rooms are much better for
only US$5 more.

⭐**Hotel Sharq** BOUTIQUE HOTEL **$$$**
(📞71-140 08 20; www.hotelsharq.uz; Rakatboshi 3a; s/d US$85/105; ❋🤖🏊; Ⓜ Kosmonovtlar) This recommended place is just what Tashkent needs – a well-located, upmarket but affordable hotel that has style, security and good service. It has a big pool and garden (perfect for breakfast in the sun), spacious and well-decorated rooms and staff who fall over themselves to be helpful. Ask for a garden-view room.

⭐**Hotel Bek** BOUTIQUE HOTEL **$$$**
(📞71-215 58 88; www.bek-hotel.uz; Yusuf Khos Khodjib 64a; s/d from US$60/80, ste US$100-120; ❋🤖🏊; Ⓜ Kosmonovtlar) With friendly and professional English-speaking staff, spotless rooms, stylish touches and a small but very welcome plunge pool, this hotel is a great choice for business travellers or those looking for some comfort. King-sized beds, reliable wi-fi and a relaxed and friendly atmosphere are this place's hallmarks, and about the only complaint is that you're a good 15-minute walk from the nearest metro station.

Hyatt Regency BUSINESS HOTEL **$$$**
(📞71-207 12 34; www.tashkent.regency.hyatt.com; Navoi 1a; r US$190-250; ❋🤖🏊; Ⓜ Abdulla Qodiriy) One of Tashkent's five-star options is a huge fortress of a place, taking up an entire city block. It's easily the best hotel in town, featuring a top-notch Italian restaurant (with a gelato bar), a slinky modern bar, 24-hour gym and a fine terrace. It's worth paying a little extra for one of the six balcony rooms.

Ichan Qala BOUTIQUE HOTEL **$$$**
(📞71-231 98 98; www.ichanqala.uz; Yusuf Khos Khojib 75/10; s/d US$90/100; ❋🤖🏊) An impressive place built in a faux medressa style with 60 rooms in five villas, nice outdoor seating and clever touches like a poolside clicker to call for service. Rooms are modern with a blingy decor that feels more nouveau Russian than old Central Asian, but all in all it's a good choice. You'll never find it with the official address; it's actually on Taffakur 57.

Hotel Uzbekistan HOTEL **$$$**
(📞71-113 11 11, 71-113 10 12; www.hoteluzbekistan.uz; Tarakkiyot 45; s/d from US$100/150; ❋@🤖; Ⓜ Amir Timur Hiyoboni) This old dinosaur towering over central Amir Timur maydoni has reinvented itself as Tashkent's best-value top-end hotel. Helpful receptionists have replaced the scowling *babushkas* and most of the rooms are sleek and modern with flat-screen TVs and plush comforters (the bathrooms still need some work). You are here for the location and the ex-Soviet vibe, so don't expect international standards of management.

This is one place to push for a hefty discount, with online rates around US$80 for a double.

✖️ Eating

You'll eat better in Tashkent than anywhere else in Uzbekistan. Tashkent's burgeoning middle class loves to dine out on everything from sushi and Italian food to more traditionally popular cuisines such as Russian, Caucasian and Central Asian. The large Korean population means that there's plenty of authentic Korean food on offer. Most restaurants add on a 15% to 20% service charge.

Western-style supermarkets and minimarkets are abundant, but for fresh produce you are much better off at a farmers market. **Oloy Bazaar** (Alaysky Bazaar; Amir Timur; ⏰7am-7pm; Ⓜ Abdulla Qodiriy) lacks the character of Chorsu, but locals say it has the best, if priciest, produce. Near the train station, **Mirobod Bazaar** (Gospitalny Bazaar; cnr Mirabod & Nukus; ⏰7am-6pm; Ⓜ Toshkent) is fiesta of fruit bathing in the teal-green glow of its giant, octagonal flying saucer of a roof.

Central Asian Plov Centre UZBEK **$**
(cnr Abdurashidov & Ergashev; plov 7000S; ⏰10am-2pm) To sample *plov* (pilaf) styles from various regions of Uzbekistan head to the celebration of *plov* that is the Central Asian Plov Centre. Walk past the mob of people crowding around steaming *kazans* (large *plov* cauldrons) and take a seat inside, where your group's order will arrive Uzbek-style on a single plate from which everybody eats. Get here before noon for the best selection.

Ovqat Bozari UZBEK **$**
(Chorsu Bazaar; ⏰6am-8pm; Ⓜ Chorsu) After some shopping in Chorsu Bazaar head for this arcade draped with colourful *ikat* fabrics. It's a good place to get *plov*, but the various family-run stalls also sell such Uzbek specials as *naryn* (noodles with horsemeat), *hosip* (sausage) and some excellent shashlyk.

PLOV, GLORIOUS PLOV

Few things excite the Uzbek palate like *plov* (pilaf), that delicious conglomeration of rice, vegetables and meat bits swimming in lamb fat and oil. This Central Asian staple has been elevated to the status of religion in Uzbekistan, the country with which it's most closely associated. Each province has its own style, which locals loudly and proudly proclaim is the best in Uzbekistan – and by default the world.

That *plov* is an aphrodisiac goes without saying. Uzbeks joke that the word for 'foreplay' in Uzbek is '*plov*'. Men put the best cuts of meat in the *plov* on Thursday; not coincidentally, Thursday's when most Uzbek babies are conceived. Drinking the oil at the bottom of the *kazan* (large *plov* cauldron) is said to add particular spark to a man's libido.

B&B Coffee House
CAFE $

(Usmon Nosir (Shota Rustaveli) 30a; coffee 6000-12000S, snacks 20,000S; ⊘8am-10pm; ✸) 'Beans & Brews' is perhaps our favourite cafe in town, with good espresso coffee, juices and sandwiches, plus French toast and oatmeal that knocks the socks off your free hotel breakfast. The decor is modern and hip, with monochrome exposed brick design and outdoor tables. If only it had wi-fi.

★ National Food
UZBEK $$

(Milliy Taomlar; Gafur Gulom 1; dishes 5000-15,000S; ⊘6am-10pm; Ⓜ G'afur G'ulom) You'll be hard pressed to find a restaurant with more local colour than this bustling eatery opposite the Circus. As you walk through the entrance you'll be greeted by giant *kazans* (cauldrons) filled with various national specialities. In addition to the requisite *plov* and *laghman,* you can sample *beshbarmak* (noodles with meat and broth), *dimlama* (braised meat, potatoes, onions and vegetables)*, halim* (meat porridge) and *naryn* (horsemeat sausage served with cold noodles).

Stuzzico
PIZZA $$

(✇71-252 33 80; www.facebook.com/stuzzico. tashkent; Mirobod 4; pizza 25,000-43,000S; ⊘11am-10.30pm; Ⓜ Kosmonavtlar) Perhaps the best pizza in town, with fresh ingredients, fresh basil and crispy crusts, and big enough for two. Also good coffee, salads and cakes and a pleasant terrace. The cute kids' pizzas are made into the shape of a face. Delivery possible.

Efendi
TURKISH $$

(✇71-233 15 02; Azimov 79A; mains 12,000-30,000S; ⊘9am-midnight; ✸🗡🅿; Ⓜ Oybek) This sprawling Turkish place has an extensive menu, or you can just saunter inside and pick out a kebab and salad from the refrigerated display case and retire to the shaded outdoor seating. The food is consistently good, from the excellent *iskender kebab* (lamb with bread, yoghurt and tomato sauce) to the *patlican* (eggplant) salad, and you can order half portions if you're not that hungry.

Shalimar Restaurant
PAKISTANI $$

(✇71-233 63 63; Tokai 1b; curries 20,000-30,000S; ⊘11am-11pm; ✸🅿; Ⓜ Amir Timur Hiyoboni) When the urge for a vegetable jalfrezi or chicken tikka masala becomes unbearable, head to this Pakistan-run place. Everything is authentic, from the nan and paratha breads to the super-sweet chai and the strains of Urdu music on the TV.

Urban Food
BURGERS $$

(Shahrisabsz 23; burgers 14,000-22,000S; ⊘10am-11pm; ✸🅿; Ⓜ Amir Timur Hiyobani) If you're *plov*ed out and need a Western food fix, Urban Food is a definite step up from your average Tashkent fast-food joint, with quality burgers, Philly cheese steaks, shakes and fries, all cooked up fresh in a modern and hip environment. Good espresso coffee is also served here.

Sunduk
FRENCH $$

(✇71-232 11 46; Azimov 63; mains 25,000-38,000S; ⊘9.30am-midnight Mon-Sat; ✸📶🗡🅿; Ⓜ Amir Timur Hiyoboni) The comfort food at this diminutive eatery, kitted out like a French country kitchen, is as perfect as the handwriting on the menus – on homemade paper, no less. The good-value business lunch (19,000S) is popular with the diplomatic set, many of whom work nearby.

Yolki Palki
RUSSIAN $$

(Shakhrisabz 5; mains 15,000-30,000S; ⊘11am-11pm; ✸🗡🅿; Ⓜ Amir Timur Hiyoboni) A sprawling Russian chain famous for all-you-can-eat hot and cold salad bars with every Ukrainian and Russian speciality imaginable. It's a good place to try such staples as *pelmeni* (dumplings) and *pirozhki* (meat-stuffed bun), and there's a good set lunch too. No service charge.

★ Afsona
UZBEK $$$

(www.facebook.com/afsonatashkent; Shevchenko 30; mains 22,000-47,000S; ☺noon-11pm; ❄️📶; ⓂMing Oriq/Oybek) This well-run restaurant aims to deliver Uzbek cuisine with a contemporary touch, breathing life into old favourites such as pumpkin *manty* (steamed dumplings), *cheburek* pastries and *hanum* (dough roll stuffed with vegetables). The decor is understated, with stylish geometric wood designs favoured over the ethnographic museum approach. The four-course set business lunch is a steal at 30,000S.

★ Jumanji
INTERNATIONAL $$$

(☎71-255 42 00; www.jumanji.uz; Yusuf Khos Khodjib 62/2; mains 25,000-60,000S; ☺noon-11pm Mon-Sat, 5-11pm Sun; ❄️📶📶📶; ⓂKosmonavtlar) A charming, laid-back and family-friendly environment reigns here. There's a varied and interesting menu that runs from Georgian specialities to Asian dishes and traditional Uzbek dishes like *kazan kebab* (beef and potatoes), and even a lunchtime salad bar (18,000S), while the coolly efficient staff ensure that this is one of Tashkent's most perennially enjoyable eating experiences.

★ City Grill
INTERNATIONAL $$$

(☎71-233 49 72; www.citygrill.uz; Shakhrisabz 23; mains 25,000-80,000S; ☺noon-11pm; ❄️📶📶; ⓂAmir Timur Hiyoboni) The central City Grill is a great spot for a sophisticated and good-value business lunch or a blow-out dinner. Specialising in steak and pasta, the menu here is varied and uses delicious fresh produce. There's also a fantastic selection of salads, soups and other meat grills. Service is discreet and efficient.

Amaretto
ITALIAN $$$

(☎71-215 55 57; Shota Rustaveli 28; mains 14,000-45,000S; ☺noon-11pm; ❄️📶; ⓂOybek) The mouth-watering Italian food, professional English-speaking service and subdued, candlelit ambience combine to make this the obvious choice for a romantic dinner. We prefer the outdoor terrace to the rather garish dining rooms inside, but wherever you eat, the excellent pizza and pasta, good salads and large (but pricey) wine list are winners.

🍷 Drinking & Nightlife

Tashkent has a lively and rapidly changing nightlife, although it's aimed largely at the Land Cruiser classes and you may well feel conspicuous arriving at some clubs' velvet ropes without designer threads, sunglasses worn at midnight and a bevvie of models by your side. Reservations are a good idea to ensure entrance.

Black Bear Kofi
COFFEE

(Shevchenko 38; ☺8am-11pm; ⓂMing Oriq/Oybek) This reliable local chain serves good coffee and cakes, lemonades and shakes from half a dozen locations across Tashkent, with larger branches like this one serving breakfasts (granola!), sandwiches and salads on a pleasant terrace. There is, however, no English menu or wi-fi.

Cafe Dudek
MICROBREWERY

(www.facebook.com/dudekuz; Muqimi 42; beer 9500S, mains 45,000-60,000S; ☺noon-11pm; 📶) The sunny outdoor terrace here is a great place to kick back over a house-brewed Czech-style pilsner or unfiltered wheat beer (the *tmavi lejak* dark beer is our favourite). Dudek also makes their own sausages and house-baked Czech bread, along with something called 'hunting vole soup' that we weren't brave enough to try, even after a couple of dark beers. There's occasional live music.

Tapas Bar
CLUB

(Shakhrisabz 33A; admission 15,000-20,000S; ☺9pm-5am Fri, Sat & Sun; ⓂAmir Timur Hiyoboni) For flat-out debauchery, it's hard to beat this hipsterish student venue, formerly known as VM. Ostensibly a warm-up (or warm-down) bar for club-goers, its small dance floor often takes on a life of its own, obviating the need to go elsewhere. Weekends bring live bands. It's accessed from it's own separate entrance inside the grounds of Le Grande Plaza Hotel.

La Terasse
CLUB

(Rakatboshi 23; admission from 15,000S; ☺from 9pm Fri & Sat; ⓂKosmonavtlar) The former KT Komba is the premier weekend playground for the young, smart local set. A restaurant earlier in the evening, it gets going after midnight and the party goes on until dawn. Music is kept interesting by guest DJs and live acts.

Brauhaus
PUB

(Shakhrisabz 5; beer from 7000S; ☺11am-midnight; 📶; ⓂToshkent) Sports fans flock here to watch big football matches on one of several screens in the cavernous basement. Upstairs features live music, German sausages and other beer hall classics, which you can wash down with several varieties of homebrew, including a *weissbier* (wheat beer).

☆ Entertainment

Opera, theatre and ballet offer mostly traditional repertoires with the exception of the Ilkhom Theatre (p212), which is arguably Central Asia's most progressive theatre. Major concerts occasionally take place in the **Dom Forum** (Ⓜ Amir Timur Hiyoboni/Yunus Rajab), hosting names like Uzbek superstar singer Sevara Nazarkhan.

For listings, check out www.facebook.com/tashkent.events.info for expatriate-oriented events news, and www.afisha.uz (in Russian) for invaluable entertainment listings. Tickets for many events are available at www.kassa.uz (in Russian).

In addition to the heavy-hitters consider the **Muqimi Musical Theatre** (Ⓙ 71-245 16 33; M Gafurov 187; tickets from 6000S; ⊘ shows 6pm; Ⓜ Bunyodkor) for traditional Uzbek folk singing, dancing and operettas, and the **Academic Russian Drama Theatre** (Ⓙ 71-233 81 65; www.ardt.uz; Ataturk 24; tickets 6000-12,000S; ⊘ shows 6.30pm Wed-Fri, 5pm Sat & Sun; Ⓜ Amir Timur Hiyoboni) for Russian-language classical Russian and Western drama as well as some more modern pieces.

For something a little sportier head out to modern **Bunyodkor Stadium** (Ⓙ 71-230 93 39; www.bunyodkor-stadium.uz; Bunyodkor Shoh; tickets 35,000S; Ⓜ Mirzo Ulughbek) to see soccer heroes Bunyodkor FC, or local matches that are held at the **Pakhtakor Stadium** (Cotton Picker stadium; www.pakhtakor.uz/en; tickets 13,000-30,000S; Ⓜ Pakhtakor) in the central park between Uzbekistan and Navoi. Tickets can be bought directly from the stadium box offices.

★ Ilkhom Theatre THEATRE

(Inspiration Theatre; Ⓙ 71-241 22 41; www.ilkhom.com; Pakhtakor 5; tickets 8000-30,000S; ⊘ box office 11am-6.30pm, shows 6.30pm Tue-Sun; Ⓜ Pakhtakor) Tashkent's main cultural highlight is this progressive theatre, whose productions often touch on gay themes and racial subjects, to consternation of the more conservative elements of Uzbek society. Alongside the cutting-edge plays (performed in Russian but often with English subtitles) there are also occasional jazz concerts and art exhibitions in the lobby.

The Ilkhom's director, Mark Weil, who founded the theatre in 1976, was tragically stabbed to death in 2007, allegedly for blaspheming the Prophet Mohammed in his Pushkin-inspired play *Imitations of the Koran. Imitations of the Koran* remains in the repertoire today.

★ Alisher Navoi Opera
& Ballet Theatre THEATRE

(Ⓙ 71-233 90 81; www.gabt.uz; Ataturk 28; ticket 10,000-30,000S; Ⓜ Kosmonavtlar) Tashkent's main opera and ballet theatre is worth a visit as much for its impressive interior as its fine opera and ballet performances. Verdi and Puccini are standards, or be bold and try a Soviet Uzbek opera by Mukhtar Ashrafi. The ticket office is hidden in one of the exterior pillars.

Tashkent State
Conservatory CONCERT VENUE

(Ⓙ 71-241 29 91; Abai 1; Ⓜ Ozbekistan) Chamber concerts and Uzbek and Western vocal and instrumental recitals in an impressive edifice. Entrance is around the back.

Circus CIRCUS

(Ⓙ 71-244 35 91; www.cirk.uz; Gofur Gulom 1; tickets 10,000-25,000S; ⊘ 3pm Sat & Sun, closed Jun-Aug; Ⓜ G'afur G'ulom) This popular kiddie diversion of clowns, jugglers and stuntmen sells out quickly.

🔒 Shopping

Tashkent has at least 16 open-air farmers markets or bazaars (Uzbek: *dekon bozori;* Russian: *kolkhozny rynok* or bazar). Chorsu, Mirobod and Oloy bazaars are the most interesting to visit.

Though selection is limited, maps can be purchased at **Sharq Ziyokori** (Bukhara 26; ⊘ 9am-6pm Mon-Sat; Ⓜ Kosmonavtlar).

It's recommended that you certify antique purchases with the vendor or at the Culture Ministry Antiques Certification Office (p279), which is roughly opposite the Latvian embassy.

★ Abulkasim Medressa ARTS & CRAFTS

(Navoi Park; ⊘ 9am-6pm; Ⓜ Milliy Bog) Close to the Oliy Majlis in Navoi Park, this medressa has been turned into an artisans' school and workshop where local wood carvers, lacquerware makers, metal workers and miniature painters ply and teach their craft. It's a great place to buy the fruits of their labour, plus souvenirs such as *suzani* (embroidery), *rospic* (lacquer boxes) and ceramics.

Chorsu Antiques ANTIQUES
(Sakichmon; ⊙10am-5pm; Ⓜ Chorsu) There
are several antique and musical instrument
shops nestled here amid a row of hard-
ware and baby cradle shops behind Chorsu Bazaar. Interesting finds include *khalat*
(cloaks) and excellent quality *suzani*. Haggle hard.

Human House CLOTHING
(✆71-255 44 11; www.humanhuman.net; Usmon
Nosir 30/9; ⊙10am-6pm Mon-Sat; Ⓜ Oybek)
This shop not only has carpets, skullcaps,
suzani and textiles from various Uzbek
provinces, but it also doubles as one of
Tashkent's most fashionable boutiques, featuring modern clothing infused with Uzbek
styles and designs.

Toshkent Univermagi DEPARTMENT STORE
(TsUM; cnr Uzbekistan & Rashidov; ⊙9am-7pm
Mon-Sat; Ⓜ Kosmonavtlar) It may not have the
atmosphere of the bazaars, but for the best
prices and a surprisingly good selection of
silk scarves (US$7) and silk by the metre, try
this old Soviet-style department store.

Tezykovka Bazaar MARKET
(Yangiobod Bazaar; Tolarik 1; ⊙Sun) The vast local flea market of Tezykovka Bazaar is also
known as Yangiobod Market. This sombre
sea of junk – 'everything from hedgehogs to
car parts' as one resident put it – is located
in the Khamza District, and reached by bus
30 from the Mustaqillik Maydoni metro, or
take a taxi from the centre for 10,000S. It's a
good place to pick up Soviet knick-knacks.

ⓘ Information

DANGERS & ANNOYANCES
Tashkent is generally a safe place. Unlike in
years gone by, the legions of *militsia* (police)
around won't bother you too much. However,
metro station entrances are the one place you'll
continue to meet police officers, most of whom
will let you continue on your way once they've
looked inside your bag. Have your passport and
valid registration slips on you when riding the
metro, and don't even think of taking photos
down there.

Tashkent's airport is a generally annoying
place. Lines at both immigration and customs
are long and disorganised and the whole process
can last two or three hours. If you are offered
'help' with your forms or luggage when going
through customs, you should politely decline
unless you're happy to pay a premium for this
service. Ask for two customs forms in English
and fill them out on your own.

INTERNET ACCESS
Nearly all hotels and many restaurants now offer
wi-fi.

MEDICAL SERVICES
In the case of a medical emergency contact
your embassy, which will be able to assist with
evacuation.

Safo Tibbiyot Clinic (✆+998 95 169 5038,
71-255 95 50; www.safouz.com; Ivliev 21; consultation US$10; ⊙9am-6pm; Ⓜ Oybek) Has
English-speaking Uzbek doctors. In Mirobod
District off Usmon Nosir.

Tashkent International Medical Clinic (TIMC;
✆71-120 11 20, 71-291 01 42, 71-291 07 26;
www.tashclinic.org; Sarikul 38; consultation
US$65, after hours US$150; ⊙8am-5pm
Mon-Fri) Has state-of-the-art medical and
dental facilities and is run by Western and
Western-trained doctors who speak English. It's
difficult to find; call for directions.

MONEY
The ATMs in town are often not working or are
cashless, so you may have to visit a couple to
find one that works. MasterCard holders should
head to ATMs at the Ramada Tashkent and
Grand Mir hotels, while Visa cardholders can
use machines at the Lotte City Hotel Tashkent
Palace, Ramada Tashkent and Hotel City Palace.
ATMs at the Hotel Uzbekistan accept both Visa
and MasterCard but are often out of order.

Asaka Bank (Abdulla Kahhor 73; ⊙9am-2pm &
3-3.30pm Mon-Fri) Offers US dollar advances
on MasterCards at 3% commission.

Kapital Bank (Nukus; ⊙9am-5pm Mon-Fri;
Ⓜ Toshkent) Charges 3% for cash advances
against Visa cards. The office is on the ground
floor to the right as you enter the building.

National Bank of Uzbekistan (NBU; ✆71-232
03 82; Gulomov 95; ⊙10am-3pm Mon-Fri;
Ⓜ Amir Timur Hiyoboni) For Visa cash advances in US dollars (3% commission), head to
room 213, where English is spoken.

POST
In addition to the **main post office** (pochta
bulimi; Shakhrisabz 7; ⊙9am-8pm; Ⓜ Abdulla
Qodiriy), there are smaller post offices scattered
around town, including a branch near Chorsu
Bazaar.

**EMERGENCY & IMPORTANT
NUMBERS**

Ambulance	✆03
Fire	✆01
Police	✆02

TELEPHONE

To get a temporary SIM card you'll need to visit the main offices of the following companies. Bring your passport. A SIM card costs less than US$2 in som.

Beeline (☑ +998 90 185 0055; www.beeline. uz; Bukhara 1; ☺ 9am-7pm)

UCell (☑ +998 93 180 0000; www.ucell.uz; Vosit Vohidov 118; ☺ 8am-7pm Mon-Fri, to 5pm Sat, 9am-4pm Sun)

UMS (☑ +998 97 130 0909; www.ums.uz; Amir Timur 24; Ⓜ Abdulla Qodiriy)

UzMobile (☑ 1099, 71-177 0909; www.uz mobile.uz; Nukus 22; Ⓜ Toshkent)

TRAVEL AGENCIES

Independent travellers will be happy to know that it's actually easy to go it alone in Uzbekistan. Even if you're organising your trip alone, travel agencies can still be useful for planning hassle-free excursions, pre-arranging train tickets and securing qualified guides for outdoor activities such as trekking, rafting and heli-skiing. Also, if you need a Letter of Invitation to apply for a visa then the assistance of a travel agency is usually essential.

Advantour (☑ 71-150 30 20; www.advantour. com; Mirobod Lane I 47A; ☺ 9am-6pm Mon-Fri; Ⓜ Oybek) Draws rave reviews for its service and can customise tours for both groups and individuals in Uzbekistan and across Central Asia. The personable and knowledgeable owners speak perfect English, and all the major services, from hotel booking to tours and transportation, can be arranged.

Arostr Tourism (☑ +998 90 186 8648, 71-256 40 67; www.arostr.com; Buyuk Turon 73, Apt 18; ☺ 9am-6pm Mon-Fri; Ⓜ Kosmonavtlar) A solid choice for individual travellers as it arranges obligation-free letters of invitation for visas, can book hotels, guides and transport and its comprehensive website is a good source of general travel advice.

Asia Adventures (☑ 71-150 62 80, 71-252 72 87; www.centralasia-adventures.com; Kunaev 27/10, Office 23; ☺ 9am-6pm Mon-Fri; Ⓜ Oybek) This adventure-travel specialist offers a range of exciting mountaineering, biking, camel safari and heli-skiing tours, with a focus on in the Chimgan mountains, as well as more traditional guided tours across Uzbekistan.

Asian Special Tourism (AST; ☑ +998 98 370 7009; www.ast.uz; Mironshoh tupik III 18; ☺ 9am-6pm Mon-Fri; Ⓜ Toshkent) Few people know the local mountains like agency lead guide Boris Karpov, who also leads the twice-monthly excursions of the Tashkent Hiking Club.

Steppe Journeys (☑ 71-235 79 06; www. steppejourneys.com; Niyozbek Yuli 1; Ⓜ Minor) Travellers recommend this agency for its professional and personal service and focus on architectural and crafts tours. Contact Odil Akhmedov.

VISAS & REGISTRATION

OVIR (☑ 71-231 45 40, 71-132 65 70; Uzbekistan 49A; ☺ 9am-5pm Mon-Fri; Ⓜ Ozbekistan) is the place to deal with any registration or visa issues. At the time of research it was not issuing extensions to tourist visas.

❶ Getting There & Away

AIR

Tashkent International Airport (☑ 71-140 28 04) is 6km south of the centre. Domestic flights leave from Terminal 3, on the southern side of the runway, a 5km drive from the international terminal. The airport is scheduled to get a new international terminal in 2020.

From Tashkent, **Uzbekistan Airways** (☑ 71-140 02 00; www.uzairways.com; Amir Timur 51; ☺ 8am-7pm; Ⓜ Toshkent) flies to Andijon (twice weekly), Bukhara (at least daily), Fergana (daily except Sunday), Nukus (twice daily), Termiz (three daily), Samarkand (at least daily) and Urgench (several daily).

Regional flights include daily services to Almaty and Astana; and twice weekly to Ürümqi, Bishkek and Dushanbe. Daily flights to Moscow fill quickly.

Uzbekistan Airways also flies to Bangkok, Beijing, Delhi, Dubai, Frankfurt, Istanbul, London, Moscow, Paris, Rome, Seoul and Tel-Aviv.

BUS & SHARED TAXI

Shared taxis (and the very occasional bus) run to Bukhara (80,000S, seven hours) and Samarkand (30,000S, three hours) when full from Tashkent's otherwise defunct **public bus station** (Tashkent Avtovokzal; ☑ 71-279 39 29; pr Bunyodkor), a couple of hundred metres across the street (northwest) from Olmazor (formerly Sobir Rakhimov) metro station.

Shared taxis to Termiz (100,000S, 10 hours) and the Tajikistan border at Sariosiyo (120,000S, 12 hours) leave from a separate stand 500m northwest of the public bus station. The highway flyovers make it difficult to access on foot so it's worth taking a taxi here.

Buses and taxis to these and other destinations also leave from the huge Abu Sakhi Bus Station behind the Ippodrom Bazaar, 3km beyond Olmazor metro on prospekt Bunyodkor.

The main departure point for shared taxis and marshrutkas to the Fergana Valley is near **Kuyluk Bazaar** (Qoyliq Bazaar), about 20 minutes east of the centre on the Fergana Hwy. Take bus 68 eastbound along Navoi from the Turkuaz stop. Alternatively it's a 8000S taxi ride from the centre. For a seat in a shared taxi figure on 50,000S to Andijon or 30,000S to Kokand.

TRAIN

The most comfortable, if not the most flexible, way to travel onwards is from Tashkent's **train station** (zheleznodorozhny vokzal; ☎71-233 84 81, 71-299 72 16; www.uzrailpass.uz; Kichik Halqa Yuli), next to the Tashkent metro station.

The super fast 'Afrosoiyob' trains to Samarkand (economy/business/VIP 58,000/78,000/112,000S, 2¼ hours) depart at 7.30am, 8am and 8.30am. Fares vary slightly according to the train. The 7.30am departure continues to Bukhara (95,000/130,000/180,000S, four hours).

A good alternative is the cheaper but still fast 'Sharq' train, which departs Tashkent at 9am daily to Samarkand (3¼ hours) and Bukhara (5¾ hours). Fares are about 30% less than the Afrosoiyob trains and tickets are generally easier to get.

A useful new service now runs twice daily from Tashkent to Kokand, Margilon and Andijon, offering the most comfortable way to get to the Fergana Valley. Trains leave Tashkent at 8.05am and 5.20pm; economy tickets cost 52,000S for Andijan (5½ hours) and 41,000S to Kokand (four hours).

Slower overnight passenger trains trundle to the following cities. The following prices are for *platskartny/kupe* (3rd-class/2nd-class sleeper) carriages:

Bukhara (60,000/80,000S, eight hours) Departs 10pm.

Nukus (106,000/158,000S, 22 hours) Departs 3.25pm or 5.15pm.

Termiz (81,000/119,000S, 15 hours) Departs 7.20pm.

Urgench (101,000/150,000S, 22 hours) Departs 12.10pm.

There are also international services to Almaty (twice weekly) and Moscow (three or four weekly).

Buying Tickets

The 24-hour main ticket office is to the left of the train station entrance. Queues generally aren't bad, but if you are in a rush head for the **VIP Ticket Office** (⊙8am-1pm & 2-8pm), signed the 'Hall of Luxury', on the right-hand side of the ticket office, where you can avoid the lines for a very reasonable 4000S per ticket commission. You'll need your passport to purchase train tickets (a photocopy won't do).

Train tickets to Samarkand can normally be bought three or four days beforehand if you are flexible with your departure time. Tour agencies and some hotels will buy tickets in advance but charge a hefty premium.

🛈 Getting Around

TO & FROM THE AIRPORT

A taxi is the easiest way from the airport, but the gaggle of taxi drivers waiting outside the terminal routinely try to rip off out-of-towners. The 15-minute taxi ride from the centre of Tashkent

UZBEKISTAN TASHKENT (TOSHKENT)

Tashkent Metro

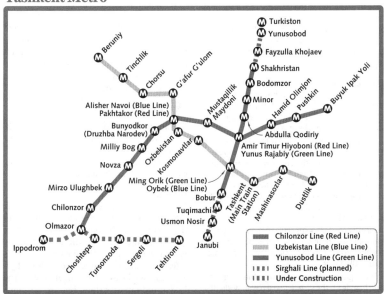

to the airport costs no more than US$1 in som, but you'll be lucky to get a ride in the other direction for less than US$5. Make sure you agree on a firm price beforehand. Budget hotels will pick you up from the airport for around US$10.

BUS & MINIBUS

The destination of public buses and marshrutkas (minibuses) is written clearly in the window. Buses and marshrutkas cost 800S, payable on board to the conductor or driver.

Between the efficient metro and cheap taxis it's rarely worth the hassle of taking local minibuses.

CAR

Any hotel or travel agency can arrange a comfortable private car and driver from about US$10 per hour. You'll pay half this on the street, but you'll usually need some basic Russian for this.

METRO

Tashkent's metro is the easiest way to get around, running between 5am and midnight. During the day you'll never wait more than five minutes for a train (1200S per trip), and the stations are clean and safe, though the security is tight. Police will want to inspect your bags twice on the way in to any station and may occasionally want to see your passport and registration slips. You'll need to buy a *zheton* (token) for each trip. Be aware that photography is strictly forbidden inside the stations.

Despite the use of Uzbek for signs and announcements, the system is easy to use, and well enough signposted that you hardly need a map. If you listen as the train doors are about to close, you'll hear the name of the next station at the end of the announcement: '*Ekhtiyot buling, eshiklar yopiladi; keyingi bekat...*' ('Be careful, the doors are closing; the next station is...').

TAXI

Every car is a potential taxi in Tashkent, but essentially there are two forms: licensed cabs and 'independent' cabs. The former have little roof-mounted 'taxi' signs. The latter are just average cars driven by average dudes.

Independent taxis generally leave it up to you to pick the price, which is fine. As long as you don't insult them with your offer, they will usually accept it. The minimum fare for a short hop is 4000S, but can be half this if there are other passengers in the cab already. Longer trips will cost 5000S to 8000S: always agree a fare before you get into the car.

Licensed cabs – especially those waiting outside bars and hotels – are a different beast, so always agree a fare in advance and expect rates to be 50% higher.

If you just want to book a taxi rather than wait and haggle on the street, you'll pay only slightly higher rates by getting your hotel to dial **City Taxi** (☑ 71-200 3330; www.citytaxi.uz), **Taksi Premier** (☑ 71-244 77 77) or **Millennium Taxi** (☑ 71-129 55 55).

Cab drivers tend not to know street names (and when they do, it's generally the Soviet-era ones), so use landmarks – big hotels and metro stations work best – to direct your driver to your destination.

AROUND TASHKENT

Chimgan Ugam-Chatkal National Park

Just over an hour northeast of Tashkent by car lies Ugam-Chatkal National Park, an outdoor haven loaded with hiking and adventure-sport opportunities as well as more relaxing pursuits. The mountains here are not quite as extreme or scenic as the higher peaks around Almaty and Bishkek, but the activities are more accessible and at least as challenging.

This entire area is known locally as Chimgan, a reference to both its biggest town and its central peak, Bolshoy Chimgan (3309m). Unesco declared the Chatkal Mountains a World Heritage Site in 2016 as part of the bi-national Western Tian Shan, shared with Kyrgyzstan.

As a major *sanatoria* centre in Soviet times, Chimgan today boasts a few newer resorts and retreats to complement the usual diet of decrepit yet still-functioning concrete Soviet hulks. And the Chorvok Reservoir offers more mellow outdoor pursuits such as fishing, swimming and canoeing – ask about these at the Chorvok Oromgohi hotel.

🏃 Activities

In the warmer months of June and July, white-water rafting trips are possible on the raging waters of the Pskem, Ugam and Chatkal rivers. Talk to **Asia Raft** (☑ 71-267 09 18; www.asiaraft.uz) in Tashkent.

Hiking

Ugam-Chatkal National Park covers the mountainous area west and southwest of the Kyrgyzstan border, from the city of Angren in the south all the way up to the Pskem Mountains in the fingerlike, glacier-infested wedge of land jutting into Kyrgyzstan, northeast of Chimgan town. The Pskem top out at 4319m, but are off limits

Around Tashkent

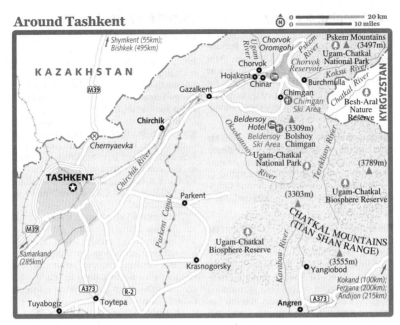

to all but well-heeled heli-skiers because of their location in a sensitive border zone.

For now, all of the national park's accessible terrain lies in the Chatkal Mountains, which stretch into Kyrgyzstan. Lacking the stratospheric height of the big Kyrgyz and Tajik peaks, the appeal of the Chatkals is their accessibility. Escaping civilisation involves walking just a short way out of the Chimgan or Beldersoy ski areas.

Asian Special Tourism (p214) can give you the scoop on day and overnight hiking possibilities around here and also hook you up with the Tashkent Hiking Club.

Several agencies in Tashkent and Samarkand offer guided hiking and trekking trips to the top of Bolshoy Chimgan peak, while Pavel at Tashkent's Art Hostel (p208) can arrange hiking day trips from Tashkent.

A guide is highly recommended for all hikes as the routes are not marked and topographical maps are about as common as Caspian Tigers (which died out from these parts in the 1970s). Guides are mandatory for multiday hikes to secure the necessary border-zone permits and ensure that you don't inadvertently walk into Kyrgyzstan (highly possible given the jigsaw borders).

Skiing & Heli-skiing

In the winter months, downhill skiing is possible at the Beldersoy and Chimgan ski areas. They encompass both the best and the worst of Soviet-style ski resorts. The best: limited grooming, excellent free-riding, some unexpectedly steep terrain, rock-bottom prices and plenty of hot wine and shashlyk. The worst: crummy lifts, limited total acreage and no snow-making to speak of.

The best terrain is way up above the tree line at Beldersoy, accessible by a lone T-bar. From the base, a long, slow double chairlift leads up to the T-bar. With just one chairlift and two trails, Chimgan is more for beginners, but also has challenging free-riding off-piste. A chairlift ride costs 15,000S. Beldersoy has surprisingly passable equipment available for hire; figure on 70,000S per day for skis, poles and boots.

While the resorts are not worth a special trip to Uzbekistan, the helicopter skiing most definitely is, as the Chatkal and Pskem Mountains are reputed to get some of the driest, fluffiest powder you'll find anywhere. Figure on paying US$500 per person per day for heli-skiing – a bargain by international standards. Book through Asia Adventures (p214) in Tashkent.

UZBEKISTAN CHIMGAN UGAM-CHATKAL NATIONAL PARK

🛏 Sleeping & Eating

Chorvok Oromgohi HOTEL $$
(☑ +998 90 188 0553; www.chorvoq.uz; Posyolok Bokachul; s/d from US$35/45) This huge pyramid on the shore of the Chorvok Reservoir will certainly catch your eye, for better or for worse. Standard rooms are pretty basic fare; you're paying for the balconies with mountain or lake views.

Beldersoy Hotel HOTEL $$$
(Best Eastern; ☑ +998 90 176 3826; www.beldersoy. com; r from US$100; ❄ ✆) This swanky four-season mountain lodge belonging to the Beldersoy ski area is just outside Chimgan and is the best bet for well-heeled skiers and hikers.

Cinara's UZBEK $$$
(☑ 71-129 90 09; http://cinaras.caravangroup.uz; Hodijent; mains 40,000-50,000S; ⊙11am-11pm) This lovely restaurant, just before Charvak village, is a popular stop en route to Chimgan. You can relax on tea-beds surrounded by ancient *chinor* (plane) trees in lovely bucolic surroundings. The shashlyk and fish are good. Ask about the nearby petroglyphs.

❶ Getting There & Away

To get to Chimgan from Tashkent, take a minibus (4000S) or shared taxi (6000S) from Buyuk Ipak Yoli metro to Gazalkent (50 minutes) and transfer to a shared taxi to Chimgan (6000S, 40 minutes). A private taxi direct to Chimgan from Tashkent from the metro costs about 100,000S.

Tashkent's budget accommodation can arrange good-value day trips for around US$50 per carload.

FERGANA VALLEY

On arrival in the Fergana Valley many visitors wonder where the valley is. From this broad (22,000 sq km), flat bowl, the surrounding mountain ranges (Tian Shan to the north and the Pamir Alay to the south) seem to stand back at enormous distances – when you can see them, that is.

Drained by the upper Syr-Darya, the Fergana Valley has the finest soil and climate in Central Asia. It is Uzbekistan's most populous and its most industrial region, as well as the country's fruit and cotton basket, meaning it has long wielded a large share of Uzbekistan's political, economic and religious influence.

The Fergana Valley's eight million people are overwhelmingly Uzbek – 90% overall and higher in the smaller towns. For visitors the main attractions are the exceptional crafts, the kaleidoscopic bazaars and the chance to see the Silk Road in action – for centuries the valley has been the centre of Central Asian silk production.

As early as the 2nd century BC the Greeks, Persians and Chinese found a prosperous kingdom (known as Davan, or Dayuan) based on farming, with some 70 towns and villages. The Russians were quick to realise the valley's fecundity, and Soviet rulers moulded it to an obsessive raw-cotton monoculture that still exists today.

Fergana was at the centre of numerous revolts against the tsar and later the Bolsheviks. In the 1990s the valley gave birth to Islamic extremism in Central Asia. President Karimov's brutal crackdown on alleged

---

NODIRA, UZBEKISTAN'S FAVOURITE POETESS

Of the pastiche of colourful characters to have emerged from Fergana Valley lore over the years, perhaps the most beloved was the beautiful poetess Nodira (1792–1842), wife of Umar Khan of Kokand. When Umar died in 1822, his son and successor, Mohammed Ali (Madali Khan), was only 12 years old. The popular Nodira took over as de facto ruler of the khanate for the better part of a decade, turning Kokand into an artistic hotbed and oasis of liberalism in a region accustomed to sadistic despots.

Unfortunately, little of this liberal spirit rubbed off on Madali, who developed a reputation for ruthlessness during a successful campaign to expand the khanate's borders. His territorial ambitions drew the ire of the notorious Emir Nasrullah Khan of Bukhara. Nasrullah would eventually get the upper hand in this battle, and in 1842 he seized Kokand and executed Madali and, when she refused to marry him (or so the story goes), Nodira. Within three months the emir's troops would be forced out of Kokand, touching off a battle for succession that would ultimately result in the rise to power of Khudayar Khan, a distant cousin of Madali.

Best known for her poetry (in both Uzbek and Tajik), Nodira remains as popular as ever today, as evidenced by the preponderance of Uzbek women named Nodira.

Fergana Valley

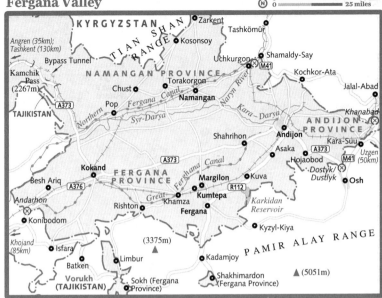

extremists eventually came to a head in the form of the 'Andijon Massacre' in 2005, the memory of which still haunts the region today.

The post-Andijon crackdown has increased the police presence in the valley, but it's not something that's likely to affect most tourists. The valley's people, overwhelmingly Uzbek and more conservative than the rest of the country, remain among the most hospitable and friendly in the country.

ⓘ Information

Standards of dress are a potential source of misunderstanding in the valley. Except perhaps in the centre of Russified Fergana town, too much tourist flesh will be frowned upon, so dress modestly (ie no shorts or tight-fitting clothes). Women travellers have reported being harassed when walking alone in cities such as Andijon, especially at night.

Security is tight compared with other parts of the country and all foreigners entering the Fergana Valley by road must register at a major roadblock west of the Kamchik tunnel separating the valley from Tashkent. Keep your passport at the ready, be agreeable when being questioned, and get a registration slip for each night you're in the valley.

ⓘ Getting There & Around

There is no public bus service on the winding mountain road between Tashkent and the Fergana Valley, but shared taxis run to and from all the major towns.

The most comfortable way to access the Fergana Valley is on the train service from Tashkent to Andijon, via Kokand and Margilon (for Fergana). The line goes through the 19km-long Chinese-built Kamchik Tunnel.

Kokand (Qo'qon)

📱 73 / POP 200,000

As the valley's first significant town on the road from Tashkent, and as one of Uzbekistan's three great 19th-century khanates, Kokand (Qo'qon) is a gateway to the region and stopping point for many travellers. With a historically interesting palace belonging to the former khans, a relaxed vibe and several medressas and mosques hidden in the old town backstreets, it makes for a worthwhile half-day visit.

This was the capital of the Kokand khanate in the 18th and 19th centuries and was second only to Bukhara as a religious centre in Central Asia, with at least 35 medressas and hundreds of mosques. But if you walk

Kokand

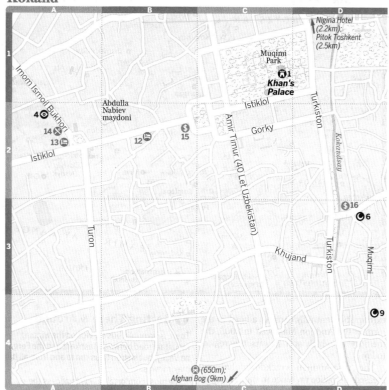

the streets today, you will find only a polite, subdued Uzbek town, its quiet old centre hedged by colonial avenues, bearing little resemblance to Bukhara.

Nationalists fed up with empty revolutionary promises met here in January 1918 and declared a rival administration, the 'Muslim Provincial Government of Autonomous Turkestan' led by Mustafa Chokaev. The Tashkent Soviet immediately had the town sacked, most of its holy buildings desecrated or destroyed and 14,000 Kokandis slaughtered.

◉ Sights

Besides the palace, a number of smaller historical buildings will be of interest to travellers with a keen interest in architecture from the khanate era.

The Bolsheviks closed the 1799 **Narbutabey Medressa** (Akbar Islamov) `FREE`, but it opened after independence only to have

Karimov shut it down again in 2008. Visitors can visit the mosque (with its original ceiling), which Stalin reopened to win wartime support from Muslim subjects, as well the non-working medressa (now named the Mir Medressa). The local caretaker will show you around for a tip. Nearby is the unrestored Modari Khan Mausoleum, built in 1825 for Umar's mother, which features unusual red, green, yellow and blue tilework.

Inside the Narbutabey graveyard's north gate, proceed straight and you'll see the 1830s **Dakhma-i-Shokhon** (Grave of Kings) – the tomb of Umar Khan and other family members – which has an elegant wooden portal carved with the poetry of Umar's wife, Nodira. Originally buried behind Modari Khan, Nodira was adopted by the Soviets as a model Uzbek woman and moved to a prominent place beneath a white stone tablet beyond Dakhma-i-Shokhon near the graveyard's south gate.

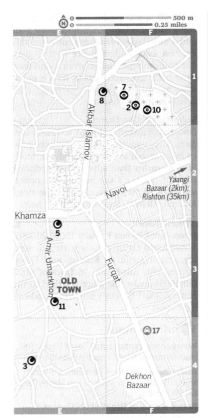

UZBEKISTAN KOKAND (QO'QON)

(1850–1903) lived and studied for the last 33 years of his life. There is a small museum in Muqimi's old room, which contains a few of his personal belongings, plus Arabic calligraphy by Muqimi himself. Hidden elsewhere down the sleepy backstreets of Kokand's old town are the Hojibek Mosque & Medressa and the small neighbourhood Zimbardor Mosque (with a welcoming chaikhana next door).

★ **Khan's Palace**   PALACE

(☑073-553 60 46; www.kokandmuseum. uz; Istiklol 2; admission/camera/guided tour 5000/6000/6000S; ☺9am-5pm) The palace of the Khan of Kokand, with seven courtyards and 114 rooms, was built in 1873, though its dazzling tiled exterior makes it look so perfect that you'd be forgiven for thinking it was as new as the modern park that surrounds it. Just three years after its completion, the tsar's troops arrived, blew up its fortifications and abolished the khan's job.

The Khan in question was Khudayar Khan, a cruel ruler who had previously cosied up to the Russians. Just two years after completing the palace, Khudayar was forced into exile by his own subjects, winding up

Anchoring the Old Town is Kokand's most impressive mosque, now the **Jami Mosque Museum** (Khamza 5; admission/camera/Russian guide 5000/2000/6000S; ☺9am-5pm), built by Umar Khan in 1812. Centred on a 22m minaret, it includes a colourful 100m-long *aivan* (portico) supported by 98 red-wood columns brought from India. The entire complex has reverted to its former Soviet guise as a museum of applied art, with one room housing a collection of *suzani* (embroidery) and ceramics from the region. A small workshop on-site makes delicious pistachio-flavoured halva (fudge-like sweet). Heading towards the **Kamal-Kazi Medressa** (Khamza), now home to a woman's organisation and so generally not open to the public, turn down Muqimi ko'chasi from Khamza ko'chasi to the truncated remnants of the 19th-century **Sahib Mian (Sohibzoda) Hazrat Medressa** (Muqimi; ☺9am-5pm), where the Uzbek poet and 'democrat' Mohammedamin Muqimi

under Russian protection in Orenburg. As his heirs quarrelled for the throne, the Russians moved in and snuffed out the khanate, in the process breaking a promise to eventually return Khudayar to the throne. The homesick khan later fled Orenburg and embarked on an epic odyssey through Central and South Asia before dying of disease near Herat.

Roughly half of the palace used to be taken up by the harem quarters, which the Russians demolished in 1919. Khudayar's 43 concubines would wait to be chosen as wife for the night – Islam allows only four wives so the khan kept a mullah at hand for a quick and short-lived marriage ceremony.

Six courtyards remain and their 27 rooms collectively house the Kokand Regional Studies Museum, which has some interesting offbeat exhibits such as the wooden lock and a pair of circus stilts.

🛌 Sleeping & Eating

Kokand has a decent range of accommodation, making it a logical place to overnight, though you can see most of the sights in a half day. There are good eating options near the Hotel Kokand and Nigina Hotel. Options beyond that are somewhat limited. For self-caters, the small **Jahon Bazaar** (Imom Ismail Bukhori) is worth a visit for fresh produce or dried fruits and nuts.

Nigina Hotel   HOTEL **$**
(☑ 73-542 85 33; Movoranakar 2b; s/d US$15/30; ✼) The location in the far north of town, 5km from the centre, is a minus for sightseeing, but there are good restaurants next door and the friendly hotel is right next to the shared taxis to Tashkent. The four new rooms are fresh and clean and the best choice.

Hotel Khan   HOTEL **$$**
(☑ 73-542 33 04, +998 90 307 6474; www.khan.uz; Istiqlol 31; r US$44-70; ✼ ☏) Perhaps the best option in town, the family-run Khan exhibits an unusual amount of panache for the Fergana Valley. Little extras such as felt slippers, free bottled water and flat-screen TVs make all the difference, while the ornate tsarist-style wallpaper adds a boutique touch. Double rooms are modern and stylish, but single rooms are tiny and overpriced.

Hotel Kokand   HOTEL **$$**
(☑ +998 95 400 4081, 73-552 20 42; www.hotelkokand.uz; Imom Ismoil Bukhori 1; s/d US$25/40; ✼ ☏) Ongoing renovations, a central location, helpful English-speaking staff and a switched-on management make this the best value budget choice in the valley. The spacious renovated superior rooms have clean bathrooms and carpets. Wi-fi is in the lobby and 1st floor only. There's room for negotiation on the room rates.

Rohatbahsh Chaikhana   TEAHOUSE **$**
(Imom Ismoil Bukhori 1; shashlyk 4000S; ⊘8am-8pm) This popular canteen-style chaikhana, also known as Jahon Chaikhana, tends to close earlier than advertised, but during daylight hours it's the best budget option in town and very convenient for the Hotel Kokand. All the Uzbek standards are here.

★**Kafe Kapriz**   CAFE **$$**
(Imom Ismoil Bukhori 1; mains 13,000-20,000S; ⊘8am-10pm) Clean premises, terrace seating and a menu of Russian and Uzbek staples, plus salads and 16 types of pizza (20,000S), make this place attached to the Hotel Kokand the city's best all-around eating option.

ℹ Information

Money changers hang out at Dekon Bazaar (the main farmers market), near the bus station.

Asaka Bank (Istiqlol; ⊘9am-2pm & 3-4pm Mon-Fri) Offers cash advances on MasterCard for 3% commission.

National Bank of Uzbekistan (Khamza; ⊘9am-5pm Mon-Fri) Offers cash advances on a Visa card.

ℹ Getting There & Around

Transport to points within the Fergana Valley leave from a **shared taxis stand** (Furqat ko'chasi) near the Dekon Bazaar. Shared taxis head to Fergana (15,000S, 1¼ hours) and Andijon (20,000S, two hours). Marshrutkas (302 to Fergana) cover the same routes but are less comfortable.

Regular minivans to Rishton (5000S, 45 minutes) leave from the suburban Uchqobrik stand on the road to Fergana, while shared taxis go from the Pitak Rishton stand past Yangi Bazaar, 2km east of the main bus station. A one-way private taxi to Rishton is a wise investment at around 20,000S.

Shared taxis to Tashkent (50,000S, four hours) congregate at what's known to locals as **'Pitak Tashkent'** (Pitok Tashkent) about 5km north of town by the defunct bus station. A taxi here from the centre of Kokand will cost 5000S.

From the **Kokand train station** (Amir Timur 40), on the southern edge of town, there is a comfortable 8am service to Tashkent (economy 43,000S, 4½ hours). Local train services to Andijon and Margilon are either overpriced or impossibly slow; you're better off taking a shared taxi.

Useful public transport options include marshrutka 2 or 4 from Dekon Bazaar to the Hotel Kokand area, and marshrutka 15, 28 or 40 north from the bazaar to the Jami Mosque Museum.

Fergana (Farg'ona)

📞 73 / POP 216,000

Tree-lined avenues and pastel-plastered tsarist buildings give Fergana (Farg'ona) the feel of a mini-Tashkent. Throw in the best services and accommodation in the region, plus a central location, and you have the most obvious base from which to explore the rest of the valley.

Fergana is the valley's least ancient and least Uzbek city. It began in 1877 as Novy Margelan (New Margilon), a colonial annexe to nearby Margilon, and became Fergana in the 1920s. It's a nice enough place to hang out, and somewhat cosmopolitan with its relatively high proportion of Russian and Korean inhabitants.

The city itself is short on sights, though the Fergana Bazaar sprawling over several blocks north of the centre is a pleasant place to explore and soak up local colour with good-natured Uzbek traders, leavened with Korean and Russian vendors selling homemade specialities. The sparse **Museum of Regional Studies** (📞 73-224 31 91; Murabbiylar 26; admission 5000S; ⊙ 9am-5pm Wed-Mon) covers the Fergana region and is of marginal interest. Visitors can inspect the WWII uniforms and a 3D map of the Fergana Valley, plus an epic set of Russian-style office furniture.

🛏️ Sleeping & Eating

Shashlyk stands occupy Al-Farghoni Park in the warm months; a cluster of them are along pedestrian Mustaqillik near the TsUM department store.

Valentina's Guesthouse   HOMESTAY **$**
(📞 +998 90 272 4072; daniol26@yahoo.com; Al-Farghoni 11, apt 10; r per person US$10; ❄️ 🎧) This unglamorous but good-value Russian-style homestay has six comfortable rooms with king-sized beds and shared bathrooms in two neighbouring Soviet apartments. The nine-floor apartment block, topped by a huge antenna, sticks out like a sore thumb; walk around the back, take the

left-hand entrance and walk to the 4th floor. Ever-patient Valentina speaks Russian but only a little English.

⭐**Taj Mahal Hotel**   HOTEL **$$**
(📞 73-224 10 86; Marifat 38/50; s/d/lux US$20/40/50; ❄️ 🎧) This modern hotel has no link to India – the owners told us they simply liked the name – but it's nevertheless the best choice in town, with a very central location, sparkling rooms, friendly staff and an epic basement club-style restaurant. There are only six single rooms so book these in advance or you'll have to pay for a double.

Hotel Ziyorat   HOTEL **$$**
(📞 73-224 0373; hotel.ziyorat@mail.ru; Kurbunjon Dodhoh 2a; s/d US$35/50, lux s/d US$40/60; ❄️ 🎧 🏊) The creaky lift and beige carpets at this former Soviet behemoth hark back to the good old bad old days, but the renovated rooms are modern, spacious and carpeted, with clean tiled bathrooms, a balcony and a fridge. The singles are a decent size and there's even a pool in summer. Lenin must be turning in his grave.

Hotel Asia Fergana   HOTEL **$$$**
(📞 73-244 13 26; www.asiahotels.uz; Navoi 26a; s/d from US$73/110; ❄️ 🎧 🏊) A comfortable, if overpriced, option aimed at groups, with 100 rooms, pleasant gardens and English-speaking staff. It's part of the Asia group owned by the Marco Polo travel agency. Visa cards accepted. The outdoor pool is a nice place to beat the heat and sip a poolside cocktail in the evening.

Café Emirates   CENTRAL ASIAN **$$**
(Sayilgoh; mains 15,000-19,000S; ⊙ 8.30am-11pm; ❄️) Emirates may not be the most atmospheric restaurant in town, but it's clean and modern, with comfy seating, good service and good-value comfort food, from Turkish-style kebabs and sausage breakfasts to pizza and espresso coffee.

Bravo   INTERNATIONAL **$$**
(Khojand 12; mains 8000-12,000S; ⊙ 9am-11pm; ❄️ 📶 🏧) Fergana's best little boho cafe was under renovation when we visited last. Hopefully the sunny patio and live jazz music will survive the *remont*.

⭐**Traktir Ostrov Sokrovish**   INTERNATIONAL **$$$**
(Treasure Island Tavern; Marifat 45; mains 10,000-40,000S; ⊙ 10am-midnight; ❄️ 🎧 📶 🏧) This

Fergana

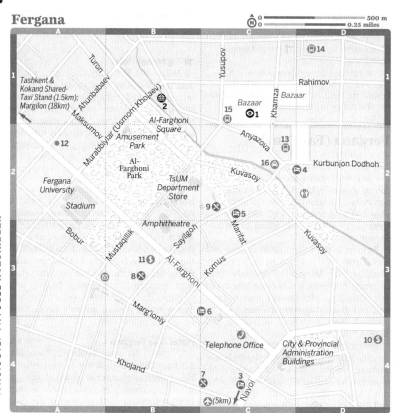

centrally located and hip place hums with locals at all times of the day, and the summer terrace with cooling misters is a delight. The food is excellent, with a luxury of choice from burgers and chicken, steaks and even salmon Caesar salad and sushi, plus espresso coffee and cocktails.

ℹ️ Information

Money changers can be found at the bazaar.

Asaka Bank (cnr Navoi & Kuvasoy; ⊗9am-5pm Mon-Fri) You can get US dollar cash advances on a MasterCard here.

National Bank of Uzbekistan (Al-Farghoni 35; ⊗9am-5pm Mon-Fri) A cash advance office for Visa cardholders is on the 3rd floor.

OVIR (Office of Visas & Registration; Ahunbaabaev 36; ⊗9am-5pm Mon-Fri) Travellers might need to visit this office if staying in a private home.

Post Office (Mustaqillik 35; ⊗7am-7pm)

Telephone Office (Al-Farghoni)

ℹ️ Getting There & Around

Trains to Tashkent run daily from nearby Margilon train station. A taxi there costs 8000S.

AIR

Uzbekistan Airways has three flights a week between Fergana and Tashkent, with a less reliable weekly flight to Bukhara. The airport is 4km southwest of the centre. The airport is a 25-minute trip on bus 6 to/from the local bus station, but check with the driver to make sure he's going all the way to the airport. A taxi costs 6000S one way.

BUS & SHARED TAXI

Shared taxis and minibus 764 to Andijon (minibus/taxi per seat 5000/12,000S, 1½ hours) depart throughout the day from the long-distance bus station, north of the bazaar. This is also a good spot to find rides to Margilon (bus/marshrutka/taxi per seat 500/1500/2500S, 20 minutes).

Fergana

Bus 30 to Rishton (3000S, 50 minutes) and bus 302 to Kokand (5000S, two hours) use the local bus station southeast of the bazaar.

Shared taxis to Kokand (10,000S, one hour) leave from this stand and from a nearby lot opposite the Hotel Ziyorat. Negotiate to get dropped in the centre of Kokand rather than the suburban Uchqobrik stand.

Minivan 10 to Margilon departs from a stop (cnr Anyazova & Yusupov) at the southwest corner of the bazaar.

A private (not shared) taxi costs around 10,000S to Margilon. For an ambitious day tour to Rishton, Kokand and Margilon, count on around US$40.

Shared taxis to Tashkent (50,000S, five hours), as well as more to Kokand, leave from a stop on the road to Margilon near Yermazar Bazaar, 2km northwest of the centre.

Around Fergana

Margilon (Marg'ilan)

📞 73 / POP 197,000

If you've been travelling along the Silk Road seeking answers to where, in fact, this highly touted fabric comes from, Margilon (Marg'ilan), 16km from Fergana, will be your answer. Uzbekistan is the world's third-largest silk producer, and Margilon is the traditional centre of the industry, boasting the large Yodgorlik Silk Factory and several smaller, family-run silk workshops.

Although there is little to show for it, Margilon has been around for a long time, probably since the 1st century BC. For centuries its merchant clans, key players in Central Asia's commerce and silk trade, were said to be a law unto themselves; even in the closing decades of Soviet rule, this was the heart of Uzbekistan's black-market economy. Margilon is also one of the country's most devoutly Islamic cities.

◎ Sights

A good tour guide should be able to get keen silk connoisseurs into the private homes of weavers whose silk is for sale at Kumtepa Bazaar. They should also be able to organise tours to one of Margilon's larger commercial silk factories.

Margilon is easily visited as a half-day trip from Fergana, but if you have a particular interest in silk weaving the **Ikat House** (📞 +998 90 303 3800; ikathouse01@gmail.com; Ipak Yuli 133; s/d US$25/40; ❈ 🛜) and **Adras Hotel** (📞 +998 95 404 0035; hoteladras@list.ru; B Margiloniy 32; s US$20-30, d US$30-40; ❈ 🛜) are both worthwhile options.

★ **Yodgorlik Silk Factory**   FACTORY
(📞 +998 91 121 2552, 073-253 67 61; yodgorlik-factory@mail.ru; Imam Zakhriddin 138; guide tip 10,000S; ⊙ 8.30am-noon & 1-5pm Mon-Fri) Margilon's main attraction is this fascinating factory, a block west of the central Dekon Bazaar. English-language guides can walk you through traditional methods of silk production from steaming and unravelling the cocoons to the tie-dyeing and weaving of the dazzling *khanatlas* (hand-woven silk) fabrics for which Margilon is famous.

After the tour you can buy silk or *adras* (silk-cotton mix) by the metre (US$8 to US$25) in the showroom, a former mosque. There are also silk scarves, clothing, carpets and embroidered items for sale. Visa cards accepted.

Sayid Ahmad Hoja Medressa   WORKSHOP
This charming medressa was converted into a crafts centre more than a decade ago, with the former *hujras* (cell-like living quarters) now housing a *suzani* embroiderer, metal worker, copper chaser and cloth block print stamper. The main attraction is the workshop of Rosuljon Mirzoakhmedov, the latest

in nine generations of master *ikat* weavers, who has a sales room in the winter mosque. A water channel flows through the medressa, an unusual design that the local cloth dyers have taken full advantage of.

The medressa is a 15-minute walk south and then east from the central crossroads.

★ Kumtepa Bazaar
BAZAAR

(⊘ Thu & Sun) The fantastic Kumtepa Bazaar, 5km west of Margilon centre, is a time capsule full of weathered Uzbek men in traditional clothing exchanging solemn greetings and gossiping over endless pots of tea. Rows of handmade *khanatlas* and *adras* silk, available from just 5000S per metre, are both the shopping and the visual highlight. It's probably the most interesting bazaar in the country. The busiest day is Sunday, but it also works on Thursday.

Margilon's traditional streak is in full view here, with Uzbek matrons dressed almost exclusively in the locally produced *khanatlas* dresses and head scarves and men in skullcaps and *chapan* (heavy quilted jacket).

Take a shared taxi (2000S per person) or 'Bozor' marshrutka (1000S) from Margilon to get here. A taxi from Fergana costs around 6000S.

❶ Getting There & Away

Marshrutkas and taxis from Fergana drop you off near the town's main intersection, diagonally across from the central Dekon Bazaar. Shared taxis run frequently from here back to Fergana (3000S).

A half-day taxi from Fergana to the Yodgorlik Silk Factory and Kumtepa Bazaar costs around 50,000S.

There are daily trains to Tashkent (five hours) departing at 7am and 4.40pm from the train station, 4km south of Margilon's main intersection.

Rishton

📔 73 / POP 22,000

Just north of the Kyrgyzstan border, Rishton is famous for the ubiquitous cobalt and green pottery fashioned from its fine clay. About 90% of the ceramics you see in souvenir stores across Uzbekistan originates here – most of it handmade. Some one thousand potters make a living from the legendary local loam, which is so pure that it requires no additives (besides water) before being chucked on the wheel.

Only a handful of these potters are considered true masters who still use traditional techniques. Among them is Rustam Usmanov, erstwhile art director of the defunct local collectivised ceramics factory. He runs the **Rishton Ceramics Museum** (📔 73-271 18 65, +998 91 681 2391; Ar-Roshidony 230; ⊘ 9am-6pm) out of his home 1km west of the centre on the main road to Kokand. Usmanov gives free tours of his workshop and can provide lunch to travellers who call ahead.

Rishton is best visited as a stop between Fergana and Kokand. It's about a 45-minute shared taxi ride from either (4000S), or take a slower bus (2500S). A private taxi from either destination costs around 20,000S.

Andijon

📔 74 / POP 580,000

Andijon – the Fergana Valley's largest city and its cultural centre – will forever be linked with the uprising and ensuing massacre of 13 May 2005. The very word 'Andijon' is a hot potato in Uzbekistan; just mentioning it is enough to stop any conversation in its tracks. That's a shame because both culturally and linguistically Andijon is probably the country's most authentic Uzbek city. For travellers it is of interest for its lively bazaars and as the valley's main gateway to Osh in Kyrgyzstan.

⊙ Sights

Jahon Bazaar
BAZAAR

(⊘ 9am-6pm) Andijon's Jahon Bazaar is the biggest bazaar on the Uzbek side of the Fergana Valley. There are silk stalls here, in case you miss Kumtepa Bazaar in Margilon. Sunday and Thursday are its busiest days. From Eski Bazaar in the old town, it's 4km north on marshrutka 394 or anything saying Жахон бозори/Jahon Bozori.

Devanboy Mosque
MOSQUE

(Oltinkul) With a new facade, twin minarets and a *taharkhana* (wash house), the 19th-century Devanboy Mosque now plays the role of Andijon's Friday mosque. The friendly imam welcomes visitors, but no photos are allowed inside. Massive redevelopment is taking place on the streets around the mosque.

Jome Mosque & Medressa
MOSQUE

(Oltinkul; admission 5000S; ⊘ 9am-4pm Tue-Sun) Across from the Eski Bazaar is the handsome 19th-century Jome Mosque & Medressa, said to be the only building to survive the 1902 earthquake. It reopened as a working medressa in the 1990s, but was turned into a vaguely interesting museum of local ethnography after a police crackdown on suspected Islamic militants. The huge interior courtyard is largely in ruins. The 700-year-old minaret was spared demolition in 2016 after an unusual campaign by locals changed the local government's plans to replace it with a fountain.

Babur Literary Museum   MUSEUM

(Bazernaya 21; admission 5000S; ⊙9am-noon & 1-5pm) This museum occupies the site of the royal apartments where Zahiruddin Babur (1483–1530) lived and studied as a boy within Ark-Ichy, the town's long-gone citadel. The mildly interesting displays focus on Babur's literary exploits, specifically his Baburnama, a vast memoir of Babur's fascinating and tumultuous life. A graph of Babur's family tree shows his descent from Timur on the male line and from Genghis Khan on his mother's side.

🛏 Sleeping & Eating

There is a large choice of chaikhanas around the bazaars and just about everywhere else.

Hotel Hamkor   HOTEL $$

(Hamkor Business Centre; ☑ 74-298 08 08; hamkorbc @mail.ru; Babur 53; r US$40-60; ❈🛜) Well located in the centre of the city, this modern business hotel boasts spacious rooms, English-speaking staff and an unusual understanding of the needs of travellers. *Lux* (deluxe) rooms are the best choice for US$50.

Hotel Villa Elegant   HOTEL $$

(☑ +998 95 202 8558; www.vellaelegant.uz; Bobur Shoh 40; s/d US$40/60; 🛜🛁) There are few fireworks at this large, modern economy business hotel, but it's comfortable and modern and the poolside seating and lobby fridge full of cold beer hint at its fun side. The location is perfect for onward transportation by train or shared taxi.

Hotel Andijon   HOTEL $$

(☑ 74-223 70 40; Fitrat 241; s/d US$25/40, ste US$45; 🛜) This friendly English-speaking, Soviet-style hotel across from Navoi Sq sports spacious, renovated rooms (even the singles are a good size), but some rooms can be smoky and wi-fi is only really reliable in the lobby. The *lux* suite can sleep six, making it a great deal.

Bosco   RUSSIAN $$$

(☑ +998 97 338 3767; Istiklol 8; mains 20,000-30,000S; ⊙9am-9pm) For something fancier than *plov,* try Bosco, which serves up a standard menu of Russian classics under a classy backdrop of dark wood, crisp linens and live music.

ℹ Information

Money changers can be found outside Eski Bazaar, while the **Asaka Bank** (Milly Tiklanish 41) offers MasterCard advances in US dollars and the **National Bank of Uzbekistan** (Navoi 42) does the same for Visa.

ℹ Getting There & Around

Andijon's airport is located 3km southwest of the train station. **Uzbekistan Airways** (☑ 74-228 18 31; www.uzairways.com; Andijon Airport) has two weekly flights between Andijon and Tashkent.

Shared taxis and minibuses to Fergana (taxi/ minibus per seat 12,000/5000S, 1¼ hours) leave from the main bus station, near the train station.

Shared taxis to the Kyrgyzstan border at Dostyk (Dustlyk; 10,000S per seat, one hour) leave from the nearby Yangi Bazaar stand.

BABUR'S EXILE

Born in 1483 in Andijon to Fergana's ruler, Umar Sheikh Mirzo (a descendant of Timur), Babur is Andijon's favourite son and one of the most fascinating figures of Central Asian history. He inherited his father's kingdom before he was even a teenager and took Samarkand at the tender age of 14, but eventually lost both Samarkand and Fergana and was driven into Afghanistan by the Uzbek Shaybanids, effectively ending Timurid rule in Central Asia.

Babur's life of exile took him across the Hindu Kush to Kabul and eventually across the Khyber Pass into India, where he founded the powerful Mughal Empire. He died aged 47, succeeded by his son Humayan, and was buried in his beloved gardens in Kabul. A cultured man who wrote in both Turkic and Persian, Babur's autobiography, the *Baburnameh,* is full of wistful longing for his lost lands of Central Asia and is a classic of medieval literature.

Shared taxis to Tashkent (40,000S to 50,000S per seat, five hours) leave from the nearby Tashkent Stoyanka.

Two daily trains depart Andijon train station in the south of town at 6.20am and 3.50pm for Tashkent (economy/business/VIP 53,000/94,000/170,000S, five hours), via Margilon and Kokand. There are also long-distance services to Moscow (twice weekly), Urgench (weekly) and Bukhara (twice weekly), all via Tashkent.

Marshrutka 33 travels from Eski Bazaar in the old town past Navoi Sq and Villa Elegant Hotel (near the train station) before passing near the airport. Any marshrutka signed 'Эски Шахар' ('Eski Shahar' or Old Town) goes to Eski Bazaar.

CENTRAL UZBEKISTAN

Central Uzbekistan covers a huge swath of the country, from the important historic cities of Samarkand, Bukhara and Shahrisabsz down to Termiz and the Surkhandarya region on the southern border with Afghanistan and Tajikistan. Defined by Central Asia's two great rivers, the Syr-Darya (Jaxartes) and Amu-Darya (Oxus), these are the lands historically known as Transoxiana, where steppe and semi-desert meets the mountain spurs of the Hissar, Fan and Nuratau Mountains.

The Timurid empire, Sheybanid Uzbeks and the emirate of Bukhara all ruled large parts of Central Asia from central Uzbekistan. For visitors Samarkand and Bukhara are the big draws and deserve a couple of days each. Shakhrisabz has some tantalising remains of Timur's summer palace, but recent renovations have destroyed much of the town's charm. Termiz is way off the beaten track but has some intriguing remains from its rich Buddhist past.

Samarkand (Samarqand)

☑ 066 / POP 596,300 / ELEV 710M

No name is as evocative of the Silk Road as Samarkand (Samarqand). For most people it has the mythical resonance of Zanzibar or Timbuktu, fixed in the Western popular imagination by imaginative poets and playwrights, few of whom saw the city in the flesh.

On the ground the sublime, larger-than-life monuments of Timur (Tamerlane) and the city's long, rich history still work some kind of magic. You can visit most of Samarkand's high-profile attractions in two or three days. If you're short on time, at least see the Registan, Gur-e-Amir, Bibi-Khanym Mosque and Shah-i-Zinda.

Away from these islands of majesty, Samarkand is a well-groomed modern city, with a large Russian town of broad avenues and parks. The recent walling off of parts of the old town and the pedestrianisation of Toshkent street has led to the 'Disneyfication' of some areas, but there's enough grandeur left to say that Samarkand remains a breathtaking place to visit.

Don't forget to pass by the main sights after dark; the Registan and Gur-e-Amir are floodlit and particularly sublime by night.

History

Samarkand (Marakanda to the Greeks), one of Central Asia's oldest settlements, was founded in the 8th century BC. It was already the cosmopolitan, walled capital of the Sogdian empire when it was taken in 329 BC by Alexander the Great, who said, 'Everything I have heard about Marakanda is true, except that it's more beautiful than I ever imagined.'

A key Silk Road city, it sat on the crossroads leading to China, India and Persia, drawing in trade and artisans. From the 6th to the 13th century it grew into a city more populous than it is today, changing hands every couple of centuries – Western Turks, Arabs, Persian Samanids, Karakhanids, Seljuq Turks, Mongolian Karakitay and Khorezmshah have all ruled here – before being obliterated by Chinggis Khan in 1220.

This might have been the end of the story, but in 1370 Timur decided to make Samarkand his capital, and over the next 35 years forged a new, almost-mythical city that became Central Asia's economic and cultural epicentre. His grandson Ulugbek ruled until 1449 and made it an intellectual centre as well.

When the Uzbek Shaybanids came in the 16th century and moved their capital to Bukhara, Samarkand went into decline. For several decades in the 18th century, after a series of earthquakes, it was essentially uninhabited. The emir of Bukhara forcibly repopulated the town towards the end of the century, but it was only truly resuscitated by the Russians, who forced its surrender in May 1868 and linked it to the Russian Empire by the Trans-Caspian railway 20 years later.

Samarkand's most famous (and infamous) modern son, Islam Karimov, the first president of Uzbekistan, is buried at a new tomb at the Hazrat-Hizr Mosque. A statue of the man is planned as the centre piece of a new plaza to the east of the Registan.

⊙ Sights

⊙ Old Town

⭐ **Registan**   PLAZA
(cnr Registan & Toshkent; admission 30,000S; ⊙ 8am-7pm Apr-Oct, 9am-5pm Nov-Mar) This ensemble of majestic, tilting medressas – a near-overload of majolica, azure mosaics and vast, well-proportioned spaces – is the centrepiece of the city, and arguably the most awesome single sight in Central Asia. The three grand edifices here are among the world's oldest preserved medressas, anything older having been destroyed by Chinggis Khan.

The Registan, which translates to 'Sandy Place' in Tajik, was medieval Samarkand's commercial centre and the plaza was probably a wall-to-wall bazaar. The three medressas have taken their knocks over the years courtesy of the frequent earthquakes that buffet the region; that they are still standing is a testament to the incredible craftsmanship of their builders. The Soviets, to their credit, worked feverishly to restore these beleaguered treasures, but they also took some questionable liberties, such as the capricious addition of a blue outer dome to the Tilla-Kari Medressa. For an idea of just how ruined the medressas were at the start of the 20th century, check out the excellent photo exhibit inside the Tilla-Kari Medressa.

The **Ulugbek Medressa**, on the western side, is the original medressa, finished in 1420 under Ulugbek who is said to have taught mathematics here (other subjects taught here included theology, astronomy and philosophy). The stars on the portal reflect Ulugbek's love of astronomy. Beneath the little corner domes were lecture halls, now housing displays on Ulugbek, including copies of the 'Zij' (his writings on astronomy) and miniatures depicting Central Asian astronomers at work. At the rear is a large mosque with a beautiful blue painted interior and an austere teaching room to one side. Police guards occasionally offer to clandestinely escort visitors to the top of the medressa's minaret for around US$10.

The other buildings are rough imitations by the Shaybanid Emir Yalangtush. The entrance portal of the **Sher Dor (Lion) Medressa**, opposite Ulugbek's and finished in 1636, is decorated with roaring felines that look like tigers but are meant to be lions. The lions, the deer they are chasing and the Mongolian-faced, Zorostrian-inspired suns rising from their backs are all unusual, flouting Islamic prohibitions against the depiction of live animals. It took 17 years to build but hasn't held up as well as the Ulugbek Medressa, built in just three years.

In between them is the **Tilla-Kari (Gold-Covered) Medressa**, completed in 1660, with a pleasant, gardenlike courtyard. The highlight here is the mosque, which is on the left-hand side of the courtyard and is intricately decorated with blue and gold to symbolise Samarkand's wealth. The mosque's delicate ceiling, oozing gold leaf, is flat but its tapered design makes it look domed from the inside. The result is magnificent. Inside the mosque is an interesting picture gallery featuring blown-up B&W photos of old Samarkand. Several shops sell prints of these old photos.

Most of the medressas' former dormitory rooms are now art and souvenir shops. Be sure to visit the Registan in the evening to see if the impressive sound and light show is being projected. If a large group has paid for the show then other visitors can watch for free.

Note that your entrance ticket is valid all day long, allowing you to come back and photograph the complex at the various times of day needed for the sunlight to be coming from the right direction. However, tell the complex security guards if you'd like to do this, otherwise they will tear your ticket and you won't be able to reuse it.

In the neighbourhoods south of the Registan are the **Hoja-Nisbatdor Mosque** (Suzangaran) featuring a large *aivan* (portico) embraced by walls inlaid with *ghanch* (carved alabaster) that has been beautiful restored, and the small 19th-century **Imon Mosque** (btwn Ali Kushchi & Suzangaran; ⊙ dawn-dusk) with an open porch, tall carved columns and a brightly restored ceiling.

⭐ **Bibi-Khanym Mosque**   MOSQUE
(Toshkent; admission/camera 22,000/5000S; ⊙ 8am-8pm) The enormous congregational Bibi-Khanym Mosque, northeast of the Registan, was financed from the spoils of Timur's invasion of India and must have

Samarkand

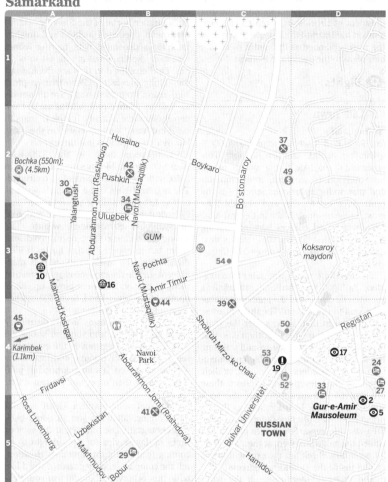

been the jewel of his empire. Once one of the Islamic world's biggest mosques (the cupola of the main mosque is 41m high and the *pishtak* or entrace portal, 38m), it pushed contemporary construction techniques to the limit, so much so that the dome started crumbling even before construction had finished.

The mosque partially collapsed in an earthquake in 1897 before being rebuilt in the 1970s and more rapidly in the years after independence.

Legend says that Bibi-Khanym, Timur's Chinese wife, ordered the mosque built as

a surprise while he was away. The architect fell madly in love with her and refused to finish the job unless he could give her a kiss. The smooch left a mark and Timur, on seeing it, executed the architect and decreed that women should henceforth wear veils so as not to tempt other men.

The interior courtyard contains an enormous marble Quran stand that lends some scale to the place. Local lore has it that any woman who crawls under the stand will have lots of children. The courtyard also contains two smaller mosques. The one on the left as you enter through the enormous

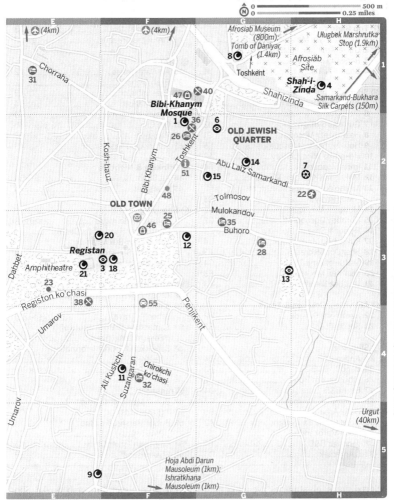

main gate has an impressive unrestored interior festooned with Arabic calligraphy.

Across from the mosque is the surprisingly plain 14th-century **Bibi-Khanym Mausoleum** (Toshkent; admission 14,000S; ☺8am-6pm), home to five tombs and some lovely interior painted stalactites, but it's quite overpriced for what it is.

Hazrat-Hizr Mosque   MOSQUE
(Toshkent; admission 12,000S; ☺8am-6pm) Across Shahizinda ko'chasi from the Siob Bazaar, the Hazrat-Hizr Mosque occupies a hill on the fringes of Afrosiab. The 8th-century mosque that once stood here was burnt to the ground by Chinggis (Genghis) Khan in the 13th century and was not rebuilt until 1854. In the 1990s it was lovingly restored by a wealthy Bukharan and today it's Samarkand's most beautiful mosque, with a fine domed interior and views of Bibi-Khanym Mosque, Shah-i-Zinda and Afrosiab from the minaret. The ribbed *aivan* ceiling drips colour.

★Shah-i-Zinda   ISLAMIC TOMB
(Shahizinda; admission/camera 10,000/7000S; ☺7am-7pm) Samarkand's most moving and

Samarkand

beloved site is this stunning avenue of mausoleums, which contains some of the richest tilework in the Muslim world. The name, which means 'Tomb of the Living King', refers to its original, innermost and holiest shrine – a complex of cool, quiet rooms around what is probably the grave of Qusam ibn-Abbas, who is said to have brought Islam to this area in the 7th century. The most stunning Timurid-era tilework dates from 14th and 15th centuries.

A shrine to Qusam, a cousin of the Prophet Mohammed, existed here on the edge of Afrosiab for around seven centuries before Timur (Tamerlane) and later Ulugbek buried their family and favourites near the sanctity of the original shrine.

The most beautiful tomb is the Shodi Mulk Oko Mausoleum (1372), resting place of a sister and niece of Timur, second on the left after the entry stairs. The exquisite majolica and terracotta work here – notice the minuscule amount of space between the tiles – was of such exceptional quality that it merited almost no restoration.

After remarkably surviving more than seven centuries with only minor touch-up work, many of the tombs were aggressively and controversially restored in 2005. As a result, much of the brilliant mosaic, majolica and terracotta work you see today is not original.

Shah-i-Zinda is an important place of pilgrimage, so enter with respect and dress conservatively. Just outside the entrance are the foundations of a 15th-century *tahorathana* (bathhouse). At the end of the pathway between the mausoleums, the complex opens up into Samarkand's main cemetery, which is a fascinating place to walk.

Ishratkhana Mausoleum   MAUSOLEUM
(Sadriddin Ayni) If you prefer your ruins really ruined, it's worth the slog out to the crumbling 15th-century Ishratkhana Mausoleum, newly topped by a tin roof. With a preponderance of pigeons and an eerie crypt in the basement, this is the place to film your horror movie. It's a 30-minute walk from the Old Town; follow Suzangaran ko'chasi from the Registan and then at the very end turn left onto Andijon ko'chasi until you hit Sadriddin Ayni ko'chasi.

Across the street is the blue-domed **Hoja Abdi Darun Mausoleum** (Sadriddin Ayni) **FREE**, which shares a tranquil, shady courtyard with a mosque and a charming *hauz* (artificial stone pool). It's a timeless site, far from the tourist chatter.

◉ Russian Town

Samarkand's Russified western downtown area tends to escape tourists' radars, which is unfortunate because it's quite un-Sovietised and charming.

★Gur-e-Amir Mausoleum   MAUSOLEUM
(Bo'stonsaroy; admission/camera 22,000/5000S; ⊙8am-7pm Apr-Oct, to 5pm Nov-Mar) The beautiful portal and trademark fluted azure dome of the Gur-e-Amir Mausoleum marks the final resting place of Timur (Tamerlane), along with two sons and two grandsons (including Ulugbek). It's a surprisingly modest building, largely because Timur was never expecting to be buried here. The tilework and dome are particularly beautiful; be sure to return at night when the building is spotlit to grand effect.

Timur had built a simple crypt for himself at Shakhrisabz, and had this one built in 1404 for his grandson and proposed heir, Mohammed Sultan, who had died the previous year. But the story goes that when Timur died unexpectedly of pneumonia in Kazakhstan (in the course of planning an expedition against the Chinese) in the winter of 1405, the passes back to Shakhrisabz were snowed in and he was interred here instead.

As with other Muslim mausoleums, the stones are just markers; the actual crypts are in a chamber beneath. In the centre is Timur's stone, once a single block of dark-green jade. In 1740 the warlord Nadir Shah carried it off to Persia, where it was accidentally broken in two – from which time Nadir Shah is said to have had a run of very bad luck, including the near death of his son. At the urging of his religious advisers he returned the stone to Samarkand and, of course, his son recovered.

The plain marble marker to the left of Timur's is that of Ulugbek; to the right is that of Mir Said Baraka, one of Timur's spiritual advisors. In front lies Mohammed Sultan. The stones behind Timur's mark the graves of his sons Shah Rukh (the father of Ulugbek) and Miran Shah. Behind these lies Sheikh Seyid Umar, the most revered of Timur's teachers, said to be a descendant of the Prophet Mohammed. Timur ordered Gur-e-Amir built around Umar's tomb.

The Soviet anthropologist Mikhail Gerasimov opened the crypts in 1941 and, among other things, confirmed that Timur was tall (1.7m) and lame in the right leg and right arm (from injuries suffered when he was 25) – and that Ulugbek died from being beheaded. According to every tour guide's favourite anecdote, he found on Timur's grave an inscription to the effect that 'whoever opens this will be defeated by an enemy more fearsome than I'. The next day, 22 June, Hitler attacked the Soviet Union.

Behind the ugly wall surrounding Gur-e-Amir is the unexpected 15th-century **Ak Saray Mausoleum** (Ok Saroy Mazar; Shohruh Mirzo; admission 5000S; ⊙8am-6pm), with some stunningly restored blue and gold decoration under the main dome and three tombs in the crypt.

Statue of Amir Timur   STATUE
(Bulver Universitet) This glowering statue of Timur seated on his throne marks the boundary between the old Uzbek town and the Russian-designed new town. It's a major landmark and spotlit at night.

Nearby is the brick **Rukhobod Mausoleum** (Registan; admission 12,000S; ⊙9am-6pm), dated 1380 and possibly the city's oldest surviving monument, which was renovated in 2015 and now serves as a souvenir and craft shop. The entry price is quite ridiculous; just look in from the door.

Hovrenko Wine Factory   MUSEUM
(☑+998 97 914 9411; www.xovrenko.uz; Mahmud Kashgari 58; tasting per person 45,000S, museum

admission free; ⊗8am-1pm Apr-Oct) Those with adventurous taste buds can sign up for a tasting of eight wines, *balzams* and cognacs from the Hovrenko Wine Factory, which has been producing wines here since 1868. The small attached museum has no signage in English, but has some interesting photos of Soviet wine production in the 1930s. Call ahead to ensure there's availability.

Regional Studies Museum   MUSEUM

(Abdurahmon Jomi 51; admission 14,000S; ⊗9am-6pm) The Regional Studies Museum occupies an old Jewish merchant's house, and has a lavish wing devoted to Jewish history, with old photos of Samarkand's once-prominent population of both European and Bukhara Jews. The rest of the museum contains the standard line-up of old ceramics, stuffed animals and historical displays.

◉ Ancient Samarkand (Afrosiab)

At a 2.2-sq-km site called Afrosiab, northeast of Siob Bazaar, excavations of Marakanda (early Samarkand) lie more or less abandoned to the elements. If it's not too hot, the best way to reach Afrosiab is on foot. Cross the intersection north of Bibi-Khanym and follow Toshkent yo'li for about 1km to the Afrosiab Museum. Ulugbek's Observatory is 1.5km beyond that.

To get to the Observatory directly take bus 45 or 99 or minibus 17 from Shahizinda ko'chasi.

Afrosiab Museum   MUSEUM

(Toshkent yo'li; admission/guide 22,000/20,000S; ⊗8.30am-6pm) The Afrosiab Museum was built around one of Samarkand's more important archaeological finds, a chipped 7th-century fresco of the Sogdian King Varkhuman (r 650–670) receiving ranks of foreign dignitaries (including Chinese envoys carrying silk), while sitting astride elephants, camels and horses. You'll see reproductions of this iconic fresco throughout the country. It was only discovered in 1965 during the construction of Toshkent yo'li.

The left-hand wall depicts red- and white-faced dignitaries leading geese and horses on a sacrificial procession, while the right wall shows the Chinese Tang emperor Gaozong hunting panthers.

The 2nd floor of the museum deals with the 11 distinct layers of the archaeological site; at the time of research it was closed due to water damage. It's worth catching the short film explaining the murals and their French-sponsored renovation.

Tomb of Daniyar   MAUSOLEUM

(Toshkent; admission 18,000S; ⊗7am-7pm Apr-Oct, 8am-5pm Nov-Mar) The restored tomb of the Old Testament prophet Daniyar (Daniel) is a long, low structure topped with five domes, containing an 18m sarcophagus – legend has it that Daniel's body grows by half an inch a year and so the sarcophagus has been enlarged over the centuries. His remains, which date from at least the 5th century BC, were brought here by Timur from Susa, Iran (suspiciously, an alleged tomb of Daniel can also be found there).

Ulugbek's Observatory   OBSERVATORY

(Toshkent; admission/camera 22,000/5000S; ⊗8am-7pm Apr-Oct, 9am-5pm Nov-Mar) The remains of Ulugbek's 15th-century observatory is one of the great archaeological finds of the 20th century. Ulugbek was probably more famous as an astronomer than as a ruler. His 30m quadrant, designed to observe star positions, was part of a three-storey observatory he built in the 1420s. All that remains now is the instrument's huge curved track, unearthed in 1908.

◉ Old Jewish Quarter

Over the last decade city planners have redesigned Samarkand to seal off older sections of town from the view of tourists. Roads have been rerouted and ugly walls have been erected around the Gur-e-Amir and behind the Registan, and virtually all access points between the old town and touristy Toshkent and Registon streets have been closed off.

Plucky travellers who do manage to persevere into the old town will be rewarded with an authentic slice of *mahalla* (neighbourhood) life. The most interesting neighbourhood is the old Jewish Quarter, accessible by a gate off Toshkent yo'li, next to the Samarkand Tourist Information Centre. From the gate, walk east along the main lane, Abu Laiz Samarkandi, and find the glorious ceiling paintings of the **Qoraboy Oqsoqol Mosque** down an alley on your right.

Continuing along Abu Laiz Samarkandi, pass the diminutive **Mubarak Mosque** on your left and proceed to the neighbourhood **Hammomi Davudi** (Abu Laiz Samarkandi; bath 5000S; ⊗5am-9pm, women Mon, Tue & Wed, men

Thu-Sun) public baths, which still provide their essential service to old town residents.

Take a left on unmarked Denau ko'chasi, opposite the *hammomi*, and look for the working 19th-century **Gumbaz Synagogue** (⌨ +998 91 552 7268; Denau) a few houses down on the left. You're welcome to visit the synagogue, which was built for the Bukharan Jews of Samarkand in 1891, but call ahead to be sure that there will be someone there. The atmospheric hall has photos of past rabbis on the walls, stars of David in the carved doors and an inner 'gumbaz' (domed hall). Approximately 250 Jews remain in Samarkand, with numbers decreasing all the time, according to Rabbi Yusuf Fakar.

Wander through the lanes south of the *hammomi* until you locate the surprisingly impressive new **Mausoleum of Abu Mansur al-Moturudiy** (Buhoro; admission 14,000S; ⊙ 6am-7pm). The entry fee is over the top; you can see the building from the outside for free.

A few blocks west of here is the more interesting **Makhdumi Khorezm Mosque** (Buhoro), with a colourful ceiling under its *aivan* (portico) and some lush interior tilework.

Other neighbourhoods worth wandering are west-southwest of Bibi-Khanym and behind the Gur-e-Amir.

⚜ Festivals & Events

During Samarkand's **Navrus festival** (⊙ Mar) you'll find dancing, live music and other performances, plus fireworks in Navoi Park. Ask travel agencies or tour guides about the annual Navrus kupkari (Tajik buzkashi; traditional polo-like game played with a headless goat carcass) match in Urgut or Koshrabot.

The city also hosts the international **Sharq Taronalari** (www.sharqtaronalari.uz; ⊙ Aug) classical and folk music competition every other year in Registan Sq. Note that the Registan has limited opening hours in the month before and during the festival.

🛏 Sleeping

Samarkand's B&Bs aren't quite up to Bukhara's lofty standards, but are preferable to the hotels laden with tour groups.

A branch of Tashkent's popular Topchan Hostel (p207) is scheduled to open in Samarkand's old town in 2018. Expect similar prices and facilities to the original.

Bahodir B&B   B&B $
(⌨ 66-235 43 05, +998 90 250 4462; Mulokandov 132; dm from US$10, s/d/tr US$14/24/33; ❄ 🖥) Just moments from the Registan, this rather dank guesthouse is cheap and popular, even if the steamy common bathroom and the ramshackle en suite rooms leave a lot to be desired. The pleasant courtyard is often full of overlanders, swapping travel tales and info on remote border crossings. Ask to see several rooms (upstairs are better), as standards vary.

Hotel Abdu Rahmon   B&B $
(⌨ 66-235 47 72; Buxoro 1/7; s/d US$14/24; ❄ 🖥) A well-signposted Old Town guesthouse, this good-value place is run by the family behind Bahodir B&B. The two-floor courtyard property has simple, clean rooms with tiny hot water bathrooms and crummy bedding, but the pleasant terrace enjoys great afternoon light and sunsets over the city skyline. English is spoken. The family is building a third guesthouse nearby, due to open as a three-star hotel with six rooms in 2018.

★**Emir B&B**   B&B $$
(⌨ 66-235 74 61, +998 91 314 0258; muhandis 2005@mail.ru; Oksaroy 142; dm/s/d/tr US$10/20/30/45; ❄ 🖥) The 12 rooms here are clean and cosy and have heated floors in their bathrooms, which is great in winter. There's a large and very pleasant communal area that's traditionally furnished with lovely carpets and embroideries on the wall. The six- and four-bed dorms are a good deal, while the upper balconies have fine Gur-e-Amir views.

★**Bibi Khanum Hotel**   BOUTIQUE HOTEL $$
(⌨ 66-210 08 12; www.hotel-bibikhanum.com; Toshkent 10; s/d/tr US$50/65/85; ❄ 🖥) This well-run place is popular for its fresh pine-clad rooms, central location and the stunning views of the next-door Bibi-Khanym Mosque from the breakfast terrace and upper balconies. Order dinner (mains 16,000S) on the terrace the morning before. The hotel is owned by Zamin Travel (p239), which has its office here.

★**Jahongir B&B**   B&B $$
(⌨ 66-235 78 99, +998 91 555 0808; www.jahongirbandb.com; Chirokchi 4; s/d/tr/q US$30/45/50/60; 🖥) This charming place in an old town neighbourhood unaltered by Samarkand's relentless modernisation has two courtyards sprinkled with vines and flowers

and a selection of 15 comfortable and inviting rooms. Each is equipped with a fridge, some have a TV and bathrooms are modern. Highly recommended. The in-house travel agency (p239) runs day trips to Shakhrisabz.

★ **Hotel Arba**   BOUTIQUE HOTEL **$$**
(☑ 66-233 60 67; www.hotel-arba.com; Mahmud Koshgari 92; s/d/tr US$50/70/90; ﹡ 🔊) This well-run place in the Russian part of town has some boutique touches, featuring exposed brickwork and colourful *ikat* silks, and the rooms have good bathrooms and big, comfortable beds. Staff are also remarkably friendly. It's a way from the Registan, but there are some good restaurants nearby. Single rooms are a bit of a let-down though.

★ **Antica**   GUESTHOUSE **$$**
(☑ 66-235 20 92, +998 93 336 1792; antica samarkand@hotmail.com; Iskandarov 58; economy s/d US$35/45, s/d/tr US$45/55/75; ﹡ 🔊) A gorgeous garden courtyard shaded by pomegranate, persimmon and mulberry trees make this family home a joy to stay at. The new rooms around the garden are more spacious, but the original 19th-century courtyard and dining room are more atmospheric, boasting original hand-carved walnut-wood doors and painted alabaster walls. Room 9 is much sought after for its upper balcony.

Hotel Marokand   BOUTIQUE HOTEL **$$**
(☑ 66-235 33 24; www.marokand-hotel.com; Chorraha 141; s/d/tr US$20/40/60; ﹡ 🔊) The eight fresh and bright rooms here have clean tiled bathrooms and good mattresses, plus there's a small but pleasant courtyard and helpful staff, all of which make this a good choice, especially for French speakers. The location in backstreets north of the Registan is a bit inconvenient and some rooms are smaller than others, so check a couple before committing.

Timur the Great   B&B **$$**
(☑ +998 93 720 1818, 66-235 19 80; timurthegreat@ mail.ru; Buhoro 84; s/d/tr US$20/30/40, ste US$30-50; ﹡ 🔊) The four simple but pleasant original rooms here surround an awning-covered courtyard. It's good value and well located on the edge of the old town. A new back block of luxury suite rooms was unveiled in 2017 and are much more comfortable for just a few dollars more.

★ **Hotel Grand Samarkand**   HOTEL **$$$**
(☑ 66-233 28 80; www.grand-samarkand.com; Yalangtush 38; s/d/ste US$85/120/140; ﹡ 🔊 ≋) Probably the best top-end option in town, with a boutique feel to the spacious, exposed brick rooms. The hotel consists of two buildings on either side of the road; the main one on the western side is perhaps better, with a pleasant courtyard. The 'superior' annexe across the road has two pools and a nice outdoor restaurant under a trellis.

L'Argamak   BOUTIQUE HOTEL **$$$**
(☑ +998 97 920 4012, 66-239 11 01; www.largamak. com; Sulton Muhamad 4; r US$110; 🅿 ﹡ 🔊) The 23 modern rooms at this French-Uzbek joint venture vary in size but all feel quite lush, with quality bedding and fluffy pillows. Breakfast on the rooftop terrace is a delight, with views of the Gur-e-Amir and jams made from the courtyard's cherry and fig trees. Rates includes free phone calls to the USA, France and Japan.

Registon Hotel   HOTEL **$$$**
(☑ 66-233 55 90; www.hotel-registon.uz; Ulugbek 16; s/d/tr US$50/80/95; ﹡ 🔊 ≋) The Registon looks good, if a little uninspiring, with 70 spacious rooms that have fridges and decent bathrooms, although some have an odd layout. Wi-fi is only in the lobby, but the pool is a real bonus in summer. You're in the Russian town, so a taxi ride from the sights, but located well for dining options.

✕ Eating

Most restaurants are in the newer Russian part of town, far removed from the touristy Registan area, where there's a surprising dearth of choice. The best of the few unappealing options across from the Registan is the two-floor **Cafe Labig'or** (Registan; mains 6000-10,000S; ⊙ 8am-11pm), which has a breezy upstairs terrace where fairly mediocre Uzbek standards are served up. On the plus side the setting is pleasant and they have cold beer.

Kyzyl Chaixona   CENTRAL ASIAN **$**
(Siob Bazaar; mains 5000S; ⊙ 7am-7pm) The clean 'red teahouse' within the confines of Samarkand's main market has pleasant outdoor *tapchans,* low prices and plenty of local colour. Expect *somsa* (samosa), shashlyk, *laghman* (noodles) and soups amid the chaotic atmosphere of the market traders.

Old City   INTERNATIONAL $$
(✉+998 93 346 8020; Abdurahmon Jomi 100/1;
mains 14,000-16,000S; ⊙10am-11pm) This
charming place in the Russian part of town
is recommended for its interesting dishes,
such as *basturma* cold smoked beef, *lavash*
(flat bread) with feta-like brinza cheese, and
over 40 salads, including a delicious beet-
root and walnut option. Service is friendly
and assured, the classy interior has a cosy
fireplace, and while it caters largely to tour-
ists, standards are high.

Cafe Magistr   CAFE $$
(Bo'stonsaroy 30/45; mains 10,000-17,000S;
⊙8am-11pm; ✻ ☎ 📶) Right in the heart of the
city, this bright two-room cafe aimed at students serves everything from real coffee to
breakfast pancakes, as well as salads, burgers and pizza (the spicy pizza comes recommended) in a breezy fast-food setting. It's a
reliable place that we kept coming back to.

Besh Chinor   UZBEK $$
(Temerchilar; mains 5000-8000S; ⊙9am-10pm)
This low-key traditional place is a great spot
for *plov* (pilaf), chicken kebab or *manty*
(steamed dumplings). There's beer on tap,
a fridge full of cold drinks and a quiet and
easily missed back garden area. It's clean
and staff are friendly, but there's no English
menu.

Samarkand Restaurant   UZBEK $$
(✉66-233 35 91; Mahmud Kashgari 54; mains
10,000-20,000S; ⊙11am-11pm; ✻ 📶) Everyone
seems to love this big bustling place. The
top-floor Russian-style room has a ski lodge
vibe with bear skins on the walls, but serves
up excellent value Gijduvan-style kebabs,
salads and even sushi rolls. Expect to get
pulled into the dancing by a conga line of
Uzbek grannies if there's a thumping wedding party on the ground floor.

Karimbek   UZBEK $$
(Gagarin 194; mains 15,000-20,000S; ⊙8am-11pm;
📶) This Uzbek theme restaurant remains
one of the most popular places for groups
and independent travellers alike. The
national- and Russian-influenced cuisine
can be enjoyed in a variety of settings, from
private country hut to airy street-side patio.
A nightly belly-dancing show jiggles to life
around 8pm. It's a 4000S cab ride from the
centre of town.

Art Cafe Norgis   UZBEK $$
(Toshkent; mains 7000-10,000S; ⊙9am-10pm;
☎ 📶) A handy place for lunch between the
Registan and the Bibi Khanym Mosque, this
'art cafe' is purely the haunt of tour groups,
but as the food is decent and there's nothing
else around, it's worth the mention. The menu
is made up of unexciting Uzbek standards,
but a pleasant yoghurt and spice side dish
and piping hot fresh bread are highlights.

★**Platan**   INTERNATIONAL $$$
(✉66-233 80 49; www.platan.uz; Pushkin 2; mains
20,000-28,000S; ⊙10am-11pm; ✻ ☎ ✎ 📶)
Possibly the best restaurant in Samarkand,
Platan has a classy interior and a summer
terrace for shady al fresco dining in the
summer. The menu includes some Middle
Eastern and Thai influences alongside re-
gional dishes like Russian-style red caviar or
cooling Uzbek *chalop* (cucumber, dill, green
onion and sour cream soup).

🍴 **Drinking & Nightlife**

Blues Cafe   BAR
(✉66-233 62 96; www.facebook.com/cafeblues
bar; Amir Timur 66; ⊙1-11pm) A surprisingly
tasteful and low-lit bar deep in the Russian
old town, Blues Cafe is one of Samarkand's
coolest spots and has live jazz and blues mu-
sic most Fridays. There's real coffee, a full
menu of Western food (mains 19,000S to
24,000S) and cocktails to be had.

Alt Stadt   BEER GARDEN
(Navoi 17; ⊙11am-11pm) On a warm summer
evening it's hard to beat a stein of unfiltered
weissbier (wheat beer) at this pleasant peo-
ple-watching terrace. The beer is a bargain
at under US$0.50 and the shashlyk (10,000S
to 20,000S) and salads are good too. Last
time we visited there were plans to change
the name.

Bochka   BEER HALL
(Ozod Sharq 2; beer 5000S; ⊙11am-11pm) Beer
fans can drink Samarkand's most famous
brew direct from the source at this wood-
lined bar just outside the Pulsar brewery.
Czech-style pilsner, weiss and black beer
flows on tap, chased down by a meaty menu
of sausages and potatoes (mains 12,000S).
The street leading up to Bochka is lined
with beer halls and shashlyk restaurants if
you fancy a bar hop.

UZBEKISTAN SAMARKAND (SAMARQAND)

WORTH A TRIP

URGUT BAZAAR

The town of Urgut, 40km south of Samarkand, is best known for its bazaar. This is one of the best places in the country to buy jewellery, *suzani* (embroidery) and antique clothing. Prices are lower and the quality is on par with anything sold in Samarkand and Bukhara, but you'll have to negotiate hard. It overflows with tourists in the high season; if you are serious go in the low season when prices drop. Arrive at the crack of dawn for the best selection.

While the bazaar is open every day, the textile and jewellery section, located at the back of the main bazaar, only happens on Sunday and Wednesday, and to a lesser extent on Saturday too. To get here from Samarkand, take a shared taxi (7000S, 45 minutes) or marshrutka (4000S) from a stand at the corner of Dagbet and Registan.

Shopping

There are souvenir shops and craft workshops of varying quality at all the big sights, in particular at the Rukhobod Mausoleum and the Registan. There are also several noteworthy antique shops in Tilla-Kari Medressa and one in Sher Dor Medressa, but textile and *suzani* buffs are better off going to Urgut (p238).

Siob Bazaar   MARKET
(Toshkent; ⊗7am-7pm) Around and behind Bibi-Khanym Mosque, Samarkand's frenetic, colourful main market is a great place for both vegetarians and photographers (vegetarian photographers will be in heaven!). There are a few souvenir stalls by the entrance, a section specialising in skullcaps and an entire quarter devoted to halva (fudge-like sweet).

**Happy Bird
Handicrafts Centre**   ARTS & CRAFTS
(www.asianart.uz; Toshkent 43A; ⊗10am-7pm) A dozen craft shops cluster around this single courtyard, making it a great place to shop for quality souvenirs, from ceramics and jewellery to wood carvings and *suzani* (embroidery). The handmade paper comes from nearby Konigil, as it has done for a

millennium. The Samarkand Tourist Information Centre (p283) runs craft tours here if you fancy learning more about the crafts on display.

Dil-Suzani Boutique   ARTS & CRAFTS
(☑+998 90 212 2297; dilsuzani@mail.ru; Tilla-Kari Medressa; ⊗9am-5pm) If you are interested in buying *suzani* (embroidery), owner Dilshod is very knowledgeable and gives an excellent free introduction to the symbolism of embroidery designs and Samarkand's traditional *sandal* heating system.

**Samarkand-Bukhara
Silk Carpets Showroom**   CARPETS
(www.silkcarpets.uz; Sher Dor Medressa; ⊗8am-7pm) Samarkand-Bukhara Silk Carpets has a Registan-based showroom with its trademark high-quality woven silk tapestries and *suzani* carpets on display. If you have a special interest you can arrange to visit the factory (☑66-235 22 73; Hujom 12A; ⊗9am-5pm Mon-Fri) east of the Shah-i-Zindah.

ⓘ Information

MONEY
Hotel Registon Plaza has an ATM but it's rarely in use.

Asaka Bank (Mustaqillik maydoni, Room 106; ⊗9am-4pm Mon-Fri) Offers US dollar cash advances on MasterCard and Maestro cards for 3% commission.

Kapital Bank (Nodira Begim 8; ⊗9-4pm Mon-Fri) Offers US dollar cash advances on Visa cards for 4% commission. It's near the Agricultural Institute.

POST
Main Post & Telegraph Office (Pochta 5; ⊗8am-5pm)

Post Office (Toshkent yo'li; ⊗10am-5pm Mon-Fri)

TOURIST INFORMATION
Samarkand Tourist Information Centre
(☑+998 91 545 0390; Toshkent 45; ⊗10am-5pm mid-Mar–mid-Nov) This volunteer organisation offers good travel advice, particularly on local transport, and sells postcards and stamps. They run some particularly interesting city tours (US$8 to US$15 per person), visiting handicraft masters, learning to cook in a local's house or touring the backstreets of the Jewish Quarter.

TRAVEL AGENCIES & TOURS
Most B&Bs double as travel agencies and/or can organise cars, guides, camel trekking and yurt-stays around Lake Aidarkul, and homestays in the Nuratau-Kyzylkum Biosphere Reserve.

Abask Travel (☑ 00 98 93 348 0102, 66-235 0098; faruhb@yahoo.com; Toshkent 41A; ⊘ 9am-6pm Mon-Fri) Well-connected Farruh Bahronov offers tours in English and French, and can organise everything from accommodation, visas and transport services to cultural and eco tours.

Jahongir Travel (☑ +998 91 555 0808; www.jahongir-travel.com; Chirokchi 4) Odil at Jahongir B&B can arrange guides, transport and day trips around Samarkand and Nurata. Combine a day trip to Shakhrisabz (from US$15 per person) with some hiking and an overnight homestay at Amankutan, or hike over the nearby pass on Timur's old invasion route from Shakhrisabz.

Sogda Tour (☑ 66-235 29 85; www.sogda-tour.com; Registan 38; ⊘ 9am-6pm Mon-Fri) This travel company has some exciting tours in the region, including excursions to the caves and mountains around Derbent and Boysun.

Zamin Travel (☑ 66-235 00 36; www.zt-ouzbekistan.com; Toshkent 10) Good local agency that specialises in off-the-beaten-track hiking between homestays in villages around Samarkand and Shakhrisabz. Trekking further afield in the Chimgan and Fan Mountains can also be organised.

The going rate for trained guides is US$35 per day, or US$5 per hour. Your B&B will almost certainly be able to hook you up with someone trusted and experienced, or go through one of Samarkand's travel agencies.

Local guides organising local and regional tours include the following:

Davlat Negmadjanov (☑ +998 90 276 1791; davlat63@mail.ru) A charming and knowledgeable English-speaking driver and guide to Samarkand and the surrounding area. He has his own car and provides reliable and affordable services.

Denis Vikulov (☑ +998 91 550 2772; denis-guide@rambler.ru) Local guide who offers tours in English and offers transfers and tours to other cities with his car.

Valentina Belova (☑ +998 91 559 6130) The grand dame of Samarkand's guides offers tours in English.

ⓘ Getting There & Away

AIR

Uzbekistan Airways flies between Samarkand and Tashkent once or twice daily except on Monday and Friday. Aeroflot has direct flights to Moscow. The airport is 6km north of the centre.

SHARED TAXI & BUS

The main departure point for shared taxis to Tashkent (bus/shared taxi per seat 20,000/35,000S, six/3½ hours) is the Ulugbek

marshrutka stop, about 200m east of the observatory. Get here on bus 45 from the northern side of Siob Bazaar.

Buses to Bukhara originate in Tashkent and pass by the highway opposite the Ulugbek marshrutka stop (20,000S, 4½ hours) every hour or so.

Shared taxis to Bukhara (40,000S to 50,000S) are a better option than the buses, though most involve a transfer in Navoi. The main departure point to Navoi (20,000S, two hours) is the Povorot marshrutka stop about 2.5km west of the WWII Crying Mother monument on Ulugbek kochasi. Take any bus signposted 'Поворот'. There are also some shared taxis from the Ulugbek stand. Shared taxis on from Navoi to Bukhara take an hour and cost a further 20,000S.

Shared taxis to Shakhrisabz congregate at the end of Suzangaran, just off Registon kochasi. You might find a direct taxi (20,000S to 25,000S, 1½ hours) but more likely you'll have to take one to Kitab (15,000S, one hour) and then take a minivan (2000S, 20 minutes) on to Shakhrisabz.

Most people headed to Khiva/Urgench take the train or travel via Bukhara, but there is normally one morning bus from the Ulugbek stop to Urgench (40,000S, 12 hours), which continues to Nukus (45,000S, 13½ hours).

Shared taxis to Termiz (40,000s to 70,000S, five hours) and Denau (80,000S, seven hours) gather at 'Grebnoy Kanal' on the city's outskirts about 6km east of the Ulugbek stop. Take bus 1 or 395 or a taxi (8000S) to get here. Staff at the Samarkand Tourist Information Centre can connect you with shared taxi drivers to both destinations and arrange to have you picked up at your hotel. A private taxi to the Tajikistan border at Sariosiyo costs around US$60.

TRAIN

You can buy tickets at the **train station** (☑ 66-229 15 32; Rudaki), 5km northwest of Navoi Park, or at the more convenient **City Train ticket office** (cnr Amir Timur & Bo'stonsaroy; ⊘ 8am-6pm) in the new town.

The super fast 'Afrosoiyob' bullet train to Tashkent (economy/business/VIP 58,000/78,000/112,000S, 2¼ hours) departs daily at 5pm, with a second service from Karshi at 6pm, and possibly also 5.30pm. The cheaper and slower 'Sharq' train leaves at 10.30am daily (economy/business 42,000/64,000S, 3¾ hours).

If you're heading to Bukhara, choose between the fast Afrosoiyob train (42,000/57,000/74,000S, 1¾ hours) at 9.40am or the slower 'Sharq' service (37,000/56,000S, 2½ hours) at 12.20pm.

For Termiz (60,000/86,000/162,000S, 11 hours) there is an overnight train at 11.30pm en route from Tashkent.

The overnight service to Urgench (82,000/121,000/240,000S, 12 hours) leaves at 12.20am.

The weekly train to Almaty (*platz/kupe* 267,000/390,000S, 29 hours) is an interesting choice, running every Thursday from Nukus.

To get to the train station take any bus that says 'Temir y'ol', such as the 73 from the Registan or 1, 3 or 10 from the Bulvar stop. The last bus is around 9pm.

A taxi to the Registan costs around US$1 in som. The new 1 tram line is scheduled to run from the train station to Siob Bazaar from 2018.

Getting Around

A taxi from the airport to the Registan will cost about US$1.50 in som, so there's little reason to mess with irregular marshrutka 60.

Minibuses (900S) run from about 6am until 8pm or 9pm. To get between the Registan stop and Navoi in the heart of the new town take any vehicle marked ГУМ (GUM), such as bus 3, 22 or 32, or marshrutka 6 or 35.

From the Bulvar stop take bus 14 or 74 to the Registan, or 1,10 or 54 to the Shah-i-Zinda.

A taxi between the old town and new town costs around 3000S, the standard charge for cabs in Samarkand.

A electric cart (1000S) shuttles up and down pedestrian Toshkent street from near the Registan to Siob Baaar.

Shakhrisabz (Shahrisabz)

075 / POP 75,000

Shakhrisabz (Shahrisabz) is a small, traditional Uzbek town south of Samarkand, across the hills in the Kashkadarya province, and is a lovely drive from Samarkand with some spectacular views. This is Timur's home town, and once upon a time it probably put Samarkand itself in the shade.

Timur was born on 9 April 1336 into the Barlas clan of local aristocrats, at the village of Hoja Ilghar, 13km to the south of Shakhrisabz. Ancient even then, Shakhrisabz (called Kesh at the time) was a kind of family seat. As he rose to power, Timur gave it its present name (Tajik for 'Green Town') and turned it into an extended family monument. Most of its current attractions were built here by Timur (including a tomb intended for himself) or his grandson Ulugbek.

In recent years the once charming centre of town was bulldozed and rebuilt as another of Uzbekistan's giant, empty plazas, with a few medieval buildings marooned in the antiseptic blandness. Despite the renovations, it's an worthwhile day trip from Samarkand, and several agencies in Samarkand offer some interesting add-on hikes and homestays in the surrounding mountains.

Sights

Between 2014 and 2016 much of the central heart of old Shakhrisabz, its historic bazaar and several old *mahalla* (residential districts), were bulldozed to create a gaping new park, leaving just a sprinkling of isolated monuments renovated to within an inch of their lives. It was a clumsy move that spurred an outraged UN to add Shakhrisabz to its list of endangered World Heritage Sites in 2016. Truth be told, Shakhrisabz is now a less interesting place to visit because of the development.

The new plaza now runs from the Ak-Saray Palace to the Kok-Gumbaz Mosque, so most visitors get dropped off at the northern end, walk down to the Kok-Gumbaz Mosque and then either get picked up there, or walk or take the electric cart back.

Just south of the palace on the eastern side of the square is the simple **Amir Timur Museum** (Ipak Yoli; admission 6000S; 9am-6pm), housed inside the renovated Chubin Medressa. Among the maps and models is a war drum, an interesting medieval polo mallet and ball, and the 14th-century doors of the Shamseddin Kulyal originally in the Dorut Tilyovat.

A few empty buildings remain marooned on the western side of the plaza and are worth keeping an eye open for as you walk south.

Starting from the north, the Mulk Ashtor Mosque was built in 1904 but has roots back to the 14th century. It's just inside the old town at the end of a road southwest of the Timur statue. Heading south through the plaza you'll also pass the locked and empty Abdu Shukur Medressa on the western side, opposite the 16th century Kuba Caravanserai (now the Kuba Restaurant). Finally just south is the Chorsu market crossroads that once marked the heart of the old bazaar.

Ak-Saray Palace RUINS
(White Palace; admission 5000S; 24hr) Just north of the centre, Timur's summer palace has as much grandeur per square centimetre as anything in Samarkand. There's actually little left except bits of the gigantic,

Shakhrisabz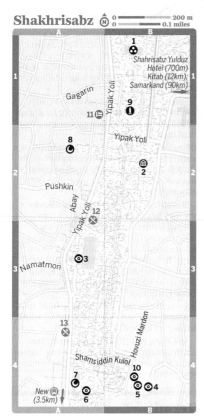

Shakhrisabz

◉ Sights
1 Ak-Saray Palace	B1
2 Amir Timur Museum	B2
3 Chorsu	A3
4 Crypt of Timur	B4
5 Dorus Siyadat	B4
6 Dorut Tilyovat	A4
7 Kok-Gumbaz Mosque	A4
8 Mulk Ashtor Mosque	A2
9 Statue of Timur	B1
10 Tomb of Jehangir	B4

⊜ Sleeping
11 Hotel Oq Saroy	A1

⊗ Eating
12 Kuba Restaurant	A2
13 Kullalik Chaikhana	A4

UZBEKISTAN SHAKHRISABZ (SHAHRISABZ)

a mob of meringue. Ak-Saray has been a Unesco World Heritage Site since 2000.

Just to the north is an impressive section of old city walls and the restored Samarkand Darwaza gate.

Dorus Siyadat MAUSOLEUM

(Seat of Power & Might; ⊙ 8am-6pm) Timur finished the 3500-sq-metre mausoleum complex of the Dorus Siyadat in 1392 and at the time it may have overshadowed even the Ak-Saray Palace. The main survivor is the tall **Tomb of Jehangir** (admission 6000S; ⊙ 8am-6pm), Timur's eldest and favourite son, who died aged just 22. It's also the resting place for another son, Umar Sheikh (Timur's other sons are with him at Gur-e-Amir in Samarkand). Today it's also a popular place to buy excellent-value embroidered bags.

In the southeastern corner of the courtyard of foundations is a bunker with a wooden door leading to an underground room, the Crypt of Timur. The room, plain except for Quranic quotations on the arches, is nearly filled by a single stone casket. On the casket are biographical inscriptions about Timur, from which it was inferred (when the room was discovered in 1963) that this crypt was intended for him. Inside are two unidentified corpses.

Next to the Tomb of Jhangir is the Khazarati-Imom Mosque with an impressive *aivan* (portico) of huge wooden pillars.

Kok-Gumbaz Mosque MOSQUE

(⊙ 8.30am-6pm) This heavily renovated, large Friday mosque was completed by Ulugbek in 1434 in honour of his father Shah Rukh (who

38m-high *pishtak* (entrance portal), covered with gorgeous, unrestored filigree-like mosaics. The crumbling relic will please critics of Samarkand's zealous restoration efforts: indeed, coming here will give you some idea of how Samarkand's buildings would have looked a century ago.

Ak-Saray was probably Timur's most ambitious project – work began in 1380 and took some 24 years to complete. Its creation followed a successful campaign in Khorezm and the 'import' of many of its finest artisans. Check to see if it's possible to climb to the top of the *pishtak*, as the stairway was closed in 2017 after an accident. The arch was a staggering 22.5m wide, and collapsed 200 years ago.

A new statue of Timur stands in what was the palace centre, giving you a sense of the huge scale of the original palace. It's not uncommon to see 10 weddings at a time posing here for photos at weekends, creating quite

was Timur's son). The name, appropriately, means 'blue dome'. The palm trees painted on the interior walls are calling cards of its original Indian and Iranian designers.

Facing Kok-Gumbaz is **Dorut Tilyovat** (House of Meditation; admission 5000S; ⊙8am-6pm), the original burial complex of Timur's forebears. Under the dome on the left is the Mausoleum of Sheikh Shamseddin Kulol, spiritual tutor to Timur and his father, Amir Taragay (who might also be buried here). The mausoleum was completed by Timur in 1374. On the right is the ornate Gumbazi Seyidan (Dome of the Seyyids), which Ulugbek finished in 1438 as a mausoleum for his own descendants (although it's not clear whether any are buried in it).

🛏 Sleeping & Eating

Hotel Oq Saroy　　　　GUESTHOUSE **$$**
(☑+998 90 316 5406; Amir Timur Sq; s/d US$20/40) Marooned on the western side of Shakhrisabz's desolate new plaza is this small place of 14 rooms with hot water and mini fridges. There's a pleasant outdoor restaurant out the front. It's the best budget option, though not much English is spoken.

Shahrisabz Yulduz Hotel　　　HOTEL **$$**
(Shahrisabz Star; ☑75-521 05 58; Ipak Yoli 2; s/d US$40/60; ✸⊛) This new, modern hotel is the only midrange accommodation in town and it has clean, if uninspiring, carpeted rooms with spacious bathrooms. It doesn't see many guests, but there's an on-site restaurant and staff are friendly.

Kuba Restaurant　　　　　UZBEK **$**
(Oilaviy Restaurant; Ipak Yoli; mains 6000-17,000S; ⊙11am-9pm) Set under the cool domes of the 16th-century Koba Caravanserai, this new restaurant is easily the most architecturally atmospheric setting in town, though it lacks the vibrancy of the local teahouses. The carpeted interior is refreshingly dark and cool in the summer heat and there's a stage for live Uzbek pop in the evenings.

Kullalik Chaikhana　　　　TEAHOUSE **$**
(Ipal Yoli; mains 10,000-15,000S; ⊙10am-7pm) Once a bustling local teahouse in the heart of the even more bustling bazaar, the Kullalik now overlooks the silent, yawning empty plaza. There is nice *tapchan* (bedlike platform) seating here and the shashlyk and salads are handled competently, making it the logical place for a local-style lunch.

ℹ Getting There & Around

Shakhrisabz is about 90km from Samarkand, over the 1788m Takhtakaracha Pass, a scenic drive that is part of the fun of a trip here. The pass is occasionally closed by snow from January to March, forcing a three-hour detour around the mountains.

Several B&Bs and most Samarkand guides can arrange day trips to Shakhrisabz for around US$15 per person, including a driver and a tour of all the main sights.

Headed back to Samarkand independently, it's easiest to take a Damas minivan north to Kitab (1500S, 20 minutes) and then pick up one of the frequent shared taxis to Samarkand (15,000S, 80 minutes).

Shared taxis on from Shakhrisabz leave from the **New Bus Station** (Yangi Vokzal), 3km south of town. Damas minivans shuttle here from 500m south of the Dorus Siyodat. Cars run frequently to Tashkent (50,000S, five hours). To get to Bukhara take a shared taxi to Karshi (20,000S, 1½ hours) and change there. For Termiz (100,000S) you may have to change in Guzar (10,000S).

A private chartered taxi costs 100,000S to Samarkand, 200,000S to Tashkent and 400,000S to Bukhara or Termiz.

An electric cart (1000S) shuttles north to south through the town's central pedestrianised plaza, from the Timur statue south to the main road at the Kok-Gumbaz Mosque.

Termiz

☑76 / POP 140,000 / ELEV 380M

The last stop in Uzbekistan on the way to Afghanistan, Termiz is a historic border town with an edgy, Wild West feel. While the present-day city bears few traces of its cosmopolitan history, the surrounding area is full of archaeological clues to the region's Buddhist and Bactrian past, and many of these come together in Termiz's excellent museum.

Termiz is the hottest place in Uzbekistan, so try to avoid coming here in July and August, when temperatures routinely exceed 40°C (104°F).

Old Termiz was a 2500-year-old Silk Road port and Buddhist centre on the banks of the Oxus, located a few kilometres to the west of the modern city. It was part of the Bactrian empire and conquered by Alexander before reaching its Buddhist heyday under the Kushan empire. The local Termizshah dynasty ruled the resurgent city in the 11th and 12th centuries before it was finally crushed by the Mongols.

Termiz

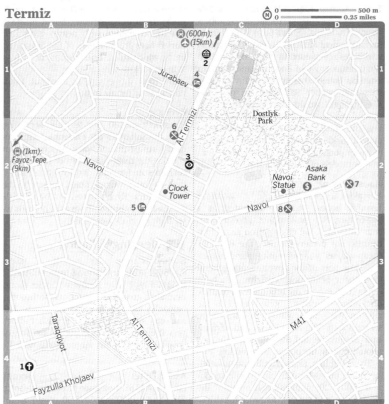

⊙ Sights

The highlight of any trip to Termiz is its excellent archaeological museum, which acts as a great primer for the surrounding sights.

There are two main cluster of sights. The Sultan Saodat Ensemble and the Kyr Kyz site are northeast of the city, while the Mausoleum of Al-Hakim al-Termizi and Fayoz-Tepe lie to the northwest on the road to Karshi, near the site of old Termiz.

The easiest way to visit the sites is to hire a taxi or minivan. Figure on around US$7 for a couple of hours' visit to either grouping or US$15 for both.

If you want an English-speaking guide ask at the Archaeological Museum or contact English-speaking **Rayhon** (☏ +998 91 580 8189), who can arrange tours of the main sights.

For insights into modern Termiz, the Yubileyny Bazaar is a useful landmark (and a

Termiz

good place to pick up local minibuses) while the gold-domed Alexander Nevsky Orthodox Church is worth a visit on a Sunday when Termiz's dwindling Russian community flock there.

Termiz Archaeological Museum   MUSEUM
(☑ 76-224 37 65; Al-Termizi 29; admission 20,000S, includes Fayoz-Tepe; ☺ 8am-6pm) The Termiz Archaeological Museum is reason enough to visit Termiz. Unveiled in 2001, the museum is a treasure trove of Buddhist and Bactrian artefacts collected from the many ravaged sites that pepper Surkhandarya province. The highlight would have to be the collection of 3rd- to 4th-century Buddhist statuary. The museum also has an excellent 3D map of Surkhandarya that depicts the area's most important archaeological sights, as well as models of individual sites.

**Mausoleum of
Al-Hakim al-Termizi**   MAUSOLEUM
Termiz's holiest sight is dedicated to a 9th-century Sufi philosopher, known locally as Al-Hakim, the city's patron saint. In a triumph for preservationists, the interior's cheap plaster *ghanch*-work, spuriously installed as part of the government's general monument beautification drive, has been removed to expose the original 15th-century brick. The mausoleum gets packed to the gills on Wednesday, when the faithful are served lunch. The Amu-Darya and Afghanistan are just behind the complex walls, but photographing the border is forbidden.

To get out here catch marshrutka 15 heading north on Al-Termizi from Yubileyny Bazaar (800S, 20 minutes), just north of the clock tower, and strike a deal with the driver to continue on to the main gates. There's plenty of transport on Wednesday.

Fayoz-Tepe   RUINS
(M39; admission incl with Termiz Archaeological Museum; ☺ dawn-dusk) The best place to glimpse Termiz's Buddhist past is at this 3rd-century-AD Buddhist monastery complex, 9km west of the bus station. Discovered only in 1968, in recent years it has been restored and a teapot dome put over the monastery's original stupa, visible through a glass window. Wander the surrounding ruins and you can make out halls with column bases, water pipes that once brought in water from the Oxus River, a kitchen and meditation halls.

Looking southwest from the site you can spot the remains of Kara-Tepe, a Buddhist cave monastery on the banks of the Amu-Darya, facing the Afghan border. The site is closed to visitors.

Sultan Saodat Ensemble   MAUSOLEUM
(☺ dawn-dusk) FREE The restored Timurid-style Sultan Saodat ensemble of mono-chrome mausoleums won't impress you if you've been to Samarkand, but it makes a fun trip combined with nearby Kyrk Kyz. Buried here are members of the Sayyid dynasty, which ruled Termiz from the 11th to 15th centuries.

By road the ensemble is about 10km northeast of Termiz centre.

Kyrk Kyz   RUINS
It's worth the 30-minute walk northwest from the Sultan Saodat Ensemble to this ruined fortified manor house, where you can wander the maze-like series of mud-walled corridors and rooms. Murky legend has it that 40 young women holed up here in the 11th century (Kyrk Kyz means 'Forty Girls'), successfully fighting off waves of nomads after their menfolk were slain.

🛏 Sleeping & Eating

Surhan Atlantic   HOTEL $
(☑ 76-221 74 24; cnr Al-Termizi & Navoi; s US$9-15, d US$14-25; ❄ ☎) The renovated Soviet rooms here are a great deal, with clean bathrooms, balconies and fairly comfortable beds. The manager speaks only basic English, but he's very friendly. The budget rooms are fine, or splash out on slightly larger rooms with TV and breakfast.

Asson Hotel   HOTEL $$
(☑ 76-224 43 66; www.asson-hotel.com; Al-Termizi 27; s/d US$40/70 ste US$70-90; ❄ ☎) Refurbished in pleasant pale green tones, the Asson is perfectly located for the archaeological museum and well situated in the thick of things. The daring decor includes the occasional leopard print bedspread. Staff is helpful, but there's not much English spoken.

Aylin Food   TURKISH $
(Al-Termizi; mains 8000-16,000S; ☺ 9am-11pm) This friendly Turkish restaurant serves up pre-cooked comfort food at lunchtime, changing daily but centred on grilled chicken and moussaka. If there's something in particular you fancy, English-speaking Turkish owner Mustafa will turn his hand to almost anything, from omelettes to pizza, including vegetarian dishes.

Restoran Farhod   UZBEK $$
(Navoi; mains 14,000-30,000S; ☺ 8am-11pm) Opposite the Navoi statue some way from the bustle of Al-Termizi is this unassuming looking place. Go inside though, and you'll find a permanently bustling local favourite where Uzbek national dishes and a range of deli-

cious kebabs are served up. There are also private booths available, should you fancy some peace and quiet.

Azizbek UZBEK **$$**
(Navoi; mains 10,000-30,000S; ◷9am-11pm)
This friendly place is worth the detour from the centre of town; its staff are charmingly friendly, there's beer on tap and the menu of grilled meat and salads makes for a perfect meal when served on the outdoor patio. Upstairs a smoky disco gets busy with locals in the evenings.

🛈 Getting There & Around

Uzbekistan Airways has three flights a day to/from Tashkent from the airport 15km north of town. On arrival in Termiz by air, you may need to register your arrival with the police, as you're entering a border zone. On seeing your foreign passport, you'll be directed to the relevant office at the airport terminal, and the process is very straightforward. To get to the airport take marshrutka 264, which runs up Al-Termizi (1000S). A taxi costs 15,000S.

Shared taxi is the way to get to Samarkand (70,000S, five hours) and Karshi (50,000S, five hours). Transfer in Karshi for Bukhara (30,000S, two hours). There are a couple of weekly buses to Tashkent (50,000S, 13 hours), but it's easiest to take a shared taxi (80,000S, nine hours) or the train.

All of the above leave from the bus station, which is little more than a taxi stand, in the southwest part of town; take marshrutka 8 here from near the clock tower.

Trains run daily between Termiz and Tashkent (*platskartny/kupeyny/SV* 81,000/119,000/228,000S, 14 hours) with stops in Boysun, Karshi and Samarkand. Trains leave Termiz at 5.35pm for the overnight trip.

Slow local trains depart at 6.40am and 6.10pm to Denau (5000S, three hours), and continue another hour to Sariosiyo at the Tajik border.

Nurata

📶 436 / POP 30,000

To the north of the featureless Samarkand–Bukhara 'Royal Road', the Pamir-Alay Mountains produce one final blip on the map before fading unceremoniously into desertified insignificance. The Nuratau Mountains, which top out at 2169m, are the focus of Uzbekistan's modest ecotourism movement.

The marginally interesting town of Nurata makes a logical base for an off-the-beaten-track loop that takes in the city's sites, an overnight stay at one of the Kazakh-style yurt camps near Aidarkul Lake and some hiking from a homestay base in the Nuratau Mountains.

Nurata itself is most famous for its old, circle-patterned *suzani* (embroidery), which can sell for thousands of dollars at international auctions, but it also has a few quirky tourist attractions.

Most notable is the **Fortress of Alexander the Great** (◷dawn-dusk), a series of eroded mud-walled fortifications and buttresses line the hill south of Nurata village, dating from Alexander the Great's founding of the town of Nur here 2300 years ago. The fort was meant to defend the settled lands of the south from the nomads of the steppe to the north. There's not a great deal to see, but the views over Nurata are good and the connection with Alexander is compelling.

Behind the fortress a path leads 4km to the Zukarnay Petroglyphs, which date from the Bronze Age. If it's too hot to walk, there are sometimes guys with motorcycles waiting near the fortress who will whisk you there for a couple of thousand som.

Beneath the fortress is the trout-filled **Chashma Spring** (admission 4000S), formed, it is said, where the Prophet Mohammed's son-in-law Hazrat Ali drove his staff into the ground. Several hundred holy trout occupy the pool, living off the mineral-laden waters of the spring. Next to the spring is a 16th-century Friday mosque and a 9th-century mausoleum.

🏃 Activities

After briefly taking in Nurata's sights (a couple of hours is enough for most people), you'll want to hightail it to the yurt camps to the north and east of Nurata.

There are several camps within shooting distance of Nurata, most of them near the shores of manmade Lake Aidarkul, formed from the diverted waters of the Syr-Darya in 1969.

All yurt camps include short camel rides in their rates and most offer fishing and a swim in the lake. Longer treks, including multiday excursions, are possible for an extra charge if arranged in advance.

The comfortable Kazakh-style camel-hair yurts, most of them tastefully decorated with carpets and *suzani*, sleep six to eight people. There's not a great deal of difference between the camps and all places charge around US$40 per person per day including three meals (there's no option but to eat in camp).

HOMESTAY HIKING IN THE NURATAU MOUNTAINS

South of Lake Aidarkul, there is great hiking and birdwatching in the mountains of the Nuratau-Kyzylkum Biosphere Reserve. Families in several villages have converted their homes into rustic guesthouses where they welcome guests. The most popular village is Sentyab (Sentob), where there have been three guesthouses since 2007, but if you want a more rural experience try the homestays in the remoter villages of Hayat, Asraf or Eski Forish. The area is ideal for hiking and horse riding, either on day trips or multiday trips between villages. In winter you can even observe authentic *kupkari* matches (a traditional polo-like game played with a headless goat carcass). This is a great opportunity to experience the traditional life of a Tajik-speaking mountain farmer family in their element – and a great way to ward off architecture burnout if you've seen one too many medressas.

For further information, contact local expert Sherzod Norbekov at **Responsible Travel** (☑ 072-452 12 00, +998 90 265 0680; www.nuratau.com; Esonqulov 34, Bog'don/ Yangiqishloq), who is based in Bog'don (former Yangiqishloq), a small town 70km west of Jizzakh. He can advise on transport and put together good hiking tours. Registration can be done in the guesthouses or in the office.

Most tour companies or B&Bs in Samarkand can also arrange a tour that takes in Nurata, Aydarkul and the Nuratau homestays.

On your own you'll have to take a shared taxi from Samarkand to Jizzakh and then another to Bog'don (Yangiqishloq), from where you'll have to hire a private taxi to Sentob or the other villages (60,000S). A taxi on to Nurata will cost 130,000S.

Camps close from November to mid-March, and sometimes during July and August. Showing up unannounced isn't a good idea; you're far better off calling ahead and arranging a deal via the office of a travel agency, that way your transfers will be taken care of and you can tailor your package to your needs where possible.

Tour agencies in Bukhara and Samarkand can arrange transport for a two-day loop of Nurata and Aidarkul for around US$90 per vehicle.

🛏 Sleeping

A stone's throw from the Chashma Spring, **Ruslan Rakhmonov** (☑ 436-523 14 04, +998 93 661 1013; ruslan.nuratau@mail.ru; Ohunbobo-yev 2, Nurata; per person incl full board US$25; 🛜) runs a good four-room homestay set around a pleasant courtyard and decorated with local-style embroideries. He can arrange excursions to the local yurt camps, a local karez (traditional well system) in the Chuya Valley and the 9th-century mosque at Gazgan village.

Sputnik Yurt Camp   YURT $$
(☑ +998 93 430 9766; www.camping.uz; Yangika-zgan; per person incl meals US$40; ⊙ Mar-Nov) The first and probably the fanciest yurt camp of the lot, with an attractive dining

yurt and lots of comforts, including real beds.

Aidar Yurt Camp   YURT $$
(☑ +998 97 929 9922; Dungalok; per person incl meals US$30-35; ⊙ mid-Mar–mid-Oct) Tucked away in a cone of sand dunes, this appealing yurt camp is located just 10km away from Lake Aidarkul. About a dozen charmingly decorated yurts have electricity, and shared bathrooms are rustic but clean with hot water. Clamber up to the top of the dunes for a pink sunset to the west, before the campfire, complete with traditional music and dance, gets going.

Food served on site is traditional nomad fare, and isn't the highlight but does the job. Camel rides are also offered.

Qizilqum Safari Yurt Camp   YURT $$
(☑ +998 95 610 4455; qizilqum-safari@mail.ru; Dungalok; per person incl meals US$40; ⊙ mid-Mar–early Oct) With 20 colourfully decorated, Kazakh-style yurts, this place is popular with groups and has electricity, hot showers and plenty of creature comforts. The owner has a second camp 300m away.

❶ Getting There & Away

To get to Nurata, make your way from Bukhara or Samarkand to Navoi and then take a shared taxi (12,000S, one hour). In Nurata sporadic marshrutkas run to Dungalok and Yangikazgan, but you'll likely have to hire a private car or arrange a transfer with your yurt camp. Negotiations start at 50,000S one way to the yurt camps.

Bukhara (Buxoro)

🖉 65 / POP 263,000

Central Asia's holiest city, Bukhara (Buxoro) has buildings spanning a thousand years of history, and a thoroughly lived-in and cohesive old centre that hasn't changed too much in two centuries. It is one of the best places in Central Asia for a glimpse of pre-Russian Turkestan.

Most of the centre is an architectural preserve, full of medressas and minarets, a massive royal fortress and the remnants of a once-vast market complex. Government restoration efforts have been more subtle and less indiscriminate than in flashier Samarkand. The city's accommodation options are by far the best and most atmospheric in the country.

You'll need at least two days to see the main sights. Try to allow time to lose yourself in the old town; it's easy to overdose on the 140-odd protected buildings and miss the whole for its many parts.

History

It was as capital of the Samanid state in the 9th and 10th centuries that Bukhara – Bukhoro-i-sharif (Noble Bukhara), the 'Pillar of Islam' – blossomed as Central Asia's religious and cultural heart. Among those nurtured here were the philosopher-scientist-medic Ibn Sina and the poets Firdausi and Rudaki – figures of a similar stature in the Persian Islamic world as, for example, Newton or Shakespeare in the West.

After two centuries under the smaller Karakhanid and Karakitay dynasties, Bukhara succumbed in 1220 to Chinggis (Genghis) Khan, and in 1370 fell under the shadow of Timur's (Tamerlane's) Samarkand.

A second lease of life came in the 16th century when the Uzbek Shaybanids made it the capital of what came to be known as the Bukhara khanate. The centre of Shaybanid Bukhara was a vast marketplace with dozens of specialist bazaars and caravanserais, more than 100 medressas (with 10,000 students) and more than 300 mosques.

In 1753 Mohammed Rahim, the local deputy of a Persian ruler, proclaimed himself emir, founding the Mangit dynasty that was to rule until the Bolsheviks came. Several depraved rulers filled Rahim's shoes; the worst was probably Nasrullah Khan (called 'the Butcher' behind his back), who ascended the throne in 1826 by killing off his brothers and 28 other relatives. He made himself a household name in Victorian England after he executed two British officers.

In 1868 Russian troops under General Kaufman occupied Samarkand (which at the time was within Emir Muzaffar Khan's domains). Soon afterwards Bukhara surrendered, and was made a protectorate of the tsar, with the emirs still nominally in charge.

In 1918 a party of emissaries arrived from Tashkent (by then under Bolshevik control) to persuade Emir Alim Khan to surrender peacefully to Soviet rule. The wily despot stalled long enough to allow his agents to stir up an anti-Russian mob that slaughtered nearly the whole delegation.

But the humiliated Bolsheviks had their revenge. Following an orchestrated 'uprising' in Charjou (now Turkmenabat in Turkmenistan) by local revolutionaries calling themselves the Young Bukharans, and an equally premeditated request for help, Red Army troops from Khiva and Tashkent under General Mikhail Frunze stormed the Ark (citadel) and captured Bukhara.

Bukhara won a short 'independence' as the Bukhara People's Republic, but after showing rather too much interest in Pan-Turkism it was absorbed in 1924 into the newly created Uzbek SSR.

⊙ Sights

◉ Lyabi-Hauz & Around

Lyabi-Hauz   PLAZA

Lyabi-Hauz, a plaza built around a pool in 1620 (the name is Tajik for 'around the pool'), is the most peaceful and interesting spot in town – shaded by mulberry trees as old as the pool. The old tea-sipping, chessboard-clutching Uzbek men who once inhabited this corner of town have been moved on by local entrepreneurs bent on cashing in on the tourist trade. Still, the plaza maintains its old-world style despite the evening pop music and family funfair feel.

Until a century ago Bukhara was watered by a network of canals and 200 stone pools (*hauz*) where people gathered and gossiped, drank and washed. As the water wasn't changed often, Bukhara was famous for

Bukhara

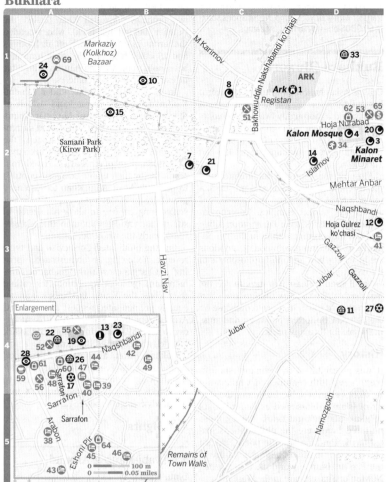

plagues and water-borne diseases; the average 19th-century Bukharan is said to have died by the age of 32. The Bolsheviks modernised the system and drained most of the pools but several, including the Lyabi-Hauz, remain.

On the eastern side of Lyabi-Hauz is a statue of Hoja Nasruddin, a semi-mythical 'wise fool' who appears in Sufi teaching-tales around the world.

Nadir Divanbegi Khanaka HISTORIC BUILDING
(Lyabi-Hauz; admission 1500S; ☉9am-6pm) On the western side of the Lyabi-Hauz is the

Nadir Divanbegi Khanaka, a Sufi cloister used for religious ceremonies, debates and instruction. Both this and the medressa opposite are named for Abdul Aziz Khan's treasury minister, who financed them in the 17th century. It's the poor relation of the medressa, but inside there's a small display of ceramics.

Nadir Divanbegi Medresse ISLAMIC SITE
(Lyabi-Hauz; ☉8am-6pm) The Nadir Divanbegi Medressa was built as a caravanserai, but was converted in 1622 after the khan mistook it for a medressa (the khan was consid-

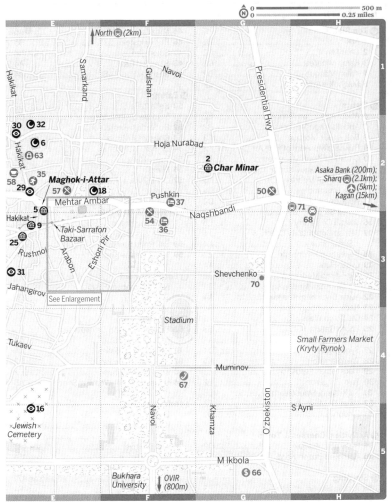

ered infallible). It's notable for its stunning exterior tilework, which depicts a pair of peacocks holding lambs either side of a sun with a human face, in direct contravention of the Islamic prohibition against depicting living creatures. Inside you'll find a dozen craft and carpet stalls.

The medressa is host most evenings at 6pm and 8pm to an hour-long **fashion show** (☏+998 90 718 6068; Lyabi-Hauz; 26,000S) of Uzbek designs, accompanied by live traditional music. It's not the most interesting show, but it's popular with groups.

Dinner is available for 40,000S, but you'll get much better food elsewhere.

Kukeldash Medressa　　ISLAMIC SITE
(Naqshbandi) The Kukeldash Medressa, built in 1569 by Abdullah II, was at the time the biggest Islamic school in Central Asia. It now hosts the occasional evening puppet show.

Those with more interest in the art of puppetry could stop for a quick visit to the displays on the history and manufacture of Bukhara's famous puppets at the nearby **Puppet Museum** (☏+998 90 514 4422; http://

Bukhara

bukharapuppets.net; Naqshbandi; ☉8.30am-7.30pm) **FREE**.

★ **Char Minar**   HISTORIC BUILDING
Photogenic little Char Minar, in a maze of alleys between Pushkin and Hoja Nura-bad, bears more relation to Indian styles than to anything Bukharan. This was the gatehouse of a long-gone medressa built in 1807. The name means 'Four Minarets' in Tajik, although they aren't strictly speaking minarets but rather decorative towers. For 4000S it's possible to climb up onto the roof of the building and come face to face with

the charming minarets. Souvenir stalls in front of the building sell some interesting Soviet memorabilia and B&W photographs of pre-Soviet Bukhara.

◉ The Covered Bazaars

From Shaybanid times, the area west and north from Lyabi-Hauz was a vast warren of market lanes, arcades and crossroad mini-bazaars whose multidomed roofs were designed to draw in cool air. Three remaining domed bazaars, heavily renovated in Soviet times, were among dozens of specialised bazaars in the town – **Taki-Sarrafon** (Moneychangers' Bazaar; Naqshbandi), **Taki-Telpak Furushon** (Cap Makers Bazaar; Mehtar Ambar) and **Taki-Zargaron** (Jewellers' Bazaar). They remain only loosely faithful to those designations today.

★ Maghok-i-Attar   MUSEUM
(Pit of the Herbalists; Arabon; admission/camera 10,000/3000S; ⊘ 9am-5pm Fri-Tue, to 3pm Thu) Between the two covered bazaars, in what was the old herb-and-spice bazaar, is Central Asia's oldest surviving mosque, the Maghoki-Attar, a lovely mishmash of 9th-century facade and 16th-century reconstruction. This is probably also the town's holiest spot: in the 1930s archaeologists found under it bits of a 5th-century Zoroastrian temple ruined by the Arabs and an earlier Buddhist temple.

According to legend, the mosque survived the Mongols by being buried by locals in sand. Indeed, only the top of the mosque was visible when the digging began in the 1930s; the present plaza surrounding it is the 12th-century level of the town. A section of the excavations has been left deliberately exposed inside. The building today ostensibly functions as an interesting museum exhibiting Solor and Ersari Turkmen carpets (so-called 'Bukhara' carpets are almost always Turkmen).

Climb a couple of stairs in the corner of the mosque for a view of the charred Zoroastrian remains. You will often find melted candles and evidence of small fires in the exterior niches of the building, a sign that Zoroastrian influence in Uzbek folk culture runs deep.

The charming staff will tell you that until the 16th century, Bukhara's Jews are said to have used the mosque in the evenings as a synagogue – a wonderful image of the cosmopolitan tolerance that was once such a part of Bukhara's identity.

The foundations surrounding the mosque once belonged to a series of bathhouses and caravanserai.

Bukhara Museum of Fine Art   MUSEUM
(Naqshbandi; admission/camera 1500/3000S; ⊘ 9am-5pm Fri-Tue, to 3pm Thu) This museum of art has a worthy collection of mostly 20th-century paintings by Bukharan and Russian artists, including the atmospheric works of Pavel Benkov. Look out for works by Zelim Saidjanov, the Bukharan artist featured in Colin Thubron's *Lost Heart of Asia* and *Shadow of the Silk Road*. It's in the former headquarters of the Russian Central Asian Bank (1912).

Photo Gallery   GALLERY
(www.uzbekistan.dk; ⊘ 9am-7pm) **FREE** This private gallery in the former Olimjon Caravanserai contains mesmerising photos of Bukhara Jews, gypsies and city life shot by Bukharan photographer Shavkat Boltaev. Prints of many of the photos are for sale.

Just beyond the gallery at the intersection of Jubar and Naqshbandi is the large 16th-century Gaukushan Medressa, with chipped majolica on its unrestored facade. It's normally closed, but the surrounding ensemble is a pleasant and quiet corner of the old town. Push a little deeper to the tiny and decrepit **Turki Jandi Mausoleum** (Namozgokh; ⊘ 7am-7pm), favoured for getting one's prayers answered. Turki Jandi's tomb is accessed through the mosque in front of the taller, second cupola. A well inside the mosque contains holy water that locals drink from a cooler near the entrance. Have the chatty mullah show you the sections of original 10th-century Arabic script on the mosque's doors, allegedly inscribed by Turki Jandi himself.

Further into the neighbourhood to the south is the 1892 house of one of Bukhara's many infamous personalities, the man who plotted with the Bolsheviks to dump Emir Alim Khan. Wealthy merchant **Fayzulla Khojaev** (☏ 224 41 88; Tukaev; admission 4500S, camera 3000S; ⊘ 9am-5pm Fri-Tue, to 3pm Thu) was rewarded with the presidency of the Bukhara People's Republic, chairmanship of the Council of People's Commissars of the Uzbek SSR, and finally liquidation by Stalin.

Ulugbek Medressa   ISLAMIC SITE
(Hoja Nurabad; admission incl Abdul Aziz Khan Medressa 5000S; ⊘ museum 9am-4.30pm Fri-Tue, to 2.30pm Thu) Built in 1417, this is

STODDART, CONOLLY & THE BUG PIT

On 24 June 1842 Colonel Charles Stoddart and Captain Arthur Conolly were marched out from a dungeon cell before a huge crowd in front of the Ark, the emir's fortified citadel, made to dig their own graves and, to the sound of drums and reed pipes from atop the fortress walls, were beheaded.

Colonel Stoddart had arrived three years earlier on a mission to reassure Emir Nasrullah Khan over Britain's invasion of Afghanistan. But his superiors, underestimating the emir's vanity and megalomania, had sent him with no gifts, and with a letter not from Queen Victoria (whom Nasrullah regarded as an equal sovereign) but from the governor-general of India. To compound matters Stoddart violated local protocol by riding, rather than walking, up to the Ark. The piqued Nasrullah threw him into jail, where he was to spend much of his time at the bottom of the so-called 'bug pit', in the company of assorted rodents and scaly creatures.

Captain Conolly arrived in 1841 to try to secure Stoddart's release. But the emir, believing him to be part of a British plot with the khans of Khiva and Kokand, tossed Conolly in jail too. After the disastrous British retreat from Kabul, the emir, convinced that Britain was a second-rate power and having received no reply to an earlier letter to Queen Victoria, had both men executed.

Despite public outrage back in England, the British government chose to let the matter drop. Furious friends and relatives raised enough money to send their own emissary, an oddball clergyman named Joseph Wolff, to Bukhara to verify the news. According to Peter Hopkirk in *The Great Game*, Wolff himself only escaped death because the emir thought him hilarious, dressed up in his full clerical regalia.

Central Asia's oldest medressa, and may well be familiar to you as it became a model for many others. The blue-tiled medressa, one of three built by Ulugbek (the others are at Gijduvan, 45km away on the road to Samarkand, and in Samarkand's Registan complex), is unrestored and in need of conservation work.

Abdul Aziz Khan Medressa　　　　ISLAMIC SITE

(museum admission 2000S; ◷ museum 9am-5pm) The student rooms at the 16th-century Abdul Aziz Khan Medressa are occupied, rather typically, by souvenir shops. This is an unrestored gem, built by its namesake to outdo the Ulugbek Medressa across the street. One *hujra* (cell-like living quarter) in the corner of the courtyard still has its original paintings and fireplace. The highlight is the prayer room, now a museum of wood carvings, with jaw-dropping *ghanch* stalactites dripping from the ceiling.

It is said that Abdul Aziz had the image of his face covertly embedded in the prayer room's mihrab (Mecca-facing niche) to get around the Sunni Muslim prohibition against depicting living beings. The only other medressa in town that depicts living beings is the Nadir Divanbegi Medressa (p248).

◉ Kalon Minaret & Around

★ Kalon Minaret　　　　ISLAMIC SITE

When it was built by the Karakhanid ruler Arslan Khan in 1127, the Kalon Minaret was probably the tallest building in Central Asia – *kalon* means 'great' in Tajik. It's an incredible piece of work, 47m tall with 10m-deep foundations (including reeds stacked underneath in an early form of earthquake-proofing), and has stood for almost nine centuries. Chinggis (Genghis) Khan was so dumbfounded by it that he ordered it spared while his troops ransacked the rest of the city.

The minaret is an architectural masterpiece. Its 14 ornamental bands, all different, include the first use of the glazed blue tiles that were to saturate Central Asia under the Timurids. Up and down the southern and eastern sides are faintly lighter patches, marking the restoration of damage caused by Soviet general Frunze's artillery in 1920. Its 105 inner stairs, accessible from the Kalon Mosque, have been closed off to tourists for several years but may reopen.

At the foot of the minaret, on the site of an earlier mosque destroyed by Chinggis Khan, is the 16th-century congregational Kalon Mosque (Hoja Nurabad; admission/camera 6000/2000S; ◷ 8.30am-7.30pm, closed noon-

2pm for Friday prayers), which is big enough for 10,000 people. Its courtyard has some spectacular tile work. Used in Soviet times as a warehouse, it was reopened as a place of worship in 1991.

Mir-i-Arab Medressa ISLAMIC SITE
(Hoja Nurabad) The working Mir-i-Arab Medressa, with its luminous blue domes, is among Uzbekistan's most striking buildings, especially in later afternoon light. The eponymous Mir-i-Arab was a 16th-century Naqshbandi sheikh from Yemen who had a strong influence on the Shaybanid ruler Ubaidullah Khan.

Tourists can technically only go as far as the foyer. However, if you ask permission you may be allowed to view the tombs of Mir-i-Arab and Ubaidullah Khan in a room under the northern dome.

◉ The Ark & Around

★ **Ark** FORTRESS
(☑65-224 38 53; Registan Sq; admission/camera/guide 15,000/3000/14,000S; ☺9am-7pm Thu-Mon, to 3pm Tue) The spectacular-looking Ark, a royal town-within-a-town, is Bukhara's oldest structure, occupied from the 5th century right up until 1920, when it was bombed by the Red Army. For centuries it was the residence of the emirs of Bukhara. It's about 80% ruins but there are still some remaining royal quarters, now housing several interesting museums.

At the top of the entrance ramp is the 17th-century Juma (Friday) Mosque, with some beautiful stalactite carved column heads. Next are the former living quarters of the emir's *kushbegi* (prime minister), where foreign ambassadors were received and now houses exhibits on the nearby archaeological sites of Paikend, Varakhsha and Romitan, once important Silk Road trading centres.

Second on the left is the oldest surviving part of the Ark, the vast Reception and Coronation Court, whose roof fell in during the 1920 bombardment. The last coronation to take place here was Alim Khan's in 1910. The submerged chamber on the right wall was the treasury and mint, and behind this was the harem.

To the right of the corridor were the open-air royal stables and the *noghorahona* – a room for drums and musical instruments used during public spectacles in the square below.

Around the Salamhona (Protocol Court) at the end of the corridor are what remain of the royal apartments. These apparently fell into such disrepair that the last two emirs preferred full-time residence at the summer palace. The most interesting displays here cover Bukhara's history from the Shaybanids to the tsars. Displays include a huge whip attributed to the mythical hero Rustam, the padlock that used to secure the Ark gates and a case used to make petitions to the emir. Another room contains the emir's throne as well as portraits of the ill-fated British officers Stoddart and Conolly (p252), who were eventually executed in front of the fortress on Registan Sq.

Northeast of the Ark and just behind it is the old **Zindon** (jail; admission 10,000S; ☺9am-6pm Fri-Tue, to 3pm Thu). Morbidly fascinating attractions include a torture chamber, shackles used on prisoners and several dungeons, including the gruesome fourth cell, the 6.5m deep *kanakhona* (bug pit), accessible only by rope, where Stoddart and Conolly languished for years in a dark chamber filled with lice, scorpions and other vermin. There are also some fabulous early-20th-century photographs of pre-Soviet Bukhara taken by Russian photographer Sergey Prokudin-Gorsky.

Across from the Ark, between Hoja Nurabad and Islamov, the interior of the 16th-century **Hoja Zayniddin Mosque** (☺7am-7pm) has a tremendous *aivan* (portico) and some of the best original mosaic and *ghanch*-work you're going to see anywhere.

Bolo-Hauz Mosque MOSQUE
(Registan Square) Beside a pool opposite the Ark's gate is the functioning Bolo-Hauz Mosque (1718), the emirs' official place of worship. The stunning painted wood and carved columns of the high *aivan* are some of the most beautiful in Central Asia. Beside it is a now-disused 33m water tower, built by the Russians in 1927.

Chashma Ayub Mausoleum MAUSOLEUM
(Samani Park; admission/camera 1500/3500S; ☺9am-5pm Thu-Mon, to 3pm Tue) The peculiar Chashma Ayub (Spring of Job) mausoleum dates from the 12th century and has a tent-like Karakhanid-style roof. Legend has it that the prophet Job struck his staff on the ground here, causing a spring to appear whose water then cured him of his many boils and ulcers. Inside is a small museum about water management in Bukhara (more

BUKHARA'S JEWS

South of Lyabi-Hauz is what's left of the old town's unique Jewish Quarter. There have been Jews in Bukhara since perhaps the 12th or 13th century. They developed their own culture with its own language – Bukhori, which is related to Persian but uses the Hebrew alphabet. Bukhara's Jews still speak it, as do about 10,000 Bukhara Jews who now live elsewhere, mainly in Israel and New York.

The Bukhara Jews managed to become major players in Bukharan commerce, in spite of deep-rooted, institutionalised discrimination. Bukhara Jews made up 7% of Bukhara's population at the time of the Soviet Union's collapse, but today only about 360 remain (and of these only a fraction read Hebrew).

The **Jewish Community Centre & Synagogue** (☑65-224 23 80, 65-510 18 33; Sarrafon 20) in the old town holds regular services and also sponsors a functioning Jewish school just around the corner. Look for the ancient torahs and photo of Hilary Clinton who visited in 1997.

A century ago there were at least seven synagogues in Bukhara, reduced after 1920 to two. The second synagogue is located southwest of the old town – from the ruined mosque on Namozgokh, take a left onto Gulzor ko'chasi, then turn right at the red garage door (number 3) and you'll find the synagogue on the right a little further down the street.

The **Jewish Cemetery** (Muminov; ⊙8am-6pm), just south of the Old Town, is perhaps the most impressive evidence of the previous size of the local Jewish community. It's a very well-maintained and huge space, with centuries of tombs on display.

interesting than it sounds) and a tap where pilgrims drink from the spring.

Ismail Samani Mausoleum MAUSOLEUM
(Samani Park) FREE This mausoleum in Samani Park, completed in 905, is the town's oldest Muslim monument and one of its most architecturally interesting. Built for Ismail Samani (the founder of the Samanid dynasty), his father and grandson, its intricate baked terracotta brickwork – which changes 'personality' through the day as the shadows shift – disguises walls almost 2m thick, helping it survive without restoration (except of the spiked dome) for 11 centuries.

Behind the park is the Talipach Gate and one of the few remaining, eroded sections (a total of 2km out of an original 12km) of the Shaybanid **town walls** (Samani Park). If you have eight minutes to spare take a ride on the nearby Ferris wheel for views over the mausoleum.

Modari Khan Medressa ISLAMIC SITE
(Mirdustim) Southeast of Samani Park are two massive medressas, one named for the great Shaybanid ruler Abdulla Khan (currently empty) and the other for his mother called Modari Khan ('Mother of the Khan'). The medressa contains some craft shops and a high wire for practising circus performers.

◉ Outskirts of Bukhara

Char Bakr ISLAMIC TOMB
(admission/camera 4000/3000S; ⊙8am-8pm) This peaceful and little-visited burial complex a few kilometres west of Bukhara is a good place to escape the tour bus crowds and has partially managed to escape Uzbekistan's dreaded renovation squads. The main mosque and *khanaga* (pilgrim resthouse) are linked by medressa cells that allow access to the rooftop. A street of tombs to the side leads to the 10th-century mausolea of Sheikh Abu Bakr Fazl and Sheikh Abu Bakr Sayid. The complex includes a *garmoba* (washroom complex) and the interesting niche of a *sakokhana,* where pilgrims once received free refreshments.

Minivans 202 and 247 run here from Markazy (Kholkhoz) Bazaar.

Sitorai Mohi Hosa PALACE
(Star-and-Moon Garden; ☑65-228 50 47; admission/camera/guide 15,000/3000/21,000S; ⊙9am-5pm Thu-Tue) For a look at the lifestyle of the last emir, Alim Khan, go to his summer palace (1912–18), 6km north of Bukhara. The three-building compound mixes Russian architecture with Central Asian design in an explosion of kitsch. A 50-watt Russian generator provided the first electricity the emirate had ever seen. In front of the harem

is a pool where the women frolicked, overlooked by a wooden pavilion from which the emir supposedly tossed an apple to his chosen bedmate.

To get here from Bukhara take bus 7 or 33 from the Vokzal stop east of the old town. The palace is at the end of the line, past the Karvon Bazaar. A taxi costs around 7000S.

🏃 Activities

★ **Hammon Bozori Kord**   BATHHOUSE
(☑ +998 93 477 1133; Hakikat; admission 120,000S; ☺ 6am-midnight Wed-Mon, noon-midnight Tue) Bozori Kord is an age-old Bukharan bathhouse where little has changed for centuries. It's now solidly oriented to tourists (hence the hefty entry fee), but otherwise totally authentic and a fantastic experience. You'll be put through an hour-long process that involves working up a sweat in the *hammam*, being washed down, massaged and stretched, and then rubbed all over with ginger and left to sweat it out again.

The baths are open to all until 6pm and then by reservation only until midnight.

Hammom Kunjak   BATHHOUSE
(☑ 65-622 45 45; Ibodov 4; admission 20,000S; ☺ 9am-6pm) This ancient Bukharan bathhouse, in the shadow of the Kalon Minaret, is for women only. It's traditionally where mothers bring their newborn babies at 40 days old for a first ritual wash. It is also available for private group rental after-hours.

🎉 Festivals & Events

Silk & Spices Festival   CULTURAL
(☺ May/Jun) The four-day Silk & Spices Festival in May or June is a celebration of local folk art as well as silk and spices, with lots of music and dance, plus acrobats and wrestling.

🛏️ Sleeping

Bukhara's wonderful, largely traditional-style B&Bs set the gold standard for accommodation in Central Asia. Most are former Jewish merchants' houses set around private courtyards tucked away in the backstreets of the old town. Several of their traditional dining rooms are considered to be part of the city's Unesco World Heritage status. Booking ahead is essential during the busy months of April, May, September and October.

Rumi Hostel   HOSTEL $
(☑ 65-221 06 21, +998 90 637 0545; http://hotel-rumi.business.site; D Sallohhona 19; dm US$10, s/d without bathroom US$18/24, s/d US$23/29; ❄ 🛜) This sprawling converted house on the southern edge of the old town is the best shoestring option and particularly popular with overlanders (there's plenty of parking outside). The mother and son owners are super-friendly and English-speaking son Bek is full of great travel advice. The house itself is a bit ramshackle, but it's a great place to meet other travellers.

There are also three-, four- and six-bed family rooms. Rates are flexible.

Sarrafon B&B   B&B $
(☑ 65-221 05 02, +998 91 402 0641; www.sarrafon-travel.uz; Sarrafon 4; dm US$15, s/d from US$20/30; ❄ 🛜) Sarrafon has forged a reputation for being great value due to its ideal location, friendly host family and quality breakfasts. It may be rather low on traditional charms, but it has some nice touches, such as local carpets on the floors and walls, and you won't get a much better deal than this just off Lyabi-Hauz. The dorms are just normal double rooms.

Hotel Samani   GUESTHOUSE $
(☑ +998 95 600 1919, 65-224 51 38; samani.bukhara@gmail.com; Husainov 6; s/d/q US$20/32/50; ❄ 🛜) Travellers rave about this budget family-run place with just 12 rooms. The bathrooms are simple (expect the floor to flood when you have a shower) and the decor is more modern than stylish, but the family couldn't be friendlier and the location is perfect. Only the son speaks English.

Arabon Hotel   B&B $
(☑ 65-221 05 19; arabonbukhara@mail.ru; Arabon 2-4; s/d US$18/30; ❄ 🛜) This small B&B in a quiet part of the old town offers budget rooms with a splash of history. The six rooms are spacious and decent – not as stylish as the pricier places (despite the *ikat* bedspreads) but comfortable enough – and there's a lovely 150-year-old dining room. Contact English-speaking Sobir.

★ **Amelia**
Boutique Hotel   BOUTIQUE HOTEL $$
(☑ 65-224 12 63; www.hotelamelia.com; Bozor Hoja 1; s/d from US$55/75; ❄ 🛜) It's the proactive and passionate management here that really propels this boutique hotel to the top of its class. Housed in a Jewish merchant's house,

the hotel's 11 rooms are all unique, including one featuring a recreation of the famous Sogdian frescoes of Varaksha. Bathrooms are spacious with heated floors, while the stunning 19th-century breakfast room and fantastic rooftop terrace are reason enough to stay here.

★ **Hovli Poyon B&B** B&B $$
(☑ 65-224 18 65; www.hovli-poyon.uz; Hoja Gulrez 13; s/d US$30/45; ✳ 🖤) Few Bukhara B&Bs are more memorable than this one, set in a 19th-century house dripping with both character and history. It was once home to the father of Emir Alim Khan, and both the grand *aivan* (portico) and huge vine-strewn courtyard are emir-worthy. The excellent-value rooms are surprisingly modern and piney – the rooms at the front of the house are the most authentic.

★ **Komil Hotel** BOUTIQUE HOTEL $$
(☑ +998 90 515 0305, 65-221 08 00; www.komiltravel.com; Barakyon 40; s/d from US$45/70; ✳ 🖤) This friendly 27-room hotel has stunning *ghanch* work and a young, laid-back owner who speaks fluent English. The rooms are gorgeous, and the 19th-century dining room is a pure pleasure to breakfast in. Even some of the modern rooms are decorated in traditional style, while the interiors of the older ones are all original. Vegetarians will find plenty on offer.

★ **Emir B&B** BOUTIQUE HOTEL $$
(☑ 65-224 49 65; www.emirtravel.com; Husainov 17; s/d/tr US$35/50/65; ✳ @ 🖤) This wonderful place consists of two old Jewish Quarter houses set around twin courtyards and run by the friendly and knowledgeable Mila. One has traditional-style rooms filled with antiques, *ghanch* and trinket-laden niches, the other is all new and shiny – both are spacious with comfy beds and good bathrooms. Highly recommended.

Amulet Hotel HISTORIC HOTEL $$
(☑ 65-224 53 42; www.amulet-hotel.com; Naqshbandi 73; s/d US$50/75; ✳ 🖤) Housed inside the converted 1861 Said Kamol Medressa, this charming eight-room place has all the comforts you need without sacrificing an inch of its traditional flavour. The traditional *sandal* (sitting area), complete with heated floor, makes for a cosy place to relax in the winter months. It's a bit overpriced, but you'll still need to book way ahead if you plan to stay here.

★ **Minzifa** BOUTIQUE HOTEL $$
(☑ 065-221 06 28, +998 93 477 0800; www.minzifa. com; Eshoni Pir 63; s US$40, d US$60-70; ✳ 🖤) Traditional Bukharan style is faithfully on display at this superb courtyard hotel, although the decor is toned down by flashes of modern art and subtler than usual colour schemes. It has some of the friendliest service in town, ultra-comfy oversized twin beds, espresso coffee and 13 uniquely decorated rooms with wooden ceilings and dripping with painted *ghanch*.

Salom Inn B&B $$
(☑ 65-224 37 33; www.salomtravel.com; Sarrafon 3; s/d US$30/55; ✳ 🖤) Housed in the courtyard of an old mansion in the Jewish Quarter, this is a charming, well-managed and good-value place. The rooms are spacious and modern rather than antique and atmospheric, but they are stuffed full of handicrafts and boast carved wooden ceilings and handmade local sheets. The vine-clad courtyard is a great place to relax.

Sasha & Son B&B B&B $$
(☑ 65-224 49 66; www.sashasonhotels.com; Eshoni Pir 3; s/d US$50/60; ✳ 🖤) Behind a beautifully carved wooden front door is a maze connecting several small buildings with new rooms elaborately done up in traditional decor. All rooms have satellite TV and snazzy bathrooms with fine tilework. The location is excellent, just moments from Lyabi-Hauz. An all-round good choice.

★ **Lyabi House Hotel** B&B $$$
(☑ 65-224 24 84; www.lyabihouse.com; Husainov 7; s/d US$60/80; ✳ 🖤) No place in town better combines authentic old-Bukhara design with modern amenities. Breakfast is served in the dignified *aivan* with carved wooden columns – which is worth stopping by to see even if you're not staying here. The newest rooms are a little bland so request an older room, and one away from the noisy reception area.

Kavsar Boutique Hotel BOUTIQUE HOTEL $$$
(☑ +998 91 406 3883; d-amir22@mail.ru; Naqshbandi 112; s/d US$45/80; ✳ 🖤) There's an intimate feel at this B&B. There are just eight comfortable and modern rooms (with good mattresses) set around a small intimate split-level central courtyard that feels either romantic or cramped depending on how busy things are. Breakfast in the 150-year-old dining room is a highlight. Online or walk-in rates are normally more like US$35/55.

Eating

The quality of restaurants in Bukhara lags far behind its accommodation. The few decent restaurants are often booked so make reservations. Some B&Bs offer meals, including to non-guests, and are more intimate than the tourist-heavy fare around Lyabi-Hauz.

For self-caterers the main farmers market is Markaziy (Kolkhoz) Bazaar, just north of the Ismaili Samani Mausoleum in the west of town.

★ **Saroy** INTERNATIONAL $$
(Sarrafon; mains 15,000-23,000S; ⊙12.30-11.30pm; ✳ 🍴) A welcome addition to the eating scene, this restaurant fronting the Lyabi-Hauz is housed in a beautifully appointed two-storey building with both traditional and European touches. The large menu has some vegetarian choices among its tasty Russian, European and Central Asian mains, and the well-trained, English-speaking staff are helpful and friendly.

★ **Minzifa** INTERNATIONAL $$
(☎65-224 61 75, +998 93 960 2326; Hoja Rushnogi 6; mains 10,000-26,000S; ⊙11am-11pm Mar-Nov; ✳ ✎ 🍴) Bukhara's most charming and professional restaurant is this perennially popular place with a fantastic roof terrace overlooking the sunset-framed domes of the Sarrafon *hammam*. The menu stretches to dishes like chicken with cream sauce and walnuts, and has plenty of meat-free options such as vegetable shashlyk. Reserve at least a day or two ahead during high season.

Be sure to save space for dessert (such as apples, pears and bananas with sour cream, honey and walnuts) or smoke a shisha while snacking on a selection of Uzbek traditional sweets like halva and sherbet.

Chinar Chaikhana UZBEK $$
(☎+998 91 373 7969; Naqshbandi; mains 10,000-16,000S; ⊙9am-10pm; 🍴) Occupying a large property just a short stroll from Lyabi-Hauz, this self-styled chaikhana is actually a full restaurant rather than just a teahouse. Come early to snag a table on the upstairs roof terrace as it gets busy. The food focuses on Uzbek classics, and a selection of salads are brought to your table to choose from.

Bella Italia ITALIAN $$
(Naqshbandi; mains 15,000-25,000S; ⊙11am-11pm, cafe from 8am; ✳ ✎ 🍴) There is surprisingly decent Italian food at this classy space on the eastern edge of the old town. The

outdoor seating is romantic and the pizza and pasta is a godsend for vegetarians. The menu even stretches to sushi rolls (16,000S to 30,000S) and there's good espresso in the attached cafe.

Budreddin Restaurant UZBEK $$
(Naqshbandi; mains 15,000-20000S; ⊙11am-11pm; ✎ 🍴) Budreddin has a great location on the western side of Lyabi-Hauz, with a small blacksmith's workshop marking the entrance. The outdoor seating in the faux medressa-style courtyard is pleasant, and there's a romantic mood that teeters on cheesy when the violinist kicks in. Vegetarian options include stuffed peppers and vine leaves, and wine is available by the glass.

Old Bukhara Restaurant UZBEK $$
(✎+998 90 185 7077; www.oldbukhara.com; Samarkand; mains 10,000-15,000S; ⊙10am-11pm; 🍴) One the better choices in Bukhara's centre has tables set around a pleasant tree-filled courtyard as well as quieter options on the terraces and roof. The menu is more interesting than your average Uzbek restaurant, featuring fish baked in puff pastry, *sumochki* (literally 'purses') of fried beef dumplings and Uzbek wine by the glass.

Bolo Hauz Chaikhana UZBEK $$
(Afrosiab; mains 6000-8000S; ⊙9am-8pm) This large chaikhana in the park opposite the Ark is an ideal place for a cheap and simple meal of Uzbek salads, soups, *plov* (pilaf) or noodles. There's pleasant outdoor seating, English is spoken and they'll bring beer if you ask for it.

Lyabi-Hauz UZBEK $$
(Lyabi-Hauz; mains 7000-20,000S; ⊙9am-11pm) Dining al fresco around the venerable pool with grey-beards, local families and Russian tourists is the quintessential Bukhara experience. The chaikhana-style restaurant serves shashlyk, plov and *kovurma laghman* (fried noodles with meat and tomato sauce), but it's more about the ambience than the food. There's also live Russian-style music most evenings. Check your bill as items can get mysteriously added.

Chashmai Mirob UZBEK $$
(Hoja Nurabad; mains 6000-7000S; ⊙10am-10pm, closed Nov-Mar; ✎ 🍴) It's known more for its fabulous view of the Mir-i-Arab and Kalon Mosque than for its home-cooked food, but you can still eat passably here, though you

may be swamped by tour groups if you're unlucky. The menu is heavy on Russian classics and you can pre-order *plov*.

🍷 Drinking & Nightlife

For anything rowdier than puppets and coffee you must head southeast of the centre into the newer part of town, but the nightclubs here are decidedly provincial (read: mostly male). Most visitors are content with a beer or two beside the Lyabi-Hauz. Bukhara's old town is eerily silent by night, which is part of its charm.

★ Silk Road Spices   TEAHOUSE
(☑ +998 93 383 4034, 65-224 22 68; www.silkroad spices.co; Halim Ibodov 5; set tea & sweets per person 20,000S; ☺ 9am-8pm) This boutique teahouse offers a delightful diversion from all that sightseeing. It has three spicy varieties of tea, as well as cinnamon or cardamom coffee, served with four types of local sweets such as halva and *nabat* (crystal sugar) in a cosy, traditional atmosphere. The owner's family has been working in the spice trade for 600 years.

Tea & Coffee Khona   CAFE
(Toki-Sarrafon; ☺ 9am-11pm) The switched-on management behind the Minzifa Restaurant opened this charming cafe in the Toki-Sarrafon bazaar. The location is dreamy, housed in a former mosque, whose traditional architecture includes some fine original wooden beams carved with Islamic calligraphy. The menu stretches to tea, coffee, cakes and cocktails.

Cafe Wishbone   CAFE
(☑ +998 93 658 4050; www.cafe-wishbone-bukhara.uz; Hakikat 1A; coffee 10,000S; ☺ 9am-8pm) A German-Uzbek coffee shop where you can get real coffee and a slice of German-style apple strudel. The interior design is a bit stark, but a cappuccino on the terrace is very welcome. Snacks include potato waffles and sandwiches. Niggles include no wi-fi and having to pay to use the toilet.

Cafe Segafredo   CAFE
(Naqshbandi; coffee 8000S; ☺ 9am-11pm; 🖼) This pioneering family-run cafe has good coffee available and well-intended, if rather slow, service. There's a selection of sweet items available too, and its central location makes it the best place for a caffeine injection in town.

Shopping

With almost every mosque and medressa stuffed with craft vendors, it's not hard to find a souvenir in Bukhara. Popular buys include embroidered bags, painted miniatures, knives, spices, skullcaps, carpets, ceramics and tea pots.

To watch artisans at work check out the **Bukhara Artisan Development Centre** (Naqshbandi; ☺ 9am-6pm Mon-Sat) for *suzani*, miniature paintings, jewellery boxes and chess set, and **Unesco Carpet Weaving Shop** (Eshoni Pir 57; ☺ 9am-5pm Mon-Sat), which was launched by, but is no longer associated with, the namesake organisation.

Feruza's Ikat Store   CLOTHING
(Toki-Sarrafon) If your itinerary isn't taking you to the Fergana Valley, check out Feruza's stall for a great collection of stylish, family-made *ikat* silks from Margilon. Asking prices start at US$5 per metre for cotton to US$20 per metre for 80% silk.

Tim Abdulla Khan   CARPETS
(Hakikat; ☺ 9am-6pm) For carpets, you couldn't ask for a better shopping atmosphere than at the silk-weaving centre in this cavernous late-16th-century building, located near Taki-Telpak Furushon Bazaar (a *tim* was a general market). Vendors will openly inform you on what's handmade and what's machine-made, and if you get overwhelmed there's an on-site cafe.

Shahriston Market   MARKET
(Hoja Nurabad; ☺ 7am-6pm) The virtually tourist-free Shahriston Market is in a large courtyard, where locals trade blingy jewellery and house-sized carpets among themselves and relative bargains can be had compared to things on sale down the street in the traveller-oriented covered markets.

ⓘ Information

MONEY
Top-end hotels will change money at set government rates.

Asaka Bank (Naqshbandi 168; ☺ 9.30am-4pm Mon-Fri) Offers US dollar cash advances on MasterCard for 3% commission.

Kapital Bank (Sarrafon; ☺ 9am-2pm & 3-4pm Mon-Fri) Gives US dollar cash advances on Visa cards for 3% commission and has a useful location by the Lyabi-Hauz.

Kapital Bank ATM (Hoja Nurabad; ☺ 24hr) Bukhara's most reliable ATM; it works about half the time.

National Bank of Uzbekistan (M Ikbola 3; ⊘9am-5pm Mon-Fri) Inconvenient location but offers US dollar cash advances on Visa cards.

POST & TELEPHONE

Post Office (Mehtar Ambar; ⊘10am-5pm Mon-Fri)

Uztelecom (Muminov 8; ⊘24hr) Offers international calls for standard Uztelekom rates.

TRAVEL AGENCIES

Besides yurtstays near Aidarkul Lake and mountain homestays in Nuratau (which just about any hotel can arrange), regional attractions include endangered Persian gazelles north of Karaul Bazaar, swimming in Tudakul Lake and the excavated remains of the pre-Islamic Silk Road city of Paikent, 60km southwest of Bukhara.

Many of the best agencies are attached to the B&Bs.

Emir Travel (☑65-224-49-65; www.emirtravel.com; Husainov 17) Contact Mila Ahmedov.

Komil Travel (☑65-221 08 00; www.travelbukhara.com) Contact Komil.

Minzifa Travel (☑+998 93 659 1107; www.minzifatravel.com; Eshoni Pir 63, Minzifa Hotel) Contact Timur Alimov.

Salom Travel (☑65-224 41 48; www.salomtravel.com; Sarrafon 3) Contact Raisa Gareeva.

ⓘ Getting There & Away

AIR

The airport is located 6km east of town. **Uzbekistan Airways** (☑65-225 39 46; Bukhara Airport) has flights from Bukhara to Tashkent at least daily.

Figure on around 6000S for the 10-minute taxi trip between the centre and the airport.

BUS & SHARED TAXI

All eastbound transport leaves from the North Bus Station, about 3km north of the centre. Here you'll find private buses to Navoi (7000S, 2½ hours), Samarkand (30,000S, 4½ hours) and Tashkent (40,000S, eight to 10 hours).

Just to the north or across the road are more reliable shared taxis to Navoi (20,000S, one hour) and Tashkent (80,000S, 6½ hours). Shared taxis to Samarkand (50,000S, three hours) often involve a change of car in Navoi.

About 1.5km north of here is Karvon Bazaar, departure point for Urgench and Khiva-bound transport. Shared taxis congregate in a lot on the less-crowded south end of the market. The going rate is 70,000S to 80,000S per seat for Urgench (five to six hours). You might find a direct ride to Khiva for a little more, but it's more likely that your driver will just put you in another shared taxi on arrival in Urgench. Sporadic morning buses to Urgench pass through from

Tashkent on the main road in front of the taxi stand, but you are better off with a shared taxi.

To get to the North Bus Station and Karvon Bazaar take bus 9 (700S) from the Lyabi-Hauz marshrutka stop in front of the Asia Hotel and Taki-Telpak Furushon Bazaar. A cab here will cost you 5000S, or 6000S to Karvon Bazaar.

The Sharq (Eastern) 'bus station' east of the centre no longer has any buses, but it's still a shared taxis departure point. Transport runs to Karshi (30,000S, two hours), Shakhrisabz (60,000S, four hours) and Denau on the Tajik border (70,000S, six hours). Change in Karshi for Termiz (from Karshi 50,000S, five hours). A taxi from the centre costs 5000S.

If you are headed to the Turkmen border make your way to the Markaziy (Kolkhoz) Bazaar and pick up a shared taxi to Karakol or Olot.

TRAIN

The **train station** (☑65-524 65 93; Kagan) is 9km southeast of Bukhara in Kagan. Luckily you can buy tickets from the more convenient **train ticket office** (⊘8am-1pm & 2-4.30pm Mon-Fri) southeast of the old town.

The superfast 'Afrosiyab' service departs at 3.50pm for Samarkand (42,000/57,000S, 1¾ hours) and Tashkent (95,000/130,000S, four hours). The cheaper but slower 'Sharq' train departs at 8am for Samarkand and Tashkent; it costs 20% less and takes 40% longer. It's generally harder to buy tickets for Tashkent than Samarkand.

An overnight service to Tashkent leaves at 10.35pm, arriving the next morning at 6.30am. Otherwise Bukhara is a bit of a backwater for trains – the main services from Tashkent to Nukus, Urgench and Russia go via Navoi, not Bukhara.

To get to Kagan take a shared taxi (3000S) from the stand just east of the Vokzal bus stop. A private taxi costs from 10,000S to 15,000S.

ⓘ Getting Around

BICYCLE

A couple of shops by the Lyabi-Hauz rent out decent bikes for around US$1 per hour or US$8 per day (bring your passport as deposit).

PUBLIC TRANSPORT

From the Lyabi-Hauz marshrutka stop in front of the Asia Hotel, bus 8 runs to the Markaziy (Kolkhoz) Bazaar and bus 9 runs to Karvon Bazaar. Both pass the Lyabi-Hauz and the useful Vokzal stop, where you can pick up transport going just about anywhere.

TAXI

You should be able to get anywhere in the centre of town in a taxi for about 3000S, so long as you avoid the taxi drivers who hang out around Lyabi-Hauz.

KHOREZM (XORAZM)

The Amu-Darya delta, stretching southeast of Urgench to the Aral Sea, has been inhabited for millennia and was an important oasis long before Urgench or even Khiva were important. What the Nile is to Egypt, the Amu-Darya has been to Central Asia. The historical name of the delta area, which includes parts of modern-day northern Turkmenistan, was Khorezm.

Today Khorezm (Xorazm) district takes in the former khanate of Khiva, the border region with Turkmenistan and the Soviet-era city of Urgench. Historically Khorezm also included the collection of ancient desert cities now collectively known as the Elliq-Qala (Fifty Fortresses). Today, these are technically in Karakalpakstan, but are most commonly visited from Khiva.

Urgench (Urganch)

☎ 62 / POP 140,000

Urgench (Urganch), the capital of Khorezm province, is a standard-issue Soviet grid of broad streets and empty squares, 450km northwest of Bukhara across the desolation of the Kyzylkum desert. When the Amu-Darya changed course in the 16th century, the people of Konye-Urgench (then called Gurganj), 150km downriver in present-day Turkmenistan, were left without water and started a new town here.

Today travellers use Urgench mainly as a transport hub for Khiva, 35km southwest. It's also the jumping-off point for the 'Golden Ring' of ancient fortresses in southern Karakalpakstan. It's not the kind of place you're likely to want to hang around in, but it can be useful as a stop over.

Accommodation in Urgench is overpriced and there's no reason to base yourself here unless you have a dawn flight or train. If you must, the previously notorious **Hotel Urgench** (☎ 62-223 14 10; Pakhlavan Mahmud 27; s/d/lux US$25/40/50; ✻ 🛜) has been renovated and now offers acceptable and clean, though somewhat overpriced, Soviet-style rooms – it's worth bargaining. Head up the main avenue from the train station, cross the bridge and take the first right a block after the main square. Four-star **Khorezm Palace** (☎ 62-224 99 99; www.khorezmpalace.uz; Al-Beruni 2; s/d/ste US$50/60/90; 🅿 ✻ 🛜 ⛳) is better on paper than reality. The pool is often shut, the wi-fi works best in the lobby and even the air-con can be hit and miss. Solo travellers are better off booking a double room. It's a short distance from the junction of Al-Beruni and Al-Khorezmi. The **Chaikhana Urgench** (Al-Khorezmi 35/1; mains

Khorezm

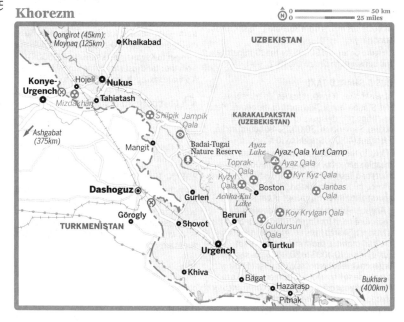

5000-10,000S; ⊗8am-10pm) serves the standards, and more shashlyk stands are located along pedestrian Uzbekistan ko'chasi. Go one short block north from the Hotel Urgench and take a left.

For getting around town, minibus 19 runs from the train station to the post office via Dekon Bazaar. Marshrutkas 3 and 13 go from the southern side of Dekon Bazaar to the airport via Al-Khorezmi.

☞ Tours

Reliable local guides offer tours from Urgench to the Elliq Qala fortresses.

Bahadir & Bakhtiyar Rakhamov (☑62-512 12 41, Bahadir 62-352 41 06, Bakhtiyar 62-517 51 33) are an English-speaking father-and-son driving team, offering excursions to the *qalas* (fortresses).

Delia Madrashimova (☑62-290 96 36; per day US$35) is an English-speaking guide who is a good bet for excursions to the *qalas* or Khiva.

ⓘ Information

National Bank of Uzbekistan (Al-Khorezmi; ⊗9am-2pm & 3-4pm Mon-Fri) Offers US dollar cash advances on a Visa card for 3% commission.

Post, Telephone & Telegraph Office (Al-Khorezmi 1; ⊗24hr)

ⓘ Getting There & Around

For getting around town, minibus 19 runs from the train station to the post office via Dekon Bazaar. Marshrutkas 3 and 13 go from the southern side of Dekon Bazaar to the airport via Al-Khorezmi.

AIR

Uzbekistan Airways (☑62-224 59 59; Al-Khorezmi 1; ⊗8am-8pm) has multiple flights daily from Urgench to Tashkent and four weekly flights to St Petersburg and Moscow. The airport is 4km north of the centre.

A taxi to the airport costs 4000S.

SHARED TAXI

Shared taxi is the favoured way of getting across the Kyzylkum desert to Bukhara and beyond. Shared taxis leave from a stand a block north of the train station to Bukhara (70,000S, seven hours) and Samarkand (100,000S, 10 hours). For Tashkent you are better off taking the train.

The **bus station** (Al-Khorezmi), near the train station, hardly functions, with elusive buses departing some mornings to Bukhara (30,000S) and Samarkand (45,000S).

Shared taxis to Nukus (30,000S, two hours) congregate at the Olympic (Olympiysky) Stadium or Raitsentr Bazaar, both about 2km northwest of the centre. From the Khiva shared taxi stand take minivan 19 or a taxi (4000S). Traffic is most frequent in the morning. If nothing's going to Nukus, go to Beruni and change there.

The stand for shared taxis to Khiva (5000S, 20 minutes) is south of Dekon Bazaar on Al-Beruni. Cars depart when full every 20 minutes or so.

TRAIN

From the **train station** (☑62-225 6111; Al-Khorezmi) daily overnight trains leave Urgench for Tashkent (*platskartny/kupeyny* 110,000/159,000S) at 2.30pm, arriving in Tashkent at 9am the next morning. There is also a 7.30pm departure for Tashkent that comes from Saratov in Russia. All Tashkent-bound trains also call at Samarkand (*platskartny/kupeyny* 82,000/121,000S, 12 hours).

There are also weekly services to Andijon and Almaty, and international services to Moscow and St Petersburg. Other transit trains, such as the Qongirot (Kungrad)–Tashkent and St Petersburg–Tashkent, pass through Turtkul.

Buy tickets in the *kassa* (ticket office) to the right of the main station building.

Around Urgench

Elliq-Qala

The enigmatic ruins of over a dozen walled towns, palaces and forts, some well over 2000 years old, stand half-forgotten in the semi-desert east and north of Urgench in southern Karakalpakstan. They are the remains of a chain of fortified settlements that once formed the boundary between the cultivated delta and the steppe nomads. With help from Unesco, local tourism officials have dubbed this area the 'Golden Ring of Ancient Khorezm'. The area's traditional name is Elliq-Qala (Fifty Fortresses).

For fans of ancient history, amateur archaeologists and anyone with an inner Indiana Jones lurking inside them, this is an area not to be missed. Outdoor and nature enthusiasts will also find things to keep them busy, from scrambling among the *qala* (fort) ruins, to camel trekking near Ayaz-Qala.

Birders will want to take their binoculars to the **Badai-Tugai Nature Reserve** (admission US$10; ⊗dawn-dusk), a *tugai* (trees, shrubs and salt-resistant plants unique to Central Asia) forest that's home to 91 bird species and 21 mammal species. It's just off the main road about 60km north of Urgench and is best visited on an early-morning trip from Khiva. At the time of writing, the central part of the reserve, containing most of the flora and fauna of interest including the Bukhara deer, was closed to visitors.

⊙ Sights

There are about 20 forts that you can explore here today, and who knows how many that have yet to be discovered (the 'Fifty Fortresses' moniker is an approximation). The most impressive *qalas* are the hilltop Ayaz-Qala and the historically significant Toprak Qala. Other forts such as Guldursun and Janbas Qalas are interesting mainly for the scale of their defensive walls.

Toprak Qala   FORT
(Topraq Qala; admission 4000S; ⊙ dawn–dusk) This fort about 10km west of Boston was the main temple complex of the Khorezm kings who ruled this area in the 3rd and 4th centuries. The many rooms of the main corner palace are still clear and you can just make out the central Zoroastrian fire temple. The fort was abandoned in the 6th century.

Ayaz-Qala   FORT
(admission 4000S) Impressive mud-walled Ayaz-Qala, located 23km north of Boston (Bustan), is a complex of three forts. Its heyday was the 6th and 7th centuries. From the car park walk up to the large hilltop ruins and then hike down to the smaller defensive manor below. It's possible to overnight or lunch at the Ayaz-Qala Yurt Camp (p262), but it's essential to call ahead.

Janbas Qala   FORT
The unique fortification walls here are punctured by hundreds of arrow slits and once garrisoned 2000 soldiers. The site overlooks an old branch of the Amu-Darya.

Koy Krylgan Qala   FORT
The oldest, most remarkable and most difficult-to-pronounce fort in Elliq-Qala is circular Koy Krylgan Qala, which archaeologists believe doubled as a temple and observatory complex. It was in use as early as the 4th century BC. Find it 18km east of Guldursun Qala.

Guldursun Qala   FORT
Guldursun Qala was built as early as the 1st century, but reached a high point in the 12th century under the Khorezmshahs. Walk through the main eastern gate and along

parts of the large city walls to the northeastern corner tower. It is normally visited en route to Koy Krylgan Qala.

🛏 Sleeping

Ayaz-Qala Yurt Camp   YURT $$
(☑ 61-532 43 61, +998 94 140 0070; per person incl meals US$45) Right next to Ayaz-Qala, this somewhat charmless yurt camp has eight concrete-based yurts lined up in a row, each big enough to hold five to eight people. Things can get very hot in summer. Tour groups often book out Ayaz-Qala, especially for lunch. At other times you're practically at one with the desert. Bring a torch. Bookings are essential.

Given some warning, the Ayaz-Qala yurt camp can arrange camels for a short ride (US$5 to US$10 per hour) into the fringes of the surrounding semi-desert.

ℹ Getting There & Away

The only way to explore Elliq-Qala is with private transport. Make absolutely sure your driver knows this area well and negotiate hard. The best strategy is to visit Guldursun Qala first and go anticlockwise.

Khiva's tourist information office (p269) offers half-/full-day tours for US$40/60 per carload, with good drivers and air-conditioned cars. The half-day trip visits Ayaz-Qala, Toprak Qala and Kyzyl Qala; the full day trip visits another three or four sites.

Murod at Hotel Islambek (p267) in Khiva arranges a similar half-/full-day trip for US$30/40, while other guesthouses offer slightly pricier trips.

If you are headed to Nukus it's possible to visit Elliq-Qala and then pay a little extra to be dropped at Nukus, stopping en route to visit the 4th-century Zoroastrian *dakhma* (Tower of Silence) at Shilpik (Chilpak).

Khiva (Xiva)
☑ 62 / POP 50,000
Khiva's name, redolent of slave caravans, barbaric cruelty, terrible desert journeys and steppes infested with raiding Turkmen tribesmen, struck fear into all but the boldest 19th-century hearts. Nowadays it's a friendly and welcoming Silk Road old town that's well set up for tourism.

The historic heart of Khiva (Xiva) has been so well preserved that it's sometimes criticised as lifeless – a 'museum city'. But walk through the city gates and wander the fabled Ichon-Qala (inner walled city) in all its monotone, mud-walled glory and it's hard not to feel like you are stepping into another era.

Try to spend at least one night in Khiva. The old town is at its best at dawn, sunset and by night, when the moonlit silhouettes of the tilting minarets and medressas, viewed from twisting alleyways, work their real magic.

History

Legend has it that Khiva was founded when Shem, son of Noah, discovered a well here; his people called it Kheivak, from which the name Khiva is said to be derived. The original well still exists in the courtyard of an 18th-century house in the northwest of the old town.

Khiva existed by the 8th century as a minor fort and trading post on a side branch of the Silk Road, but while Khorezm prospered on and off from the 10th to the 14th centuries, its capital was at Old Urgench (present-day Konye-Urgench in Turkmenistan), and Khiva remained a bit player.

It wasn't until well after Konye-Urgench had been finished off by Timur (Tamerlane) that Khiva's time came. When the Uzbek Shaybanids moved into the decaying Timurid empire in the early 16th century, one branch founded a state in Khorezm and made Khiva their capital in 1592.

The town ran a bustling slave market that was to shape the destiny of the Khivan khanate for more than three centuries. Most slaves were brought by Turkmen tribesmen from the Karakum desert or Kazakh tribes of the steppes, who raided those unlucky enough to live or travel nearby.

Russian Interest Awakens

In the early 18th century, Khiva had offered to submit to Peter the Great of Russia in return for help against marauding tribes. In a belated response, a force of about 4000, led by Prince Alexandr Bekovich, arrived in Khiva in 1717.

Unfortunately for them, the khan at the time, Shergazi Khan, had lost interest in being a vassal of the tsar. He came out to meet them, suggesting they disperse to outlying villages where they could be more comfortably accommodated. This done, the Khivans annihilated the invaders, leaving just a handful to make their way back with the news. Shergazi Khan sent Bekovich's head to his Central Asian rival, the Emir of Bukhara, and kept the rest of him on display.

In 1740 Khiva was wrecked by a less gullible invader, Nadir Shah of Persia, and Khorezm became a northern outpost of the Persian empire. By the end of the 18th century it was rebuilt and began taking a small share in the growing trade between Russia and the Bukhara and Kokand khanates. Its slave market, the biggest in Central Asia, continued unabated, augmented by Russians captured as they pushed their borders southwards and eastwards.

Russian Conquest

When the Russians finally sent a properly organised expedition against Khiva, it was no contest. In 1873 General Konstantin Kaufman's 13,000-strong forces advanced on Khiva from the north, west and east. After some initial guerrilla resistance, mainly by Yomud Turkmen tribesmen, Mohammed Rakhim II Khan surrendered unconditionally. Kaufman then indulged in a massacre of the Yomud. The khan became a vassal of the tsar and his silver throne was packed off to Russia.

The enfeebled khanate of Khiva struggled on until 1920 when the Bolshevik general Mikhail Frunze installed the Khorezm People's Republic in its place. This, like the similar republic in Bukhara, was theoretically independent of the USSR. But its leaders swung away from socialism towards Pan-Turkism, and in 1924 their republic was absorbed into the new Uzbek SSR.

⊙ Sights

Access to the buildings of Khiva's Ichon-Qala (p263) is possible only through an entry ticket that can be bought at the West Gate. The ticket is valid for two consecutive days, and includes all but a handful of smaller museums and the occasional minaret. You are free to walk around the Ichon-Qala without a ticket, you just won't be able to access any sights.

Keen photographers and anyone with a taste for beauty should head out in the late afternoon for spectacular views of Khiva's mostly west-facing facades bathed in the orange glow of the setting sun. The top of the west wall, the watchtower at the Kuhna Ark, and the Islom Hoja Minaret offer the best viewpoints.

Ichon-Qala   HISTORIC SITE

(2-day admission 51,000S, camera US$3, video US$3; ⊙ ticket booth & sights 9am-6pm) Khiva's Ichon-Qala is one of the great highlights of

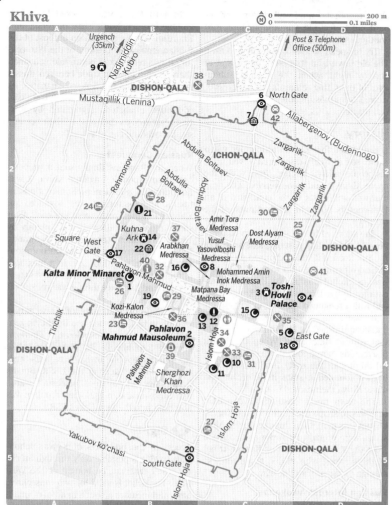

Uzbekistan. The perfectly preserved medieval walled town is home to dozens of mosques, medressas and mausolea, most of which are home to small museums. You need a whole day to see the sights, but try also to wander the streets during the cool of dawn or dusk when the town is at its most magical.

Gates are known as **North Gate** (Bogcha-Darvoza; Garden Gate), **East Gate** (Polvon-Darvoza, Strongman's Gate) and **South Gate** (Tosh-Darvoza; Stone Gate). The main ticket office for Ichon-Qala can be found in the twin-turreted **West Gate** (Ota-Darvoza; Father Gate), a 1970s reconstruction – the original was wrecked in 1920 – which is also the main entrance to the old city.

One highlight for which no ticket is needed is the walk along the northwestern section of the Ichon-Qala City Walls. The stairs can be accessed at the North Gate and are a great place to be at sunset. The 2.5km-long mud walls date from the 18th century, and were rebuilt after being destroyed by the Persians.

★ **Kalta Minor Minaret**   ISLAMIC SITE

This fat, turquoise-tiled minaret was begun in 1851 by Mohammed Amin Khan, who

Khiva

UZBEKISTAN KHIVA (XIVA)

according to legend wanted to build a minaret so high he could see all the way to Bukhara. Unfortunately the khan dropped dead in 1855, leaving the beautifully tiled structure unfinished.

East of the minaret, beside the medressa, is the small, plain **Sayid Alauddin Mausoleum** (Pahlavon Mahmud), dating from 1310 when Khiva was under the Golden Horde of the Mongol empire. You might find people praying in front of the 19th-century tiled sarcophagus.

Kuhna Ark FORT
(◎8am-8pm) To your left after you enter the West Gate stands the Kuhna Ark – the Khiva rulers' own fortress and residence, first built in the 12th century by one Ok Shaykh Bobo, then expanded by the khans in the 17th century. The khans' harem, mint, stables, arsenal, barracks, mosque and jail were all here. Apart from getting a peek at the life of the khans, the complex has some fine tilework and excellent views.

The small, low-slung building to the left of the entrance outside the main fortress is the **Zindon** (Khans' Jail; ◎8am-8pm), with a simple display of chains, manacles and weapons, suggesting how poor an idea falling foul of the khan would have been.

Once inside the Ark, the first passage to the right takes you into the 19th-century Summer Mosque – open-air and spectacularly ornate with superb blue-and-white plant-motif tiling and a red, orange and gold ceiling. There are some interesting displays on Khorezmian archaeology here.

Beside it is the old mint, now a museum that exhibits bank notes and coins that were minted here, including money printed on silk. Unfortunately labelling is only in Uzbek.

Straight ahead from the Ark entrance is the restored, open-air throne room, where the khan dispensed judgement. The circular area on the ground was for the royal yurt, which the no-longer-nomadic khans still liked to use. The tiled *aivan* (portico) is simply stunning.

At the back right corner of the throne room, a door in the wall leads to a flight of steps up to the **watchtower** (admission 6000S), the original part of the Kuhna Ark, set right against the Ichon-Qala's massive west wall. It's well worth paying the fee to climb up here – the city views are extraordinary, especially at sunset.

East of the Kuhna Ark, across an open space that was once a busy palace square (and place of execution), the 19th-century **Mohammed Rakhim Khan Medressa** (⊘9am-6pm) is named after the khan who surrendered to Russia in 1873. The history museum within is partly dedicated to this khan and his son, Isfandiyar. Mohammed Rakhim Khan was also a poet under the pen name Feruz.

Juma Mosque MOSQUE

(Pahlavon Mahmud; ⊘9am-6pm) Almost in the centre of the Ichon-Qala, the large and atmospheric Juma Mosque is interesting for the 218 wooden columns supporting its roof – a concept thought to be derived from ancient Arabian mosques. Six or seven of the columns date from the original 10th-century mosque (see if you can spot them), though the present building dates from the 18th century.

From inside, you can climb 82 dark and narrow steps up to the pigeon-poop-splattered gallery of the 47m **Juma Minaret** (admission 5000S), for fine views over the city. The minaret is apparently starting to lean and so access may be restricted in the future.

★Pahlavon Mahmud Mausoleum MAUSOLEUM

(Islom Hoja; admission 6000S; ⊘8am-6pm) This revered mausoleum, with its sublime courtyard and stately tilework, is one of the town's most beautiful spots. Pahlavon Mahmud was a poet, philosopher and legendary wrestler who became Khiva's patron saint. His 1326 tomb was rebuilt in the 19th century and then requisitioned in 1913 by the khan of the day as his family mausoleum.

The beautiful Persian-style chamber under the turquoise dome at the northern end of the courtyard holds the tomb of Mohammed Rakhim Khan. Pahlavon Mahmud's tomb, to the left off the first chamber, has some of Khiva's loveliest tiling on the sarcophagus and the walls. Tombs of other khans stand unmarked east and west of the main building, outside the courtyard.

Islom Hoja Medressa ISLAMIC SITE

(Islom Hoja; ⊘9am-6pm) Walk south from the Abdulla Khan Medressa to the Islom Hoja Medressa and minaret – Khiva's newest Islamic monuments, both built in 1910. You can climb the **minaret** (6000S; ⊘8am-8pm) any time but morning light is best. With bands of turquoise and red tiling, it looks rather like an uncommonly lovely lighthouse. At 57m tall, it's Uzbekistan's highest.

The medressa holds Khiva's best museum, the Museum of Applied Arts. It exhibits Khorezm handicrafts through the ages – fine woodcarving, metalwork, Uzbek and Turkmen carpets, stone carved with Arabic script (which was in use in Khorezm from the 8th to the 20th centuries) and fine tilework from the nearby Pahlavon Mahmud Mausoleuem.

Islom Hoja himself was an early-20th-century grand vizier and a liberal (by Khivan standards): he founded a European-style school, brought long-distance telegraph to the city and built a hospital. For his popularity, the khan and clergy had him assassinated.

★Tosh-Hovli Palace PALACE

(⊘9am-8pm) This palace, which means 'Stone House', contains Khiva's most sumptuous interior decoration, dense with blue ceramic tiles, carved wooden pillars and elaborate *ghanch*. Built by Allakuli Khan between 1832 and 1841 as a more splendid alternative to the Kuhna Ark, it's said to have more than 150 rooms off nine courtyards, with high ceilings designed to catch the slightest desert breeze. Allakuli was a man in a hurry – the Tosh-Hovli's first architect was executed for failing to complete the job in two years.

Two separate entrances take you into two separate wings of the palace. The northern harem wing has some handicrafts exhibitions. Don't miss the harder-to-spot and labyrinthine south wing, where the throne room, two brick yurt bases and a sumptuous *aivan* (covered portico) are located, along with a wonderful carriage dating from 1872. You'll have to avoid the young Uzbek couples canoodling in the dark corners.

Isfandiyar Palace PALACE

(Mustaqillik; ⊘9am-6pm) The Isfandiyar Palace (also called the Palace of Nurullabay) was built between 1906 and 1912, and like the emir's summer palace (p254) in Bukhara displays some fascinatingly overwrought decorations that straddle the messy collision of East and West. The rooms are largely empty, allowing one to fully appreciate the gold-embroidered ceilings, ceramic chimneys and lavish 4m-high mirrors and chandeliers.

THE BUILDER KHAN

Just east of the Juma Mosque, a lane leading north from Pahlavon Mahmud ko'chasi contains some of Khiva's most interesting buildings, most of them created by Allakuli Khan – known as the 'builder khan' – in the 1830s and '40s. First there's the tall Allakuli Khan Medressa, with some stunning blue tilework, and the earlier Kutlug Murod Inoq Medressa (1804–12), facing each other across the street, with nearly matching facades. The latter now houses an art museum.

North of the Allakuli Khan Medressa is the Allakuli Khan Bazaar & Caravanserai. The entrance to both is through tall wooden gates beside the medressa. The bazaar is a domed market arcade, catering to both traders and tourists, which opens onto Khiva's modern Dekon Bazaar at its east end.

Opposite the Allakuli Khan Medressa to the south are the 1855 Abdulla Khan Medressa, which holds a tiny nature museum, the tiny Ok (White) Mosque (1657) and the closed Anusha Khan Baths.

The East Gate (p264), a long, vaulted 19th-century passage with several sets of immense carved doors, bridges the baths and the bazaar area. The slave market was held here, and niches in the passage walls once held slaves for sale. Just outside the gate is a working mosque that overflows with wizened old men on Friday.

Despite being located just outside the walls of the Ichon-Qala (p263), admission here is included on the two-day ticket.

🛏 Sleeping

Negotiating often bears fruit at Khiva hotels. In high season (April, June, September and October), it's a good idea to book ahead, or you won't be able to stay in the better options, many of which are booked up weeks ahead. Only the larger hotels stay open from December to February.

★ Hotel Islambek HOTEL $
(☑62-375 30 23, +998 91 999 3322; islambek_hotel@rambler.ru; Zargarlik 60; dm US$10, s/d from US$14/24; P ✳ 🛜) This 20-room place (and 13-room annexe) is perhaps the best budget option in the Ichon-Qala. The migraine-inducing wallpaper in the rooms may not scream style but there's much to like here, including a spacious airy courtyard, parking for overlanders, great rooftop views, flexible pricing and good-value single rooms.

Hostel Lali-Opa HOSTEL $
(☑+998 91 998 8999; Obvodnaya; dm US$10; 🛜) This hostel run by the Guest House Lali-Opa is 2km north of the Ichon-Qala in the owners' spacious home. The four quiet dorms here are much more comfortable than the main Lali-Opa, if you don't mind making the daily commute; the owners sweeten the deal with free transfers and use of a bike.

Mirzoboshi B&B $
(☑+998 95 602 4713, 62-375 27 53; mirzaboshi@inbox.ru; Pahlavon Mahmud 1; s/d/tr US$25/40/50; ✳ 🛜) This mud- and brick-walled B&B is located right in the heart of the Ichon-Qala (the entrance is around the back). There are just three renovated rooms, and a large roof terrace with a fine view of the Kalta Minor. For more privacy and comfort but less traditional charm, opt for their clean and modern **annexe** (☑62-375 91 88; Zargarlik 24; dm/s/d/tr US$15/20/35/40; ✳ 🛜).

Guest House Lali-Opa B&B $
(☑+998 91 998 8999, 62-375 44 49; www.laliopa.com; Rahmonov 11A; dm/s/d US$10/20/30; ✳) This friendly little guesthouse, located just a few steps outside the West Gate, is firmly aimed at shoestringers. The grungy four-bed dorms share cramped bathrooms and the ramshackle rooms are fairly charmless, but there's a pleasant balcony and what it lacks in character it makes up for in friendly service and plenty of travel advice. Vegetarian meals are available.

Otabek B&B B&B $
(☑62-375 61 77, +998 91 912 9224; barnush@mail.ru; Islom Hoja 68; s/d US$10/20; ✳ 🛜) The Otabek sits somewhere between a guesthouse and a homestay. The nine rooms are spacious and bright and there's one three-bed dorm room. It's superbly located in the middle of the Ichon-Qala and comes with a friendly resident family to look after you, though it helps if you speak some Russian.

★ **Meros B&B** B&B $$
(☑ 62-375 76 42, +998 94 315 3700; www.mer-oskhiva.com; Boltaev 57; s/d/tr US$25/35/45; ❄ 🛜) Staying at this gorgeous, professionally run place is an absolute treat: four of the seven rooms have charming balconies and all have modern bathrooms. The rooms share access to a superb roof terrace where you can book a romantic dinner overlooking great Ichon-Qala views. The ornate dining room was personally decorated by the owner, a restoration master. Reservations advised.

Hotel Orient Star HISTORIC HOTEL $$
(☑ 62-375 68 59, +998 943 152 600; doniyoraa@rambler.ru; Pahlavon Mahmud 1; s/d US$60/80; ❄ 🛜) This unique hotel offers the rare opportunity of staying inside the 19th-century Mohammed Amin Khan Medressa. Accommodation in the 78 converted *hujra* (cell-like living quarters) is somewhat austere, but with cable TVs, domed roofs and fancy stone bathrooms you need not live a completely hermit-like existence. It's definitely Khiva's most atmospheric hotel, despite lacklustre staff: room 242 has the best views.

Arkanchi Hotel HOTEL $$
(☑ 62-375 2974; www.hotel-arkanchi.uz; s/d/tr US$45/60/75; ❄ 🛜) The Arkanchi is probably the best hotel in the Ichon-Qala. The spacious and modern carpeted rooms come with good bathrooms and there's a pleasant bar and an espresso machine in the lobby. Guests can rent bicycles to explore outside the Ichon-Qala. Ask for a discount in July and August, and from November to March.

Hotel Shahrizada Khiva BOUTIQUE HOTEL $$
(☑ 62-375 95 65, +998 91 572 7070; www.kh-ivashaherezada.uz; Islom Hoja 35; s/d/tr from US$25/50/70; ❄ 🛜) Popular with tour groups, the Shahrizada is a spacious hotel with high ceilings and fresh, clean rooms set around an oddly decorated dining room. There is lots of carved wood on display, including the memorable front door, which was hand-carved in the owner's workshop. Single rooms are a bit pokey.

The huge new Shahrizada Plus is scheduled to open in 2018 outside the city walls.

✗ Eating

Despite its ever-growing tourism industry, Khiva has a limited selection of restaurants to choose from. Leave the Ichon-Qala and prices suddenly halve.

Tokhir-Zukhra Chaikhana UZBEK $
(Mustaqillik; mains 6000-20,000S; ⊘ 11am-11pm) The best place for a chaikhana-style meal of freshly grilled kebabs and beer on tap is this laid-back spot just northwest of the Ichan Qala. The giant mutton and beef shashlyk are a meal by themselves and better than anything you'll find in the old town.

Bir Gumbaz UZBEK $
(Pahlavon Mahmud; mains 7000-12,000S; ⊘ 8am-11pm) This place serves up homemade Uzbek standards and real coffee on a terrace with superb Kalta Minor minaret views. There's an inside dining room if you're in Khiva during the colder months.

★ **Terasse Cafe** UZBEK $$
(☑ 62-375 20 23, +998 91 993 9111; www.terrassa-khiva.com; mains 10,000-16,000S; ⊘ 10am-10pm; ❄ 🛜 ✏ 📶) Dining experiences in Khiva don't get better than on a cool summer evening in the rooftop terrace of this well-run place, surrounded by the spotlit medressas and palace walls of the old town. The coffee is the best in town and the food ranges from good local shashlyk to eggplant salad and grilled vegetables. Reserve a table on the rooftop.

★ **Khorezm Art Restaurant** UZBEK $$
(☑ +998 95 606 9270; www.khorezmart.uz; Allakuli Khan Medressa; mains 10,000-15,000S; ⊘ 10am-10pm; ❄ ✏ 📶) Charmingly located in a low-lit and cosy stone building in front of the Allakuli Khan Medresa, this is definitely one of the best choices in town, with attentive service and an atmospheric rooftop terrace, despite the large number of groups. The menu includes Khorezmian specialities like pumpkin *manty* (steamed dumplings) and *tuxum barak* (ravioli filled with egg and yoghurt).

Cafe Zerafshan UZBEK $$
(mains 15,000-25,000S; ⊘ 10am-10pm) You can choose between outdoor seating on *tap-chans* (bedlike platforms) in the shadow of the Islom Hoja minaret, or the more formal interior of the converted Tolib Mahsum Medressa. The food is the standard Khivan menu of Uzbek and Khorezmian dishes, but it's all pretty good. There's also espresso coffee.

Mirzobashi Teahouse UZBEK $$
(mains 15,000S; ⊘ 10am-11pm; 📶) A pleasant, spacious and breezy teahouse-style restaurant right in the heart of the old town.

There's a good range of Central Asian dishes, including local specialities like *qiyma zarafshan* (a meat roll).

Kheivak Restaurant UZBEK $$

(Islom Hoja; mains 7000-16,000S; ⏰7am-11pm; 🛜🍴📶) The Malika Kheivak hotel has a pleasant sun-dappled courtyard covered with traditional *tapchan* and tables. It's a very handy spot for lunch in the Ichon-Qala, offering local-style egg and pumpkin-stuffed ravioli, as well as passable pizza and a fridge full of cold beer.

☆ Entertainment

Fashion & Traditional
Dance Show DANCE

(☑+998 90 719 5643; admission US$5; ⏰first show 6pm) This rather touristy music and dance show takes place in the Allakuli Khan Medressa nightly in the high season, normally around 6pm. Book tickets through the tourist information office or at the gate, and be sure to ask for a discount, which is often granted to individual tourists.

🛍 Shopping

Khiva is particularly known for its Turkmen-style woollen and fleece hats and carved wood. Souvenir and craft shops line the streets of the Ichon-Qala and are wedged into many attractions. The best quality is to be found in the Kutlimurodinok Medressa, which contains several handicraft workshops.

In the **Khiva Silk Carpet Workshop** (www.khiva.info/khivasilk; Pahlavon Mahmud; ⏰9am-7pm) carpet makers hand-weave high-quality silk rugs, not in traditional carpet patterns but in unique designs inspired by Khivan tilework, carved doors and miniature paintings. There's usually someone there to give you an introduction to the weaving process and the natural dyes used. Expect to pay US$2300 for a 1.3m by 2m carpet. There are also fine *suzani* (embroidery) for sale.

ℹ Information

MONEY

Bring plenty of cash to Khiva – if the somewhat unreliable MasterCard ATM in the Arkanchi Hotel isn't working, then the nearest place to get cash is in Urgench.

POST

Post & Telephone Office (Amir Timur 23; ⏰9am-7pm Mon-Sat) Located 650m north of the North Gate.

TOURIST INFORMATION

Tourist Information Office (☑62-375 69 28; www.khivamuseum.uz; Pahlavon Mahmud; ⏰8am-7pm) This helpful centre organises tours and guides for Khiva, little visited architectural sites around Khiva and the Elliq-Qala fortresses, as well as selling maps and information booklets. A useful service for non-Russian speakers is the organisation of taxis to Bukhara and the purchase of air and train tickets (with commission).

TOURS

The following guides offer tailored tours to Khiva and the area nearby. They all speak English, with the exception of Amon who speaks French.

Ali Madaminov (☑+998 91 279 2829)
Amon (☑+998 90 713 1383, 62-719 80 50)
Anush Boltaeva (☑+998 91 436 3780)
Muhammad Yunusov (☑+998 91 916 6632; muhammad-987@inbox.ru)
Temur Madaminov (☑+998 91 431 5799)

ℹ Getting There & Away

AIR

The nearest airport to Khiva is in Urgench, a 30-minute drive away. Shared taxis will drop you at the airport for 7000S.

BUS

A couple of daily buses depart Khiva for Tashkent (50,000S, 21 hours) via Samarkand and Bukhara, but they overnight en route at a roadside chaikhana, causing registration headaches for foreigners.

SHARED TAXI

The best way to travel between Urgench and Khiva is by shared taxi (5000S, 20 minutes), which leave from just outside the North Gate. Life is too short to bother with the interminable trolleybus (1½ hours).

If you're heading to Bukhara, your best bet is a shared taxi from Urgench (80,000S). Alternatively, the tourist information office can often match you with other travellers to share a taxi direct to your hotel in Bukhara (100,000 per seat), or ask at your guesthouse.

Shared taxis to Nukus only run from Urgench (20,000S per seat, 1½ hours). From Khiva you can get a private taxi (150,000S) from the Dekon Bazaar shared taxi stand. Guesthouses and the tourist information office can arrange a taxi for a higher fee.

TRAIN

Train services run only from nearby Urgench. Tickets are normally available a couple of days beforehand at the **ticket office** (⊘ 8am-1pm & 2-6pm) north of the Ichon-Qala. This may shift when the Khiva's new train station is opened.

A new train link to Khiva is scheduled to open in 2018, with fast services to/from Bukhara, Samarkand and Tashkent. This should reduce travel time to Bukhara to four hours. The new station is under construction 1km outside the East Gate.

KARAKALPAKSTAN (QARAQALPAQSTAN)

If you're attracted to desolation, you'll love the Republic of Karakalpakstan (Qaraqalpaqstan), a theoretically autonomous republic inside Uzbekistan. The destruction of the Aral Sea has rendered Karakalpakstan one of Uzbekistan's most depressed regions. The capital, Nukus, feels half deserted, and a drive into outlying areas reveals a region of dying towns and blighted landscapes. What once thrived as a rich delta, a branch of the Silk Road and a great Islamic centre of learning, now feels like the end of the world.

So why come here? Art lovers are drawn to the famous Savitsky Museum in Nukus for its great collection of Soviet avant-garde art. Adventurers come for the remote 4WD trip to bathe in the dying Aral Sea. Overlanders come looking for remote border crossings to Turkmenistan and western Kazakhstan. And beyond that, it's a quirky region full of friendly people. Plus it's kind of another 'stan to add to your list!

A good website about the region is www.karakalpak.com.

Nukus (No'kis)

☑ 61 / POP 260,000

The isolated Soviet creation of Nukus (No'kis) is one of Uzbekistan's least appealing cities and gets few visitors compared to its attractive Silk Road cousins. With its giant boulevards and decaying apartment blocks, in many ways it feels like Uzbekistan 25 years ago. However, as the gateway to the fast-disappearing Aral Sea and home to the remarkable Savitsky Museum – one of the best collections of Soviet art in the world – there is actually a reason to come here, apart from sampling the general sense of hopelessness and desolation.

The annual **Pakhta-Bairam** (⊘ late Nov/early Dec) festival takes place on the first Sunday after Karakalpakstan meets its cotton-picking quota, usually in late November or early December. Competitions are held in traditional sports such as wrestling, ram-fighting and cock-fighting.

◉ Sights

A **Karakalpak State Museum of Regional Studies** (Kamalov) is planned to house the region's main ethnographic and jewellery displays, and focus on the history and archaeology of Khorezm.

★**Savitsky Museum**   MUSEUM
(☑ 61-222 25 56; www.savitskycollection.org; Rzaev 127; admission/camera/guide 38,000/120,000/40,000S; ⊘ 9am-1pm & 2-5pm Mon-Fri, 10am-4pm Sat & Sun) The Savitsky Museum houses one of the most remarkable art collections in the former Soviet Union. About half of the paintings were brought here in Soviet times by artist and ethnographer Igor Savitsky, who managed to preserve an entire generation of avant-garde work that was proscribed and destroyed elsewhere in the country for not conforming to the socialist realism of the times.

The paintings found protection in these isolated backwaters (Nukus, after all, being literally the last place you'd look for anything) and it's interesting to hear how this nonconformist museum survived during the Soviet era. An English-language guided tour can really help to contextualise the collection and acts as an introduction to the fascinating stories behind many of the paintings.

The museum owns some 90,000 artefacts, including more than 15,000 paintings, only a fraction of which are actually on display. The museum also has some archaeological displays from the Elliq-Qala fortresses, including Zoroastrian ossuaries from Shilpik (Chilpak) and a bodhisattva statue from Guldursan. There are also some ethnographic displays, with a fine collection of jewellery, camel bags and wedding jewellery.

When we visited there was talk of closing the museum on Monday so check the website if you plan to be in Nukus for only one day. Tuesday and Friday are free for school groups and so can be very busy. For more on the Savitsky Museum visit http://museum.kr.uz.

🛏 Sleeping & Eating

Kizil-Kum Hotel
GUESTHOUSE $

(📋61-223 26 26, +998 90 593 2888; kizil_kum.
hotel@mail.ru; Qaraqalpaqstan Alpish Jilliq; s
US$10-15, d US$20) Surely the winner of Central Asia's 'least likely location for a budget hotel', the Kizil-Kum is southwest from the centre in a truly forlorn stretch of Nukus' suburbs. But once you're here it's a great deal, with clean and quiet rooms, hot water, shower curtains and even showerhead holders in the tiny bathrooms! There's also a small plunge pool and sauna.

The little cafe serves meals if ordered in advance. Add US$5 if you want breakfast.

To get here take minibus 53 from the bazaar. It loops down to the station and back into town, passing the hotel. Look for the big yellow building on an otherwise very ramshackle street.

★ Jipek Joli
HOTEL $$

(📋61-222 85 00; www.ayimtour.com; Jibek Joli 4; s/d from US$35/60, half lux US$45/70, lux US$55/80; ❄️🛜) Exactly what a struggling backwater like Nukus needs – a well-run hotel with enthusiastic and responsive English-speaking staff to help you make onward travel plans. This extremely comfortable 18-room place is well furnished and spacious, set around an excellent courtyard restaurant and brightened by local Karakalpak art. It's by far the best place in town. The courtyard yurt doubles as a dorm (US$20).

There's a second even more modern **annexe** (📋61-224 25 25; Kamalov/Tatibayev 50; s/d/tr US$30/50/65; ❄️🛜) just a block and a half away, should the main building be full. It has a plush dining room and espresso machine and the rooms are very comfortable, but it lacks the cosy courtyard of the main building.

Rahnamo Hotel
HOTEL $$

(📋61-222 47 43; http://hotelrahnamo.uz; Qaraqalpaqstan; s/d US$25/40; ❄️🛜) This study in beige offers 13 rooms, all of which are comfortable, spacious and excellent value, though lacking in atmosphere. It's very well located, however, and staff are polite. Discounts can bring the rates down to US$20/30.

Argo
CAFETERIA $

(Qaraqalpaqstan 6; mains 6000S; ⏱10am-10pm; 🛜) This self-service restaurant isn't exactly haute cuisine but it's cheap and easy, with good salads, pleasant outdoor seating and

---

no pesky Cyrillic menus to wrestle with. Come before 1pm for the best selection of fresh food; at other times the cafeteria-style mains can get a bit stewed.

Cinnamon Cafe
CAFE $$

(Jipek Joli; pizza 20,000S; ⏱8am-11pm; ❄️🛜📋) This unexpectedly modern and hip place has real coffee and a tempting array of cakes and house-made gelato. They also make pizzas (big enough for two) and a small selection of meals if you want something heartier. The location across from the Savitsky Museum makes it the perfect place for a reviving espresso after several hours spent staring at Soviet art.

Sheraton Cafe
RUSSIAN $$

(Gharezsizlik 53; mains 10,000-23,000S; ⏱10am-11pm; ❄️📋) With its red-and-cream upholstered dining room, this chintzy place may not live up to its hotel namesake, but it's a pretty sophisticated dinner venue and the staff do a good job. The menu is dominated by Russian classics, but there are also some Korean dishes such as *bibimbap* (rice, vegetables and egg in a stone pot) and fried beef.

ℹ Information

Asaka Bank (cnr Qaraqalpaqstan & Dostlyk; ⏱9am-4pm Mon-Fri) US dollar cash advances on MasterCards for 3% commission.

Kapital Bank (Aimurzaev; ⏱9am-4pm Mon-Fri) US dollar cash advances on Visa cards for a 3% commission.

Post & Telephone Office (Qaraqalpaqstan 7; ⏱post 7am-7pm, telephone 24hr) Centrally located.

ℹ Getting There & Away

AIR

Nukus airport is being upgraded, meaning that flights to Moscow (three weekly) are suspended

MIZDAKHAN

On a hill 20km west of Nukus, near Hojeli, are the remains of ancient Mizdakhan, once the second-largest city in Khorezm. Inhabited from the 4th century BC until the 14th century AD, Mizdakhan remained a sacred place even after Timur (Tamerlane) destroyed it; tombs and mosques continued to be built here right up to the 20th century.

The most impressive of the tombs is the restored underground vault of the Mausoleum of Mazlum Khan Slu, dating from the 12th to 14th centuries, and the seven-domed Mausoleum of Shamun Nabi.

On the neighbouring hill towards the Turkmen border are the remains of a 4th- to 3rd-century BC fortress called Gyaur-Qala, which is worth checking out if you missed the forts of Elliq-Qala.

To get here, take a shared taxi or minivan from Nukus' Konye Qala bus stand to Hojeli (5000S, 20 minutes), crossing the Amu-Darya (Oxus River) en route. From Hojeli take a shared taxi (2000/8000S per seat/car) bound for the Turkmen border and get off after 8km in Mizdakhan. A private taxi from Nukus will cost around 50,000S return with waiting time.

until 2019; flights to Tashkent are still running. Security staff at the airport may want to see all of your registration receipts when flying out of the city. The airport is 2.5km northwest of the centre.

Uzbekistan Airways has twice-daily flights from Nukus to Tashkent. The **ticket office** (☑ 61-222 79 95; Pushkin 43; ☺ 9am-1pm & 2-7pm) is hidden in the back of an apartment block in the centre of town.

SHARED TAXI

Shared taxis to Urgench (25,000S, two hours) and Tashkent (120,000S, 14 hours) via Samarkand (120,000S, eight hours) and Bukhara (100,000S, five hours) depart from a stand near the **South (New) Bus Station** (☑ 61-223 22 93; Yuzhny Avtovokzal), 6km south of town. For Khiva take a shared taxi to Urgench and change there.

A single daily bus lumbers from the South Bus Station to Tashkent (70,000S, 20 hours, 1pm), but overnights at a teahouse near Navoi and so creates registration problems for foreigners. It's much better to take the train.

Shared taxis to Khojeli, Mizdarkhan and the Turkmen border leave from the Konye Qala bus stand in Nukus' old town.

TRAIN

Nukus' **train station** (☑ 61-223 29 58) is located 5.5km south of the town centre. There are daily trains to Tashkent (*platskartny/kupeyny* 106,000/158,000S, 22 hours) that stop in Samarkand (99,500/119,000, 14 hours).

Four trains a week stop in Nukus en route from Tashkent to Saratov and Volgograd in Russia. There's also a Tuesday train to Almaty (*platskartny/kupeyny* 383,000/577,000S) via Tashkent and a daily Nukus–Benau train in remotest western Kazakhstan.

🛈 Getting Around

A taxi around town, including to the airport, costs around 4000S. Marshrutkas 1, 3, 4 or 48 from the bazaar go to the train station. To get to the South (New) Bus Station take marshrutkas 34, 74 or 94 from the bazaar or the train station. Marshrutka 5 runs from the Konye Qala bus stand to the bazaar, and numbers 31, 27 and 11 to/from the train station.

Moynaq (Mo'ynoq)

☑ 61 / POP 12,000

Moynaq (Mo'ynoq) encapsulates more visibly than anywhere else the absurd tragedy of the Aral Sea. Once one of the sea's two major fishing ports, it now stands almost 200km from the water. What remains of Moynaq's fishing fleet lies rusting on the sand in the former seabed.

The mostly Kazakh residents have moved away in droves, and today Moynaq is a virtual ghost town populated by livestock herders and the elderly looking after grandchildren whose parents have left to find work elsewhere. The few who remain suffer the full force of the Aral Sea disaster, with hotter summers, colder winters, debilitating sand-salt-dust storms, and a gamut of health problems.

⦿ Sights

Moynaq used to be on an isthmus connecting the Ush Say (Tiger's Tail) peninsula to the shore of the Aral Sea. You can appreciate this on the approach to the town, where the road is raised above the surrounding land.

Poignant reminders of Moynaq's tragedy are everywhere: the sign at the entrance to the town has a fish on it; a fishing boat stands as a kind of monument on a makeshift pedestal near Government House.

From the Aral Sea memorial you can spot a lake southeast of town, created in an attempt to restore the local fish industry and the formerly mild local climate. It didn't quite work, but it's at least given the locals a source of recreation.

The town itself consists of one seemingly endless main street linking the bus station at its southeast end with the Oybek Hotel and the ships graveyard to the northwest.

The beached ships are a five-minute walk from the Oybek Hotel, at the northwest end of town, across the main road and beyond the collection of homes. Once difficult to find, most ships have now been moved to a centralised location beneath the Aral Sea memorial, which occupies a bluff that was once the Aral Sea's bank. Inside city hall, the **Moynaq Museum** (Main Rd; admission/camera 5000/5000S; ⊗9am-6pm Tue-Sun) has some interesting photos and paintings of the area prospering before the disaster.

🛏 Sleeping & Eating

Spending the night in Moynaq shouldn't be done unless you have to. Bring your own food and water (don't drink the local water in Moynaq). Drivers often know the best homestays and places to get lunch. The town's only hotel, the Oybek, was not operating at the time of research but it may

---

VISITING THE ARAL SEA

Catching a glimpse of the notorious Aral Sea's receding southern shoreline holds no small amount of appeal for adventurous travellers. It's a very remote area so it's essential to go with an experienced driver with a good 4WD vehicle and an intimate knowledge of the route.

From Moynaq the route heads west along the sea's former shoreline and then sets out across the dried-up seabed, where oil refineries belch fire and black smoke in an eerie scene reminiscent of a Mad Max movie. The former seabed has been dry for so long that it is already a forest of sage brush, which soon peters out into a stretch of interminable salt flats receding into mirages in every direction.

From here you can see the Ustyurt Plateau, stretching into Kazakhstan to the north and all the way to the Caspian Sea to the west. At the end of the asphalt road dirt tracks climb the plateau, past cliffs and canyons, to eventually reveal your first sight of the intensely blue Aral Sea. Against the barren backdrop of the dried-up seabed and the rocky Ustyurt Plateau it looks profoundly beautiful, all the more so for what it represents – the dangers inherent in human's attempts to subjugate nature.

It's possible to drive to the water's edge where the sea's eternal tide exposes bits of seabed rendered in various shades of grey. There are a couple of beach areas, otherwise swimming here involves wading through knee-deep muck. The water is salty enough to suspend a brick, giving you a similar feeling to floating in the Dead Sea. Every approach to the sea is different as the waters are moving approximately 200m further away each year.

Most people visit the Aral on an organised two-day trip from Nukus, camping at a spot overlooking the sea or staying in the yurt camp of Bes Qala Tours. It's also possible to do a three-day trip, driving closer to the remote Kazakh border and overnighting on the second night at Sudochie Lake. It's not a cheap trip, at around US$250 per person in a group of three for a two-day trip.

Whichever way you do it, this is the trip of a lifetime, and one that you should see, while you still can.

The two best tour operators in Nukus are **Bes Qala Tours** (☑+998 91 377 7729, 61-224 51 69; www.besqala.com), run by Tazabay Uteuliev, and **Ayim Tour** (☑61-224 25 25; www.ayimtour.com; Rzaev, Jipek Joli Hotel; ⊗9am-5pm Mon-Sat). The overnight trips cost US$480 for a Land Cruiser (less for a much less comfortable Russian UAZ jeep), plus US$40 per person for food, US$120 for a guide (if needed) and US$15 per person for a sleeping bag and tent. Others doing similar tours are **Ayap Ismayilov** (☑+998 93 363 0088) and **Oktyabr Dospanov** (☑+998 90 575 3228; oktyabrd@gmail.com).

reopen in the future. If you do decide to overnight here, the homestay of **Makhmud-jan Aitzhanov** (☏ +998 93 920 0155, +998 93 489 3090; Amir Timur 2; per person incl full board US$15-20) is an easy walk from the bus station and his family cooks filling *plov* dinners. There's no central plumbing but there's a tap and shower outside. Call ahead to check he's taking guests as registration (p282) can be a problem.

ℹ Getting There & Away

BUS

A single 8am bus makes the trip to Moynaq from Nukus (10,000S, four hours) via Qongirot (Kungrad), departing from Nukus' Konye Qala bus stand in the old town. The bus returns from Moynaq in the afternoon (check times with the bus driver). All buses to Moynaq are stand-ing-room only; board early if you want a seat.

SHARED TAXI

Shared taxis are much quicker than the bus. You might find a direct shared taxi to Moynaq (25,000S per seat), but you'll more likely have to take a shared taxi to Qongirot (15,000S) from a stop opposite the train station, and transfer at Qongirot's train station to another shared taxi (15,000S). Arrive back in Qongirot by mid-after-noon to ensure an onward ride.

A day trip from Nukus in an ordinary taxi should cost around 250,000S, and more like US$75 through an agency.

UNDERSTAND UZBEKISTAN

Uzbekistan Today

Any account of contemporary Uzbekistan has to begin with the Andijon Massacre of 13 May 2005, which was sparked off when two dozen powerful local businessmen were jailed for being members of Akram-iya, an allegedly extremist Islamic move-ment banned by the Uzbek government. A group of their allies stormed the prison where they were being held, touching off a massive but largely peaceful demonstration in Andijon's main square. The authorities responded; over the next few hours, gov-ernment troops killed somewhere between 187 and 1000 civilians, depending on which source you believe.

When Uzbekistan refused to allow an in-dependent international investigation, the USA withdrew most of its aid and the EU enforced sanctions and an arms embargo. Karimov evicted American forces from the strategically important Karshi-Khanabad (K2) airbase near Karshi and the US Peace Corps and high-profile NGOs were forced to leave in the face of 'registration problems' or similar technicalities.

Karimov used the Andijon events to launch what Human Rights Watch called an 'unprecedented' crackdown against op-position political activists and independent journalists. Today it remains extremely dif-ficult for a Western journalist to get a visa to Uzbekistan.

Relations with the West have slowly im-proved, largely because Uzbekistan remains a key player in regional security and as a transit for NATO operations in Afghanistan. With such tight control inside the country, many radical Uzbeks appear to have left to join Islamist organisations abroad, tak-ing major roles in the New Year's Eve 2016 nightclub shootings in Istanbul and the Stockholm truck attack in 2017.

Despite a constitutional two-term limit, Karimov quietly won third and fourth suc-cessive terms in 2007 and 2015, garnering over 90% of the vote each time. Karimov was only forced out of power in 2016 by his death. He was laid to rest in Samarkand and a tomb is under construction at the Khazret Khizr Mosque.

The then Prime Minster Shavkat Mirzi-yoyev was duly elected president with 89% of the vote in a rubber stamp election. There have been signs that there may be some po-litical reforms, especially after Uzbek jour-nalist Muhammad Bekjanov was released from prison after 18 years, but few Uzbeks are holding their breath.

Uzbekistan remains a tightly controlled state, with almost no opposition, no free media, arbitrary detention and arrest, and reports of systematic human rights abuse and torture.

Gulnara, Karimov's daughter, a former pop star, socialite, diplomat, multi-mil-lionaire businesswoman and one time heir apparent to the presidency, saw a spectac-ular fall from grace in 2014. After a public bust-up with her mother (who she accused of being a witch), she was put under investi-gation for corruption for receiving hundreds of millions of dollars in bribes and at the time of writing remains under house arrest in Tashkent.

One piece of good news was the 2016 Rio Olympics, where Uzbekistan topped the boxing medal table, winning three golds and two silvers. Photos of the wildly popular athletes now advertise fruit juice across the country.

Two encouraging recent reforms were the deregulation of the national currency in September 2017 and the official end of student and teacher forced labour in the cotton harvest, both of which hint at more economic reforms to come.

History

The land along the upper Amu-Darya (Oxus River), Syr-Darya (Jaxartes River) and their tributaries has always been different from the rest of Central Asia – more settled than nomadic, with a sophisticated oasis and trading culture that has dominated the region from the time of the Achaemenids (6th century BC) to the present day. An attitude of permanence and proprietorship still sets the people of this region apart.

Ancient Empires

The region was known to the Persians as Bactria, Khorezm and Sogdiana and loosely formed part of the Persian empire. In the 4th century BC Alexander the Great entered Cyrus the Great's Achaemenid empire. He stopped near Marakanda (Samarkand) and then, having conquered the Sogdians in their mountain fortresses, married Roxana, the daughter of a local chieftain.

Out of the northern steppes in the 6th century AD came the Western Turks – the western branch of the empire of the so-called Kök (Blue) Turks. They soon grew attached to life here and abandoned their wandering ways, eventually taking on a significant role in maintaining the existence of the Silk Road. The Arabs brought Islam and a written alphabet to Central Asia in the 8th century, but found the region too big and restless to govern.

A return to the Persian fold came with the Samanid dynasty in the 9th and 10th centuries. Its capital, Bukhara, became the centre of an intellectual, religious and commercial renaissance. In the 11th century the Ghaznavids moved into the southern regions. For some time the Turkic Khorezm-shahs dominated Central Asia from present-day Konye-Urgench in Turkmenistan, but their reign was cut short by Chinggis (Genghis) Khan in the early 13th century.

Central Asia again became truly 'central' with the rise of Timur (also known as Tamerlane), the ruthless warrior and patron of the arts who fashioned a glittering Islamic capital at Samarkand.

The Uzbeks

Little is known of early Uzbek history. At the time the Golden Horde was founded,

---

UZBEKISTAN & COTTON

For better or for worse, the Uzbek economy hums to the tune of the 'White Gold'. The country is the word's fifth largest producer of cotton and the crop earns the state over US$1 billion a year. Truth be told, cotton is – and always was – a poor match for much of Uzbekistan; it's a thirsty crop in a parched land. Decades of monoculture that has led to the drying up of the Aral Sea has also exhausted the land and saturated it with salt. Poor yields and low government-controlled prices leave farmers too poor to pay for machinery or labour. Yet the government won't let them rotate their crops or convert to fruit. It's all cotton, all the time.

The whole system would collapse entirely but for the country's policy of forcibly sending students, doctors, government employees and others, including children, into the fields every autumn to harvest cotton. The practice has drawn international condemnation and boycotts of products made with Uzbek cotton by Wal-Mart and other juggernauts of the Western apparel industry.

The Uzbek government, which has always denied all accusations, finally passed a law in 2009 banning the forced labour of children under 16. The law has had no effect on forced adult labour according to the Cotton Campaign, which estimates that four million adults are forced to work in Uzbekistan's cotton fields, each of whom are given a daily quota of 60kg of cotton they have to pick. Travel through Uzbekistan or Karakalpakstan in the autumn and you'll see thousands of people in the fields.

Shibaqan (Shayban), a grandson of Chinggis Khan, inherited what is today northern Kazakhstan and adjacent parts of Russia. The greatest khan of these Mongol Shaybani tribes (and probably the one under whom they swapped paganism for Islam) was Özbeg (Uzbek; 1313–40). By the end of the 14th century these tribes had begun to name themselves after him.

The Uzbeks began to move southeast, mixing with sedentary Turkic tribes and adopting the Turkic language; they reached the Syr-Darya in the mid-15th century. Following an internal schism (which gave birth to the proto-Kazakhs), the Uzbeks rallied under Mohammed Shaybani and thundered down on the remnants of Timur's empire. By the early 1500s, all of Transoxiana ('the land beyond the Oxus') from the Amu-Darya to the Syr-Darya belonged to the Uzbeks, as it has since.

The greatest (and indeed last) of the Shaybanid khans, responsible for some of Bukhara's finest architecture, was Abdullah II, who ruled from 1538 until his death in 1598. After this, as the Silk Road fell into disuse, the empire unravelled under the Shaybanids' distant cousins, the Astrakhanids. By the start of the 19th century the entire region was dominated by three weak, feuding Uzbek city-states – Khiva, Bukhara and Kokand.

The Russians Arrive

In the early 18th century the khan of Khiva made an offer to Peter the Great of Russia to become his vassal in return for help against marauding Turkmen and Kazakh tribes, stirring the first Russian interest in Central Asia. But by the time the Russians got around to marching on Khiva in 1717, the khan no longer wanted Russian protection, and after a show of hospitality he had almost the entire 4000-strong force slaughtered.

The slave market in Bukhara and Khiva was an excuse for further Russian visits to free a few Russian settlers and travellers. In 1801 the mentally unstable Tsar Paul sent 22,000 Cossacks on a madcap mission to drive the British out of India, along with orders to free the slaves en route. Fortunately for all but the slaves, the tsar was assassinated and the army recalled while struggling across the Kazakh steppes.

The next attempt, by Tsar Nicholas I in 1839, was really a bid to pre-empt expansion into Central Asia by Britain, which had just taken Afghanistan, although Khiva's Russian slaves were the pretext on which General Perovsky's 5200 men and 10,000 camels set out from Orenburg. In January 1840, a British officer, Captain James Abbott, arrived in Khiva (having travelled from Herat in Afghan disguise) offering to negotiate the slaves' release on the khan's behalf, thus nullifying the Russians' excuse for coming.

Unknown to the khan, the Russian force had already turned back, in the face of a devastating winter on the steppes. He agreed to send Abbott to the tsar with an offer to release the slaves in return for an end to Russian military expeditions against Khiva. Incredibly, Abbott made it to St Petersburg.

In search of news of Abbott, Lieutenant Richmond Shakespear reached Khiva the following June and convinced the khan to unilaterally release all Russian slaves in Khiva and even give them an armed escort to the nearest Russian outpost, located on the eastern Caspian Sea. Russian gratitude was doubtlessly mingled with fury over one of the Great Game's boldest propaganda coups.

When the Russians finally rallied 25 years later, the khanates' towns fell like dominoes – Tashkent in 1865 to General Mikhail Chernyaev, Samarkand and Bukhara in 1868, Khiva in 1873, and Kokand in 1875 to General Konstantin Kaufman.

Soviet Daze

Even into the 20th century, most Central Asians identified themselves ethnically as Uzbek-speaking Turks or Tajik-speaking Persians. The connection between 'Uzbek' and 'Uzbekistan' is very much a Soviet definition. Following the outbreak of the Russian Revolution in 1917 and the infamous sacking of Kokand in 1918, the Bolsheviks proclaimed the Autonomous Soviet Socialist Republic of Turkestan. Temporarily forced out by counter-revolutionary troops and *basmachi* (Muslim guerrilla fighters), they returned two years later and the Khiva and Bukhara khanates were forcibly replaced with 'People's Republics'.

Then in October 1924 the whole map was redrawn on ethnic grounds, and the Uzbeks suddenly had a 'homeland', an official identity and a literary language. The Uzbek Soviet Socialist Republic (SSR) changed shape and composition over the years as it suited Moscow, losing Tajikistan in 1929, acquiring Karakalpakstan from Russia in 1936, taking parts of the steppe from Kazakhstan in 1956 and 1963, then losing some in 1971.

For rural Uzbeks, the main impacts of Soviet rule were the forced and often bloody collectivisation of the republic's mainstay (agriculture) and the massive shift to cotton cultivation. The Uzbek intelligentsia and much of the republic's political leadership was decimated by Stalin's purges. This and the traditional Central Asian respect for authority meant that by the 1980s *glasnost* (openness) and *perestroika* (restructuring) would hardly trickle down here and few significant reforms took place.

Independence

Uzbekistan's first serious noncommunist popular movement, Birlik (Unity), was formed by Tashkent intellectuals in 1989 over issues that included having Uzbek as an official language and the effects of the cotton monoculture. Despite popular support, it was barred from contesting the election in February 1990 for the Uzbek Supreme Soviet (legislature) by the Communist Party. The resulting communist-dominated body elected Islam Karimov, the first secretary of the Communist Party of Uzbekistan (CPUz), to the new post of executive president.

Following the abortive coup in Moscow in August 1991, Karimov declared Uzbekistan independent. Soon afterwards the CPUz reinvented itself as the People's Democratic Party of Uzbekistan, inheriting all of its predecessor's property and control apparatus, most of its ideology, and its leader, Karimov.

In December 1991, Uzbekistan held its first direct presidential elections, which Karimov won with 86% of the vote. His only rival was a poet named Muhammad Solih, running for the small, figurehead opposition party Erk (Will or Freedom), who got 12% and was soon driven into exile (where he remains to this day). The real opposition groups, Birlik and the Islamic Renaissance Party (IRP), and all other parties with a religious platform, had been forbidden to take part.

A new constitution unveiled in 1992 declared Uzbekistan 'a secular, democratic presidential republic'. Under Karimov, Uzbekistan would remain secular almost to a fault. But it would remain far from democratic.

Onward to Andijon

The years after independence saw Karimov consolidate his grip on power. Dissent shrivelled thanks to control of the media, police harassment and imprisonment of activists. Through it all, the economy stagnated and the devastating cotton monoculture continued.

A new threat emerged in February 1999 when a series of bomb attacks hit Tashkent. This led to a crackdown on radical Islamic fundamentalists – *wahabis* in the local parlance – that extended to a broad spectrum of opponents. Hundreds of alleged Islamic extremists were arrested. The IRP, with support in the Fergana Valley, was forced underground and Erk was declared illegal.

After extending his first term by referendum, Karimov won a second term as president in January 2000, garnering 92% of the votes. Foreign observers deemed the election a farce and international condemnation was widespread. But the 9/11 attacks on the USA gave Karimov a reprieve. The Uzbek president opened up bases in Termiz and Karshi to the USA and NATO for use in the war in Afghanistan, then sat back and watched the US aid money – US$500 million in 2002 alone – start flowing in.

As an added bonus for Karimov, solidarity with the USA in the 'War on Terror' effectively gave him a licence to ratchet up his campaign against the *wahabis*. According to human rights groups, Karimov used this licence to brand anyone he wanted to silence a 'terrorist'. Another rigged election in 2004, this one parliamentary, drew only modest international criticism.

Such was the situation on 13 May 2005 when events in the eastern city of Andijon rocked the country and instantly demolished Uzbekistan's cosy relationship with the USA.

People

Centuries of tradition as settled people left the Uzbeks in a better position than their nomadic neighbours to fend off Soviet attempts to modify their culture. Traditions of the Silk Road still linger as Uzbeks consider themselves good traders, hospitable hosts and tied to the land.

Population

By far the most populous country in Central Asia, Uzbekistan boasts almost 30 million people, creating an ethnically and linguistically diverse jigsaw puzzle. Uzbeks make up around 80% of the population, while Tajiks make up 5%, as do ethnic Russians. Kazakhs, Koreans, Tatars, Karakalpaks and Ukrainians make up the other major ethnic minorities. There is still a minuscule Jewish population in Bukhara and an even smaller one in Samarkand.

Tashkent is Uzbekistan's biggest city and the Fergana Valley is home to Uzbekistan's largest concentration of people, a quarter of the population. About three-quarters of people there are ethnic Uzbek. Samarkand, the second city, is Tajik-speaking, as are many of the communities surrounding it, including Bukhara and Karshi. The further west you travel the more sparsely populated the land becomes. Karakalpakstan – home to Kazakhs, Karakalpaks and Khorezmians – has seen its population dwindle as a result of the Aral Sea disaster.

Religion

Close to 90% of Uzbeks claim to be Muslim, although the vast majority are not practising. Most are the moderate Hanafi Sunni variety, and there are strong strains of Sufism. About 9% of the population (mostly Russians) are Christian (mostly Eastern Orthodox).

Since the 1999 bomb attacks in Tashkent, mosques have been banned from broadcasting the azan (call to prayer) and mullahs have been pressured to praise the government in their sermons. Attendance at mosques, already on the decline, fell drastically in the wake of the 2005 Andijon incident but is again on the rise under the government's watchful eye.

Arts

Traditional art, music and architecture – evolving over centuries – were placed in a neat little box for preservation following the Soviet creation of the Uzbek SSR. But somehow, in the years to follow, two major centres of progressive art were still allowed to develop: Igor Savitsky's collection of lost art from the 1930s, stashed away in Nukus'

Savitsky Museum, and the life stories told inside the late Mark Weil's legendary Ilkhom Theatre in Tashkent.

Contemporary art is, like the media, tightly controlled by the state. Renegade artists who push buttons, such as Weil and photographer Umida Ahmedova, find themselves in trouble. Ahmedova, whose work captures the lives and traditions of ordinary Uzbeks, drew international attention in 2009 when she was arrested and convicted of 'slandering the Uzbek nation' for a series that eventually ran on the BBC website.

While Karimov pardoned her, a glance at the seemingly harmless photos reveals much about the president's artistic ideal: Uzbekistan should be portrayed as clean, orderly, prosperous and modern. This ideal has also had an impact on urban planning – witness the makeover of Samarkand, where planners have cordoned off the old town from tourists' view, and the demolition of Amir Timur maydoni in Tashkent.

Environment

Uzbekistan spans several ecosystems, and topographic and geographic shifts. Its eastern fringes tilt upwards in a knot of rugged mountains – Tashkent's Chatkal and Pskem Mountains run into the western Tian Shan range, and Samarkand's Zarafshon Mountains and a mass of ranges in the southeast flow into the Pamir Alay range. This isolated, rocky and forested terrain makes up an important habitat for the bear, lynx, bustard, mountain goat and even the elusive snow leopard.

To the west of the well-watered mountains are vast plains of desert or steppe. The Amu-Darya (Oxus River) drops out of Tajikistan and winds its way westward along the Turkmen border for more than 2000km before petering out short of Moynaq, cleaving the landscape into two: the Karakum (White Sands) desert and the Ustyurt Plateau to the west; and the Kyzylkum (Red Sands) desert to the east. Despite its bleakness, this land is far from dead; the desert is home to the gazelle, various raptors and other critters you'd expect to find – monitors, scorpions and venomous snakes.

There are some 15 nature reserves in Uzbekistan, the largest of which is the Hissar Nature Reserve (750 sq km), due east of Shakhrisabz.

Environmental Issues

Much of this protected territory is threatened by Uzbekistan's lacklustre environmental protection laws and the deterioration of its national park system, which lacks the funds to prevent illegal logging and poaching. The faltering of the reserves, however, pales in comparison to the Aral Sea disaster, which has been dubbed by some experts as the 'greatest man made environmental disaster in history'.

Food & Drink

Plov, a Central Asian pilaf consisting of rice and fried vegetables, is the national staple and every region prepares its own distinct version.

Every region also has its own variation of *non* (nan bread); the raised rim of Kokand's speciality makes it a particularly fine shashlyk plate, while Samarkand's *non* resembles a giant bagel without the hole.

Regional staples such as *laghman* (long, flat noodles), *beshbarmak* (noodles with horse meat and broth), *halim* (porridge of boiled meat and wheat) and *naryn* (horse meat sausage with cold noodles) are all popular. *Moshkichiri* and *moshhurda* are meat and mung-bean gruels, respectively. *Dimlama* is a ragout of meat, potatoes, onions and vegetables braised slowly; the meatless version is *sabzavotli dimlama*. *Buglama kovok* (steamed pumpkin) is a light treat.

Uzbeks love their ubiquitous *kurut* (small balls of tart, dried yoghurt) and their *noz* (finely crushed chewing tobacco). *Somsa* (puff pastry stuffed with lamb meat and onion) are also ubiquitous but vary greatly; the good ones are a great snack, but most are full of fat and smell of the Soviet Union.

Chaikhanas are the best place for a pot of green or black tea, while espresso coffee can be found in all the main tourist centres. Other nonalcoholic drinks include *katyk*, a thin yoghurt that comes plain but can be sweetened with sugar or jam.

Despite the country's Muslim veneer, it's easy to find beer, and to a lesser extent wine and spirits, and there's no taboo about drinking it.

Locally brewed beers include Czech-style Pulsar, local Qibray brand and Sarbast, a joint-venture made with Carlsberg.

SURVIVAL GUIDE

 **Directory A–Z**

ACCOMMODATION

Uzbekistan has some charming accommodation (especially B&Bs), but it's important to book them well in advance during high season, especially in Bukhara, Khiva and Samarkand, where all the best places will normally be full. Lesser options are unfortunately a big step down in comfort and atmosphere. Homestays are possible in the Nuratau Mountains, with yurtstays north of Nurata.

Hotels generally price their rooms in US dollars, but in the wake of currency reforms in 2017 tourists will have to pay for hotel rooms in Uzbek som.

Homestayers and campers face a range of potential problems related to registration (p282).

ACTIVITIES

Camel trekking, usually combined with a yurt-stay, is the most intriguing activity, though most trips are relatively short jaunts around one of the for-tourist yurt camps. Other potential outdoor activities are rafting, skiing and hiking, all remarkably accessible from Tashkent. Uzbekistan is said to offer the best birding in Central Asia.

Good places for hiking include the Chimgan region and the Nuratau Mountains, while a couple of agencies in Samarkand offer hiking in the villages around Shakhrisabz in southern Uzbekistan.

CUSTOMS REGULATIONS

On arrival in Uzbekistan you will need to fill out two identical customs declarations forms, one to turn in and one to keep (which must be handed in upon departure, so don't lose it). Declare every cent of every type of money you bring in on your customs form, or face possible penalties. When entering overland the forms will likely be in Uzbek so you'll need some help filling them in.

You should also declare all your prescription medicines and preferably bring the prescriptions with you. Customs officials seems particularly interested in sleeping pills and painkillers, particularly anything with codeine or pseudoephedrine (eg Sudafed), so don't bring these unless you have to (and then bring a prescription). For a list of banned medications see www.advantour.com/uzbekistan/travel.htm.

Handicrafts over 50 years old cannot be taken out of Uzbekistan. If in doubt get a clear receipt from the vendor or get pre-clearance from the **Culture Ministry Antiques Certification Office** (☑ 71-237 07 38; Lashkarbegi 19; ⊗ 9am-5pm Mon-Fri; Ⓜ Hamid Olimjon) in Tashkent.

Arriving and leaving overland, overland customs officials will likely want to see your phone and check the photos for pornography or any other sensitive material.

DANGERS & ANNOYANCES

As in many totalitarian states, the main danger is the police and authorities. Petty crime and robbery are quite rare.

→ Keen to encourage tourism, President Mirziyoyev has curbed the once common *militsia* (police) habit of shaking down travellers for bribes at bus stations and roadside checkpoints.

→ You may still be stopped, particularly when entering Tashkent's metro, in the sensitive Fergana Valley and in border towns like Termiz.

→ Always carry your passport.

→ The main annoyances are the need to obsessively collect flimsy and utterly pointless registration slips, and the need to carry around huge piles of cash due to the worthlessness of the som.

EATING

Central Asia is no place for foodies and Uzbekistan is no exception. You won't have any problem finding food, but the range is limited and there is a tendency towards blandness. Vegetarians will likely order most of their food from the salad menu, which often lists 20 different types of cold dishes.

Restaurants are split between traditional-style chaikhanas, smarter restaurants in tourist cities and fast-food places in smaller towns.

EMBASSIES & CONSULATES

For details of Uzbek missions abroad see the website of the Ministry of Foreign Affairs (www.mfa.uz).

Uzbekistan has embassies in Kazakhstan (p365), Kyrgyzstan (p135), Tajikistan (p193) and Turkmenistan (Map p382; ☑ 97 10 62; Görogly köçesi 50A; ⊙10am-1pm & 2-6pm Mon, Wed & Fri).

Embassies & Consulates in Uzbekistan

Most embassies and consulates are located in Tashkent. For additional embassy listings see www.goldenpages.uz. Hours of operation listed for regional embassies are for visa applications only.

Afghan Embassy (☑71-226 73 81, 71-226 73 80; afghanemb_tashkent@yahoo.com; Batumskaya 1, Shaihan Tahur, Tashkent; ⊙drop-off 9am-noon & 1.30-4pm Mon-Fri, pick-up 3-4pm)

Chinese Embassy (☑71-233 80 88; http://uz.chineseembassy.org; Gulomov 79, Tashkent; ⊙9am-noon Mon, Wed & Fri, pick-up 3-5.30pm Tue, Thu & Fri)

French Embassy (☑71-233 51 57, 71-233 53 82; www.ambafrance-uz.org; Istikbol 25, Tashkent; ⊙9am-noon & 3-5pm Mon-Fri)

German Embassy (☑71-120 84 40, 24hr emergency line 71-181 54 06; www.taschkent.diplo.de; Rashidov 15, Tashkent; ⊙8-11am & 2-4pm Mon-Thu, 8am-11am Fri)

Iranian Embassy (☑71-268 38 77; Parkent 20, Tashkent; ⊙9am-noon Mon-Thu)

Kazakhstan Embassy (☑71-252 16 54; www.kazembassy.uz; Chekhov 23, Tashkent; ⊙dropoff 10am-1pm, pick-up 4-5pm Mon, Tue, Thu & Fri)

Kyrgyzstan Embassy (☑71-237 47 94; www.kgembassy.uz; Niyozbek Yuli 30, 6 Tor, Tashkent; ⊙10-11.30am & 2.30-4pm Mon-Fri, closed Tue morning & Thu)

Russian Embassy (☑71-120 35 04; www.russia.uz; Nukus 83, Tashkent; ⊙drop-off 10am-12.30pm, pick-up 3-4pm Mon-Fri)

Tajikistan Embassy (☑71-254 99 66; Abdulla Kahhor Lane VI 61, Tashkent; ⊙9am-1pm Mon-Fri)

Turkmenistan Embassy (☑71-256 94 01; www.uzbekistan.tmembassy.gov.tm; Afrosiab 19, Tashkent; ⊙10am-noon Mon-Thu)

UK Embassy (☑71-120 15 00; www.gov.uk/government/world/uzbekistan; Gulomov 67, Tashkent; ⊙9am-5pm Mon-Fri)

US Embassy (☑71-120 54 50; https://uz.usembassy.gov; Moyqorghon 3, Block V, Tashkent; ⊙9am-6pm Mon-Fri)

ETIQUETTE

In general respect is shown to the elderly, especially men who are known as *aksakal* (white beards).

Greetings Shake men's hands with the greeting 'salom' or 'salom aleikum'. For added respect place your left hand over your chest.

Amin At the end of a shared meal run your hands over your face in the *amin* gesture to signify thanks.

Tea There is formalised etiquette when pouring out tea. Rinse out your *piala* (small tea bowl) with a drop of hot tea, then return a *piala*-ful to the pot three times before the tea is considered ready to drink.

FESTIVALS & EVENTS

There are colourful celebrations throughout the country during the vernal equinox festival of Navrus (celebrated on 21 March). Festivities typically involve parades, fairs, music, dancing in the streets, plenty of food and, in some places, a rogue game of *kupkari* (traditional polo-like game played with a headless goat carcass). Samarkand has a good one, although the best place to enjoy Navrus is in the countryside.

INTERNET ACCESS

Wi-fi is now ubiquitous in tourist hotels and in many restaurants and cafes, so there's little need to resort to internet cafes. Speeds vary from glacial to lightning fast, but in general are quite adequate.

Some websites, notably politically sensitive Uzbek-language sites, are blocked but social media sites like Facebook and Twitter work fine. Communication apps like Skype and WhatsApp often don't work properly.

LGBTIQ TRAVELLERS

Uzbekistan is a conservative Muslim country. Gay sex between men is technically illegal, and while there is a small gay scene in Tashkent, most gay men are discreet. Lesbians tend to be overlooked by the authorities. Travellers will find little overt hassle but, again, discretion is wise in this tightly monitored country.

MEDICAL SERVICES

Health insurance is strongly advised for Uzbekistan.

Be careful not to bring any sleeping pills or painkillers into Uzbekistan as they are illegal and customs officials are on the look-out for medications such as codeine, Valium, Xanax and Temazepam. All medicines should be in their original packaging.

No vaccinations are legally required in order to enter Uzbekistan.

Doctors recommend all travellers are current with immunisations against hepatitis A, typhoid and tetanus, and some travellers should consider hepatitis B and rabies.

Uzbekistan requires HIV testing for foreigners staying more than three months. Foreign tests are accepted under certain conditions, but make sure you check with the Uzbekistan embassy before travelling.

The Tashkent International Medical Clinic (p213) is the only international-standard clinic in the country. Outside the capital health facilities are few and far between and should be considered for emergency use only. For anything serious you will want to be evacuated to Europe.

All towns have pharmacies that will sell you most forms of antibiotics.

MONEY

ATMs

ATMs can be found in most of Tashkent's top-end hotels, in a couple of hotels outside the capital and in a few banks, but they are frequently out of order. Try to avoid using ATMs on a Sunday, when they are almost always out of cash. Banks in major cities can give you a US dollar cash advance on a Visa or MasterCard for a 3% commission but these can take time to track down. Most midrange and top-end hotels accept Visa cards.

In the provinces, cash advances are generally possible at Asaka Bank for MasterCard holders and at Kapital Bank or the National Bank of Uzbekistan (NBU) for Visa cardholders. If these are not working, try Orient Finanz Bank for MasterCard, or Ipak Yuli Bank for Visa. Commissions is generally 3%.

Banks in major cities can give you a US dollar cash advance on a Visa or MasterCard for a 3% commission but these can take time to track down. Most midrange and top-end hotels accept Visa cards.

Bargaining

Bargaining is sensible at souvenir stalls and with taxi drivers, common in bazaars and sometimes necessary with shared taxis. You can often get a reduction on hotel rates, especially in the shoulder and off seasons. That said, most local people will offer a fairly sensible starting price so don't expect to half the price.

Cash

The currency in Uzbekistan is the som (S), sometimes spelled s'om or soum. It's easy to feel rich in Uzbekistan – the highest Uzbek note (50,000S) was only introduced in 2017 and is currently worth around US\$6.

Until recently tourists used to have to pay for accommodation in hard currency, meaning you had to bring wads of cash US dollars with you, but since September 2017 tourists now have to pay in Uzbek som, meaning you now have to travel with large wads of Uzbek som.

Cash US dollars are still the easiest way to change money into som. Make sure they are pristine notes with no marks on them. Euros can also be used and changed, but it's not as easy.

Changing Money

Official exchange booths at airports, hotels and the National Bank of Uzbekistan and several private banks will change most currencies into Uzbek som, though US dollars and euros are the easiest currencies.

OPENING HOURS

Many tourist-oriented hotels, restaurants and craft shops shut between November and March.

Banks 9.30am to 2pm and 3pm to 4.30pm Monday to Friday

Museums Generally closed on Monday in Tashkent and Wednesday in Bukhara.

Offices 9am to 1pm and 2pm to 5pm Monday to Friday

Restaurants & chaikhanas 10am to 11pm

POST

The **Uzbekistan Post Office** (O'zbekiston Pochtasi; www.pochta.uz/en) is fairly reliable, though for important items it's better to use a courier service such as DHL, which has an office in Tashkent.

THE BLACK MARKET & CURRENCY REFORMS

Until 2017 Uzbekistan had a thriving currency black market that offered travellers 50% more som for their dollars than the artificially low fixed government rate.

In September 2017 the currency was deregulated and instantly lost half of its value, bringing it on a par with the former black market, which effectively disappeared overnight. A black market might return, since Uzbeks can still can not freely convert som into US dollars, but it is unlikely to have the prevalence or advantages of the old black market.

In September 2017, the Uzbekistan government introduced major currency reforms, bringing the previously artificially low Uzbek som in line with free market rates and thus effectively doing away with the black market.

It also reversed the law requiring foreigners to pay for their accommodation in foreign currency, meaning that foreigners are now required to pay in Uzbek som. The rate you pay will be similar to the amount previously listed in US dollars, but will have to be paid in Uzbek som converted at the current bank rate.

In general, prices in som for hotels, food and transportation have remained the same since the reforms and the currency remains relatively stable, but be prepared for price variances, especially for entry fees, which will likely rise in many places, as these were previously calculated using the government's artificially low som rate.

One anomaly is domestic flights with Uzbekistan Airlines, which at the time of writing were still being priced in Uzbek som using the artificially low pre-reform government rate. It's unlikely that this system can be maintained, but as long as it is, travellers can enjoy bargain-priced domestic flights.

PUBLIC HOLIDAYS

1 January New Year's Day

14 January Day of Defenders of the Motherland

8 March International Women's Day

21 March Navrus

9 May Day of Memory and Honour (formerly Victory Day)

1 September Independence Day

1 October Teachers' Day

8 December Constitution Day

REGISTRATION

Registration rules are stricter in Uzbekistan than in most former Soviet countries. The law states clearly that you must register somewhere within three days of arriving in Uzbekistan.

Checking into a hotel licensed to take foreigners means automatic registration, so if you're staying in hotels for your entire trip there's nothing to worry about. Your hotel or B&B will give you a small slip of paper that you must keep until you have left the country.

If you are camping or staying in a private home, the rules get hazy.

If you spend a night in a private home you are supposed to register with the local Office of Visas & Registration (OVIR), but this can create more problems than it solves for you and your hosts. Asking the next hotel you stay at to supply missing registration slips is a possibility, but they may demand a fee for this service or refuse your request outright.

Officially you don't need to register if you are staying in a given town for less than three nights. But like everything else in Uzbekistan, this rule is open to interpretation. If the authorities decide you need to be registered for shorter stays, well then you need to be registered. Failure to comply with the 'law' can result in anything from a small bribe being demanded, to a fine of up to a couple of thousand US dollars and deportation.

Such harsh fines are unlikely, but if you go several consecutive days without registering you are asking for trouble. Bottom line: the authorities like to see at least some registration slips in your passport. The more you have, the better, and the only way to be completely safe is to ensure that every night of your stay is accounted for by a registration slip or overnight train ticket.

Tashkent hotels in particular can be a real pain in the backside about this – most will not register someone without a registration slip for every night of their stay, so have your paperwork in order!

If you plan to camp your way around Uzbekistan, resign yourself to staying in hotels at least every third night to accumulate some registration slips. If headed to Tashkent try to stay in a hotel the night before arriving so that you have a registration slip.

When you leave the country or take a domestic flight, border officials may thoroughly scrutinise your registration slips or they may not look at them at all. However, the main thing is to be able to produce a convincing bundle when asked. Authorities may also check your registration slips when you are in the country, so carry them with you alongside your passport at all times.

If you are missing only a few registration slips upon departure from the country, you should be in the clear – in theory. In practice, police sometimes hassle departing tourists over just one or two missing registration slips. If this happens, stand your ground and argue forcefully that you were in some towns for less than three nights, and were not required to register for those nights.

Travellers reports suggest that this is less of a problem when departing Uzbekistan overland, especially if you are clearly travelling by bicycle.

SHOPPING

Uzbekistan offers Central Asia's best shopping. Almost every corner of every historic building in Samarkand, Bukhara and Khiva is stuffed with crafts and souvenirs. The best buys include *doppi* (skullcaps), Turkmen-style wool hats, *chapon* cloaks, carved wood, ceramics, embroidered bags, carpets and *suzani* (embroideries).

TELEPHONE

Uzbekistan's antiquated fixed-line system is creaky and most people prefer to use mobile phones. Local calls cost peanuts and domestic long-distance calls are cheap.

➡ To place a call to a mobile phone, dial ☑83 (from a land line) or ☑+998 (from another mobile phone), followed by the two-digit code and the seven-digit number.

➡ To place a call to a land line, dial ☑83 (from either a land line or a mobile phone) followed by the two-digit city code and the seven-digit number. If the city code is three digits, drop the 3 and just dial 8.

➡ If dialling from any Tashkent number (mobile or fixed) to any other Tashkent number, regardless of carrier, just dial the seven-digit number (no code).

➡ To place an international call from a land line, dial 8, wait for a tone, then dial 10.

International phone calls with Uztelecom (www.uztelecom.uz) cost 1265/1140S per minute to the USA/Europe, or 500S to the neighbouring Central Asian republics.

There are four main Uzbek mobile phone providers: Ucell, Uzmobile, UCell and Beeline. Getting a SIM card isn't all that difficult, but is easiest done at the provider's main Tashkent office. Bring your passport.

Call charges are minuscule and 3G internet coverage is generally fast and cheap. It's fast and easy to add to your balance at any of the hundreds of Paynet booths in every town.

TIME

Uzbekistan is GMT/UTC plus five hours, which is the same as the other Central Asian republics,

EMERGENCY & IMPORTANT NUMBERS

Ambulance	☑103
Country Code	☑998
Fire	☑101
Police	☑102

apart from central and eastern Kazakhstan. There is no daylight savings time.

TOILETS

➡ Public toilets generally cost around 1000S, but they are mostly nasty and best avoided.

➡ Where toilet paper is provided it is normally of sandpaper-like consistency, so carry a stash of tissues with you at all times.

➡ In general used toilet paper should be placed in the small bin beside the toilet.

TOURIST INFORMATION

There are helpful privately run tourist information centres in Samarkand (p228) and Khiva (p269). Beyond this the private travel agencies and B&Bs are your best source of information.

The government-run Uzbektourism is not interested in independent travellers.

TRAVEL WITH CHILDREN

Uzbekistan is not an obvious choice for children, who seem surprisingly immune to the charms of early medieval Islamic architecture. Tashkent has a couple of amusement parks, a water park, bowling alleys and malls if your kids need a dose of the familiar. Yurt camps and camel rides help break up the normal sightseeing routine.

Baby-change facilities and high chairs are mostly non-existent, though nappies (diapers) are available in the cities. Prams can tackle the modern streets of Tashkent and Samarkand, but the old towns of Bukhara and Khiva will prove a problem.

VISAS FOR UZBEKISTAN

Uzbek visa rules depend on the state of Uzbekistan's relations with your country's government. At the time of writing, citizens of the following countries were exempt from letters of invitation (LOI): Austria, Belgium, France, Germany, Italy, Japan, Spain, Switzerland, the UK and the USA. Everybody else needs an LOI, as do (sometimes) citizens of the above countries who are applying for visas outside their country of citizenship.

Visa-free travel for 21 Western countries (including Australia but not New Zealand) is scheduled to be introduced in 2021. Travellers will be able to enter the country for 30 days after paying US$50 at the airport. The regulation

ℹ TRAVEL PERMITS

Border permits are required for remote mountain areas near the Tajik and Kyrgyz borders, including most of Ugam-Chatkal National Park, the Zarafshon and Hissar Mountains, and Zaamin National Park. It's unlikely you'll be headed into these regions unless you are on an expedition-style trek. You'll need the help of a travel agency to get a border permit.

was supposed to be introduced in 2017 but was delayed, so check whether it has actually been implemented.

If there is no Uzbek embassy in your country, you should be eligible for 'visa on arrival' at Tashkent International Airport if you arrange special LOI support for this several weeks in advance through a travel agency or inviting business.

Any Uzbek travel agency can arrange LOI support, but most demand that you also purchase a minimum level of services – usually hotel bookings for at least three nights. A few agencies and hotels still provide LOI support with no strings attached, including Arostr Tourism (p214) and Topchan Hostel (p207). They charge US$40 to US$50 for a LOI for a single-entry 30-day tourist visa. Tack on another US$10 per entry for visa-on-arrival support. Allow five to 10 business days for LOI processing, or pay double for four-to five-day 'rush' processing.

The standard tourist visa is a 30-day, single-entry or multiple-entry visa. They cost US$60 to US$100 for most nationalities, and US$160 for US citizens. Additional entries cost US$10 per entry. Tourist visas lasting more than 30 days are very difficult to obtain; for a longer trip you are better off arranging a business visa. Three-day transit visas are possible without an LOI, but often cost as much as a tourist visa.

Most embassies can issue same-day visas when you present an LOI. Visa processing without an LOI usually takes three to 10 days, depending on the embassy. Be aware that when you apply for your visa in person at an Uzbek embassy, you must have filled in your application form and uploaded a photograph digitally beforehand – this can not be done at the Uzbek embassy. Application forms are available online at http://evisa.mfa.uz.

You may also need to provide a photocopy of every page in your passport, even the blank ones!

Extensions are not given to tourist visa holders so your only option in this case is to travel to neighbouring Kazakhstan or Kyrgyzstan to buy a new visa. Business visas are easier to extend.

VISAS FOR ONWARD TRAVEL

The website Caravanistan (www.caravanistan.com) has excellent information on visas and letters of invitation (LOI) for onward travel. Most embassies require you to show an onward ticket if you are applying for a transit visa.

Azerbaijan

Most tourists can now get an e-visa online at www.evisa.gov.az. A 30-day tourist visa from the Azerbaijan embassy requires two passport photos, a copy of your passport and a LOI.

China

The Chinese embassy (p280) prefers you get your China visa in your home country and is generally reluctant to issue visas to tourists. If things change you'll need a copy of your passport and Uzbek visa on a single page, plus copies of hotel bookings in China and an air ticket from Tashkent to China. Proof of employment or a LOI is also sometimes required. Bishkek is an easier place to get a China visa.

Iran

First you must apply for an authorisation through an Iranian agent. This costs around US$50 and takes one to two weeks to arrive, after which you can apply for a 30-day tourist visa (valid for entry within three months) at the Iranian embassy you elected for collection. The cost of visa processing in Tashkent (p280) varies from US$50 to US$100 and takes a week to process (though a same-day service is available for a fee).

Russia

Begin by filling out a visa application form online at http://visa.kdmid.ru. You'll need to bring your original passport and a copy of its photo page, a passport photo, a travel voucher/LOI (original not copy) and proof of insurance to apply for a single- or double-entry 30-day tourist visa at the Russian embassy (p280). Processing takes four days and you pay for the visa at the time of application. Prices vary depending on nationality, but figure on around US$50.

Tajikistan

Tourist visas and permits for the Gorno Badakhshan region are easily available online without an invitation, so there's little reason to schlepp out to the embassy. If you do need to go, the consulate is actually across the road from the embassy (p280) proper.

Turkmenistan

The entrance to the visa section is behind the main embassy (p280) to the left. Come early (6am if you can face it) and add your name to the waiting list (you can then go for breakfast and return at 10am when the gates open). Whether you actually get a tourist visa is very hit-and-miss these days and authorisation seems quite random. Five-day transit visas cost around US$55, with tourists visas ranging from US$30 to US$115. Processing takes a week for transit visas and up to 10 days for tourist visas.

WATER
Tap water in Uzbekistan isn't safe to drink, especially in Karakalpakstan. Bottled water is available cheaply everywhere. Long-term visitors should bring a filter.

ⓘ Getting There & Away

ENTERING & EXITING UZBEKISTAN
As long as your papers are in order, entering Uzbekistan is relatively easy, long lines at the airport notwithstanding. It's important that you fill in two identical customs forms and declare every penny of foreign currency on them.

AIR
The main international gateways to Tashkent are Moscow and Istanbul, through there are direct flights from most European and Asian cities.

Departure tax is included in the price of a ticket.

If arriving by air, your grand entrance into Uzbekistan will most likely occur at Tashkent International Airport (p214). A few flights from Russia arrive in regional hubs such as Samarkand, Bukhara and Urgench.

The numerous aviakassa (private ticket kiosks) scattered around major cities can help book international tickets on national carrier Uzbekistan Airways (p214) as well as other airlines.

In 2017 air links were reintroduced between Tashkent and Dushanbe for the first time in over 20 years. Uzbekistan Airways flies once a week.

LAND

To & From Afghanistan
The Friendship Bridge linking Termiz with northern Afghanistan has been opened to tourist traffic since 2005, though the Uzbeks have been known to close their side of the border for security reasons or other concerns. Contact a reliable travel agency in Tashkent to make sure it's open before setting out. Travel to Afghanistan was not considered safe at the time of research.

To get to the *tamozhnya* (border, or 'customs house') at Hayratan from Termiz, take a taxi (25,000S) or track down marshrutka 255 from near Yubileyny Bazaar (1500S, 20 minutes). The bridge is 15km southeast of Termiz. There's a fair bit of walking involved to get between the various checkpoints on the Uzbek side, and then across the bridge. From the Afghan side you're looking at about a 30-minute taxi ride to Mazar-e-Sharif (US$10).

To & From Kazakhstan
Despite their very long common border there are just two main places to cross from Uzbekistan into Kazakhstan: Chernyaevka between Tashkent and Shymkent, and the remote Qongirot (Kungrad)–Beyneu crossing from Karakalpakstan into Kazakhstan's far west.

Crossing at Chernyaevka is the easiest from the point of view of public transport, but it can sometimes involve long lines, so go early and be patient. To get to Chernyaevka from Tashkent is a 30,000S taxi ride, or you can take a shared taxi (5000S, 20 minutes) or marshrutka from Yunusobod Bazaar.

If you have your own vehicle, Yallama (60km southwest of Tashkent) is where you should cross, as private cars cannot cross at Chernyaevka.

The other crossing is by train or road between Karakalpakstan and Beyneu in western Kazakhstan. Train 917 departs daily at 9.20am from Nukus to Beyneu (10 hours). Other trains crossing this border include Tashkent–Volgograd (weekly) and Tashkent–Saratov (twice weekly).

A twice-weekly Tashkent-Almaty fast train started in 2017. The Spanish-built Talgo train leaves Tashkent at 3pm on Tuesday and Sunday, arriving at 9.30am the next morning, with a three-hour wait at the border. There are three classes (two with two berths per compartment, and economy with four berths). Fares cost 80,000/200,000/260,000S in economy/*kupe*/VIP.

To & From Kyrgyzstan
The only border crossings into Kyrgyzstan that are open to foreigners are at Uchkurgon/Shamaldy-Say (northeast of Namangan) and Dostyk (Dustlyk), between Andijon and Osh. They are generally hassle-free, although long lines do occur.

Most travellers use the Osh crossing. In Andijon, frequent shared taxis to the border at Dostyk (10,000S, one hour) depart from the Yangi Bazaar stand, southeast of the train station. Walk across the border and pick up a minivan or taxi for the short trip to Osh.

Limited public transport and taxis are available at the Uchkurgon crossing.

To & From Tajikistan
There are two main border crossings between Uzbekistan and Tajikistan: Oybek between Tashkent and Khojand and the Denau–Tursanzade crossing in southeastern Uzbekistan. The once popular Samarkand–Penjikent crossing has been shut for years now, and shows no signs of reopening.

Those heading from Tashkent to Dushanbe normally drive to Khojand via the pain-free Oybek border crossing and then take a shared taxi from Khojand to Dushanbe (US$20). To get to this border from Tashkent, take a marshrutka or shared taxi from Kuyluk Bazaar to Bekobod and get off at Oybek (15,000S, 1½ hours), about 35km shy of Bekobod, near Chanak village. An ordinary taxi between Tashkent and Oybek costs about US$30. Once across the border take a taxi to Khojand (US$15), or a taxi to nearby Bostan (US$1) and then a minibus to Khojand.

The fairly remote Denau–Tursanzade crossing near Sariosiyo can see long lines. Denau is a 1½-hour drive from Termiz or a five-hour drive from Samarkand. You can get shared taxis to the border from either city. A private taxi from Samarkand to the border costs around US$60. From Termiz regular shared taxis head to Denau (25,000S) from the bus station and some carry on to Sariosiyo (30,000S) and the actual border (35,000S). There are also two daily local trains directly to the border town of Sariosiyo (5000S, four hours), 15km north of Denau, but this is a slow way to travel. From Denau, take a minivan to Sariosiyo, cross the border and proceed by taxi from Tursanzade to Dushanbe (US$10, 45 minutes).

A third, little-used crossing is at Andarhon, between the towns of Kokand and Khojand in the Fergana Valley. Shared taxis and buses run from the Afghan Bog road junction, 9km southwest of Kokand, to the Tajikistan border, which is situated between the Uzbek town of Besh Ariq and the Tajik town of Kanibodom. A taxi for the 50km drive costs around 100,000S and is a wise investment. Check in advance that the border crossing is open.

To & From Turkmenistan

The three border crossings between Uzbekistan and Turkmenistan are reached from Bukhara, Khiva and Nukus. Each crossing requires a potentially sweltering walk of 10 to 20 minutes across no man's land due to the absurdly designed border posts. Shared taxis or minibuses are sometimes available to ferry travellers across, but don't count on them.

From Bukhara the easiest option is to take a taxi (100,000S, 1½ hours) to the border at Farab. Shared taxis (8000S, 40 minutes) make the trip from Bukhara's Markaziy (Kolkhoz) Bazaar to Olot (Alat), about 20km short of the border (p259). If there are no taxis to Olot then you'll have to change in Karakol. From Olot another shared taxi to the border costs from 10,000S. There are slow local trains to Olot from Kagan (3000S, two hours, twice daily), but it's much quicker to take a taxi. You'll need to take two short minibus rides to cross no man's land but be prepared to walk if they aren't operating. Once over the border, take a shared taxi to Turkmenabat (40 minutes).

From Khiva it costs about 50,000S to hire a taxi to the border (one hour), from where you'll have to take a taxi across no man's land then a short taxi ride to Dashogus. In the other direction drivers often ask for up to US$30. By shared taxi you'll likely have to change at Koshkapur (5000S) and then probably again at Shavat, the nearest town to the border. Ask around at the shared taxi stand (p269) beside Dekon Bazaar. There are buses to Shavat (2000S, one hour, three daily) from Dekon Bazar.

From Nukus it's about a 20km ride to the Konye-Urgench *tamozhnya* (30,000S). Alternatively take a shared taxi to Hojeli from Nukus' Konye Qala bus stand and then take a taxi from there to the border (12,000S). Once you've walked across the border you can pick up a shared taxi to Konye-Urgench (US$2).

ℹ Getting Around

AIR

Travelling by air is good value in Uzbekistan and it's a great way to cover the large distances between big cities. Flights do fill up though, so try to book at least several days in advance during high season.

Uzbekistan Airways has convenient booking offices in Tashkent, but elsewhere it's easier to buy tickets online or in one of the many *aviakassa* (travel agencies).

At the time of writing, Uzbekistan Airways had just changed its pricing system for foreigners from fares quoted in US dollars to fares paid in Uzbek som converted at the *old* exchange rate. This means that domestic airfares were halved. The airline will probably adjust these fares over time, but if you are lucky you might still get a bargain-priced domestic flight. Either way, if paying in cash you will have to pay for tickets in Uzbek som.

BICYCLE

An increasing number of people are cycling across Uzbekistan, though there are some disadvantages, including monotonous desert landscapes, the intense summer heat and the registration hassles involved with camping en route.

BUS, SHARED TAXI & ORDINARY TAXI

Clapped-out state buses have almost disappeared from Uzbek roads and long-distance buses of any kind are increasingly hard to find.

For shorter distance between towns you will find 11- to 14-seat Russian-made 'Gazelle' vans. For shorter suburban trips you'll find cramped seven-seat Daewoo Damas minivans.

In general you are almost always better off with a shared taxi, if there is one.

Shared taxis are easily the best way to get around Uzbekistan, and most of Central Asia in general. They ply all the main intercity routes and also congregate at most border points. They leave when full from set locations – usually from near bus stations – and run all day until late afternoon. Prices fluctuate somewhat and there is always room for negotiation. One advantage to shared taxis over buses is that they will often drop you off at your hotel rather than a suburban bus station (though this depends on the destination and the driver).

You can always buy extra seats (or even all four seats) if you're in a hurry or prefer to travel in comfort. This is the standard way most travellers with a midrange budget get around in Uzbekistan and it's much cheaper than hiring a car and driver through a travel agency.

CAR & MOTORCYCLE

Driving your own vehicle across Uzbekistan is possible, provided you have insurance from your home country and a valid international driving licence. Be prepared for the same kind of hassles you'll experience anywhere in the former Soviet Union: lots of random stops and traffic cops fishing for bribes. Driving is on the right.

There are no car-rental agencies, so you'll need to hire a taxi and driver, either from the bazaar or through a B&B or a tour agency. Costs are generally affordable even for several days on end; budget around US$50 per day (excluding petrol). A cheaper option is to pay for all seats in a shared taxi between towns.

TRAIN

Trains are perhaps the most comfortable and safest method of intercity transport. The express (*skorostnoy*, or 'high-speed') trains between Tashkent, Samarkand and Bukhara (and from Khiva as of 2018), with airplane-style seating, are faster than a shared taxi and a *lot* more comfortable. Book at least a couple of days in advance, and preferably longer, as they are popular. These have economy, business and VIP classes, though there's not much between them.

Other long-haul trains are of the slow but comfortable Soviet variety, with *platskartny* (hard sleeper) and *kupeyny* (soft sleeper) compartments available. Some long-distance trains offer deluxe 'SV' class (private compartment) seating.

Slow, dirt-cheap local *prigorodny* trains, with bench-style seating, are worth avoiding as they take twice as long as a shared taxi.

You can buy tickets for any Uzbek train service at any train station; you will need your passport and you pay in som. Only locals can buy train tickets online, but this service should eventually extend to tourists. For schedules visit www.uzrailpass.uz; the Russian version works better than the English version.

Some tour agencies can book train tickets in advance for you (45 days in advance is the maximum), which can be useful during high season, though you can expect to end up paying two or three times the actual ticket price for this service.

Tickets can be particularly hard to obtain in September when students return to Tashkent from the cotton harvest.

Kazakhstan

♪ 7 / POP 17.8 MILLION

Best Places to Eat

➡ Olivia (p318)
➡ Line Brew (p300)
➡ Tandoor (p299)
➡ My Cafe (p300)
➡ Izumi Tai (p342)
➡ Gosti (p299)

Best Places to Stay

➡ Rixos Khadisha Shymkent (p317)
➡ Wild Nature (p321)
➡ Orbita Boutique Hotel (p317)
➡ Rixos Almaty (p298)
➡ Zhanara's Homestay (p311)
➡ Hostel Astana (p339)

Why Go?

The world's ninth-biggest country is the most economically advanced of the 'stans', thanks to its abundant reserves of oil and most other valuable minerals. This means generally better standards of accommodation, restaurants and transport than elsewhere in Central Asia. The biggest city, Almaty, is almost reminiscent of Europe with its leafy avenues, chic ALZhiR Museum-Memorial Complex, glossy shopping centres and hedonistic nightlife. The capital Astana, on the windswept northern steppe, has been transformed into a 21st-century showpiece with a profusion of bold futuristic architecture. But it's beyond the cities that you'll find the greatest travel adventures, whether hiking in the high mountains and green valleys of the Tian Shan, searching for wildlife on the lake-dotted steppe, enjoying homespun hospitality in village guesthouses, or jolting across the western deserts to remote underground mosques.

When to Go
Almaty

Apr–Jun Naturalists' heaven as the steppe and hills blossom and migrating birds flock in.

May–Sep The weather is perfect; from July it's hiking season.

Nov–Apr It's cold, but skiers enjoy Central Asia's best facilities at Chimbulak.

Visas & Permits

Citizens of 45 countries, including EU states, Australia, Canada, Israel, Japan, New Zealand, Norway, South Korea, Switzerland, the USA and some other countries can travel to Kazakhstan without a visa for up to 30 days; as always in this region it is best to check that this arrangement continues. For most other visas you must obtain a letter of invitation (LOI) before applying, available through most travel agencies in Kazakhstan and Central Asia travel specialists in other countries.

Registration is required if you are staying in Kazakhstan more than five days – only if you enter by land or sea and your entry form is stamped once rather than twice. If it's stamped twice, you don't need to register. It is not necessary to register if you enter by air.

COSTS

Relative Cost
Slightly more expensive than Uzbekistan, but cheaper than Turkmenistan.

Daily Expenses
⇒ Hostel dorm (Almaty or Astana): 2800–3500T

⇒ Comfortable hotel double:12,000–20,000T

⇒ *Stolovaya* (canteen) meal 1000T, restaurant dinner: 5000–7000T

⇒ Admission to museums: 500–1000T

Train: Almaty to Astana: *platskartny* (hard-sleeper)/*kupeyny* (soft-sleeper) 4443/9774T, high speed 13,567T

Price Ranges

Sleeping (double room with bathroom, including breakfast): **$** <8200T, **$$** 8200–22,800T, **$$$** >28,000T

Eating (main course): **$** <1500T, **$$** 1500–3000T, **$$$** >3000T

Itineraries

⇒ **One week** Explore Almaty and take four or five days to explore Kolsai Lakes , the Charyn Canyon and the Altyn-Emel National Park.

⇒ **Two weeks** Extend the weeklong itinerary with time in southern Kazakhstan: Shymkent, lovely Aksu-Zhabagyly Nature Reserve, the splendour of Turkestan and the spectacular arid scenery and eerie Soviet boat wrecks on the bank of the Aral Sea.

⇒ **One month** You can get round the whole country, visiting remote destinations such as the ancient underground mosques of Mangistauin, the pristine Altay Mountains and the glitz of 21st-century architecture in Astana, the capital.

Fast Facts

⇒ **Area** 2.7 million sq km

⇒ **Capital** Astana

⇒ **Currency** Tenge (T)

⇒ **Languages** Kazakh, Russian

KAZAKHSTAN

Exchange Rates

Australia	A$1	255T
Canada	C$1	257T
China	¥10	510T
Euro zone	€1	400T
Japan	¥100	304T
NZ	NZ$1	237T
Russia	R10	56T
UK	UK£1	450T
USA	US$1	324T

Resources

⇒ **Edge** (www.edgekz.com)

⇒ **Visit Kazakhstan** (www.visitkazakhan.kz)

⇒ **Lonely Planet** (www.lonelyplanet.com/kazakhstan)

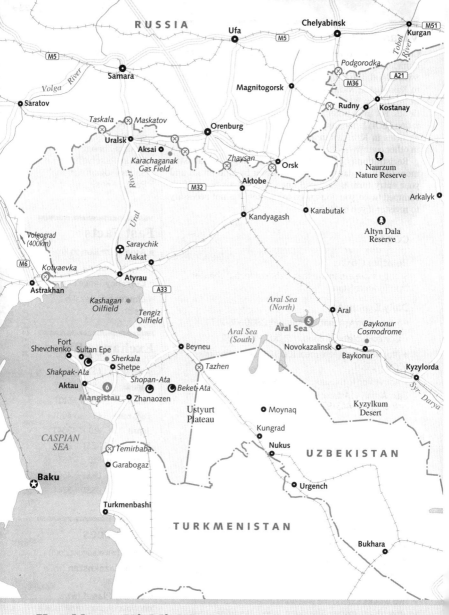

Kazakhstan Highlights

① **Almaty** (p292) Dining out in the leafy, sophisticated metropolis and hiking in the spectacular mountains on its doorstep.

② **Kolsai Lakes** (p311) Staying in hospitable

homestays and trekking amid gorgeous alpine scenery.

③ **Turkestan** (p322) Being awed by the beautiful Timurid architecture at Kazakhstan's holiest site.

④ **Aksu-Zhabagyly** (p320) Hiking, horse riding and looking for tulips in the forests and mountains.

⑤ **Aral Sea** (p325) Checking out Soviet boat wrecks and an

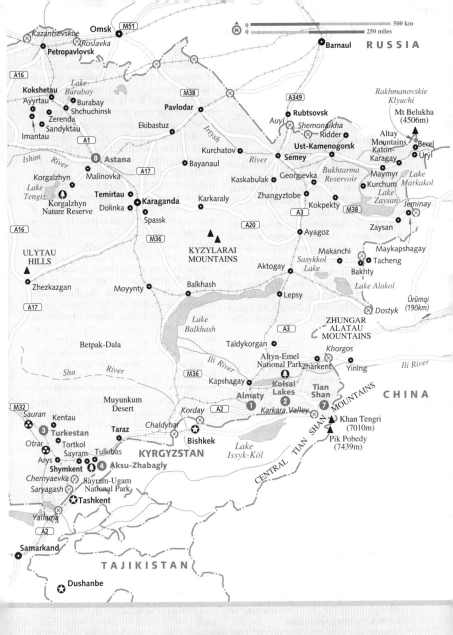

arid canyon on the banks of the returning sea.

6 Mangistau (p330) Exploring remote desert country, honeycombed with canyons, underground mosques and ancient necropolises.

7 Tian Shan (p313) Trekking and taking helicopter flights above glaciers in Kazakhstan's highest and most spectacular mountain range.

8 Astana (p333) Enjoying 21st-century fantasy architecture and a lively dining scene.

ALMATY АЛМАТЫ

📍 727 / POP 1.7 MILLION / ELEV 850M

The leafy city of Almaty (Alma-Ata), with a backdrop of the snowcapped Zailiysky Alatau, has always been among the more appealing Russian creations in Central Asia. Today Almaty's new rich have expensive suburban apartments, large SUVs, glitzy shopping malls, Western-style coffee lounges, expensive restaurants, dance-till-dawn nightclubs and new ski resorts to help them enjoy life to the full. Meanwhile, others from the city's outer districts and the countryside squeeze into packed buses and rickety marshrutkas around the Green Market (Zelyony Bazar) or Sayakhat bus station.

Almaty is Kazakhstan's main transport hub and a place many travellers pass through. Stay a few days and you'll find that it is a sophisticated place – one for enjoying green parks and excellent museums, shops and markets, and for eating, drinking and partying in Central Asia's best selection of restaurants, cafes, bars and clubs. And great mountain hiking and skiing are right on the doorstep.

History

Almaty was founded in 1854, when the Kazakhs were still nomads, as a Russian frontier fort named Verny, on the site of an old Silk Road oasis called Almatu, which had been laid waste long before by the Mongols. Cossacks and Siberian peasants settled around Verny, but the town was almost flattened by earthquakes in 1887 and 1911. In 1927 it became the capital of Soviet Kazakhstan, with the name Alma-Ata (Father of Apples). The Turksib (Turkestan–Siberia) railway arrived in 1930 and brought big growth – as did WWII, when factories were relocated here from Nazi-threatened western USSR and many Slavs came to work in them. Numbers of ethnic Koreans, forcibly resettled from the Russian Far East, arrived too.

In the 1970s and '80s Kazakhstan's leader Dinmukhamed Kunayev, the only Central Asian member of the Soviet Politburo, managed to steer lots of money southeast from Moscow to transform Alma-Ata into a worthy Soviet republican capital. Hence the number of imposing late-Soviet buildings such as the Arasan Baths (p296), the **Hotel Kazakhstan** (Dostyk 52; 🚇 12) and the **Academy of Sciences** (Shevchenko; Ⓜ Abay).

In 1991 Alma-Ata was the venue for the meeting where the USSR was finally pronounced dead and all five Central Asian republics joined the Commonwealth of Independent States. The city's name was changed to Almaty, close to that of the original Silk Road settlement, soon afterwards.

Almaty was replaced by Astana as Kazakhstan's capital in 1998 but remains the country's business, social and cultural hub. Office towers, apartment blocks and shopping centres continue to push skyward, especially in the south of the city.

FESTIVALS & EVENTS IN ALMATY

As well as regular annual events, frequent one-off festivals of music, food, cinema and more brighten up Almaty's calendar; check afisha.kz or www.timeout.kz.

Nauryz (Navrus; ⊙ 22 Mar) The big spring festival, celebrated throughout Central Asia, sees colourful parades in the city, and horse racing and often *kokpar* (*buzkashi;* the traditional Central Asian pololike sport played with a headless goat carcass) at the **Hippodrome** (📞 727 294 86 00; Zhansugirov; ⊙ 10am-8pm; 🚇 8) several kilometres north of the centre.

Kazakhstan Fashion Week (http://kfw.kz) Young Kazakh designers show off their latest creations on the catwalk in Almaty. Check website for dates.

International Jazz Festival (www.jazz.kz; ⊙ Apr) International artists jam it up in various venues over several days.

Eurasia International Film Festival (⊙ Sep) Free screenings of dozens of films, mostly from Commonwealth of Independent States (CIS) countries but some from Western Europe, over several days, plus occasional fly-ins by Hollywood celebs.

Almaty Day (⊙ 16 Sep) The annual city festival sees numerous indoor and outdoor musical events and exhibitions (usually with one dedicated to locally grown apples), and fireworks.

◉ Sights

More than anything, Almaty is a city to stroll. Make your way to the pedestrianised stretch of **Zhibek Zholy** (Arbat; 🚌 7, 92) for Almaty's (sort of) version of Moscow's Arbat, dotted with inexpensive cafes, a few buskers and kitsch art stands. Though it has been sanitised in recent years, the two-level **Green Market** (Zelyony Bazar, Kok Bazar; Zhibek Zholy 53; ⊙8am-6pm Tue-Sun; 🚌9, 11, 19) has a true flavour of Central Asia and is worth putting on your itinerary even if you're not really food shopping. There's an entire row dedicated to horsemeat.

★Central State Museum   MUSEUM
(📞727 264 55 77; www.csmrk.kz; Furmanov; foreigner/local 500/300T, tour in English 1000T; ⊙9.30am-6pm Wed-Mon; 🚌2, 63, 73, 86) Almaty's best museum takes you through Kazakhstan's history from Bronze Age burials and nomadic culture to WWII sacrifices, telecommunications and the transfer of the capital to Astana, with many beautiful artefacts on display. A large replica of the Golden Man (a national symbol of Kazakhstan; a 3rd- or 4th-century warrior whose gold-clad remains were uncovered in 1969) stands in the entrance hall.

★Kazakhstan Museum of Arts   MUSEUM
(📞727 394 57 18; www.gmirk.kz; Satpaev; 200T; ⊙11am-7pm Tue-Sun; 🚌95, Ⓜ Auezov) This is the best art collection in the country, with Kazakh, Russian and some Western European art and a room of top-class modern Kazakh handicrafts, with much explanatory material in English. Particularly interesting is the room on Russia's Mir Iskusstva movement, and also the large collection of paintings by Kazakh Abylkhan Kasteev (1904–73).

★Kök-Töbe   HILL
(Green Hill) This 1100m hill on the city's southeast edge is crowned by a 372m-high TV tower visible from far and wide, and affords great views over the city and the mountains, plus an assortment of attractions at the top. The easy way up is by the smooth **cable car** (Lugansky; one way/return 1000/2000T; ⊙10am-midnight Mon-Fri, 10.30am-1am Sat & Sun; 🚌5, 12, Ⓜ Abay).

At the top you'll find several cafes and restaurants, craft shops, a roller coaster, a minizoo, an 'I Heart Almaty' sign, a children's playground and life-sized bronze statues of the four Beatles, placed here on the initiative of local fans in 2007. The work of Almaty sculptor Eduard Kazaryan, this is claimed to be the world's only monument showing all the Fab Four together. You can sit beside a guitar-strumming John on the bench.

The cable car and other facilities may close early, or not open at all, in poor weather. The cheaper way up Kok-Tobe is by bus 95 (opposite Ramstor on Furmanov) or 99 (south up Abylay Khan, east on Abay, south on Dostyk) to their terminus on Omarova, where a shuttle minibus (one way/return 350/600T, every few minutes from 10am to 1am) runs the final 1.25km up the hill.

★Kazakh Museum of Folk Musical Instruments   MUSEUM
(📞727 291 69 17; Zenkov 24; 500T; ⊙10am-6pm Tue-Sun; 🚌1, 12) In a striking 1908 wooden building (designed by cathedral architect Zenkov) at the east end of Panfilov Park, the city's most original museum is a must for musicians. As well as a fine collection of traditional Kazakh instruments (wooden harps and horns, bagpipes, the lute-like two-stringed *dombra* and the viola-like *kobyz*), there are also Turkish, Uzbek and Kyrgyz folk instruments for comparison and it's possible to attend the occasional performance of traditional music.

Panfilov Park   PARK
(btwn Gogol & Kazybek Bi) This large and attractive rectangle of greenery is one of central Almaty's most popular strolling and hang-out places for all ages. At its heart stands the candy-coloured **Zenkov Cathedral** (⊙services 8am & 5pm; 🚌1, 12). Kazakhstan's nearest (albeit distant) relative to St Basil's Cathedral in Moscow and one of Almaty's few surviving tsarist-era buildings. Designed by AP Zenkov in 1904, the cathedral is built entirely of wood (including the nails). Used as a museum and concert hall in Soviet times, it was returned to the Russian Orthodox Church in 1995.

The park is named for the Panfilov Heroes, 28 soldiers of an Almaty infantry unit who died fighting off Nazi tanks in a village outside Moscow in 1941. They are commemorated at the fearsome **WWII War Memorial** (🚌1, 12) east of the cathedral, which depicts soldiers from all 15 Soviet republics bursting out of a map of the USSR. An eternal flame honouring the fallen of 1917–20 (the Civil War) and 1941–45 (WWII) flickers in front of the giant black monument. Nearby, a monument depicting three ragged

Almaty (Alma-Ata)

Almaty-II Train Station

89

Rayymbek

26

Rayymbek

Rayymbek

Seyfullin

Seyfullin

Nauryzbay Batyr

Zheltoksan

Abylay Khan

Mametova

Kunaev

Suyunbay

32 59

68

87 65 16

31

Mukanov

Muratbaev

Shagabutdinov

Adi Sharipov

Gogol

Baytursynov

Zhibek Zholy

28

Gogol

75

Zhibek Zholy

69

51 79 61 17

76 70

29

47

Ayteke Bi

Kazybek Bi

66

Tole Bi (Komsomolskaya) 42

71

Panfilov

Furmanov

Tulebaev

38 41

25

23

49

Masanchi

Bogenbay Batyr

Coffeedelia

73

Almaly

18 36

84

27 60

48

81

Karasay Batyr

56

Shagabutdinov

Adi Sharipov

Dosmukhamedov

Kabanbay Batyr

Zhambyl

Zheltoksan

Nauryzbay Batyr

Bayseitova

Shevchenko

83 67

77

Abaya

54

35

Kurmangazy

63

45

46

62

Teatr imeni Auezova

Baykonur

Abay

Seyfullin

8

5

13

Central State Museum

Zhandosov

33 72

21

Kazakhstan Museum of Arts

3

10

1

82

Baytursynov

Bayzakov

30

Timiryazev

12

64

Markov

24

Furmanov

soldiers honours Kazakh soldiers who'd fallen in Afghanistan.

Respublika Alany PLAZA
(Satpaev; 🚌2, 63, 73, 86) This broad, Soviet-created ceremonial square provides a panoramic view of the snowcapped mountains on a clear morning and is surrounded by several landmark buildings and monuments.

Its focus is the tall **Independence Monument** (Ⓜ Abay). The stone column is surmounted with a replica Golden Man standing on a winged snow leopard. Around its base are statues of a Kazakh family; behind is a semicircular wall of low-relief bronze sculptures depicting scenes from Kazakhstan's history, from Golden Man times at the left end to President Nazarbayev at the right.

Overlooking the square from the south is the neoclassical-style **Maslikhat** (City Council; 🚌2,63,73,86) building. Southeast of here, opposite the Central State Museum, is a large official **Presidential Residence** (Furmanov 205; 🚌2, 63, 73, 86). At the top of Zheltoksan, the striking **Dawn of Freedom Monument** (Ⓜ Abay) honours those killed and injured on Respublika alany on 17 December 1986 during the Zheltoksan (December) protests, the first unrest unleashed in Central Asia by the Gorbachev era of glasnost. Possibly as many as 250 people were killed when police opened fire on rioters protesting against the appointment of a Russian, Gennady Kolbin, as head of the Kazakhstan Communist Party.

🏃 Activities & Tours

Almaty is the most popular destination in Kazakhstan, and justifiably so, given the wealth of attractions easily reachable from the city: Kolsai Lakes, Charyn Canyon, Altyn-Emel National Park and more. Numerous tour operators offer trips to these attractions, but the vast majority (with some notable exceptions recommended here) prefer to deal with groups of travellers and can be downright unhelpful when it comes to solo travellers or couples.

⭐**Walking Almaty** WALKING
(📞778 574 15 24; www.walkingalmaty.com; Tole Bi 130B; 2hr walking tour per person $30; 🚌37, 48) Visitors rave about walking tours of Almaty run by enthusiastic Central Asia expert, polyglot and Californian expat Dennis Keen. He knows everything there is to know about the city, from its history to what kinds of weeds grow here, and he's also the man to come to if you're interested in eagle hunters.

Almaty (Alma-Ata)

★ **Arasan Baths**   BATHHOUSE
(☎727 390 10 10; http://arasan-spa.kz; Tolebaev

78; 2hr session weekdays/weekends 2700/4700T;
⊙8am-midnight Tue-Sun; 🚌1, 12) Built in the

1980s in a modernistic Soviet style, this is perhaps the finest bathhouse in Central Asia. If you fancy trying a traditional bathhouse experience, go with a friend or two and you'll find the routine easy to pick up. Choose from Russian-Finnish or oriental baths, each with men's and women's sections. There's an attached detox and spa centre.

★ **Trekking Club** TREKKING, CLIMBING

(☑ 727 229 31 04, 777 260 56 32; www.trekkingclub. kz; Svezhest 217; 📱 28) Expert agency offering hikes, treks and climbs in the mountains south of Almaty and treks in and around the Turgen Gorge east of the city, where the club has a well-equipped tent camp. The office is on the road towards Ozero Bolshoe Almatinskoe, about 15km southwest of the city centre.

★ **Outfitter KZ** OUTDOORS

(☑ 727 391 11 55; www.outfitter.kz) This enthusiastic new operator arranges excellent tours to the Kolsai Lakes, Charyn Canyon, Altyn-Emel National Park, Tamgaly Petroglyphs and other attractions in the area. It also does day trips to Big Almaty Lake, complete with ascents of Big Almaty Peak. Unlike the majority of other tour operators in town, it's happy to work with individual travellers.

SilkOffRoad MOTORCYCLING

(☑ Marat 707 717 31 66, Sergey 705 419 55 22; www.silkoffroad.kz; Satpaev 29/1; 📱 18, 121, Ⓜ Baykonur) These motorcycling pioneers organise superb biking tours of Kazakhstan and Central Asia in general, from the Pamir Hwy and the Ustyurt Plateau to the Great Silk Road. Even if you don't join one of their tours, they are happy to help with advice and technical support and there are motorbikes and rugged cars for rent.

Karlygash Makatova ADVENTURE SPORTS

(Karla Makatova; ☑ 701 755 20 86; kmakatova@ yahoo.com) Independent one-woman operator who has long organised trips for the expat community and travellers: city walking tours, day hikes, treks, climbs, drives, rafting trips, helicopter flights, wine tours and more to Kyrgyzstan, and Mongolia. Her trips are spirited, not too expensive, and a good way to meet locals and expats. Contact her via WhatsApp (same as mobile number) or email.

Kazakhstan Travel Agency OUTDOORS

(☑ 727 328 04 29; www.almaty-travel.kz; Dostyk Ave 103/10; 📱 5, 29) Organises a good range of tours to Charyn Canyon, Turgen Canyon, Kolsai Lakes, Big Almaty Lake and other attractions around Almaty.

Silk Road Adventures OUTDOORS

(☑ 727 268 27 43; www.silkadv.com; Adi Sharipov 117/44; ⊙ 9am-6pm Mon-Fri, to 2pm Sat; 📱 112) Long-established, highly experienced operator offering all kinds of long and short, individual and group trips throughout Kazakhstan and Central Asia, including hiking in the mountains near Almaty and the Altay, Mangistau 4WD tours, and Baikonur Cosmodrome visits.

🛏 Sleeping

Almaty has plenty of accommodation options to suit all budgets. These range from severa- dozen hostels catering to budget travellers to immaculate high-end hotels with a full range of amenities. In between there's a solid smattering of midrange and boutique hotels.

★ **Interhouse Almaty** HOSTEL $

(☑ 777 836 27 94; www.interhouse.life/ interhouse-almaty/; Khodjanov 55/1; dm/d 3500/10,454T; ⊛ ❄; 📱 56, 63, 86) This three-storey house on the outskirts of the city hides one of the country's best hostels. The warm welcome from the owner makes guests feel like family, the bathrooms are huge (and there's a good ratio of guests per bathroom), a hearty breakfast is included in the price and there's a rose- and jasmine-filled garden to chill in. Occasional barbecues.

★ **Sky Hostel** HOSTEL $

(☑ 727 225 59 32; www.facebook.com/Sky-Hostel-Almaty-565745803551826/; Kurmangazy 107; dm/d 3500/14,369T; ⊛❄🛜; 📱 9, Ⓜ Baikonur) Vying for the title of 'Almaty's Top Hostel', this friendly place has earned a steady stream of guests for its pop-arty decor, helpful English-speaking staff, and its stupendous roof terrace, because it's best to observe the city from on high. If you don't fancy bedding down in a 12-bed dorm, book a private room in advance. Guest kitchen available.

Nomad's Guesthouse HOSTEL $

(☑ 775 726 30 32; http://nomads-gh.com; Tulebayev 38/61; dm/d 2500/6500/8000T; ⊛❄🛜; 📱 2, 63, 86) This large, friendly hostel represents the best value when it comes to a supercentral stay near the Green Market and Panfilov Park. The private rooms have

SUNKAR FALCON CENTRE

Run by ornithologist and respected falconer Pavel Pfander, this **falcon centre** (☑727 269 12 35; 300T; ☉10am-last client; ☐28) ✎, near Ile-Alatau National Park (p305), breeds critically endangered birds of prey, such as saker falcons and golden eagles, and releases them into the wild. If you don't get to meet Kazakhstan's elusive eagle hunters, it's well worth coming here for the professional display of trained raptors in flight (1000T) at 5pm daily except Monday.

their own bathrooms, the dorms are very spacious and the staff do their best to help even though not all speak English.

Almaty Backpackers   HOSTEL $

(☑778 951 17 11; www.facebook.com/almatybackpackerskz; Markov 46A; dm/s/d 3200/6800/8300T; ⊜⊛; ☐79) This hostel is one of the best in town. It's certainly the most spacious, with large rooms and a good outdoor area with a sociable atmosphere. All rooms, including the dorms (three to six bunks), have their own bathrooms, there's a good kitchen and the washing machine is free. Helpful staff can arrange tours of the region.

Hotel D'Rami   BOUTIQUE HOTEL $$

(☑777 234 01 22; http://dramihotel.com; Ablay Khan 123; r 19,000T; ⊜⊛⊜; ☐9) The eight rooms in this new minihotel are low-key, but absolutely spotless, and the central location makes this an ideal base from which to launch yourself into the dining/nightlife melee of Almaty.

Lessor Apartments   APARTMENT $$

(☑727 279 50 74; www.lessor.kz; office Zheltoksan 74; apt from 8890T; ☉office 10am-9pm; ⊛⊜; ☐1, 12) Lessor rents out ordinary city-centre apartments for two to four people with kitchen and bathroom, most within a five-minute walk of its office. The apartments have normal local home furnishings, so you get some sense of what local living is like. If you book ahead then call on arrival in Almaty, staff will explain how to reach your apartment and will meet you there. The office entrance is on Zhibek Zholy.

Hotel Astra   HOTEL $$

(☑727 246 86 88; www.astra-hotel.kz; Zheltoksan 12; s/d incl breakfast from 13,520/16,400T; ⊜⊛⊜⊜; Ⓜ Rayimbek batyr) A short walk from Almaty-II train station, this is a relatively good-value place with professional, English-speaking reception and pleasant, carpeted rooms that are unlikely to make your social-media posts. The restaurant serves all meals and the bar never closes.

Hotel Otrar   HOTEL $$

(☑727 250 68 69; www.group.kz; Gogol 73; s/d incl breakfast from 16,000/17,000T; ℗⊜⊛⊜⊜; ☐1, 12) Well situated facing Panfilov Park, the Otrar is a Soviet masterpiece of marble, dim lighting and flimsy-looking, tiny balconies, whose well-kept rooms are equipped with comfy beds, red carpets, polished wood furniture and bath-tubs. Price includes a buffet breakfast and two hours in the pool/sauna.

★ Rixos Almaty   DESIGN HOTEL $$$

(☑727 300 33 00; http://almaty.rixos.com; Kabanbay Batyr 510; r/ste from €191/497; ℗⊛@⊜⊜; ☐7, 9) The rooms at Almaty's most luxurious hotel are suitably sumptuous but surprisingly understated and decked out in neutral shades. The Olympic-sized swimming pool, however, is all marble and underwater lighting, there's an excellent spa on-site and the hotel's Brasserie restaurant serves refined takes on Kazakh food, as well as Pan-Asian dishes. Faultless multilingual service to boot.

★ Hotel Kazzhol   HOTEL $$$

(☑727 250 50 16; www.hotelkazzhol.kz; Gogol 127/1; s/d incl breakfast from 22,950/27,200T; ℗⊜⊛@⊜⊜; ☐1, 12, Ⓜ Zhibek Zholy) The cheaper rooms in this efficient, sparkling-clean hotel on a quiet lane off Zhibek Zholy are the best value at this price level. Desk staff speak English, and the smart rooms all have writing desks and international satellite TV. Breakfast is a good buffet and the fitness centre has a 20m pool. Airport and station transfers available.

Grand Hotel Tien Shan   BUSINESS HOTEL $$$

(☑727 244 96 99; www.tienshanhotels.com; Bogenbay Batyr 115; s/d/ste incl breakfast from 28,000/36,000/68,000T; ℗⊜⊛@⊜⊜; ☐112) An elegant hotel in the handsome former Geology Ministry building, with attractive, good-sized rooms and friendly staff. Rates include an excellent spa with saunas and a good pool.

Eating

You won't find a better range of good restaurants anywhere else in Central Asia. A large range of international cuisines is represented and there's also plenty of variety at the budget end. The majority of midrange and top-end restaurants offer inexpensive business-lunch deals on weekdays.

There are plenty of large, well-stocked supermarkets with both local and imported goods on their shelves. **Yubileyny** (cnr Gogol & Abylay Khan; snacks from 300T; ⊙24hr; Ⓜ Zhibek Zholy) is one of the biggest, with a huge wine section among other temptations, and there are several quick-eat and takeaway food options out front. For fresh produce, don't miss the Green Market (p293).

Fakir
UZBEK $

(☑727 273 87 89; Kaldayakov 17; mains 600-1200T; ⊙11am-midnight; 🚌5, 22) Cheerful Uzbek cheapie near the Green Market, with heaped helpings of *manty* (steamed dumplings), *plov* (pilaf), noodle dishes and *chorba* (stew). Popular with office workers. Waiting staff vary from cheerful and welcoming to surly and uncommunicative, Soviet-style.

Kaganat
CAFETERIA $

(☑727 261 75 22; Abylay Khan 105; mains 450-1000T; ⊙8am-10pm; 🍴; Ⓜ Almaly) This popular cafeteria chain will feed you satisfactorily and cheaply all day. Soups, salads, breads, assorted hot mains and desserts are on offer.

Dastarkhan Food
CAFETERIA $

(☑727 267 37 37; Nauryzbay Batyr 122/124; mains 450-1200T; ⊙24hr; 🕿; 🚌32, 92) This superior cafeteria with attractive decor and spacious layout serves up a big choice of well-prepared dishes, from salads, soups and *bliny* (crepe) to *laghman* (long, stout noodles), *plov* (pilaf), Korean *kuksi* (noodle, meat and vegetable soup) and assorted fish and meat mains. Draught beer too. Long lunchtime queues Monday to Friday.

★Tandoor
INDIAN $$

(☑707 388 99 33; www.facebook.com/tandoorkz; Tole Bi 102; mains 1700-2800T; ⊙11am-midnight; 🕿🍴📶; 🚌16, 37) This authentic Indian restaurant is well worth seeking out. Sultry decor and crimson ceilings combined with such classic northern Indian dishes as *bhuna gosht* (meat curry) and *aloo gobi* (cauliflower and potatoes) make for an atmospheric meal. The *pudina* chicken tikka (chicken marinated in yoghurt and mint)

is among the best chicken dishes we've ever had, anywhere.

★Gosti
RUSSIAN $$

(☑727 341 07 61; http://abr.kz/restaurants/gosti; Kunaev 78; 1800-3500T; ⊙11am-midnight; 🕿; 🚌37, 48) The owners of this restaurant decided on a 19th-century Russian-country-mansion theme and then ran with it a few kilometres. Expect lots of samovars, chintzy curtains, a menu full of refined Russian standards, such as meat in aspic, *pelmeni* (dumplings), *vareniki* (other dumplings), *draniki* (potato fritters) and beef stroganoff, and kvass to wash it down.

Manga Sushi
SUSHI $$

(☑701 952 80 00; www.manga-sushi.kz; Gogol 201/92; sushi 1000-2400T; ⊙noon-midnight; ✳🕿📶; 🚌1, 12) It's worth travelling all the way to the outskirts of Almaty to sample some of Kazakhstan's most imaginative sushi rolls amid floor-to-ceiling manga art'; our favourite sushi rolls are called *Ghost in the Shell*. The service is young and sweet, and there are slurpable bowls of ramen as well.

Venetsia
CENTRAL ASIAN $$

(☑727 293 81 67; cnr Kayyrbekov & Tole Bi; mains 1200-2200T; ⊙11am-midnight; 🚌9, 11, 29) Popular Venetsia sits beside the little Malaya Almatinka River and its outdoor terrace is a great place to eat on a summer evening. There's a huge choice of Central Asian and Caucasian dishes, including Kazakh *beshbarmak* (flat noodles with meat cooked in a vegetable broth which is eaten separately), and the many varieties of shashlyk are among the best choices.

Daredzhani
GEORGIAN $$

(☑727 313 24 15; http://abr.kz/restaurants/daredzhani/; Kazybek Bi 40/85; mains 1900-3400T; ⊙noon-midnight; 🕿🍴📶; 🚌16, 37) The pick of the city's Georgian establishments, Daredzhani serves numerous favourites from the Caucasus, including *pkhali* (cold, fragrant, herb-rich vegetarian starter), *khinkali* (giant seamed dumplings), chicken in plum sauce, shashlyk, and four types of *khachapuri* (Georgian bread with melted cheese). The decor is all earthy colours, pottery and farm implements and there's a solid Georgian wine menu, too.

Khodja Nasreddin
UZBEK $$

(☑727 264 23 15; Lugansky 54; mains 1300-2800T; ⊙noon-midnight; 🚌5, 12, 29) This is one of

Almaty's best Uzbek restaurants and especially nice in summer when you can sit around the courtyard. Go for the *plov prazdnichny* (festival pilaf), *kazan kebab* (lamb ribs and fried potatoes) or a good old shashlyk with spicy *adzhika* (hot pepper, garlic, herb and spice) sauce. The *pichini* (potato and cheese pies) make a good side dish.

Coffeedelia   CAFE $$

(☑727 272 64 09; www.facebook.com/pages/ Coffeedelia/110394802375412; Kabanbay Batyr 79; mains 1300-2700T; ☺8am-midnight Sun-Fri, 9am-1am Sat; 🔊; 🚌2, 63, 73, 86) This fashionable coffee house with a relaxed atmosphere, fabulous cakes and pastries and good coffees, teas, juices and breakfasts is an evergreen chart-topper on the big Almaty cafe scene. This branch is busy and has a great pavement terrace.

★Line Brew   INTERNATIONAL $$$

(☑701 742 06 86; http://line-brew.kz/line-brew-almaty; Furmanov 187A; mains 1650-6800T; ☺noon-1am; 🔊📶; 🚌2, 63, 73, 86, Ⓜ Abay) This branch of the popular nationwide microbrewery attracts the carnivorously inclined with stone-cooked meats, an assortment of steaks, some of the juiciest shashlyk in the region and a supporting cast of salads and hot and cold appetisers. The beer on tap is the best in Kazakhstan and there's a pleasant summer terrace upstairs.

★My Cafe   INTERNATIONAL $$$

(☑701 755 88 33; www.mycafe.kz; Furmanov 128/104; mains 2500-5200T; ☺10am-midnight; 🌸🔊📶; 🚌2, 63, 73, 86) Yes, this place is self-consciously trendy, with pulsing ambient music, hip young staff and decor comprising giant steel feathers, but the food is imaginative and excellent. The *okroshka* (cold summer soup) is the best we've ever had, the flavourful lamb burger comes in a charcoal bun and the buckwheat noodles with grilled eel hit the spot.

Crudo   STEAK $$$

(☑727 291 11 45; http://parmigiano-group.com/ en/restaurants/crudo; Abay 17; mains 2540-4980T; ☺noon-midnight; 🌸🔊📶; Ⓜ Abay) Trendy without being snooty, this bare-brick-walled, industrial-themed place attracts meat lovers with the best steaks in Almaty. Ribeyes, T-bones, flank steaks, filet mignons and New York steaks are expertly seared to your specifications, with horse steak adding a local touch. Good-value lunch deals, too.

Korean House   KOREAN $$$

(☑727 318 76 03; http://korean-house.kz; Gogol 2; mains 1900-6900T; ☺noon-midnight; 🌸🔊📶; 🚌1, 12) In a green and leafy part of old Almaty, this popular, upmarket chain serves a smorgasbord of spicy, flavourful dishes from the Korean peninsula, from *bulgogi* and udon with seafood to squid in chilli sauce and *bibimbap*. Service is attentive and professional and there's an obligatory sushi and pan-Asian soup section.

La Barca Fish & Wine   INTERNATIONAL $$$

(☑778 582 88 88; www.facebook.com/labarcaf-ishandwine/?rf=772217756142106; Abylay Khan 145; mains 2700-12,000T; ☺noon-11pm; 🌸🔊📶; Ⓜ Abay) Local professionals swear by the fish and seafood here – the grilled seabass, the oysters! – but the rest of the menu is also refreshingly different from most other restaurants in the city and includes such gourmet delights as quinoa salad and baked bone marrow. If you order the steak, make sure you have a fat bank account.

🍷 Drinking & Nightlife

Finding a drink for any budget isn't difficult in Almaty, as the distinction between cafes, restaurants and bars is blurred. Beer gardens under sunshades sprout around the city in summer. There are some superb coffee shops, too.

The nouveau riche crowd and Almaty's students and 20-somethings have spawned a hedonistic nocturnal scene. There are lots of special events and parties: www.timeout. kz, www.afisha.kz and www.night.kz all have good listings (in Russian).

★Sova Espresso Bar   COFFEE

(☑707 474 25 26; www.facebook.com/sova.al-maty/; Abylay Khan 113; ☺9am-11pm; 🔊; 🚌5, Ⓜ Almaty) The brainchild of award-winning baristas from Moscow, Sova not only serves some of the city's best lattes, espressos and frappuccinos, but it also goes the extra mile, with an inventive international menu, great cakes and an extensive selection of sangrias and inexpensive cocktails. Great all-rounder.

★Chukotka   CLUB

(☑727 273 39 74; www.chukotka.kz; Gogol 40; ☺noon-1am Tue-Thu, to 5am Fri & Sat; 🔊; 🚌13, 71) Good rock bands from around 9pm and DJs spinning house, soul, hip hop and disco after midnight make sure the dance floor is never still at this ever-hip Almaty nightspot inside Panfilov Park. The crowd is open-minded, student-to-30s and gay friendly. The free admission helps, as do the relatively reasonable drink prices.

Bowler Coffee Roasters COFFEE
(☑707 730 09 10; www.facebook.com/bowler. coffee.roasters/; Kabanbay Batyr 65; ⊗8am-8pm; ☜; ⬛5, 29, 48) Thimble-sized coffee shop with three tiny tables, an extensive collection of teas and coffees kept in smart wooden drawers and a barista who really knows the difference between a *ristretto*, an *espresso doppio* and a *café bombón*.

Vzletnaya CLUB
(☑707 706 59 18; www.facebook.com/vzletnaya music/; Valikhanov 27; ⊗7-10pm Thu, 11pm-7am Fri & Sat; ☜; ⬛17) The latest club du jour caters to Almaty's young and beautiful crowd, as well as serious techno and trance enthusiasts. Quality local DJs get rave reviews for their sets.

Shakespeare Pub PUB
(☑727 291 94 22; www.shakespeare.kz; Dostyk 40; ⊗noon-1am Sun-Thu, to 2am Fri & Sat; ☜; ⬛5, 29, 48) Almaty's premier expat drinking hole is a large pub-like space always with a lively atmosphere (especially Friday and Saturday nights), a big drinks selection, Line Brew and a new Shakespeare Special microbrew on tap, and soccer on the (not too obtrusive) screens. Locals also like it, and there's fish and chips, shepherd's pie and roast beef for homesick Brits.

Stalker BAR
(☑727 291 20 46; Dostyk 30; ⊗6pm-1am; ☜; ⬛48) Dark, wood-panelled, unassuming bar that serves a good selection of local and imported beers to a mixed expat and local crowd that likes to avoid the circus of the local Irish pubs.

Pivnitsa BAR
(☑727 246 47 60; Zhambyl 174; ⊗noon-midnight; ☜; ⬛9) No 'pub' decor, no expat prices, no loud music – this beer bar is a place where you can just sit and chat over a variety of local and foreign brews, and that's just what the predominantly local clientele enjoy doing.

☆ Entertainment

Almaty has a good theatre and musical scene. Check www.timeout.kz, afisha.kz and night.kz for listings, and keep an eye open for concerts by Kazakh folk-music ensembles such as Sazgen Sazy (www.sazgen-sazy. kz). For traditional music performances, it's best to enquire at the Kazakh Museum of Folk Musical Instruments (p293).

Abay State Opera & Ballet Theatre OPERA, BALLET
(☑727 272 79 34; www.gatob.kz; Kabanbay Batyr 110; 800-4500T; ⊗ticket office 10am-2pm & 3-6pm; ⬛2, 63, 73, 86) Almaty's top cultural venue stages three or four performances a week at 5pm or 6.30pm. Some get sold out a week or more ahead. Popular favourites such as *Swan Lake, La Bohème, La Traviata, Aida* and *Carmen* are among the regular shows. Also look out for Kazakh operas such as *Abay* and *Abylay Khan.* Tends to close in July and August.

🛍 Shopping

Malls such as **RamStor** (☑727 530 54 01; Furmanov 226; ⊗10am-10pm), **Silk Way City** (☑707 558 30 93; Tole Bi 71; ⊗24hr) and **Mega Alma-Ata** (☑727 232 25 01; Rozybakiev 247A; ⊗10am-10pm) are stocked with expensive, often imported, goods, and there are international brand stores dotted all around the city centre. There isn't much in the way of crafts, though the **Central State Museum** (Mikrorayon Samal-1, No 44; ⊗9.30am-6pm Wed-Mon) gift shop stands out as an exception. There are also several good bookshops with some English reading material, including those inside **Rahat Palace** (☑727 250 12 34; www.rahatpalace.com; Satpaev 29/6; r/ste incl breakfast from 53,760/98,560T; ☏◐❄ @☜❄; ⬛18, 121), **InterContinental Almaty** (☑727 250 50 00; www.inter continental.com; Zheltoksan 181; r incl breakfast from 56,800T, ste from 116,000T; ☏◐❄☜❄; ⬛32, Ⓜ Abay) and Otrar (p298) hotels, plus trekking and maps at **Akademkniga** (Furmanov 91; ⊗10am-8pm Mon-Fri, to 7pm Sat & Sun).

LGBTIQ ALMATY

There is a gay scene in Almaty but the scene is pretty low-key and bars and clubs often open, close and change location quickly.

The nearest thing to a typical gay bar in the West, **Studio 69** (☑727 250 74 01; Kurmangazy 125; ⊗9pm-6am; Ⓜ Abay) primarily welcomes gay men and has a fairly relaxed atmosphere and a not especially good drag show. It's been the subject of local controversy and doesn't publicise its events terribly well.

If you're into camping, skiing or trekking, sports gear is available for purchase at **Limpopo** (Seyfullin 534; ⊙10am-7.30pm Mon-Sat, 10am-6pm Sun; 🚍112) and **Robinson** (Abylay Khan 60; ⊙10am-7pm Mon-Fri, to 6pm Sat; 🚍2, 63, 73, 86) or to rent at **Snowshop** (☑771 407 33 31; http://snowshop.kz; Makataev 32; per day snowboard & boots 3000T, mountain bike 2000T; ⊙9am-9pm; 🚍73) and **Fischer** (Furmanov 124; per day set ski gear 3500T, snowboard & boots 5000T, mountain bike 2500T; ⊙10am-8pm; 🚍2, 63, 73, 86).

Amanulla Shafii   ARTS & CRAFTS
(Hotel Saulet, Furmanov 187; ⊙10am-6pm Mon-Fri) Amanulla's little shop has a decent range of reasonably priced Kazakh carpets and dearer ones from Turkmenistan and Afghanistan.

ℹ Information

Almost all foreign embassies are in Astana, but there are plenty of consulates in Almaty. See p364 for details.

DANGERS & ANNOYANCES

Almaty is a pretty safe town, but you should still exercise normal precautions. The most common emergencies for Westerners here concern late-night activities – people robbed in taxis after emerging inebriated from bars and nightclubs, and the like. Also beware of being overcharged in taxis, particularly if you don't speak the language; agree on a price before setting off.

LEFT LUGGAGE

Left-luggage offices in the airport (ground floor) and Almaty-II station are open 24 hours, charging 800T and 450T respectively, per item for 24 hours.

MEDICAL SERVICES

Keep the number of your country's embassy handy in case you need to contact them regarding an emergency evacuation.

AMC Assist (☑708 983 30 00; www.amc centers.com; ⊙24hr) American Medical Center specialising in 24/7 emergency medical care and evacuation.

Apteka No 2 (cnr Furmanov & Gogol; ⊙7am-1am; 🚍2, 63, 73, 86) Well-stocked central pharmacy.

International Medical Centre (IMC; ☑727 378 64 64; www.imcalmaty.com; Mukanov 235; ⊙9am-7pm Mon-Fri, 10am-2pm Sat; 🚍112) Nonemergency medical care provided by English-speaking doctors.

MONEY

There are exchange kiosks at the transport terminals and on most main streets. An ATM is never far away: the airport, all shopping malls, most banks and some supermarkets and shops have them.

ATF Bank (Furmanov 100; ⊙9am-1pm & 2-6pm Mon-Fri; 🚍2, 63, 73) One of many banks with ATMs. Possibly the only bank that still exchanges travellers cheques.

POST

Central Post Office (Bogenbay Batyr 134; ⊙8am-7pm Mon-Fri, 8.30am-5.30pm Sat, 9am-2pm Sun; Ⓜ Almaly)

DHL (☑727 258 85 88; www.dhl.kz; Gogol 99; ⊙10.30am-7pm Mon-Fri; Ⓜ Zhibek Zholy) International delivery.

REGISTRATION

Migration Police (OVIR; ☑727 263 86 81; Karasay Batyr 109A; ⊙9am-1pm & 3-6pm Mon-Fri, 9am-1pm Sat; 🚍18, 48) This is where you register with the migration police. The entrance is actually between Baytursynuly 61 and 63. Processing is free and normally takes 15 to 30 minutes, but you should arrive close to morning opening time in case of delays.

A notary's office outside the entrance can help you fill in the application form for 150T, and makes photocopies.

TELEPHONE

Almaty has numerous outlets of the four mobile-phone companies. The most useful ones for travellers:

Beeline (☑771 141 96 24; www.beeline.kz; cnr Furmanov & Tole Bi; ⊙9am-8pm; 🚍2, 63, 73, 86)

KCell (☑727 258 83 00; www.kcell.kz; Gogol 58; ⊙9am-9pm; Ⓜ Zhibek Zholy) Centrally located KCell store.

TOURIST INFORMATION

Almaty Info Centre (☑727 272 39 60; www.almaty-info.net; Tolebaev 174; ⊙9am-1pm & 2-6pm Mon-Fri; 🚍112) General information on the city and the country.

Altyn-Emel National Park Office (☑727 250 04 51; altynemel.almaty.office@mail.ru; Room 244, Hotel Zhetisu, Abylay Khan 55; ⊙9am-noon & 2-6pm Mon-Fri, 9am-1pm Sat; 🚍63) Book accommodation in the park and arrange permits.

Ecotourism Information Resource Centre (EIRC; ☑727 272 53 63; www.eco-tourism.kz; Tolebaev 174; ⊙9am-1pm & 2-6pm Mon-Fri; 🚍112) Info and bookings of homestays in villages, plus tours.

Kazakhstan Tourism Association (☑727 272 40 30; www.kaztour-association.com;

Shevchenko 14; ⊘9am-5pm Mon-Sat; 🚌9)
Moderately helpful info on the country.

Tourist Information Center (☎727 390 88 86; www.visitkazakhstan.kz; Kurmangazy 33; ⊘9am-6pm Mon-Fri; Ⓜ Abay) Staff answer questions and have plentiful info on Almaty.

Tourist Information Center (www.visitalmaty. kz; Almaty International Airport; ⊘24hr; 🚌92) Helpful booth at the airport.

Valentina Guesthouse (p305) A guesthouse out in Almaty's southwest suburbs that functions as a travel agency, providing ticketing, accommodation bookings, inexpensive tours and visa support for guests and nonguests.

ℹ️ Getting There & Away

Almaty is Kazakhstan's main air hub and is linked to most major Kazakhstan cities by daily trains. Minibuses and shared taxis run to many places in the southeast of the country. Longer hauls are generally more comfortable by train.

AIR

The **airport** (www.alaport.com; Maylin 2; 🚌92) is 13km north of the centre; its website gives schedules and daily flight information. Domestic destinations include the following:

DESTINA-TION	AIRLINE	COST (T)	FREQUEN-CY
Aktau	Air Astana, Bek Air, SCAT	37,200	4-5 daily
Aktobe	Air Astana	79,700	1-2 daily
Astana	Air Astana, Bek Air, Qazaq Air, SCAT	19,000	up to 16 daily
Atyrau	Air Astana, Bek Air	46,800	3 daily
Kara-ganda	Air Astana, SCAT	23,700	2 daily
Kyzylorda	Air Astana, Bek Air	45,000	1-3 daily
Semey	SCAT	35,000	daily
Shymkent	Air Astana, Bek Air, SCAT	22,800	4-5 daily
Taraz	Qazaq Air	12,500	2 weekly
Uralsk	Air Astana, Bek Air	46,800	1-2 daily
Ust-Kameno-gorsk	Air Astana, SCAT	25,900	2-3 daily

BUS, MINIBUS & TAXI

Long-distance buses use **Sayran bus station** (☎727 396 70 63; cnr Tole Bi & Utegen Batyr; 🚌16, 37, 48, 🚌19), 5km west of the centre.

Destinations (schedules subject to change) include the following:

DESTINA-TION	COST (T)	FREQUENCY	DURATION (HR)
Astana	5500	2 daily	19
Bishkek, Kyrgyzstan	1500	2 daily	5
Karaganda	4500	2 nightly	16
Semey	5900	nightly at 7.10pm	20
Shymkent	3000	10 nightly	11
Taraz	3000	20 daily	8
Turkestan	4500	6 daily	14
Ürümqi, China	16,000	daily at 7am	24
Ust-Kameno-gorsk	6000	2 daily	22
Yining, China	6500	daily at 7am	12

Quicker minibuses and shared taxis to some of the nearer destinations wait at the front of the bus-station building or on Utegen Batyr at the side. To Taraz it's 3500T (seven hours) by minibus and 6000T (six hours) by shared taxi.

Most nearby destinations are served by the ramshackle **Sayakhat bus station** (☎727 380 74 44; Rayymbek; 🚌2), on the northern edge of the city centre. A minibus to Kegen (1500T, five to six hours) leaves between 7am and 9am (when it fills with passengers); a shared taxi runs to Zhalanash (2500T, five hours) and Saty (2500T, six hours) and goes from the street outside the station's east side between 6am and 7am. Ask around Sayakhat a day or two ahead and get there early on departure day. Numerous minibuses run to Esik (Issyk; 400T, 45 minutes).

CAR & MOTORCYCLE

If you're planning to do much travelling outside Almaty, self-drive rental is an option provided you are prepared for possible encounters with the traffic police. Self-drive rates for one or two days start around $70 to $80 per day. Check all the small print very carefully, including daily kilometre limits and restrictions on where you can take the car. **Dixie Travel** (☎727 327 10 10; www.dixie.kz; Zheltoksan 59; ⊘9am-6pm Mon-Fri; 🚌63) is a midrange local rental agency, while Europcar is an international high-end option, with branches at the **airport** (☎727 270 30 72; ⊘9am-1pm & 2.30-6.30pm; 🚌92) and **in town** (☎727 263 59 37; Office 3, Mikrorayon Samal-2, No 30; ⊘9am-1pm & 2.30-6.30pm Mon-Fri; 🚌2, 63, 86).

Motorcyclists in need of help or advice should head to **Car & Bike Rental Marat** (☑ Marat 701 717 31 66, Sergei 705 419 55 22; www.silk-offroad.kz; Satpaev 29/1; ☺ 9am-5pm; ☐ 121, Ⓜ Baikonur), owned by the founder of the local Motorcycle Travel Club who is happy to provide advice and technical support.

TRAIN

Many long-distance trains stop at both **Almaty-I station** (☑ 727 296 33 92; Seyfullin; ☐ 2, 73), 8km north of the centre at the end of Seyfullin, and the central **Almaty-II station** (☑ 727 296 15 44; Zheltoksan; ☐ 5, Ⓜ Raiymbek Batyr), at the north end of Abylay Khan. The latter is by far the most convenient and popular point of departure. A few trains only go to one or the other.

Destinations served from Almaty-II include Aktau (daily), Aralsk (one to three daily), Astana (three to four daily), Karaganda (four to five daily), Kyzylorda (two to three daily), Shymkent (three to five daily), Taraz (three to five daily) and Turkestan (two to three daily). Other destinations are served less frequently. Astana, Karaganda, Kyzylorda and Tashkent are served by high-speed, Spanish-built Talgo trains.

ⓘ Getting Around

TO/FROM THE AIRPORT

If flying into Almaty airport (p303), you can catch bus 92 immediately outside the arrivals hall; the bus runs west on Rayymbek, south on Nauryzbay Batyr, west on Abay (returning to the airport, it heads north on Zheltoksan instead of Nauryzbay Batyr). Alternatively, walk out of the airport, walk 300m along the main Maylin street, and catch bus 79 or 86 into the centre; 86 runs south along Furmanov. The journey takes 30 to 40 minutes.

You can also take one of the official taxis for around 2500T, although drivers will try for as high as 5500T; call the inexpensive Econom Taxi and get a ride for 1300T; or negotiate with freelance, unofficial cabs likely to want around 1000T to 1500T.

BICYCLE

There are numerous automated Almaty Bike (www.almatybike.kz) points around the city. Register on the website (you need a Kazakhstani mobile number for this) and then borrow bicycles for 30 minutes/one hour/two hours (free/100T/250T) for short hops.

BUS, TRAM & TROLLEYBUS

Buses, trolleybuses and trams run from 6am or 7am to 10pm. They can get crowded, so if you have much baggage or are short of time, it's easier to take a taxi. A ride costs T80 if you use a refillable Onay transport card (purchased at kiosks) or 150T in cash. A hugely useful app that shows all transport routes in Almaty is www.2gis.ru.

TRAINS FROM ALMATY

* high-speed service, ** 1st/2nd class, *** 1st/2nd/3rd class

DESTINATION	TRAIN NO	COST (T) 2ND/3RD CLASS	DEPARTURE	DURATION (HR)
Aktau (Mangyshlak)	377	11,377/7273	11.18pm daily	61¼
Aktobe	007	10,730/6887	7.14am, every other day	40¾
Aralsk	007	8,347/5367	7.14am, every other day	30¾
Astana-1*	705	22,107/15,379**	5.21pm daily	13½
Astana Nurly-Zhol*	003	9774/4443**	8am daily	14¾
Karaganda	003	11,874/8554/3866***	8am daily	12
Kyzylorda	077	13,170 (2nd class only)	5.58pm every other day	17
Novosibirsk, Russia	302	32,497/23,476	4.20pm every other day	39¾
Semey (Semipalatinsk)	302	5292/3404	4.20pm every other day	22
Shymkent	011	6579/2707	10.11pm, 5 weekly	11
Taraz	377	3190/2073	11.18pm daily	10½
Tashkent	001	15,087/5603	10.11pm Mon & Sat	16¾
Turkestan	377	4570/2950	11.18pm daily	19½
Ürümqi, China	014	37,382 (2nd class only)	12.14am Tue & Sun	32
Ust-Kamenogorsk	352	5292/3404	7.15pm every other day	25¾

Useful Routes

In the central area, Furmanov is the main artery for north–south routes (buses 2, 63, 73 and 86 are particularly useful), along with Nauryzbay Batyr (southbound) and Zheltoksan (northbound). Gogol and Abay are the principal east–west arteries.

Bus 29 Sayakhat bus station, Zhangeldin, Kaldayakov, Bogenbay Batyr (Kabanbay Batyr northbound), Dostyk, Butakovka.

Bus 48 Sayran bus station, Tole Bi, Dostyk.

Bus 66 Gogol (north side of Panfilov Park), Kaldayakov, Tole Bi (Kazybek Bi northbound), Dostyk, Abay, Zhandosov.

Bus 105 Furmanov, Abay, Baytursynuly, Timiryazev.

Trolleybus 1 Gorky Park, Gogol, Auezov, Timiryazev.

Trolleybus 12 Gorky Park, Gogol, Auezov, Zhandosov.

METRO

Almaty's shiny, clean, air-conditioned metro runs from Rayymbek station, near Almaty-II train station, about 3km south beneath Furmanov as far as Maskau, to the southwest of the city centre. It's useful for some cross-city trips. There are seven intermediate stations; Sayran is handy for the long-distance bus station. Rides cost 80T and trains run about every 10 minutes, 6.30am to 11.30pm. Use a designated, refillable Almaty card (sold at all metro stations) or swipe in with the multitransport Onay card. Police no longer check ID at stations, but it's a good idea to carry your passport on you anyway.

TAXI

There are some official taxis – marked with chequerboard logos or other obvious signs. Official taxi prices vary wildly; **Econom Taxi** (☎ 727 245 47 47; www.economtaxi.kz; ⊗ 24hr) is an economical and reliable option, while **Almaty Taxi** (☎ 727 225 27 27; www.almatytaxi.kz; ⊗ 24hr) is pricier. Many private cars also act as freelance taxis. Stand at the roadside with your arm slightly raised and you'll rarely have to wait more than six or eight cars before one stops. Just say where you're going and how much you're offering. If you can't agree on a price, let the car go and wait for another.

A ride in the centre of Almaty should cost 300T to 500T depending on distance (sometimes a bit more at night). Uber (www.uber.com) is also an option.

AROUND ALMATY

There are some great outings to be made right on Almaty's doorstep, notably into the

WORTH A TRIP

TURGEN GORGE

Part of the Ile-Alatau National Park and located 70km east of Almaty, this beautiful, densely forested gorge, carved out of rock by the white water of Turgen River, is a hiker's wonderland. The gorge sees relatively few visitors, so the half a dozen waterfalls (the most impressive of which is the 55m Buzgul), meadows and surrounding mountains remain relatively pristine. You can get here with your own wheels or else do a hiking or mountain-biking tour with Kazakhstan Travel Agency (p297).

Zailiysky Alatau range, a beautiful spur of the Tian Shan to the south of the city. The main access routes into the Zailiysky Alatau are the Malaya (Little) Almatinka valley, where the winter-sports centres Medeo and Chimbulak are found, and the Bolshaya (Big) Almatinka valley, leading up to Ozero Bolshoe Almatinskoe (Big Almaty Lake). Both are part of the vast **Ile-Alatau National Park** (www.ile-alatau.kz 200T). Note that foreigners are not allowed to walk into Kyrgyzstan through these mountains, and permits are officially required on some routes approaching the border.

🏃 Activities

Hikes

The higher reaches of the Zailiysky Alatau are beautiful and spectacular, with many peaks over 4000m, deep river valleys, many glaciers, and Tian Shan firs on the steep valley sides. The Kazakhstan–Kyrgyzstan 'green border' – foot trails through the mountains – is closed for foreigners, with border guards patrolling the access routes, so it's no longer possible to trek all the way across the mountains to Lake Issyk-Köl in Kyrgyzstan. Some routes that approach the border without crossing it also tend to fall foul of the border guards, but it is still possible to take a hike of one or a few days in the Zailiysky Alatau. To avoid problems with the border guards, go with a knowledgeable guide, or at least get the most reliable information possible from Almaty sources (such as trekking agencies) beforehand.

Agencies such as Trekking Club (p297), Silk Road Adventures (p297), Kan Tengri (p313), Karlygash Makatova (p297)

Ile-Alatau National Park

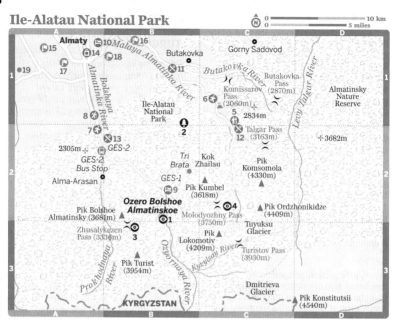

or **Valentina Guesthouse** (☑777 668 63 99, 727 360 30 92; http://valentina-gh.narod.ru; Zhabaev 62A, Akzhar; ☐22) in Almaty can provide guides and organisational support for mountain treks. Rates for small-group treks of more than one day with English-speaking guides start at 40,000T to 50,000T per day, including car transfers.

Medeo & Chimbulak
Медео, Чимбулак

Medeo and Chimbulak are Almaty's winter-sports playgrounds in the Malaya Almatinka valley. The facilities were comprehensively upgraded for Almaty's hosting of the 2011 Asian Winter Games. Medeo, about 15km southeast of central Almaty at an altitude of 1700m, is a scattering of buildings around the huge Medeo ice rink. Chimbulak, further up the valley at 2200m, is Central Asia's top skiing centre. The two are connected by road and a cable car. Medeo is always several degrees cooler than Almaty, and Chimbulak is cooler still. Except in summer, rain in Almaty means snow and zero visibility at the higher elevations.

What looks like a dam in the main valley above Medeo ice rink is actually there to stop avalanches and mudslides.

🏃 Activities

★ Medeo Ice Rink   SKATING
(☑727 386 95 33; www.medey.kz; adult/child 2200/600T; ◷10am-4pm & 6-11pm Thu-Sun Nov-late Mar) The 10,500-sq-metre Medeo ice rink, built in 1972, is made for speed and figure skating and many champion skaters have trained here, though you certainly don't need to be an expert to skate here. The rink is built to hold up to 1000 skaters and ice-skate rental is 1200T per two hours (bring your passport). Outside the ice-skating season plenty of people still come to Medeo for a stroll, hike, picnic or mountain biking in the surrounding valleys and hills.

Chimbulak Ski Resort   SKIING
(Shymbulak; ☑727 331 77 77; www.shymbulak. com; 1-day skier's lift pass adult 5500-8000T, child 2500-5000T; ◷ski lifts in ski season 10am-5pm Mon-Fri, tp 7pm Sat & Sun) Central Asia's best ski resort has a total of 14 runs (mostly reds), two cable cars, a chairlift and a drag lift. If you're feeling breathless at the top, it's because you're above 3200m. The ski season lasts from approximately November to mid-April; there's great powder snow in winter and plenty of off-piste action. Skis and snowboards rent for 6000T to 15,000T per day depending on condition (bring your

Ile-Alatau National Park

passport). In summer the place turns into a mountain-biking playground.

Nonskiers can take a return trip on the Combi 1 and Combi 2 **cable cars** (round trip adult/child 2500/1500T, combined round-trip ticket with Chimbulak cable car, Combi 1 & Combi 2 lifts 3500/2000T; ⊙ ski season 9.30am-6pm Mon-Wed & Fri, 9.30am-midnight Thu, 8.30am-midnight Sat, 8.30am-6pm Sun, other months 9.30am-6pm Mon-Thu, to 8pm Fri-Sun; 🚌29) from Chimbulak up to the Talgar Pass. You're likely to spot visitors from snow-free countries, rolling in the snow at the summit and taking selfies. The lifts also operate some days outside the ski season, from June to sometime in September (weather permitting).

🛏 Sleeping & Eating

There are several (overpriced) hotels en route to Chimbulak, as well as at the foot of the ski ranks, but there's little need to stay in the mountains unless you're a very serious skier. If that's you, the large **Hotel Chimbulak** (📞727 390 93 93; www.shymbulak hotel.kz; r weekday/weekend incl breakfast from 15,200/18,000T; ⓟⓟ🛎) has a great location at the foot of the ski lifts but the rooms are bland.

Chalet Shymbulak
Meat Restaurant   INTERNATIONAL $$
(📞727 225 13 51; www.chalet-shymbulak.kz; mains 2200-5000T; ⊙10am-6pm Mon-Fri, to 8pm Sat & Sun; 🛎) Rustic kitsch meets carnivore-enticing fare. The shashlyks are particularly good. Park yourself by the window for great mountain views.

★ Bellagio   ITALIAN $$$
(📞727 368 79 60; http://bellagio.kz/; Gornaya 197; mains 3350-19,950T; ⊙noon-midnight; ❄🛎✎▥; 🚌12) There's no denying that the setting is idyllic: yurts with dining tables against a snowy mountain backdrop, a glacial stream crossing the property. The dishes are a mix of Italian and international ones, and there are some seriously good Italian and French wines. This place is a favourite with Nazarbayev, Putin and Bill Clinton, so you're in good/bad company.

ℹ Getting There & Around

Bus 12 runs to Medeo (80T, 30 minutes) every 30 to 45 minutes (6.30am to 8pm) from Dostyk, opposite the Hotel Kazakhstan, in Almaty. If you're heading straight on up to Chimbulak in the cable car, get off at the cable-car station, 1km before Medeo ice rink. The last bus back down leaves Medeo at 8.40pm.

Ozero Bolshoe Almatinskoe Area

West of and parallel to the Malaya Almatinka valley lies its 'big sister', the Bolshaya Almatinka valley (Долина БольшойАлматинки). The paved road south up this valley starts beside the colonnaded entrance to the First President's Park on Al-Farabi on the southern edge of Almaty. After 7km you reach the entrance to the Ile-Alatau National Park (p305).

About 1km past the park gate is the restaurant complex Tau Dastarkhan (p309). The road forks 250m past here, at a spot

HIKING AROUND ALMATY

On any mountain hike or trek, you *must* be equipped for bad conditions. The trekking season lasts from about mid-May to mid-September; July and August have the most reliable weather, but at any time it can rain or snow in the mountains, even when it's warm in Almaty. If you're caught unprepared by a sudden storm, it could be fatal. There is also year-round avalanche danger wherever you see snow. Altitude sickness can affect anyone who ascends rapidly above 2500m, so spending a night to acclimatise on the way up is advisable.

Medeo to Butakova

This is a relatively leisurely hike of three to four hours, through wooded hills in the middle section, with buses at both ends. Start by heading east up the paved side road 100m downhill from the Medeo ice rink. After about 1.5km take the track up to the left between two large properties with high stone perimeter walls. About 800m up here, take the path heading left up through the trees for 500m to the Komissarov Pass (2060m).

Cross straight over the little pass and descend the valley path about 1.5km to the paved road at Berezovaya Roshka. You then have a 5km road walk down the valley to Butakovka village, passing a couple of picnic spots and shashlyk joints and some enormous high-walled mansions. From Butakovka bus 29R heads back to Almaty (Dostyk) once or twice an hour.

Medeo to Kok Zhailau, Peak Kumbel & Tri Brata

This is a fairly straightforward day hike. There's a turn-off to the right just before the bus stop before the ski lift for Chimbulak. Take it and follow along the river for 100m until a green arrow points you right towards Kok Zhailau. Follow the steep track through the forest until it flattens out into the Kok Zhailau meadow a couple of hours and a 700m ascent later.

It takes another two hours or so to ascend the steep trail that leads up to Tri Brata (Three Brothers), three craggy bluffs on the western flank of Peak Kumbel, and then on to the peak itself, from which you get tremendous views over Almaty. From here, you can go back the way you came or descend into the Almarasan Valley, to the main road, where there are umpteen shashlyk restaurants.

known as GES-2 after a small hydroelectric station nearby. The right branch heads to the settlement of Alma-Arasan (4km). The left branch follows the Bolshaya Almatinka River upstream, passing another small hydroelectric station, GES-1, after 8km, and reaching Ozero Bolshoe Almatinskoe (after a further 7km).

This picturesque turquoise lake, 1.6km long, rests in a rocky bowl at 2500m altitude, reflecting the Tian Shan mountains and the giant fir trees in its still depths. Border guards are present around the lake and climbing on the dam is forbidden. You can't get too close to the lake and the border guards will ask for and register your passport.

The best time to visit the lake is in May/June or September/October. Avoid weekends, as the place is overrun with locals. Some of the surrounding peaks require permission from the local Migration Police

(OVIR) office, while others, such as the Pik Bolshoe Almatinsky, can be climbed without. Outfitter KZ (p297) offers day trips to the lake, with the climb thrown in ($75 per person).

At the head of the Zhusalykezen Pass (3336m), 6km up to the southwest from the observatory, is Kosmostantsia – mostly wrecked buildings belonging to scientific research institutes.

🛏 Sleeping & Eating

Alpen Rose HOTEL $$
(☑ 701 888 00 00; http://alpenrose.kz; r incl breakfast weekdays/weekends 12,000/15,000T, without bathroom weekdays/weekends 9,000/12,000T; 🅿 🛜) Rooms at this pink chalet-style hotel are very plain for the price, with prehistoric furniture and cold-water showers, but its location just 4km down the road from Ozero Bolshoe Almatinskoe makes it a potentially handy base for hikers. It's open all

Day Walks from Chimbulak

In summer, it's a 3km hike (or ride in the gondola) from Chimbulak up to the Talgar Pass at 3163m, where you can see glacier-flanked Pik Komsomola (4330m) rising 3km to the south. Or you can head on up the valley road from Chimbulak. It continues upward for 8km, with some steep sections, to end at about 3500m, beneath the glaciers ringing the top of the valley. If you are going up to these high elevations it's advisable to spend a night acclimatising first.

Chimbulak to Alpen Rose hotel

This two-day route doesn't stray too close to the Kyrgyzstan border or Ozero Bolshoe Almatinskoe so is unlikely to fall foul of border guards. From Chimbulak, hike up the valley road to the Tuyuksu meteorological station (where it's possible to sleep) then ascend westward and cross the Molodyozhny Pass (3750m). Descend the scree on the west side of the pass, cross the Kumbel River (in the morning, before it rises with meltwater), cross the next ridge west and follow the Chukur (Shukyr) river down to the Alpen Rose (p308).

Big Almaty Lake & the Zhusalykezen Pass Loop

The road up to the Zhusalykezen Pass is now paved all the way, but if you prefer to do this traditionally popular route (or just part of it) on foot, it's still a fine walk – about 22km all the way from the **GES-2 bus stop** (🚌 28) to the pass, with an ascent of nearly 1900m. For acclimatisation reasons it's a good idea to give it two days, with a night en route.

You can start walking where bus 28 terminates at GES-2, or save 8km by taking a taxi to GES-1 (around 5000T from central Almaty). Here climb the metal steps beside the broad water pipe rising sharply up the valley, then walk up beside the pipe for the most direct route to Ozero Bolshoe Almatinskoe (two to three hours). From the lake, follow the road uphill to the right to the observatory (40 minutes). From the observatory it's about 2½ hours up the road to Kosmostantsia at the Zhusalykezen Pass (3336m). From here you can continue 2km north to Pik Bolshoy Almatinsky (3681m), which affords great views back down to Almaty (smog permitting); or 2km south to Pik Turist (3954m), which is easier walking though higher. Unfortunately it's no longer possible to return to Almaty by descending westward to the Prokhodnaya valley, as the route through Alma-Arasan has been blocked.

year and has a restaurant/bar with a warming fireplace. Its *banya* (public bath) is its saving grace.

Tau Dastarkhan INTERNATIONAL **$$**
(📞727 275 91 40; mains 1800-3700T; ⊙noon-midnight; 🚌28) The Tau Dastarkhan complex offers half a dozen midrange and top-end restaurants in a pretty water-garden setting; it's a good spot for a meal in the Bolshaya Almatinka valley.

ℹ Getting There & Away

From central Almaty, buses 63 and 86 run south on Furmanov and along Al-Farabi to the First President's Park. Here you can switch to bus 28, heading up the valley about every 30 minutes from 7am to 7pm, as far as the GES-2 fork. To walk from GES-2 to the lake takes four or five hours, with a rise of nearly 1100m.

A taxi from the city centre costs around 6000T one way to the lake and around 10,000T to Kosmostantsia, plus around 2000T per hour

for any waiting time; it's cheaper to go with Uber. Almost any Almaty travel agency can organise a day trip to the lake (prices start around 30,000T per carload).

SOUTHEAST KAZAKHSTAN

The region from Almaty to Lake Balkhash is known as Zhetisu (Russian: Semirechie), meaning Land of Seven Rivers. There are actually more than 800 rivers, many fed by glaciers in the mountains along the Kyrgyz and Chinese borders. It's also known as the 'Golden Triangle' for its trio of major natural attractions: Kolsai Lakes, Charyn Canyon and Altyn-Emel National Park. The three are located near one another and it's easy to organise a multiday tour of the 'Golden Triangle' from Almaty. This is one of Kazakhstan's most varied regions: landscapes vary from

Southeast Kazakhstan

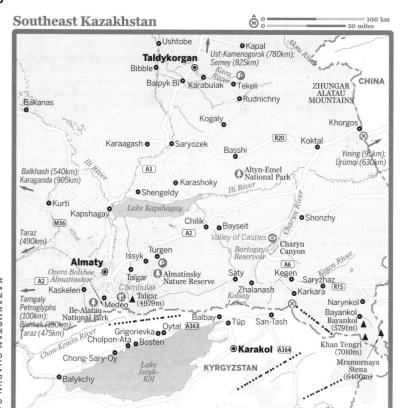

Utah-like rock formations and arid moonscapes to lush greenery, waterfalls, lakes fed by glacial meltwater and dense forest. The forbidding, snow-peaked Tian Shan range straddles the border with Kyrgyzstan, offering Kazakhstan's most challenging hiking.

Trekking in the Tian Shan range is limited to July and August. The summer months are a good time to visit the Kolsai Lakes, whereas Altyn-Emel and the Charyn Canyon are best visited in spring, early summer and September, before and after the searing heat of July and August.

Charyn Canyon
Чарынский каньон

Sculpted by the wind, water and sun over millions of years, and some 300m deep in places, **Charyn Canyon** (per person per day 750T) is Kazakhstan's answer to the Grand Canyon, with some truly spectacular and varied landscapes. There are the red rock formations of the Valley of Castles (Dolina Zamkov; the canyon's most popular destination), the canyon's most popular destination – reminiscent of Utah or Arizona, with a dirt road snaking down to the fast-flowing, glacial Charyn River. Other parts of the canyon are less explored; the intrepid roam there in 4WDs, armed with GPS. It's well worth seeking out the arid moonscape of the Yellow Canyon, or try to spot the nimble-footed mountain goats through binoculars above a particularly precipitous river bend. While many visitors dash to and from the Valley of Castles on day trips from Almaty, it really pays to stay for two or three days, camping under the stars and exploring off the beaten track.

From the car park where you pay the entry fee, a rough 3km road descends into the Valley of Castles, before ending at the

Charyn River. It's an idyllic spot, but apart from having a quick and very cold dip near the shore, swimming is dangerous, as the river is deceptively fast. April, May, June, September and October are the best months to come: in the summer it gets seriously hot.

There is only one place to stay in the Charyn Canyon – a catch-all collection of rooms, yurts and huts at **Eco-Park Charyn Canyon Tourist Complex** (☑ 701 777 20 84, 777 200 03 21; http://eco-park.kz/index_en.html; huts 7000T, rooms 10,000T, yurts for up to 8 people 40,000T; ☺ May-Sep) in the bottom of the Valley of Castles that also has an on-site restaurant. Camping wild is allowed in the canyon.

You can take a long day trip from Almaty for around 45,000T per carload through agencies such as the highly recommended Outfitter KZ (p297), plus 15,000T for English-speaking guide, or 5000T per person on weekend bus trips through the Ecotourism Information Resource Centre (p302). Eco-Park tours range from 5000T cheapies to 100,000T Jeep tours (up to three people).

Getting here by public transport is doable, but not as a day trip. Take the morning minibus from Almaty's Sayakhat bus station to Kegen, and get out at the signposted turn-off to the canyon about 190km from Almaty, just before the road starts descending into the Charyn valley. From here it's 10km east along a fairly flat dirt road to a parking area and then 3km (about one hour) down through the Valley of Castles to the river.

If you have your own vehicle, the Valley of Castles can be visited in a regular car, but you need a 4WD to visit the other parts of the canyon.

Kolsai Lakes
Кольсайские озёра

Upon seeing the three deep-blue Kolsai Lakes squeezed in between the steep, spruce-covered foothills of the Küngey Alatau, you can be forgiven for thinking that you're in Canada or Switzerland. This is some of Kazakhstan's most dramatic scenery, and these glacial bodies of water lie 110km southeast of Almaty as the crow flies, but almost 300km by road, via Chilik (Shelek) and Zhalanash. They are strung along the Kolsai River, about 1800m to 2800m high, 10km southwest of the village of Saty.

Take appropriate precautions in May and June when ticks are present, raising a risk of tick-borne encephalitis.

 Activities

As you hike through **Kolsai Lakes National Park** (per person per day 800T; ☺ 24hr), graze on wild strawberries and raspberries in summer and take frigid dips in the clear waters. The hiking trails between the lakes are steep in places and can get very muddy. You need your own wheels to reach the lakes, or go as part of a tour from Almaty.

From 1km-long Nizhny (Lower) Kolsai lake (1800m) it's a 6km hike (about three house) to Sredny (Middle) Kolsai lake (2250m) – the biggest and most beautiful. From the middle lake to the smaller Verkhny (Upper) Kolsai lake at 2800m, where the forests give way to alpine grasslands, is about 4km and three hours' walking; enquire at the entrance about permission to visit Verkhny lake, since it's part of the border zone with Kyrgyzstan.

If travelling with a 4WD, build in time to also visit cerulean **Kaiyndy Lake** (per person per day 800T; ☺ 24hr) 10km south of the village of Saty. Fed by a glacial river, it's notable for its forest of drowned spruces, the branches below the water beautifully preserved by the cold water. There's a nice little beach for bathing, and a short trail through spruce forest to the end of the lake.

In addition to hiking, it's possible to arrange a day's picturesque **horse riding** around the lower and middle lakes. If coming as part of a tour, Outfitter KZ (p297) arranges rides for 24,000/40,000T for one/three people. It's 8000T per person, plus 8000T each for the guide/interpreter and the horse driver.

Sleeping & Eating

Camping (per person 750T) wild is allowed in the lakes area and is the best way to go if you're an adventurous, independent traveller. Otherwise, choose between a set of cottages run by **Jibek Joly** (☑ 727 277 66 44; www.facebook.com/JibekJolyCompany/; Nizhny Kolsai Lake; r per person Sun-Thu 6250T, Fri & Sat 10,500T, without bathroom Sun-Thu 4550-5250T, Fri & Sat 5500-7500T; ⓟ) ✿, one of many yurts that pop up seasonally, or full-board village **homestays** (☑ 72777 2 77 18; per person incl 3 meals 3500-4000T) ✿ in Saty, with friendly **Zhanara** (☑ 72777 2 77 28, mobile 777 022 27 21; Instagram saty_saumal kolsaj; ☎) among the best, with its comfortable rooms and delicious traditional Kazakh food, including fresh river trout and homemade kumys (fermented mare's milk). There's no shower

KAZAKHSTAN KOLSAI LAKES

ISSYK KURGANS

Some 69km east of Almaty, the main road into the settlement of Esik/Issyk is lined with a dozen or so **Saka burial mounds** (museum admission 250T; ⊘ museum 9am-6pm Tue-Sun) dating back to the early Iron Age period. This is where Kazakhstan's most significant archaeological find – the Golden Man – was unearthed, and though the intricate jewellery, gold suit and headdress from the *kurgan* (burial mound) now reside in Astana, the excellent museum lets you admire copies of the exquisite finds. Frequent marshrutkas run from Almaty (400T, 45 minutes).

here, but a traditional *banya* (public bath, 1000T) instead gets you squeaky clean.

There are no restaurants in the area, though self-caterers will find small supermarkets in Saty.

❶ Getting There & Away

A shared taxi to Saty (2500T, six hours) normally leaves Almaty's Sayakhat bus station between 6am and 7am. The return journey departs from Saty at 5am. Alternatively, take a taxi to Saty for around 12,000T from Sayakhat, or find a shared taxi to Zhalanash (2500T; ask at Sayakhat a day or two before you plan to go), then take a taxi to Saty (25km) or the first lake. Taxis from Saty to the first lake cost 1000T.

Many people visit the lakes on two-night tours or multiday tours that take in the Charyn Canyon and Altyn-Emel National Park as well. Outfitter KZ (p297) arranges two-day trips that involve hiking to Kaiyndy Lake on the first day, then two of the main Kolsai Lakes on the second day for around 40,000T.

Altyn-Emel National Park
Алтын-Эмель

The 4600-sq-km Altyn-Emel National Park, stretching northeast from Lake Kapshagay, is worth visiting if you like beautiful desolation and unusual natural and archaeological attractions. Apart from the striking landscapes, such as the white, red and ochre of the fossil-rich Kakutau mountains, the park is famous for the Singing Dune, which hums like an aircraft engine when the weather is suitably windy and dry. Archaeology fans will be absorbed by the Terekty Petroglyphs and the 31 Besshatyr burial mounds – one of the biggest groups of Scythian tombs known anywhere. In spring and early autumn you can hope to see rare goitred gazelles (*zheyran*), argali sheep and wild ass (*kulan*), as well as shy Bukhara deer, lynx and Tian Shan brown bears (bring binoculars!).

Unless you're an adventurous traveller with your own wheels and good language skills, the easiest way to visit is via Almaty agencies. Typical prices from Outfitter KZ (p297) for a two-day trip range from 60,000T to 100,000T for transport (up to four people) plus around 10,000T per person for accommodation, food and park fees (less if you camp).

You need to be in a vehicle to visit the park and visitors must stick to three linear routes of between 80km and 160km (one way) each. The western route (No 2), accessed through Shengeldy village, is the easiest reached from Almaty and includes the Terekty Petroglyphs and Besshatyr burial mounds. The central (No 1) and eastern (No 3) routes are both accessed through Basshi village inside the park's northern edge and are more popular than No 2: No 1 reaches the Singing Dune, while No 3 gets into some of the park's most remote territory, in the Katutau and Aktau mountains. It's difficult to cover more than one route in one day.

Cyclists don't need a guide, but are only allowed to do the tough cycle ride to the Singing Dune and back.

Five simple hotels (glorified guesthouses, really) ranging from 2500T to 5000T per person (breakfast/lunch/dinner 500/1500/1000T) are bookable via the park offices. You can camp for free at one location on each route. The guesthouses offer full board, but the food quality is nothing to get excited about. Bring your own supplies if camping.

The park's Almaty office (p302) provides information, takes hotel bookings and can issue the necessary permits for all three routes. The **head office** (☑ 705 610 25 11; altynemel.kadr@mail.ru; Askarbeka 73) in Basshi issues permits for routes 1 and 3 only. Obligatory daily fees are 1027T per person for park entry, 200T ecological charge per vehicle, and 600T per group for a park guide.

Karkara Valley
Долина Каркара

The beautiful, broad valley of the Karkara River is an age-old summer pasture for herds from both sides of what's now the Kazakhstan–Kyrgyzstan border.

From Kegen, 250km by road east of Almaty, a scenic road heads south up Karkara Valley to Karkara village, and then on to the border post about 28km from Kegen. From May to October, this laid-back border crossing offers an alternate route between Almaty and Lake Issyk-Köl in Kyrgyzstan. Karkara Valley is the jumping off-spot for exploring Kazakhstan's tallest and wildest mountain range, the Tian Shan.

No public transport reaches the Kazakhstan–Kyrgyzstan border from either side, but a shared taxi leaves Almaty's Sayakhat bus station between 7am and 9am daily for Kegen (1500T, five hours), and from Kegen you can get up the valley to the border by hitching (although this is never entirely safe, and we don't recommend it) or by taxi (around 5000T). A taxi directly from Almaty to the border should cost around 8000T to 10,000T. You may also be able to find shared taxis to Kegen from Sayakhat. If travelling in steps, arrange transport in advance from Kyrgyzstan's Karkyra (p84) border post.

Central Tian Shan

Kazakhstan's highest and most magnificent mountains rise in the country's far southeastern corner where it meets Kyrgyzstan and China. Mt Khan Tengri (7010m) on the Kyrgyz border is widely considered the most beautiful and demanding peak in the Tian Shan, and there are many more 5000m-plus peaks around it, including Mramornaya Stena (Marble Wall, 6400m) on the Kazakh–Chinese border.

Khan Tengri is flanked by two long, west-running glaciers: the North Inylchek Glacier on its Kazakh side and the South Inylchek Glacier on its Kyrgyz side.

Mountain-tourism firm **Kan Tengri** (☑ 727 291 02 00; www.kantengri.kz; Kasteev 10, Almaty; ☉ office 9am-6pm Mon-Fri) offers a variety of exciting one- to three-week trek trips and full-scale mountaineering expeditions in this area in July and August, using base camps on the Inylchek Glaciers at altitudes of around 4000m. Access is often by helicopter, using the Karkara Valley base camp as a staging post. A typical two-week trekking trip costs around €2500. Many trips include helicopter flights around the main peaks and glacier hikes to the foot of Khan Tengri and/or Pik Pobedy on the Kyrgyzstan–China border. Note that helicopter flights are often grounded if there is poor visibility. The major peak accessible to trekkers is Karly Tau (5450m), a three-day expedition out of the North Inylchek base camp.

SOUTHERN KAZAKHSTAN

This is the most Kazakh part of Kazakhstan: Kazakhs are generally the great majority in the population, having been settled here in large numbers during Soviet collectivisation. It is also the only region of Kazakhstan that was within the sphere of the Silk Road

---

TAMGALY PETROGLYPHS

The World Heritage–listed **Tamgaly Petroglyphs** (Петроглифы Тамгалы) are the most impressive of many petroglyph groups in southeastern Kazakhstan. Set in a lushly vegetated canyon near Karabastau village, 170km northwest of Almaty, they number more than 6000 separate carvings from the Bronze Age and later, in several groups. Many Almaty agencies can organise day trips for around 35,000T per carload; Outfitter KZ (p297) has expert historian guides (English-speaking guide 20,000T) and takes customers to an additional petroglyph site not visited by other operators.

The varied images include sun-headed idols, women in childbirth, hunting scenes and a big variety of animals, and are best seen in the afternoon when most sunlight reaches them. The canyon was a ritual site for nomadic peoples from at least 3000 years ago. Don't confuse Tamgaly with Tamgaly Tas, which is a smaller and more recent petroglyph site on the Ili River.

and the settled civilisations of Transoxiana in medieval times. Chief among its varied attractions are the pristine mountain country of Aksu-Zhabagly and the splendid Islamic architecture of the Yasaui Mausoleum at Turkestan, Kazakhstan's most sacred Muslim shrine and a fine piece of Timurid architecture. For those arriving in Shymkent from the relative wilderness of Aral and Kyzylorda, the city's excellent dining scene is a feast for the starving.

Taraz   Тараз

📋 7262 / POP 362,993

Situated on the route from Tashkent and Shymkent to Bishkek and Almaty, Taraz is one of Kazakhstan's oldest cities, going back 2000 years to a fortress built in the valley. In the 11th and 12th centuries it was a wealthy Silk Road stop and capital of the Turkic Karakhanid state, but it was comprehensively levelled by Chinggis (Genghis) Khan and effectively disappeared until the existing town was founded in the 19th century, as a northern frontier town of the Kokand khanate. Today it's a pleasant, mostly Soviet-built place with leafy boulevards, a large ceremonial square surrounded by off-pink governmental buildings, one of Kazakhstan's best regional museums and a couple of medieval mausoleums.

The town has changed its name eight times; in Soviet times it was called Dzhambul, after the locally born Kazakh bard Zhambyl Zhabaev, and still appears as such on train timetables.

◉ Sights

One of Kazakhstan's best local museums, the **Taraz Regional Museum** (📋 7262 43 25 85; Tole Bi 55; 250T; ☺ 9am-6pm Tue-Sun) houses an unusually impressive collection of *balbals* (totem-like stone markers with the carved faces of honoured warriors or chieftains) and a respectable array of chunky Kazakh jewellery and a yurt lavishly decked out in the style of a century ago.

For historic Taraz, visit a wooded park on Ybyraev (700m east of Dostyk alany) that contains reconstructions of two small mausoleums. The **Karakhan Mausoleum** (Ybyraev; ☺ 9am-6pm), originally built in the 12th century, contains the tomb of a revered Karakhanid potentate known as Karakhan or Aulie-Ata (Holy Father). The **Dauitbek Mausoleum** (Ybyraev; ☺ 9am-6pm), built for a 13th-century Mongol viceroy, is said to have been built lopsided in revenge for the man's infamous cruelty. These are Islamic holy sites, so leave shoes outside.

For a taste of the bazaar atmosphere for which Taraz used to be celebrated, have a wander round busy **Shakhristan Market** (Tole Bi; ☺ 7am-7pm) across the road from the now-boarded-up Green Market.

🛏 Sleeping & Eating

Hotel Uyut   HOTEL **$**

(📋 7262 46 11 17; gostinitsa.uyut@mail.ru; Bayzak Batyr 245; s/d from 6000/8000T; ❄✳🛜; 📶1, 47) A five-minute walk from the train station, this cosy new hotel has spotless rooms, satellite TV, comfortable beds and arctic air-con which is a blessing in summer. The staff

KAZAKHSTAN TARAZ

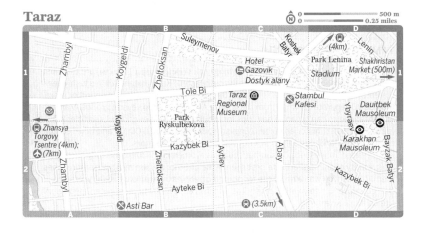

Taraz

0 — 500 m
0 — 0.25 miles

are sweet and helpful; the only downside is lack of on-site restaurant.

Hotel Gazovik
HOTEL $$
(⏰7262 45 36 81; hotel_gazovik@mail.ru; Sulemenov 7A; s/d incl breakfast from 10,500/19,000T; P✲🛜) Still the best central hotel, the 'Gasman' is a modern, 21-room affair with carpeted rooms boasting paintings, international TV channels and bath-tub. The half *lux* (semideluxe) rooms are considerably larger than the boxlike standard singles. Reception staff speak some English and there's a Russian/European restaurant on the ground floor.

Stambul Kafesi
TURKISH $
(Cafe Istanbul; ⏰7262 45 39 79; Abay 117A; mains 800-1300T; ⏰11am-11pm) Step into this clean, efficient Turkish cafe for pizzalike *pide,* shashlyk and excellent doner kebabs. Fresh pomegranate juice available sometimes.

Asti Bar
INTERNATIONAL $$
(Koygeldi 227; mains 1500-2800T; ⏰4pm-4am; 🛜) Doubling as a karaoke joint in the evenings, this restaurant is worth checking out for its unusual decor and some surprisingly imaginative dishes with an international bent.

ⓘ Getting There & Away

Taraz' **Aulie-Ata International Airport** (⏰7262 54 26 00; 🚌37), 8km from the centre off the Shymkent road, has two weekly flights to Almaty with Qazak Air (from 12,500T), daily flights to Astana with SCAT and Air Astana (from 37,000T) and one Saturday flight to Moscow with S7.

From the **bus station** (⏰7262 45 53 40; Zhambyl; 🚌46), 4km northeast of the centre, minibuses leave when full for Almaty (3500T, eight hours, 6am to 6pm), Shymkent (1200T, three hours, 8am to 8pm) and Bishkek (1500T, five hours, 8am to 8pm). There are also a few full-size buses to Almaty (3000T) leaving between 9pm and 11pm from the bus station and from Hotel Lirona. Shared taxis to Almaty (6000T, seven hours) and Bishkek (4000T, four hours) leave from outside the bus station until early evening. Shared taxis to Shymkent (2500T, 2½ hours) go until about 10pm from **Zhansaya Torgovy Tsentr** (Tauke-Khan; 🚌40), a small shopping centre 5km west of the centre.

The **train station** (⏰7262 96 01 15; Baluan Sholak; 🚌1, 47) is 4km south of the centre. At least five daily trains run to Almaty (3189T to 5433T, 7¼ to 11 hours, two to four daily) and 10 or more to Shymkent (1898T to 7003T, three to 4¼ hours, seven to 13 hours), plus four to nine a day to Turkestan, two to six daily to Aral, and at least five weekly to Astana.

WORTH A TRIP

AYSHA-BIBI & BABAZHA-KATUN MAUSOLEUMS

In Aysha-Bibi village, 16km west of Taraz, are the **tombs** (⏰24hr) of two 11th- or 12th-century women, legendary protagonists of a local Romeo and Juliet tale. The Aysha-Bibi Mausoleum, though heavily restored in 2000–2002, is probably the only authentically old building around Taraz. Made of delicate terracotta bricks in more than 50 different motifs forming lovely patterns, the building looks almost weightless.

Shymkent-bound minibuses will drop you in the village, along the main road; the mausoleums are 300m (signposted) south.

ⓘ Getting Around

You can get a taxi from the airport to Taraz' centre for aorund 1000T.

Bus fares are 65T. For a map of all bus and marshrutka routes, check out www.taraz-bus.kz. Useful routes include the following:

1 & 47 Train station to Tole Bi along Abay.

37 Westbound along Kazybek Bi to the airport.

40 Kazybek Bi (westbound), Kolbasshy Koygeldi (northbound) and Tole Bi (westbound) and on out west to Zhansaya Torgovy Tsentr.

46 Bus station to Tole Bi and Kazybek Bi in the centre.

Shymkent
Шымкент

⏰7252 / POP 885,799 / ELEV 510M

Southern Kazakhstan's most vibrant city, with bustling bazaars and a lively downtown, Shymkent (Chimkent) has more of a Central Asian buzz on its leafy streets than anywhere else in the country. The Mongols razed a minor Silk Road stop here; the Kokand khanate built a frontier fort in the 19th century; Russia took it in 1864; and the whole place was rebuilt in Soviet times. Little more than 100km from Uzbekistan's capital Tashkent, today Shymkent is a thriving trade centre that refines oil and brews two of Kazakhstan's best beers, Shymkentskoe Pivo and the Bavarian-style microbrew Sigma. Its population is about 65% Kazakh and about 14% Uzbek. It's mostly modern and brash, with a couple of good museums, but southeast of the main part of the city, across

Shymkent (Chimkent)

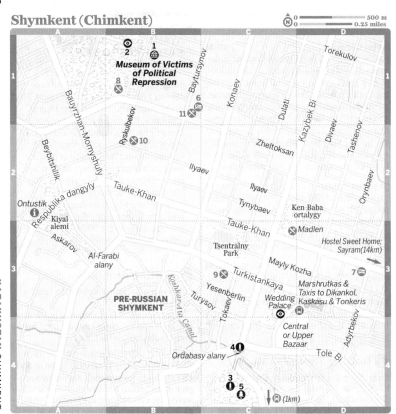

the small Koshkar-Ata canal, you'll find the few remaining streets of pre-Russian Shymkent – a quiet, village-like area of wooden houses.

◎ Sights

Of several new markets around the fringes, **Bazar Samal** (Ryskulov; ⊙8am-8pm Tue-Sun; ⊠58, 92) next to Samal bus station is the biggest and most interesting, with a particularly colourful array of rugs and textiles.

★Museum of Victims
of Political Repression   MUSEUM
(Sayasi kugyn-surgin kurbandary muzeyi; ☑7252 21 05 25; Ryskulbekov; 150T; ⊙9am-1pm & 2-6pm Mon-Fri, 9am-1pm Sat; ⊠74) This small museum documents Soviet oppression in Kazakhstan, from the dekulakisation (Soviet campaign of political repression from 1929 to 1932) and Stalinist repressions of the 1930s to the victims of Zheltoksan in Almaty in 1986. There

are some heartbreaking personal effects of ALZhIR (p335) inmates in the small room adjoining the main hall, and photos of victims surround a powerful central sculpture showing freedom-striving figures restrained by a Soviet banner, their bodies pierced by a broken Communist star. Booklet (200T), partly in English, may be available.

Across the street in Abay Park two tall concrete pillars lean on each other above an eternal flame in the central monument of **Alleya Slavy** (Alley of Glory; Abay Park; ⊠74), and the alley is lined with plaques bearing the names of the more than 140,000 people from the south Kazakhstan region who lost their lives during WWII. A simple memorial consisting of an army helmet honours Kazakh servicemen who died in Afghanistan.

Tauelsizdik sayabagy   PARK
(Independence Park; Kabanbay batyr; ⊠27) Tauelsizdik sayabagy, accessed by footbridge from the tall, Mother Earth–topped Inde-

Shymkent (Chimkent)

pendence Monument (Ordabasy alany; 🖵 27, 58), was inaugurated in 2011 for the 20th anniversary of Kazakhstan's independence. It focuses on Ramizder alany (Symbols Sq) which contains assorted national and ethnic-Kazakh symbols designed to inspire feelings of national unity, dominated by the tall **Altyn Shanyrak** (Golden Shanyrak; 🖵 27) monument, representing the central roof opening of a yurt.

**Regional Museum of
Southern Kazakhstan**   MUSEUM
(📞 7252 47 60 01; http://ukomuseum.kz; Baydibek Bi 118/2; 200T; ◷ 10am-7pm Tue-Sun; 🖵 71) In its shiny new quarters on the northern outskirts of the city, this regional museum has well-presented, trilingual displays on local geology, Iron Age burial mounds (check out the human bones buried in a large clay pot) and archaeological finds from famous sites such as Otrar (silver jewellery) and Sayran (13th-century Chinese vase). There's an excellent ethnography section, with elaborate horse tackle and shamanistic implements, a splendid collection of 19th-century heavy silver jewellery, and some fine traditional musical instruments.

🛏 Sleeping & Eating

★ Hostel Sweet Home   HOSTEL $
(📞 705 716 86 38; Shalgyndy 18; dm/d 4320/7000T; ⊕ 🛜; 🖵 26) With its individually decorated rooms and friendly, incredibly helpful, English-speaking host Albina, this hostel gets rave reviews from backpackers. The attention to detail, the tranquil location, the summer terrace and the superclean, airy doubles and dorm are all pluses. Albina can pick you up from the train station and bus 26 stops three blocks away.

ShymCity Hostel   HOSTEL $
(📞 778 251 38 05; www.facebook.com/shymcity/; Tauke-Khan 72; d/q 7000/12,000T; ⊕ 🛜 🖵; 🖵 5, 26, 74) A house converted into a hostel, this place is popular with international backpackers, and justifiably so. The owner speaks English and is very helpful when it comes to making onward travel arrangements, there are three friendly cats and the garden with a small pool is a tranquil space in which to chill. Our one quibble is with the uncomfortable mattresses.

★ Orbita
Boutique Hotel   BOUTIQUE HOTEL $$
(📞 7252 40 72 71; http://orbitahotel.kz; Abay dangyly 27; s/d incl breakfast from 18,000/22,000T; 🅿 ⊕ ✳ 🛜; 🖵 20, 26, 74) This little gem 2km west of the centre has just a handful of rooms, all individually and pleasingly designed with features like half-timbering and exposed brick – one even has an African theme – and equipped with tea/coffee makers and well-stocked minibars. Young, attentive receptionists, fluent in English, inhabit the conservatory-like upstairs lobby. Price includes one of the best breakfasts in Kazakhstan.

★ Rixos Khadisha
Shymkent   DESIGN HOTEL $$$
(📞 725 261 01 01; http://khadishashymkent.rixos.com/; Zheltoksan 17; s/d/ste from €108/127/539; 🅿 ⊕ ✳ 🛜 🖵; 🖵 27, 74) This showstopper five-star hotel is Shymkent's answer to the Ritz. Expect plenty of marble, a stunning atrium with soaring golden eagles and Golden Man statues, friendly multilingual service that's not stuffy, and splendid rooms – all plush fabrics and chandeliers – that put you in mind of 19th-century Europe. Two superb restaurants, two bars and spa seal the deal.

Madlen   CAFE $
(📞 7252 21 06 91; http://madlen.kz; Ilyaev 17; dishes 400-900T; ◷ 9am-midnight; 🛜; 🖵 12, 26, 74) Good cafe with excellent breakfasts (stuffed *bliny*, rice porridge, omelettes), pasta and pizza dishes, tasty cakes, croissants and good coffee, and a leafy pavement terrace too.

DON'T MISS

NAVRUS IN SHYMKENT

Shymkent's **Navrus** (Nauryz) celebrations, on 22 March, are among the biggest in the country. *Kokpar* (local traditional polo played with a goat carcass), horse races, *audaryspak* (horseback wrestling) and *kyz kuu* (a boy-girl horseback chase) all happen at the Ippodrom (Hippodrome) on the northern edge of the city.

Ladushki   CAFETERIA **$**

(☑ 7252 54 54 05; www.ladushki.kz; Tokaev 27; items 80-300T; ⊙ 8am-9pm; ☑ 43) With decor like a kids' restaurant, this is a central branch of a popular chain of good-value cafeterias where you can get a serve of *manty* (steamed dumplings) or *bliny*, or two pastries and a coffee, for under 400T.

★**Kok-Saray**   UZBEK **$$**

(☑ 7252 43 22 30; Tauke-Khan 121; mains 900-1800T; ⊙ 11am-midnight; 🛜 🅿; ☑ 26, 74) Atmospheric multiroomed Kok-Saray, with carved-wood pillars, murals and an airy front terrace, serves the best Uzbek food in town (and in Kazakhstan, claim aficionados). Don't miss the perfect *plov* (*tashkentsky* with white rice, *andizhansky* with black) or the superb *samsas* (samosas), which include a delicious pumpkin (*s tykvoe*) variety (in autumn only). You can't miss its bright lights after dark.

Bar Villa   INTERNATIONAL **$$**

(☑ 701 581 06 59; Zheltoksan 9/2; mains 1800-3500T; ⊙ noon-midnight; 🛜; ☑ 74) Overlooking the park behind Kinoteatr Kakakhstan, Bar Villa's two levels of mostly sofa seating have big windows to enjoy the leafy view, and there's a three-level garden terrace for summer. The well-prepared fare focuses on pasta, salads and grills including several sausage varieties, and an excellent picture menu makes up for the lack of an English-language version.

★**Olivia**   ITALIAN **$$$**

(☑ 725 261 01 01; http://khadishashymkent.rixos.com; Rixos Khadisha Shymkent Hotel, Zheltoksan 17; mains 2800-6500T; ⊙ 6pm-midnight; ❄🛜🅿; ☑ 27, 74) Visually a sultry cross between a stone-walled cellar and a library, with plenty of books on art and design on surrounding shelves, this gorgeous restaurant serves beautifully executed pasta dishes, risottos

and grilled meats from a short but sweet menu put together by the Michelin-starred chef. An excellent Euro-centric wine list and professional service make this place hard to fault.

ⓘ Information

Exchange offices at the train station and on Tauke-Khan in the centre (between Kazybek Bi and Dulati) trade Uzbek, Kyrgyz and Russian cash.

Ontustik (☑ 7252 40 07 00; www.ontustik-travel.kz; Respublika dangyly; ⊙ 9am-6pm Mon-Sat; ☑ 26, 74) Helpful tourist office with info on the city, maps, and contact information of local tour operators. English spoken.

ⓘ Getting There & Away

AIR

From the **airport** (☑ 7252 45 50 31; www.air-server.kz; ☑ 12), 10km northwest of the centre, there are two to four daily flights with Air Astana or SCAT to Almaty (from 14,000T), two or three daily flights to Astana with SCAT and Qazaq Air (from 21,700T), plus two or three weekly with SCAT to Aktau (30,700T), three weekly Moscow flights with SCAT (57,400T) and three weekly Istanbul flights with SCAT and Atlas Global (from 74,300T).

BUS, VAN & TAXI

From the main **Avtovokzal Samal** (☑ 7252 45 12 41; http://samal.avokzal.kz; Ryskulov; ☑ 40, 58, 92), 4km north of the centre, there are departures to Almaty (2500T to 4000T, 11 hours, six daily) via Taraz, leaving between 6.30pm and 8.30pm; and Kyzylorda (1500T to 2000T, eight hours, two daily) via Turkestan (700T). Book tickets in advance.

For Taraz, minibuses (1000T, three hours) depart Samal when full from around 8am to 7pm, and shared taxis (2500T) go from just outside Samal's entrance. Samal also has minibuses running to Turkestan (1200T, 2½ hours).

For Chernyaevka on the Uzbek border, minibuses (1000T, two hours) leave Samal when full between 9am and 6pm; less frequently in the afternoon. For Bishkek there's at least one bus (2500T, eight hours) leaving at 6.30pm or later from Samal.

Avtovokzal Koktem (☑ 7252 57 15 93; cnr Zhibek Zholy & Aymautov; ☑ 26, 27), 3km northeast of the centre, also has buses serving Almaty (2500T to 4000T, 11 hours), leaving between 7pm and 7.30pm.

ⓘ Getting Around

Taxis to the centre cost 1000T to 1300T from the airport and 500T to 600T from **Samal**

TRAINS FROM SHYMKENT

From the **train station** (☎ 7252 95 21 20; Kabanbay Batyr; ☐ 5, 12, 71), 1.5km southeast of Ordabasy alany, trains run to the following destinations:

DESTINATION	COST (T) 2ND/3RD CLASS	FREQUENCY	TIME (HR)
Aktau (Mangyshlak)	8428/5402	5 weekly	46
Aktobe	21,151/14,138	3 weekly	27¼-31½
Almaty	6579/2709	3-5 daily	10½-17¼
Aral	5308/3432	1-5 daily	16¾-19¾
Astana	6972/4492	5-10 weekly	23¾-25¾
Kyzylorda	2822/1839	6-8 daily	6½-11½
Moscow	70,850/53,841	2 weekly	61¾
Taraz	1898/1256	10-13 daily	3½-5½
Tashkent	7304/2880	2 weekly	5¾
Turkestan	1991/1315	7-10 daily	3½-4¼

(p318) or Ayna (cnr Zhibek Zholy & Aymautov, 3km northeast of the centre) bus stations. In the city, almost any taxi will take you anywhere for 300T to 400T. Smartphone users can download the hugely useful 2gis.ru app that shows all the transport routes from every bus stop in the city.

Some useful buses (fare 70T; all running both directions along their routes):

5 Train station, Ordabasy alany, Tashenov, Tauke-Khan, Respublika dangyly.

12 Airport, Tauke-Khan, Kazybek Bi, Ordabasy alany, train station.

19 Ordabasy alany, Avtovokzal Koktem.

69 Ordabasy alany, Kazybek Bi, Tauke-Khan, Baytursynuly, Avtovokzal Samal.

Around Shymkent

Sayram   Сайрам

POP 38,000

The busy little town of Sayram 14km east of Shymkent, was a Silk Road stop long before Shymkent existed and dates back possibly 3000 years. Kozha Akhmed Yasaui (the first great Turkic Muslim holy man) was born here and Sayram's several notable mausoleums are a stop for many pilgrims en route to Yasaui's mausoleum at Turkestan. Sayram's population today is almost entirely Uzbek.

Most of Sayram's main monuments can be seen in a walk of about 1½ hours starting from the town's central traffic lights. Take the eastern (slightly uphill) street, Amir Temur, and then the first (narrow) street on the right after 300m. About 120m along, in a fenced field on your right, is **Kydyra Minaret** (Khyzyr Munarasy; ⊙9am-5pm) FREE. Return to the central crossroads and continue

straight ahead, passing the bazaar on your left. Just after the bazaar, on the right, is the 13th-century Karashash-Ana Mausoleum. Continue 250m, passing the modern Friday Mosque on your right, to the large Mirali Bobo Mausoleum.

Now turn back towards the central crossroads but turn into the first street on the left, marked Botbay Ata Kesenesi. The high bank on your right along here is part of the old city walls. Fork right after 180m, and the street ends at a larger street, Yusuf Sayrami. To your right is a double-arched gate erected in 1999 for Sayram's official 3000th birthday. Head left along the street and in 90m you'll reach a green and yellow sign marking the spot where, according to legend, Kozha Akhmed Yasaui's mentor Aristan Bab handed him a sacred persimmon once received by Aristan Bab from the Prophet Mohammed (notwithstanding the five-century gap between the lives of the Prophet Mohammed and Akhmed Yasaui). About 250m past this spot, turn left into a cemetery to the three-domed Abdul-Aziz Baba Mausoleum.

Several central *chaikhanas* (teahouses) serve inexpensive shashlyk, tea, *lavash* (Turkish flat bread), soups and *plov* (pilaf).

Absurdly overcrowded marshrutkas to Sayram (110T, 40 minutes) leave Shymkent's Ayna bus station about every 15 minutes until around 7pm. Alternatively, a round-trip taxi with waiting time should cost around 5000T.

Sayram-Ugam National Park

This mountainous park abutting the Uzbek border immediately southwest of the

Aksu-Zhabagly reserve is less well known than its neighbour, but offers similar attractions and is generally cheaper to visit. A community-tourism program provides homestays in the villages of Kaskasu, Dikankol and Tonkeris, in beautiful foothill country where grasslands meet wooded foothills, and in the main access town Lenger. The park entrance fee is 500T per person per day.

Good outings include horse or 4WD trips to the western end of the spectacular Aksu Canyon from Tonkeris, foot or horse day trips into Kaskasu Canyon from pretty Kaskasu village, and the highlight two-to-three-day camping trip by foot or horse to beautiful Susingen Lake from Kaskasu or Dikankol.

It's best to make contact in advance with the community tourism organisation **Ugam Public Association** (☑director 701 222 03 28, director's English-speaking son Askar 701 111 81 92, office 75247 6 29 92; www.ugam.kz; Tole Bi, Lenger; ☺9am-6pm Mon-Fri) 🖉, directed by ex-air-force pilot Alikhan Abdeshev. The office, down a lane beside the Ostanovka Voenkomat bus stop in Lenger, is about 15 minutes' walk from Lenger bus station. Community-tourism prices are 3000T per day for a guide, 1500T per hour for an English translator, 3000T per day per horse. Ecotourism Information Resource Centre (p302) in Almaty can also help you book your trip.

Local homestays (with meals 5000T) have comfortable beds in clean rooms, and traditional *banyas* (public baths), and serve good local food. Except at Lenger, toilets are outside. At Kaskasu and Lenger you can sleep in yurts (5800T per person, including full board). Camping (4000T per person including full board) is also possible.

Lenger is 27km southeast of Shymkent; Dikankol is 47km, Kaskasu is 57km and Tonkeris is 70km. Ugam Public Association offers car transfers for 60T per kilometre. Marshrutkas (250T, 45 minutes), shared taxis (300T) and much slower buses to Lenger leave frequently (7am to 6pm) from the Voenkomat bus stop on Tole Bi in Shymkent. For Dikankol, Kaskasu and Tonkeris, marshrutkas (600T, one to 1½ hours, every two to three hours), buses (around 350T, 1½ to two hours, three times daily) and occasional shared taxis go from Tashenov near Shymkent's Central Bazaar.

Shared taxis run to Kaskasu from Lenger's market.

Aksu-Zhabagly

This beautiful 1319-sq-km patch of green valleys, rushing rivers, snowcapped peaks and high-level glaciers is the oldest (1926) and one of the most enjoyable of Kazakhstan's nature reserves. Sitting at the west end of the Talassky Alatau (the most northwesterly spur of the Tian Shan), it stretches from the steppe at about 1200m up to 4239m at Pik Sayram. The main access point is Zhabagly village, 70km east of Shymkent as the crow flies.

The diversity of life here, where mountains meet steppe, is great for botanists, birders and nature lovers. Some of Kazakhstan's best nature guides live locally, making this a good base for visiting other regional attractions including the Karatau mountains (rich in endemic plants), steppe lakes, deserts and historical/cultural sites such as Turkestan and Otrar.

Wildlife you may see includes ibexes, argali sheep, red marmots, paradise flycatchers, golden eagles, Tian Shan brown bears and the elusive snow leopard.

You can visit at any time, but the best weather is from April to September. For birders and botanists, April and May are the favourites. The famous, bright-red Greig's tulip is one of over 1300 flowering plants in the reserve. It dots the alpine meadows, and is quite common even in villages, from mid-April to early May. Spring is also the best time to spot the Tian Shan brown bears.

⊙ Sights & Activities

From Zhabagly village it's 6km southeast to the nearest reserve entrance, then 6km (about 1½ hours' walk) to Kshi-Kaindy, a mountain refuge near a waterfall at 1700m, then a further 6km to Ulken-Kaindy, a second refuge. From Ulken-Kaindy it's 10km to a group of some 2000 stones with petroglyphs up to 900 years old, below a glacier descending from the 3800m peak Kaskabulak. A good way to visit these sites is by horse, spending two nights at Ulken-Kaindy. More demanding treks will take you over 3500m passes with nights spent in caves. Another great spot is the 300m-deep Aksu Canyon at the reserve's western extremity, a 25km drive from Zhabagly village.

Obligatory daily fees for entering the **Aksu-Zhabagly reserve** (http://aksu-jabagly.kz) are 6500T per person, plus 9500T per group for an accompanying ranger. The excellent local

SAURAN

Some 48km northwest of Turkestan (p322) stand the best-preserved and most atmospheric **ruins** (⊙24hr) FREE of all the many ruined Silk Road cities in the Syr-Darya valley. Its circuit of baked-earth walls, plus remains of some bastions, residential buildings and gates, still stand despite conquerors and the elements. You're likely to have the ruins all to yourself. A taxi from Turkestan should cost around 8000T round trip: ask for Krepost (Fortress) Sauran to distinguish it from Sauran village.

Sauran was capital of the Mongol White Horde in the 14th century, and 16th-century writers described it as a 'pleasant' and 'cheerful' city with two high minarets and a sophisticated water-supply system.

Sauran is visible as a long, low mound about 2.5km southwest from the Turkestan–Kyzylorda highway, some 50km out of Turkestan and about 13km past the village of Sauran. Closer up, the ruins loom like something out of *The Lord of the Rings* (but remember: this is Sauran, not Sauron).

accommodation options will deal with these for you and offer a range of well-run trips in the reserve and further afield – their websites are great information sources. Typical local trip prices include an English-speaking guide 28,500T per day; horse 3000T per hour or 19,000T to the Kshi-Kaindy waterfall; three-passenger 4WD vehicle to Aksu Canyon and back 51,000T; camping in the reserve including meals 7500T per person.

🛏 Sleeping & Eating

There are several friendly guesthouses/homestays, which also provide delicious home-cooked meals and can arrange transport and tours. It's best to contact these places in advance to give them time to make plans for your visit.

English-speaking **Misha Norets** (✆701 693 15 47; norets_1969@mail.ru; Satpaev 25/2, Tulkibas; per person with 3 meals 10,000T; P🐕🛜) offers homestay accommodation with good meals in his simple family home in Tulkibas, 18km west of Zhabagly village. He charges a guiding fee of 15,000T per day, per group.

Run by a Kazakh-Dutch family, **Turbaza Ruslan** (✆701 189 52 83; www.zhabagly.com; Abay 24, Zhabagly; r 12,000T, 3 meals per person 7000T; 🛜) has six good rooms at their main house in the village, and four twin-bed rooms in a lovely property on the edge of the nature reserve, 7km from the village (1000T per car, or two to three hours' walk).

Cosy **Zhenja & Lyuda's Boarding House** (Dom Zheni i Lyudy; ✆701 717 58 51, 72538 5 55 84; www.aksuinn.com; Abay 36, Zhabagly; per person with 3 meals 28,500T; P🐕🛜) on Zhabagly's main street has rooms with two comfy single beds and private bathroom, and vegetarian meals can be arranged.

NGO **Wild Nature** (Dikaya Priroda; ✆72538 5 56 86, 775 793 22 46; www.wildnature-kz. narod.ru; Taldybulak 14, Zhabagly; Kazakh-style homestay with 2 meals per person 24,000T, simple homestay without meals per person 7600T, camping per person 2000T) 🕊 runs one of Kazakhstan's longest-running community tourism programs, with comfortable homestays in houses with hot showers and good local meals. A camping option is available for budget travellers. Wild Nature director Svetlana is a highly knowledgable biologist and great guide who speaks excellent English, and offers a variety of short local trips and longer nature-focused trips.

ℹ Getting There & Away

Marshrutkas to Zhabagly village (450T, two hours) leave Shymkent's Ayna bus station around 11am. Alternatively, there are marshrutkas about every half-hour, 7.30am to 3pm, from Ayna to Turar-Ryskulov (also called Turarkent or Vanovka; 400T, 1½ hours) on the Taraz highway, where you can get a taxi from the market for the 20km trip to Zhabagly (250/1000T shared/whole).

From Shymkent, up to 11 trains per day stop at Tulkibas (from 1553T, 1¾ to two hours). From Almaty (via Taraz), there are three or four trains daily (from 3800T, 9¼ to 15 hours). Wild Nature (p321) offers pick-ups from both Turarkent and the Tulkibas railway station for 8000T for up to three people. It's possible to arrange a pick-up for up to four people from Shymkent (35,400T) and Taraz (40,500T).

Turkestan Туркестан

🎣 72533 / POP 159,634

At Turkestan stands Kazakhstan's greatest architectural monument and most important pilgrimage site: the mausoleum of Kozha Akhmed Yasaui. It was built by Timur (Tamarlane; 1336–1405) in the late 14th century on a grand scale comparable with his magnificent creations in Samarkand, and has no rivals in Kazakhstan for human-made beauty.

Turkestan was already an important trade and religious centre when the revered Sufi teacher and mystical poet Kozha Akhmed Yasaui came to live here in the 12th century. Yasaui was born at Sayram, probably in 1103, underwent ascetic Sufi training in Bukhara, then lived in Turkestan, dying here about 1166. He founded the Yasauia Sufi order and had the gift of communicating his understanding to ordinary people through poems and sermons in a Turkic vernacular, a major reason for his enduring popularity.

Turkestan makes an ideal base for day trips to Sauran and Otrar.

◉ Sights

★ **Yasaui Mausoleum** MAUSOLEUM
(foreigner/local 500/200T, photo inside 500T; ⊙ 7am-9pm May-Sep, 9am-1pm & 2-6pm rest of year) This astoundingly beautiful, tiled mausoleum with a turquoise dome is home to Kozha Akhmed Yasaui. The main chamber is capped with an 18m-wide dome, above a vast, 2000kg, metal *kazan* (cauldron) for holy water, given by Timur, who had the tomb built in the 14th century. Yasaui's tomb lies behind an ornate wooden door at the end of the main chamber: you can view it through grilles from corridors on either side.

The right-hand corridor contains the tomb of Abylay Khan, leader of Kazakh resistance to the Zhungars in the 18th century. Off the main chamber's far left corner is the mausoleum's carpeted mosque, with a beautifully tiled mihrab (Mecca-facing niche). Except in the mosque, visitors to the mausoleum don't usually remove shoes though women normally wear headscarves (available at the entrance).

The glorious blue, turquoise and white tiling on the outside of the building is the highlight for most and merits close inspection. Note the particularly lovely fluted rear dome, above Yasaui's tomb chamber.

Yasaui's original small tomb was already a place of pilgrimage before Timur ordered a far grander mausoleum built here in the 1390s. Timur died before it was completed and the main facade was left unfinished – today it remains bare of the beautiful tilework that adorns the rest of the building, with scaffolding poles still protruding.

Inside the attractive grounds of the Yasaui Mausoleum are several smaller monuments. Directly south of the main structure are the 19th-century **Friday Mosque** (Zhuma meshiti; ⊙ 7am-9pm) – the wooden column in the corner and wall outside of which allegedly date back to Yasaui's time – and the 12th- to 15th-century **Hilvet semi-underground mosque** (⊙ 9am-7pm) FREE, with the cell to which Kozha Akhmed Yasaui is said to have withdrawn towards the end of his life and a 14th-century coverlet

Turkestan

from his tomb. Southeast of the main mausoleum, the small mausoleum of Rabigha-Sultan Begum with a tiled turquoise dome is actually a replica of the 15th-century original (which was torn down in 1898). Rabigha-Sultan Begum was a great-granddaughter of Timur whose husband, Abylkayyr Khan, a 15th-century leader of the then-nomadic Uzbeks, put the finishing touches to the structure of the Yasaui Mausoleum's facade.

Just near the entrance to the grounds, outside the historical defensive wall, is a small **History Museum** (with ticket to the Yasaui Mausoleum free; ⊘9am-1pm & 3-6pm) with some English-language labeling.

Historical-Cultural-Ethnographic Centre   MUSEUM
(Tarikhi-Madeni-Etnografiyalyk Ortalyk; Tauke Khan; 300T; ⊘9am-7pm) This big, proud new museum has three floors of colourful exhibits on regional history, from prehistoric petroglyphs and household implements of the Kazakh nomads to the obligatory Nazarbayev homage on the top floor. Much of the material is paintings, maps and dioramas, since the collection of actual artefacts is sparse before the 19th century. Explanatory information is in Kazakh only, but free tours in English are available.

🛏 Sleeping & Eating

⭐**Hotel Edem**   HOTEL $
(☑72533 3 35 71; http://edemhotel.kz/index2.html; Sultanbek Kozhanov 6A; r incl breakfast 7500-14,500T; ❄❅❈) One of the two best sleeping options, the Edem has pleasant rooms with wood-and-wrought-iron beds and cane furnishings. Thoughtful touches like lamps reachable from your bed are combined with helpful management. Also here is the town's best **restaurant** (mains 900-2700T; ⊘8am-midnight; ❈) serving good shashlyk, sushi, pasta, salads and beer, with a courtyard garden that turns into Turkestan's most popular nightspot in summer. Tours to Sauran and Otrar arranged.

Around the corner from Hotel Edem is a tiny **nameless restaurant** (Amir Temir; mains from 350T; ⊘noon-10pm) in a hole-in-the-wall, serving *plov* (pilaf) and grilled meats, cooked in a clay oven. Your nose will lead you there.

Hotel Khanaka   HOTEL $$
(☑72533 59 1 59; www.khanakahotel.kz; Bayburt 3a; s/d 15,000/18,000T; ❄❅❈❆) Turkestan's first upmarket offering, new in 2017, has spotless rooms and more perks than any other hotel in town: flat-screen TVs, plunge pool, sauna, gym... Staff are friendly and speak some English, and the on-site restaurant looks encouraging.

ℹ Information

There are Visa, MasterCard and Maestro ATMs in the gable-roofed building opposite Hotel Yassy on Tauke Khan. For currency exchange, enquire at **Kazkom** (Tauke Khan 371; ⊘9am-noon & 2-6pm Mon-Fri).

ℹ Getting There & Around

Two bus/minibus terminals are strung close together along Tauke Khan 2km west of the Yasaui Mausoleum. Vehicles to Shymkent leave when full and are most frequent before 10am. **Avtovokzal Merey** (Tauke Khan), first up on the left, has minibuses to Shymkent (600T, 2½ hours) and some services to Taraz and Almaty. **Avtovokzal Altyn Orda** (Tauke Khan), almost opposite, has more comfortable Shymkent vans (900T), a bus to Bishkek (2800T, 11 hours) at 6pm, and comfortable buses to Taraz (1500T), Shymkent (500T) and Almaty (4500T).

Coming by road from Shymkent, you can disembark your minibus when the mausoleum looms into view on your left as you enter Turkestan.

Marshrutkas 2 and 10 (50T) run between Sultanbek Kozhanov and the bus and train stations.

The **train station** (Tauke Khan), at the far end of Tauke Khan, is 3km past the bus stations. Train services include:

DESTINATION	COST (T)	FREQUENCY	TIME (HR)
Aktobe	19,024	Tue & Thu	23¼
Almaty	3432-11,535	1-4 daily	13½-21
Aral	3836-12,626	3-5 daily	12¾-15¼
Bishkek	11,978	Tue & Sun	16
Kyzylorda	2088-3416	6-10 daily	3½-7½
Shymkent	1758-2837	6-10 daily	2¾-3¾
Tashkent	10,690	daily	8½

Otrar   Отрар

About 44km south of Turkestan lie the ruins of Otrar, a once-prosperous Silk Road town that brought Chinggis (Genghis) Khan to Central Asia. Much of the rest of Asia and

Europe might have been spared Mongol carnage if Otrar's Khorezmshah governor had not had Chinggis Khan's merchant-envoys murdered here in 1218. As retribution, the following year Chinggis' forces mercilessly trashed Otrar, which until then had been one of the most important Silk Road towns in the fertile Syr-Darya valley. It was rebuilt afterwards but eventually abandoned around 1700 after being trashed again by the Zhungars (Oyrats). Today it's just a large dusty mound, known as **Otyrar-Tobe** (200T; ⊙8am-dusk; FREE), 4km northeast of the small town of Bayaldir, worth visiting for the numerous archaeological finds that have been uncovered here. Technically there's an entry fee but it is rarely collected.

In its heyday Otrar spread over nearly 10 times the area of the mound itself. Archaeologists have exposed a now unsympathetically reconstructed bastion, piece of city wall, the pillar stumps of the main mosque, low walls of the 14th-century Palace of Berdibek (where another great pillager, Timur, died, en route to conquer China, in 1405), a few residential areas and a bathhouse. The **Otrar Museum** (⌨72544 2 11 50; Zhibek Zholy 1; T200; ⊙9am-6pm) in Shauildir village is a good introduction to the ruins.

Several kilometers west of Otyrar-Tobe is the mausoleum of **Aristan Bab** (200T; ⊙dawn-dusk), a religious mystic and early mentor of Kozha Akhmed Yasaui whose tomb pilgrims should visit before that of Yasaui in Turkestan. Much of the existing domed, brick building dates from 1907, though the tomb has been here since the 12th century. Heed the rules of good tombside conduct and refrain from 'slaughtering at the tomb' and 'tightening fabric on trees'.

The easiest way to visit is by hiring a driver/taxi in Turkestan; it costs around 8000T round trip to visit the two sites.

It's also possible to visit from Shymkent, though it's considerably further away. Minibuses (800T, 2½ hours) to Shauildir leave about hourly, 7am to 6pm, from Shymkent's Samal bus station. Shared taxis from Samal cost 1200T.

There's no direct public transport between Shauildir and Turkestan, but a one-way taxi costs about 4000T including an hour's stop at Otyrar-Tobe.

A taxi from Shauildir to Otyrar-Tobe, Aristan-Bab and back shouldn't cost more than 2500T.

Kyzylorda   Қызылорда

⌨7242227,499 / POP 227,499

On the Syr-Darya 290km northwest of Turkestan, Kyzylorda became capital of Soviet Kazakhstan in 1925 but was replaced by cooler Almaty when the Turksib railway reached there in 1929. Oil and gas operations in the South Turgay Basin, mainly Chinese-owned, underpin its economy today. The most ethnically Kazakh of Kazakhstan's regional capitals, Kyzylorda is a charmless town that's brutally hot in summer; its most attractive feature are the heroic Soviet-era mosaics on the side of the train-station building. Kyzylorda's chief role for most travellers is as a staging post for Aral or Baykonur.

The **Regional Museum** (⌨7242 27 62 74; Auezov 20; foreigner/local 500/200T; ⊙9am-1pm & 3-7pm Tue-Sun) traces the history of the region, from archaeological finds from the nearby Silk Road settlement of Syganak and the ecological devastation wreaked on the Aral Sea, to the 15th-century khanates (look out for the dragon-adorned Dzhungar helmet), Kyzylorda's brief stint as the capital of Soviet Kazakhstan, and renowned local musicians, writers and Olympic champions. Labelling mostly in Kazakh makes the displays a little less engaging, however.

There are several hotels scattered around the city centre that'll do in a pinch. The **Hotel Kayr** (⌨7242 27 67 97; Aytbaeva 29; s/d 9500/12,000T, without bathroom 7000/7500T incl breakfast; ⊕※🛜), 1km southeast of the train station, is at the cheap end of the price scale by Kyzylorda standards and has well-kept, comfy rooms. Shared bathrooms are good and clean though the rooms that go with them are smallish.

Of the several decent restaurants serving Kazakh, Uzbek and Turkish dishes, **Registan** (⌨7242 27 25 59; Korkyt-Ata 18; mains 800-1800T; ⊙10am-2am; 🛜) does a reliable job and serves good draught beer too.

❶ Getting There & Around

From the **airport** (⌨702 565 77 27; http://aeroport.kz/city/kyzylorda), 21km from the city, there are one or two flights daily with Air Astana and Bek Air to Almaty (from 30,900T) and Astana (from 36,500T), as well as weekly flights to Karaganda (from 26,500T) with SCAT.

The **train station** (Auelbekov), on the northern edge of the centre, has departures to Aral (2397T to 3032T, 7¼ to 8¼ hours, two to five daily), as well as five to nine departures to Turk-

BAYKONUR COSMODROME

The Baykonur Cosmodrome, a 6717-sq-km area of semidesert about 250km northwest of Kyzylorda, has been the launch site for all Soviet and Russian manned space flights since Yury Gagarin, the first human in space, was lobbed up here in 1961. In fact the cosmodrome is 300km southwest of the original town of Baykonur, but the USSR told the International Aeronautical Federation that Gagarin's launch point was Baykonur, and that name also stuck to the real site. The military town built to guard and service the cosmodrome, formerly called Leninsk, has now acquired the name Baykonur too. The Kyzylorda–Aral road and railway pass between the town and the cosmodrome, some of whose installations are visible (the whole site stretches about 75km north). The town's train station is called Toretam (Russian: Tyuratam).

Since the collapse of the USSR, Kazakhstan has leased the cosmodrome and town to Russia until 2050. Baykonur today has nine launch complexes and sends up astronauts from many countries, including space tourists, as well as unmanned spacecraft. Following the end of the USA's space-shuttle program in 2010, it's the world's only launch centre for human space flight apart from China's Jiuquan.

Visitors to the cosmodrome and Baykonur town require advance permission from the Russian space agency, Roscosmos (www.roscosmos.ru), and the only practicable way in is through a well-connected travel agency. Among the few agencies offering visits on a regular basis are Almaty-based Silk Road Adventures (p297) and Karaganda-based Nomadic Travel Kazakhstan (p347). Three-day trips, not including flights to Kyzylorda, cost 16,000T/30,000/75,000T for one/three/five people. These include visits to the actual cosmodrome, the cosmonaut museum and Gagarin's memorial house. Tours that take in actual rocket launches cost more. Launch dates are known three to six months ahead and the paperwork needs to be submitted at least two months in advance. Note that rocket launches are often cancelled at the last minute if the weather is unfavourable for take-off, but you don't get your money back.

estan (2088T to 7548T, 3¾ to 5¾ hours) and Shymkent (2588T to 3579T, seven to 10 hours).

A bus to Aral (1500T, nine hours) leaves at 10pm from about June to September only, from the southeast corner of the square in front of the train station. Three daily buses to Turkestan (1200T, five hours) and Shymkent (1500T to 2000T, eight hours) and one to Almaty (5000T, 20 hours), plus marshrutkas to Turkestan (1400T) and Shymkent (1800T), go from the shabby **Avtovokzal Saltanat** (☎ 7242 23 52 08; Bokeykhan 64), 3.5km south of the centre. Bus 1 (65T) travels slowly between the train station and Avtovokzal Saltanat via the city centre.

Aral   Арал

☎ 72433 / POP 32,097

Four decades ago, Aral (Aralsk), 450km northwest of Kyzylorda, was an important fishing port on the shores of the Aral Sea, with a population twice its current size. A large mosaic inside its train station depicts how in 1921 Aral's comrades provided fish for people starving in Russia – a scene that preceded the Aral Sea ecological disaster that took water from its lifelines,

the Syr-Darya and Amu-Darya rivers, and pushed the shoreline 60km out from Aral. For those who wish to witness the ecological disaster first-hand, grim, semidilapidated Aral, where locals are wary of strangers, makes a decent base for a day or two. Aral is easier to visit than similarly defunct ports in Uzbekistan – and less gloomy, as efforts to save the northern part of the Aral Sea are succeeding and its fishing industry is growing again.

There are several ATMs on the main square, just north of Abilkayyr Khan.

◉ Sights & Activities

A trip to the slowly replenishing Aral Sea is the main – the only! – reason to come to Aral. Near its northern shore rise the sculpted rock formations of a magnificent canyon, in shades of ochre and yellow reminiscent of Utah or Arizona. Four Soviet shipwrecks lie on the seashore amidst dense growth of samphire, and the medicinal spring near a fishing village draws visitors from afar.

Aral's small **history museum** (Yesetov; 300T, each photo 100T; ⊙ 9am-noon & 3-7pm

Mon-Sat) has a few desiccation photos, some imaginative oil paintings and around 15 jars preserving different Aral Sea fish species – all now again present in the North Aral except for the sturgeon.

Beside Aral's former harbour, near the town centre, four fishing boats stand on pedestals as a tribute to fallen heroes. The biggest of the four now forms part of the **Fishermen's Museum** (Makataev; 200T; 9am-noon & 3-7pm Mon-Sat), which has fishing gear, paintings, photos and maps from Soviet times, and a 10-minute video. The boat's interior has been partly refurbished and you can climb up on deck.

Also possible through the highly-recommended NGO **Aral Tenizi** (705 449 37 32, 701 662 71 63, 72433 2 22 56; serik_duisen@mail.ru; Makataev 10-13; office 9am-6pm Mon-Fri) is a day trip to Zhalanash (the former ship graveyard), with a drive along the dry seabed and on to tiny Tastubek, 25km further and the nearest village to the seashore (4km), for 60,000T. You can swim in the sea from an earth beach near Tastubek, and short outings (up to an hour) in fishers' boats can be arranged for around 10,000T.

Try to make contact ahead, to allow time to make your arrangements.

Sleeping & Eating

Guesthouses (with full board) arranged by Aral Tenizi for 3500T offer the best insight into local life, but the family-run **Asem Hotel** (701 310 52 01, 724 332 45 21; Yesetov; r 3000-7000T;), near the museum, and small **Shattyk Guesthouse** (72433 2 32 56; shattyq@bk.ru; Yesetov 16; per person incl breakfast/3 meals 4000/7000T;) rent out rooms as well.

For tasty Kazakh-Korean dishes seek out **Chin-Son** (Makataev; mains 800-1500T; 11am-midnight), across from the Aral Tenizi office, or **Infinity Cafe** (mains 800-1700T; 11am-2am), near the main square, for salads, shashlyk, and dumpling soup.

Getting There & Away

A bus to Kyzylorda (1500T, nine hours) leaves from the bus stop near the bazaar in the centre of town at 10pm year-round, and twice daily from May to September. No public transport runs along the good 600km road to Aktobe. Aral

THE ARAL SEA: ON ITS WAY BACK TO ARAL

Four decades after they last saw the Aral Sea in their harbour, the people of Aral have real hope that it will be back soon.

Helped by international aid and lending agencies, Kazakhstan has revived the northern Aral by building the 14km-long Kok-Aral Dam, completed in 2005, across the last channel connecting the northern and southern parts of the sea. With no outlet to the south, the North Aral has risen again with water from the Syr-Darya. Rehabilitated waterworks along the river have helped by increasing the water flow into the sea, and by 2016 the North Aral had crept back to within 25km of Aral.

Now a second dyke, 4m higher than the Kok-Aral Dam, is to be built across the mouth of Saryshyganak Bay, the sea's northeastern arm which used to reach Aral. At the same time a new channel will be cut from the Syr-Darya to feed water into Saryshyganak Bay. Construction began in 2017, and it's hoped that the waters will reach Aral in 2020.

In the 1990s the fishing catch in the North Aral was limited to flounder, the only species able to survive the sea's extreme salinity then. Since 2005, at least 15 types of freshwater fish have returned to the North Aral via the Syr-Darya. Fishers travel from their villages, often now 25km or 30km from the shore, to take out small boats from which they catch carp, catfish, pike and the valuable pike-perch, which is exported to Russia and Poland. The total annual catch is up to around 11,000 tonnes (about half of what the Aral provided in its heyday). Four fish-processing plants are operating again around the North Aral, with more expected to open.

Locals also hope that revival of the North Aral and Saryshyganak Bay will help reduce the noxious sandy, salty windstorms that plague communities such as Aral.

The Kok-Aral Dam has condemned the supersaline, fishless remnants of the South Aral to accelerated evaporation, but most experts consider that already a lost cause, with no hope of more water from its main source, the Amu-Darya, which flows through Turkmenistan and Uzbekistan.

Tenizi can provide taxis to or from Kyzylorda for 50,000T to 70,000T (five to six hours).

Aral's **train station** (☏ 72433 9 50 72), called Aralskoe More, is 1km northeast of the central square. Departures include the following:

DESTINATION	COST (T) 2ND/3RD CLASS	TIME (HR)	FREQUENCY
Aktobe	3683/ 2384	10-12	1-4 daily
Almaty	7146/ 4585	29½- 34	1-2 daily
Bishkek	25,177/ 20,033	28½	2 weekly
Kyzylorda	2636/ 1723	7-8	3-5 daily
Shymkent	4570/ 2950	15½- 17¾	2-4 daily
Turkestan	3836/ 2484	12¼- 14¼	2-5 daily

In July and August tickets often sell out a week ahead: buy your onward or return tickets in advance.

WESTERN KAZAKHSTAN

Western Kazakhstan – so far west that the part beyond the Ural River is in Europe – is a hot, arid gateway to Central Asia from the Caucasus and the Volga and Ural regions of Russia. For those with a taste for adventurous exploring, the deserts outside the Caspian-side city of Aktau, dotted with underground mosques, ancient necropolises, wandering camels and spectacular rock formations, are just the ticket. The other main cities – Atyrau, Aktobe and Uralsk – have limited interest for travellers except as overland transit points.

Kazakhstan's biggest oil and gas fields – Tengiz (oil), Karachaganak (gas) and the offshore oil of Kashagan beneath the Caspian Sea – and a glut of other mineral resources have brought boom times to the west's main cities, but elsewhere the human population is sparse and the landscape is chiefly desert and steppe. The region is one hour behind Astana time.

Aktau

☏ 7292 / POP 183,233

An entry point into Central Asia by air from the Caucasus and İstanbul, and by an irreg-

ular ferry from Baku (Azerbaijan), Aktau (Актау) perches on Kazakhstan's Caspian shore. With some sandy beaches, low-key summer tourism and a temperate climate (several degrees above zero in January), this spread-out, dusty town is pleasant enough for a day or two – but the area's main interest, other than transport connections, is the natural and human-made wonders of the surrounding region, Mangistau.

Local uranium and oil finds were the reason Soviet architects began to lay out a model town of wide, straight streets in this remote location in 1958. The uranium, from an open-cast mine 30km northeast, fed Aktau's nuclear fast breeder reactor, which generated the town's electricity, powered its desalination plant and produced uranium concentrate for military purposes. Today, Aktau is a centre for oil and gas operations, both onshore and offshore.

The only significant street with a name is Kazakhstan Respublikasy Prezidentininy dangyly (you can understand why many people still call it Lenina). Aktau addresses are based on *mikrorayon* (MKR; microdistrict) building numbers: 4-17-29 means Microdistrict 4, Building 17, Apartment 29.

Aktau has an Azerbaijan consulate (p364) as well a **Migration Police** (☏ 7292 47 45 03; Dom 123, Mikrorayon 3; ☉ 9am-noon Mon-Thu & Sat) office which can handle visa registration.

◉ Sights & Activities

From the MiG fighter plane memorial you can descend steps to the breezy seafront, a mixture of low cliffs, rocks and thin sandy strips, with assorted cafes and bars that are lively in summer (when some of them double as open-air discos). A narrow street followed by a pedestrian promenade parallel the coast for 1km southeast from here. Halfway, a statue of Ukrainian poet and exile Taras Shevchenko stands looking mournfully out to sea on the boundary between Mikrorayons 4 and 5.

Straight inland from the MiG fighter, a striking **WWII Memorial** (Kazakhstan Respublikasy) consists of an eternal flame surrounded by five enormous white panels (all inscribed with sorrowful scenes from each year of the war) that make an enormous open yurt. Just up from the monument is the small **Regional Museum** (☏ 7292 42 66 15; Dom 23A, Mikrorayon 9; foreigner/local 400/200T; ☉ 9am-1pm & 2-6pm Tue-Fri, 10am-5pm Sat & Sun), with moderately inter-

Aktau

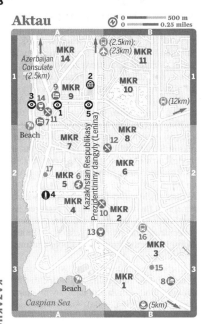

esting exhibits focusing on regional history and ecology ranging from pickled Caspian fish to the Kazakh khanates in the region, the arrival of Russians in the 19th century, World War II losses and the early Mangistau oil industry.

When you tire of exploring the city by foot, take a sail with **Briz-Aktau** (☑701 913 40 77, 7292 52 30 50; www.marin.kz; Dom 1, Mikrorayon 5; per hour 30,000-45,000T; ⊙office 9am-6pm Mon-Fri) on the blue Caspian waters in a beautiful 12m French-built sail/motor catamaran. Briz' professionally skippered boats, for up to 10 passengers, can go for any period from an hour upward (including overnight). All boats have four two-person cabins, plus a galley area.

🛏 Sleeping

Hotel Keremet
HOTEL $

(☑7292 50 15 69; Dom 20, Mikrorayon 3; s/d 1800/3800T; ❄🛜) Recently renovated, rooms at this budget option are seriously cheap without being skanky or unsafe, which makes them a terrific backpacker option. There's a cafe adjoining and staff cheer up if you can manage some words of Russian for them.

Hotel Kaspiysky Bereg
HOTEL $$

(Caspian Shore Hotel; ☑7292 51 17 18; kaspiimangistau@mail.ru; Mikrorayon 7; r incl breakfast 10,000-12,000T; ❄🛜) This homey small hotel near the seashore has good-sized, carpeted rooms. The most expensive boast attractive Chinese silk 'paintings' and have glassed-in terraces facing the sea (through trees). The breakfast spread is unimaginative, the beds are Soviet-hard and to get extra towels you have to throw yourself at the receptionist's mercy.

★ Renaissance Aktau Hotel
HOTEL $$$

(☑7292 30 06 00; www.marriott.com; Mikrorayon 9; r incl breakfast Sun-Thu from 28,500T, Fri & Sat 35,650T; ℗⊜❄🛜🏊) The favourite of Western business-folk, the metallic, contemporary Renaissance provides very comfy, brightly decorated, well-equipped rooms, plus a great sea-view terrace, good outdoor pool, health club with heated pool, and a host of other facilities.

🍴 Eating & Drinking

Several seafront cafes below the MiG monument serve up fried chicken, *manty* (steamed dumplings) and meat/fish/

vegetable shashlyk (700T to 2000T), and have outdoor tables in summer. Aktau's oil wealth has resulted in a good selection of international restaurants scattered about the city.

Modigliani   GEORGIAN $$
(☑ 7292 51 08 83; www.facebook.com/modigliani. aktau; Mikrorayon 7; mains 1100-4600T; ⊘ noon-midnight; ☎ ✐) Near the promenade and the MiG plane, this Georgian place has a medieval-cellar ambience. Standout dishes include slow-cooked lamb and veal *chakhushuly* (spicy soup) with herbs and vegetables, *lobio* (beans with walnuts, herbs and spices) baked in a clay pot and *manty* (steamed dumplings). There's a good business-lunch deal on weekday lunchtimes, too.

Fusion   FUSION $$
(☑ 7292 54 51 91; Dom 476, Mikrorayon 2; mains 1200-3400T; ⊘ noon-midnight; ☎) Fusion is exactly that: a melange of sushi, pan-Asian noodle dishes, salads, shashlyk and vaguely international meat and fish dishes. It's a bit of a catch-all place, but it's all well-prepared and the service is sweet and helpful.

Shashlyki u Dyadyi Gadima   KAZAKH $$
(☑ 707 600 71 77; Dom 38B, Mikrokayon 8; mains 800-1400T; ⊘ noon-midnight; ☎) Considered by locals to serve some of the best shashlyk in the city, Uncle Gadim's place really delivers when it comes to large skewers of delicious grilled meat. There's a summer terrace, too.

Guns & Roses   BAR
(☑ 7292 52 49 41; www.facebook.com/pages/Guns-N-Roses-Bar-Aktau-Kazakhstan/240831312606604; Kazakhstan Respublikasy, Dom 66, Mikrorayon 2; ⊘ 11am-2am Sun-Thu, to 4am Fri & Sat; ☎) The best of Aktau's handful of British-style pubs, Guns & Roses serves generous burgers, steaks and pizzas, shows sport on TV and hosts a live rock/jazz/pop band from 10pm Thursday to Saturday.

Lido   CAFE
(☑ 7292 33 09 72; Mikrorayon 7; ⊘ noon-3am) Lido's two open-air decks are packed for summer-night drinks and there's an assortment of grilled dishes to go with your beer.

❶ Getting There & Away

AIR

From **Aktau Airport** (☑ 7292 60 97 55; www.aktau-airport.kz), 23km north of the centre, there are flights to the following destinations:

DESTINATION	COST (T)	FREQUENCY	AIRLINE
Almaty	28,250	up to 5 daily	Air Astana, Bek Air, SCAT
Astana	39,300	up to 4 daily	Air Astana, Bek Air, SCAT
Astrakhan	45.400	4 weekly	SCAT
Atyrau	19,500	up to 3 daily	Air Astana, SCAT
Baku, Azerbaijan	30,400	1-2 daily	Azal, SCAT
Moscow, Russia	60,300	6 weekly	Aeroflot, SCAT
Shymkent	32,000	5 weekly	Bek Air, SCAT
Tbilisi, Georgia	43,600	5 weekly	SCAT
Yerevan, Armenia	56,600	weekly	SCAT

BOAT

A car ferry to Baku (Azerbaijan) with some passenger spaces leaves roughly weekly (when full) from the **seaport** (http://portaktau.kz) in the southeast of town. The journey takes 30 hours and costs 27,000T per passenger. Buy your ticket at the **paromnaya kassa** (Ferry Ticket Office; ☑ 777 490 46 63; Office 1, Dom 29, Mikrorayon 5; ⊘ 9am-1pm & 2-6pm Mon-Fri) in town, or at the port itself: at the first gate, go to the first building on the right and keep right.

MINIBUS & SHARED TAXI

From the **avtovokzal** (☑ 7292 40 02 28; Mikrorayon 28A), in the north of town, minibuses leave when full, until 7pm, to Shetpe (650T, 2½ hours) and Zhanaozen (680T, 2½ hours). Shared taxis to Shetpe (2000T, two hours) go from the street immediately north of the bus station; shared taxis to Zhanaozen (2000T, two hours) go from the street to the south.

TRAIN

Aktau's train station, called Mangyshlak or Mangistau, is 12km east of the centre. It lies near the end of a branch line off the Atyrau–Uzbekistan line, so journeys to anywhere are long. There are one or two daily trains to Astana, and three or four weekly departures for Nukus, Uzbekistan; other destinations are served daily. A newly built line crossing the Kazakhstan–Turkmenistan border is for freight trains only. Destinations include:

DESTINATION	TRAIN NO	COST (T) 2ND/3RD CLASS	DEPARTURE	TIME (HR)
Aktobe	309	5138/3311	2.04pm	29½
Atyrau	313	4201/2712	6.55pm	22¼
Almaty	377	11,377/7273	10.34pm	60¾
Astana	037/237	12,162/7793	11.28am	47¼
Nukus, Uzbekistan	309	10,492 (3rd class only)	2.04pm every other day	29

ⓘ Getting Around

City buses cost 55T. The frequent bus 3 runs north up Kazakhstan Respublikasy Prezidentininy dangyly then east to the bus station (the second stop after the big gold-domed mosque), and vice versa. Bus 4 runs about every half-hour (7am to 8pm) from the seaport to the centre; going out to the port you can catch it on the north side of Mikrorayon 3 (MKR 3).

Taxis within town cost 200T to 300T. For the train station expect to pay 1000T, for the airport 2000T, and the seaport 500T.

Hard-working Azeri fixer **Ramil** (☑ 775 513 10 00) offers taxi services to/from the airport himself and works with various drivers in the area, arranging trips to Beket-Ata and elsewhere in Mangistau. He doesn't speak English, but uses the translator app on WhatsApp to great effect.

Around Aktau

Mangistau   Маңғыстау облысы

The stony deserts of the Mangistau region stretch 400km east from Aktau to the Uzbekistan border. This labyrinth of dramatic canyons, weirdly eroded, multicoloured rocky outcrops, mysterious underground mosques and ancient necropolises is only beginning to be explored, even by archaeologists. A minor branch of the Silk Road once ran across this inhospitable wilderness, and centuries-old sacred sites – some with strong Sufic associations – are located where people buried their dead or where holy men dwelt. The underground mosques may have originated as cave hermitages for ascetics who retreated to the deserts.

Take food with you to all Mangistau attractions; most are in the middle of nowhere. It's polite to bring food to share with the rest of the pilgrims to Beket-Ata and Shopan-Ata.

ⓘ Getting There & Away

For many of Mangistau's attractions, particularly in the north of the region, you'll need a 4WD with a driver who knows where they are going. Beket-Ata is well-signposted and reachable in a city car, though the road is only paved up to the turn-off beyond Zhanaozen, and the journey is considerably more comfortable in a 4WD. Getting to these places across the other-worldly desertscapes, with only the occasional herd of camels or sheep for company, is definitely part of the fun.

Tashkent-based **Advantour** (Map p204; ☑ +998 71 150 3020; 47A, Mirobod-1, Tashkent; ⊗ 9am-6pm Mon-Fri, to 1pm Sat) and Almaty-based **Stantours** (☑ 727 247 61 29, 705 118 46 19; www.stantours.com) and **Silk Road Adventures** (☑ 727 268 27 43; www.silkadv.com; Adi Sharipov 117/44; ⊗ 9am-6pm Mon-Fri, to 2pm Sat; 🖵 112) are experienced operators offering trips. Day trips from Aktau in a 4WD for up to four passengers generally cost 60,000T to 80,000T; itineraries of several days, camping most nights, are also available. If you have the relevant language skills, going with a local driver from Aktau, organised by Ramil, can be a really interesting experience.

MANGISTAU NECROPOLISES

All of Kazakhstan is dotted with picturesque cemeteries or necropolises set outside villages and towns, and Mangistau has a notable concentration of them: locals boast the figure 362. Many of these date back to nomadic times, when tribes would bury their dead at special sites. Fascinating carvings adorn many of the older stone monuments – the most common forms are the *kulpytas,* a stone column often depicting the life of the deceased; the *koitas,* a stylised ram; the *koshkar-tas,* a more realistic ram; and the sarcophagus-like *sandyk-tas.* One of the most interesting necropolises is Koshkar Ata, a skyline of miniature domes and towers that resembles some fairy-tale city. Just inside the entrance is a fine old *koshkar-tas*. It's located at Akshukur, beside the main road 15km north of Aktau.

NORTHERN MANGISTAU

The arid land north and northeast of Aktau is rich in both natural sights and ancient necropolises, without the crowds that flock to Beket-Ata. In a 4WD it's possible to combine the sights around the town of Shetpe with the pilgrimage places of Shakpak-Ata and Sultan Epe in one long day trip, but it's best to make it two, and linger.

Some 133km north of Aktau and another 37km northwest of Taushlik, the nearest settlement, 10th century Shakpak-Ata is a beautiful underground mosque cut into a honeycombed cliff and preceded by an arched portal, carved with inscriptions in Arabic and etchings of horses. Unusually, the interior is cruciform and there are burial niches carved into the cliff face.

Around 7km past the Shakpak-Ata turn-off along the Taushlik–Shevchenko road is the turn-off for the necropolis of Sultan Epe, a holy man and protector of sailors. His tomb is rich in carvings and there's a small underground mosque nearby, consisting of several low rooms and dating back to sometime between the 10th and 12th centuries. About 1km before you reach Sultan Epe, you pass the Kenty Baba necropolis, consisting of three towerlike buildings with tombs inside, and some wonderful, centuries-old etchings of hunters and their prey on the wall of one of the towers.

The small town of Shetpe is 150km northeast of Aktau by paved road (2½ hours by minibus from Aktau bus station). About 35km towards Shetpe from the crossroads where the Shetpe and Taushik roads divide, a signposted 4km side road leads up to Otpan Tau, Mangistau's highest hill (532m), where a modern 'historical-cultural complex', affording great panoramas, includes three gold-domed towers, a she-wolf monument (by legend the first Kazakhs were born from a wolf), and a symbolic torch commemorating the legendary use of this site for warning beacons.

The awesome 332m-high, 1km-long chalk outcrop Sherkala (Lion Rock) rises mysteriously from the desert about 22km northwest from Shetpe by paved road. A three-hour taxi round trip from Shetpe bazaar should cost 6000T, including a couple of other interesting spots nearby. Shortly before you reach the track turn-off to Sherkala, a 'Kyzylkala Kalashygy' sign indicates a 1km track to the remnants of the small Silk Road settlement of Kyzylkala, beside a small green oasis with trees. Over to your right as you approach Sherkala from the road is the abandoned, little-known Temir Abdal Ata cave-shrine, with the carved stones of an abandoned necropolis scattered in front of it. Not far from Sherkala is the tranquil oasis of Samal Canyon, with greenery shading a clear stream.

Beket-Ata

Beket-Ata, 285km east of Aktau, is an underground mosque to which the clairvoyant and teacher Beket-Ata (1750–1813) retreated in the later part of his life, ultimately dying and being buried here. A Mangistau native, Beket-Ata studied in Khiva (Uzbekistan) and on his return he is believed to have set up four mosques, including this one where he founded a Sufi school. Every day dozens of pilgrims – and hundreds on holidays – make the bumpy journey across the deserts to pray and receive Beket-Ata's inspiration. The underground mosque (three caves) is set in a rocky outcrop near the bottom of a desert canyon, with shaded resting places along the picturesque walkway to facilitate the descent and ascent.

Aktau tour companies run two-day 4WD trips to Beket-Ata costing around 80,000T to 100,000T for up to four people. Private drivers will do it for much less; ask at your hotel and check the Beket-Ata ads in *Tumba* newspaper or online, where you'll find Toyota LandCruisers that may cost 30,000T to 40,000T round trip and rickety Soviet minibuses charging as little as 5500T per person. One reliable option is Ramil (p330), who can organise a (non-English-speaking) driver to take you on a long day trip in a comfortable jeep for around 40,000T. Alternatively, take an early public minibus or shared taxi from Aktau bus station to the dusty oil town of Zhanaozen, 150km east by paved road. From Zhanaozen bazaar, 4WDs (4500/30,000T per person/vehicle round trip) and more uncomfortable minibuses (5000T per person) leave in the morning for Beket-Ata. You'll spend most of the five- or six-hour, 135km trip lurching and bumping along steppe and desert tracks. En route, vehicles stop at Shopan-Ata, an underground mosque and large necropolis dating back to at least the 10th century, where Shopan-Ata, a disciple of Kozha Akhmed Yasaui, dwelt. Most groups sleep (free) in the pilgrim hostel-cum-mosque-cum-dining hall at Beket-Ata, before leaving early next morning. Expect to share the room with 200 pilgrims or so; the Ritz this ain't. Zhanaozen has

KAZAKHSTAN AROUND AKTAU

passable hotels, including centrally located cheapie **Hotel Sherkala** (☎72934 5 20 36; Dom 66, Mikrorayon Orken; r from 3000T) and more upmarket **Hotel Aksaray** (☎72934 2 73 00; http://aksarayhotel.kz; Mikrorayon 3; r 11,000-15,000T; ❄🛜), with rather intense wallpaper but also cable TV and bathrobes. Best in town is **Hotel Temirkazyk** (☎72934 5 69 46; www.temirkazykhotel.kz; ulitsa 2, Mikrorayon Aray 1; s/d incl breakfast from 11,000/13,000T; P❄🛜), with good, big, comfy rooms and a decent cafe/restaurant. Dining-wise, Zhanaozen has some excellent shashlyk joints and several low-key restaurants serving Kazakh specials.

On arrival at Shopan-Ata and Beket-Ata all visitors are expected to purify themselves by using the squat toilets. If you're travelling with pilgrims, be ready to join in prayers, ritual walks around sacred trees and communal meals of the Kazakh national dish *beshbarmak* and slaughtered lamb in the evenings.

Uralsk   Уральск

☎7112 / POP 232,943 / ELEV 35M

Originally a settlement called Yaitsky Gorodok, established by Cossacks in 1584 at the confluence of the Ural and Chagan Rivers, Uralsk (Oral) is both historically significant and aesthetically appealing, with vintage wooden houses surviving in the leafy southern part of the city, Kureni, where Cossacks originally settled. Yaitsky Gorodok played a major role in the Pugachev Rebellion in the 1770s: this is where renegade Cossack Yemelyan Pugachev declared himself the rightful tsar and gathered an army of Cossacks and peasants, some 10,000 strong, before being defeated by Russia's imperial forces and delivered to the tender mercies of Empress Catherine the Great in a small cage. She renamed the town 'Uralsk' to erase Pugachev's legacy, though Pushkin later came to visit, to chronicle the rebellion.

It's possible to get a visa at the Russian Consulate (p365) here if you have three weeks to spare.

⊙ Sights

House-Museum of
Yemelyan Pugachev   MUSEUM
(☎7112 26 49 86; Dostyk-Druzhba 35; 100T; ⊙10am-6pm Wed-Sun) This log cabin was owned by the father of the Kazakh bride who married Cossack rebel Yemelyan Pugachev during his short stint in the city.

One room shows off some personal effects, as well as coins of 'Tsar Peter III', Pugachev's throne and the small cage in which the tsar-imposter was eventually delivered to Empress Catherine the Great upon his defeat and capture. Other rooms depict a typical Cossack kitchen and there's a yard full of ye olde farm implements.

House-Museum of
Manshuk Mametova   MUSEUM
(☎7112 50 46 93; Saraychik 51; 150T; ⊙10am-6pm Tue-Sun) This museum chronicles the life of Hero of the Soviet Union Manshuk Mametova, who lived here with her adoptive parents between 1932 and 1934. Her father, a doctor, was shot in 1938 as part of the Stalinist repressions, and Manshuk went on to become a machine gunner, dying at her post during the 1943 battle in Pskov region, giving her comrades cover as they retreated. The collection of personal possessions on display is touching, as is Manshuk's simple childhood room.

WWII War Memorial   MEMORIAL
(Pugachev) This particularly striking WWII memorial comprises a wall, with the faces of various Heroes of the Soviet Union, including Uralsk's most famous daughter, machine-gunner Manshuk Mametova, depicted in relief. In front of it, two tall white panels reach for the sky, and there's a wall inscribed with the names of the many local dead beyond the eternal flame.

🛏 Sleeping & Eating

Hotels scattered around the city range from revamped Soviet cheapies and excellent self-catering accommodation to business hotels.

The cheaper rooms in the **Hotel Ural** (☎7112 50 79 32; Kurmangazy 80; s/d 6000/7000T, without bathroom 3500/3800T; P❄) are an acceptable, basic, budget option.

Comprising just four spacious, fully equipped studio apartments, **Apart-Hotel Vegus** (☎7112 50 58 95; Prospekt Yevraziya 46; studio 10,000T; P⊖❄🛜) is both great value and an excellent choice in terms of proximity to attractions and public-transport links.

One of the nicest places in town is the **Hotel Pushkin** (☎7112 51 35 60; www.pushkin hotel.com; Dostyk 148B; s/d incl breakfast from 18,810/22,657T; P❄🛜), restored and furnished by an Italian company, with impressionist paintings adorning its walls.

For food, basement restaurant **Zolotoy Vek** (☎7112 50 95 80; Temir Masin 44/1; mains

615-2115T; ⏰noon-2am; ❄🛜) is a bit of a catch-all crowd-pleaser: the extensive menu offers dozens of salads, grilled meats and pizzas. We can vouch for its excellent shashlyk. At **Khutorok** (📱702 943 85 09; http://xytorok.kz; Chagano-naberezhnaya 78; mains 1100-3300T; ⏰11am-2am; ❄✏), views of the Chagan River complement a hearty menu of Ukrainian dishes.

ℹ Getting There & Away

From the **airport** (📱711 293 96 66; http://aeroport.kz/city/uralsk), 15km south of the city, there are flights to Aktau (from 19,467T, up to two daily) with Bek Air and SCAT; Almaty (69,200T, daily) with Air Astana; Astana (from 24,352T, two daily) with Air Astana and Bek Air; and Atyrau (14,157T, five weekly) with Qazaq Air.

Minibuses to Atyrau (6000T, five hours) and shared taxis to Aktobe (9000T, five hours) leave from the train station. From the **avtovokzal** (📱7112 28 31 09; http://uralsk.info/bus/; Syrym Datov), comfortable, air-conditioned buses also run to Atyrau (4000T, four daily) and Aktobe (3350T, daily at 11am), with international departures to Orenburg (3000T, eight hours, daily at 8am), Samara (2750T, six hours, four daily) and Saratov (4200T, nine hours, two daily). Unlike the railway, the road between Uralsk and Aktobe stays inside Kazakhstani territory.

From the **train station** (📱7112 51 86 47; Zhukov) there are trains to Aktobe (3015T to 3053T, 11 to 13 hours, one or two daily), Almaty (12,213T to 13,137T, 50½ to 59 hours, four weekly) and Aktau (Mangyshlak; 5367T, 3rd class only, 40½ hours, every other day). Note that trains to or from Aktobe (including those to/from Almaty) duck into Russia en route; reports are that you need a Russian visa for that stretch.

ℹ Getting Around

Public transport costs 60T. Handy bus routes include the following:

2 Down Dostyk and past the WWII memorial.
12 Between the airport and city centre via the bus and train stations.
39 Down Dostyk to Kureni.

NORTHERN KAZAKHSTAN

This is the most Russified part of Kazakhstan but it's also the location of the eye-catching new capital, Astana, chief showpiece of President Nazarbayev's vision of the prosperous, cosmopolitan Kazakhstan of the future.

The northern steppes also harbour surprising areas of natural beauty: the flamingo-filled lakes of Korgalzhyn; the hills, forests and lakes around Burabay; and the picturesque Kyzylarai mountains southeast of Karaganda.

This is the most poignant part of Kazakhstan when it comes to dark tourism. The remnants of two of the most notorious gulags in the country, ALZhIR and KarLag, near Astana and Karaganda, respectively, are a touching memorial to the thousands who perished in Stalinist forced labour camps.

History

Until the 19th century, this region was largely untouched except by Kazakh nomads and their herds. As Russia's hand stretched southwards, Russian and Ukrainian settlers came to farm the steppe – a million or more by 1900. In Soviet times, the Kazakhs were forced into collective farms, and industrial cities such as Karaganda and Kostanay sprouted to exploit coal, iron ore and other minerals, while over a million political prisoners suffered in the huge KarLag labour-camp complex around Karaganda. In the 1950s vast areas of steppe were turned over to wheat in Nikita Khrushchev's Virgin Lands scheme, bringing in yet more settlers, though the scheme never came to fruition.

In the 1950s most of the labour camps were closed, but a lot of survivors stayed. After the Soviet collapse many ethnic Germans, Russians and Ukrainians emigrated, but Kazakhs still number less than one-third in several areas.

Climate

The climate is sharply continental and the most pleasant months to travel are May to September. In January and February average temperatures in Astana range between -11°C (12.2°F and -22°C (-7.6°F), and bitter steppe winds can make it feel colder still.

Astana Астана

📱7172 / POP 872,655 / ELEV 373M

The country's new capital has risen fast from the northern steppe and is already a showpiece for 21st-century Kazakhstan. Astana is scheduled to go on rising and spreading into a city of over one million people by 2030. Its skyline grows more fantastical by the year as landmark buildings, many of them by leading international architects, sprout along the wide boulevards in a variety of Asian, Western, Soviet and wacky futuristic styles. Several spectacular structures are open to visitors and it's hard not be impressed by the very concept of this 'Singapore of the steppe'.

Though characterised by its bitter, windy winters and hot, dusty summers, Astana is a pleasant city with a young, forward-looking vibe. Kazakhstan's ambitious and talented youth are increasingly drawn here, and if you spend a few days, the capital will really begin to get under your skin, too.

Astana began life in 1830 as a Russian fortress called Akmola (Kazakh for 'White Tomb'). In the 1950s Akmola became the headquarters of the Virgin Lands scheme and in 1961 was renamed Tselinograd (Virgin Lands City), but after the collapse of the USSR it returned to its original name. Akmola was a medium-sized provincial city known primarily for its bitter winters when President Nazarbayev named it out of the blue in 1994 as Kazakhstan's future capital. It formally took over from Almaty in 1997. Nazarbayev claimed that the change was due to Astana's more central and less earthquake-prone location than Almaty, and its better transport links with Russia. He may also have wanted to head off secessionist sentiments among northern Kazakhstan's large ethnic Russian population. In 1998 the city was renamed again, as Astana – Kazakh for 'Capital'.

◎ Sights

◉ New City

'New' Astana, south of the river, is centred on the showpiece of Nurzhol Bulvar, a 2km line of gardens and plazas leading east from iconic Khan Shatyr to the presidential palace, flanked by a sequence of imaginative contemporary buildings and anchored by the 97m-high Bayterek Monument.

★**Khan Shatyr**   ARCHITECTURE
(www.khanshatyr.com; Turan dangyly 37; ◎10am-10pm; ⊛; ☐10, 32, 43, 46, 50) Astana's most extraordinary building (so far), the Khan Shatyr is a 150m-high, translucent, tentlike structure made of ethylene tetrafluoroethylene (ETFE), a heat-absorbing material that produces summer temperatures inside even when it's -30°C outside. Touted as a

'lifestyle centre with world-class shopping', from outside it resembles nothing so much as a drunkenly leaning circus tent, while the multilevel interior contains a high-end shopping mall, food court, and various attractions.

There's a drop tower, flume ride and 500m-long monorail (admission for all three 2000T) and, on the top level, the **Sky Beach Club** (☑7172 58 51 03; http://khanshatyr. com/en/sky-beach-club; adult/child Mon-Fri 10,000/6000T, Sat & Sun 15,000/6500T; ◎10am-10pm; ☐10, 32, 46, 50, 53) with a big swimming pool, sandy beach, palm trees and water slide, where those who can afford it can imagine they're on a tropical coast in the middle of the Eurasian steppe. Opened in 2010, the Khan Shatyr was designed by celebrated British architect Norman Foster and marks, for the moment, the western end of the main axis of new Astana.

City Park   PARK
(Turan dangyly; ☐12, 17, 21, 32, 50) The large, somewhat-untidy city park abuts the south side of the Ishim river. On its southern edge you'll find the **Atameken** (☑7172 22 16 36; www.atamekenmap.kz; Korgalzhyn taszholy; 400T; English tour 500T; ◎9am-9pm; ☐21, 32, 44, 50), a 200m-long, walk-around country map with models of major buildings, and **Duman** (☑7172 24 22 22; www.duman.kz; Korgalzhyn taszoly 2; oceanarium adult/child 1500/700T; ◎10.30am-10.30pm May-Sep, to 8.30pm rest of year), an amusement centre most worth visiting for its oceanarium, which has over 2000 creatures from the world's oceans and a 70m shark tunnel.

◉ Nurzhol Bulvar

Just to the south of the boulevard between the two are the four-minaret **Nur Astana** (Kabanbay Batyr 36; ◎sunrise-sunset; ☐10, 12, 32, 40) mosque (and inside the exquisite multidomed prayer hall with inscriptions and geometrical patterning), the egg-domed **National Archive** (Aqmeshit; ☐12, 18, 28, 32, 50) building, and three undulating light-green apartment towers known as the **Northern Lights** (☐12, 18, 28, 32, 40). On the opposite side of Nurzhol Bulvar stand **Kaz-MunayGaz** (Kabanbay Batyr; ☐32, 43, 46, 50, 53), headquarters of the state energy company; the gleaming copper **Transport & Communications Ministry** (☐32, 46, 50), dubbed the 'Lighter' by irreverent locals,

ALZHIR MUSEUM-MEMORIAL COMPLEX

During the Stalin years, Akmol, 35km west of Astana, housed **ALZhIR** (http://alzhir.kz/en/; admission 200T; ☉10am-6pm Tue-Sun), a notorious camp for wives and children of men who were interned elsewhere as 'betrayers of the motherland'. The ALZhIR Museum-Memorial Complex poignantly evokes the camp's horrors, displaying a transportation wagon, a replica guard post and photos and possessions of the prisoners, as well as explanatory material in English on the Gulag system in Kazakhstan. Minibuses to Akmol (400T, one hour) leave Astana bus station eight times daily.

Some of the most heart-rending exhibits are letters – from children to their imprisoned mothers, from mothers determined to survive and see their families again, as well as unusual possessions: a coffee grinder inscribed with 'When a man is tired of London, he's tired of life'.

A five-minute walk along the road from the museum, opposite the church, is another memorial to the prisoners of ALZhIR in the form of a broken Communist star. On the outskirts of town another memorial marks the mass grave where thousands of women who perished here are seeing out eternity.

The museum is just around the corner from the bus stop on the highway. Coming back from Akmol, you can wait for a bus or get a shared taxi (400T) behind the blue Sauda Uyi building 600m along the street from the museum entrance.

and made more ironic by a fire inside the building soon after its completion;, and the **Emerald Towers** (🖳10, 12, 21, 28, 70), striking office blocks whose tops splay outward like the pages of opening books.

The eastern half of Nurzhol bulvar starts with the **Ploshchad Poyushchykh Fontanov** (Singing Fountains Square; 🖳12, 18, 32, 40), which springs to life with music-and-water shows at 9pm on summer evenings. Further east stand twin golden-green, conical business centres: the southern one contains the headquarters of **Samryk-Kazyna** (Prospekt Mangilik; 🖳12, 18, 21, 32, 40), Kazakhstan's sovereign wealth fund. Curving away left and right from these towers are the two wings of the House of Ministries – **northern wing** (Prospekt Mangilik; 🖳12, 18, 21, 32, 70) and **southern wing** (Prospekt Mangilik; 🖳12, 18, 21, 32, 70) – flanked by the **Senate** (Prospekt Mangilik; 🖳12, 18, 21, 32, 40) and **Mazhilis** (Prospekt Mangilik; 🖳12, 18, 21, 32, 70), the towers of parliament. Straight ahead stands the white-pillared **Ak Orda** (Presidential Palace; Nurzhol bulvar; 🖳12, 18, 21, 28, 70).

★**Bayterek Monument**　　　MONUMENT
(☎7171 24 08 35; adult/child 700/300T; ☉10am-10pm; 🖳12, 18, 28, 32, 50) Nurzhol bulvar's centrepiece is this 97m-high monument, a white latticed tower crowned by a large glass orb. This embodies a Kazakh legend in which the mythical bird Samruk lays a golden egg

containing the secrets of human desires and happiness in a tall poplar tree, beyond human reach. Lifts glide visitors up inside the egg, where you can ponder the symbolism, enjoy expansive views and place your hand in a print of President Nazarbayev's palm while gazing towards his palace.

◉ East of Nurzhol Bulvar

The new city's axis continues east across the Ishim River behind the Ak Orda, where there are two of Astana's biggest attractions: the Palace of Peace and Reconciliation and National Museum of the Republic of Kazakhstan, as well as the squat **Palace of Independence** (Dvorets Nezavisimosti; ☎7172 70 03 89; www.indepalace.kz; Tauelsizdik; tours 500T; ☉10am-6pm Tue-Sun; 🖳4, 14, 21), worth a visit for its huge scale model of how Astana is planned to look in 2030. In between the three is the 91m **Kazak Yeli Monument** (Kazakh Country Monument; Prospekt Tauelsyzdyk; 🖳4, 14, 21), intended to symbolise the historic destiny of Kazakhstan's people, and just behind it the lens-shaped **Shabyt Art Palace** (Prospekt Tauelsyzdyk; 🖳14, 21), currently an arts university. Just north of the square is the **Hazrat Sultan Mosque** (Tauelsizdik; ☉sunrise-sunset; 🖳4, 14, 19, 40), boasting Kazakhstan's largest dome as well as beautifully marbled interiors. Look out for a splendid old copy of the Quran.

Astana

KAZAKHSTAN ASTANA

Inset

0.25 miles
500 m

Soviet
Grain
Silo
6

Respublika dangyly

Auezov

Maskeu

Druzhby
(Dukenuly)

30

Zhangeldin

Bogenbay Batyr dangyly

Zhangeldin

Yesenberlin

Muldagulova

Zheltoksan

Zhenis dangyly

Gyote

Astana
Train
Station

71
70

Konstitutsii

ploshchad 310
Gvardeyskoy
divizii

Tarkhan

Kenesary

Imanov

Kravtsova

Tashenova

65

Sembinov

Omarova

Abay dangyly

Kenesary

Imanov

Baraeva

Tashenova

Valikhanov

35
44
41
42
29
50

Otyrar

68
31

Sabyr Rakhimov
(Koshkarbaeva)

Gabdullin

Gabdullin

3 Museum of the
Armed Forces

66

Respublika dangyly

58
38

See Inset

59

Auezov

52

Bokeykhan

Omarova

Beybitshilik

18

6

Kabanbay Batyr

19

Zheltoksan

Zhenis dangyly

Bigeldinov

Ryskulov

46

Kenesary

8

28

10

Zhangeldin

Seyfullin

Radisson
Hotel

51

Saryarka dangyly

53

MIKRORAYON
KARAOTKEL
2

Ayagoz

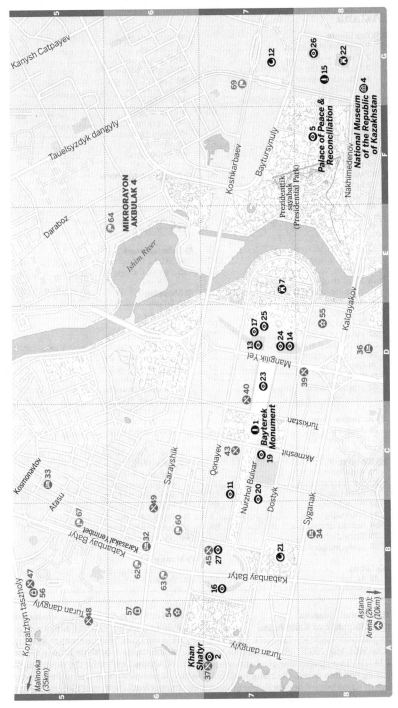

Astana

★ **National Museum
of the Republic of Kazakhstan**   MUSEUM
(www.nationalmuseum.kz; Tauelsizdik 54; 1500T,
photo 500T, tour 2000T; ⊙10am-6pm Tue-Sun;
▣14, 21) This huge blue-glass-and-white-
marble museum covers the history and culture of Kazakhstan from ancient to modern
times. Themed halls comprise interactive
displays and artifact exhibits, ranging from
a yurt in the Hall of Ethnography to a chronicle of the capital's modern history in the
Hall of Astana. Don't miss the Golden Hall,
which houses several thousand Bronze Age
ornaments from the famed 'Golden Man' (a

national symbol of Kazakhstan) – a 3rd- or 4th-century warrior whose gold-clad remains were uncovered in 1969.

★ Palace of Peace & Reconciliation

ARCHITECTURE

(Dvorets Mira i Soglasya; ☑ 7172 74 47 44; Tauelsizdik; tours adult/child 500/300T; ☺ tours every 30min, 10am-7.30pm, to 6pm Oct-Apr; ☑ 4, 14, 21, 29, 40) This beautiful glass-and-steel pyramid was opened in 2006 as the home for the triennial Congress of World and Traditional Religions, hosted by Kazakhstan. The 30-minute tour (English-speaking guides available) shows you a 1350-seat opera hall, the 3rd-floor atrium where the congress was held, and the apex conference room with windows filled with stained-glass doves (by British artist Brian Clarke). Full of symmetry and symbolism, the pyramid is beautifully illuminated and a highlight of the city.

◎ Old City

'Old' Astana, north of the river, has a couple of worthwhile museums including the Nazarbayev-centric **Museum of the First President** (☑ 7172 75 12 92; Beibitshilik 11; ☺ 10am-6pm Tue-Sun; ☑ 1, 9, 17, 23, 32) **FREE**, a succession of lavish galleries displaying gifts to President Nazarbayev from foreign governments and grateful citizens. See if you can spot a walrus carving (Canada), ram-horn dagger (Tajikistan), silver wine set (Uzbekistan) and an elaborate bone carving (China).

★ Museum of the Armed Forces

MUSEUM

(☑ 7172 44 25 73; Respublika dangyly 2; ☺ 10am-6pm Tue-Sun; ☑ 1, 3, 10, 20, 32, 52) **FREE** The yurt-shaped museum showcases beautifully presented exhibitions on weaponry and warfare, with striking murals greeting visitors. On the ground floor, chainmail armour, powder flasks and swords surround the atrium with its heroic statues of Kazakh notables (including President Nazarbayev). The Hall of Ancestry is an intriguing look at weapons through the ages, including detailed diagrams on the construction of medeival bows and the cavalry tactics of Turkic, Mongol and Kazakh armies. Mines and machine guns on the 3rd floor are skippable.

★ Soviet Grain Silo

NOTABLE BUILDING

(☑ 3, 10, 12, 22, 48) This rare relic of the 1950s may be gone in a few years' time, banished

ASTANA DAY

Astana Day (www.astanaday.kz; ☺ 6 Jul), the day that Astana became the capital of Kazakhstan, is celebrated in a big way. The square behind the Palace of Peace & Reconciliation usually serves as the focus for concerts, a fairground and fireworks. Other events take place around the city. The date (also a national holiday) coincides with President Nazarbayev's birthday.

by the relentless recking ball, but for now you can see this enormous, decaying grain silo, inscribed with 'The Virgin Lands have been raised. The heroic deed continues.' It's a remnant of Nikita Khrushchev's ill-advised plans to make Tselinograd the breadbasket of the Soviet Union, in spite of the unsuitability of the local soil for intensive cultivation.

🛏 Sleeping

Astana has a good range of accommodation to suit all budgets. For backpackers, there are over half a dozen decent hostels in the old part of town, as well as numerous options on various room-sharing websites. Midrange and boutique hotels have recently taken off, and there are also numerous high-end business hotels, mostly in old Astana.

★ Hostel Astana

HOSTEL $

(http://hostel-astana.hoteleastana.com/en/; Kenesary 42, apt 96; dm/s/d 5000/9500/12,500; ☻@🛜; ☑ 2, 9) The pick of Astana's hostels comes with a wonderful roof terrace, featuring panoramic views of the city. The two dorms are gender-segregated, there's a spacious double and smaller room with bunks, and even a fully equipped separate apartment. Lots of nice touches: hypo-allergenic beds, ample luggage storage and a huge kitchen. The staff are happy to advise about the city's attractions.

Apple Hostel

HOSTEL $

(☑ 707 847 3836; www.apple-hostel.kz; Sabyr Rakhimov 22; dm 2500T; ✳@🛜; ☑ 1, 2, 9, 48, 70) This friendly, well-kept little hostel in the old city is unsigned and hard to find, so contact them ahead of arrival. It offers spacious four- and six-bed dorms, a well-equipped kitchen and two bathrooms. The entrance is up a small staircase next to Akku drycleaners, just inside the southernmost archway into the courtyard of a huge apartment block.

The hostel will pick you up from the bus or train station for 1000T.

Nomad Hostel   HOSTEL **$**
(📞707 557 07 56; www.facebook.com/nomad hostel; Kvartira 112, 5th fl, podezd 3, Zhiloy Kompleks Nomad, Syganak 10; dm/s/d from 3300/6200/9150T; ⊖@🛜; 🚌10, 12, 21, 32, 46) Popular with solo travellers and with a very helpful owner, Nomad occupies a modern, clean apartment with a good kitchen and sitting area, a mixed eight-person bunk dorm, a ladies only four-bed one and two small, comfy doubles. Only one bathroom. Call ahead to make sure someone will be there to help you get in (there are no signs).

Belon-Land Hotel   BUSINESS HOTEL **$$**
(📞7172 32 83 08; http://belon.kz; Bagenbay Batyr 45; s/d from 18,300/22,500T; ❄🛜; 🚌2, 16, 36, 106) Well-located for train-station access and within easy reach of attractions in the old part of town, this friendly business hotel is part of a local minichain. Rooms are fairly compact but spotless and comfortable, staff are very helpful and boons include a small pool, gym and sauna.

**Seven Inn
Boutique Hotel**   BOUTIQUE HOTEL **$$**
(📞7172 65 00 01; http://seven-inn-boutique-hotel. hoteleastana.com; Enbekshiler 21; r 22,000 incl breakfast; ❄🛜; 🚌12, 18, 40, 46, 56) There's

excellent service at this seven-room hotel, with staff going out of their way to be helpful. Decor is somewhat reminiscent of old-world European hotels, with wood-panelled rooms, grand mirrors and chandeliers. Close to Ak Orda, the pyramid and the National Museum.

Otyrar Hotel   HOTEL **$$**
(📞776 111 65 01; www.otyrar-hotel.hoteleastana. com; Otyrar 10; s/d 9800/14,400T; ⊖🛜; 🚌1, 2, 13, 24, 70) Cosy little hotel, tucked away down a little side street. Staff are very helpful (though not much English spoken), and the compact, spotless en suites come with flat-screen TVs and bug netting – essential for summer. Wi-fi works best in the lobby and dining room.

Hotel Ulpan   HOTEL **$$**
(📞7172 57 16 83; http://ulpan.ucoz.ru; Khalel Dos-mukhammeduly 11; s/d 11,000/16,200T; ⊖❄🛜; 🚌18, 21, 28, 50, 70) As much a guesthouse as a hotel, this small, family-run establishment on a quiet street is as close as you'll get to the left-bank attractions at midrange prices. The bright rooms have shiny bedspreads and little flower prints. Breakfast is available in your room for 1000T. One family member speaks some English.

Hotel Jumbaktas   BUSINESS HOTEL **$$$**
(📞7172 57 97 77; www.jumbaktas.kz; Karasakal Ye-rimbet 65; s/d incl breakfast from 32,400/34,600T; 🅿⊖❄🛜; 🚌18, 21, 28, 52, 70) The building is a modern, 10-storey glass cylinder but the in-

---

EXPO 2017 ASTANA

Taking place between June and September 2017, the World Expo gave Astana its biggest boost yet. Perhaps surprisingly in a country whose economy relies heavily on oil, gas and other minerals, the theme of Expo 2017 Astana (www.expo2017astana.com) was 'Future Energy', with numerous talks, workshops, musical performances and parades taking place on the theme of alternative energy sources and energy-saving technologies. Kazakhstan officialdom had been at pains to argue that the country is ultimately committed to a green economy. The Expo site, in the southeast of the city, was built to be energy self-sufficient, with solar cells and its own wind farm. Of the 100 plus participant countries, many showcased their own commitment to green energy in the purpose-built grounds, while others took the opportunity to promote their country as a tourism destination.

With almost a quarter of a million visitors to the Expo in the first week, the event was certainly a big boost for Astana's development. Three new motorways were built and Astana acquired a new train station to accommodate high-speed services to Almaty and other major cities, as well as a fleet of new, energy-efficient buses.

While it is not clear what the Expo grounds will be used for in future, new infrastructure aside, the Expo's biggest achievement has been to expose locals to cultures and developments from around the world.

side has an elegant air, with chandeliers, patterned marble floor and sizeable, comfortable rooms in golds and russets. Reception is welcoming and English-speaking and the location is ideal for exploring modern Astana.

✗ Eating

Astana's dining scene spans the globe and is unrivalled in Kazakhstan outside Almaty. Dining options run the gamut from 24-hour cheapies serving kebabs, to international fast food chains in the food courts of shopping malls like **Mega Astana** (http://astana.megacenter.kz/eng/foodcourt; Korgalzhin taszholy 1; mains from 1000T; ⊙ food court 10am-midnight), to excellent Japanese, Korean, Indian, Georgian, Chinese, Russian, Italian, Ukrainian and Central Asian cuisine.

Eagilik Books & Coffee CAFE $

(☑7172 20 08 01; www.facebook.com/eagilik/; Kenesary 61/1; snacks 300-600T; ⊙10am-9pm Tue-Sat, 2-9pm Sun; 🛜🖉; 🚍1, 2, 9, 19, 48) The relaxed cafe at this friendly English bookshop, a bit of an expat hang-out, does a very welcome range of homemade quiches, pies, cheesecakes and cinnamon rolls. The coffee's fine, too. The shop sells a good range of English-language books on Central Asia.

★ Hot Spot CAFE $$

(☑7172-20 20 17; www.facebook.com/hotspotastana/?rf=709283589204027; Kenesary 63; mains 1700-2500; ⊙9am-midnight; 🛜; 🚍1, 2, 9, 19, 48) Popular with a young, laptop-wielding crowd, this trendy cafe has something for everyone: good coffee, ample breakfasts, some of the best burgers in town, a great take on *syrniki* (cottage cheese fritters) and a handful of craft beers. Young, friendly service.

Melnitsa UKRAINIAN $$

(☑701 531 06 07; Turan dangyly 31; mains 1800-5400; ⊙noon-2am; 🛜; 🚍12, 32, 43, 46, 53) The owners of this restaurant chose a 'Ukrainian peasant inside a windmill' theme and then decided to run with it a few miles. Expect hay wagons, pitchforks and a menu full of gut-busting Ukrainian favourites, such as *deruny* (potato fritters), *golubtsy* (stuffed cabbage leaves), *vareniki* (cherry dumplings) and *salo* (lard). Service sometimes moves at a glacial pace.

Epoch RUSSIAN $$

(☑7172 21 01 57; http://rest.pucha.kz/epoxa/; Valikhanov 9; mains 1600-3600T; ⊙noon-midnight; 🚍1, 2, 9, 26, 48) Walk in past the vintage Soviet cars by the entrance and you're free to indulge your communist fantasies. The decor is OTT USSR – Stalin portraits, hammer-and-sickle emblems, red brick walls lined with books. Servers are dressed in Pioneer uniforms, and the extensive menu features such classics as borscht, Lenin-style beefsteak and meat in aspic. Live music most evenings. Kitsch fun.

Fusion Guru INDIAN $$

(☑701 877 55 44; www.facebook.com/thefusionguru/; Qonayev 14; mains 1600-3600T; ⊙noon-11.30pm; 🖉🌐; 🚍10, 12, 32, 52, 70) Cavernous restaurant specialising in authentic Indian food – mostly from the north, with tandoori chicken, lamb rogan josh and other favourites, but with the odd southern dish thrown in (Goan fish curry). Ask the staff to amp up the spice levels if you're a chilli fiend. Service is friendly but scatty.

Divan TURKISH $$

(☑7172 97 17 00; www.divan-restaurant.kz; Qonayev 14; mains 1800-2900T; ⊙9am-11pm; 🚍12, 18, 32, 46, 51) The menu at this friendly Turkish eatery has a series of lamb/chicken/beef kebabs and shashlyk, as well as *pide* (Turkish pizza), steak and hearty soups. It's all good – as are the views of the Bayterek monument and dancing fountains from the window tables. No alcohol.

Caramel CAFE $$

(☑7172 29 33 00; Zhiloy Kompleks Nursaya 2, Dostyk 13; cakes & pastries 500-1000T; breakfast 1000-1800T; ⊙11am-2am; 🛜; 🚍12, 18, 28, 46, 52) A tasteful, spacious and relaxed coffee house that's great to drop into for a late breakfast (including English and continental) or a caffeine-and-strudel pick-me-up.

Assorti INTERNATIONAL $$

(☑7172 57 88 58; www.assorti.kz; Turan dangyly 37; mains 1200-3900T; ⊙10am-11pm; 🛜; 🚍10, 29, 32, 46, 56) Inside Khan Shatyr, this popular chain restaurant serves up nice enough pizzas and grilled meats. Two other branches around the city.

★ Pane & Vino ITALIAN $$$

(☑7172-72 96 03; www.panevinoastana.com; Sarayshyk 5; mains 2400-14,900; ⊙noon-1am; ❄🛜🖉; 🚍18, 21, 28, 52, 70) Decorated with framed recipes from different regions of Italy, this refined, contemporary restaurant really delivers when it comes to pasta, risotto and grilled meat dishes. Homemade gnocchi and *prosecco* and shrimp risotto stand out. Wood-fired pizzas are a bargain.

★ Izumi Tai
JAPANESE $$$

(Изуми Тай; ☎700 888 09 91; www.facebook.com/izumi.astana/; Kabanbai Batyr 32; mains 3100-13,000; ⊗noon-2am; 🛜📶; 🚌10, 12, 32, 46, 51) Tasteful minimalist decor and friendly service greet you as you enter, and the extensive menu of Japanese dishes – from sashimi to cold soba noodles – doesn't let the side down. The scallop sushi rolls are among the best we've ever tasted, anywhere.

★ Astana Nury
GEORGIAN, AZERBAIJANI $$$

(☎7172-43 93 39; www.a-n.kz; Respublika dangyly 3/2; mains 1800-9900T; ⊗noon-3am; 🛜📶; 🚌1, 2, 10, 20, 32) This top-class Azerbaijani/Georgian restaurant has two lovely decks overlooking the river as well as an inside dining room with beautiful Azeri decor. The many varieties of shashlyk, coal-grilled meats and Azeri *pilaw (plov)* dishes are among the best on the menu.

🍺 Drinking & Nightlife

Microbreweries now have a foothold in Astana, with new wine and cocktail bars lending the established nightlife scene some sophistication. 'Face control' (bouncers deciding whether you look pretty enough to be allowed in) and dress codes are the norm at the better clubs, but don't go before midnight, as the action doesn't kick off before then.

★ Espresso Bar
COFFEE

(☎707 733 30 95; www.facebook.com/Espresso BarAstana/; Mukhtar Auezov 2; ⊗9am-11.30pm Mon-Fri, from 9.30am Sat & Sun; 🛜; 🚌1, 2, 10, 32, 52) Latte art has made it to Kazakhstan! This friendly cafe has won many fans with what is, arguably, Astana's best coffee. Ample breakfasts and snacks are additional enticements.

Barley
BEER HALL

(☎701 952 1777; http://ariahm.kz/projects/the-barley/; Amangeldi Imanov 20; ⊗noon-2am; 🛜; 🚌1, 20, 38, 70) This glass-and-brick club and restaurant complex is a place to see and be seen; the food is hit-and-miss, but the two own brews – a Belgian-style wheat beer and a classic barley pilsner – get rave reviews, and plenty of clients from the US embassy.

Provino
WINE BAR

(☎778 425 2221; www.provino.com.kz; Kenesary 30; ⊗10am-2am Mon-Sat, to midnight Sun; 🚌1, 9, 17, 32) Cute little wine bar with 10 or so international wines by the glass and many more by the bottle, including a number of Kazakh vintages. There's a full menu of bar snacks and even substantial dishes, but the tipples are the main draw.

Pivnitsa
BAR

(☎7172 99 05 00; www.radissonblu.com/hotel-astana/restaurants-and-bars/pivnitsa; Saryarka dangyly 2; ⊗noon-2am; 🛜; 🚌12, 21, 36, 46, 53) This dark Czech cellar-bar – stone walls, wooden booths and long wood tables – is a convivial place for mugs of the unfiltered house beer, Kelly (800T for 0.5L), which comes in two types: light and dark. There are also sausages, steaks and other meaty fare to soak it up. The bar is entered from the riverside just below the Radisson Hotel.

Chocolate Room
CLUB

(Shokolad; ☎701 550 00 17; Saryarka dangyly 2; ⊗11pm-5am; 🛜; 🚌12, 21, 36, 46, 53) Once past the face control (look your very best) you'll have a wild time dancing to hip hop, dance and '80s DJs with Astana's beautiful 20-somethings at what is still one of the coolest clubs in town. Admission is free; pay for a table or perch at the bar. It's entered from the riverside below the Radisson Hotel.

☆ Entertainment

As befitting any capital worth its salt, Astana has several theatres, including the brand new Opera House, which stages opera and ballet performances. All shopping malls have multiplex cinemas that screen international blockbusters; most are dubbed, but there are some screenings in English.

Astana Opera House
OPERA

(☎7172 70 96 00; www.astanaopera.kz; Qonayev 1; ⊗box office 10am-6.45pm Mon-Fri, to 5.45pm Sat & Sun; 🚌10, 29, 32, 46, 56) Astana's gleaming Opera House stages excellent performances by global opera and ballet companies, as well as Universal Ballet, chamber-orchestra concerts and more.

Central Concert Hall
CLASSICAL MUSIC

(☎7172 70 52 56; www.qazaqconcert.kz; Prospekt Mangilik 10/1; ⊗box office 9am-6pm Mon-Fri; 🚌12, 18, 21, 32, 70) This turquoise-tiled concert hall, designed by Italian architects Manfredi and Luca Nicoletti, has a swirling, circular design intended to evoke the petals of a flower. Symphony orchestra and traditional Kazakh music concerts are held here.

Shopping

Astana has half a dozen luxury shopping malls, mostly stocking Italian fashions, though some stores also feature local designers.

Sary Arka MALL
(☑7172 51 56 06; www.saryarka.com; Turan dangyly 24; ☉10am-10pm; ☒12, 32, 46, 53) This mall is worth visiting for two stores. Red Carpet features ladies' fashion and accessories by Kazakhstan designers such as Aida Kaumenova, Gulnara Kassym and Aseem Nurseitova. Dresses and accessories at Dinara Satzhan are more outlandish, and there are some beautiful woven wall hangings there as well.

Empire GIFTS & SOUVENIRS
(☑7172-68 80 00; www.empire-ltd.kz; Korgalzhyn taszholy 1, Mega Astana KeruenCity; ☉9am-6pm; ☒12, 21, 32, 46, 53) These (mostly) tasteful, high-end gifts include framed traditional silver belt ornaments and necklaces, locally designed crystal goblet sets, chess sets, jewellery boxes, leather wallets and fairly garish, nomadic-themed porcelain. There are four more branches in Astana's other main shopping malls.

Talisman GIFTS & SOUVENIRS
(☑7172 43 94 28; Respublika dangyly 7; ☉10am-8pm; ☒1, 2, 10, 27, 52) A mind-boggling array of all things Kazakhstan: felt yurts, hats and booties, replica nomadic objects, such as the phallic-looking vessels for carrying fermented mare's milk, models of the Bayterek Monument, porcelain, wall hangings and more.

❶ Information

Astana is home to nearly all the foreign embassies in Kazakhstan. See p364 for a list.

There is no tourist office, so your best bet are hotel desks and travel agencies, such as **Akmolaturist** (☑7172 22 26 72; www.facebook.com/profile.php?id=100015924251080&ref=br_rs; Office 22, Hotel Abay, Respublika dangyly 33; ☉10am-6pm Mon-Fri; ☒1, 2, 19, 38, 70).

The website www.edgekz.com has some up-to-date, interesting articles on Astana.

There are ATMs at all the shopping malls, the two train stations and the airport. They are also found along Respublika dangyly and other main streets in the old part of the city.

There are pharmacies in all the shopping malls, plus 24-hour pharmacies along the main streets. Look for the green cross.

The **International SOS Astana Clinic** (☑7172 47 69 11; www.internationalsos.com/locations/cis/kazakhstan; Kosmonavtov 62A; ☒18, 27, 32, 44, 70) is a private clinic with English-speaking doctors and 24-hour emergency care.

❶ Getting There & Away

Astana is well connected with the rest of the country and the world. The old train and bus stations are side by side, 3km north of centre, while the new Nurly Zhol train station is to the east of modern Astana. **Astana International Airport** (TSE; ☑7172-70 29 99; www.astana-airport.com; ☒10, 12, 100, 200) is 14km south of the city.

AIR

Domestic destinations are served by Air Astana and the cheaper budget carriers, SCAT and Bek Air. The airport website has full schedules.

From Astana International Airport, domestic services include the following:

DESTINATION	COST (T)	TIME (HR)	FREQUENCY
Aktau	25,200	2½	1-3 daily
Aktobe	22,000	1½	2-3 daily
Almaty	15,000	1½	4-10 daily
Atyrau	26,600	2-2½	2 daily
Semey (Semipalatinsk)	29,000	2	4 weekly
Shymkent	16,200	2	5 daily
Taraz (Zhambyl)	24,700	1½	1 daily
Ust-Kamenogorsk	20,300	1½	3 daily

Astana also has numerous direct flights to European and Asian capitals.

BUS, MINIBUS & SHARE TAXI

From the **bus station** (☑7172 38 11 35; www.saparzhai.kz; Gyote 5; ☒10, 12, 19, 21, 27, 48, 100, 200), buses and minibuses travel slowly to many destinations, including those in the table overleaf.

Private minibuses and shared taxis to Karaganda (minibus/shared taxi 1500/2500T, three

KAZAKHSTAN ASTANA

hours), Shchuchinsk (1800T, 2¾ hours) and Burabay (2000T, three hours) wait outside the bus station.

Bus destinations include:

DESTINATION	COST (T)	TIME (HR)	FREQUENCY
Almaty	5500	19	2 daily
Karaganda	1500	4½	every 30 minutes, 7am to 9pm
Novosibirsk (Russia)	1050	15	9.05pm Thu & Fri
Omsk (Russia)	5400	11	2 daily
Petropavlovsk	3700	10	3 daily
Semey	4700	15	5 daily
Shchuchinsk (for Burabay)	1900	3	19 daily
Shymkent	6000	24	2 daily
Taraz	4700	20	1 daily

TRAIN

Astana has two train stations: the old **Astana-1 train station** (☑ 7172 38 07 07; Gyote 7; 🚋 10, 12, 19, 21, 27, 48, 100, 200) in the old part of the city and the new **Astana Nurly Zhol train station** (☎; 🚋 2, 14, 32, 48, 50, 57, 201, 500), which opened in June 2017, located east of modern Astana. The old train station handles international departures, while Nurly Zhol is responsible for most of the cross-country high-speed (Talgo) services. Some of the Nurly Zhol departures also call at the old train station.

Between them, the two stations have services to Almaty (three daily) and Karaganda (at least 13 daily), as well as daily trains to Petropavlovsk, Shymkent, Aktobe, Kyzylorda and Omsk, with several weekly services to Semey (Semipalatinsk), Yekaterinburg and Moscow. Some of the most convenient are listed below.

ⓘ Getting Around

A taxi from the airport into town costs around 2000T to 3500T. Taxi drivers are reluctant to

DESTINATION	TRAIN NO.	COST (2ND/3RD CLASS)	DEPARTURE	TIME (HR)
Almaty (via Karaganda)	705/706*	20,122/14,703T**	8.48pm daily	13
Bishkek (Kyrgyzstan)	305/306	4262/3243 RUB	7.15pm Fri & Sun	27
Karaganda	83/84	2158/1424T	8.44am every other day	4
Kokshetau	55/56	13,900/8556T	7.40am daily	4½
Kyzylorda	55/56	55,840/35,815T	11.59pm daily	32
Moscow (Russia)	83/84	15,501/11,338 RUB	11.26am Wed & Sun	56
Omsk (Russia)	145/146	4183/3042 RUB	4.20am daily	14½
Petropavlovsk	75/76	18,335/11,496T	8.20am every other day	8½
Semey (Semipalatinsk)	375/376	4499/2898T	2.20pm Mon-Fri	17¼
Shymkent	55/56	8271/5312T	11.59pm daily	23
Tashkent (Uzbekistan)	315/316	5767/4542 RUB	7.15pm Tue	35
Uralsk	57/58	5921/4789 RUB	10.45pm every other day	38
Yekaterinburg (Russia)	305/306	5256/3879 RUB	6pm Wed & Fri	24

From Astana Nurly Zhol, services include the following:

DESTINATION	TRAIN NO.	COST (2ND/3RD CLASS)	DEPARTURE	TIME (HR)
Almaty	3/4*	13,567/9774/4443T***	9.22am daily	14¾
Atyrau	19/20*	27,100/18,021T**	7.20pm every other day	22½
Karaganda	853/854	1070T (seat)	11.10am daily	3¼
Kokshetau	805/806	1426T (seat)	6.30am daily	4¾
Kyzylorda	89/90*	28,370/21,695T**	11.50pm Mon & Sat	22½
Mangistau	37/38	11,595/7435T	7pm daily	48
Shymkent	707/708*	19,082/14,938T**	11.50pm every other day	15¾

* high-speed service / ** 1st/2nd class / *** 1st/2nd/3rd class

use meters, so prices must be negotiated before setting off. Uber also works in Astana.

A new light railway system is due to come into operation in 2018.

BICYCLE

There are numerous **Astana Bike** (www.velobike.kz; 100/250/500T for 1/2/3 hours) docking stations all over the city. You need to register online and pay a 500T daily access fee before borrowing a bike. They're free if you use one to go from one docking station to another within 30 minutes, otherwise you'll be charged per hour.

BUS

Astana has an excellent city bus network, with bus route maps shown at many bus stops. Buses start between 6am and 7am and finish between 10pm and 11pm. Single-trip tickets cost 90T; for express routes they cost 150T. The very useful Astra Bus app helps you plot your route and shows you in real time which buses are due to arrive at which bus stop.

Useful bus routes include the following:

10 Astana-1 train station to airport via Khan Shatyr and Qonayev bulvar

9 & 12 Astana-1 train station via Beibitshilik, Seyfullin, Zhengis and Kenesary

21 Astana-1 to Bayterek Monument, Ak Orda, the pyramid and National Museum, via Zhengis, Sarayka, Qabanbay Batyr, Qonayev and Mangilik

25 Astana-1 south to the river via Zhengis and Respublika dangyly

32 Astana Nurly Zhol to the old city via the pyramid, Ak Orda, Nurzhol bulvar, Turan dangyly and Respublika dangyly

40 Astana-1 to the pyramid and Khan Shatyr via Seyfullin and Kenesary in old Astana, and Sarayshyk, Mangilik and Dostyk in modern Astana

100 Express bus from Astana-1 to the airport

500 Express bus from Astana Nurly Zhol to the airport

505 Express bus from Astana Nurly Zhol to Khan Shatyr, via the pyramid

TOUR BUS

The hop-on, hop-off **Astana Bus Tours** (7172 77 90 99; www.redbus.kz; adult/student/child 3000/2000/2000T; 9am-9pm Mar-Nov) tourist service in open-top double-deckers – the first of its kind in Central Asia – provides an easy option for getting round Astana's sights. Buses depart every 40 minutes from Duman, opposite Keruen City mall, stopping at the Khan Shatyr, Bayterek Monument, Palace of Peace and Reconciliation, the Expo 2017 site, and other attractions. Tickets are valid for 24 hours.

Around Astana

Korgalzhyn   Қорғалжын

Korgalzhyn is home to the Unesco World Heritage–listed Korgalzhyn Nature Reserve, which attracts wildlife lovers, particularly birding enthusiasts. The area's 200-plus lakes are a vital stop on major bird-migration routes from Africa, the Middle East and India to summer breeding grounds in Siberia.

Lake Tengiz is particularly interesting as the salty lake is home to the world's most northerly flamingo colony from April to September. Some 4000 of the world's 10,000 critically endangered sociable lapwings spend their summers in the area too. Birdwatchers from flock in during May and June for the northward migration.

The on-site **Korgalzhyn Nature Reserve Visitors' Centre** (71637 2 16 50, 71637 2 10 13; Madin Rakhimzhan 20; park entry 400T; 10am-1pm & 2-5pm Mon-Fri) has exhibits on local birdlife and issues permits.

Travellers staying overnight base themselves in Korgalzhyn village, which is 38km from the entrance to the actual nature reserve. Little Lake Tengiz – the most accessible part of the reserve for flamingowatching, is another 20km or so beyond that, so you'll need to arrange transport. The village has several simple but clean guesthouses whose owners will organise trips into the reserve and to other nearer bird-rich lakes outside the reserve. Contact **Gostevoy Dom U Nadezhdy** (71637 2 11 59, 702 923 92 48; Chokan Ualikhanov 12/2, Korgalzhyn; per person incl meals 7000T), **Timur Iskakov** (71637 2 10 64, 701 622 48 00; timur_iskak@mail.ru; Gorky 9, Korgalzhyn; per person incl meals 7000T;), or especially the highly recommended **Bibinur Alimzhanov** (702 453 61 28, 71637 2 18 00; alimzhanov@gmail.com; Abay 10/2, Korgalzhyn; per person incl meals 7000T;). All offer full board.

The Almaty-based Ecotourism Information Resource Centre (p302) can help make trip/homestay arrangements.

Minibuses to Korgalzhyn (1700T, three hours) leave Astana bus station eight times daily from 10am. Buy your ticket in advance for the first departure. Shared taxis to Korgalzhyn (2000T, two hours) go from outside the bus station. Uzbekistan-based Advantour (p330) runs day trips from Astana to Korgalzhyn Nature Reserve (from US$140 per person).

Lake Burabay
Озеро Бурабай

☑ 71630

Lake Burabay (formerly Borovoe), 240km north of Astana, is the focus of **Burabay National Nature Park** (www.gnpp.kz), a picturesque 835-sq-km area of lakes, hills, pine forest and strange rock formations that have given birth to several Kazakh legends. It's very popular with weekenders from Astana and holidaymakers from Russia, and development is fairly rampant, with new hotels constantly popping up in town and around the lakes.

The small town of Burabay stretches about 2.5km along the lake's northeast shore. It can get very crowded here, particularly on summer weekends, with bungee trampolines, bouncy castles and nightclubs providing entertainment for all ages.

◉ Sights & Activities

In town, stop by the **Burabay National Nature Park Visitor Centre** (Vizit-Tsentr & Tabigat Murazhayy; ☑ 71636 7 17 80; www.burabay-damu.kz; Kenesary; adult/child 700/500T; ☉10am-7pm Tue-Sun) for a diverse display of taxidermied wildlife from Kazakhstan's national parks (including a demented-looking fox), two ATMs, and a souvenir shop selling a park map for 350T. Entry includes an adjoining outdoor zoo with fairly content maral and reindeer, camels, wild boar, argali sheep and yaks. Predators in tiny enclosures are not a sight for animal lovers, however.

A well-made walking path parallels the main road for 9km from the lake's southeast to northwest corners via Burabay town. Heading west from the town it's 4km to picturesque **Goluboy Zaliv** (Blue Bay), where you can rent a **rowing boat** (per 30/60min 1500/3000T; ☉9am-8pm) to paddle out to Zhumbaktas. The most celebrated Burabay legend links Zhumbaktas, the Sphinx-like rock sticking out of the lake, with Okzhet-pes, the striking 380m-tall rock pile rising on the shore behind it.

Continue 1.75km further round the lake to reach **Polyana Abylay Khana** (Abylay Khan's Clearing), a clearing 6km south of Burabay where the warrior hero reputedly once assembled his forces during his Zhungar campaigns. A tall, eagle-topped monument, with good old Ab astride a snow leopard, stands in the clearing.

A path from the back of the clearing leads up 947m Mt Kokshetau, the highest peak in Burabay National Nature Park (about 1½ hours to the top). A few steps along the trail lead you to Abylai Khan's Throne – several rocks perched on a broad flat one. Local lore suggests that if you walk around it seven times anticlockwise and then hug a pine tree, your wish will come true.

A gentler climb, with good views of both Lake Burabay and Lake Bolshoe Chebachie to its north, is Mt Bolektau. This short, easy ascent takes around half an hour. The track leads up to the right just before the Km 4 post heading west from Burabay town.

It's possible to cycle along parts of the lakeside path; if cycling on the main road, bear in mind that motorists are not terribly respectful of bicycles. To rent a bike, look for '*Prokat Velosipedov*' (прокат велосипедов) signs along the main road in Burabay. Bike hire typically costs around 500T per hour, 2000T per day.

🛏 Sleeping & Eating

The choice of hotels in and near Burabay town is wide and good, though lodgings on or near the main street are 'entertained' by the pounding bass from clubs until the wee hours. It's easy to rent a room, cabin, apartment or yurt for 1200T to 2800T per person: look for signs saying '*sdam komnatu/domik/kvartiru/yurtu*' (сдам комнату/домик/квартиру/юрту) along the main street, Kenesary. All-inclusive sanatoriums are near the lakes, further south.

By the roundabout at the entrance to Burabay from Shchuchinsk, **Baza Otdykha Akmolaturist No 1** (☑ 71630 7 15 11; www.touring.kz; Kenesary 55; per person 3000-3750T) provides cosy rooms for two to six people, with a shared kitchen and clean shared bathrooms.

Almost directly opposite the museum, intimate 20-room **Hotel Gloria** (☑ 71630 7 23 66; Kenesary 4; r from 10,000T, f 22,000T; ✳🕸) has a lot going for it, from a supercentral location to well-equipped rooms.

Kokshebel Lake Resort (☑ 71636 7 11 97; sales-kokshebel@mail.ru; Kenesary 2A; incl breakfast cabins 15,000-35,000T, r 18,000-28,000T; ⓅⓈ✳🕸🏊) is a well-built, well-run hotel with attractive pine-wooded grounds stretching down to the lakeshore (with private beach) at the west end of town.

Burabay's main smattering of nonhotel eateries is along Kenesary near the central bus and taxi stop and next to (and inside) the market. Expect plenty of shashlyk, *plov* (pilaf) and *manty* (steamed dumplings).

Just beyond the south end of the market, hole-in-the-wall **Ayzhar** (Kenesary; mains 600-1200T; ⊘9am-11pm) serves inexpensive shashlyk, salads and hearty breakfasts. In front of the market, popular **Asia Kafe** (🗂702 991 99 93; Kenesary 21; mains 1000-1800T; ⊘11am-midnight) is a solid choice if you're looking for shashlyk, as well as more imaginative meaty mains such as duck with cranberry sauce and baked veal with mushrooms.

ℹ️ Getting There & Away

Minibuses (1800T to 2200T, three hours) and shared taxis (3000T) to Burabay leave from outside Astana's bus station when full. Daytime departures are plentiful in summer and at weekends. More plentiful transport (at least 19 buses or minibuses) runs from Astana to Shchuchinsk, on the Astana–Kokshetau road 15km south of the lake. From Shchuchinsk small white buses (180T, 30 minutes) run every 40 minutes (7am to 8pm) to Burabay, or there are shared/charter taxis for 350/1500T. In Burabay, the stop is just off the main street, Kenesary, towards the west end of town.

There are six to nine trains daily from Astana to the Kurort-Borovoye (Курорт-Боровое) train station in Shchuchinsk (from 1450T, three hours). Shchuchinsk bus station is in front and to the right of the train station.

Karaganda   Қарағанды

🗂7212 / POP 497,824 / ELEV 550M

Smack in the steppe heartland, 220km southeast of Astana, Karaganda (Karagandy) is most famous for two things: coal and labour camps. The two are intimately connected, as the vast 'KarLag' network of Stalin-era camps around Karaganda was set up to provide food and labour for the mines. Prison labour also built much of Karaganda itself.

During the depressed 1990s many of Karaganda's ethnic-German residents (descendants of Stalin-era deportees) emigrated to Germany. But Karaganda has bounced back and today the central areas of the city are a pleasant surprise, with a lively buzz, good dining scene and plenty of parks and broad tree-lined streets, all prettily illuminated after dark. Bukhar Zhyrau dangyly, the main street, heads north through the centre from the train and bus stations.

If you want to explore the steppe heartland with English-speaking guides, climb its

hills, photograph saiga or birds, visit remote archaeological and historic sites and experience vast panoramas, the dynamic young travel enthusiasts of **Nomadic Travel Kazakhstan** (🗂7212 99 61 65; www.nomadic.kz; Office 209, Bukhar Zhyrau dangyly 49; ⊘9am-6pm Mon-Fri) 🏖 are just the ticket. The office is a good place for regional tourist information, and it has an excellent city and regional tourist map available.

⊙ Sights

Off the main drag, leafy **Central Park** (off Bukhar Zhyrau dangyly) stretches over 2km from north to south around a large lake.

Karaganda Ecological Museum   MUSEUM
(🗂7212 41 33 44; http://ecomuseum.kz; Bukhar Zhyrau dangyly 47; admission per person without tour 150T, with tour 200-300T; ⊘9am-7pm Mon-Fri, by arrangement Sat & Sun) The Karaganda Ecological Museum, run by a dedicated, campaigning environmental NGO, is aimed at local schoolchildren and is the most imaginative museum in the country. Everything can be touched, and this includes large rocket parts that have fallen on the steppe after Baykonur space launches, and debris collected from the Semipalatinsk Polygon (p357). Other display topics include the saiga antelope and chemical safety in

Karaganda (Karagandy)

pressions of the 1930s. Guided tours (300T) available in English.

⎇ Sleeping & Eating

Karaganda has plenty of *stolovayas* (canteens) for budget travellers, as well as a good selection of more upmarket international restaurants catering to the business set. In summer, open-air shashlyk-and-beer cafes are strung all along Abdirov.

There are several lively bars in the city centre. One of the city's best restaurants – **Line Brew** (☎ 721 256 31 80; http://line-brew.kz/line-brew-karaganda/; Beibitshilik bulvar 24; mains 1400-5300T; ❈ ☎ ▣) – is also part of the award-winning national chain.

Metelitsa Hotel HOTEL $$
(☎ 721 240 00 04; http://metelitsa-hotel.kz; Bukhar Zhyrau dangyly 56a; r from 18,000T; ❈ ☎ ❈) Intimate hotel tucked away in a quiet cul-de-sac, with cosy, carpeted rooms, helpful staff and a decent restaurant on-site.

Hotel Ar-Nuvo HOTEL $$$
(☎ 7212 42 02 84; www.arnuvo.kz; Beibitshilik bulvary 4A; s/d incl breakfast from 22,000/24,000T; ℙ❈☎) This attractive, well-run hotel provides cosy, solidly comfy rooms (that could be dragged into the 21st century, ideally) with nice big white bath-tubs. Desk staff

Kazakhstan. Labelling is in Russian only; request an English tour in advance.

Karaganda Oblast Museum MUSEUM
(☎ 7212 56 48 62; Yerubaev 38; 200T; ⊙ 9am-6pm) Displays at this regional museum run the gamut from stuffed local wildlife and a model of an Iron Age *kurgan* (burial mound) to letters from Middle Horde Kazakhs, offering their vassalship to the Russian Empire, and the creation of the 458km Irtysh-Karaganda canal in the 1970s to supply the city's ever-hungry heavy industry. There's a poignant section on KarLag and the Stalinist re-

GULAG MEMORIALS AROUND KARAGANDA

Dolinka, about 45km southwest of Karaganda, was the administrative centre for the whole KarLag system, whose territory extended over 1200 sq km. The excellent 14-room **KarLag Museum** (Museum of the Victims of Political Repressions; ☑ 72156 5 82 22; Shkolnaya 39, Dolinka; 500T; ☺9am-6pm Mon-Sat) here, housed in the old KarLag headquarters building, gives a vivid idea of the conditions and suffering of the victims through re-creations of cells and other rooms, dioramas and paintings, as well as memorabilia such as photos, letters and furnishings. KarLag death rates reached 30% a year at times. There is much explanatory material in English but the English-language tour (1000T per group) is well worthwhile; call ahead to book one. Also in the village are other KarLag relics including a hospital, a clinic, the officers' club and the Mamochkino children's cemetery. Get to Dolinka by Shakhtinsk-bound bus 121, leaving Karaganda bus station every 10 to 20 minutes. Get off at the Vtoroy Shakht stop after about one hour (150T), walk or take a shared taxi into Dolinka (1.5km) and ask for the *muzey* (museum).

Spassk, 35km south of Karaganda on the Almaty highway, was the site of a KarLag camp where foreign prisoners of war were kept after WWII. There's little to see here, besides the mass grave of some 5000 prisoners near the highway, and lives lost marked with eerie groups of crosses and country-specific monuments scattered around the site. A round-trip taxi to Spassk costs about 5000T from Karaganda.

Nomadic Travel Kazakhstan (p347) takes trips to both these sites for 27,000T per group of up to five.

are welcoming, speak decent English, and there's a good 24-hour restaurant. As the name implies, it has art nouveau touches.

Rational CAFETERIA $
(Yermekov 58/6; mains 500-1100T; ☺24hr) Rational bills itself a 'business-class *stolovaya* (canteen)' and serves up a range of typical Russian and Central Asian staples that are indeed a cut above the general run of self-service restaurants. This branch is bright and popular and set in the side of the bus-station building.

Moi Tbilisi GEORGIAN $$
(☑721 247 77 58; Abdirov dangyly 32/3; mains 1500-3200T; ☺noon-2am; ☺☑) Georgian classics such as chicken *satsivi* (in walnut sauce), *pkhali* (cold, herb-infused vegetable starters), *khinkali* (steamed, meat-filled dumplings) and grilled meats are served in a log-cabin-style interior with cosy booths. Solid list of Georgian wines complements the hearty food.

Pivovaroff INTERNATIONAL $$$
(☑721 241 15 62; www.facebook.com/pages/Pivovaroff/351811084977319; Beibitshilik bulvary 1; mains 1800-3700T; ☺noon-2am; ☺) Set in a stone-walled basement not unlike a castle cellar, with high-back wooden booths, Pivovaroff is a good choice for dining on salads and grills (including shashlyk and German

sausages) and quaffing unfiltered Staronemetskoe beer.

🍷 Drinking & Entertainment

Elvis LIVE MUSIC
(☑7212 31 97 40; www.music-club.kz; Yerubaev 50A; ☺7pm-3am) Elvis is a fun place to listen to live rock and roll, jazz or blues (nightly from 10pm), drink some beer and eat good food – especially in the open air in summer.

ⓘ Getting There & Around

Karaganda's **airport** (☑7212 42 85 42; www.kgf.aero), 24km southeast of the centre (3000T by taxi), has up to six daily flights to Almaty (from 28,200T) with Air Astana and SCAT, and three or four times weekly to Kyzylorda (from 16,000T) with SCAT. There are up to four daily flights to Moscow with Aeroflot (87,435T) and twice-weekly flights with AtlasGlobal to Antalya (147,000T). Taxis from the airport cost around 4000T.

Destinations from the **bus station** (☑7212 43 18 18; www.avokzal.kz; Yermekov 58/6) include Almaty (6500T, 16 to 19 hours, three daily), Astana (1500T, 4½ hours, every half-hour, 6.30am to 8pm), Semey (3900T, 16 hours, daily) and Ust-Kamenogorsk (5000T, 20 hours, daily). Other daily buses head as far as Petropavlovsk, Omsk, Yekaterinburg and Barnaul (Russia). Minivans (1800T) and shared taxis (3000T) outside the bus station will whisk you to Astana in three hours.

The **train station** (☏ 7212 43 36 36; Yermekov; ☎) has at least 15 daily trains to Astana (2025T to 5326T, 2½ to 4½ hours), plus an additional four or five trains to Astana Nurly Zhol, and up to six trains daily to Almaty (5782T to 13,071T, 10½ to 19½ hours). There are also daily trains to Petropavlovsk and Shymkent, and departures to Semey, Moscow and various Siberian cities several days a week. Book ahead as Karaganda is a midroute station.

Bus 1 (70T) from the train station runs north along Bukhar Zhyrau dangyly then east along Beibitshilik.

EASTERN KAZAKHSTAN

Ust-Kamenogorsk, a relatively prosperous regional capital, is the gateway to this large region full of mountains, lakes and villages with good hiking, horse riding, biking, rafting and other activities. The Altay Mountains, at the eastern extremity, are one of the most beautiful corners of Kazakhstan but you must plan well ahead to get a border-zone permit to visit them.

The region's other main city, Semey, is best known for the infamous Polygon nuclear-testing zone nearby, but is one of Kazakhstan's most culturally and historically interesting cities.

Ust-Kamenogorsk
Усть-Каменого́рск

☏ 7232 / POP 321,536 / ELEV 280M

Ust-Kamenogorsk (Öskemen) is a lively city with generally low-key Soviet architecture, at the confluence of the Irtysh and Ulba Rivers. Founded as a Russian fort in 1720, 'Ust' has grown from a small town since the 1940s, when Russians and Ukrainians began arriving to mine and process the area's copper, lead, silver and zinc. These industries still keep Ust out of the economic doldrums, but are bad news for air quality. The city's proximity to Altai makes it a decent stopover on the way to some of Kazakhstan's most beautiful mountains.

◉ Sights

★ **Levoberezhny Park** PARK
(Left-Bank Park; adult/child 350/150T; ⊙ 10am-7pm; ☐ 17, 26, 60) This large park on the south bank of the Irtysh contains several interesting exhibits and is well worth a couple of hours of your time. Moving west from the entrance through still-growing botanical gardens you reach the Ethnographical Exhibition, which comprises houses in the traditional styles of over a dozen of Kazakhstan's

Ust-Kamenogorsk (Oskemen)

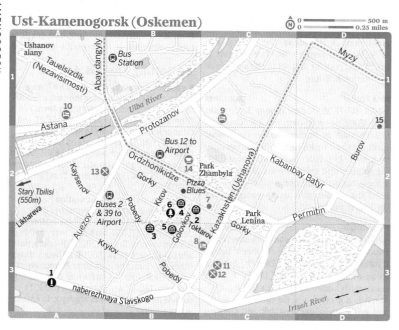

ethnic groups, from Chechens and Tatars to Koreans and Uyghurs.

Strelka VIEWPOINT

(📍2, 23) A pedestrian/cyclist promenade runs to the Strelka (Arrow), the point of land where the Irtysh and Ulba meet, marked by a large Heroes of the Soviet Union memorial.

Afghan War Monument MONUMENT

(naberezhnaya Slavskogo) This poignant memorial is inscribed with a poem, dedicated to the mothers of soldiers who never returned from Afghanistan.

Park Zhastar PARK

(☺daylight) The pretty, beautifully maintained central park makes for a pleasant stroll, and several of Ust-Kamenogorsk's oldest buildings and some worthwhile museums are clustered around it.

The **Ethnography Museum** (📞7232 26 46 61; Golovkov 59; admission per branch 200T; ☺9am-5pm) is in two buildings facing opposite corners of Park Zhastar. The branch on the northeast corner of the park exhibits the traditional culture of the Kazakhs of east Kazakhstan region, with a plethora of household objects devoted to nomadic life and a fully furnished yurt. The second, more worthwhile, **branch** (📞7232 26 85 29; www. vkoem.kz; Kaysenov 67; 200T; ☺10am-6pm; 📍10, 53) to the southwest is devoted to the many different ethnic groups in the region, with traditional embroidery, birch-bark craft and more.

Filling the southeast corner of the park is the good **History Museum** (📞7232 25 54 60; Kaysenov 40; foreigner/local 500/250T; ☺9am-5pm Wed-Mon; 📍10, 53), with a natural-history section with stuffed regional wildlife, including a snow leopard and a giant maral deer,

and human history exhibits that reveal the huge number of ancient burial mounds in the region. Maps and documents trace Ust-Kamenogorsk's growth as a city and there's a large cluster of *balbals* (stone pagan deities) outside.

In the northern part of Park Zhastar, you can check out a number of **historic log cabins** (Park Zhastar; 200T; ☺9am-5pm; 📍25, 53), furnished and decorated in period style.

👉 Tours

Altai Expeditions OUTDOORS

(📞7232 26 97 64, 7232 24 57 09; www.altai expeditions.kz; Office 122, Gorky 46; ☺10am-7pm Mon-Fri; 📍1,2,3,4) Run by experienced, enthusiastic Andrey Yurchenkov, highly recommended Altai Expeditions offers a big range of active trips and nature tours with English-speaking guides. Trips run in the Kazakh, Russian, Mongolian and Chinese Altay and areas nearer to Ust-Kamenogorsk, from day trips to serious foot or horse treks or 4WD tours with hotel or guesthouse accommodation.

🛏 Sleeping & Eating

De Luxe Hotel HOTEL $$

(📞7232 24 09 93; Kaysenov 28A; r from 12,000T; ❄🍴📶♿; 📍10, 53) This hotel has two things going for it: a supercentral location convenient for checking out the city's attractions, and sweet and helpful staff, which almost allows you to overlook erratic wi-fi and missing light bulbs.

Shiny River Hotel HOTEL $$

(📞7232 76 65 25; www.shinyriverhotel.kz; Astana 8/1; s/d incl breakfast from 10,000/14,000T; 🅿❄📶; 📍2, 39, 📍3) This excellent modern hotel overlooking the Ulba has sober but tasteful and very comfy rooms, with shiny silk cushions and bedspreads, plus

KAZAKHSTAN UST-KAMENOGORSK

Ust-Kamenogorsk (Oskemen)

two bars, two classy restaurants and an in-house travel agency. Avoid the cheapest rooms that face the corridor.

Hotel Ust-Kamenogorsk
HOTEL $$

(☏7232 26 18 01; www.hotel-oskemen.kz; Kaban-bay Batyr 158; r incl breakfast from 8500T; ※ 🛜) A large Soviet-era hotel with somewhat-dated rooms in decent condition. All have bathrooms, carpets and thick leopard-spot or tiger-stripe blankets. The wi-fi signal comes and goes like a stray cat.

Pizza Blues
PIZZERIA $

(☏7232 25 23 66; http://pizza-blues.kz; Kazakhstan 64; pizzas 1340-3480T; ⊙11am-midnight; ※ 🛜 ✏ 🅿; 🚌10) A branch of the popular local chain that serves decent pizza, Russian meat and fish dishes, *bliny* and more.

Teplitsa
CAFETERIA $

(☏7232 20 89 59; http://teplica.pizza-blues.kz; Auezov 43; mains 500-900T; ⊙9am-11pm; 🚌2, 39) Teplitsa (Greenhouse) is a stylish update on the old *stolovaya* (cafeteria) concept. There's plenty of freshly prepared food to choose from, and it's hard to beat the tasty sausages grilled to order in front of you. Terrific value.

Imbeer
SUSHI $$

(☏7232 25 95 02; http://imbeer.pizza-blues.kz/; Kazakhstan 64; mains 990-2440T; ⊙11am-midnight; ※ 🛜 ✏ 🅿 ♿; 🚌10) Ticking all the boxes when it comes to foreigner-friendliness, this shiny, casual place is part of the Pizza Blues franchise but specialises in perfectly palatable sushi, noodle dishes and the ubiquitous shashlyk. A glossy, trilingual picture menu, friendly service, kiddie menu and a bright interior add to the appeal.

Stary Tbilisi
GEORGIAN $$

(☏7232 25 63 92; Protozanov 117/1; mains 1100-3400T; ⊙11.30am-1am; 🛜 ✏; 🚌2) *Khachapuri* (Georgian bread with melted *sulguni* cheese), chicken *satsivi* (in walnut sauce), *lobio* (hot, fragrant bean dish) and other Georgian favourites are present and correct. Clichéd name aside, the food is very good; be prepared for a leisurely evening if you order the shashlyk.

🍷 Drinking & Nightlife

★ Sova Espresso Bar
COFFEE

(☏777 269 98 31; www.facebook.com/coffee.shop.sova/; Kirov 64; ⊙8.30am-8pm; 🛜; 🚌1, 2, 3, 4) This branch of the Almaty cafe, founded by award-winning baristas from Moscow,

brings a slice of latte art to the wilds of Ust-Kamenogorsk. Best coffee in town, easily.

ℹ Getting There & Away

From the **airport** (☏7232 77 84 84; 🚌2, 12, 39) there are up to three flights daily with Bek Air, SCAT and Air Astana to Astana (from 22,900T) and Almaty (from 20,700T), and twice weekly SCAT flights to Karaganda (from 16,000T) and Zaysan (8000T). S7 flies to Moscow four times weekly (99,000T) and to Novosibirsk twice-weekly (51,350T).

From the **main bus station** (☏7232 76 66 26; Abay dangyly; 🚌1, 2, 3, 4) buses run to Semey (1600T, 3½ to four hours, 10 daily), Almaty (6000T, 24 hours, daily), Astana (5000T, 23 hours, twice daily), Karaganda (4000T, 21 hours, daily). Destinations in Russia include Barnaul (5000T, 12 hours, twice daily), Novosibirsk (6300T, 18 hours, four daily), and Omsk (9500T, 20¼ hours, daily). Shared taxis to Semey from the bus station cost 2800T – you're most likely to find one earlyish in the morning.

Buses to Ürümqi, China (18,000T, 28 hours) also go from the bus station, at 6.15pm Tuesday, Thursday and Sunday, via the border at Maykapshagay.

Ust-Kamenogorsk's main **train station** (🚌1, 8, 19, 🚌3) is Zashchita, off Tauelsizdik 7km northwest of the centre. Trains run every other day to Almaty (5292T to 12,462T, 17 to 24¾ hours). There are also daily trains to Astana (5681T, 27¼ hours), but the train line leading to the capital initially heads north into Russia to meet the Semey–Novosibirsk line, so travellers need a Russian visa. If your final destination is in Russia, it is not clear whether you need a multiple-entry visa; best to err on the safe side. From Zhangyztobe, 150km southwest and reachable by taxi (shared/charter 3000/10,000T, 2½ hours) or occasional bus (600T, three hours) from Ust-Kamenogorsk bus station, there are up to four daily trains heading to Almaty (4499T to 10,520T, 13¾ to 19¼ hours).

ℹ Getting Around

Buses 2, 12 and 39 (90T) run to the airport from Auezov in the centre. A taxi costs around 1000T; if your hotel hails a taxi, it should use a meter.

From Abay dangyly outside the bus station, trams 1, 2, 3 and 4 (65T) run to Ordzhonikidze and Kazakhstan on the east side of the Ulba; bus 6 (90T) will take you to Auezov for the Hotel Irtysh. Buses 1, 8 and 19 and tram 3 link Zashchita station with the city centre.

If you have a smartphone, 2gis is an excellent app that shows all the transport routes around the city, lets you plot A-to-B travel and even tells you when the next bus/tram is due to arrive at any given stop.

EXCURSIONS AROUND UST-KAMENOGORSK

Even if you have left it too late to get the border-zone permit needed to visit the Altay Mountains proper or other areas near the Chinese border, there's still plenty of good country within reach of Ust-Kamenogorsk that's good for hiking, horse or bike riding, rafting or just exploring. Public transport around the region is limited; it's easier if you organise trips through an Ust-Kamenogorsk agency such as Altai Expeditions (p351) or **Imperia Turizma** (☎ 7232 26 11 08; www.imper-tour.kz; Burov 20, Ust-Kamenogorsk; ⊙ 9am-6pm Mon-Fri; ▣ 13).

The mining town of Ridder, 110km northeast of Ust-Kamenogorsk, is the gateway to beautiful mountain country abutting the Russian border, including the Zapadno-Altaysky (Western Altay) Nature Reserve. There are several camping grounds with cabins along the road heading east through the nature reserve from Ridder to the border, and good, not-too-demanding hiking and trekking in the Ivanovsky Khrebet hills south of the road. (Note: foreigners are not allowed to cross into Russia by this road.) Altai Expeditions charges around €75 per person per day for Ivanovsky Khrebet trips with English-speaking guides. Imperia Turizma offers two-/three-day treks in the Ridder area for 13,000/16,000T per person including transport and meals, or a day's rafting for 25,000T per person not including transport or meals. Eleven buses a day run to Ridder (1000T, three hours) from Ust-Kamenogorsk bus station.

Within easy day-trip distance south of Ust-Kamenogorsk are the intriguing Akbaur Bronze Age astronomical and petroglyph complex (Altai Expeditions charges 7000T per car for a half-day trip), and the ruined medieval Buddhist monastery Ablainskit.

About 200km east of Ust-Kamenogorsk, Maymyr village is a good base for hikes and rides around the broad Naryn valley and the high mountains to the south. Altai Expeditions offers comfy cottage or yurtstays here, and good horse riding. Further south and southeast the highly varied terrain ranges from deserts and dramatic rock formations on the north side of Lake Zaysan to the pristine, 35km-long, 1400m-high Lake Markakol, accessible in summer by a hairy mountain-pass 4WD track from Katon-Karagay, the 'Austrian Road'. Altai Expeditions' wide-ranging 10-day 'Nomad' 4WD tour (around €1900/1500 per person for two-/four-person groups) encompasses this area. You do need a border-zone permit for Markakol, however.

Altay Mountains   Алтай

In the far eastern corner of Kazakhstan the magnificent Altay Mountains spread across the borders to Russia, China and, 50km away, Mongolia. Altay sees few tourists, so intrepid travellers who make it this far can feel like true pioneers.

The hassle of getting to this sparsely populated region is certainly well worth it. Rolling meadows, snow-covered peaks, forested hillsides, glaciers, pristine lakes and rivers, archaeological sites, and rustic villages with Kazakh horsemen riding by make for scenery of epic proportions. Twin-headed Mt Belukha (4506m), on the Kazakh–Russian border, has many mystical associations and Asian legends refer to it as the location of the paradisaical realm of Shambhala.

There are a couple of rustic hiking trails along the southern shore of gorgeous Lake Markakol, a thriving habitat of more than 200 different bird species accessible from the village of Urunkhaika. Near Berel you can visit the excavations of a famous group of Scythian burial mounds, where in 1997 archaeologists discovered the amazingly preserved body of a 4th-century-BC prince, buried with several horses and carriages.

The season of easiest movement and decent weather is short in the Altay: mid-June to the end of September. Caravanistan (www.caravanistan.com) works with several local tour operators in Altay and can organise pretty much any tailor-made trip you want, from treks and rafting to horse riding and homestays. Imperia Turizma (p353) offers 12-day trips from Ust-Kamenogorsk, with a week's trekking in the Belukha foothills, for 75,000T per person in groups of around 10 (bring your own tent and sleeping gear). Altai Expeditions (p351) offers a trip to the foot of Belukha with packhorses, English-speaking guide, cook, tents and sleeping mats

ℹ️ BORDER PERMITS

As of 2017, visitors who are not Kazakh citizens need to apply for a border permit if they wish to travel pretty much anywhere in Altay, even Ridder. Top destinations such as Lake Markakol, Mt Belukha, Rakhmanovskie Klyuchi and the West Altay National Reserve near Poperechnoe village all require a permit. A permit takes 10 business days to process, costs US$50 and requires you to submit your proposed route and dates of travel. The easiest way to get it is via Caravanistan (www.caravanistan.com).

included, and some nights in guesthouses or hotels, for €2430/1890/1440 per person in two-/four-/six-person groups. It also does a 13-day 'Altai Lakes' trip, with eight days on horseback, for €3200/2550 per person in two-/four-person groups.

🛏️ Sleeping

Accommodation in Altay consists almost exclusively of homestays in villages such as Urunkhaika (the gateway to Lake Markakol) and Poperechnoe (northeast of Ridder). Home-cooked meals can be organised at all village homestays.

There is also an appealing spa hotel, **Rakhmanovskie Klyuchi** (Rakhmanov's Springs; ☑ 705 798 53 56, 7232 56 02 32; www.altaytravel.ru; office pr Nezavisimosti 92/2, Ust-Kamenogorsk; s/d/tr without bathroom 10,000/16,000/21,000T, 2-/4-person cottages 25,000/50,000T, full board per person 6000T; ⊙ office 9am-6pm Mon-Fri), located in a remote corner of Altay, near the famed Mt Belukha. Views of the peak are possible from the Radostny Pass, a one-hour walk up from the resort.

ℹ️ Information

Tourism in Altay is still in its infancy, and very little English is spoken, so travellers may visit the region either as part of an organised tour or have to be very self-sufficient. Planning ahead and making arrangements well in advance is essential. Caravanistan (www.caravanistan.com) has an excellent online guide to Altay, tips on what to do and staff can help you organise your trip. Ust-Kamenogorsk-based Altai Expeditions (p351) and Imperia Turizma (p353) also run various trips into the region.

ℹ️ Getting There & Away

Ust-Kamenogorsk is the gateway to Altay. In Altay there is little public transport, though there are frequent marshrutkas from Ust-Kamenogorsk to Ridder, and infrequent ones from Ridder to the village of Poperechnoe. The village of Urunkhaika on the shores of Lake Markakol is a seven-hour drive from Ust-Kamenogorsk along a fairly decent road; the most direct route requires a ferry crossing.

Semey

☑ 7222 / POP 318, 053 / ELEV 200M

Though sadly best known to the world for the Soviet nuclear-testing ground nearby (the Polygon) Semey (Semipalatinsk; Семей), has an unusually rich cultural heritage that makes it one of Kazakhstan's most interesting provincial cities. Founded in 1718 as a Russian fortification against the Zhungars, it stands 200km down the Irtysh from Ust-Kamenogorsk, in the heartland of the Kazakh Middle Horde, noted for their eloquence and intellect. The area has produced several major Kazakh writers and teachers, notably the national poet Abay Kunanbaev (1845–1904), and Semey was a home in exile to the great Russian writer Fyodor Dostoevsky.

Between 1949 and 1989 the Soviet military exploded some 456 nuclear bombs in the Semipalatinsk Polygon, an area of steppe west of the city. Not even villagers living close by were given protection or warning of the dangers. An unprecedented wave of popular protest, the Nevada-Semipalatinsk Movement, was largely instrumental in halting the tests in 1989, and President Nazarbayev closed the site in 1991. While much of the Polygon site is now considered safe to visit, the tragic effects linger in the generations exposed to the effects of the testing: genetic mutations, cancers, weakened immune systems and mental illness continue to destroy lives and occupy hospitals and clinics in and around Kurchatov and Semey. The UN Development Programme has calculated that over 1.3 million people have been adversely affected by the tests.

⊙ Sights

Most visitors use Semey as a jumping-off point for macabre Polygon visits, but the clutch of local museums is enough to keep you entertained for a day or two.

★ **Lenin Statues** MONUMENT
(Zhamakaev) A curious collection of 15 communist busts and statues, mostly Lenins – including Kazakhstan's tallest Lenin! – stands in a small park behind Hotel Semey. Spot the three Kirovs and one Karl Marx lurking among the Lenins.

Abay Museum MUSEUM
(☑7222 52 24 22; Lenin 12; ⊙10am-1pm & 2-6pm Tue-Sat) **FREE** This museum is dedicated to the 19th-century humanist poet Abay Kunanbaev, whose forward-looking vision of Kazakhstan is not necessarily shared by his followers. Along with displays about Abay's life and work, the museum has many 19th-century artefacts, and sections on the Kazakh nomadic tradition and Abay's literary successors, including Mukhtar Auezov (1897–1961), author of the epic novel *Abay Zholy* (The Path of Abay). Displays are in Kazakh only and guided tours in Russian are grudgingly provided.

Stronger than Death Memorial MEMORIAL
(Polkovnichy Island) On the left, 600m past the end of the bridge that takes you south of the centre, across River Irtysh, is the sombre and impressive Stronger than Death Memorial erected in 2002 for victims of the nuclear tests. Designed by architect Shota Valikhanov, it has a marble centrepiece of a mother covering her child, while above billows a Polygon mushroom cloud, etched into a 30m-high black tombstone.

Fine Arts Museum MUSEUM
(☑7222 52 31 84; Pushkin 108; foreigner/local 600/300T; ⊙10am-6pm Tue-Sat) The collection here, one of the country's best, covers Kazakh, Russian and Western European art from the 16th century onwards, including a not-to-be-missed Rembrandt etching and landscapes, portraits and still-life paintings by top 19th-century Russians such as Levitan, Kramskoy and Kiselev. There's an engaging contemporary-art section and temporary exhibitions include works by up-and-coming local artists.

Dostoevsky Museum MUSEUM
(☑7222 52 19 42; Dostoevskogo 118; 200T; ⊙9am-6pm Mon-Sat) This well laid-out museum incorporates the wooden house where the exiled writer lived from 1857 to 1859 with his wife and baby. The displays range over Dostoevsky's life and works, including his five years in jail at Omsk (and a model of the prison barracks) and five years of enforced military service at Semey. His rooms have been maintained in the style of his day. Tours, in English, Russian or Kazakh, cost 200T extra.

**History & Local
Studies Museum** MUSEUM
(☑7222 52 07 32; www.semeymusey.kz; Abay 90; foreigner/local 500/150T; ⊙9am-5pm Mon-Sat) Displays at this regional museum run the gamut from prehistoric finds to some rare archaeological pieces, a collection of traditional Kazakh artefacts, the development of Semipalatinsk, local involvement in WWII and the tragedy of the Polygon. Founded in 1883, it claims to be the oldest museum in Kazakhstan. There's an appealing collection of *balbals* (stone carvings) outside. Tours in Kazakh/Russian are 300T.

Anatomical Museum MUSEUM
(Lenin 1; ⊙8.30am-5pm) **FREE** In an unmarked building that's part of Semey Medical University, this one-room museum exhibits the usual pickled organs you might expect medical students to look at – but also a gruesome collection of babies and embryos with appalling deformities (though not, allegedly, caused by nuclear radiation from Polygon). Not for the squeamish. It's in room 28, upstairs. Ask nicely for the key in room 22.

⌇ Sleeping & Eating

Hotel Semey HOTEL **$**
(☑7222 56 36 04; www.semey.semstar.com; Kabanbay Batyr 26; incl breakfast s/d from 4000/6000T, f 20,000T; P ❂ ❄ ☎) Well-located Hotel Semey has that unmistakable Soviet aura but staff are reasonably helpful (and speak a little English) and the rooms have been modernised. The cheapies share facilities, while some of the semi-deluxe rooms have air-con.

LOCAL KNOWLEDGE

PEACE MUSEUM

This **museum** (Polokovnichy Island), dedicated to the victims of the Polygon, was due to open in 2018, to coincide with the 200th anniversary of Semey's founding. It will be encased in a 24m-diameter glass sphere resting on a pair of giant stone hands.

KAZAKHSTAN SEMEY

Semey (Semipalatinsk)

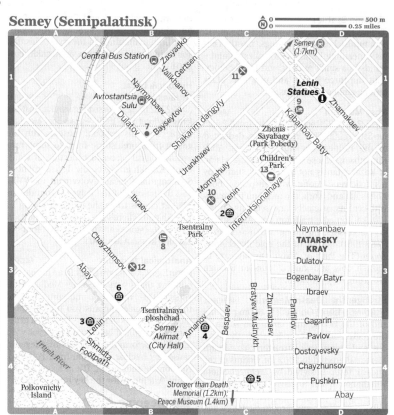

Hotel Nomad
HOTEL **$$**

(☑ 7222 52 04 44; www.hotelnomad.kz; Ibraev 149; s/d incl breakfast from 17,000/23,000T; P❄🛜) The best hotel in town overlooks the central park. For a place of this quality the prices are excellent. Rooms are unfussy but tasteful and well equipped, desk staff speak English, and room rates include a proper breakfast.

Vostok
KAZAKH **$**

(☑ 7222 56 16 77; Momyshuly 8; mains 700-1500T; ☉ noon-midnight) Shashlyk straight off the grill, *laghman* (long, stout noodles) and other Kazakh staples are served in garden booths at this relaxed local joint.

Abat
RUSSIAN **$**

(☑ 7222 56 85 33; Dulatov; terrace mains 800-1500T, cafeteria dishes 200-600T; ☉ terrace 11am-1am, cafeteria 9am-10pm) The outdoor terrace cafe here has a fun atmosphere in summer and serves reasonable shashlyk, other meat dishes, salads and desserts. The indoor cafeteria is inexpensive and run-of-the-mill, with offerings such as *plov* (pilaf), pizza, *manty* (steamed dumplings) and fried chicken.

Ribeye Art & Grill
STEAK **$$$**

(☑ 7222 52 02 01; http://ribeye.kz; Kabanbay Batyr 21; mains 1800-7000T; ☉ 11am-1am; 🛜) The vast triangular bar in the centre of this hangar-like space serves sangrias and imaginative cocktails, but the main draw here is the meat. Ribeyes, skirt steaks and striploins are grilled to your specifications, along with a supporting cast of burgers.

🍷 Drinking & Nightlife

Kofeman
COFFEE

(☑ 7222 56 55 38; Internatsionalnaya 43; dishes 300-2000T; ☉ 10am-1am; 🛜) Semey's fashionable coffee lounge, with proper latte art, an ambitious menu that overreaches itself by

Semey (Semipalatinsk)

trying to provide American and Mexican breakfasts, pasta, burgers, steaks, cheesecake and alcoholic drinks, and erratic service. Stick to the coffee and skip the rest.

ⓘ Getting There & Away

From the **airport** (✆ 7222 36 02 22), 11km south of the centre, SCAT flies at least once daily to Almaty (27,600T), while Air Astana flies four times weekly to Astana (29,600T).

From the **main bus station** (Tsentralniy Avtovokzal; ✆ 7222 52 08 15; www.avtovokzalsemey.kz; Valikhanova 167), next to the busy bazaar, eight daily buses run to Ust-Kamenogorsk (1600T, four hours), three to Astana (3800T, 14 hours) and two to Karaganda (3900T, 19 hours). Shared taxis to Ust-Kamenogorsk (2800T, 2½ hours) gather here too. Two daily buses to Barnaul, Russia (4200T, 11 hours), and three a week to Ürümqi, China (10,600T, 32 hours), go from the **Mezhdunarodny Avtovokzal** (International Bus Station; ✆ 7222 51 47 97; Karzhaubayuly 249) in the north of the city, and there is at least one nightly departure for Novosibirsk (5000T, 11 hours) from **Avtostantsia Sulu** (Naymanbaev).

The **train station** (✆ 7222 38 12 32; Privokzalnaya 1), just off the north end of Shakarim dangyly, has two or more daily departures to Almaty (5363T to 5747T, 19¾ to 20½ hours), eight weekly (not daily) to Astana (4499T to 11,572T, 11½ to 17 hours), four weekly trains north to Bar-

naul (15,086T, 11 hours) and two to Novosibirsk (19,980T, 17 hours).

ⓘ Getting Around

Buses 11 and 13 (65T) run from the train station to the centre along Shakarim dangyly. Bus 33 heads from the train station to the main bazaar (near the main bus station) then along Kabanbay Batyr and Internatsionalnaya to Tsentralnaya ploshchad, then eventually to the airport. Buses 35 and 41 also run between Tsentralnaya ploshchad and the bazaar. Taxis cost around 1000T to or from the airport.

Around Semey

Kurchatov (Курчатов) & the Polygon

The town of Kurchatov, 120km west of Semey, was the command centre for the Semipalatinsk Polygon, the Soviet Union's primary nuclear test sites. The nuclear testing zone itself stretched some 100km to 120km south and west from Kurchatov. Today, the rather desolate town is home to Kazakhstan's National Nuclear Centre (p358), which, among other things, works on the development of nuclear power in Kazakhstan. You can travel freely to the town and have a walk around; the central square is dominated by the large, Stalinist-neoclassical town hall (formerly the Polygon's headquarters), and a rather manic-looking statue of Igor Kurchatov himself, the director of the Soviet atomic-bomb program. But to visit desolate Polygon, parts of it still emitting dangerous levels of radiation, you need to organise a tour in advance.

◎ Sights

In the Kurchatov **Radiation Safety & Ecology Institute Museum** (✆72251 2 34 13; www.irse-rk.kz; ⊙9am-6pm Mon-Fri) **FREE**, a guide leads you around, showing off the exhibits: the model of the Experimental Field where the effects of nuclear explosions were measured on buildings, aircraft, and live animals; jars with picked and charred animal tissue – the result of the damage; the controls that would have set off the explosions, where you can sit in the chair and flip the switches; the grainy black-and-white film of the explosions.

Then you're rattling through the steppe in a rugged Soviet minivan, stopping every now and then for a scramble down into the underground bunkers and the remains of the metro. Everywhere, the guide compares radiation levels to those in Kurchatov; in most places, the radiation levels are the same. Much of the 18,000-sq-km Polygon territory has at least partially recovered from the 456 nuclear tests conducted here between 1949 and 1989, though heightened levels of cancer still blight the local population. By a round, craterlike lake, the guide makes you don a radiation suit, face mask, and two pairs of booties of the kind you put over your shoes in some museums. The radiation here is 10 times higher than in the city.

On your way to or from Semey, you can turn off the main road and visit another spectre of Soviet presence – the ghost town of Chagan, where the bombers used in Polygon testing were based until the collapse of the Soviet Union. As you walk between the gutted apartment buildings, giant flocks of rooks and crows take off – the only sign of life and a mildly sinister presence.

Though some parts of the Polygon itself can be visited safely, it would be lunacy to wander in without an expert guide. Several agencies in Semey organise visits, as does the Karaganda-based Nomadic Travel Kazakhstan (p347); give it two weeks to make arrangements. You won't get into the museum, institute or the Polygon site itself unless you organise a trip through an agency such as **Togas Inturservis** (☐ 7222 56 63 68; Dulatov 145; ◷ 9am-5pm Mon-Sat) in Semey, which charges around US$250 per person for everything – less if you don't need an English-speaking guide – including guide, entry fees, plus the 60,000T that the **National Nuclear Centre** (Natsionalny Yaderny Tsentr; ☐ 72251 3 33 33; www.nnc.kz; Zdanie (Bldg) 054B, Krasnoarmeyskaya 2, Kurchatov) charges for the Soviet-style minibus that takes up to six visitors around the Polygon site. You can try obtaining permission yourself by email (in English is OK) a week or more ahead to the Director at the National Nuclear Centre.

ⓘ Getting There & Around

Four buses a day run to Kurchatov (900T, three hours) from Semey's Avtostantsia Sulu (p357). A round-trip taxi from Semey with an hour or two in Kurchatov costs around 14,000T. A tour is considerably pricier, but everything is organised, and you can visit the ghost town of Chagan en route.

UNDERSTAND KAZAKHSTAN

Kazakhstan Today

Born into a rural peasant family in 1940, President Nursultan Nazarbayev has ruled Kazakhstan since late Soviet times, and still garners Soviet-style percentages of the vote – 97.7% in 2015, an election criticised by international observers (like every other post-Soviet election here) for its irregularities. Nazarbayev has fostered a strong personality cult – his picture and words of wisdom greet you on billboards everywhere you go – and there is nothing to stop him staying at the top for as long as his health holds. In 2010 parliament named him 'Leader of the Nation', enabling him to exert a strong influence over government if he ceases to be president.

Nazarbayev doesn't hide his belief that the economy comes first and democracy second. He has certainly delivered on the economy, using international investment to help develop Kazakhstan's vast resources of oil, gas and almost every other known valuable mineral. As of 2016, Kazakhstan was the world's 16th-biggest oil producer, pumping 1.6 million barrels per day.

Nazarbayev certainly does not welcome political opposition – in fact, protests require police permission which is never granted and any opposition press tends to get shut down by excessive fining – but he has managed to forge a largely peaceful and increasingly prosperous country, which keeps him popular enough among the population at large. In the main cities it's easy to see – from the ostentatious imported motors, the expensive restaurants and the nightclubs where some locals will happily plonk down the equivalent of hundreds of dollars to reserve a table – that Kazakhstan's new rich are quite numerous. And there's a sizeable middle class developing. Yet those who are excluded from the networks of the new wealthy have begun to get disgruntled about corruption and poor health and education services as well as poverty. This was brutally highlighted in 2011 when a strike by government oil workers in the western town of Zhanaozen ended with security forces shooting dead at least 14 demonstrators and jailing the rest – the first time independent

Kazakhstan had seen social unrest and violence on such a scale. Nazarbayev's popularity waned somewhat in wake of the oil price crash of 2014, and the subsequent downturn in Kazakhstan's economy.

Even though Nazarbayev signed a decree in 2017 that theoretically gives parliament greater power, he still has the final say, and there is still no apparent strategy in place for a transition to multiparty democracy, nor – despite Nazarbayev's age and rumours of health problems – any obvious heir apparent, which fuels a lot of gossip and shadowy manoeuvrings behind the scenes. Rival clan leaders in Shymkent are engaging in some discreet sabre-rattling in anticipation of an eventual power struggle after he dies.

Critics of Nazarbayev continue to be put out of action. Prominent human-rights activist Yevgeny Zhovtis finished serving a four-year manslaughter sentence in 2013 after a driving accident, and in the wake of the Zhanaozen events, opposition politician Vladimir Kozlov spent almost five years in prison for attempting to overthrow the government by encouraging strikes. Both trials were condemned as unfair by human-rights groups. In 2015, Nazarbayev's ex-son-in-law-turned-political-enemy, Rakhat Aliyev, allegedly committed suicide in a prison cell in Vienna. In 2016, Kazakh beer tycoon Tokhtar Tuleshov was jailed for 21 years after a closed trial for allegedly planning a coup against the president. The media-rights body Reporters Without Borders ranked Kazakhstan 157th out of 179 countries in its 2017 Press Freedom Index.

Kazakhstan's Soviet state-run economy was dismantled in the 1990s, but corruption remains a barrier to a true free-market economy: Kazakhstan ranked 131st out of 174 countries in the 2016 Corruption Perceptions Index of Transparency International.

History

Kazakhstan as a single entity with defined boundaries was an invention of the Soviet regime in the 1920s. Before that, the great bulk of this territory was part of the domain of nomadic horseback animal herders that stretched right across the Eurasian steppe. At times some of its various peoples fell under the sway of regional or continental potentates; at other times they were left to sort themselves out. From around the 9th centu-ry AD the far south came within the ambit of the settled Silk Road civilisations of Transoxiana (the area between the Amu-Darya and Syr-Darya rivers). A people who can be identified as Kazakhs first emerged in southeastern Kazakhstan in the 15th century. Over time they came to cover a territory roughly approximating modern Kazakhstan, though some of this continued to be governed periodically from elsewhere and/or occupied by other peoples. The borders of Soviet Kazakhstan excluded some Kazakh-populated areas and included some areas with non-Kazakh populations.

Early Peoples

Kazakhstan's early history is a shadowy procession of nomadic peoples, most of whom moved in from the east and left few records. By around 500 BC southern Kazakhstan was inhabited by the Saka, part of the vast network of nomadic Scythian cultures that stretched across the steppes from the Altay to Ukraine. The Saka left many burial mounds, in some of which fabulous hoards of gold jewellery, often with animal motifs, have been found (many examples can be seen in Kazakhstan's museums). Most splendid of all is the 'Golden Man', a warrior's costume that has become a Kazakhstan national symbol.

From 200 BC the Huns, followed by various Turkic peoples, arrived from what are now Mongolia and northern China. The early Turks left totemlike carved stones known as *balbals,* bearing the images of honoured chiefs, at sacred and burial sites, and these too can be seen in many Kazakhstan museums. From about AD 550 to 750 the southern half of Kazakhstan was the western extremity of the Manchuria-based Kök (Blue) Turk empire.

The far south was within the sphere of the Bukhara-based Samanid dynasty from the mid-9th century, and here cities such as Otrar and Yasy (Turkestan) developed on the back of agriculture and Silk Road trade. The Karakhanid Turks from the southern Kazakh steppe ousted the Samanids in the late 10th century, taking up the Samanids' settled ways (and Islam) and constructing some of Kazakhstan's earliest surviving buildings (in and around Taraz).

Chinggis (Genghis) Khan

Around AD 1130 the Karakhanids were displaced by the Khitans, a Buddhist people driven out of Mongolia and northern China. The Khitan state, known as the Karakitay empire, stretched from Xinjiang to Transoxiana, but in the early 13th century it became prey to rising powers at both extremities. To the west, based in Khorezm, south of the Aral Sea, was the Khorezmshah empire, which took Transoxiana in 1210. To the east was Chinggis Khan, who sent an army to crush the Karakitay in 1218, then turned to the Khorezmshah empire, which had misguidedly murdered 450 of his merchants at Otrar. The biggest-ever Mongol army (200,000 or so) sacked the Khorezmian cities of Otrar, Bukhara and Samarkand, then swept on towards Europe and the Middle East. Central Asia became part of the Mongol empire.

On Chinggis Khan's death in 1227, his enormous empire was divided between his sons. The lands furthest from the Mongol heartland – north and west of the Aral Sea – went to the descendants of his eldest son Jochi and became known as the Golden Horde. Southeastern Kazakhstan was part of the Chaghatai khanate, the lands that went to Chinggis' second son Chaghatai. In the late 14th century far southern Kazakhstan was conquered by Timur from Samarkand, who constructed Kazakhstan's one great surviving Silk Road building, the Yasaui Mausoleum at Turkestan.

The Kazakhs

The story of the Kazakhs starts with the Uzbeks, a group of Islamised Mongols named after leader Özbeg (Uzbek), who were left in control of most of the Kazakh steppe as the Golden Horde disintegrated in the 15th century.

In 1468 an internal feud split the Uzbeks into two groups. Those who ended up south of the Syr-Darya ruled from Bukhara as the Shaybanid dynasty and ultimately gave their name to modern Uzbekistan. Those who stayed north remained nomadic and became the Kazakhs, taking their name from a Turkic word meaning 'free rider' or 'adventurer'. The Kazakh khanate that resulted was a confederation of nomadic peoples that by the 18th century stretched over most of southern, western and central Kazakhstan, descendants of the Mongols and earlier Turkic inhabitants.

The Kazakhs grouped into three 'hordes' (zhuz), with which Kazakhs today still identify: the Great Horde in the south, the Middle Horde in the centre, north and east, and the Little Horde in the west. Each was ruled by a khan and comprised a number of clans whose leaders held the title axial, bi or batyr.

The Zhungars (Oyrats), a warlike Mongol clan, subjugated eastern Kazakhstan between 1690 and 1720 in what Kazakhs call the Great Disaster. Abylay Khan, a Middle Horde leader who tried to unify Kazakh resistance to the Zhungars after 1720, was eventually elected khan of all three hordes in 1771, but by that time they were well on the way to becoming Russian vassals.

The Russians Arrive

Russia's expansion across Siberia ran up against the Zhungars, against whom they built a line of forts along the Kazakhs' northern border. The Kazakhs sought tsarist protection from the Zhungars, and the khans of all three hordes swore loyalty to the Russian crown between 1731 and 1742. Russia gradually extended its 'protection' of the khanates to their annexation and abolition, despite repeated Kazakh uprisings. By some estimates one million of the four million Kazakhs died in revolts and famines before 1870. Meanwhile, the abolition of serfdom in Russia and Ukraine in 1861 stimulated peasant settlers to move into Kazakhstan.

Communist Takeover & 'Development'

In the chaos following the Russian Revolution of 1917, a Kazakh nationalist party, Alash Orda, tried to establish an independent government, based in Semey. As the Russian Civil War raged across Kazakhstan, Alash Orda eventually sided with the Bolsheviks, who emerged victorious in 1920 – only for Alash members soon to be purged from the Communist Party of Kazakhstan (CPK). Meanwhile, several hundred thousand Kazakhs fled to China and elsewhere.

The next disaster to befall the Kazakhs was denomadisation, between 1929 and 1933. Under Soviet government, the world's biggest group of seminomadic people was pushed one step up the Marxist evolutionary ladder to become settled farmers in new collectives. Unused to agriculture and with the land not suited to intensive farming, they died in their hundreds of thousands from famine and disease.

In the 1930s and '40s more and more people from other parts of the USSR – prisoners and others – were sent to work in labour camps and new industrial towns in Kazakhstan. They included entire peoples deported en masse from western areas of the USSR around the time of WWII. Kazakhstan was only second to Siberia in terms of gulag notoriety. A further 800,000 migrants arrived in the 1950s when Nikita Khrushchev decided to plough up 250,000 sq km of north Kazakhstan steppe to grow wheat in the Virgin Lands scheme.

The labour camps were wound down in the mid-1950s, but many survivors stayed on, and yet more Russians, Ukrainians and other Soviet nationalities arrived to mine and process Kazakhstan's coal, iron and oil. The proportion of Kazakhs in Kazakhstan's population fell below 30%.

During the Cold War the USSR decided Kazakhstan was 'empty' and 'remote' enough to use for its chief nuclear-bomb testing ground (the Semipalatinsk Polygon). In 1989 Kazakhstan produced the first great popular protest movement the USSR had seen: the Nevada-Semey (Semipalatinsk) Movement, which forced an end to nuclear tests in Kazakhstan.

Independent Kazakhstan

Nursultan Nazarbayev began to rise up the CPK ranks in the 1970s. He became the party's first secretary in 1989 and has ruled Kazakhstan ever since. In 1991 Nazarbayev did not welcome the breakup of the USSR, and Kazakhstan was the last Soviet republic to declare independence. Multiparty elections in 1994 returned a parliament that obstructed Nazarbayev's free-market economic reforms, and he dissolved it in 1995, with new elections returning an assembly favourable to him. Soon afterwards an overwhelming referendum majority extended his presidential term until 2000.

In 1997 Nazarbayev moved Kazakhstan's capital from Almaty to Astana, then a medium-sized northern city, citing Astana's more central and less earthquake-prone location, and greater proximity to Russia. Astana has been transformed into a capital for the 21st century with some spectacular new buildings and is a key symbol of Nazarbayev's vision of Kazakhstan as a Eurasian economic and political hub, though some decry it as a shining monument to clanism and nepotism.

Nazarbayev's economic program was based on developing Kazakhstan's vast mineral resources. Western companies paid huge amounts to get a slice of Kazakhstan's large oil and gas reserves, and by the dawn of the 21st century the country was posting 9% to 10% economic growth year after year, which kept Nazarbayev popular enough and helped maintain ethnic harmony too.

In 1999 Nazarbayev was assured of victory in new presidential elections after the main opposition leader, Akezhan Kazhegeldin, was barred from standing. Nazarbayev won new seven-year presidential terms in 2005, and then in 2011, both with over 90% of the vote. His political rivals and critics were frequently sacked, jailed or even, in two cases in 2005 and 2006, found shot dead. The government denied any involvement in the deaths.

People

Although Kazakhs form the majority of Kazakhstan's population, this is a multiethnic country, made so by the sheer diversity of peoples deported to Kazakhstan under Stalin from every corner of the Soviet Union, from Greeks and Koreans to Chechens and Jews. Interethnic harmony generally reigns, and the government encourages everyone to think of themselves as Kazakhstanis as well as ethnic Kazakhs, Russians, Ukrainians etc. Of the 17 million population, 65.5% are Kazakhs – a big upswing since Soviet times. Since independence in 1991, over three million Russians, Germans and Ukrainians have left Kazakhstan and over 800,000 *oralman* (ethnic Kazakhs repatriating from other countries) have arrived. Other ethnic groups are Russians (21.5%), Uzbeks (3%), Ukrainians (1.8%), Germans, Tatars and Uyghurs (1% to 1.4% each), and more than 100 others. Southern areas of Kazakhstan today are about 90% Kazakh, while in some northern towns the majority population is ethnic Russian.

Kazakh culture, rooted in oral tradition, survives most strongly in the countryside, although urban Kazakhs are also showing a growing interest in their roots. City-dwellers often still decorate their homes with colourful, yurt-style carpets and tapestries.

Family, respect for elders and traditions of hospitality remain very important to Kazakhs. Ancestry determines a person's *zhuz*

KAZAKHSTAN PEOPLE

(horde) and clan. The best ancestor of all is Chinggis Khan, and right up to the 20th century the Kazakh nobility consisted of those who could trace their lineage back to him.

Kazakh tradition is most on display during the spring festival Nauryz (Navrus; 22 March), when families gather, don traditional dress, eat special food, and enjoy traditional music and games rooted in their equestrian traditions, such as *kokpar* (local traditional polo played with a goat carcass) and *kyz kuu* (a boy–girl horse chase: if he wins he gets to kiss her, if she wins she beats him with her riding whip). Falconry (hunting with birds of prey) is another still-beloved Kazakh tradition. Also lingering from the past is the practice of bride stealing (with or without the bride's consent), which can still happen in some rural areas and the more Kazakh-dominated towns in the south.

Religion

Islam, Kazakhs' predominant faith, is at its strongest in the deep south and has a strong Sufic strain. Pilgrimages to the mausoleum of Kozha Akhmed Yasaui at Turkestan and the desert shrine of Beket-Ata, east of Aktau, are important ways for Kazakh Muslims to affirm their faith. The younger generation tends to be more religious than their Soviet-born parents, and some – to the concern of the general population – are turning to the more severe form of Sunni Islam, exported by Saudi Arabia, that funds some of Kazakhstan's mosques. Christianity (mainly Russian Orthodox) claims about a quarter of the population. The government stresses Kazakhstan's tradition of religious tolerance.

Arts

Film

The seeds of Kazakhstan's feisty film industry were sown when Stalin relocated the main Soviet film studios to Almaty during WWII. The biggest recent productions have been two lavish historical epics aimed at fostering national pride: *Nomad* (2005) and Oscar-nominated *Mongol* (2007). Young Kazakhstani directors are also making thought-provoking movies tackling more sensitive realities. The best include Sergey

Dvortsevoy's *Tulpan* (2008), about a young man returning from the Russian navy to a shepherd's life in the Betpak-Dala; *Song from the Southern Seas* (2008), directed by Marat Sarulu, focused on contemporary Kazakh-Russian interethnic relations; and the Oscar-shortlisted *Kelin* (2009) by Ermek Tursunov, a silent movie whose erotic scenes upset some in Kazakhstan.

The highest-grossing Kazakh film ever (US$1 million) was Akhan Sataev's *The Racketeer* (2007), about a young man drawn into the post-Soviet gangster world in Almaty. Sadly, many other Kazakh-made films, despite garnering awards at international festivals, are largely ignored by their home audiences, who much prefer Hollywood productions. Globally better known than anyone working in Kazakhstan is Timur Bekmambetov, who was born in Atyrau in 1961 but has made his film career in Moscow and Hollywood, directing international successes *Night Watch, Wanted* and *9. Harmony Lessons* (2013) explores the teenage psyche and relationships and won an award for an outstanding artistic contribution.

The annual Eurasia Film Festival, held in Astana, showcases recent films from throughout Central Asia.

Music & Literature

Kazakh traditional music is popular, but you are more likely to hear it at organised concerts; buses and minibuses tend to play contemporary pop instead. The music is largely folk tunes: short on pounding excitement, it captures the soulful rhythms of nomadic life on the steppe. The national instrument is the *dombra*, a small two-stringed lute with an oval box shape. Other instruments include the *kobyz* (a two-stringed fiddle), whose sound is said to have brought Chinggis Khan to tears, and the *sybyzgy* (two flutes strapped together like abbreviated pan pipes). Keep an eye open for shows by the colourfully garbed Sazgen Sazy and Otrar Sazy folk orchestras. Roksonaki and Ulytau are groups that provide an interesting crossover between indigenous sounds and imported rhythms like rock, pop and jazz.

The most skilled singers or bards are called *akyns*, and undoubtedly the most important form of Kazakh traditional art is the *aitys*, a duel between two *dombra* players who challenge each other in poetic lyrics.

You might catch one of these live during Nauryz (Navrus) or other holidays.

Kazakhstan has a rich literary heritage, with folk stories, heroic legends, long narrative poems and love ballads handed down orally and traditionally performed by *jyrau* (lyric poets).

Art & Crafts

In pre-Soviet times the Kazakhs developed high skills in the crafts associated with nomadic life: brightly woven carpets, wall hangings and ornate wooden chests for yurts, chunky jewellery, elaborate horse tackle and weaponry, and splendid costumes for special occasions. You can admire these in almost any museum in Kazakhstan. Sadly, unlike its neighbours, Kazakhstan now makes very little in terms of crafts – much of what you see is mass-produced in China.

Environment

The Land

Except for mountain chains along its southeastern and eastern borders, Kazakhstan is pretty flat. At 2.7 million sq km, it's about the size of Western Europe. Southeast Kazakhstan lies along the northern edge of the Tian Shan, where Mt Khan Tengri (7010m) pegs the China–Kazakhstan–Kyrgyzstan border. In the northeast, some peaks in the Altay top 4000m.

The north of the country is mostly treeless steppe, with much of its original grassland now turned over to wheat or other agriculture. A surprising number of lakes and scattered ranges of hills break up the steppe. Further south and west it is increasingly arid, becoming desert or semidesert.

The most important rivers are the Syr-Darya, flowing across the south of Kazakhstan to the Aral Sea; the Ili, flowing out of China into Lake Balkhash; and the Irtysh, which flows across northeast Kazakhstan into Siberia. Lake Balkhash in the central east is now (following the demise of the Aral Sea) the largest lake in Central Asia (17,000 sq km), though nowhere more than 26m deep.

Wildlife

Kazakhstan's mountains are rich in wildlife, including bears, lynx, argali sheep, ibexes, wolves, wild boar, deer and the elusive snow leopard, of which an estimated 200 roam mountainous border areas from the Altay to Aksu-Zhabagyly Nature Reserve. Two types of antelope – the saiga and the goitred gazelle (zheyran) – roam the steppe in much smaller numbers than they used to. The saiga's numbers fell from over a million in the early 1990s to about 40,000 by 2002, largely due to uncontrolled hunting for meat and horn after the Soviet collapse. It's staged a bit of a comeback with the help of a combined government-NGO program to conserve steppe habitats in central Kazakhstan and in the Uralsk region, but in 2015 the conservation efforts suffered a blow due to a disease that felled thousands of saiga. As of 2017, the population hovers around 108,000. In Altyn-Emel National Park, Przewalski's horses, extinct in Kazakhstan since 1940, have been reintroduced from zoos in Europe. For some encouraging wildlife conservation news check out the Association for the Conservation of Biodiversity in Kazakhstan (http://acbk.kz).

The golden eagle on Kazakhstan's flag is a good omen for ornithologists. Hundreds of bird species are to be seen, from the paradise flycatchers of Aksu-Zhabagyly and the flamingos and sociable lapwings of Korgalzhyn to the relict gulls of Lake Alakol.

Environmental Issues

Kazakhstan is still grappling with the fearful legacy of Soviet exploitation and mismanagement. The Aral Sea catastrophe is well known, and the country also continues to suffer from the fallout, literal and metaphorical, of Soviet nuclear tests, conducted mainly near Semey. Industrial air pollution continues at high rates in most of the Soviet industrial centres, including Ust-Kamenogorsk, Karaganda, Ekibastuz and Kostanay.

The development of Kazakhstan's oil reserves in and near the Caspian Sea is adding to concerns for the world's largest lake. Nearly 1500 oil wells lie within reach of Caspian storm-surge floods, and there have already been leaks from wells submerged by the sea's 3m rise since the 1970s (the Caspian's level oscillates periodically, as a result, it's thought, of climatic factors). The pumping of the giant offshore Kashagan field is now well under way, and environmentalists fear that it could put paid to the last natural breeding ground of the beluga (white) sturgeon, source of the world's best caviar, and threaten the breeding grounds of the endangered Caspian seal, one of the world's smallest seals.

SURVIVAL GUIDE

 Directory A–Z

ACCOMMODATION

All Kazakhstan cities have a broad range of hotels, from basic, revamped Soviet places to comfortable modern establishments. Some hotels operate on a 24-hour basis, meaning that if you check in at 4pm, you don't have to check out until 4pm the following day. There are now dozens of backpacker hostels in Almaty and Astana, with a few more in Shymkent. Near national parks there are good guesthouse options with meals included.

ACTIVITIES

The mountain regions abutting the Kyrgyz, Chinese and Russian borders offer the greatest outdoor excitement. The best areas for multiday adventurous trekking are the Tian Shan range to the south and the Altay Mountains to the east, though the mountains around Almaty, Kolsai Lakes, Aksu-Zhabagyly Nature Reserve and Sayram-Ugam National Park offer excellent day hikes.

Ascents of Belukha in the Altay, and Khan Tengri and other peaks in the central Tian Shan, are superb challenges for climbers in July and August.

Cycling among Kazakhstan's central steppes and hills is offered by Karaganda-based Nomadic Travel (p347). Kazakhstan Bike Tours (www.biketours.kz), an affiliate of Kan Tengri (p313), and **Spice Roads** (www.spiceroads.com) are just two of the operators who offer multiday cycle tours of Kazakhstan. There are mountain-biking enthusiasts in Almaty, with plenty of potential for the sport in the surrounding mountains, but mountain-biking tourism hasn't taken off yet.

Kazakhstan is an emerging birdwatching destination, lying on early-summer migration routes from Africa, India and the Middle East to Siberia, with hundreds of species to be seen. The mountains south of Almaty and the deserts northwest of the city are good areas, as are the Aksu-Zhabagyly and Korgalzhyn Nature Reserves.

In winter skiers and snowboarders enjoy Central Asia's best facilities at the modern Chimbulak resort near Almaty as well as a couple of others. There's good skiing in Altay as well, but you need a border permit to visit the area.

CUSTOMS REGULATIONS

Customs declaration forms don't need to be filled on entering the country unless you're carrying goods above normal duty-free limits. Up to US$3000 cash in any currency can be taken in or out of the country without a written declaration.

EMBASSIES & CONSULATES

Most embassies are in Astana, although a few remain in Almaty.

Afghan Consulate (☑727 255 56 63; farahi@ mail.ru; Dom 21, Mikrorayon Dubok-2, Momyshuly, Almaty; ⊗9.30am-4pm Mon-Fri; ▣37)

Azerbaijan Embassies & Consulates Astana embassy (☑7172 75 55 27; www.azembassy. kz; Diplomatichesky Gorodok B-6; ⊗10.30am-4pm; ▣18, 21, 52, 70); Aktau consulate (☑7292 42 23 00; http://aktau.mfa.gov.az/; Dom 30, Mikrorayon 15; ⊗10am-1pm Mon-Fri)

Chinese Embassies & Consulates Astana embassy (☑7172 79 35 76; http://kz.chineseembassy.org; Kabanbay Batyr 37; ⊗visa applications 9am-noon Mon, Wed & Fri; ▣21, 27, 28, 37, 70); Almaty consulate (☑727 270 02 07; http://almaty.chineseconsulate.org; Baytasov 12; ⊗10am-4pm Mon-Fri; ▣65)

French Embassies & Consulates Astana embassy (☑7172 79 51 00; www.ambafrance-kz.org; Kosmonavtov 62; ⊗9.30am-5pm Mon-Thu, to 4pm Fri; ▣18, 28, 32, 52, 70); Almaty consulate (☑727 396 98 00; www.ambafrance-kz.org; Furmanov 99; ⊗9am-4pm Mon-Fri; Ⓜ Zhibek Zholy)

German Embassies & Consulates Astana embassy (☑7172 79 12 00; www.kasachstan.diplo.de; Kosmonavtov 62; ⊗9am-5pm Mon-Fri; ▣18, 28, 32, 52, 70); Almaty consulate (☑727 262 83 41; www.kasachstan.diplo.de; Ivanilov 2, Mikrorayon Gorny Gigant; ⊗9am-5pm Mon-Fri; ▣2)

Iranian Embassies & Consulates Astana embassy (☑7172 79 23 25; http://astana.mfa.ir; Daraboz 21, Mikrorayon Akbulak 4; ⊗9am-5pm Mon-Fri; ▣60, 61); Almaty consulate (☑727 254 19 74; Lugansky 31; ⊗9am-5pm Mon-Fri; ▣5)

Japanese Embassy Astana embassy (☑7172 97 78 43; www.kz.emb-japan.go.jp; 5th fl, Kosmonavtov 62; ⊗9am-5pm Mon-Fri; ▣18, 28, 32, 52, 70)

Kyrgyz Embassies & Consulates Astana embassy (☑7172 24 20 40; www.kyrgyzembs.kz; Diplomatichesky Gorodok B-5; ⊗10-4pm Mon-Thu; ▣18, 28, 32, 52, 70); Almaty consulate (☑727 264 22 12; www.consulkg.kz; Lugansky 30A; ⊗visa applications 9am-12.30pm Mon-Fri; ▣5)

Mongolian Embassies & Consulates Astana embassy (☑7172 96 51 55; www.monembassy.gov.mn; Daraboz 35, Mikrorayon Akbulak 2;

⊗9am-6pm Mon-Fri; ▣60); Almaty consulate (☑727 269 35 36; almaty@mfat.gov.mn; Musabaev 1; ⊗9am-1pm & 2-6pm; ▣103)

Russian Embassies & Consulates Astana embassy (☑7172 44 08 06, consular section 7172 44 07 83; www.rfembassy.kz; Baraeva 4; ⊗visa applications 3.30-5.30pm Tue & Thu); Almaty consulate (☑727 274 71 72; www.almaata.mid.ru; Zhandosov 4; ⊗visa applications 9.30am-12.30pm Tue & 3-5pm Fri; ▣18); Uralsk consulate (☑7112 51 16 26; www.uralsk.mid.ru; Mukhita 78; ⊗visas 9.30-11am Tue & Thu)

Tajik Embassies & Consulates Astana embassy (☑7172 24 13 15; embassy_tajic@mbox.kz; Karasakal Yerimbet 15; ⊗10am-1pm Mon-Thu; ▣18, 21, 28, 52, 70); Almaty office (☑727 269 70 59; tajconsalmaty@mfa.tj; Sanatornaya 16, Mikrorayon Baganashyl; ⊗visa applications 9am-noon Mon-Fri, visa issuance 2-5pm Mon-Fri; ▣63, 86) For the Almaty office, take bus 63 south from Furmanov as far as the Pediatria Instituty stop on Al-Farabi. Walk 100m further and continue straight over where Al-Farabi bends right at traffic lights. The consular-section entrance is on the left, 200m up this road, Syrgabekov.

Turkmen Embassies & Consulates Astana embassy (☑7172 31 27 67; www.turkmen embassy.kz; Otyrar 8/1; ⊗10am-1pm Mon-Thu; ▣1, 2, 19, 38, 48); Almaty consulate (☑727 272 69 44; Furmanov 137; ⊗visa applications 10am-1pm Mon-Thu; Ⓜ Almaly)

UK Embassies & Consulates Astana embassy (☑7172 55 62 00; http://gov.uk/world/kazakhstan; 6th fl, Kosmonavtov 62; ⊗9am-5.30pm Mon-Thu, to 4pm Fri; ▣18, 28, 32, 52, 70); Almaty office (☑727 250 61 91; http://gov.uk/world/kazakhstan; 7th fl, Rahat Palace Hotel Business Centre, Satpaev 29/6; ⊗8.30am-5pm Mon-Thu, to 3pm Fri; Ⓜ Tulpar)

US Embassies & Consulates Astana embassy (☑7172 70 21 00; http://kazakhstan.us embassy.gov; Koshkarbaev 3; ⊗9.30am-5pm Mon-Fri; ▣3, 4, 14, 19, 40); Almaty consulate (☑727 250 76 12; http://kazakhstan.us embassy.gov; Zholdasbekov 97, Mikrorayon Samal-2; ⊗9am-5pm Mon-Fri; ▣48)

Uzbek Embassy (☑727 291 17 44; www.uz embassy.kz; Baribaev 36, Almaty; ⊗visa applications 2-6pm Mon, Tue, Thu & Fri; ▣1, 12)

FESTIVALS & EVENTS

The biggest festivities around the country are for Nauryz (Navrus), the Muslim spring festival on 22 March, with traditional sports, music festivals and family get-togethers. Shymkent is a particularly good place to be for Nauryz. Major religious festivals – the Muslim Qurban Ait and Eid al-Fitr, and Russian Orthodox Christmas (7 January) – are widely celebrated though they're not official holidays.

FOOD & DRINK

The food culture of Kazakhstan is rooted in the Kazakhs' nomadic past, where the most readily available food was usually horses and sheep.

The cuisines of some non-Kazakh groups – Russian, Korean, Uyghur, Dungan – are also prominent. A sign in Arabic script usually indicates a Uyghur restaurant and good *laghman* (long, stout noodles) to be had inside. Major cities have excellent, varied dining scenes for all budgets, from cheapie *stolovayas* (canteens) to high-end Japanese.

The 'business lunch' (*biznes lanch, kompleksny obed*) offered by many restaurants is usually a good-value set meal, typically comprising soup or salad, main course, dessert and drink.

The Kazakh national dish is *beshbarmak*, chunks of long-boiled mutton, beef, or perhaps horsemeat, served in a huge bowl atop flat squares of pasta with onions and sometimes potatoes. The broth from the meat is drunk separately.

In bazaars and some restaurants you'll come across horsemeat in various forms. Menus may offer a plate of cold horsemeats as a starter, and horse steak as a main dish. *Kazy, shuzhuk/shuzhak* and *karta* are all types of horsemeat sausage, in horse-intestine casing. *Kuurdak* (or *kuyrdak*) is a fatty stew of potatoes, meat and offal from a horse, sheep or cow, boiled in a pot for two to three hours.

Across the country you'll find ubiquitous Central Asian dishes such as shashlyk, *laghman* (long, stout noodles), *manty* (steamed dumplings), *plov* (pilaf) and *samsa* (samosa). Kazakhs make a sweet *plov* with dried apricots, raisins and prunes. In summer open-air beer and shashlyk bars, with glowing (or flaming) grills out front, spring up in every town.

A favourite local snack is *baursaki*, fried dough balls or triangles, not unlike heavy doughnuts. Kazakhstan is reckoned to be the original source of apples, and wild apple trees still grow in parts of the southeast.

KAZAKHSTAN DIRECTORY A-Z

366

Kymyz (fermented mare's milk) is a popular drink. It's mildly alcoholic with a sour, slightly fizzy taste. You can buy it, as well as *shubat* (fermented camel's milk), in many supermarkets as well as in markets and the countryside.

Sophisticated cafes with award-winning baristas and latte art have become an established feature in Almaty and Astana, as have microbreweries, English- and Irish-style pubs and glitzy bars.

INTERNET ACCESS

Kazakhstan is a wired country. Internet cafes have largely gone out with the dinosaurs, and the few that remain are usually used for online gaming by teenage boys. With the exception of cheapest, down-at-heel hotels in remote towns, it is now rare to encounter accommodation that doesn't offer free wi-fi. Free wi-fi is ubiquitous in cafes, bars and restaurants. If you have an unlocked smartphone or tablet, it's easy and inexpensive to purchase a local SIM card with oodles of data.

LGBTIQ TRAVELLERS

The gay scene in Kazakhstan in largely underground and low-key. It exists only in large cities, such as Almaty, Astana and Karaganda, and gay-friendly venues are few. Homosexuality is frowned upon by the general population, so overt displays of affection are best avoided.

MAPS

Kasachstan, published by Reise Know-How, is an excellent traveller's map, printed on waterproof, rip-resistant paper. The best local source of country, regional and hiking maps is Akademkniga (p302) in Almaty.

MEDICAL SERVICES

It's advisable to travel to Kazakhstan with comprehensive health insurance.

If you're bringing prescription drugs to Kazakhstan, make sure to bring a copy of each prescription and a letter from your physician.

The quality of health care in hospitals across Kazakhstan is variable. State-owned, public hospitals are woefully underfunded. There are also pricey private hospitals and clinics, particularly in Astana and Almaty, with English-speaking doctors and a good standard of medical care, though for anything particularly serious it's best to be airlifted to Europe. If you call an ambulance, odds are that the operator won't speak English, and it may be faster to just take a taxi to the nearest hospital. Pharmacies are easy to come by but some over-the-counter medications common in other countries may not be easily available.

MONEY

The national currency is the tenge (T).

ATMs abound at banks, shopping centres, supermarkets, hotels, some train stations and elsewhere. Look for 'Bankomat' signs. Most accept at least Maestro, Cirrus, Visa and MasterCard.

Tenge (T) notes come in denominations of 200, 500, 1000, 2000, 5000, 10,000 and 20,000T. There are also 1, 2, 5, 10, 20, 50 and 100T coins. 1T and 2T are not legal tender on public transport. If you have 10,000T or – heaven forbid! – 20,000T bills, get change as soon as you can and hold on to smaller bills, as public transport, taxis and small convenience stores find it difficult to deal with larger bills. Prices in hotels are usually quoted in the national currency, but occasionally US dollars or euros.

You can make purchases with credit cards (Visa and MasterCard preferred) at a fair number of shops, restaurants, hotels and travel agencies. There is sometimes a surcharge for doing so.

Exchange offices (marked 'Obmen Valyuty') are common on city streets. Dollars, euros and roubles are the most widely accepted currencies.

Bargaining

Bargaining is sensible in markets and when agreeing on taxi prices. In shops, prices are fixed. Asking for a discount on hotel accommodation during low and shoulder seasons is a good tactic.

Tipping

Tipping is not customary in Kazakhstan, as hotel and restaurant bills often include a service charge. However, since the restaurant service charge doesn't go to the waiter, a tip is always appreciated.

OPENING HOURS

Banks 9.30am to 1pm and 2pm to 4.30pm Monday to Friday

Museums Generally closed on Mondays

Offices 9am to 1pm and 2pm to 5pm Monday to Friday

Restaurants 11am or noon to midnight

POST

There are post offices in all towns, and the postal service is reasonably reliable, if slow. If you have anything of importance to post it's generally safer and quicker to use an international courier firm. DHL (p302) has a particularly wide network of drop-off centres around the country.

REGISTRATION & TRAVEL PERMITS

Registration

Registration is a confusing, ever-changing and headache-inducing subject. When you arrive at the country's international airports, two entry stamps (one is not enough) on your migration card are the indication that registration has taken place and is valid until you leave the country.

Travellers entering by land or sea typically receive only one entry stamp and have to register with the migration police (Migratsionnaya Politsia, Koshi-Kon Politsiyasi, OVIR) no later than the fifth day of their stay in the country if they are staying in Kazakhstan beyond that day (counting the arrival date as the first day). If you leave the country before day five is finished, registration is not necessary. Confusingly, some travellers arriving by land or sea are granted two entry stamps, while others are not. Also, we have heard of travellers being shaken down for bribes by police even if they have registered properly, so beware.

If you have to register, you can either while away your precious time at an OVIR office at Almaty, Astana, or one of Kazakhstan's 14 regional capitals. Almaty is the best of the lot. Alternatively, many upmarket hotels and travel agencies can handle your registration for a fee of around 5000T. Registration is free and valid for three months. Migration-police offices are generally open for limited hours, often in the morning only, and some close completely on certain weekdays as well as weekends. They also close on public holidays and often on Mondays following public holidays that fall on a weekend. Take your migration card and passport, photocopies of the migration card and the passport's personal-details and Kazakhstan-visa pages, and the address of your hotel (don't give a private address). You will have to fill in a form in Russian, available at the migration-police office and often also at nearby photocopy shops (which can often help you fill it in). You'll be told when to come back and collect your documents, which could be any time from 15 minutes to two working days later. Bring a Russian-speaking friend to make the process easier. The official fine for registering late is US$100.

Note that if you have a double-entry or triple-entry visa, you must be registered again each time you re-enter Kazakhstan (unless you are leaving again within five days).

The registration rules change from time to time and may be interpreted differently in different places: check the situation when you get your visa and again when you reach Kazakhstan. Immigration police outside Almaty, even in Astana, will often only register you for five to 10 days, meaning that you will have to re-register elsewhere if you stay in the country longer.

If your visa was obtained with a letter of invitation (LOI), you will have to register regardless of whether you have one or two entry stamps on your migration card. If the OVIR office tells you to go away, insist on registering or face heavy fines on departure. If you are registering at a migration-police office, they may want to see not just the LOI itself but also extra paperwork from the LOI issuer. If you can't obtain this (for example if the issuer is in Almaty and you are on the other side of the country), provincial migration police will often only register you for five days or even refuse to register you at all – check with your LOI provider in advance if this is a possibility.

Travel Permits

A special border-zone permit is needed for travel to areas near the Chinese border, notably the Altay Mountains and Mt Khan Tengri. The only way to obtain these is through tour firms taking you to these areas, who will normally include the permit charge (about 7500T) in their trip cost. Processing can take up to 45 days, so plan well ahead.

A permit is also officially required for areas near the Kyrgyz border in the mountains south of Almaty. Local guides in Almaty know the score.

Baykonur Cosmodrome and the Semipalatinsk Polygon can only be visited on tours organised through agencies. You need to start the paperwork at least two months ahead for Baykonur and about two weeks ahead for the Polygon.

Entry to nature reserves usually requires a permit, normally arranged quickly through the local reserve office, for anything up to 2000T.

TELEPHONES

International Calls

You can cut costs for international calls from landlines or mobile phones by using prepaid cards such as the Nursat i-Card+, sold at mobile-phone shops, petrol stations, kiosks and some supermarkets in units from 5 to 50. You scratch off a PIN then dial a local access number given on the card. Calling instructions are then available in English. Calls cost around 10T per minute to the USA, Canada or China; 15T per minute to Uzbekistan or Russia; 30T to 80T per minute to other Central Asian countries, Britain, Germany, Italy and France.

Alternatively, get a local SIM card with data and use Skype or another VoIP service to call home for free.

KAZAKHSTAN DIRECTORY A–Z

EMERGENCY & IMPORTANT NUMBERS

Ambulance	103
Emergency	112
Police	102

Mobile Phones

Almost everyone in Kazakhstan has a mobile (cell) phone and it's easy to get a local SIM card for your phone if you have an unlocked GSM-900 frequency phone (this includes most European mobiles and North American smartphones). Shops and kiosks selling SIM cards with call credit and plenty of data for a few hundred tenge are everywhere. Take your passport when you go to buy. The same outlets often sell inexpensive phones too, and will top up your credit for cash or with PIN cards.

➡ KCell and Beeline are the best networks for nationwide coverage; Beeline works better in the countryside around Almaty.

➡ Typically 1000T credit gives you at least two hours of talking to a combination of mobile and landline numbers.

Telephone Numbers

➡ Mobile numbers have 10 digits.

➡ Landlines have a three-, four- or five-digit area code followed by a local number: the area code plus the local number always totals 10 digits.

➡ The Kazakhstan country code is 7.

How to Dial from Kazakhstan Phones

FROM	TO	DIAL
Any phone	Mobile in Kazakhstan or Russia	🗹 8 + mobile number *or* 7 + mobile number
Landline	Other countries except Russia	🗹 8 + 10 + country code + area code + local number
Landline	Landline in other Kazakh city or Russia	🗹 8 + area code + local number
Landline	Landline in same city	local number only
Mobile	Landline in Kazakhstan or Russia	🗹 8 + area code + local number *or* 7 + area code + local number
Mobile	Other countries except Russia	country code + area code + local number

TIME

Kazakhstan is GMT plus six hours, with the exception of western Kazakhstan, which is GMT plus five hours. Daylight savings time is not observed.

TOILETS

Public toilets range from sanitary and flushing (both Western-style and squat toilets), with some industrial wood-chip toilet paper provided when you pay a small fee (50T or so) to revolting holes in the ground in some rickety shack. Bring your own toilet paper, just in case.

VISAS

Kazakhstan visa rules and practices change quite frequently; information on recent changes is available from recommended travel agents and the websites of Kazakhstan embassies and consulates.

Citizens of 45 countries may travel visa-free for 30 days. These are EU states, Australia, Brazil, Canada, Israel, Japan, Jordan, Saudi Arabia, Liechtenstein, Monaco, New Zealand, Norway, Oman, Qatar, Singapore, Switzerland, South Korea, the UAE and the US. Likewise, no visa is needed for visits up to 14 days for Hong Kong citizens, 30 days for Turkish citizens, or 90 days for CIS or Georgian citizens.

For other visas, or if you are not from one of the visa-free states, you must obtain 'visa support' in the form of a letter of invitation (LOI). This is available, usually by email, through most travel agencies in Kazakhstan, Central Asia travel specialists in other countries, or Kazakh businesses. You'll need to submit a copy of the LOI in your visa application to the embassy or consulate. Agents' fees for providing LOIs normally range from around US$30 to US$100 depending on the visa required. LOIs must be applied for at least two weeks before the date of your first entry into Kazakhstan, and you should allow one to two weeks to obtain the LOI before you apply for the visa itself (but note that LOIs cannot normally be issued more than two months before your arrival in Kazakhstan).

Single-entry tourist or business visas on arrival for a stay of up to 30 days can be obtained only by nationals arriving from a country without a Kazakh diplomatic mission. The fee is approximately US$80, and you must hold a LOI. The visa on arrival is available at the airports of Aqtau, Almaty, Astana, Atyrau and Uralsk. If you request a LOI from a travel agency for this purpose, tell them why: not all agencies can provide LOIs suitable for visas on arrival. Also check with the agency about any other paperwork you must provide on arrival and about currently acceptable means of payment: you may be required to pay in cash US dollars or tenge.

The maximum length of a tourist visa is 90 days (triple entry with three visits of a maximum 30 days each). It is no longer possible to get either a business or tourist visa for more than 30 days in Kazakhstan at a time.

Fees for the visa itself depend on the type of visa and your nationality, and with the on-arrival visas – on the mood of the immigration officer. A single-entry, one-month tourist visa is normally US$45 to US$100 (but US$160 for US citizens). Some consulates will deal with visa applications by mail; others, including most in Asia, require you to apply for and collect your visa in person. Processing time at consulates in the West is normally two to five working days.

As of 2017, visitors may only apply for a Kazakhstan visa in their country of residence (unless their country does not have a Kazakh consulate). If you are in a country without a Kazakh embassy or consulate (such as Australia, Ireland, New Zealand or Sweden), you can apply to Kazakh missions in other countries; those in Brussels and Vienna are among the more efficient and less expensive in Europe.

Overstaying your visa, even by a single day, carries the penalty of US$5000 or 20 days in jail – your choice!

Extending a Kazakh visa is generally only possible with a medical certificate stating you are unable to travel.

VISAS FOR ONWARD TRAVEL

Azerbaijan

The best option is a 30-day tourist e-visa which you can get online for US$23 at https://evisa.gov.az/en/, no strings attached (note that there are also similar sites which force you to book hotels and tours; you should avoid these). You receive the visa by email (within about a week), and there is no need to bother with any consulate. No confirmed hotel bookings are needed, normally.

Paper 30-day tourist visas may also be available within five working days from the Azerbaijan Astana embassy (p364) or the Aktau consulate (p364) if you have a LOI (letter of invitation), but this affects few travellers. Visa on arrival may be an option again shortly.

China

Getting a Chinese visa in Kazakhstan and elsewhere in Central Asia remains difficult-to-impossible. Policy and practice change frequently; at the time of writing, visas were not being issued at the Chinese Almaty consulate (p364) for nonresidents, and only a few people succeeded in getting tourist visas (in five to seven days) at the embassy (p364) in Astana in the past; showing proof of sufficient funds (for example bank statements), flight bookings in and out of China, hotel bookings and an itinerary for their whole stay, and proof of employment. No LOI needed but don't say you are going to Xinjiang. You can try your luck but in general, China insists that visa applicants apply in their own country of residence.

It's much better to get your Chinese visa before you leave home (bearing in mind you have to enter China within three months), or in Hong Kong, where procedures are easy and inexpensive.

Kyrgyzstan

For those who still need visas, the Kyrgyzstan Almaty consulate's (p365) 'normal' processing time is 10 working days, with most visas costing US$55 to US$80; but same-day express processing is usually available for US$100 to US$150. Take your passport, a photocopy and one photo. Some nationalities also have to provide a LOI which must be used within a month's issuance. You have to make three visits to the consulate: one to put in the application, one to come back with the bank receipt for payment, and one to pick up the visa.

Russia

The Russian Almaty consulate (p365) and Astana embassy (p365) have reluctantly been issuing tourist visas again for up to 30 days, and still issue transit visas for those they deem unworthy of a tourist visa. Travellers have obtained transit visas in one or two days without LOIs for around 15,000T. You may have to show an onward ticket out of Russia and a visa for the onward country. Visa duration is up to 10 days depending on the duration of your transit in Russia; you may have to enter Russia within three days of the visa being issued. Opening hours for applications are just one or two mornings a week: no one speaks English but if you can manage to call ahead for an appointment it should help. Application forms are available online (only), at http://visa.kdmid.ru. Astana is generally less unfriendly than Almaty. It's worth checking in advance via email whether you're likely to be issued a tourist visa given your Kazakhstan visa status. Stantours (p330) has been successfully helping travellers with LOIs for tourist visas in both Almaty and Astana.

Tajikistan

Most travellers are now able to get a flexible online e-visa and GBAO permit (for travel in the Pamirs) for up to 45 days at www.evisa.tj for US$50 with a few days' processing. Be careful to get all details correct and exactly as in your copies, otherwise the application may fail and you lose your money.

Paper tourist visas are issued in Tajikistan's friendly Almaty embassy office (p365) without LOIs. For a one-month tourist visa (US$100 for same-day processing), provide photocopies of your passport and Kazakh visa and a written request to the ambassador. This office also issues the GBAO permit, hassle-free.

Turkmenistan

To get a Turkmen visa you either need to book a tour through a travel agency, or have visas for the bordering countries from which you will enter Turkmenistan and leave Turkmenistan (these can include Azerbaijan), enabling you to get a transit visa. Transit visas are also available if you fly in or fly out (but not normally both). You have to go in person with your passport to the Turkmen embassy (p365) or consulate (get there before opening time). Transit visas cost US$55 for most nationalities and processing takes five to 20 working days: it's sometimes possible to apply in one city and pick up your visa in another, as you don't have to hand over your original passport with the application.

Uzbekistan

Citizens of some, mostly Western, countries can obtain visas without a LOI but processing for these at the Uzbek Almaty embassy (p365) takes much longer – typically four or five working days, against on-the-spot processing if you have a LOI. Some Almaty travel agents can provide Uzbek LOIs hassle-free if given enough time – US$70 for about two weeks' processing at Stantours (p330). Go to the embassy at least 30 minutes before opening time, put your name on a list and you'll probably get in before the door closes. In the peak summer travel season you may need to get there in the morning. All applicants should take their passport, a photocopy of it, their Kazakh visa and registration (or migration card with entry stamp), one photo, a LOI and a completed application form (normally supplied with an LOI or available at http://evisa. mfa.uz). Tourist visas cost US$55/65/75 for seven/15/30 days, US$95 for three months; for more than one entry, add US$10 per entry. US citizens pay US$160 for any visa. Payments must normally be in US dollars at the bank indicated by the embassy.

VOLUNTEERING

United Nations Volunteers (www.unv.org) is active in Kazakhstan in health, poverty and environmental fields and in coordinating local volunteer projects.

Crossroads (www.crossroads.org.hk) seeks volunteers to work in many fields, from drug and alcohol rehab and distribution of supplies to the destitute to working with the homeless.

WATER

In general, tap water is not safe to drink in Kazakhstan. Some locals do, or have filters attached to their taps, but it's best to err on the side of caution and either boil the water or buy bottled water.

WORK

The majority of expats in Kazakhstan work in the oil and gas industries. Teaching English is also a possibility if you are a native speaker; it helps if you have done an international TEFL course. Getting a work visa is relatively straightforward.

❶ Getting There & Away

ENTERING KAZAKHSTAN

As long as you have your visa organised, you should have no problems getting into Kazakhstan. Keep the migration card you receive in your passport: you have to hand it in when you leave the country. What you must pay special attention to is registration (p367).

AIR

Kazakhstan has excellent international air connections through numerous carriers including the good national airline, **Air Astana** (KC; www. airastana.com). Between them, Astana Airport (p343) and Almaty Airport (p303) have numerous direct connections to Europe, Asia and Central Asia, as well as the Gulf States. Aktau (p329) and **Atyrau** (☑ 702 237 21 71) serve the Caucasus, and several cities, including Atyrau, Shymkent, Semey and Ust-Kamenegorsk, have direct Moscow flights.

LAND

To & From China

Buses run daily to Ürümqi (24 hours) and Yining (12 hours) from Almaty's Sayran bus station (p303), via the border at Khorgos. Sleeper buses leave for Ürümqi at 7am (16,000T) daily. You can book three days ahead but tickets are usually available on departure day: be ready to show your Chinese visa. Sleeper buses to Yining

---

WILDLIFE TOURS

Svetlana Baskakova of Wild Nature (p321), based at Aksu-Zhabagly Nature Reserve, is an expert biologist and great guide for almost any nature-focused trip you like, including exciting brown-bear-spotting and snow-leopard-tracking trips in Aksu-Zhabagly itself.

Kasachstan Reisen (☑ in Germany 0173-62 65 136, in Kazakhstan 701 407 96 11; www. kasachstanreisen.de) offers good ornithological, entomological, botanical (especially wild tulips in spring) and a variety of other tours, normally led by multilingual Kazakhstan expert Dagmar Schreiber.

Rubythroat Birding Tours (http://rubythroatbirding.com; Aitykov 8, Ust-Kamenogorsk) 🪶, based in Ust-Kamenogorsk, is recommended for birdwatchers and has expert guides.

(6500T, 12 hours), about 100km beyond Khorgos, also depart daily at 7am. The crossing is often crammed with Kazakh and Uyghur families and traders with vast amounts of baggage.

Train 014 departs Almaty-II station (p304) for Ürümqi at 12.14am on Sunday and Tuesday, taking a scheduled 32 hours and crossing the border at Dostyk (Druzhba). Kupeyny (2nd-class couchette) tickets cost 37,200T. Tickets are sold in the main ticket hall at Almaty-II and are usually still available in the last few days before departure: press 'Mezhdunarodnaya Kassa' on the machine next to the information bureau to get a number for the ticket queue. Be ready to show your Chinese visa. The trains have restaurant cars but the food is poor and overpriced. At Dostyk, you have to wait four or five hours while the train bogies are changed and customs checks take place. The train toilets are locked during this time except for the 20-minute dash between the Kazakhstan and China border posts: get in line early for this!

To get to the border at Khorgos, go to Almaty-I (p304) and either take daily train 702 at 8.01am (3483T, 3¾ hours) or train 394 at 11.51pm (2422T, 5¼ hours). A 15-minute bus transfer to the Khorgos border is included in the fare. From the border you will need a bus or taxi for the 100km on to Yining, from which there are three daily trains to Ürümqi. The return trains 701 and 393 depart Altynkol at 3.10pm and 10pm, respectively.

Ürümqi also has bus connections with Ust-Kamenogorsk and Semey. Cyclists may cross into China via Khorog on bicycles, but are obliged to take the bus from Semey or Ust-Kamenogorsk.

To & From Kyrgyzstan

Official Kazakh–Kyrgyz border crossings are largely hassle-free, but the 'green border' – trails through the mountains, without border posts – has been closed for several years.

From Almaty's Sayran bus station (p303), there are plenty of minibuses (1500T, three to four hours, hourly 6am to 11pm) and shared taxis (3500T) to Bishkek in Kyrgyzstan, crossing the border at Korday. Minibuses and shared taxis also run from Taraz to Bishkek, and there are also buses from Shymkent and Turkestan to Bishkek – all crossing the border at Chaldybar.

From May to October the scenic and laid-back Karkara valley (p313) border crossing offers an alternate route between Almaty and Issyk-Köl, but no public transport makes this crossing.

To & From Turkmenistan

The remote Temirbaba border point is 165km south of Zhanaozen, which is 150km east of Aktau. Turkmen 4WDs from Zhanaozen bus station take around 10 hours, including two to three hours at the border, for the trip to Turkmenbashi (6000/24,000T per person/vehicle). You're most likely to find a shared vehicle early in the morning. The road is unpaved for about the last 45km to the border and 30km south of it.

To & From Uzbekistan

The main road border between Shymkent and Tashkent, at Chernyaevka (Zhibek Zholy/Gisht Koprik), is connected with Shymkent's Avtovokzal Samal (p318) bus station by fairly frequent marshrutkas (1000T, two hours) – more frequent in the morning. Queues of four to six hours are not uncommon for crossing into Kazakhstan, due to the numbers of Uzbeks heading north in search of work; waits are generally shorter going southbound. For the short ride between the border and central Tashkent you need a taxi.

Crossing the border by train is a way to avoid queues. The railway border at Saryagash, a few kilometres north of Tashkent, is crossed by about a dozen trains each way per week, the majority heading to/from Moscow or the Urals via Turkestan, Kyzylorda and Aktobe, but two or three heading to/from Shymkent and Almaty. From Almaty, the new high-speed train 001 (18,065T, 16¾ hours) departs from Almaty-I (p304) via Almaty-II (p304) on Mondays and Saturdays.

For travellers with their own vehicles, the Yallama crossing, about 60km southwest of Tashkent, is a quicker option than Chernyaevka.

A remote desert road and rail crossing exists at Tazhen (also called Oazis) between Beyneu, western Kazakhstan, and Nukus, Uzbekistan. Trains from Russia to Tashkent via Samarkand (three weekly) use this route, coming into Kazakhstan via Atyrau, and there is a handy daily service between Aktau and Nukus for 10,492T, platskartny (3rd class) only; 24 hours. The little-used road is paved on the Uzbek side but unpaved (and terrible) between the border and Beyneu.

SEA
To & From Azerbaijan

A ferry sails roughly weekly between Aktau and Baku (in Azerbaijan). It's a cargo ship that carries some passengers and a small number of vehicles and leaves when its hold fills, and there can be anything from two days to two weeks between sailings (on average it's about once a week in summer). Tickets (20,000T for a bunk in a windowless four-person cabin) go on sale at the Paromnaya Kassa (p329) when the ship leaves Baku for the 30-hour crossing – in theory that's about 24 hours before it departs Aktau. 'In theory' because the ship sometimes waits a long time outside Aktau – three days is not unknown (and the same can happen arriving at Baku).

KAZAKHSTAN GETTING THERE & AWAY

OVERLAND TO RUSSIA

Kazakhstan's 6846km border with Russia has 18 'multilateral' road crossings (open to all nationalities), and around 15 rail crossings.

Buses & Shared Taxis

Bus services, and in some cases shared taxis, connect cities within striking distance of the border. Daily bus services include Astrakhan–Atyrau (3400T, eight hours), Samara–Uralsk (2750T, six hours), Orenburg–Aktobe (2200T, six hours), Tyumen–Petropavlovsk (4500T, 10 hours), Barnaul–Semey (4200T, 11 hours) and Novosibirsk–Ust-Kamenogorsk (6300T, 18 hours).

Road Crossings

The main multilateral road crossings (listed from west to east):

➡ Kotyaevka (between Astrakhan and Atyrau) The westernmost entry point, but some roads on the Kazakh side are very poor, notably the appalling 230km Makat–Bayganin stretch between Atyrau and Aktobe.

➡ Taskala (between Saratov and Uralsk)

➡ Mashtakov (between Samara and Uralsk)

➡ Zhaysan (between Orenburg and Aktobe)

➡ Podgorodka (Kayrak; between Chelyabinsk and Kostanay)

➡ Kazantsevskoe (between Kurgan and Petropavlovsk)

➡ Roslavka (Karakoga; between Omsk and Petropavlovsk)

➡ Auyl (between Rubtsovsk and Semey)

➡ Shemonaikha (between Rubtsovsk and Ust-Kamenogorsk)

Leave a photocopy of your passport and a contact number at the Paromnaya Kassa and they'll call you when tickets become available. Take food for the voyage: the food on board is expensive and of poor quality. Note that immigration officials may require all travellers leaving Aktau on the ferry to have registered their Kazakhstan visas, even if they are leaving within the normal five-day registration-free period.

In Baku, tickets are only sold on the day of departure: you must check with the ticket office near the Turkmenistan ferry dock every morning to find out if there's a sailing. The ferry actually leaves from one of two places: either the old seaport or the roll-on, roll-off port about 7km further east, and you will only know which one on the day.

❶ Getting Around

AIR

A good network of domestic flights links cities all around Kazakhstan and fares are reasonable. The main airlines are the pricier international-standard **Air Astana** (KC; www.airastana.com), and inexpensive **SCAT** (DV; www.scat.kz). **Bek Air** (www.bekair.aero) and **Qazaq Air** (www.flyqazaq.com) serve more limited destinations. All Kazakh airlines now meet international safety standards. All airlines issue e-tickets online, payable with international credit cards.

BICYCLE

There are challenges to cycling in Kazakhstan, from the enormous distances between places to intense heat in summer. But there is little traffic outside the main cities and some parts of the country, such as its southern and eastern fringes, make for challenging but beautiful routes, and more and more cyclists are taking up the challenge.

In cities such as Almaty, Astana and Shymkent there has been a move to introduce more and more cycle lanes. Each of the cities has numerous automated bicycle-rental points, ideal for travelling short distances.

BUS

With a few exceptions such as the busy Shymkent–Almaty, Astana–Karaganda, Atyrau–Uralsk, Semey–Ust-Kamenogorsk and Uralsk–Aktobe routes, intercity bus services are unlikely to thrill you, with less frequent departures in increasingly aged buses from ramshackle bus stations. Nevertheless, buses are an option for trips of up to five or six hours – generally a bit faster than trains and with fares similar to plat-skartny (3rd class) on trains – typically around 500T per 100km. For longer trips trains are generally more comfortable.

Note that most bus companies require you to pay a fee for storing luggage in the luggage

Train

Most main Kazakhstan cities have train service to/from Moscow via other Russian cities, daily or every two days; direct services from Almaty have been discontinued.

Many Kazakh cities also have trains to/from Siberian cities. Daily trains along the 'Turksib' line take 37 to 39 hours between Novosibirsk and Almaty (US$85), via Semey. Daily trains from Moscow's Kazansky station to Astana take around 56 hours for US$258.

The major rail routes:

➡ Moscow–Saratov–Uralsk–Aktobe

➡ Moscow–Samara–Orenburg–Aktobe–Kyzylorda–Tashkent/Bishkek

➡ Moscow–Volgograd–Atyrau–Beyneu–Uzbekistan (Nukus, Samarkand, Tashkent)

➡ Moscow–Chelyabinsk–Petropavlovsk/Kostanay–Astana–Karaganda

➡ Novosibirsk–Barnaul–Semey–Almaty (the 'Turksib')

➡ Vladivostok–Irkutsk–Novosibirsk–Omsk–Petropavlovsk (from the east)

Western Europe–Western China Highway

The new 'Western Europe–Western China' highway, a massive project to boost trans-Asia commerce, will provide the best driving option from European Russia into Kazakhstan when it is completed. The 8445km highway runs from St Petersburg to Moscow, Kazan and Orenburg, then across Kazakhstan via Aktobe, Kyzylorda, Shymkent, Taraz and Almaty, into China at Khorgos then across China via Ürümqi to the seaport Lianyungang. Long sections of new four- and two-lane highway are open across Kazakhstan, with the Almaty–Khorgos section in the process of being completed at the time of research.

compartment – typically around 10% of the total fare. When purchasing your bus ticket, ask about *provoz bagazha*.

CAR & MOTORCYCLE

Traffic police and poor roads (in that order) are the main hazards of driving in Kazakhstan. Main intercity roads may have bad, potholed stretches but are mostly in decent condition. Huge infrastructure projects are massively improving some major trunk routes.

Traffic police may stop motorists just to check their papers, and have a reputation for finding irregularities that they may then overlook if bribed. Go very slowly past any parked police vehicle or police observation post. The blood-alcohol limit is zero. Don't run red lights and do stick to speed limits (usually 50km/h in cities and 90km/h outside them). The standard bribe rate in the Mangistau region is 5000T.

You should carry an International Driving Permit as well as your home-country licence.

For many trips it is easier, and no more expensive, to take a taxi or tour than to rent a self-drive car, but there are self-drive options if that suits your needs best. In fact, Kazakhstan rewards those intrepid and adventurous people with plenty of time on their hands and a love for driving, since many of the country's natural and cultural attractions often lie in the middle of nowhere and are reachable by rugged roads. **Europcar** (www.europcar.com) has rental offices in Almaty and Astana. You can also rent through local agencies or travel agencies. Short-term self-drive rates start at around US$60 per day; expect to pay US$80 to US$100 for a 4WD. Renters must normally be aged 25 or older and have held their licence at least one year (three years with some firms). Check the small print very carefully: some companies, for example, don't allow vehicles to be taken out of the local *oblast* (region).

Those in favour of two-wheeled exploration can find kindred spirits via **SilkOffRoad Motorcycle Club** (www.silkoffroad.kz), a pioneer of motorcycle tourism across Central Asia. Motorcycle rent, expert advice and technical support is provided by Car & Bike Rental Marat (p304) in Almaty.

MARSHRUTKA & MINIBUSES

Many short and medium-length intercity routes (up to three or four hours) are now covered more frequently by modern, relatively comfortable minibuses (and a few marshrutkas – less comfortable, Russian-built, combi-type vehicles). These generally cost about 50% more than buses and go quicker.

TAXIS, SHARED TAXIS & UBER

For many intercity trips, taxis offer a much faster alternative to buses and minibuses. They're generally found waiting outside bus and train stations and you can either rent the whole cab or share it with three other passengers at a quarter of the price (about double the corresponding bus fare). Sharing may involve some time waiting around for other passengers to materialise.

In cities, some taxis use meters, others refuse to, so often your fare depends on your bargaining skills. Uber (www.uber.com) is a cheaper alternative for those with smartphones and relevant language skills.

Car-sharing is popular, with locals heading to another city posting their destination, departure time and price per passenger online, either on **BeepCar** (www.beepcar.ru) or **BlaBlaCar** (www.blablacar.ru).

TRAIN

Trains serve all cities and many smaller places. They're a good way to experience Kazakhstan's terrain, vast size and people. Except for small local trains, tickets are best bought in advance. In summer, the best tickets for popular trains may sell out a couple of weeks in advance. The official, trilingual www.tickets.kz site allows you to purchase tickets online (and book your favourite seat/berth) using international Visa and MasterCard. Tickets may also be cancelled online for a small fee. Some international trains don't show up on www.tickets.kz, but appear on the www.tatu.ru site. If you purchase a ticket through www.tatu.ru, make sure that there's a '3P' symbol under the train logo that indicates that you can print the e-ticket off yourself. All others must be collected from a train-ticket machine *in Russia*.

Tickets may also be purchased or printed off at all major train stations using the ticket machines provided. Note that they will not print tickets for departures within 24 hours, though showing the carriage attendant an electronic ticket on your smartphone (if you have one) is usually sufficient. Station ticket queues can be slow, but all cities also have downtown train-booking offices, called *zheleznodorozhnaya kassa* (Russian) or *temir zhol kassasy* (Kazakh), where you can buy tickets at a small commission, though most travellers have little use for them now that it's possible to buy online. Always take your passport when buying tickets.

Trains are generally slower than road travel but for longer intercity trips are the only option other than flying. Fares in *platskartny* (3rd-class open-bunk carriages) are similar to bus fares. *Kupeyny* (2nd-class four-person couchettes) costs about 50% more – typically 300T to 400T per hour of travel. We have quoted *kupeyny* fares, unless stated otherwise.

Timetable information is available in English at www.tickets.kz, www.poezda.net (with fares in Russian roubles) and in Russian and Kazakh at temirzholy.kz and epay.railways.kz. This last company has an online booking facility that accepts international credit cards but is still only in Russian and Kazakh (users collect tickets from machines or ticket counters at stations). Bear in mind that all train departures are shown in Astana time (GMT plus five hours). If you're travelling in western Kazakhstan (GMT plus four hours), remember to get to the station an hour early.

Turkmenistan

☎ 993 / POP 5.3 MILLION

Best Places to Eat

➡ Coffee House (p384)

➡ Hotel Ýyldyz Panoramic Restaurant (p384)

➡ Şa Kofe (p384)

Best Places to Shop

➡ Altyn Asyr Marketing Centre (p385)

➡ Altyn Göl (p385)

➡ Tolkuchka Bazaar (p385)

➡ Berkarar (p385)

Why Go?

By far the most mysterious and unexplored of Central Asia's 'stans, Turkmenistan became famous for the truly bizarre dictatorship of Saparmyrat Niyazov, who ruled as 'Turkmenbashi' ('leader of the Turkmen') until his death in 2006. Niyazov covered this little-known desert republic with grandiose monuments and golden statues of himself. Although many of these statues have since been dismantled, plenty of visitors still think of Turkmenistan as a sort of totalitarian theme park. But the least-visited of Central Asia's countries is far more than this – it's an ancient land of great spirituality, tradition and natural beauty.

The ancient cities of Merv and Konye-Urgench inspire visions of caravans plodding along the ancient Silk Road, while the haunting beauty of the Karakum desert and other quirky natural phenomena are equally mesmerising. The full Turkmen experience is ultimately about mingling with the warm and fascinating people themselves, whose hospitality is the stuff of legend.

When to Go

Ashgabat

Apr–Jun Bright sunshine and cool temperatures combine to create the best climate for travel.

Sep–Nov The fierce summer heat gradually cools and the winter approaches.

Dec Wrap up warmly; expect to see snow in the desert and very few other travellers!

TOP TIPS

➡ Spending time in Ashgabat means you don't have to be with a guide, and is a good way to cut costs, although you do still need to be on an organised trip.

➡ The other way to avoid travelling with a guide is to get a transit visa, although they tend to only be valid for three to five days, depending on your route across the country.

Fast Facts

➡ **Area** 488,100 sq km

➡ **Capital** Ashgabat

➡ **Currency** manat (M)

➡ **Languages** Turkmen, Russian, Uzbek

Exchange Rates

Australia	A$1	2.80M
Canada	C$1	2.73M
China	¥10	5.53M
Euro zone	€1	4.34M
Japan	¥100	3.27M
NZ	NZ$1	2.54M
Russia	R100	6.09M
UK	£1	4.88M
USA	US$1	3.50M

For current exchange rates, see www.xe.com.

Resources

➡ **Lonely Planet** (www.lonelyplanet. com/turkmenistan)

➡ **Caravanistan** (http:// caravanistan.com)

➡ **Gundogar** (www. gundogar.org)

➡ **News & Information** (www.turkmenistan.gov.tm)

Visas & Permits

Everyone requires a visa for Turkmenistan, and unless you're on a transit visa, you need to be accompanied by a guide throughout your stay.

COSTS

Relative Cost
The most expensive country in Central Asia.

Daily Expenses
➡ Basic hotel room: US$60
➡ Midrange hotel room: US$120
➡ Kebab lunch: US$5
➡ Pizza and a beer: US$8
➡ Dinner at hotel: US$30
➡ Museum entry: US$10
➡ Bus ride in Ashgabat: US$0.10
➡ Taxi ride within Ashgabat: US$3
➡ Domestic flight: US$100

Price Ranges
Sleeping (for two people): **$** <US$50, **$$** US$50–100, **$$$** >US$100

Eating (main course): **$** <20M, **$$** 20–50M, **$$$** >50M

Itineraries

➡ **One Week** Spend at least three days in and around Ashgabat before heading east to visit the ancient sites of Merv and Gonur Depe. From here, return to Ashgabat and travel north to Konye-Urgench, camping en route at the unforgettable Darvaza Gas Craters.

➡ **Two Weeks** Along with the sights mentioned above, take the time for some activities, such as horseback riding in Geok-Dere or a visit to the Köw Ata Underground Lake and make a trip to the Yangykala Canyon and Turkmenbashi.

➡ **Three Weeks** Arriving on a transit visa, spend a day in fascinatingly weird Ashgabat, cross the Karakum desert and spend the night camping by the Darvaza Gas Craters and then wrap things up with a visit to historic Konye-Urgench.

ASHGABAT

♪ 12 / POP 1 MILLION

With its lavish marble palaces, gleaming gold domes and vast expanses of manicured parkland, Ashgabat ('the city of love' in Arabic) has reinvented itself as a showcase city for the newly independent republic and is definitely one of Central Asia's – if not the world's – strangest places. Built almost entirely off the receipts of Turkmenistan's oil and gas revenues, the city's transformation continues at breakneck speed, with whole neighbourhoods facing the wrecking ball in the name of progress, and gleaming white marble monoliths springing up overnight like mushrooms.

Originally developed by the Russians in the late 19th century, Ashgabat became a prosperous, sleepy and largely Russian frontier town on the Trans-Caspian railway. However, at 1am on 6 October 1948, the city vanished in less than a minute, levelled by an earthquake that measured nine on the Richter scale, killing more than 110,000 people (two-thirds of the then population).

After the earthquake Ashgabat was rebuilt in the Soviet style, but its modern incarnation is somewhere between Las Vegas and Pyongyang, with a mixture of Bellagio fountains, Stalinist ministries of state and national monuments. There are some decent restaurants and no shortage of quirky sights, making it a pleasant place to absorb Turkmenistan's bizarre present before heading into the rest of the country to discover its fascinating past.

◉ Sights

Ashgabat has plenty to occupy visitors for a day or two, though its often very good museums are overpriced, which will put many travellers off going. Despite this, some sights are free (such as wandering the new city, or a visit to Tolkuchka Bazaar) or very reasonably priced (eg the Turkmenbashi Cableway), so you won't always spend a fortune.

◉ Central Ashgabat

In addition to the marble-clad monumental buildings of note, including even the Circus, which has been 'Turkmenised' with a coating of white marble, three mosques in the centre deserve a look. The modern mosque of **Khezrety Omar** (Map p382), off Atamurat Niyazov köçesi, is worth visiting for its wonderfully garish painted ceilings.

The angular, futuristic **Iranian mosque** (Tehran köçesi), illuminated with green neon, is on Görogly köçesi on the western outskirts of the city.

The **Azadi mosque** (Map p380; Shevchenko köçesi), similar in appearance to the Blue Mosque in İstanbul, stands just south of Magtymguly şayoli, 600m east of the junction with Turkmenbashi.

Independence Square   SQUARE

(Map p382) At the centre of Ashgabat is the enormous Independence Square, on which sits the golden-domed Palace of Turkmenbashi (the place of work of the former president), the Ministry of Fairness, the Ministry of Defence and Ruhyyet Palace, all of which were built by the French corporation Bouygues Construction, one-time court builder to Niyazov. Just opposite the square is the Majlis parliament building.

Statue of Lenin   STATUE

(Map p382; off Azadi köçesi) The statue of Lenin, in a small park off Azadi köçesi, is a charmingly incongruous assembly of a tiny Lenin on an enormous and very Central Asian plinth surrounded by fountains. Its walls feature modernist concrete sculptures made by Ernst Neizvestny, a Russian artist who lived and worked in Ashgabat during the 1970s. Across the road from the statue is an austere concrete building that was once the Archive of the Communist Party of Turkmenistan.

Museum of Fine Arts   MUSEUM

(Map p382; ♪ 39 61 42; Alishera Navoi köçesi 88; US$10; ⊙ 9am-6pm Wed-Mon) The Museum of Fine Arts is located in an impressive building with a big rotunda, two tiers and lots of gold. The collection contains some great Soviet-Turkmen artwork: happy peasant scenes with a backdrop of yurts and smoke-belching factories. There is also a collection of Russian and Western European paintings and a fine selection of Turkmen jewellery and traditional costumes. Guided tours in English are available for a further US$20 per group.

TURKMENISTAN ASHGABAT

ℹ **UPDATE**

Due to extenuating circumstances, our writer was not able to visit Turkmenistan. This chapter was updated remotely. Travellers should check circumstances on the ground and with their travel agency before departure.

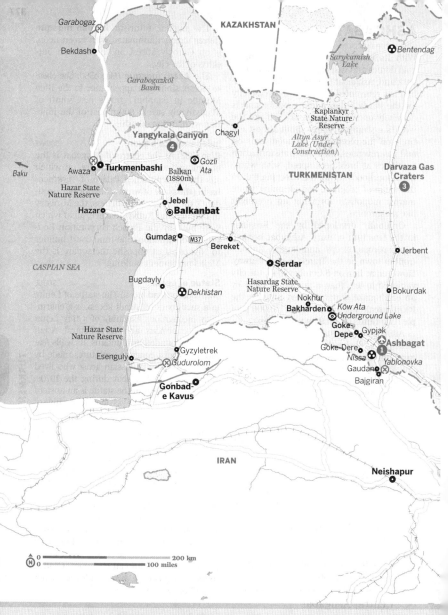

Turkmenistan Highlights

1 Ashgabat (p377)
Exploring the extraordinary, ever-changing Turkmen capital laden with marble palaces, bizarre monuments and more fountains than Las Vegas.

2 Konye-Urgench
(p393) Discovering ancient minarets and turquoise-tiled mausoleums, a testament to the former glories of the Khorezmshah empire.

3 Darvaza Gas Craters
(p392) Witnessing the bizarre combination of human accident and natural phenomenon; a vision of hell amid the lunar landscapes of the Karakum desert.

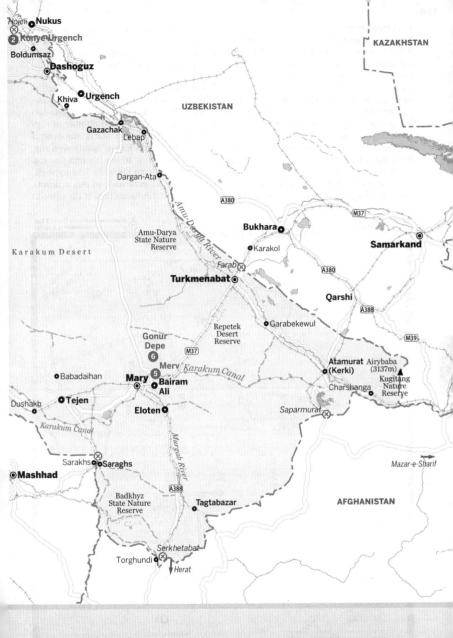

Karakum Desert

④ Yangykala Canyon
(p395) Wandering the painted desert that wouldn't look out of place in a John Ford film; great for camping and exploration.

⑤ Merv (p388)
Exploring the most famous archaeological site in Turkmenistan, which is still covered with ancient foundations and pottery shards.

⑥ Gonur Depe (p386)
Marvelling at the largest archaeological excavation in the Near East.

Halk Hakydasy
Memorial Complex   MEMORIAL

(Bikrova köçesi) Unveiled in 2014, this vast complex features three memorials honouring those that died in the 1948 earthquake, soldiers who perished in WWII and those killed in other Turkmen battles. The Earthquake Memorial features a bombastic bronze rendering of a bull and child (said to be the baby Niyazov).

There is also a museum (entrance US$10) featuring two exhibits: one covering the earthquake and the other focusing on war. The earthquake hall is perhaps Ashgabat's most touching museum and the display includes once-banned photos of pre-1948 earthquakes as well as information about the five-year clean-up effort, the burying of 110,000 bodies and the building of a new city.

Carpet Museum   MUSEUM

(Map p380; ☑ 44 68 09; Atamurat Niyazov şayoli 58; US$12; ⊙ 9am-6pm Mon-Fri, to 2pm Sat) While there's a limit to the number of rugs the average visitor can stand, the central exhibit, the world's largest handwoven rug, really is something to see (though you can see it hanging from the lobby when you enter – you don't even have to buy a ticket). The 'expert commission' here is the place to

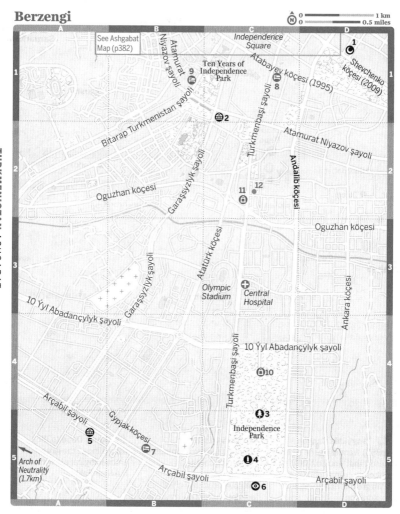

Berzengi

See Ashgabat Map (p382)

have your carpets valued and taxed, and the necessary documentation issued for export.

Circus
LANDMARK

(Map p382) This Soviet-era circus building, which resembles a flying saucer, has been 'Turkmenised' with a coating of white marble. It's definitely worth a look if you're collecting snaps of quirky landmarks, but we don't recommend seeing the circus itself, which features performing animals.

◉ Berzengi

South of Moskovsky şayoli the surreal world of Berzengi begins – an entirely artificial brave new world of white-marble tower blocks, fountains, parks and general emptiness that culminates in the Berzengi Hwy (Archabil şayoli), which is home to a number of hotel complexes, museums and ministries.

Independence Park
PARK

(Map p380) The Altyn Asyr Shopping Centre (p385) is the curious pyramidal shopping centre at the northern end of Independence Park. The Monument to the Independence of Turkmenistan, known to some expats as 'the plunger' (for reasons obvious as soon as you see it), is another monument in the park. Nearby is a trippy giant copy of Niyazov's once ubiquitous Ruhnama ('Book of the Soul').

Palace of Knowledge
NOTABLE BUILDING

(Map p380) Beyond the southern end of Independence Park is the huge, golden domed Palace of Knowledge: three large buildings that include a library, concert hall and the **Turkmenbashi Museum** (Map p380; ☑48 95 79; Archabil şayoli; US$10; ☺9am-6pm Wed-Mon).

Taking a leaf out of Kim Jong-il's book, the museum houses all the gifts and awards presented to former President Niyazov by various people around the world. Expect to see lots of gold.

National Museum
MUSEUM

(Map p380; ☑48 25 90; Archabil şayoli 30; per museum US$10; ☺9am-5pm Wed-Sun) Looking like a lost palace in the urban desert, the National Museum occupies a striking position in front of the Kopet Dag. It's actually a collection of three pricey museums – the History Museum, the Nature & Ethnographic Museum and the Presidential Museum. The History Museum is the only one that approaches value for money.

Arch of Neutrality
MONUMENT

(☺9am-8pm) Once the centrepiece of Niyazov's Ashgabat, the Arch of Neutrality was erected to celebrate the Turkmen people's unsurprisingly unanimous endorsement of Turkmenbashi's policy of neutrality in 1998. Above the arch itself is the real gem, a 12m-high polished-gold statue of Niyazov, which revolved to follow the sun throughout the day. Now in exile, overlooking his beloved city, Niyazov no longer rotates, but his comedic posture makes it clear why the monument was nicknamed 'batman' by locals.

🏃 Activities

Geok Depe Horse Farm
HORSE RIDING

(adults $15, $25 per hour per horse) Travellers report that this horse farm is run by a family and offers riding experiences. It can also be a little bit like a homestay experience – you can have lunch or dinner here, which will be a homemade meal and you might be offered the chance to eat with the family.

Turkmenbashi Cableway
CABLE CAR

(2M) For some spectacular views of Ashgabat and the surrounding desert, take a ride up the Turkmenbashi Cableway. The US$20 million cable-car system, opened in 2006, starts from the base of the Kopet Dag, south of the National Museum, and climbs to a

---

Berzengi

height of 1293m above sea level on a lower peak of the Kopet Dag. The upper terminal has souvenir shops, a restaurant, cafe, picnic spots, several high-powered telescopes for sightseeing and an 80m-high artificial waterfall.

It takes 10 minutes to travel the 3.5km-long cableway. To get here your only option is to take a cab. Ask to be taken to the *kábelnaya daróga* (in Russian) or *asma ýoly* (in Turkmen). You'd be best off paying the driver to wait as there's no passing traffic here.

🛏 Sleeping

Ashgabat has no budget accommodation and even its midrange offerings are fairly bleak. Many tour companies suggest their clients stay in Berzengi, although it can be isolated and overpriced.

Although you can roam the capital without a guide, your accommodation will be booked in advance through your agency. Even if you're on a transit visa, it is technically illegal to book hotel stays directly, although some places will turn a blind eye.

Most hotels offer international direct dialling (IDD) and fax facilities, and floor maids

Ashgabat

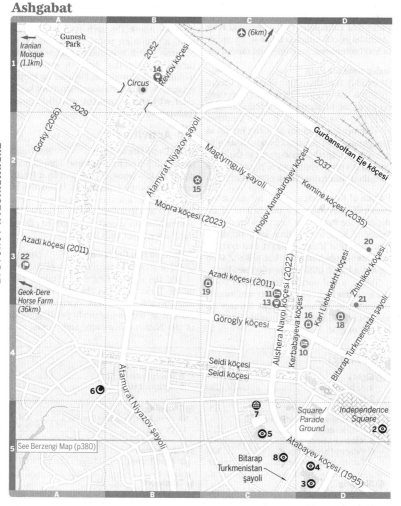

TURKMENISTAN ASHGABAT

at most hotels will do a load of laundry for around 10M.

Hotel Aziya
HOTEL **$$**

(Map p380; ☑ 48 01 80; Archabil şayoli 31; s/d incl breakfast US$55/65; ⓟ ✱) Offering the best value in the city at this price, the Hotel Aziya's rooms are enormous and come complete with flat-screen TV, good Turkmen carpets and eye-wateringly tasteless furniture. Despite the hotel's large size, there are just eight rooms – the rest of the building houses offices. To get into town, take bus 19 to Görogly köçesi or bus 34 to the station.

There's a good Chinese restaurant here too, but otherwise you're somewhat out of the city centre on the edge of Berzengi.

Hotel Daýhan
HOTEL **$$**

(Map p382; ☑ 93 23 72; Azadi köçesi 69; r US$60; ✱) This tired old Soviet joint downstairs has surprisingly good accommodation upstairs and enjoys a great location. Around half the rooms have been renovated (though prices are the same whether the room has been redone or not!) and have nice paint jobs, decent beds, TV, fridges and hot water, although bathrooms have been tidied up rather than transformed. The *lux* (deluxe) rooms are two normal rooms joined together and are no newer in design.

Oguzkent Hotel
LUXURY HOTEL **$$$**

(Map p380; ☑ 44 95 00; Bitarap Turkmenistan şayoli; s/d US$180/200; ⓟ ⊖ ✱ ⓦ ⌘) Effortlessly Ashgabat's best hotel, this gleaming palace is perhaps Central Asia's single most impressive place to stay. It combines the local fashion for marble and fountains with the solid management of the French Sofitel hotel chain and what is definitely Turkmenistan's best breakfast buffet (even if you're not staying here, treat yourself to the US$20 feast).

This is a full five-star experience with 299 fabulous rooms that include touches such as TVs in the bath, rain showers, fast and free wi-fi, three pools, a gym, spa and sauna.

Nusay Hotel
LUXURY HOTEL **$$$**

(Map p380; ☑ 22 10 25; nusay-hotel@online.tm; 1995 köçesi 70; s/d US$145/165; ✱ ⓦ ⌘) The Nusay is Ashgabat's best-value luxury option. It's perfectly located between the new and old city, and overlooks the presidential palace (which unfortunately gives the area a rather sterile and uptight atmosphere). Rooms are spacious, comfortable and luxuriously appointed. Wi-fi costs US$5 per 24 hours and works in the lobby only. There have been reports that some travellers feel uncomfortable staying here because of the constant military presence outside the hotel.

Grand Turkmen Hotel
HOTEL **$$$**

(Map p382; ☑ 92 05 55; grandhtl50@gmail.com; Görogly köçesi 50; s/d incl breakfast US$74/120; ⓟ ✱ @ ⓦ ⌘) Blessed with a fantastic location, the Grand Turkmen is a great choice. The standard rooms are in good shape (if perhaps a little small for the price) and all have balconies. It's a lively downtown place, within easy walking distance of many restaurants and sights, and in-house amenities include a gym and sauna.

Ashgabat

🍴 Eating & Drinking

With the best range of eating options in the country, after a long trip through the desert the hungry traveller will be spoiled for choice. Nightlife is thin on the ground, however, and you can hear a pin drop after 11pm when nearly all the bars and cafes close.

Coffee House　　　　　INTERNATIONAL **$$**
(Güzer; Map p382; ☑ 39 60 06; Turkmenbashi şayoli 15A; dishes 24-110M; ☺9am-11pm; ❋🅟) This place may be a masterwork of kitsch, but its breakfasts are solid and its coffee is decent, making it a prime hang-out for the foreign community. Salads, soups and burgers complete the menu.

Şa Kofe　　　　　　　　　　　CAFE
(http://shakofe.com; Berkarar Mall; mains 25-50M) This hip cafe gets rave reviews from travellers for its excellent coffee, tasty pizza, crunchy salads and sophisticated decor.

Hotel Ýyldyz
Panoramic Restaurant　　　CENTRAL ASIAN
(☑39 09 00; www.yyldyzhotel.com; Bagtyyarlyk köçesi 17; mains 50-100M) Perched on the 18th floor of the hotel, this is a popular place for sundowners or a special dinner with great views over Ashgabat. Credit cards are accepted.

Cafe Güneş　　　　　　　　　　BAR
(Map p382; Alishera Navoi köçesi) In a courtyard behind the Hotel Daýhan, this place serves up the cheapest beer in town and does tasty kebabs, with outdoor tables and a friendly atmosphere. If you're taking a taxi here or seeking directions, ask for Zip Bar – locals use its nickname.

Iceberg Bar　　　　　　　　　　BAR
(Map p382; cnr Kemine & Revfov köçesis; ☺10am-11pm) This tranquil beer garden, located behind the circus, serves up frothy pints of local beer and sticks of shashlyk. It's known locally as Berk Bar, named for the beer brand it sells.

⭐ Entertainment

Ashgabat is a great place for horse-lovers. Every Sunday from the end of March until May, then again from the end of August until mid-November, the Hippodrome plays host to dramatic Turkmen horse races. It's 5km east of the city centre – take bus 4 down Magtymguly or a 5M taxi ride. The local football team is **Kopet Dag** (Map p382). You should have no trouble picking up a ticket on match days.

🛍 Shopping

Even after renovations, Ashgabat's traditional bazaars are worth visiting, if just for the bustle. The central **Russian Bazaar** (Map p382) is good food of all kinds, especially fresh fruit and vegetables, while the **Tekke Bazaar** (Map p382) complements foodstuff with flowers as well.

For travellers of a more modern bent, several malls around town may be of interest as well. Huge **Berkarar** (Atatürk köçesi; ⊙9am-11pm) features stores galore, a bowling alley, movie theatre and Western-style cafes; while **Altyn Asyr Shopping Centre** (Map p380; Independence Park) – reputedly home to the biggest fountain in the world – is an all but empty two-floor shopping centre, though it is possible to take the lift up to the 6th floor restaurant for great city views. Turkish shopping centre **Yimpaş** (Map p380; ☑45 42 66; Turkmenbashi şayoli 54; ⊙7am-11pm) has among the best supermarkets in town, carrying everything from frozen lobster to Doritos over several floors.

Turkmen bookshops are little more than propaganda shopfronts to promote national glory, but the best selection of books can be found at **Miras Bookshop** (Map p382; Turkmenbashi şayoli 29; ⊙10am-7pm). Find some novels in Russian among copies of the Ruhnama and various other pieces of dictatorship ephemera.

Tolkuchka Bazaar   MARKET
Once one of Central Asia's most spectacular sights, Ashgabat's legendary Tolkuchka Bazaar is now sadly unregonisable following a government relocation from its time immemorial location in 2010. Now housed in a collection of characterless hangar-style buildings and surrounded by car parks, the new Tolkuchka, or the Altyn Asyr Market as it's officially known, has none of the old market's mercantile soul or chaotic charm.

Altyn Asyr
Marketing Centre   SHOPPING CENTRE
(Map p382; Görogly köçesi) If you want to buy carpets, Turkmenistan tracksuits or inexpensive cotton clothing, visit the Altyn Asyr Marketing Centre, opposite the Grand Turkmen Hotel, which has outlet shops for the carpet and textile industry. The carpets are sold with all the documentation needed to be exported from the country, making it a lot simpler to buy them here. The best selection is available in **Altyn Göl** (☑39 21 56; ⊙9am-7.30pm Mon-Fri, to 6pm Sat & Sun).

ℹ Information

DANGERS & ANNOYANCES
Take care when photographing public buildings in Ashgabat as you may be shouted at by a police officer. Do not attempt to photograph the Palace of Turkmenbashi or any other ministry; the government quarter in Ashgabat is off-limits for photography, but there are no signs to this ef-fect. Keep your distance around the government buildings lining Independence Sq.

INTERNET ACCESS
There are a few internet cafes in Ashgabat, and an increasing number of hotels and restaurants offer free wi-fi. When using internet cafes, bring your passport, know that anything you view or write can be monitored and expect news websites to be blocked.

Although the situation has improved, wi-fi connections are often terrible, if they work at all. A far better way to use the internet is to buy a local SIM card for your unlocked smartphone. MTS will sell these to you from their main office in the Russian Bazaar; you'll just need to bring along your passport.

MEDICAL SERVICES
The large and excellent **Central Hospital** (Map p380; ☑45 03 03, 45 03 31; Yunus Emre köçesi 1) is the main medical provision in Ashgabat. There's an emergency department and pharmacy, both of which are open 24 hours a day.

MONEY
There are several banks in the city centre, but they're not of much use to travellers as they don't have ATMs and don't change travellers cheques. Most places change US dollars, and euros too, even though the euro rate is not always displayed. As the exchange rate is fixed, there's no advantage in going to one place over another although there is a black market in operation. There are just two banks that can do credit and debit card advances.

TRAVEL AGENCIES
Any traveller not simply in transit through Turkmenistan will need to organise their trip through a travel agency. Agencies can organise a letter of invitation (LOI) and arrange guides, drivers, hotel bookings, city tours and excursions. The following agencies all offers comprehensive services including LOIs, guides, drivers, hotel bookings, city tours and other excursions.

Ayan Travel (Map p380; ☑22 70 05; www.ayan-travel.com; Turkmenbaşi şayoli 81)
DN Tours (Map p382; ☑27 04 39, 27 06 21; www.dntours.com; Magtymguly şayoli 50)
Tourism-Owadan (Map p382; ☑95 76 73; www.owadan.net; Oguzkhan köçesi 207) Offers services throughout the entire country.

ℹ Getting There & Away
Independent travel is not possible in Turkmenistan unless you're on a transit visa, and the only way to reach most places is via a prearranged private driver or guided tour.

WORTH A TRIP

GONUR DEPE

Long before Merv raised its first tower, Bronze Age villages were assembling along the Murgab River in what is called the Margiana Oasis. The greatest of these ancient settlements, currently being excavated around Gonur Depe (Gonur Hill), has stunned the archaeological world for its vast area and complex layout. The Royal Palace and necropolis are the most fascinating sites to visit.

The discoveries were first made in 1972 by Russian-Greek archaeologist Viktor Sarianidi, who still works at the site, continually uncovering new findings. Sarianidi considers Gonur to be one of the great civilisations of the ancient world and while this claim may be disputed, it is a fascinating site. What is certain, is that Gonur is one of the oldest fire-worshipping civilisations, parallel to the Bactrian cultures in neighbouring Afghanistan. The first agricultural settlements appeared in the area around 7000 BC, developing a strong agriculture. It is believed the city was slowly abandoned during the Bronze Age as the Murgab River changed course, depriving the city of water. The current excavations have been dated back to 3000 BC.

Sarianidi believes that Gonur was the birthplace of the first monotheistic religion, Zoroastrianism, being at some point the home of the religion's founder, Zoroaster. The adjacent sites have revealed four fire temples, as well as evidence of a cult based around a drug potion prepared from poppy, hemp and ephedra plants. This potent brew is almost certainly the haoma (soma elixir) used by the magi whom Zoroaster began preaching against in Zoroastrian texts.

Gonur is a two-hour drive from Mary and you'll need at least two hours there. A 4WD is required as the final 20km of road is little more than a rough track in the dirt.

AIR

Flights arrive and depart from Ashgabat International Airport, approximately 6km from the centre of town.

Within Central Asia, the only flights to Ashgabat are from Almaty (Kazakhstan), operated twice a week by Turkmenistan Airlines.

Domestic Turkmenistan Airlines flights are heavily subsidised for locals, making the ticket prices amazingly low. Consequently, demand is high and flights need to be booked in advance. Every day there are four flights from Ashgabat to Dashoguz (US$80), Turkmenabat (US$83) and Mary (US$70), and three daily flights to Turkmenbashi (US$94).

The easiest way to get into central Ashgabat from the airport is to take a taxi. They are both plentiful and cheap, especially if you choose to go with a shared one. You should expect to pay 15M, but agree before getting in, as drivers are likely to try their luck and ask for much more. Buses 1, 18 and 58 leave from outside the airport and go into the centre of Ashgabat (0.3M). However, as many flights to Ashgabat arrive in the middle of the night, the buses may not be running.

ⓘ Getting Around

A fleet of sparkling, modern buses serves Ashgabat along some 70 routes, making getting around the city a doddle. Any ride costs just 0.3M (you just toss the money into the box by the driver as you get on, or give the driver a note if you need change; there are no physical tickets). There is, however, no single map listing all the routes, so you'll need to improvise and check the nearest bus stop, which will only have information about buses stopping there. It's quite easy to do, as the routes are depicted on a city map, but sadly the print quality is usually so bad that it's hard to be sure which bus goes where, and there are no street names on the map. If in doubt, try asking locals.

As with almost every other city in the former Soviet Union, you can just hold out your arm on the street and a car will soon stop and give you a lift to wherever you need to go. Short hops in the city cost 5M, rising to 10M for longer journeys. Agree a price before you get in, or hand over the money with supreme confidence when you get out.

EASTERN TURKMENISTAN

Squeezed between the inhospitable Karakum desert and the rugged Afghan frontier, the fertile plains of eastern Turkmenistan have long been an island of prosperity in Central Asia. The rise of civilisations began in the Bronze Age, reaching their climax with the wondrous city of Merv. In the 13th century invading Mongols put paid to centuries of accumulated wealth, but even today the region continues to outpace the rest of Turkmenistan, thanks mainly to a thriving cotton business.

There is not much left of Merv today, but its crumbling ruins are well worth a visit, assuming you travel with a knowledgeable guide.

Mary

📞 522 / POP 123,000

The capital of the Mary region is a somewhat spartan Soviet confection of administrative buildings and vast gardens disproportionate to the size of the city. Mary (pronounced MAH-ree) is the centre of the major cotton-growing belt, which gives the city an air of prosperity; the markets bustle on weekends and commerce is surprisingly brisk. Get your fill of local colour as well as your shopping done at the enormous **Zelyony Bazaar** (Mollanepes köçesi).

Mary's history dates back to the 1820s when the Tekke Turkmen erected a fortress here, preferring the site to ancient Merv, 30km east. In 1884 a battalion of Russian troops, led by one Lieutenant Alikhanov, convinced the Turkmen to hand over control of the fort before things got bloody. Cotton production quickly picked up and the guarantee of continued wealth came in 1968 when huge natural gas reserves were found 20km west of the city.

The excellent **regional museum** (Gowshuthan köçesi) with superb archaeological collection on the upper floor, full of discoveries from Margush (Gonur) and Merv, as well as impressively detailed models of both sites. Otherwise there is nothing much of note to see in the town itself, although it makes for a handy base from which to explore the nearby ancient cities of Gonur and Merv.

Pokrovskaya Church (Seydi köçesi), a handsome red-brick affair surrounded by pleasant parkland and crammed with religious icons, was built in 1900 and is worth a stop. Cross the river on Mollanepes, then take the left hand road from the roundabout. The second street you'll get to is Seydi köçesi; turn right into it and the church is at the end.

🛏 Sleeping & Eating

Mary has a small selection of comfortable-enough hotels, but don't come expecting all of the creature comforts. Eating and drinking options are similarly limited, but there are several options for kebabs or shashlyk and you can usually find beer and wine in the local restaurants or hotel bars.

TURKMENISTAN MARY

Mary

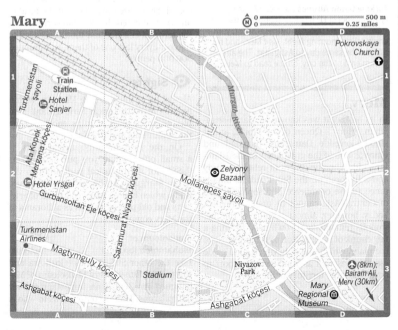

Hotel Sanjar HOTEL $

(Mollanepes köçesi 58; ❄) A standard Soviet-era hotel that has seen far better days. Appropriate only for budget travellers looking for a crash pad.

Hotel Yrsgal HOTEL $$

(📞22 53 976; Ata Kopek Mergana köçesi 2; s/d incl breakfast US$60/80; ❄@) This friendly and modern option in the centre of town is pricey for what it is, but has English-speaking staff, and comfortable, clean and spacious rooms with private bathrooms and little seating areas by the windows. Breakfast can be taken in the cafe next door, or served in your room.

Hotel Mary HOTEL $$$

(Mollanepes köçesi; s/d $100/120) Opened in 2014, this is one of Mary's most expensive hotels. Travellers report that it is centrally located and has comfortable, clean rooms and adequate bathrooms.

Cafe Gyzylgum CENTRAL ASIAN

(Garassyzlyk köçesi; 📱) Travellers report that this restaurant is among Mary's better eating options, with a wide-ranging menu of Central Asian standards and a few western dishes, cold beer and a pleasant terrace.

ⓘ Getting There & Away

Turkmenistan Airlines (📞3 27 77; Magtymguly köçesi 11) has four flights per day to/from Ashgabat (US$70). If time is short, you could take a morning flight, visit Merv and return on the same day to Ashgabat. The airport is 8km east of the city, on the road to Merv.

Merv

In its heyday it was known as Marv-i-shahjahan, 'Merv – Queen of the World', and it stood alongside Damascus, Baghdad and Cairo as one of the great cities of the Islamic world. A major centre of religious study and a linchpin on the Silk Road, its importance to the commerce and sophistication of Central Asia cannot be underestimated. Today, however, almost nothing of the metropolis remains, and you'll need to bring a fair chunk of imagination to get any sense of the place, which makes having a good guide essential, as well as your own transport to cover the large territory of the site.

History

Merv was known as Margiana or Margush in Alexander the Great's time. Under the Persian Sassanians, it was considered religiously liberal, with significant populations of Christians, Buddhists and Zoroastrians cohabiting peacefully. As a centre of power, culture and civilisation, Merv reached its greatest heights during the peak of the Silk Road in the 11th and 12th centuries, when the Seljuq Turks made it their capital. Legendary Merv may even have been the inspiration for the tales of Scheherazade's *One Thousand and One Nights*.

Merv suffered a number of attacks over the course of its history, but instead of rebuilding on top of the older ruins, Merv slowly spread west. In total, five cities were constructed next to each other, largely because of the shifting rivers. The oldest section was the Erk Kala; in later centuries most people lived in the vast walled city called Sultan Kala.

All of this was completely eradicated in 1221 under the onslaught of the Mongols. In 1218 Chinggis (Genghis) Khan demanded a substantial tithe of grain from Merv, along with the pick of the city's most beautiful young women. The unwise Seljuq response was to slay the tax collectors. In retribution Tolui, the most brutal of Chinggis Khan's sons, arrived three years later at the head of an army, accepted the peaceful surrender of the terrified citizens, and then proceeded to butcher every last one of them, an estimated 300,000 people.

⊙ Sights

Almost all of the sights in Merv are within Ancient Merv Historical Park, a giant complex of archaeological ruins encompassing the Sultan Kala and Erk Kala.

On the road towards ancient Merv is a small office where you purchase tickets (US$5) for the historical park and can visit the **Margush Archaeological Museum** **FREE**, which houses a tiny collection of artefacts and old photos, as well as a diorama of the Merv complex.

**Mausoleum of
Mohammed ibn Zeid** MAUSOLEUM

Like the other Sufi shrines (Gozli-Ata and Kubra), the 12th-century Mausoleum of Mohammed ibn Zeid is an important site for Sufi pilgrims. There's confusion as to who is

Merv

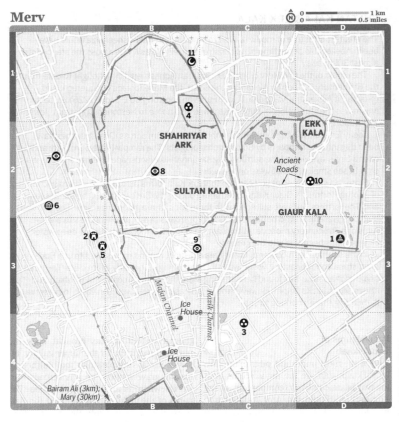

actually buried under the black marble cenotaph in the centre of the cool, dark shrine. It's definitely not Ibn Zeid, a prominent Shiite teacher who died four centuries before this tomb was built and is known to be buried elsewhere.

Great Kyz Kala FORTRESS
This crumbling 7th-century *koshk* (fortress) outside the walls of Merv is interesting for its 'petrified stockade' walls. Constructed by the Sassanians in the 7th century, it was still in use by Seljuq sultans, 600 years later, as a function room. Great Kyz Kala, along with its pair, Little Kyz Kala, are some of the most symbolic and important structures in western Merv archaeology and they have no analogues anywhere else.

Ice House RUINS
South of Sultan Kala and Giaur Kala, this is one of three ice houses built during the

Merv

⊙ Sights

Timurid era. The giant freezers, made from brick and covered by a conical-shaped roof, were used to keep meat and other foods frozen during the summer. This ice house, the closest to Giaur Kala, is perhaps the best-preserved structure.

SULTAN KALA & ERK KALA

The greatest structure of medieval Central Asia, Sultan Kala's sheer size would have been unbelievable at the time of its construction, visible as it was across the steppe from almost 30km away.

The oldest of the five Merv cities is Erk Kala, an Achaemenid city thought to date from the 6th century BC. Led by Alexander the Great, the Macedonians conquered it and renamed it Alexandria Margiana. Under Parthian control (250 BC to AD 226) Zoroastrianism was the state religion, but Erk Kala was also home to Nestorian Christians, Jews and Buddhists.

Today Erk Kala is a big earthen doughnut about 600m across. Deep trenches have been dug into the ramparts by Soviet archaeologists. The ramparts are 50m high, and offer a bird's-eye view of the surrounding savannah-like landscape. On the ramparts it's easy to see small hills that were once towers.

From this vantage point you can see that Erk Kala forms part of the northern section of another fortress – Giaur Kala, constructed during the 3rd century BC by the Sassanians. The fortress walls are still solid, with three gaps where gates once were. The city was built on a Hellenistic grid pattern; near the crossroads in the middle of the site are the ruins of a 7th-century mosque. At the eastern end of the mosque is an 8m-deep water cistern that's been dug into the ground.

In the southeastern corner of Giaur Kala a distinct mound marks the site of a Buddhist stupa and monastery, which was still functioning in the early Islamic era. The head of a Buddha statue was found here, making Merv the westernmost point to which Buddhism spread at its height. However, the stupa has been re-covered in earth to preserve it, meaning there's nothing to see.

Mausoleums of Two Askhab
MAUSOLEUM

One of the most important pilgrimage sites in Turkmenistan are the mausoleums built for two Islamic *askhab* (companions of the Prophet), Al-Hakim ibn Amr al-Jafari and Buraida ibn al-Huseib al-Islami. The two squat buildings sit in front of reconstructed Timurid *aivans* (iwans, portals) that honour the tombs of the two *askhab*. In front of the mausoleums is a still-functioning water cistern.

Mausoleum of Sultan Sanjar
MAUSOLEUM

The best remaining testimony to Seljuq power at Merv is the 38m-high Mausoleum of Sultan Sanjar, located in what was the centre of Sultan Kala. The building was restored with Turkish aid and rises dramatically in the open plain.

Sanjar, grandson of Alp-Arslan, died in 1157, reputedly of a broken heart when, after escaping from captivity in Khiva, he came home to find that his beloved Merv had been pillaged by Turkic nomads.

The mausoleum is a simple cube with a barrel-mounted dome. Originally it had a magnificent turquoise-tiled outer dome, said to be visible from a day's ride away, but that is long gone. Interior decoration is sparse, though restoration has brought back the blue-and-red frieze in the upper gallery. Inside is Sanjar's simple stone 'tomb' although, fearing grave robbers, he was actually buried elsewhere in an unknown location. The name of the architect, Mohammed Ibn Aziz of Serakhs, is etched into the upper part of the east wall. According to lore, the sultan had his architect executed to prevent him from designing a building to rival this one.

Shahriyar Ark
RUINS

The Shahriyar Ark (or Citadel of Sultan Kala) is one of the more interesting parts of Merv. Still visible are its walls, a well-preserved koshk (fort) with corrugated walls, and the odd grazing camel.

Mosque of Yusuf Hamadani
MOSQUE

North of the Shahriyar Ark, outside the city walls, lies the Mosque of Yusuf Hamadani, built around the tomb of a 12th-century dervish. The complex has been largely rebuilt in the last 10 years and turned into an important pilgrimage site; it is not open to non-Muslims.

🛈 Getting There & Around

The only way to see the Merv site without an exhausting walk is by car. From Mary expect to pay US$10 for a car and driver for four hours (the minimum amount of time needed to see the main monuments). Buses go between Mary and Bairam Ali every half-hour or so; the journey takes about 45 minutes. Guided tours are available from any travel agency and this is the way most people see Merv.

Turkmenabat

📞 422 / POP 254,000

Lying on the banks of the mighty Amu-Darya, between the Karakum desert and the fertile plains of Uzbekistan, sprawling Turkmenabat, the country's second largest city, sits at a crossroads of cultures. These days Turkmenabat essentially serves as a transit hub for those making overland journeys to and from Uzbekistan, as well as a jumping-off point for the few travellers venturing into the country's far eastern mountains.

The town itself feels as if it's in the geographic centre of nowhere, yet after the mind-numbing drive through the desert, it's something of a surprise to find such a large city appear out of the sand. There are a couple of bustling bazaars, the most convenient being Zelyony Bazaar.

The ridiculously ornate **Lebap Regional Museum** (Niyazov şayoli; US$10) is worth a stop for travellers passing through, housing a solid collection of archeological findings from the Lebap region and a good ethnographic display including a full reconstruction of a Silk Road market. The canary yellow 19th-century St Nicholas **Russian Orthodox Church** (Magtymguly şayoli) is decorated on the interior with a rich collection of icons that may also be of some interest.

Turkmenabat's sleeping and dining options will not leave you wanting to linger, but there are a few hotels that are clean and comfortable enough for a night or two (including the Jeyhun Hotel) and several solid choices for a meal (of which travellers report **Traktir** (off Puskin köçesi; 🖉 📶) is among the best).

ⓘ Getting There & Away

The train station, in the centre of town, has daily trains to Ashgabat via Mary. Outside the train station you can catch marshrutki or taxis to Mary and Ashgabat. The road to Dashoguz is in such bad condition that it's not recommended unless you have a 4WD and plenty of time. There are around four flights a day between Turkmenabat and Ashgabat (US$83, one hour). The airport is 2km east of Hotel Turkmenabat.

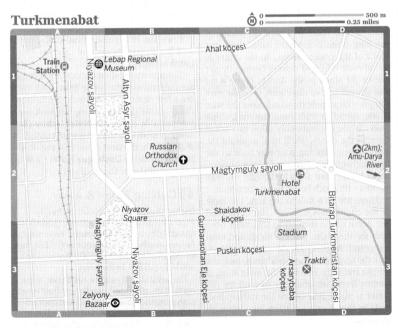

Turkmenabat

KARAKUM DESERT

The Karakum desert is a sun-scorched expanse of dunes and sparse vegetation in the centre of Turkmenistan. It's Central Asia's hottest desert, but manages to support a handful of settlements, including the oasis town of Jerbent 160km north of Ashgabat. A ramshackle collection of homes, battered trucks, yurts and the occasional camel, it doesn't look like much, but the village does offer a glimpse of rural Turkmen life, and you can watch traditional cooking methods and sit down for tea inside a yurt. All buses and marshrutkas heading from Ashgabat to both Konye-Urgench and Dashoguz go through Jerbent and pass nearby the turn-off for the Darvaza Gas Craters on the main road.

One of Turkmenistan's most unusual sights, the **Darvaza Gas Craters** are the result of Soviet-era gas exploration in the 1970s. The three craters are artificial. One has been set alight and blazes with an incredible strength that's visible from miles away, while the other two contain bubbling mud and water. There have been rumours for years that the burning gas crater will be put out to enable gas exploration in the area, but it was still burning in 2017.

Of the three, the fire crater is the most impressive, and it's best seen at night, when the blazing inferno can only be compared to the gates of hell. There is a naturally sheltered camping place behind the small hill, just south of the crater. Getting to the crater is an off-road ride and drivers frequently get lost or get stuck in the dunes. There is no one around to give directions, so make sure you go with somebody who knows the way. If you intend to walk from the road, think twice. While the walk only takes two hours through the dunes, you'll have to spend the night here, as finding your way back to the road without the reference of a huge burning crater is very hard. Even in daylight you may get lost – it's much better to pay for a tour.

There are no hotels in the area, but most of the chaikhanas that line the main road just north of the turn-off to the crater offer beds for the night, provide meals and even sell petrol. As there are no signposts for either the turn-off or the chaikhanas; look out for the train line crossing the main road. If coming from Ashgabat, the turn-off for the crater is about 1km before the railway line, and the chaikhanas are a few kilometres afterwards.

NORTHERN TURKMENISTAN

Stalin's modus operandi in Central Asia sought the division of its people, thus resulting in the split of the Khorezm (an ancient kingdom centred on the Amu-Darya delta) oasis – the northern section around Khiva going to Uzbekistan and the southern portion going to Turkmenistan. As part of historic Khorezm, the Turkmen portion still contains a sizeable Uzbek minority and retains a culture apart from the rest of the country.

Attractions in this part of the country are scarce, but those with an interest in history must visit Konye-Urgench, which is rich in Islamic relics dating back to the 11th, 12th and 13th centuries.

Sadly the region has not escaped the Aral Sea disaster and suffers from air, soil and water pollution. It's also the poorest part of the country, with little commerce apart from the smuggling of subsidised petrol to Uzbekistan.

Dashoguz

📋 322 / POP 210,000

A creation of the Soviet Union, Dashoguz is a sprawling industrial city with a neat, soulless centre and nothing to attract visitors. The main reason travellers find themselves here is as a stop-off point between the Darvaza Gas Craters and Uzbekistan.

For some local colour, head to the excellent Bai Bazaar, where you can buy pretty much anything.

The accommodation options in Dashoguz are nothing to write home about, but there are a few clean, friendly hotels. There aren't many eating options either, but look for a few passable cafes near **Hotel Uzboy** (Turkmenbashi şayoli 19/1; s/d incl breakfast US$62/74; P ❄ @ 🛜) in the west of town or the on-site restaurant in the **Dashoguz Hotel** (❄ @ 🛜) to the south (near the stadium).

ⓘ Getting There & Away

Dashoguz airport is 14km south of the city. Flights from Ashgabat to Dashoguz (US$80, four daily) take about 50 minutes. Turkmenistan Airlines also flies to Turkmenbashi (US$98, four weekly), Turkmenabat (US$90, once weekly) and Mary (US$94, two weekly).

The bus station is near the Bai Bazaar, in the north of the city. Buses regularly go from here to Konye-Urgench (5M, two hours) and once a day at 6am to Ashgabat (31M, nine hours). Due to the bad state of the road, buses for Turkmenabat were not running at the time of research. Shared taxis go from outside the train station to Ashgabat.

The train station is about 600m east of Gurbansoltan köçesi. At least one slow train per day goes from here to Konye-Urgench and one goes to Ashgabat daily.

Konye-Urgench

📋 347 / POP 30,000

Konye-Urgench (from Persian 'Old Urgench') is a rural backwater with livestock wandering its chaotic, unpaved roads. Yet centuries ago this was the centre of the Islamic world, not the end of it. Today most of Old Urgench lies underground, but there is enough urban tissue to get an idea of its former glories. Its uniqueness was acknowledged in 2005 when Unesco named it a World Heritage Site.

The modern town is somewhat short on tourist facilities and the majority of travellers drop through overland on the way from Khiva or Nukus in Uzbekistan. You can also overnight in Dashoguz and fly in for the day.

History

Khorezm fell to the all-conquering Seljuq Turks, but rose in the 12th century, under a Seljuq dynasty known as the Khorezmshahs, to shape its own far-reaching empire. With its mosques, medressas, libraries and flourishing bazaars, Gurganj (the Persian name for Konye-Urgench) became a centre of the Muslim world, until Khorezmshah Mohammed II moved his capital to Samarkand after capturing that city in 1210.

Chinggis (Genghis) Khan arrived in 1221, seeking revenge for the murder of his envoys in Otrar as ordered by Mohammed II. Old Urgench withstood the siege for six months, and even after the Mongols broke through the city walls the residents fought them in the streets. The Mongols, unused to cities, burnt the houses but the residents still fought from the ruins. In the end the Mongols diverted the waters of the Amu-Darya and flooded the city, drowning its defenders.

The Mongol generals went in pursuit of Mohammed II who eluded them for months until he finally died of exhaustion in 1221 on an island in the Caspian Sea. The tombs of his father, Tekesh, and grandfather, Il-Arslan, survive and are two of Old Urgench's monuments. In the following period of peace, Khorezm was ruled as part of the Golden Horde, the huge, wealthy, western-most of the khanates into which Chinggis Khan's empire was divided after his death. Rebuilt, Urgench was again Khorezm's capital, and grew into what was probably one of Central Asia's most important trading cities – big, beautiful, crowded and with a new generation of monumental buildings.

Then came Timur (Tamerlane). Considering Khorezm to be a rival to Samarkand, he comprehensively finished off old Urgench in 1388. The city was partly rebuilt in the 16th century, but it was abandoned when the Amu-Darya changed its course. Modern Konye-Urgench dates from the construction of a new canal in the 19th century.

👁 Sights

The ancient city's monuments are dotted like a constellation across a large site (admission/still camera/video camera US$5/2/25) straddling the Ashgabat road, 1km south of the main town. One ticket covers all the sites.

Konye-Urgench Museum   MUSEUM
(admission 11.40M; ⏱8am-6pm) The simple Konye-Urgench Museum is housed in the early-20th-century Dash Medressa, just before the main mausoleum complex. It includes some ancient Arabic texts and a few interestingly labelled artefacts from Old Urgench (eg 'blue polished eight-cornered thing'). Note the Christian symbols carved onto some of the stone pieces. Off the medressa courtyard are several rooms containing ethnographic displays of Turkmen culture, including a pottery workshop and carpet looms. To one side of the mosque is the Matkerim-Ishan Mausoleum, which is also early 20th century.

Turabeg Khanym Complex   HISTORIC BUILDING
Turabeg Khanym Complex, opposite the Konye-Urgench ticket office, is still the subject of some debate. Locals and some scholars consider this a mausoleum, though no one is too sure who is buried here. Some archaeologists contend that it was a throne room built in the 12th century (it appears to have a heating system, which would not have been used in a mausoleum). Whatever its function, this is one of Central Asia's most perfect buildings. Its geometric patterns are in effect a giant calendar signifying humanity's insignificance in the march of time.

There are 365 sections on the sparkling mosaic underside of the dome, representing the days of the year; 24 pointed arches immediately beneath the dome representing the hours of the day; 12 bigger arches below representing the months the year; and four big windows representing the weeks of the month. The cupola is unusual in early Islamic architecture and has its equal only in Shiraz, Iran.

Gutlug Timur Minaret ISLAMIC SITE

Across the road from the Turabeg Khanym Complex (p393), a path through a modern cemetery and the 19th-century Sayid Ahmed Mausoleum leads to this minaret, built in the 1320s. It's the only surviving part of Old Urgench's main mosque. Decorated with bands of brick and a few turquoise tiles, its 59m-tall minaret is not as tall as it once was, and leans noticeably.

Sultan Tekesh Mausoleum MAUSOLEUM

Instantly recognisable by its conical turquoise dome, the Sultan Tekesh Mausoleum is one of Konye Urgench's most beautiful monuments. Tekesh was the 12th-century Khorezmshah who made Khorezm great with conquests as far south as Khorasan (present-day northern Iran and northern Afghanistan). It is believed that he built this mausoleum for himself, along with a big medressa and library (which did not survive) on the same spot. However, some scholars theorise that the building had earlier existed as a Zoroastrian temple.

Kyrk Molla HILL

(Forty Mullahs Hill) The mound of graves called the Kyrk Mollais a sacred place where Konye-Urgench's inhabitants held their last stand against the Mongols. Here you might see young women rolling down the hill in a fertility rite – one of Konye-Urgench's more curious attractions.

Il-Arslan Mausoleum MAUSOLEUM

The Il-Arslan Mausoleum is Konye-Urgench's oldest standing monument. The conical dome, with a curious zigzag brick pattern, is the first of its kind and was exported to Samarkand by Timur. Il-Arslan, who died in 1172, was Tekesh's father. The building is small but well worth a close look. The conical dome with 12 faces is unique, and the collapsing floral terracotta moulding on the facade is also unusual.

Mamun II Minaret ISLAMIC SITE

South of the Il-Arslan Mausoleum lies the base of the Mamun II Minaret, which was built in 1011. It was reduced to a stump by the Mongols, rebuilt in the 14th century and finally toppled by an earthquake in 1895. Nearby you'll see the so-called 'portal of an unknown building', sometimes also referred to as the Gate of the Caravanserai. The structure is now thought to have been the entrance to the palace of Mohammed Khorezmshah, due to its ornateness and the thickness of its walls.

Nejameddin

Kubra Mausoleum MAUSOLEUM

Nejameddin Kubra (1145–1221) was a famous Khorezm Muslim teacher and poet who founded the Sufic Kubra order, with followers throughout the Islamic world. His tomb is believed to have healing properties and you may find pilgrims praying here. The building has three domes and a tiled portal that appears on the brink of forward collapse. The tombs inside – one for his body and one for his head (which were kindly separated by the Mongols) – are extraordinarily colourful with floral-pattern tiles.

🛏 Sleeping & Eating

Most travellers visit Konye-Urgench as a day trip, as there are very few sleeping options in town. Though there are almost no places to eat here, some travellers have reported finding decent meals at Suleyman Bag, near the central market.

ℹ Getting There & Around

The main sights of Konye-Urgench are spread out so it's best to use a car. There is no public transport as such, but you can flag down a taxi on the main roads or by the market. The trip to the southern monuments and back, with waiting time, should be no more than 20M.

WESTERN TURKMENISTAN

Driving west from Ashgabat, the main road skirts the edges of the Kopet Dag and the Iranian border before opening up into a vast, featureless landscape that is wonderfully Central Asian.

Highlights of the region include the magnificent Yangykala Canyon and the Köw Ata Underground Lake, where you can swim in warm waters, 65m beneath the desert.

Köw Ata Underground Lake LAKE

(40M; ⊘ dawn-dusk) Like entering Milton's underworld, only with changing rooms and a staircase, a visit to the Köw Ata Underground Lake is a unique experience. You enter a cave at the base of a mountain and walk down a staircase, 65m underground, which takes you into a wonderfully sulphurous subterranean world. At the bottom awaits a superb lake of clear water naturally heated to about 36°C (96.8°F).

Underground swimming is one of Central Asia's more unusual activities, and is worth it if you don't mind the steep entry fee – particularly annoying given the facilities here are all in poor condition.

The turn-off to the lake is clearly marked along the main Ashgabat–Balkanabat road. By marshrutka or bus from Ashgabat to Balkanabat or Turkmenbashi you could easily ask the driver to stop at the Köw Ata turn-off, although it's a good 90-minute walk from the road. There's a trio of good shashlyk restaurants on-site here, making this a great lunch stop.

Gozli Ata Mausoleum   MAUSOLEUM
(N 40°20.051', E 54°29.249') A respected Sufi teacher in the early 14th century, Gozli Ata had a large following until his untimely death at the hands of Mongol invaders. His mausoleum, located in a natural depression of rocky desert, is now a popular place of pilgrimage.

Gozli Ata's wife is buried in an adjacent mausoleum and, according to custom, visitors must first pray at her last resting place. A cemetery has sprung up nearby; gravestones here contain a notch in the top where water can collect to 'feed' the soul of the deceased.

Gozli Ata is 135km north of Balkanabat; an experienced driver is needed to find it.

Yangykala Canyon   CANYON
With bands of pink, red and yellow rock searing across the sides of steep canyon walls, Yangykala is a breathtaking sight and one of the most spectacular natural attractions in Turkmenistan. Just as alluring as the beautiful views is its solitary isolation in the desert. It's possible to camp on the plateau above the canyon, although it can get windy there.

Canyons and cliffs slash for 25km towards the Garabogazköl basin and lie approximately 165km north of Balkanabat and about 160km east of Turkmenbashi, making it easy to slot in a trip to the canyon between the two cities. While most tour companies run trips to Yangykala Canyon, not all include it on their standard itineraries, so make enquiries when planning your trip.

From the turn-off to Gozli Ata (marked with a 9km sign), another road continues north to the canyon.

Turkmenbashi

☑ 243 / POP 73,000

Turkmenbashi is Turkmenistan's only major port and the end of the line for travellers heading on to the Caucasus via the ferry to Baku. There's nothing much to keep you here for any length of time, but it's a pleasant and friendly town with a more Russian feel than most Turkmen cities and an enjoyable Caspian Sea location.

The beaches near town are a bit rocky and not great for swimming, considering the proximity of the town oil refinery. There are better beaches at Awaza, 8km west of the city. North of Awaza it's a 20-minute drive to some spectacular sand dunes, sea views and an abandoned lighthouse, but you'll need a 4WD and a driver who knows the way.

There are precious few accommodation options in Turkmenbashi, and most hotels are not of a high international standard. **Hotel Çarlak** (Sagadam köçesi; s/d incl breakfast US$75/95; P✳☎❄) is the best bet for most, though the **Hotel Hazar** (Azadi köçesi; ✳) could do for budget travellers wanting a crash pad and nothing more. Finding a restaurant is also tough, but there are one or two fine options near the Hotel Çarlak, including Tolkun. Check near the train station for a few small cafes and places for a quick bite.

❶ Getting There & Around

Turkmenistan Airlines flies to and from Ashgabat (US$94) twice daily and to Dashoguz (US$98) on Tuesday, Wednesday, Friday and Sunday. The airline office is in the same building as the Hotel Hazar. The airport is 8km east of the ferry terminal. There is a daily bus (31M, nine hours) to Ashgabat.

From the Turkmenbashi ferry terminal there are frequent untimetabled cargo ships to Baku in Azerbaijan, most of which take passengers (US$60 to US$80 per person), although there's always the chance that there won't be a departure for several days. The **Caspian Shipping Company** (www.acsc.az) website gives some idea on when the next departure will be and theoretically offers an online booking system.

Bring all the food you'll need for the 24-hour crossing, and be aware that you may have to wait several days for a departure, which can bring serious stress and woes if your Turkmen visa is about to run out. If your visa is due to expire, you'll have to be stamped out at immigration and wait in limbo at the port.

Turkmenbashi's local bus station is just off Balkan köçesi, about 500m west of the museum. From here you can catch infrequent transport to the airport, the seaport and Awaza at prices that are almost negligible. Taxis also hang around here, as well as near the train station, and charge around 1M for most destinations around town, or 2M for a ride to Awaza.

UNDERSTAND TURKMENISTAN

Turkmenistan Today

In 2007, following the death of Saparmyrat Niyazov (Turkmenbashi), Turkmenistan's bizarre dictator of more than 20 years, Gurbanguly Berdymukhamedov assumed the presidency. Berdymukhamedov made initial reforms that toned down some of his predecessor's policies: the most egregious initiatives, such as renaming the months of the year and the days of the week after Turkmenbashi's family members, a ban on ballet and the prohibition on listening to music in cars, were all lifted. Yet despite these small signs of reform, no further changes have been forthcoming. While the pathological state paranoia that so thrived under Niyazov has also been toned down, travellers wishing to visit the country continue to go through the same rigorous visa channels and must be accompanied by guides in most cases.

The most recent phase of Turkmenistan's development is dubbed 'the New Era', superseding Niyazov's 'Golden Age', and while the personality cult of Turkmenbashi still survives in the form of monuments and statues throughout the country, there's a mood of moving on in the air, with few people even wanting to talk about the man who dominated every aspect of daily life for the past two decades. And while the new president hasn't exhibited the same lust for adoration as his predecessor, portraits of Berdymukhamedov are ubiquitous and he himself enjoys no meagre personality cult.

Berdymukhamedov won an unsurprising re-election as president in 2012, with some 97% of the vote and unanimous praise from his 'rivals'. However, 2010 Wikileaks cable transcripts from the US Embassy in Ashgabat suggested that this high opinion of the president wasn't held by all: '[Berdymukhamedov] does not like people who are smarter than he is. Since he's not a very bright guy... he is suspicious of a lot of people.'

In 2016 a new draft constitution was established that removed the 70-year age limit for presidential candidates and extended the term of office from five years to seven years. The new rules essentially allow Berdymukhamedov to remain in power for the rest of his life. Elections were held in February 2017 and Berdymukhamedov, who is increasingly becoming known as Arkadag – the Great Protector – once again secured 97% of the vote.

Berdymukhamedov is known for his love of fitness and in January 2016 reports emerged that the sale of all tobacco products would be banned in the country. A total ban has not been installed, but the purchase and use of tobacco products is heavily regulated.

Although Berdymukhamedov expressed disappointment that the Turkmenistan team failed to win any medals in the 2016 Rio Olympics, local sportspeople had the chance to redeem themselves when Ashgabat hosted the 5th Asian Indoor & Martial Arts Games in September 2017 – an event that is rumoured to have cost more than US$5 billion. They delivered, winning 245 medals to top the tally.

History

From Conquerors to Communists

Stone Age sites have been identified in the Big Balkan Mountains, but the first signs of agricultural settlements appeared in Kopet Dag in the 6th millennium BC. More Bronze Age sites have been located in the Margiana Oasis, where archaeologist Viktor Sarianidi has identified a sophisticated culture that encompassed several villages and an extensive capital. Rivers that shifted over the centuries caused the abandonment of these settlements, but paved the way for a great civilisation around Merv. Alexander the Great established a city here on his way to India.

Around the time of Christ, the Parthians, Rome's main rivals for power in the West, set up a capital at Nissa, near present-day Ashgabat. In the 11th century the Seljuq

Turks appropriated Merv, Alexander's old city and a Silk Road staging post, as a base from which to expand into Afghanistan.

Two centuries later Chinggis (Genghis) Khan stormed down from the steppes and through Trans-Caspia (the region east of the Caspian Sea) to lay waste to Central Asia. Entire city-states, including Merv and Konye-Urgench, were razed and their populations slaughtered. Unlike Samarkand and Bukhara, the cities to the south failed to recover.

It's not known precisely when the first modern Turkmen appeared, but they are believed to have arrived in modern Turkmenistan in the wake of the Seljuk Turks some time in the 11th century. A collection of displaced nomadic horse-breeding tribes, possibly from the foothills of the Altay Mountains, they found alternative pastures in the oases fringing the Karakum desert and in Persia, Syria and Anatolia (in present-day Turkey). Being nomads, they had no concept of, or interest in, statehood and therefore existed in parallel to the constant dynastic shifts that so totally determined Central Asia's history.

Terrorising the Russians, who had come to 'civilise' the region in the early 19th century, Turkmen captured thousands of the tsar's troops, and sold them into slavery in Khiva and Bukhara. This invited the wrath of the Russian Empire, which finally quelled the wild nomads by massacring thousands of them at Geok-Depe in 1881.

After the Bolshevik revolution in 1917, the communists took Ashgabat in 1919. For a while the region existed as the Turkmen *oblast* (province) of the Turkestan Autonomous Soviet Socialist Republic, before becoming the Turkmen Soviet Socialist Republic (SSR) in 1924.

The Turkmen SSR

Inflamed by Soviet attempts to settle the tribes and collectivise farming, Turkmen resistance continued and a guerrilla war raged until 1936. More than a million Turkmen fled into the Karakum desert or into northern Iran and Afghanistan rather than give up their nomadic ways. The Turkmen also fell foul of a Moscow-directed campaign against religion. Of the 441 mosques in Turkmenistan in 1911, only five remained standing by 1941.

Waves of Russian immigrants brought with them farming technology and blueprints for cotton fields. Turkmenistan's arid climate was hardly conducive to bumper harvests, and to supply the vast quantities of water required the authorities began work in the 1950s on a massive irrigation ditch – the Karakum Canal. The 1100km-long gully runs the length of the republic, bleeding the Amu-Darya (Oxus River) to create a fertile band across the south. Cotton production quadrupled, though the consequences for the Aral Sea have been catastrophic.

In 1985 the relatively unknown Saparmyrat Niyazov was elected General Secretary of the Communist Party of Turkmenistan (CPT) and retained power until the collapse of the Soviet Union. Although totally unprepared for the event, Niyazov was forced to declare independence for Turkmenistan on 27 October 1991.

Independence & the Golden Age

Determined to hold on to power, Niyazov renamed the CPT the Democratic Party of Turkmenistan, before banning all other parties. His cult of personality began to flourish, starting with an order that everyone call him Turkmenbashi, which translates as 'leader of the Turkmen'. The president erected gold statues of himself and plastered buildings with his image. His slogan 'Halk, Watan, Turkmenbaşi' ('People, Nation, Me' – an eerie echo of Hitler's 'Ein Volk, Ein Reich, Ein Führer) was ubiquitous.

Tapping Turkmenistan's vast oil and gas reserves, Niyazov promised a Kuwait-style economy with enormous private wealth. Most of the profits, however, ended up funding ostentatious public-works projects. Public dissent was somewhat placated by large government subsidies for gas, water and electricity. The free ride was part of Niyazov's much touted 'Turkmen Golden Age' (Altyn Asyr), though its less benevolent side was the Orwellian control of the media that caused Reporters Without Borders to rank Turkmenistan second to last in its press freedom index (ahead only of North Korea).

Despite avoiding an assassin's bullet in 2002, Turkmenbashi proved mortal when he passed away on 21 December 2006, aged 66, of a massive heart attack. Having groomed no heir, his death left a power vacuum that for a brief moment opened the door for democratic reform and the return of exiled dissidents. Instead a surprisingly smooth transfer of power occurred when Deputy Prime Minister Gurbanguly Berdymukhamedov grabbed the reins of power and won backing from Niyazov's inner circle. He was rubber stamped into office after elections in February 2007 (having won 90% of the popular vote in elections where only the Democratic Party of Turkmenistan fielded candidates, and even Berdymukhamedov's 'rivals' openly supported him). Berdymukhamedov had been Turkmenistan's health minister and rumours that he is the former president's illegitimate son have being doing the rounds for some time. While this is unlikely – Niyazov was only 17 years old when Berdymukhamedov was born – the two men do bear an uncanny resemblance.

People

Turkmen remain nomadic at heart, if not still in practice, and carry themselves in a simple yet dignified manner that reflects their rural lifestyle. Nomadic rules, including the treatment of guests, still dominate home life.

Turkmen are guided spiritually by a unique form of Central Asian animism. Holiday breaks are thus used for pilgrimage time. Women in particular use these pilgrimages as an opportunity to take a break from their home life, and you may see caravans of women on buses, headed to shrines around the country where they'll camp, cook and pray.

By the standards of many Muslim societies, women in Turkmenistan enjoy a good amount of freedom and choice. In most cases they tend to be home-makers and mothers, as well as often working in the fields to cultivate crops. Bucking this

trend is an urban elite of educated, Westernised women in Ashgabat who work in all areas and enjoy most of the freedoms of their male counterparts. Very few women wear the veil in Turkmenistan, though traditional colourful headscarves are ubiquitous.

Population

The population of Turkmenistan is estimated to be just over five million; a census was undertaken in 2012, but its results were never officially published. Uzbeks, who make up about 5% of the population, live in the border cities of Konye-Urgench, Dashoguz and Turkmenabat. Russians have left in huge numbers since independence, as it becomes increasingly hard to work without speaking Turkmen, and dual citizenship was phased out in 2013.

Religion

Turkmen are deeply spiritual people without being particularly religious compared with people in nearby Iran or Afghanistan. Their traditional animist beliefs have been blended over the centuries with Islam, and evidence of this is clear at mosques and mausoleums, which are often decorated with animist features such as snakes and rams' horns. Likewise, pilgrims arrive at these sites bearing tokens such as miniature cribs, indicating a desire for children.

Sunni Islam is the state religion. Despite Turkmenistan's constitutional guarantee of free practice for all faiths, in reality Islam and Orthodox Christianity are the only freely practised religions.

RECOMMENDED READING

➡ *Daily Life in Turkmenbashy's Golden Age* (2010) by Sam Tranum. Engaging and perceptive account of two years' work and travel in Turkmenistan from a Peace Corps volunteer. The best of a crop of volunteer memoirs from Central Asia.

➡ *Unknown Sands: Journeys Around the World's Most Isolated Country* (Dusty Spark, 2006), by John W Kropf. A travel memoir by an American who spent two years living in Ashgabat. Despite living within the confines of the diplomatic community, Kropf managed to sneak away from the capital to give us a perspective of life on the ground for ordinary Turkmen.

➡ *Tribal Nation: The Making of Soviet Turkmenistan* (2006), by Adrienne Lynn Edgar. A scholarly account of the Soviet creation of Turkmenistan, with well-researched details on Soviet nation building of the 1920s and 1930s. The book also provides an understanding of Turkmen language and tribal law.

Arts

Turkmen carpets are world famous and can be seen just about everywhere, although the best place to see them is in the bazaar. Silk, embroidery, silver and jewellery are other crafts that have been perfected over the centuries.

The arts have not thrived since the end of Soviet rule. Theatres remain active, albeit with Turkmen-only song-and-dance acts, concerts and drama performances. The most impressive traditional singing, *bakhshi,* deals with folklore, battles and love, and is accompanied by a *dutar* (two-stringed guitar).

Between the Soviets and Niyazov, contemporary Turkmen literature has been all but destroyed. Rahim Esenov was Turkmenistan's best literary hope until he was jailed (in 2004) following the publication of his book *The Crowned Wanderer.* Turkmen are encouraged to read the writings of poet Magtymguly Feraghy (1733–83) and, increasingly, those of President Berdymukhamedov, whose voluminous contributions to literature include a book on wildflowers.

Environment

Effectively a giant desert ringed by oases along the country's borders, Turkmenistan is home to far more varied landscapes than you might expect. To the east are the canyons and lush mountains of the Kugitang Nature Reserve, while to the south the Kopet Dag range rises up in a line towards the Caspian Sea. The territory along the Caspian is particularly unusual – vast mud flats, coloured canyons and the enormous bulk of the Big Balkan massif make this one of the more bleakly beautiful places in the country.

Wildlife

The most famous of Turkmenistan's many interesting species is the Akhal-Teke horse, a beautiful golden creature that is believed to be the ancestor of today's thoroughbred. The horses are a symbol of national pride, adored by the president, revered by the people and featured on emblems and statues throughout the country.

Dromedaries (Arabian camels) are everywhere, wandering scenically between villages and towns. Many of the Karakum's nastiest inhabitants are really exciting to see in real life – most importantly the *zemzen,* or *varan,* a large monitor lizard – though these are extremely rare. Despite its large size and particularly painful bite, Turkmen have traditionally welcomed the giant lizard as it devours or scares away snakes (such as cobras), eats mice and eradicates colonies of sandflies.

You are also likely to see desert foxes, owls and the very common desert squirrel.

Tarantulas and black widow spiders are both indigenous to Turkmenistan, although you are unlikely to see them. Cobras, vipers and scorpions can all be found in the desert, so tread with caution.

Environmental Issues

Turkmenistan has paid a heavy price for the irrigation of its southern belt, using source water bound for the Aral Sea. While the Aral Sea is in Uzbekistan and Kazakhstan, its disappearance has led to desperate environmental problems in northern Turkmenistan, with the salination of the land taking its toll on the health of local people. Overfishing is another concern, as caviar-bearing sturgeon become rarer in the Caspian Sea. There is very little environmental consciousness in Turkmenistan, where no one bothers to save gas, electricity or water because all are subsidised by the government.

SURVIVAL GUIDE

ⓘ Directory A–Z

ACCOMMODATION

As a rule hotels are divided into dilapidated Soviet-era behemoths and newer three- and four-star ventures built since independence. Turkmen citizens pay around 60% to 80% less than foreigners, so while you may have to pay for the lodging of your guide, this shouldn't cost more than a few dollars. Foreigners have to pay for hotels in cash in US dollars, except in the few hotels that accept credit cards.

Camping is often the only option in remote places such as the Yangykala Canyon and the Darvaza Gas Craters, and most guides can provide tents and sleeping bags.

ACTIVITIES

Horse-lovers from around the world flock to Turkmenistan to ride the unique Akhal-Teke thoroughbreds. Many travel agencies offer specialist horse-trekking tours with these beautiful creatures.

CUSTOMS REGULATIONS

In Turkmenistan official regulations state that you need permission to export any carpet over 6 sq metres, though trying to export a smaller one without an export licence is also likely to be problematic. In all cases it's best to take your carpet to the Carpet Museum (p380) in Ashgabat, where there is a bureau that will value and tax your purchase, and provide an export licence. This can take up to a few days. There are several fees to pay. One certifies that the carpet is not antique, which usually costs US$10 to US$30, while a second is an export fee that costs around US$50 per sq metre. As with all government taxes on foreigners, these are paid in US dollars. When you buy a carpet at a state shop, these fees will be included in the price, but double-check before handing over your money. Those in a hurry are best advised to buy from one of the many government shops in Ashgabat, where all carpets come complete with an export licence. Despite being more expensive than purchases made at Tolkuchka Bazaar, this still works out as very good value.

DANGERS & ANNOYANCES

➡ Take care when photographing public buildings, especially in Ashgabat. Local police take this seriously and you may have your documents checked even if simply strolling near the Presidential Palace with a camera in your hand. There are no 'no photo' signs anywhere, so you'll need to ask the nearest policeman if it's OK to take a picture.

➡ Smoking is heavily regulated – if in doubt, smoke only where locals are doing so as there can be serious penalties for smoking outside of designated areas.

FOOD & DRINK

Similar to other Central Asian countries, shashlyk is the staple dish across Turkmenistan and is considered at its best when cooked over the branches of a saxaul tree. Other favoured snacks include *samsa* (samosa; meat-filled pastries), *plov* (pilaf; meat, rice and carrots) and a variation on the meat pastry called *fitchi,* which is larger and round in shape.

Dograma, made from bread and pieces of boiled meat and onions, is a traditional Turkmen meal. Other soups include *chorba* (soup of boiled mutton with potato, carrot and turnip, known elsewhere in the region as *shorpa*). *Manty* (steamed dumplings) served with sour cream is another popular dish.

INTERNET ACCESS

Internet access, once horrendously slow, expensive and limited to top hotels in Ashgabat, is now available in all big towns through state-run internet cafes. Free wi-fi is becoming more common, although some places still charge – expect to pay around 5M per hour. As all internet access is via the state-run www.online.tm, bear in mind that outgoing emails may be monitored and many websites (mainly news and politics sites, but also Facebook and Twitter) are blocked, so save any plotting to overthrow the government until you're back home.

MEDIA

Newspapers The main daily newspapers are *Turkmenistan* and the Russian-language *Nevtralny Turkmenistan (Neutral Turkmenistan).* There is also a weekly edition of *Neutral Turkmenistan* in English. All papers glorify the president, as is obvious from the pictures on the front pages. There is no independent or privately owned press.

TV The six national TV channels show scenes of Turkmen culture and nature. Satellite TV is widely available in larger cities, and remains the main source of objective news for all Turkmen.

MONEY

Bring enough cash to cover your entire stay. ATMs are non-existent and cards rarely accepted, so keep a supply of both US dollars and manat.

Changing Money

The currency in Turkmenistan is the manat (M), which is made up of 100 tenne. All exchange offices change dollars at the fixed rate of 3.5M to the US dollar. Exchange offices are everywhere, take no commission, and will freely exchange US dollars and euros back and forth (you don't need to worry about having official certificates in order to change your money back when you leave the country, for example). There is also a black market in operation. At the time of writing, the black market exchange rate was 6M to the US dollar.

US dollars remain the currency of choice for Turkmenistan, and it's best to bring them in various denominations. Notes often need to be in very good condition to be accepted. Euro are also generally easy to change, though less so outside Ashgabat. Don't bring other currencies.

Credit Cards

Cash advances on credit cards are only available at two banks in Ashgabat. Outside Ashgabat, emergency money can be wired through Western Union only. Credit cards are accepted by a few luxury hotels in Ashgabat but by few other places.

Travellers Cheques

Travellers cheques are not accepted anywhere. Tour agencies recommend that you bring all spending money in US dollars as relying on cards is highly risky.

POST

Your post may be read first, but at some stage it should be delivered unless your postcard is truly offensive. Sending a postcard anywhere in the world costs 3M and a 20g letter costs around 3.50M. There are post offices in all towns, usually in the same place as the international phone centre and state-run internet cafe.

PUBLIC HOLIDAYS

Turkmenistan has a great number of holidays, though the country largely continues to work as normal during most of them.

1 January New Year

12 January Remembrance Day (Battle of Geok-Depe)

19 February Flag Day (President's Birthday)

8 March Women's Day

21 March Navrus (spring festival); date varies

April (first Sunday) Drop of Water is a Grain of Gold Day

April (last Sunday) Horse Day

9 May Victory Day

18 May Day of Revival and Unity

19 May Magtymguly Poetry Day

May (last Sunday) Carpet Day

August (second Sunday) Melon Holiday

6 October Remembrance Day (1948 Earthquake)

27 & 28 October Independence Day

November (first Saturday) Health Day

November (last Sunday) Harvest Festival

7 December Good Neighbourliness Day

12 December Neutrality Day

SMOKING

Laws are strict in Turkmenistan and smoking in public spaces is banned. Ask your guide where you're allowed to smoke or follow the lead of the locals. You can only bring two packets of cigarettes into the country and buying cigarettes on the black market can be extremely costly.

TELEPHONE

You can call internationally and nationally from most big towns at the main telegraph office, often referred to by its Russian name, *glavny telegraf*.

EMERGENCY & IMPORTANT NUMBERS

Turkmenistan country code	☏ 993
Ambulance	☏ 03
Fire	☏ 01
Police	☏ 02

The major mobile phone provider is MTS (look for the sign MTC). Prepaid SIM cards (which allow internet use through a smartphone) are available very cheaply from its offices, though at the time of writing foreigners were only able to purchase them at the main MTS office in the Russian Bazaar (p384) in Ashgabat.

TIME

The whole country falls into the same time zone, which is five hours ahead of GMT/UTC. Turkmenistan does not observe daylight saving time.

TRAVEL AGENCIES

Kalpak Travel (www.kalpak-travel.com) Swiss-Kyrgyz husband-and-wife-run travel agency that specialises in tours to Central Asia, with several Turkmenistan itineraries.

Stantours (www.stantours.com) Based in Kazakhstan but offering adventures such as camel treks across the Karakum desert, markhor-watching and climbing in Kugitang, plus a week-long expedition on Akhal-Teke horses in the Kopet Dag mountains.

Young Pioneers (www.youngpioneertours.com) While budget travel is not a thing in Turkmenistan, Young Pioneers try to keep costs down where possible. As well as guided tours of Turkmenistan, they offer trips through all the surrounding 'Stans.

VISAS

Visas for Turkmenistan

All foreigners require a visa to enter Turkmenistan and transit visas are the only visas issued without a letter of invitation (LOI). Prices for visas vary enormously from embassy to embassy, though it is usually cheaper than acquiring the visa on arrival. A full list of Turkmen embassies abroad can be found at www.mfa.gov.tm/en/articles/63?breadcrumbs=no.

Permits are required to visit national parks and visas need to be endorsed to permit travel in various border zones, so it's important to know your itinerary before you begin the visa application process.

As a general rule, plan on getting a visa at least six weeks ahead of entry to Turkmenistan, as the process (even for transit visas) is lengthy. On entry every visa holder will need to pay an additional US$14 fee for an entry card that will list your exit point in Turkmenistan.

Tourist or business visas on arrival are hassle-free these days, and are processed quickly at Ashgabat airport (around US$100), as well as being available at certain border crossings. You must have an LOI in order to be issued a visa. For people arriving by boat from Azerbaijan the visa is available on arrival in Turkmenbashi (by arrangement with the consul, who needs to be present), but the Azeri authorities will not let a person without a valid Turkmenistan visa board the ferry in Baku.

It is worth noting that approval rates for visas can be higher around the times of certain festivals, including Navrus and the Horse Festival. Approval rates tend to be lower for trips scheduled around Independence Day (October).

Transit Visas

The only visa that allows unaccompanied travel for tourists is the transit visa. They are normally valid for three to five days, but are becoming increasingly difficult to acquire, with travellers reporting a rejection rate of over 50%. Allow between two and four weeks for your visa to be processed.

Transit visas can be obtained at any Turkmen consulate, and you do not need an LOI, but you must already have valid visas for the countries you'll be visiting before and after Turkmenistan. Your route must also be a legitimate way to get from one country to the next – a transit visa will not be issued if you can easily travel between countries without passing through Turkmenistan. Acceptable routes are between Iran and Kazakhstan, Iran and Uzbekistan, and Uzbekistan and Azerbaijan. Theoretically, you can also obtain a transit visa if you're travelling between Afghanistan and Kazakhstan or Azerbaijan, but travellers report that there is a higher rejection rate if travelling to or from Afghanistan.

No transit visa is extendable, save in the case of serious illness. The penalty for overstaying a transit visa is US$200, and you may be taken back to Ashgabat and deported on the next available flight at your expense.

Your route will normally not be indicated on the visa, but your entry and exit point (unchangeable) will be, and you may therefore run into trouble going anywhere not obviously between the two points, though document checks on the roads are few and far between these days. You cannot get a transit visa if you plan to fly out of Ashgabat.

Tourist Visas

Tourist visas are a mixed blessing in Turkmenistan. While they allow the visitor to spend a decent amount of time in the country (up to three weeks as a rule), they require accompaniment by an accredited tour guide, who will meet you at the border and remain with you throughout your trip.

This obviously has cost implications, as you will have to pay your guide a daily rate (usually between US$30 and US$50), as well as pay for their meals and hotels. The latter cost is very low, however, as Turkmen citizens pay a local rate that is at least 60% to 80% less than the foreigner rate. Guides will allow you to roam freely in Ashgabat and the immediate environs unaccompanied, as well as around any other large town – there's no legal requirement for them to be with you throughout the day, but you're not legally allowed to travel in Turkmenistan without them. Most tour companies insist you travel in private transport with the guide.

You can only get a tourist visa by going through a travel agency, as only travel agencies with a licence from the Turkmen government can issue LOIs. Many unaccredited agencies still offer LOI services, however, simply by going through an accredited agency themselves. The LOI will be issued with a list of all restricted border regions you are planning to visit. In turn, these are the places that will be listed on your visa, therefore it's essential you decide what you want to see before applying so that the appropriate restricted regions can be listed. It takes around three weeks for an LOI to be issued and the earliest you can apply is 90 days before the start of your trip.

Anyone working in the media or human rights fields, or for political organisations had better not state this on their application, as it's certain to be rejected. Employers are rarely called and asked to verify an applicant's position, but it can happen, so have a good cover story if you work in one of these fields.

Once the LOI is issued (usually emailed to you by your travel agent), you can take it to any Turkmen embassy to get your visa. The issuing of the visa itself is purely a formality, once the LOI has been issued. Normal processing time is three to seven working days depending on the embassy, but most Turkmen embassies offer an express service for a hefty surcharge, reducing processing time to between 24 hours and three days.

Armed with an LOI there is also the possibility of getting a visa on arrival at Ashgabat airport or the Farab border post by prior arrangement with your travel agent. In the case of Farab, the agent needs to arrange for the consul to be present. In any case the original LOI must be taken to the relevant border and the visa will be issued then and there.

Visas for Onward Travel

Turkmenistan is generally a poor place to pick up visas, with long processing times and embassies that aren't used to independent travellers. Although embassies do have official opening hours, it's wise to call ahead if you want to apply for an onward visa to ensure that someone will be there to assist.

Travel Permits

Permits are needed to visit the border regions of Turkmenistan. These will be arranged by the tour company helping with your letter of introduction. Given that the centre of the country is largely uninhabited desert and the population lies on the periphery, permits are necessary for some of the most interesting areas. Ashgabat,

Mary, Merv, Turkmenabat and Balkanabat are not restricted, but anywhere outside these areas should be listed on your visa, thus giving you permission to go there. Travellers on transit visas can usually transit the border zones along the relevant main road, if they correspond to the country they are supposed to exit to. If you get a tourist or business visa on arrival, you'll automatically have your visa endorsed for all areas of the country.

The following areas are termed 'class one' border zones and entry without documentation is theoretically not possible, though there's actually little chance you'll have your documents checked:

Eastern Turkmenistan Farab, Atamurat (Kerki) plus adjoining areas, Kugitang Nature Reserve, Tagtabazar and Serkhetabat.

Northern Turkmenistan Entire Dashoguz region including Konye-Urgench, Dargan-Ata and Gazachak.

Western Turkmenistan Bekdash, Turkmenbashi, Hazar, Dekhistan, Yangykala, Gyzyletrek, Garrygala, Nokhur and surrounding villages.

❶ Getting There & Away

ENTRY & DEPARTURE TAX

For entry into Turkmenistan there is a US$14 fee per person, depending on your nationality. Bring cash in US dollars for this; change is normally available.

International air departure tax is now included in all airline ticket prices. There is no departure tax for domestic travel, nor by land or sea.

ENTRY & EXIT FORMALITIES

Entering the country overland tends to invite more scrutiny than arriving by air. Baggage checks can be very thorough at lonely border posts, while the understaffed airport in Ashgabat seems more interested in processing people quickly rather than pawing through your underwear. You'll need to pay your arrival tax and collect your Entry Travel Pass if you're travelling on a tourist or business visa.

In 2017 the government introduced a new tourism tax. Visitors pay US$2 per day for the duration of their stay. Expect to see the charge on your hotel bill.

AIR

The only international airport with passenger flights in Turkmenistan is Ashgabat International Airport.

Lufthansa (📞 23 41 31, 23 20 37; www. lufthansa.com; Main Concourse, Ashgabat International Airport) Offers six flights per week to Frankfurt via Baku.

S7 Airlines (Map p382; 📞 92 30 21; www.s7.ru; Grand Turkmen Hotel, Görogly köçesi 50) Flies between Ashgabat and Moscow twice a week.

Turkish Airlines (Map p380; 📞 airport 23 20 59, main office 45 66 48; www.turkishairlines. com; Yimpaş Business Centre, Turkmenbashi şayoli 54) Two daily flights from İstanbul to Ashgabat.

LAND

Visitors with visas can enter Turkmenistan from all bordering countries, although the borders with Uzbekistan and Iran are the most frequently used. There are no international train or bus services to or from Turkmenistan. All land borders are open from 9am to 6pm daily but many close for lunch.

To & From Afghanistan

Serkhetabat (formerly known as Gushgi) is the border town with Afghanistan. Crossing here is now a fairly hassle-free prospect, although be prepared to be thoroughly searched by both Turkmen and Afghan border guards. It is recommended that you only tackle this crossing in daylight hours; if you do arrive late you'll need to overnight with a local family as there are no hotels in town.

The border post is 3km south of Serkhetabat. Leaving Turkmenistan, there's a 1.5km walk to the first Afghan village of Torghundi and it's a two-hour taxi journey onward to Herat. If you are coming to Turkmenistan, you'll need to catch a ride from Herat to Torghundi (US$30 in a shared vehicle). Here you need to pay a US$14 customs fee at a bank in town (1.5km south of the border), or you might be able to pay an extra 'tip' to the border guard to do this for you.

The Saparmurat border crossing (called Imam Nazar) near Atamurat (also known as Kerki) is used by UN staff, but was not recommended for independent travellers at the time of writing.

To & From Iran

The simplest exit point is Gaudan/Bajgiran, due south of Ashgabat and a corridor between the Kopet Dag into Iran. From Ashgabat, take a taxi (40M to 50M) for the 20km ride to Yablonovka checkpoint. Here you'll have your passport checked, after which you take a marshrutka shuttle to the border. Once through, it's a taxi (US$2.50) across some 20km of no man's land to Bajgiran where you can get buses or taxis (US$20, four hours) to Mashhad.

There are also borders with Iran at Saraghs (there is a Mashhad–Saraghs train, but no international trains into Turkmenistan) and Gudurolum (which is reachable by car or taxi only).

To & From Kazakhstan

Shared taxis (120M/480M per seat/car) go from Turkmenbashi, via Garabogaz, across the Kazakh border and on to Zhanaozen (Novy Uzen), where there is further transport to Aktau. From Garabogaz to the border the road's a rough dirt track. Delays at the border can occur when caravans of traders appear together. Note that there is absolutely nothing on either side of this remote border – do not try to save money by paying for a taxi to the border post alone, as you'd be extremely lucky to find any onward transport from here.

To & From Uzbekistan

There are three crossings into Turkmenistan from Uzbekistan. Each crossing requires a walk of about 10 to 20 minutes across a ridiculously wide band of no man's land. Shared taxis are sometimes available to shuttle travellers across, the cost of which is approximately US$1. Whether they are operating or not when you visit is a matter of luck.

The Farab crossing is closest to Bukhara (Uzbekistan) and Turkmenabat (Turkmenistan). The 45km taxi ride to Farab from Turkmenabat should cost 15M for a taxi or 4M for a seat in a shared taxi. From the border, take a taxi (US$25) to Bukhara, or hire a taxi as far as Uzbek Olot (or Karakol), where you can change to a shared taxi.

The Dashoguz crossing is best if you are headed for Khiva or Urgench. A taxi from Dashoguz to the Uzbek border is no more than 5M. From the border to Khiva expect to pay around US$20.

Less used is the Hojeli crossing, a 10-minute taxi ride (6M) from Konye-Urgench. Once across the border it's a half-hour drive to Nukus in Karakalpakstan. From the border, take public transport to Hojeli (US$2) or a taxi all the way to Nukus (US$10).

SEA

You can leave and enter Turkmenistan at Turkmenbashi by ferry to/from Baku in Azerbaijan. Travellers report that the ferry is unreliable and could lead to your visa expiring while waiting to leave or enter at this crossing.

ⓘ Getting Around

Travellers on tourist visas will have to travel with a guide, and guides usually have their own cars or 4WDs, so getting around Turkmenistan will always be comfortable and straightforward, though not very cheap. It's rare for guides to travel by public transport with you, but it can happen, and will save you some money if it does: try requesting this option in good time with a travel agency, but be aware that it's not normal. Transit visa holders will be able to make full use of the public transport options while those on a

business visa should be accompanied by their sponsor at all times.

Due to falling oil prices and the subsequent dip in income for Turkmenistan, petrol costs have risen considerably in recent years. Transport is still fairly cheap by international standards, but expect continued price increases.

AIR

Air transport is well priced and generally reliable, and well worth considering if you're in a hurry. Domestic Turkmenistan Airlines flights are heavily subsidised for locals (although not foreigners). Consequently demand is high and flights need to be booked in advance. Turkmenistan Airlines serves the country's main cities with a fleet of modern Boeing 717s. As the main hub, most flights go in and out of Ashgabat, though there are also flights from Dashoguz to Turkmenbashi, Mary and Turkmenabat; from Mary to Turkmenbashi; and from Turkmenbashi to Turkmenabat.

CAR & MOTORCYCLE

Driving through Turkmenistan is perfectly possible if you arrive with your own vehicle, but it's expensive and full of hassles (road blocks, poor roads) and extra charges. Significantly, there's also a road tax calculated by the kilometre for your route through the country.

MARSHRUTKAS, MINIBUSES & SHARED TAXIS

Marshrutkas and minibuses are the most effective way to get around, though they're cramped for long journeys and you'll often have to wait for some time until they're full for them to depart. Shared taxis are a good alternative to marshrutkas, being faster and more comfortable (and you can even buy the remaining seats in a vehicle if you're in a hurry to get going).

Buses are a slow but cheap way to get around. The Ministry of Motor Transport lists routes, timetables and fares – all, rather remarkably, in English: http://www.awtomenzil.gov.tm.

TRAINS

Trains are slow but comfortable and a great way to see the countryside and meet people.

Train fares are likely to be charged in US dollars, although some travellers have reported paying in manat. You can expect to pay US$15 to US$20 for a journey of around eight hours.

Understand
Central Asia

Central Asia Today

For the people of ex-Soviet Central Asia it's been a turbulent quarter-century since independence in 1991. Each of the republics have grappled with economic collapse, population shifts and resurgent Islam. All are reinventing their past, rehabilitating historical heroes and reinforcing their national languages in an attempt to redefine and shore up what it means to be Central Asian. Despite years of political repression and faltering economies, life is improving slowly, if unevenly, across the region.

Best in Print

The Lost Heart of Asia (Colin Thubron; 1994) Our favourite travel writer captures the region in beautiful prose. Also try his more recent *Shadow of the Silk Road* (2007).

The Great Game (Peter Hopkirk; 1990) Fast-paced and immensely readable account of 19th-century Victorian derring-do.

The Land that Disappeared (Christopher Robbins; 2008) Excellent contemporary account of Kazakhstan.

The Silk Road: A Travel Companion (Jonathan Tucker; 2015) A mixture of history, culture and architecture, focusing on Central Asia, Afghanistan and Iran.

Best on Film

The Desert of Forbidden Art (2010) Excellent documentary about Igor Savitsky and the 40,000 items of Soviet art he secretly collected in Karakalpakstan.

Orlando (1992) Sally Potter's film of the Virginia Woolf novel has some spectacular scenes filmed in Khiva.

Borat (2006) Kazakhstan's most famous fake citizen is ridiculous, but he's also hilarious and the satire is biting at times.

Tulpan (2008) Kazakh drama about life on the steppe, as the main character tries to woo his prospective wife Tulpan.

A New Orientation

It's not all political dictatorship and economic hardship. After the confusion and social turmoil of the 1990s life has settled for many Central Asians. Economies are growing and standards of living are rising. Grassroots community tourism projects are flourishing in much of the region. International crossings have been retied with China, Afghanistan and Iran, opening up new opportunities for trade and tourism, and are fast reconnecting the region to the rest of the world.

All this reflects the redrawing of Central Asia. Where once Tashkent and Ashgabat looked north to distant Moscow for economic and political direction, modern Central Asians now turn also to China, Turkey, Iran, Europe and the US, all of whom are equally intent on redefining spheres of influence long blocked by the Iron Curtain. The US-led 'War on Terror' simply raised the stakes in a preexisting geopolitical game that envelops everything from transcontinental gas pipelines to US and Russian military bases in the region.

The death of Uzbekistan President Karimov in 2016 has ushered in some positive economic and political changes in Uzbekistan, from currency and visa reform to new regional transport connections. The region's main political question mark is whether the new Uzbek regime will continue these modest liberalisations and improve regional ties with neighbouring Tajikistan and Kyrgyzstan, as well as international relations with the outside world.

Differing Paths

In addressing their shared postindependence challenges the Central Asian governments are forging quite different paths. Turkmenistan and Kazakhstan are the only republics that seem to have bright economic prospects – sitting pretty on enormous reserves of oil and gas but deeply vulnerable to recent drops in the price of oil and gas.

Kazakhstan in particular has developed its economic base, and the cosmopolitan cities of Almaty and Astana sit at the cutting edge of Central Asia's cultural, culinary and nightlife scenes, despite limited political reform.

Tajikistan is the only one to have experienced the horror of civil war, while the others are all in dread that they will be next to succumb to Islamic fundamentalism and political meltdown. Uzbekistan and Turkmenistan have faced this challenge by sliding into repressive states, where political abductions, torture and trumped-up charges are commonplace.

Only Kyrgyzstan has embraced democracy, with mixed results. The street demonstrations and political violence that unseated Kyrgyz president Bakiev and pushed Kyrgyzstan to the brink of civil war in 2010 revealed deep clan-based fault lines that have weakened the country.

Political Tensions

The Central Asian republics (particularly Uzbekistan) point south to turbulent Afghanistan and the threat of Islamic insurgency to justify their increasingly repressive policies. Isolated bombings in Uzbekistan, Turkmenistan and Tajikistan have underscored the threat but it's hard to say whether armed attacks are the cause for repression, or rather a result of it.

Despite claims of Central Asian fraternity, tensions persist among the 'stans. Disputes over water, electricity and gas supplies are increasingly rising to the surface. Uzbekistan, Kazakhstan and Turkmenistan are rich in energy reserves but are chronically lacking in water, while mountainous Kyrgyzstan and Tajikistan control the upstream taps but regularly run out of electricity. The chronic lack of trust means that regional issues such as the Aral Sea, the drug trade from neighbouring Afghanistan and economic cooperation rarely get the international attention they so desperately require.

The Future

As Central Asia's new economic and cultural ties strengthen, as oil and gas reserves are discovered and as Chinese-funded transcontinental trade routes are rebuilt, this little-understood corner will undoubtedly become increasingly important to the security, economy and politics of Russia, China and the world beyond.

The challenge for the future governments of Central Asia is to meet the religious, secular and economic desires of its people, while treading the tightrope between authoritarianism and Islamisation. As long as the issues of reform, reconstruction, poverty, development, corruption and succession remain unaddressed, Central Asia will continue to be a potential powder keg.

AREA: **4 MILLION SQ KM**

HIGHEST MOUNTAIN: **KOH-I SOMONI (7495M)**

LOWEST POINT: **KARAGIYE DEPRESSION (-132M)**

POPULATION: **67 MILLION**

HELLO: **SALOM** (UZBEK, TAJIK); **SALAM** (TURKMEN, KYRGYZ); **SALAMATSYZ BE** (KAZAKH)

if Central Asia were 100 people

40 would be Uzbeks   6 would be Kyrgyz
12 would be Tajiks   **6** would be Turkmen
17 would be Kazakhs   **19** would be Others

belief systems
(% of population)

Islam   Russian Orthodox   Other

population per sq km

UZBEKISTAN   KYRGYZSTAN   KAZAKHSTAN

≈ 7 people

History

Central Asia's epic history is of great continent-spanning empires, of invasions by Turkic nomads and their subsequent interactions with settled Persian farmers and traders. Over the centuries peoples, conquerors, cultures, religions and ideas have traversed the region's steppes, deserts and mountain passes, creating a unique and sophisticated culture and swinging the region alternately from the heartland of Asia to the middle of nowhere.

Early History

Cultural continuity in Central Asia begins in the late 3rd millennium BC with the Indo-Iranians, speakers of an unrecorded Indo-European dialect related distantly to English. The Indo-Iranians are believed to have passed through Central Asia and Afghanistan on their way from the Indo-European homeland in southern Russia. From Central Asia, groups headed southeast for India and southwest for Iran. These peoples herded cattle, forged iron, invented the wheeled chariot and buried their dead nobles in burial mounds *(kurgans)*. The Tajik people are linguistic descendants of these ancient migrants. One of these subsequent Indo-European groups was the Sakas (part of a people known as Scythians), who have left *kurgans,* rock carvings and other remains across Central Asia. The most spectacular Saka-era remnant is Kazakhstan's famous 'Golden Man' find, found within a 5th-century *kurgan* outside Almaty.

Central Asia's recorded history begins in the 6th century BC, when the large Achaemenid empire of Persia (modern Iran) created client kingdoms or *satrapies* (provinces) in Central Asia: Sogdiana (Sogdia), Khorezm (later Khiva), Bactria (Afghan Turkestan), Margiana (Merv), Aria (Herat) and Saka (Scythia). Sogdiana was the land between the Amu-Darya and Syr-Darya, called Transoxiana (Beyond the Oxus) by the Romans, where Bukhara and Samarkand would later flourish. Khorezm lay on the lower reaches of the Amu-Darya, south of the Aral Sea, where one day the 19th-century khans of Khiva would rule it from their walled city. Saka, the steppe and desert extending north of the Tian Shan and Syr-Darya rivers, was the home of nomadic warriors until their way of life ended in the early 20th century.

Excavations of Scythian *kurgans* (burial mounds) in Kazakhstan have revealed skeletons of female warriors and priestesses, raising connections with classical tales of the Amazons.

TIMELINE	40,000 BC	3500 BC	3000 BC
	Remains of Neanderthal man found at Aman-Kutan cave near Samarkand date from 100,000 BC to 40,000 BC.	The Botai culture of northern Kazakhstan is one of the first to domesticate horses, as horse-based nomadism becomes the dominant steppe culture.	The Bronze Age site of Gonur-Depe in the Margiana Oasis (Turkmenistan) is considered by some archaeologists to be one of the great cities of the ancient world and an early centre of Zoroastriansim.

Alexander the Great

In 330 BC Alexander the Great, a former pupil of Aristotle, from Macedonia, led his army to a key victory over the last Achaemenid emperor, Darius III, in Mesopotamia. With the defeat of his Persian nemesis, Alexander (356–323 BC) developed a taste for conquest. In 329 BC, aged 28, he reached Bactria, crossed the Oxus (Amu-Darya) on inflated hides and proceeded via Cyropol/Cyropolis (Istaravshan) and Marakanda (Samarkand) towards the Jaxartes (Syr-Darya), which he crossed in order to crush Saka defenders. Perhaps in celebration he founded his ninth city, Alexandria Eskhate (Farthest Alexandria), on the banks of the Jaxartes, where today's Khojand stands.

Alexander met the most stubborn resistance of his career in the Sogdians, who in concert with the Massagetes, a Saka (Scythian) clan, revolted and under the leadership of Spitamenes held the mountains of Zerafshan until 328 BC. After an 18-month guerrilla war, the rebels' fall was a poignant one: attacked and defeated after Greek troops scaled the cliffs of their last redoubt, the 'Rock of Sogdiana' (its location today in the Hissar Mountains remains a mystery). Their leader eventually

EURASIA'S NOMADIC EMPIRES

The vast steppes of Central Asia and Mongolia were the heartland of one of this planet's most formidable and successful forms of statehood, the nomadic empire. The domestication of the horse in northern Eurasia 5000 years ago, and the subsequent inventions of the saddle and war chariot by the Scythians a millennium later gave Eurasian nomads an early technological edge. Stirrups in particular allowed them to fire their powerful composite bows in all directions from horseback. The Eurasian grasslands fed horses by the millions, allowing mounted archers to become the unstoppable acme of open-ground warfare for more than 2500 years. It is estimated that Mongol troops had access to half the world's horses during their invasions.

Accounts of nomads by settled communities are notoriously negative, painting them as rampaging barbarians, but in fact many nomads lived a comfortable and sophisticated life. Leaders lined their fur cloaks with silk derived from the horse trade with China and made extensive use of richly cast gold jewellery and animal-shaped totems. Kazakhstan's famous Golden Man, a high-ranking Saka warrior or priest (and most likely a woman) was buried with over 4000 gold objects. Some historians even credit Eurasian nomads with the invention of bowed musical instruments through their horsehair-stringed qobuz.

It was only the introduction of gunpowder-based weapons in the 15th century that turned the tide back towards the settled fortified cities. It was a technological change that marked the end of Eurasia's great nomadic empires.

2000 BC	329–327 BC	300 BC	138–119 BC
During the 2nd millennium BC, the Amu-Darya (Oxus) river changes flow, draining north into the Aral Sea, instead of west to the Caspian Sea. The resulting Khorezm delta becomes a major centre of development.	Alexander the Great campaigns in Central Asia, founding Khojent (in modern Tajikistan), conquering Marakanda (Samarkand) and marrying the Bactrian princess Roxana.	Parthians rule Iran and southern Central Asia from 300 BC to 200 AD, building their first capital at Nissa in Turkmenistan. Theirs is one of the three greatest empires in the world and rivals Rome.	First Chinese diplomatic mission to Central Asia under Zhang Qian visits the Pamir Alay and Fergana Valley (Kyrgyzstan) and brings back reports of Central Asia's 'heavenly horses' and a kingdom called Daqin (Rome).

yielded both the fortress and the beautiful Bactrian princess Roxana (Roshanak), whom Alexander married in Balkh in 327 BC.

The brilliant Macedonian generalissimo's three-year sojourn in Central Asia was marked by a growing megalomania. It was at Marakanda (modern Samarkand) that Alexander murdered his right-hand general, Cleitus. He tried to adopt the dress and autocratic court ritual of an Oriental despot, until his Greek and Macedonian followers finally refused to prostrate themselves before him.

When he died in Babylon in 323 BC, Alexander had no named heir (despite fathering a son with Roxana). But his legacy included nothing less than the West's perennial romance with exploration and expansion.

East Meets West

The aftermath of Alexander's short-lived Macedonian empire in Central Asia saw an explosion of East–West cultural exchange and a chain reaction of nomadic migrations. The Hellenistic successor states of the Seleucid empire in Bactria disseminated the aesthetic values of the classical world deep into Asia. Hellenistic cities and Buddhist monasteries of the 2nd century BC, such as Ai-Khanoum (Alexandria-Oxiana), Takht-i-Sangin and Kobadiyan on the borders of Tajikistan, Uzbekistan and Afghanistan (former Bactria), reveal a fascinating fusion of Greek, Persian and local art forms. Ai-Khanoum boasted not only Greek-style baths, but also a theatre and gymnasium, right on the banks of the Amu-Darya.

Several thousand kilometres east, along the border of Mongolia and China, the expansion of the warlike Xiongnu (Hsiung-nu) confederacy (probably the forebears of the Ephalites, or Huns) uprooted the Yuezhi of western China. The Yuezhi (Yüeh-chih) were sent packing westward along the Ili River into Saka (the borders of Kazakhstan and Kyrgyzstan), whose displaced inhabitants in turn bore down upon the Sogdians to the south.

The Xiongnu were irritating more important powers than the Yuezhi. Although protected behind its expanding Great Wall since about 250 BC, China eagerly sought tranquillity on its barbarian frontier. In 138 BC the Chinese emperor sent a brave volunteer emissary, Zhang Qian, on a secret mission to persuade the Yuezhi king to form an alliance against the Xiongnu.

Alexander the Great (Iskander or Sikander) is a popular figure in Central Asia and several lakes and mountains are named after him.

When he finally got there, 13 years later, Zhang found that the Yuezhi had settled down in Bactria/Tokharistan (southern Tajikistan and northern Afghanistan) to a peaceable life of trade and agriculture, and no longer had an axe to grind with the Xiongnu. But Zhang Qian's mission was still a great success of Chinese diplomacy and exploration, and the stage had been set for the greatest of all East–West contacts: the birth of the Silk Road.

105 BC	107 BC	AD 78–144	440–568
Parthia and China exchange embassies and inaugurate official bilateral trade along the caravan route that lies between them. The Silk Road is born.	Chinese armies arrive in the Fergana Valley to 'persuade' the king to sell them horses. They fail but four years later return with 30,000 soldiers, leaving the region with 3000 horses.	King Kanishka rules the Kushan empire from modern-day Afghanistan. Buddhist monasteries bloom in southern Uzbekistan and Tajikistan as the first human images of Buddha are created.	The Hephthalites (White Huns) migrate from the Altai region to occupy Transoxiana, Bactria, Khorasan and eastern Persia, conquering the Kushans and eventually carving the Buddhas at Bamiyan.

DRAGON HORSES

Central Asia has been famed for its horses for millenniums. The earliest Silk Road excursions into the region were designed to bring back the famous 'blood-sweating' (due to parasites or skin infection) horses of Fergana to help Han China fight nomadic tribes harassing its northern frontier. Much of the highly coveted silk that made its way into Central Asia and beyond originally came from the trade of steeds that the Chinese believed were descended from dragons.

The Kushans

The peaceable Yuezhi finally came into their own in the 1st century BC when their descendants, the Kushan dynasty, converted to Buddhism. The Kushan empire (250 BC–AD 226) grew to control northern India, Afghanistan and Sogdiana from its base at Kapisa, near modern-day Bagram in Afghanistan. At its height in the first three centuries AD, it was one of the world's four superpowers, alongside Rome, China and Parthia.

Vigorous trade on the Silk Road helped fuel and spread Kushan and Buddhist culture, and it was under the Kushans that the first images of Buddha appeared. The rich Kushan coinage bears testament to the Silk Road's lively religious ferment, with coins bearing images of Greek, Roman, Buddhist, Persian and Hindu deities. Indian, Tibetan and Chinese art were permanently affected and the spread of Buddhism changed the face and soul of Asia.

> The Sogdians (from modern Tajikistan and Uzbekistan) were the consummate Silk Road traders, so much so that their language became the lingua franca of the Silk Road.

Sassanids, Huns & Sogdians

The Silk Road's first flower faded by about 200 AD, as the Chinese, Roman, Parthian and Kushan empires went into decline. As the climate along the middle section of the Silk Road became drier, Central Asian nomads increasingly sought wealth by plundering, taxing and conquering their settled neighbours. The Persian Sassanids (Sassanians) lost their Inner Asian possessions in the 4th century to the Huns, who ruled a vast area of Central Asia at the same time that Attila was scourging Europe.

The Huns were followed south across the Syr-Darya by the western Turks, who in 559 made an alliance with the Sassanids and ousted the Huns. The western Turks were a branch of the so-called Kök Turks or Blue Turks, whose ancestral homelands were in southern Siberia.

The Arrival of Islam

When the western Turks faded in the late 7th century, an altogether new and formidable power was waiting to fill the void – the army of Islam. Exploding out of Arabia just a few years after the Prophet Mohammed's

630	642–712	719	787–850
Chinese Buddhist pilgrim Xuan Zang travels to India via Issyk-Köl, Tashkent, Samarkand, Balkh and Bamiyan in search of Buddhist texts. En route he visits the summer capital of the Blue Turks at Tokmok, Kyrgyzstan.	Arab conquest of Central Asia by General Qutaybah ibn Muslim brings Islam to the region. Central Asia is called Mawarannhr in Arabic – the 'Land Beyond the River'.	The Sogdians under their ruler Devastich stage a major revolt against Arab rule. Devastich flees to the mountains of northern Tajikistan but the Arabs catch and crucify him three years later.	Mathematician Al-Khorezmi (Latinised as Algorismi), who gave his name to the mathematical process called an algorithm, lives in this period. The title of his mathematical work Al-Jebr reaches Europe as 'algebra'.

death, the Muslim armies rolled through Persia in 642 to set up a military base at Merv (modern Turkmenistan) but met stiff resistance from the Turks of Transoxiana. The power struggle to control the lands between the Amu-Darya and Syr-Darya ebbed and flowed but Arab armies under the brilliant General Qutaybah ibn Muslim gradually gained ground, taking Bukhara in 709 and Samarkand three years later.

China, meanwhile, had revived under the Tang dynasty and expanded into Central Asia, murdering the khan of the Tashkent Turks as it flexed its imperial muscles. It was perhaps the most costly incident of skulduggery in Chinese history. The enraged Turks were joined by the opportunistic Arabs and Tibetans; in 751 they squeezed the Chinese forces into the Talas Valley (in present-day Kazakhstan and Kyrgyzstan) and sent them flying back across the Tian Shan, defining the outer limits of the Chinese empire for good.

After the Battle of Talas, the Arabs' Central Asian territories receded in the wake of local rebellions. By the 9th century, Transoxiana (now known by the Arabic name Mawarannahr, or the 'Land Beyond the River') had given rise to the peaceful and affluent Samanid dynasty. It generously encouraged development of Persian culture while remaining strictly allied with the Sunni caliph of Baghdad. It was under the Samanids that Bukhara grew into a vanguard of Muslim culture to rival Baghdad, Cairo and Cordoba, garnering it the epithet 'The Pillar of Islam'. Some of the Islamic world's best scholars were nurtured in the city's 113 medressas and the famous library of Bukhara shone as one of the world's great centres of intellectual development.

Samanid Central Asia produced some of history's most important scientists, as well as great writers such as court poet Rudaki. Bukharan native and court physician Abu Ali ibn-Sina (Latinised as Avicenna) was the greatest medic in the medieval world, while Al-Biruni, from Khorezm, was the world's foremost astronomer of his age. Confused schoolchildren around the world can thank mathematician Al-Khorezmi (Latinised as Algorismi) for the introduction of algebra (*Al-Jebr* was the title of one of his mathematical works). He also gave his name to the mathematical process known as an algorithm.

Lost Enlightenment (2013), by S Frederick Starr, looks at Central Asia's golden intellectual age between 800 AD and 1200 AD, when it led the world in the fields of science, astronomy, mathematics and the arts.

Karakhanids to Karakitay

By the early 10th century, internal strife at court had weakened the Samanid dynasty and opened the door for two Turkic usurpers to divide up the empire: the Karakhanids held sway from three mighty capitals: Balasagun (Burana in Kyrgyzstan) in the centre of their domain, Talas (Taraz in Kazakhstan) in the west, and Kashgar in the east. It is the Karakhanids who are credited with finally converting the populace of Central Asia to Islam. Further south the Ghaznavids, under Mahmoud

819-1005	858–941	980–1037	999–1211
The heyday of the Samanid dynasty in Bukhara. Its greatest ruler, Ismail Samani, is buried in a beautiful tomb in Bukhara and is celebrated as Tajikistan's founding father.	Life of Rudaki, court poet of the Samanids, born near modern Penjikent in Tajikistan and considered to be the founder of Tajik/Persian literature.	Life of Abu Ali ibn-Sina (Latinised as Avicenna), from Bukhara, the greatest medic in the medieval world, whose *Canon of Medicine* was the standard textbook for Western doctors until the 17th century.	The Turkic Karakhanids wrest control of Transoxiana from the Persian Samanids. Dynastic founder Nasr ibn Ali is buried in a mausoleum in Uzgen (Özgön) in the Fergana Valley.

LOST BATTLE, LOST SECRETS

The Chinese lost more than just a fight at the Battle of Talas in 751. To add insult to injury, some of the Chinese rounded up after the battle were experts in the crafts of paper-making and silk-making. Soon China's best-kept secrets were giving Arab silk-makers in Persia a commercial advantage all over Europe. It was the first mortal blow to the Silk Road. The spread of paper-making to Baghdad and eventually Europe sparked a techno-logical and intellectual revolution; the impact of this on the development of civilisation cannot be overestimated.

the Great, ruled Samarkand and Bukhara from Ghazni in southern Af-ghanistan. They in turn are credited with snuffing out Buddhism in the region and introducing Islam to India.

The Karakhanids and Ghaznavids coveted each other's lands. In the mid-11th century, while they were busy invading each other, they were caught off guard by a third Turkic horde, the Seljuqs, who annihilated both after pledging false allegiance to the Ghaznavids. In the Seljuqs' heyday their empire was vast: in the east it bordered the lands of the Buddhist Karakitay, who had swept into Balasagun and Kashgar from China; to the west it extended all the way to the Mediterranean and Red Seas.

An incurable symptom of Inner Asian dynasties through the ages was their near inability to survive the inevitable disputes of succession. The Seljuqs lasted a century before their weakened line succumbed to the Karakitay and to the Seljuqs' own rearguard vassals, the Khorezm-shahs. From their capital at Gurganj (present-day Konye-Urgench), the Khorezmshahs burst full-force into the tottering Karakitay. At the end of the 12th century the Khorezmshahs emerged as rulers of all Transoxiana and much of the Muslim world as well.

And so Central Asia might have continued in a perennial state of forgettable wars. As it is, the Khorezmshahs are still remembered pri-marily as the unlucky stooge left holding the red cape when the angry bull was released.

From the 9th to 11th centuries the fringes of Central Asia saw a baffling array of shadowy nomadic groups – Oghuz Turks, Pechenegs, Kimaks, Kipchaks, Cumans and Karluks, as well as slave-trading Nogoi Horde – about whom little is known.

Mongol Terror, Mongol Peace

Chinggis (Genghis) Khan felt he had all the justification in the world to destroy Central Asia. In 1218 a Khorezmian governor in Otrar (modern-day Kazakhstan) received a Mongol delegation to inaugurate trade relations. Scared by distant reports of the new Mongol menace, the governor assassinated them in cold blood. Up until that moment Chinggis had been carefully weighing the alternative strategies for

1077–1220	12th century	1141	1220–21
Khorezmshah empire rises from its capital in Gurganj (Konye-Urgench), shrugging off Seljuq and Karak-itay domination to briefly control most of modern-day Iran, Cen-tral Asia and western Afghanistan.	Merv in Turkmenistan is the largest city in the world, known as the Queen of the World, as the Seljuqs reach the height of their glory. The Seljuq leaders Alp Arslan and Sultan Sanjar are buried here in huge mausolea.	The Shamanic-Buddhist Karakitay and Khorezmshahs defeat the Muslim Seljuqs at the battle of Qatwan, north of Samarkand. The news filters back to Crusader Europe as the legend of Prester John.	Chinggis (Genghis) Khan's army destroys Bukhara, killing 30,000. That city rebels and 160,000 of its inhabitants are killed in a week.

The Karakitay lent their name to both Cathay (an archaic name for China) and Kitai (the Russian word for China).

expanding his power: commerce versus conquest. Then came the crude Otrar blunder, and the rest is history.

In early 1219 Chinggis placed himself at the head of an estimated 200,000 men and began to ride west from his stronghold in the Altay. By the next year his armies had sacked Khojand and Otrar (the murderous governor had molten silver poured into his eyes in Chinggis' presence), and Bukhara soon followed.

It was in that brilliant city, as soldiers raped and looted and horses trampled Islamic holy books in the streets, that the unschooled Chinggis ascended to the pulpit in the chief mosque and preached to the terrified congregation. His message: 'I am God's punishment for your sins'. Such shocking psychological warfare is perhaps unrivalled in history. It worked and news eventually filtered back to Europe of the Tartars, an army of 'Devil's Horsemen', sent from the Gates of Hell (Tartarus) to destroy Christendom.

Bukhara was burned to the ground, and the Mongol hordes swept on to conquer and plunder the great cities of Central Asia – Samarkand, Merv, Termiz, Urgench, Herat, Balkh, Bamiyan, Ghazni – and, eventually under Chinggis' generals and heirs, most of Eurasia. No opposing army could match their speed, agility and accuracy with a bow.

Settled civilisation in Central Asia took a serious blow, from which it only began to recover 600 years later under Russian colonisation. Chinggis' descendants controlling Persia favoured Shiite Islam over Sunni Islam, a development which over the centuries isolated Central Asia even more from the currents of the rest of the Sunni Muslim world.

But there was stability, law and order under the Pax Mongolica. In modern terms, the streets were safe and the trains ran on time. The resulting modest flurry of trade on the Silk Road was the background to several famous medieval travellers' journeys, including the most famous of them all, Marco Polo.

One overlooked Silk Road commodity was the trade in slaves. Slaves dominated the global workforce between the 8th and 11th centuries and Turkmen raiders kept the slave markets of Khiva and Bukhara stocked well into the 19th century.

On Chinggis Khan's death in 1227, his empire was divided among his sons. The most distant lands, stretching as far as the Ukraine and Moscow and including western and most of northern Kazakhstan, went to Chinggis' grandsons Batu and Orda, and came to be known collectively as the Golden Horde. Chinggis' second son, Chaghatai, got the next most distant portion, including southern Kazakhstan, Uzbekistan, Afghanistan and western Xinjiang; this came to be known as the Chaghatai khanate. The share of the third son, Ögedei, seems to have eventually been divided between the Chaghatai khanate and the Mongol heartland inherited by the youngest son, Tolui. Tolui's portion formed the basis for his son Kublai Khan's Yuan dynasty in China.

1227	1273	1336–1405	1383–1404
The death of Chinggis Khan sees the Mongol Empire divided among his sons. Central Asia forms the heart of the Chaghatai Khanate.	Marco Polo travels through the Wakhan Valley en route to China, writing of Badakhshani (Pamir Tajik) rubies, long-horned 'Marco Polo' sheep and the high Pamir plateau.	Life of Timur (Tamerlane), whose campaigns resulted in the deaths of more than one million people. He becomes infamous for building towers or walls made from the cemented heads of a defeated army.	Timur's military campaigns conquer much of the known world, including Isfahan (1387), the Volga (1391), the Caucasus (1394), Delhi (1398), Baghdad (1401) and Aleppo (1402).

Unlike the Golden Horde in Europe and the Yuan court in Beijing, the Chaghatai khans tried to preserve their nomadic lifestyle, complete with the khan's roving tent encampment as 'capital city'. But as the rulers spent more and more time in contact with Muslim collaborators who administered their realm, the Chaghatai line inevitably began to settle down. They even made motions towards conversion to Islam. It was a fight over this issue, in the mid-14th century, that split the khanate in two, with the Muslim Chaghatais holding Transoxiana and the conservative branch retaining the Tian Shan, Kashgar and the vast steppes north and east of the Syr-Darya, an area collectively known as Moghulistan.

Timur-i-Leng (Timur the Lame), or Tamerlane, walked with a pronounced limp after a fall from a horse in 1363 left him disabled in his right leg. He also lost two fingers during one battle.

Timur & The Timurids

The fracturing of the Mongol empire immediately led to resurgence of the Turkic peoples. From one minor clan near Samarkand arose a tyrant's tyrant, Timur ('the Lame', or Tamerlane). After assembling an army and wresting Transoxiana from Chaghatai rule, Timur went on a spectacular nine-year rampage which ended in 1395 with modern-day Iran, Iraq, Syria, eastern Turkey, the Caucasus and northern India smouldering at his feet.

From across his realm, Timur plundered riches and captured artisans and poured them into his capital at Samarkand. The city blossomed, in stark contrast to his conquered lands, into a lavish showcase of treasure and spectacle. Much of the postcard skyline of today's Samarkand dates to Timur's reign. Foreign guests of Timur's, including the Spanish envoy Ruy Gonzales de Clavijo, took home stories of Oriental enchantment and barbarity which fed the West's dreams of a remote and romantic Samarkand.

Timur claimed indirect kinship with Chinggis Khan, but he had little of his forerunner's gift for statecraft. History can be strange: both conquerors savagely slaughtered hundreds of thousands of innocent people, yet one is remembered as a great ruler and the other not. The argument goes that Timur's bloodbaths were insufficiently linked to specific political or military aims. On the other hand, Timur is considered the more cultured and religious of the two men. At any rate, Timur died an old man at Otrar in 1405, having just set out in full force to conquer China.

For a scant century after Timur's death his descendants ruled on separately in small kingdoms and duchies. A Timurid renaissance was led by Timur's son Shah Rukh (1377–1447) and his remarkable wife Gowhar Shad, who moved the capital from Samarkand to the cultured city of Herat, populated by artistic luminaries such as the Sufi poets Jami and Alisher Navoi, and the miniaturist painter Behzad, whose work had a huge influence on subsequent Persian and Mughal miniatures.

1395	1424	1441–1501	1468
Timur defeats the army of the Golden Horde in southern Russia, fracturing the Mongol empire and allowing the rise of its vassals, the fragmented Russian princes. This marks the predawn of the Russian state.	Timur's grandson Ulugbek builds a world-class observatory in Samarkand, plotting 1018 stars before he is beheaded in 1449 as part of a religious backlash.	Life of poet Alisher Navoi, who wrote in Chaghatai Turkic and is considered the founder of Turkic and Uzbek literature.	Uzbek khan Abylkayyr is killed by a family rival, splitting the clan into the Uzbek Shaybanids to the south and the Kazakh khanate to the north.

Babur never returned to his beloved Fergana Valley and his wistful memoirs, the *Baburname*, are full of nostalgic laments to the joys of his lost homeland; mostly melons and women, in that order.

From 1409–49, Samarkand was governed by the conqueror's mild, scholarly grandson, Ulugbek (Ulugh Bek). Gifted in mathematics and astronomy, he built a large celestial observatory and attracted scientists who gave the city a lustre as a centre of learning for years to come.

In addition to Persian, a Turkic court language came into use called Chaghatai, which survived for centuries as a Central Asian lingua franca.

Uzbeks & Kazakhs

Modern-day Uzbekistan and Kazakhstan, the two principal powers of post-Soviet Central Asia, eye each other warily across the rift dividing their two traditional lifestyles: sedentary agriculture (Uzbeks) and nomadic pastoralism (Kazakhs). Yet these two nations are closely akin and parted ways with a family killing.

The family in question was the dynasty of the Uzbek khans. These rulers, one strand of the modern Uzbek people, had a pedigree reaching back to Chinggis Khan and a homeland in southern Siberia. In the 14th century they converted to Islam, gathered strength and started moving south. Under Abylkayyr Khan they reached the north bank of the Syr-Darya, across which lay the declining Timurid rulers in Transoxiana. But Abylkayyr had enemies within his own family. The two factions met in battle in 1468; Abylkayyr was killed and his army defeated.

After this setback, Abylkayyr's grandson Mohammed Shaybani brought the Uzbek khans to power once more and established Uzbek control in Transoxiana; modern-day Uzbekistan. Abylkayyr's rebellious kinsmen became the forefathers of the Kazakh khans.

The Uzbeks gradually adopted the sedentary agricultural life best suited to the fertile river valleys they occupied. Settled life involved cities, which entailed administration, literacy, learning and, wrapped up with all of these, Islam. The Shaybanid dynasty, which ruled until the end of the 16th century, attempted to outdo the Timurids in religious devotion and to carry on their commitment to artistic patronage. But the Silk Road had withered away, usurped by spice ships, and Central Asia's economy had entered full decline. As prosperity fell, so did the region's importance as a centre of the Islamic world.

The Great Horde roamed the steppes of the Zhetisu region (Russian: Semireche), north of the Tian Shan; the Middle Horde occupied the grasslands east of the Aral Sea; and the Little Horde took the lands to the west, as far as the Ural River.

The Kazakhs, meanwhile, stayed home on the range, north of the Syr-Darya, and flourished as nomadic herders. Their experience of urban civilisation and organised Islam remained slight compared with their Uzbek cousins. By the 16th century the Kazakhs had solidly filled a power vacuum on the old Scythian steppes between the Ural and Irtysh Rivers and established what was to be the world's last nomadic empire, divided into three hordes: the Great Horde, the Middle Horde and the Little Horde.

15th century	1501–07	1635–1758	1717
The end of the century sees the decline of the overland trade routes, including the Silk Road, due to a new emphasis on trade by sea. Trading cities such as Bukhara start a slow decline.	The Uzbek Shaybanids capture Samarkand and Bukhara, bringing to an end the Timurid dynasty and forcing Babur to flee south to Kabul and Delhi, eventually to found the Mughal empire in India in 1526.	Zhungarian (Dzungarian; Oyrat) empire terrorises Kazakhstan, Kyrgyzstan and China. When the Oyrats are finally defeated by Manchu China, Kyrgyzstan comes nominally under Chinese rule.	First Russian expedition to Khiva ends in a massacre of 4000 tsarist troops; the decapitated Russian leader's head is sent to the Emir of Bukhara as a gift.

The Zhungarian Empire

The Oyrats were a western Mongol clan who had been converted to Tibetan Buddhism. Their day in the sun came when they subjugated eastern Kazakhstan, the Tian Shan, Kashgaria and western Mongolia to form the Zhungarian (Dzungarian or Jungarian) empire (1635–1758). Russia's frontier settlers were forced to pay heavy tribute and the Kazakh hordes, with their prize pasturage filling the mountain gap known as the Zhungarian Gate, were cruelly and repeatedly pummelled until the Oyrats were liquidated by Manchu China. Stories of this dark period live on in the Alpamish and *Manas* epic poems.

The Russians had by this time established a line of fortified outposts on the northern fringe of the Kazakh Steppe. Reeling from the Zhungarian attacks, the Kazakhs (first the Little Horde, then the Middle Horde, then part of the Great Horde) gradually accepted Russian protection over the mid-18th century. It was a clear sign of things to come.

The Khanates of Kokand, Khiva & Bukhara

In the fertile oases now called Uzbekistan, the military regime of a Persian interloper named Nadir Shah collapsed in 1747, leaving a political void which was rapidly occupied by a trio of Uzbek khanates.

The three dynasties were the Kungrats, enthroned at Khiva (in the territory of old Khorezm), the Mangits at Bukhara and the Mins at Kokand; all rivals. The khans of Khiva and Kokand and the emirs of Bukhara seemed able to will the outside world out of existence as they stroked and clawed each other like a box of kittens. Boundaries were impossible to fix as the rivals shuffled their provinces in endless wars.

Unruly nomadic clans produced constant pressure on their periphery. Bukhara and Khiva claimed nominal control over the nomadic Turkmen, who prowled the Karakum desert and provided the khanates with slaves from Persia and the Russian borderlands. Kokand spread into the Tian Shan mountains and the Syr-Darya basin in the early 19th century, while Bukhara further exercised nominal control over northern Afghanistan and much of modern-day Tajikistan.

The khans ruled absolutely as feudal despots. Some of them were capable rulers; some, such as the last emir of Bukhara, were depraved and despised tyrants. In the centuries since Transoxiana had waned as the centre of Islam, levels of education and literacy had plummeted, and superstition and ignorance pervaded even the highest levels of government.

It was no dark age, however – trade was vigorous. This was especially true in Bukhara, where exports of cotton, cloth, silk, Karakul fleece and other goods gave it a whopping trade surplus with Russia. Commerce

Genetic testing has revealed that over 16 million men in Central Asia have the same Y-chromosome as Chinggis (Genghis) Khan.

1731	1835–65	1842	1848
Lesser Kazakh Horde places itself under Russian protection, opening up the ensuing annexation of Kazakhstan by tsarist forces and settlers.	Life of Shokan Ualikhanov – Kazakh ethnographer, explorer, spy, painter, Renaissance man, friend of Dostoevsky and the first person to record a fragment of the *Manas* epic.	Britain suffers disaster in the First Anglo-Afghan War. Later that year British officers Conolly and Stoddart are beheaded in front of the Ark (citadel) by the Emir of Bukhara, as the Great Game kicks off.	Russia abolishes the Great Horde, ending the last line of rulers directly descended, by both blood and throne, from Chinggis Khan.

THE MONGOL KISS OF DEATH

Alongside the exchange of silk, jade, paper and Buddhism, historians rank disease as one of the Silk Road's less salubrious gifts to the world. One school of thought has it that the Black Death plague spread in 1338 from a diseased community of Nestorian Christians at Lake Issyk-Köl in current Kyrgyzstan. Disease-ridden rat fleas then followed merchant caravans along Silk Road trade routes to the Mongol capital of Sarai in the Russian Volga.

By 1343 Mongol Khan Jani Beg of the Golden Horde was famously catapulting the plague-riddled corpses of his dead soldiers over the city walls of Kaffa, in the Crimea peninsula, in one of the world's first examples of biological warfare. The outbreak caused the Genoese population to flee by boat to the Mediterranean coast, spreading the disease deeper into Europe.

In the ensuing six years the Black Death pandemic went on to kill between 30% and 60% of Europe's population and around 100 million people across Asia. It was the Mongols' farewell kiss of death to the world.

brought in new ideas, with resulting attempts to develop irrigation and even to reform civil administrations. European travellers in the 19th century wrote best-selling travelogues marvelling at the exotic architectural splendour of these distant glimmering capitals.

In many respects, the three khanates closely resembled the feudal city-states of late-medieval Europe. But it is anybody's guess how they and the Kazakh and Kyrgyz nomads might have developed had they been left alone.

The Russians Are Coming!

By the turn of the 19th century Russia's vista to the south was of anachronistic, unstable neighbours, who had a nasty habit of raiding southern settlements, even taking Christian Russians as slaves. Flush with the new currents of imperialism sweeping Europe, the empire found itself embarking willy-nilly upon a century of rapid expansion across the steppe.

The first people to feel the impact were the Kazakhs. Their agreements in the mid-18th century to accept Russian 'protection' had apparently been understood by St Petersburg as agreements to annexation and a few decades later Tatars and Cossacks were sent to settle and farm the land. Angered, the Kazakhs revolted. As a consequence, the khans of the three hordes were, one by one, stripped of their autonomy, and their lands were made into bona fide Russian colonies, sweet psychological revenge, no doubt, for centuries of invasion by nomadic armies from the east. Kokand was the first of the three Uzbek khanates to be absorbed, followed by Bukhara (1868) and then Khiva (1873).

At its height the Mongol empire formed the largest contiguous land empire in human history, marking the greatest incursion by steppe nomads into settled society.

1862–84	1877	1881	1885
Tsarist Russia takes Bishkek (1862), Aulie-Ata (1864), Tashkent (1865), Samarkand (1868), Khiva (1873), Kokand (1877) and Merv (1884), ruled by the Governor-General Konstantin Kaufman in Tashkent.	German geographer Ferdinand von Richthofen coins the term 'Silk Road' to describe the transcontinental network of trade routes between Europe and China.	Siege of Goek-Tepe in modern Turkmenistan marks the last stand of the Turkmen against Russian annexation. Over 15,000 Tekke are killed.	Britain and Russia go to the brink of war after the Russians annex the Pandjeh Oasis at the height of the Great Game. The British are convinced the Russians have their eyes on Herat and British India beyond.

The last and fiercest people to hold out against the tsarist juggernaut were the Tekke, the largest and most independent of the Turkmen clans. The Russians were trounced in 1879 at a major battle of Teke-Turkmen, but returned with a vengeance in 1881 with a huge force under General Mikhail Dmitrievich Skobelev (who famously rode a white horse and dressed only in white). The siege and capture of Geok-Tepe, the Tekkes' last stronghold, resulted in the death of around 15,000 Tekke and only 268 Russians.

With resistance crushed, the Russians proceeded along the hazily defined Persian frontier area, occupying the Pandjeh Oasis on the Afghan border in 1885 at the southernmost point of their new empire. Throughout the conquest, the government in St Petersburg agonised over every advance. On the ground their hawkish generals took key cities first and asked for permission later.

When it was over, Russia found it had bought a huge new territory – half the size of the USA, geographically and ethnically diverse, and economically rich – fairly cheaply in terms of money and lives, and in just 20 years. It had not gone unnoticed by the world's other great empire further south in British India.

> For more on the Mongols see the excellent book *Storm from the East* by Robert Marshall (1993).

The Great Game

What do two expanding empires do when their ill-defined frontiers draw near each other? They scramble for control of what's between them, using a mix of secrecy and stealth.

The British called the ensuing struggle for imperial power the 'Great Game'; in Russia it was the 'Tournament of Shadows'. In essence it was the first cold war between East and West. All the ingredients were there: spies and counterspies, demilitarised zones, puppet states and doom-saying governments whipping up smokescreens for their own shady business. All that was lacking was the atom bomb and a Russian leader banging his shoe on the table.

As the Russians spread into Central Asia, the British turned towards their northwestern frontier. The disastrous 1842 First Afghan War took the wind out of the British sails, but only temporarily. By 1848 the British had defeated the Sikhs and taken control of the Punjab and the Peshawar valley. With a grip now on the 'Northern Areas' Britain began a kind of cat-and-mouse game with Russia across the vaguely mapped Pamir and Hindu Kush ranges. Agents posing as scholars, explorers, hunters, merchants – and even Muslim preachers and Buddhist pilgrims – criss-crossed the mountains, mapping the passes, spying on each other and courting local rulers. In 1882 Russia established a consulate in Kashgar and in 1877 a British agency at Gilgit (present-day

1888	1890	1898	1916
The Trans-Caspian railway from Krasnovodsk reaches Samarkand. The Orenburg–Tashkent line is completed seven years later, tying Central Asia firmly to the Russian heartland.	Captain Francis Younghusband is thrown out of the Pamirs by his Russian counterpart, much to the outrage of the British.	Rebellion in Andijon in Uzbekistan against the Russians. The insurrection is put down and steps are taken to Russify urban Muslims.	An uprising over forced labour conscription during WWI leads to over 200,000 Kazakhs and Kyrgyz fleeing to China.

For more on the extraordinary life of Timur see *Tamerlane: Sword of Islam, Conqueror of the World* by Justin Marozzi (2006).

Pakistan) was urgently reopened when the *mir* (hereditary ruler) of Hunza entertained a party of Russians.

Imperial tensions continued with the Russian annexation of Bukhara and Samarkand but it was the Russian occupation of Merv in 1884 that really sent blood pressures through the roof in Britain and India. Merv was a crossroads leading to Herat, an easy gateway to Afghanistan, which in turn offered entry into British India. The British government finally lost its cool the following year when the Russians went south to control Pandjeh.

Then in 1890, Francis Younghusband (later to head a British incursion into Tibet) was sent to do some politicking with Chinese officials in Kashgar. On his way back through the Pamirs he found the range full of Russian troops, and was told to get out or face arrest.

This electrified the British. They raised hell with the Russian government and invaded Hunza the following year; at the same time Russian troops skirmished in northeast Afghanistan. After a burst of diplomatic manoeuvring, Anglo-Russian boundary agreements in 1895 and 1907 gave Russia most of the Pamirs and established the Wakhan Corridor, the awkward finger of Afghan territory that divides the two former empires.

The Great Game was over. The Great Lesson for the people of the region was: 'No great power has our interests at heart'. The lesson has powerful implications today.

Colonisation of Turkestan

In 1861, the outbreak of the US Civil War ended Russia's imports of American cotton. To keep the growing textile industry in high gear, the natural place to turn to for cotton was Central Asia. Other sectors of Russian industry were equally interested in the new colonies as sources of cheap raw materials and labour, and as huge markets. Russia's government and captains of industry wisely saw that their own goods could not compete in Europe but in Central Asia they had a captive, virgin market.

In the late 19th century, European immigrants began to flood the tsar's new lands, a million in Kazakhstan alone. The new arrivals were mostly freed Russian and Ukrainian serfs hungry for land of their own. Central Asia also offered a chance for enterprising Russians to climb socially. The first mayor of Pishpek (Bishkek) left Russia as a gunsmith, married well in the provinces, received civil appointments, and ended his life owning a mansion and a sprawling garden estate.

The Russian middle class brought with them straight streets, gas lights, telephones, cinemas, amateur theatre, parks and hotels. All these were contained in enclaves set apart from the original towns. Through their lace curtains the Russians looked out on the Central Asian masses with a fairly indulgent attitude. The Muslim fabric of life was left alone

1917	1920	1920–26	1924
The Bolshevik October Revolution in Russia leads to the creation of the Tashkent Soviet. The Alash Orda movement in Kazakhstan creates an independent state until crushed by the Bolsheviks three years later.	Soviet troops seize Khiva and Bukhara, replacing the respective khanate and emirate with People's Soviet Republics.	Basmachi rebel movement in Central Asia reaches a peak, with as many as 16,000 armed men fighting the Soviet army.	The Uzbek Soviet Socialist Republic (SSR; comprising modern Uzbekistan and Tajikistan) and the Turkmen SSR are created out of the Turkestan SSR.

and development, when it came, took the form of small industrial enterprises, irrigation systems and a modest program of primary education.

In culture it was the Kazakhs, as usual, who were the first to be influenced by Russia. A small, Europeanised, educated class began for the first time to think of the Kazakh people as a nation. In part, their ideas came from a new sense of their own illustrious past, which they read about in the works of Russian ethnographers and historians. Their own brilliant but short-lived scholar, Shokan Ualikhanov (Chokan Valikhanov), was a key figure in Kazakh consciousness-raising.

The 1916 Uprising

The outbreak of WWI in 1914 had disastrous consequences in Central Asia. In southeastern Kazakhstan massive herds of Kazakh and Kyrgyz cattle were requisitioned for the war effort, whereas Syr-Darya, Fergana and Samarkand provinces had to provide cotton and food. Then, in 1916, as Russia's hopes in the war plummeted, the tsar demanded men. Local people in the colonies were to be conscripted as noncombatants in labour battalions. To add insult to injury, the action was not called 'mobilisation' but 'requisition', a term usually used for cattle and material.

Exasperated Central Asians just said no. Starting in Tashkent, an uprising swept eastwards over the summer of 1916. It gained in violence, and attracted harsher reprisal, the further east it went. Purposeful attacks on Russian militias and official facilities gave way to massive rioting, raiding and looting. Colonists were massacred, their villages burned, and women and children carried off.

The resulting bloody crackdown is a milestone tragedy in Kyrgyz and Kazakh history. Russian troops and vigilantes gave up all pretence of a 'civilising influence' as whole Kyrgyz and Kazakh villages were brutally slaughtered or set to flight. Manhunts for suspected perpetrators continued all winter, long after an estimated 200,000 Kyrgyz and Kazakh families had fled towards China. The refugees who didn't starve or freeze on the way were shown little mercy in China.

Revolution & Civil War

For a short time after the Russian Revolution of 1917, which toppled the tsar, there was a real feeling of hope in some Central Asian minds. The Central Asian society which the West, out of ignorance and mystification, had labelled backwards and inflexible had actually been making preparations for impressive progress. The Young Bukharans and Young Khivans movements agitated for social self-reform, modelling themselves on the Young Turks movement which had begun transforming Turkey in 1908. The Jadidists, adherents of educational reform, had

The English word 'horde' comes via French from the Turkic word *ordu*, meaning the yurt or pavilion where a khan held his court.

1928–30	1929	1930s	1936
Latin script replaces Arabic script in Central Asia, divorcing the region from its Muslim heritage and rendering millions illiterate overnight. Latin is replaced by Cyrillic script in 1939–40.	Tajik SSR created after borders are rejigged and redrawn to create the new republic's requisite minimum one-million population.	Stalin's genocidal collectivisation programs strike the final blow to nomadic life. Around 20% of Kazakhs leave the country with their flocks and a similar number die in the ensuing famine.	Kazakh and Kyrgyz SSRs created. Stalin's 'Great Purge' results in the arrest and execution of political leaders across the Soviet Union.

Memory of the Oyrat legacy has been preserved in epic poetry by the Kazakhs and Kyrgyz, who both suffered under the Oyrats' ruthless predations.

made small gains in modernising Uzbek schools, despite objections from the conservative khanate officials.

In 1917 an independent state was launched in Kokand by young nationalists under the watchful eye of a cabal of Russian cotton barons. This new government intended to put into practice the philosophy of the Jadid movement: to build a strong, autonomous Pan-Turkic polity in Central Asia by modernising the religious establishment and educating the people. Within a year the Kokand government was smashed by the Red Army's newly formed Trans-Caspian front. More than 5000 Kokandis were massacred after the city was captured. Central Asians' illusions about peacefully coexisting with Bolshevik Russia were shattered.

Bolshevik Conquest

Like most Central Asians, Emir Alim Khan of Bukhara hated the godless Bolsheviks. In response to their first ultimatum to submit, he slaughtered the Red emissaries who brought it and declared a holy war. The emir conspired with White (anti-Bolshevik) Russians and even British political agents, while the Reds concentrated on strengthening party cells within the city.

In December 1918 a counter revolution broke out, apparently organised from within Tashkent jail by a shadowy White Russian agent named Paul Nazaroff. Several districts and cities fell back into the hands of the Whites. The bells of the cathedral church in Tashkent were rung in joy, but it was short-lived. The Bolsheviks defeated the insurrection, snatched back power and kept it. Nazaroff, freed from jail, was forced to hide and flee across the Tian Shan to Xinjiang, always one step ahead of the dreaded secret police.

The end came swiftly after the arrival in Tashkent of the Red Army commander Mikhail Frunze. Khiva went out with barely a whimper, quietly transforming into the Khorezm People's Republic in February 1920. In September, Mikhail Frunze's fresh, disciplined army captured Bukhara after a four-day siege of the Ark (citadel). The emir fled to Afghanistan, taking with him his company of dancing boys but abandoning his harem to the Bolshevik soldiers.

The Soviet Era

From the start the Bolsheviks changed the face of Central Asia. Alongside ambitious goals to emancipate women, redistribute land and carry out mass literacy campaigns, the revolutionaries levied grievous requisitions of food, livestock, cotton, land and forced farm labour. Trade and agricultural output in the once-thriving colonies plummeted. The ensuing famines claimed nearly a million lives; some say many more.

1937	1941–45	1948	1949
The entire Kyrgyz Soviet government (140 people) are shot to death and their bodies dumped in a brick kiln at Chon-Tash outside Bishkek, as part of Stalin's purges.	Over 22 million Soviet citizens die in WWII, known locally as the Great Patriotic War. Kazakhstan and Uzbekistan each receive over one million refugees.	Ashgabat is destroyed in an earthquake; 110,000, almost two-thirds of the city, perish.	The USSR detonates its first nuclear device at the Polygon outside Semipalatinsk in Kazakhstan, following up with 460 tests over the next 40 years.

Forced Collectivisation

Forced collectivisation was the 'definite stage of development' implicit in time-warping the entire population of Central Asia from feudalism to communism. This occurred during the USSR's grand First Five Year Plan (1928–32). The intent of collectivisation was first to eliminate private property and second, in the case of the nomadic Kazakhs and Kyrgyz, to put an end to their wandering lifestyle.

The effect was disastrous. When the orders arrived, most people simply slaughtered their herds and ate what they could rather than give them up. This led to famine in subsequent years, and widespread disease. Resisters were executed and imprisoned. Evidence exists that during this period Stalin had a personal hand in tinkering with meagre food supplies in order to induce famines. His aims seem to have been to subjugate the people's will and to depopulate Kazakhstan, which was good real estate for Russian expansion.

Political Repression

Undeveloped Central Asia had no shortage of bright, sincere people willing to work for national liberation and democracy. After the tsar fell they jostled for power in their various parties, movements and factions. Even after they were swallowed into the Soviet state, some members of these groups had high profiles in regional affairs. Such a group was Alash Orda, formed by Kazakhs and Kyrgyz in 1917, which even held the reins of a short-lived autonomous government.

By the late 1920s, the former nationalists and democrats, indeed the entire intelligentsia, were causing Stalin serious problems. From their posts in the communist administration they had front-row seats at the Great Leader's horror show, including collectivisation. Many of them began to reason, and to doubt. Stalin, reading these signs all over the USSR, foresaw that brains could be just as dangerous as guns. Throughout the 1930s he proceeded to have all possible dissenters eliminated. Alash Orda members were among the first to die, in 1927 and 1928.

Thus began the systematic murder, called the Purges, of untold tens of thousands of Central Asians. Arrests were usually made late at night. Confined prisoners were rarely tried; if any charges at all were brought, they ran along the lines of 'having bourgeoisie-nationalist or Pan-Turkic attitudes'. Mass executions and burials were common. Sometimes entire sitting governments were disposed of in this way, as happened in Kyrgyzstan.

Construction of Nationalities

The solution to the 'nationality question' in Central Asia remains the most graphically visible effect of Soviet rule: it drew the lines on the

Central Asia is strewn with ancient petroglyphs, the best of which are at Saimaluu Tash in Kyrgyzstan and Tamgaly in southeastern Kazakhstan, the latter a Unesco World Heritage Site.

1954	1961	1966	1959–82
Virgin Lands campaign in Kazakhstan leads to Slav immigration and, eventually, massive environmental degradation.	Four years after the Sputnik satellite, Yuri Gagarin blasts off from the Baykonur Cosmodrome in Kazakhstan to become the first man in space. The first woman in space sets off three years later.	Tashkent is levelled in an earthquake, leaving 300,000 homeless. Plans for a new Soviet showcase city are drawn up.	Rule of Sharaf Rashidov ushers in an era of corruption and cotton-related scandal in Soviet Uzbekistan, though many locals praise him for promoting Uzbek regional interests and nationalism.

map. Before the Russian Revolution the peoples of Central Asia had no concept of a firm national border. They had plotted their identities by a tangle of criteria: religion, clan, valley or oasis, way of life, even social status. The Soviets, however, believed that such a populace was fertile soil for dangerous Pan-Islamism and Pan-Turkism and that these philosophies were threats to the regime.

So, starting in about 1924, nations were invented: Kazakh, Kyrgyz, Tajik, Turkmen, Uzbek. Each was given its own distinct ethnic profile, language, history and territory. Where an existing language or history was not apparent or was not suitably distinct from others, these were supplied and disseminated. Islam was cut away from each national heritage, essentially relegated to the status of an outmoded and oppressive cult, and severely suppressed throughout the Soviet period.

Some say that Stalin personally directed the drawing of the boundary lines. Each of the republics was shaped to contain numerous pockets of the different nationalities, and each with long-standing claims to the land. Everyone had to admit that only a strong central government could keep order on such a map. The present face of Central Asia is a product of this 'divide and rule' technique.

World War II

'The Great Patriotic War Against Fascist Germany' galvanised the whole USSR and in the course of the war Central Asia was drawn further into the Soviet fold. Economically the region lost ground from 1941–45 but a sizeable boost came in the form of industrial enterprises arriving ready-to-assemble in train cars: evacuated from the war-threatened parts of the USSR, they were relocated to the remote safety of Central Asia. They remained there after the war and kept on producing.

For many wartime draftees, WWII presented an opportunity to escape the oppressive Stalinist state. One Central Asian scholar claims that more than half of the 1.5 million Central Asians mobilised in the war deserted. Large numbers of them, as well as prisoners of war, actually turned their coats and fought for the Germans against the Soviets.

Agriculture

The tsarist pattern for the Central Asian economy had been overwhelmingly agricultural; so it was with the Soviets. Each republic was 'encouraged' to specialise in a limited range of products, which made their individual economies dependent on the Soviet whole. Tajik SSR built the world's fourth-largest aluminium plant but all the aluminium had to be brought in from outside the region.

The Uzbek SSR soon supplied no less than 64% of Soviet cotton, making the USSR the world's second-largest cotton producer after the USA.

Before the arrival of Islam, Central Asia sheltered pockets of Zoroastrianism, Manichaeism, Judaism, Nestorian Christianity and Buddhism. In the 8th century there were even Nestorian bishoprics in Herat, Samarkand and Merv.

1979–89	1988	1989	8 Dec 1991
Soviet army invades Afghanistan. The ensuing war with the mujaheddin results in the death of 15,000 Soviets, 1.5 million Afghans, and the exodus of six million refugees.	Half a million saiga antelope die suddenly on the Turgay Steppe, northeast of the Aral Sea. Locals blame a nearby biological-weapons testing site or the dumping of rocket fuel from Baykonur Cosmodrome.	Nevada Semey Movement forces an end to nuclear tests in Kazakhstan. It is the first great popular protest movement in the USSR. Ethnic violence breaks out in the Fergana Valley.	Collapse of the Soviet Union, as Russia, Ukraine and Belarus found the Commonwealth of Independent States (CIS). Two weeks later the Central Asian ex-Soviet republics join; Gorbachev resigns three days later.

Into the cotton bowl poured the diverted waters of the Syr-Darya and Amu-Darya, while downstream the Aral Sea was left to dry up. Over the cotton-scape was spread a whole list of noxious agricultural chemicals, which have wound up polluting waters, blowing around in dust storms, and causing serious health problems for residents of the area.

In 1954 the Soviet leader Nikita Khrushchev launched the Virgin Lands campaign. The purpose was to jolt agricultural production, especially of wheat, to new levels. The method was to put Kazakh SSR's enormous steppes under the plough and resettle huge numbers of Russians to work the farms. Massive, futuristic irrigation schemes were drawn up to water the formerly arid grassland, with water taken from as far away as the Ob River in Siberia. The initial gains in productivity soon dwindled as the fragile exposed soil of the steppes literally blew away in the wind. The Russians, however, remained.

The Soviet-Afghan War

In 1979 the Soviet army invaded Afghanistan, determined to prop up a crumbling communist regime on their doorstep. In retrospect, someone should have consulted the history books beforehand, for the lessons of history are clear; no one wins a war in Afghanistan.

Of the 50,000 Soviet troops engaged in Afghanistan, up to 20,000 were Central Asians, mainly Tajiks and Uzbeks, drafted into the war to liberate their backward relatives. They faced a poorly equipped but highly motivated guerrilla force, the mujaheddin, united for once in their jihad against the godless invaders.

Funding for the mujaheddin soon poured in from the USA, determined to bleed the USSR and create a 'Soviet Vietnam'. The biggest covert CIA operation of all time funnelled funds through the Pakistan secret service (Inter-Services Intelligence, or ISI), and the Afghans quickly found themselves in the middle of a proxy Cold War.

In the end, after 10 years of brutal guerrilla war that claimed the lives of 15,000 Soviets and 1.5 million Afghans, the Soviets finally pulled out, limping back over the Amu-Darya to Termiz. They weren't quite massacred to a man as the British before them, but the strains of war indelibly contributed to the cracking of the Soviet empire. Over six million Afghans had fled the country for refugee camps in neighbouring Iran and Pakistan. Afghanistan was shattered and the USSR would never recover.

Benefits of the Soviet Era

In spite of their heavy-handedness, the Soviets made profound improvements in Central Asia. Overall standards of living were raised considerably with the help of health care and a vast new infrastructure. Central Asia was provided with industrial plants, mines, farms, ranches

HISTORY THE SOVIET ERA

1992–97	1997	1999	13 May 2005
Clan-based civil war in Tajikistan claims 60,000 lives and displaces 500,000.	Astana replaces Almaty as the capital of Kazakhstan, shifting focus to the centre of the steppe. An ambitious program of architectural projects is initiated.	Uzbek president Karimov narrowly escapes assassination when car bombs explode in Tashkent. Blame falls on the Islamic Movement of Uzbekistan (IMU) as thousands are arrested in the ensuing crackdown.	Massacre of between 200 and 1000 unarmed protesters by government troops in Andijon, Uzbekistan. The incident sours relationships between Uzbekistan and the USA and Europe.

and services employing millions of people. Outside the capitals, the face of the region today is still largely a Soviet one.

Education reached all social levels (previously education was through the limited, men-only network of Islamic schools and medressas), and pure and applied sciences were nurtured. Literacy rates hit 97% and the languages of all nationalities were given standard literary forms. The Kyrgyz language was given an alphabet for the first time.

Soviet women had 'economic equality' and although this meant that they had the chance to study and work alongside men *while* retaining all the responsibilities of home makers, female literacy approached male levels, maternity leave was introduced and women assumed positions of responsibility in middle-level administration as well as academia.

Artistic expression was encouraged within the confines of communist ideology, and cinemas and theatres were built. The Central Asian republics now boast active communities of professional artists who were trained, sometimes lavishly, by the Soviet state. And through the arts, the republics were allowed to develop their distinctive national traditions and identities (within bounds).

Post-Soviet Central Asia

One Russian humorist has summed up his country's century in two sentences: 'After titanic effort, blood, sweat and tears, the Soviet people brought forth a new system. Unfortunately, it was the wrong one'.

By the spring of 1991 the parliaments of all five Central Asian republics had declared their sovereignty. However, when the failure of the August coup against Gorbachev heralded the end of the USSR, none of the republics were prepared for the reality of independence.

With independence suddenly thrust upon them, the old Soviet guard was essentially the only group with the experience and the means to rule. Most of these men are still in power today. All the Central Asian governments are still authoritarian to some degree, running the gamut from pure ancien régime–style autocracy (Turkmenistan), to a tightly controlled mixture of neocommunism and spurious nationalism (Uzbekistan), to a marginally more enlightened 'channelled transition' to democracy and a market economy (Kazakhstan and Kyrgyzstan).

In some ways, not much has changed. In most of the republics the old Communist Party apparatus simply renamed itself using various (unintentionally ironic) combinations of the words 'People', 'Party' and 'Democratic'. Political opposition was completely marginalised (Turkmenistan), banned (Uzbekistan), or tolerated but closely watched (Kazakhstan, Kyrgyzstan and Tajikistan). Kazakhstan suddenly found itself with a space program and nuclear weapons (which it promptly handed

The Persian historian Juvaini summed up the Mongol invasions succinctly: 'They came, they sapped, they fired, they slew, they looted and they left.'

2005	2006	Jun 2010	2011
Kyrgyzstan's Tulip Revolution sweeps President Akaev from power, forcing curbs on the new president's power.	Turkmenistan's 'President for life' Niyazov (Turkmenbashi) dies, ending one of the modern era's great personality cults. President Gurbanguly Berdymukhamedov continues Niyazov's repressive regime.	At least 200 killed and 400,000 displaced in ethnic clashes between Kyrgyz and Uzbeks in Osh in the Kyrgyz Fergana Valley. Tens of thousands of Uzbek refugees flee to the Uzbekistan–Kyrgyzstan border.	A turbulent year in Kazakhstan sees suicide bombings in Taraz, Atyrau and Aktobe, riots in western Kazakhstan and the reelection of President Nazarbayev with 95% of the vote.

back to Russia, making it the only country ever to voluntarily return to nuclear-free status). All the republics swiftly formed national airlines from whatever Aeroflot planes happened to be parked on their runways on the day after independence.

Yet in most ways, everything has changed. The end of the old Soviet subsidies meant a decline in everything from economic subsidies to education levels. The deepest economic trauma was/is felt in the countryside. Most heart-rending were the pensioners, especially the Slavs, whose pensions were made worthless overnight with the devaluation of the rouble. Throughout the 1990s, one of the most common sights across Central Asia was watery-eyed *babushkas* (old women) sitting quietly on many street corners, surrounded by a few worthless possessions for sale, trying not to look like beggars. Suddenly the Soviet era began to look like a golden age.

The New Great Game

Central Asia and the Caspian region is a mother lode of energy and raw materials, representing perhaps the most concentrated mass of untapped wealth in the world, a wealth measured in trillions of dollars. It is this fact that quietly drives many countries' Central Asian policies.

All eyes are on Kazakhstan, Central Asia's brightest economy, sitting pretty on what is estimated to be the word's third-largest oil reserves; but don't forget Turkmenistan, which boasts the world's fourth-largest reserves of natural gas. Kazakhstan and Uzbekistan also have major natural-gas reserves.

As Western energy firms jockey to strike high-stake deals in a region of interlocking interests, this scramble is taking on a geopolitical significance. Russia's traditional stranglehold on supply routes has been challenged in recent years by new pipelines to Turkey and more pipe dreams are planned through Afghanistan.

China has also become a major player in the scramble for influence. It recently spent billions of dollars to become the main shareholder of PetroKazakhstan and build a 3000km-long pipeline to Ürümqi. There are epic plans to continue this along the former Silk Road to Japan, making China the energy corridor of the east.

Governments are well aware of the dangers of laying major oil pipelines through volatile Central Asia, but the strategic need to ensure fuel supplies and the financial rewards are simply too fantastic to walk away from. This superpower competition for oil and gas in the region – dubbed 'round two of the Great Game' – is a rivalry which will have increasing resonance over the ensuing decades.

So many Russian Slavs were captured or sold into slavery by nomadic invaders or slave traders that the word entered the English language as the source of the word 'slave'.

For more on that quintessential Great Gamester, Francis Young-husband, read Patrick French's excellent biography *Younghusband* (1995).

Jul 2012	2014	2 Sep 2016
Fighting in the streets of Khorog in Tajikistan's Gorno-Badakhshan region leaves 40 people dead as President Rakhmonov ('Rahmon') tries to reassert control over regional commanders.	US and NATO troops transport 70,000 vehicles and 120,000 shipping containers across Central Asia as part of a withdrawal from Afghanistan, paying hundreds of millions of dollars in transit fees.	President Islam Karimov of Uzbekistan dies after 25 years in power. He is buried in Samarkand. Prime Minister Shavkat Mirziyoyev assumes control.

The Silk Road

For centuries, the great civilisations of East and West were connected by the Silk Road, a fragile network of shifting intercontinental trade routes that threaded across Asia's highest mountains and bleakest deserts. The heartland of this trade was Central Asia, whose cosmopolitan cities grew fabulously wealthy. Traders, pilgrims, refugees and diplomats all travelled the Silk Road, exchanging ideas, goods and technologies in what has been called history's original 'information superhighway'.

Silk Routes

It was only in the 19th century that the term 'Silk Road' was thought up, coined for the first time by German geographer Ferdinand von Richthofen.

The first thing to understand is that there was actually no such thing as a single 'Silk Road' – routes changed over the years according to local conditions. Parts of the network might be beset by war, robbers or natural disaster: the northern routes were plagued by nomadic horsemen and a lack of settlements to provide fresh supplies and mounts; the south by fearsome deserts and frozen mountain passes.

Though the road map expanded over the centuries, the network had its main eastern terminus at the Chinese capital Chang'an (modern Xi'an) and extended through the desert and mountains of Central Asia into Iran, the Levant and Constantinople. Major branches headed south over the Karakoram range to India and north via the Zhungarian Gap and across the steppes to Khorezm and the Russian Volga.

Caravans & Trade

Silk was certainly not the only trade on the Silk Road but it epitomised the qualities – light, valuable, exotic and greatly desired – required for such a long-distance trade. China's early need for horses to battle nomads on its northern border was actually the main impetus for the early growth of the Silk Road; the silk was traded to the nomads in exchange for a steady supply of mounts.

Though the balance of trade was heavily stacked in favour of China (as it is today!), traffic ran both ways. China received gold, silver, ivory, lapis, jade, coral, wool, rhino horn, tortoiseshell, horses, Mediterranean coloured glass (an industrial mystery as inscrutable to the Chinese as silk was in the West), cucumbers, walnuts, pomegranates, golden peaches from Samarkand, sesame, garlic, grapes and wine, plus – an early Parthian craze – acrobats and ostriches. Goods arriving at the western end included silk, porcelain, paper, tea, ginger, rhubarb, lacquerware, bamboo, Arabian spices and incense, medicinal herbs, gems and perfumes.

And in the middle lay Central Asia, a great clearing house that provided its native beasts – horses and two-humped Bactrian camels – to keep the goods flowing in both directions. There was in fact little 'through traffic' on the Silk Road; caravanners were mostly short- and medium-distance haulers who marketed and took on freight along a given beat. The earliest exchanges were based on barter between steppe nomads and settled towns. Only later did a monetary economy enable long-distance routes to develop.

Bukhara and Samarkand marked the halfway break, where caravans from Aleppo and Baghdad met traders from Kashgar and Yarkand. A network of *rabat* (caravanserais) grew up along the route, offering lodgings, stables and stores. Middlemen such as the Sogdians amassed great fortunes, much of which went to beautifying cosmopolitan and luxuriant caravan towns such as Gurganj, Merv and Bukhara. The cities offered equally vital services, such as brokers to set up contracts, banking houses to offer lines of credit, and markets to sell goods.

The Cultural Legacy

The Silk Road gave rise to unprecedented trade, but its true legacy was the intellectual interchange and refining of ideas, technologies and faiths that the trade routes facilitated. It's interesting to note that while the bulk of trade headed west, religious ideas primarily travelled east.

Buddhism spread along the trade routes to wend its way from India to Central Asia, China and back again. It's hard to imagine that Buddhist monasteries once dotted Central Asia. Today only the faintest archaeological evidence remains: at Adjina-Tepe in Tajikistan, Kuva in the Fergana Valley, and Fayoz-Tepe and the Zurmala Stupa around Termiz in Uzbekistan.

The spread of Buddhism caused Indian, Chinese, Greek and Tibetan artistic styles to merge, forming the exquisite Serindian art of Chinese Turkestan and the Buddhist Gandharan art of Pakistan and Afghanistan. Musical styles and instruments (such as the lute) also crossed borders as artists followed in the wake of traders, pilgrims and missionaries.

To religion and art can be added technology transfer. Sogdian traders revealed the skills behind chain mail, fine glass, wine and irrigation. The Chinese not only taught Central Asia how to cast iron but also how to make paper. Prisoners from the Battle of Talas established paper production in Samarkand and then Baghdad, from where it gradually spread into Europe, making it culturally the most important secret passed along the Silk Road.

The Death of the Silk Road

The Silk Road received a major blow when China turned its back on the cosmopolitanism of the Tang Dynasty (618–907) and retreated behind its Great Wall. The destruction and turbulence wreaked by Chinggis (Genghis) Khan and Timur (Tamerlane) and the literal and figurative drying up of the Silk Road led to the further abandonment of cities in desert regions. The nail in the coffin was the opening of more cost-effective maritime trading routes between Europe and Asia in the 16th century.

The Rebirth of the Silk Road

Since the fall of the Soviet Union, Central Asia has seen a minirevival in all things Silk Road. The reestablishment of rail links to China and Iran, the growth of border trade over the Torugart, Irkeshtam, Qolma and Khunjerab passes, the rebuilding of bridges to Afghanistan and the increase in vital oil and gas pipelines along former silk routes have all reconnected the 'stans with their ethnic and linguistic relatives to the south and east, while offering a means to shake off ties with Moscow. Goods from Turkey, Iran and China now dominate local bazaars as they did centuries ago. Even drug runners use former silk routes to transport their heroin from Afghanistan to Europe.

Future Silk Road dreams include constructing a rail line from the Fergana Valley over the Tian Shan to Kashgar. China's new multibillion dollar Belt and Road initiative is aimed squarely at Silk Road transportation links. Railway cars may have replaced camel trains and scrap metal replaced silk, but the Silk Road remains as relevant as ever.

Silk Road Reading

Silk Road: Monks, Warriors & Merchants by Luce Boulnois (2012)

The Ancient Silk Road Map by Jonathan Tucker & Antonia Tozer (2011)

The Silk Road in World History by Xinru Liu (2010)

THE SILK ROAD THE CULTURAL LEGACY

'The history of the Silk Road is neither a poetic nor a picturesque tale; it is nothing more than scattered islands of peace in an ocean of wars.' Luce Boulnois, *Silk Road: Monks, Warriors & Merchants* (2012)

The Silk Road

SAMARKAND

From its earliest days as Afrosiab/Marakanda to its glory days under Timur, Samarkand has been a great trade centre for 2500 years and has became a literary symbol of Silk Road exotica.

FERGANA VALLEY

It was China's desire for horses to battle its northern nomads that prised open the Silk Road. China's first expeditions west were to Fergana to source its famed 'blood-sweating' Heavenly Horses.

KONYE-URGENCH

Astride a Silk Road branch following the Amu-Darya en route to the Volga region, Konye-Urgench (Gurganj) grew rich on transcontinental trade until the destruction of its irrigation canals shifted the capital to Khiva.

Sarai

Istanbul
(Constantinople)

RUSSIA

Astrakhan

KAZAKHSTAN

BLACK
SEA

Aral
Sea

TURKEY

Trabzon

CASPIAN
SEA

UZBEKISTAN

Konye-Urgench
(Gurganj)

Otrar

Antioch

SYRIA

Palmyra

Tabriz

TURKMENISTAN

Bukhara

Tashkent

Tyre
Gaza

Damascus

Rey
(Tehran)

Margiana
(Merv)

Samarkand

Kokand

Osh

JORDAN

EGYPT

Baghdad

Ecbatana
(Hamadan)

Hecatompylos
(Damghan)

Herat

Balkh

TAJIKISTAN

Ctesiphon

Mashhad

Bamiyan

MEDITERRANEAN
SEA

IRAQ

Kapisa (Kabul)

Basra

IRAN
(PERSIA)

AFGHANISTAN

Peshawar

PENJIKENT

The Sogdians were the Silk Road's consummate middlemen and their communities dotted the Silk Road as far as Xi'an (Chang'an). This Sogdian city was once a thriving bazaar town with a rich mix of artistic influences.

Hormuz

PAKISTAN

External boundaries shown reflect the requirements of the Government of India. Some boundaries may not be those recognised by neighbouring countries. Lonely Planet always tries to show on maps where travellers may need to cross a boundary (and present documentation) irrespective of any dispute.

- – – – Main Silk Road in approx the 2nd century AD
- – – – Main Silk Road in approx the 7th century AD
- – – – Main Silk Road in approx the 13th century AD
- ······· Modern Day International Border

THE WAKHAN

A side branch led through the Pamirs from Tashkurgan towards Balkh and the Indian borderlands beyond. This was the path taken by Marco Polo and Buddhism as it spread east.

N
0 ——— 800 km
0 ——— 500 miles

TASH RABAT

The Silk Road was once lined with *rabat*, or caravanserais, built to offer food and shelter to passing caravans. This 'Stone Caravanserai' in the high pastures of Kyrgyzstan is Central Asia's best.

KASHGAR

This great Central Asian entrepôt remains a vital Silk Road hub at the junction of trade routes to Fergana, the Wakhan, Hunza and the jade markets of Khotan (China).

NORTHERN ROUTE

This route through the Zhungarian Gap, along the north of the Tian Shan, offered easier travel and better pasture for caravans but was also more prone to nomadic raids.

XI'AN (CHANG'AN)

The beginning and end of the Silk Road, Tang China's capital was home to a cosmopolitan mix of Central Asian traders, musicians and such exotica as Samarkand's famed golden peaches.

RUSSIA

Karakoram

MONGOLIA

Lake
Balkash

Gobi
Desert

Hami

Turpan

Balasagun

KYRGYZSTAN

Kucha

Loulan

Jade
Gate

Gansu
Corridor

Luoyang

Aksu

Miran

Dunhuang

Kashgar

Taklamakan
Desert

Yarkand

Xi'an
(Chang'an)

Khotan

CHINA

Leh

DUNHUANG

The best example of Silk Road artistic fusion, with Central Asian, Tibetan, Indian and Chinese influences blending in spectacular Buddhist cave murals on the edge of the desert.

Lhasa

TIBET

Delhi

NEPAL

BHUTAN

INDIA

JADE GATE

Jade from Khotan was as important a Silk Road product as silk. This customs gate and defensive garrison marked the division between the Central Asian and Chinese worlds.

BANGLADESH

INDIA

TASHKURGAN

The 'Stone Tower' was one of the great trading posts of the Silk Road, halfway along the route and a place of pause before the tough mountain or desert crossings to come.

SOUTHERN ROUTE

A string of oases along the fringes of the Taklamakan Desert made this tough desert stretch feasible, until climate change dried wells and covered its cities with shifting sand.

People

From gold-toothed Turkmen in shaggy, dreadlocked hats to high-cheekboned Kyrgyz herders whose eyes still hint at their nomadic past, Central Asia presents a fascinating collection of portraits and peoples. The most noticeable divide is between the traditionally sedentary peoples, the Uzbeks and Tajiks, and their formerly nomadic neighbours, the Kazakhs, Kyrgyz and Turkmen. In total the population of former Soviet Central Asia is about 67 million. Few areas of its size are home to such tangled demographics and daunting transitions.

Peoples of the Silk Road

Central Asian identity has always centred as much on oases and mountain valleys as it has on the concept of a modern nation state.

Centuries of migrations and invasions, and a location at the crossroads of Asia are the roots behind Central Asia's ethnic diversity. A trip from Ashgabat (Turkmenistan) to Almaty (Kazakhstan) reveals an absorbing array of faces from Turkish, Slavic, Chinese and Middle Eastern to downright Mediterranean – surmounted, incidentally, by an equally vast array of hats.

Before the Russian Revolution of 1917, Central Asians usually identified themselves 'ethnically' as either nomad or *sarts* (settled), as Turk or Persian, as simply Muslim, or by their clan. Later, separate nationalities were 'identified' by Soviet scholars as ordered by Stalin. Although it is easy to see the problems this has created, some Kazakhs and Kyrgyz say that they owe their survival as a nation to the Soviet process of nation building.

Each independent republic inherited an ethnic grab bag from the Soviet system. Thus you'll find Uzbek towns in Kyrgyzstan, legions of Tajiks in the cities of Uzbekistan, Kazakhs grazing their cattle in Kyrgyzstan, Turkmen in Uzbekistan – and Russians and Ukrainians everywhere. Given the complicated mix of nationalities across national boundaries, Central Asia's ethnic situation is surprisingly tranquil, for the main part at least.

Kazakhs

The Kazakhs were nomadic horseback pastoralists until the 1920s; indeed the name Kazakh is said to mean 'free warrior' or 'steppe roamer'. Kazakhs trace their roots to the 15th century, when rebellious kinsmen of an Uzbek khan broke away and settled in present-day Kazakhstan. They divide themselves into three main divisions, or *zhuz,* corresponding to the historical Great (southern Kazakhstan), Middle (north and east Kazakhstan) and Little (west Kazakhstan) Hordes. To this day family and ancestry remain crucial to Kazakhs. 'What *zhuz* do you belong to?' is a common opening question.

Kazakhs make up 64% of Kazakhstan, Kyrgyz 71% of Kyrgyzstan, Uzbeks 80% of Uzbekistan, Tajiks 84% of Tajikistan and Turkmen 85% of Turkmenistan.

Most Kazakhs have Mongolian facial features, similar to the Kyrgyz. Most wear Western or Russian clothes, but you may see women – particularly on special occasions – in long dresses with stand-up collars or brightly decorated velvet waistcoats and heavy jewellery. On similar occasions, men may sport baggy shirts and trousers, sleeveless jackets and wool or cotton robes. This outfit may be topped with either a skullcap or a high, tasselled felt hat resembling nothing so much as an elf's hat.

Kazakh literature is based around heroic epics, many of which concern themselves with the 16th-century clashes between the Kazakhs and Kalmucks, and the heroic *batyr* (warriors) of that age. Apart from various equestrian sports, a favourite Kazakh pastime is *aitys,* which involves two people boasting about their own town, region or clan while running down the other's, in verses full of puns and allusions to Kazakh culture. The person who fails to find a witty comeback loses.

Kazakhs adhere rather loosely to Islam. Reasons for this include the Kazakhs' location on the fringe of the Muslim world and their traditionally nomadic lifestyle, which never sat well with central religious authority. Their earliest contacts with the religion, from the 16th century, came courtesy of wandering Sufi dervishes or ascetics. Many were not converted until the 19th century, and shamanism apparently coexisted with Islam even after conversion.

Having a longer history of Russian influence than other Central Asian peoples, and with international influences now flooding in thanks to Kazakhstan's free-market economy and oil wealth, Kazakhs – in the cities at least – are probably Central Asia's most cosmopolitan people. The women appear the most confident and least restricted by tradition in Central Asia – though the custom of bride-stealing (with or without her collusion) has not altogether disappeared in rural areas and Kazakhstan's south.

The 10 or so million Kazakhs have only recently become a majority in 'their' country, Kazakhstan.

Kyrgyz

As far back as the 2nd century BC, ancestors of the modern Kyrgyz are said to have lived in the upper Yenisey Basin (Ene-Sai, or Yenisey, means 'Mother River' in Kyrgyz) in Siberia. They migrated to the mountains of what is now Kyrgyzstan from the 10th to 15th centuries, some fleeing wars and some arriving in the ranks of Mongol armies.

Many Kyrgyz derive their name from *kyrk kyz,* meaning '40 girls', which fits with oral legends of 40 original clan mothers. Today, ties to such clans as the Bugu (the largest clan), Salto (around Bishkek), Adigine (around Osh) and Sary-Bagysh (northern Kyrgyzstan) remain relevant and politicised. Clans are divided into two federations, the Otuz Uul (30 Sons) of the north and the Ich Kilik of southern Kyrgyzstan. The southern and northern halves of the country remain culturally, ethnically and politically divided, as demonstrated in the violent political upheaval of 2010.

During special events older Kyrgyz women may wear a large white wimple-like turban (known as an *elechek*) with the number of windings indicating her status. Kyrgyz men wear a white, embroidered, tasselled felt cap called an *ak kalpak*. In winter, older men wear a long sheepskin coat and a round fur-trimmed hat called a *tebbetey*.

Most Kyrgyz now live in towns and villages, but herders still do make the annual trek with their yurts up to *jailoos* (summer pastures). Traditions such as the *Manas* epic, horseback sports and eagle hunting remain important cultural denominators. One lingering nomadic custom is that of wife-stealing, whereby a man may simply kidnap a woman he wants to marry (often with some collusion, it must be said), leaving the parents with no option but to negotiate a *kalym* (bride price).

PEOPLE PEOPLES OF THE SILK ROAD

Kazakhs in...

Kazakhstan:
10 million

China:
1.4 million

Russia:
600,000

Uzbekistan:
500,000

Mongolia:
140,000

Turkmenistan:
80,000

Kyrgyzstan:
40,000

Kyrgyz in...

Kyrgyzstan:
three million

Tajikistan:
300,000

Uzbekistan:
180,000

China:
143,000

Afghanistan:
3000

Tajiks

With their Mediterranean features and the occasional green-eyed redhead, the Tajiks are descended from an ancient Indo-European people, the Aryans, making them relatives of present-day Iranians. The term 'Tajik' is a modern invention. Before the 20th century, *taj* was merely a term denoting a Persian speaker (all other Central Asian peoples speak Turkic languages).

Tracing their history back to the Samanids, Bactrians and Sogdians, Tajiks consider themselves to be the oldest ethnic group in Central Asia and one that predates the arrival of the Turkic peoples. Some Tajik nationalists have even demanded that Uzbekistan 'give back' Samarkand and Bukhara, as these cities were long-time centres of Persian culture.

There are in fact many regional Tajik subdivisions and clans (such as the Kulyabis and Khojandis), which is one reason why the country descended into civil war after the fall of the USSR.

Badakhshani (Pamir Tajik; sometimes called mountain Tajiks) are a distinct group, speaking a mix of languages quite distinct from Tajik and following a different branch of Islam. Most Tajiks are Sunni Muslims, but Pamiri Tajiks of the Gorno-Badakhshan region belong to the Ismaili sect of Shiite Islam, and therefore have no formal mosques. Most Badakhshani define themselves primarily according to their valley (Shugni, Rushani, Yazgulami, Wakhi and Ishkashimi), then as Pamiris and finally as Tajiks.

Traditional Tajik dress for men includes a heavy, quilted coat *(chapan),* tied with a sash that also secures a sheathed dagger, and a black embroidered cap *(tupi),* which is similar to the Uzbek *doppe.* Tajik women could almost be identified in the dark, with their long, psychedelically coloured dresses *(kurta),* matching headscarves *(rumol),* striped trousers worn under the dress *(izor)* and bright slippers.

There are almost eight million Tajiks in Afghanistan (about one quarter of the population) and their language Dari (very similar to Tajik) has served as the language of government for centuries. There are also around 33,000 Sarikol and Wakhi Tajiks in China's Tashkurgan Tajik Autonomous County. Wakhi Tajiks also live in northern Pakistan.

Tajiks in...

Tajikistan:
4.4 million

Afghanistan:
7.7 million

Uzbekistan:
630,000

Kazakhstan:
100,000

China:
33,000

Turkmen

Legend has it that all Turkmen are descended from the fabled Oghuz Khan or from the warriors who rallied into clans around his 24 grandsons. Most historians believe that they were displaced nomadic horse-breeding clans who, in the 10th century, drifted into the oases around the Karakum desert (and into Persia, Syria and Anatolia) from the foothills of the Altay Mountains in the wake of the Seljuq Turks.

Turkmen men are easily recognisable in their huge, shaggy sheepskin hats *(telpek),* either white (for special occasions) or black with thick ringlets resembling dreadlocks, worn year-round on top of a skullcap, even on the hottest days. As one Turkmen explained, they'd rather suffer the heat of their own heads than that of the sun. Traditional dress consists of baggy trousers tucked into knee-length boots, and white shirts under the knee-length *khalat,* a cherry-red cotton jacket. Older men wear a long, belted coat.

Turkmen women wear heavy, ankle-length velvet or silk dresses, the favourite colours being wine reds and maroons, with colourful trousers underneath. A woman's hair is always tied back and concealed under a colourful scarf. Older women often wear a *khalat* thrown over their heads as protection from the sun's rays.

The Turkmen shared the nomad's affinity for Sufism, which is strongly represented in Turkmenistan alongside the cult of sheikhs (holy men),

Turkmen in...

Turkmenistan:
3.6 million

Iran:
one million

Afghanistan:
650,000

amulets, shrines and pilgrimage. The Turkmen language is closest to Azeri. Interestingly, there was a Turkmen literary language as early as the mid-18th century.

Uzbeks

The Uzbek khans, Islamised descendants of Chinggis (Genghis) Khan, left their home in southern Siberia in search of conquest, establishing themselves in what is now Uzbekistan by the 15th century, clashing and then mixing with the Timurids. The Uzbek Shaybanid dynasty oversaw the tricky transition from nomad to settler, although the original Mongol clan identities (such as the Kipchak, Mangits and Karluks) remain.

The focal point of Uzbek society is still the network of tight-knit urban *mahalla* (districts) and *kishlak* (rural villages). Advice on all matters is sought from an *aksakal* (revered elder, literally 'white beard'), whose authority is conferred by the community. In general Uzbeks resisted Russification and emerged from Soviet rule with a strong sense of identity and cultural heritage.

Uzbek men traditionally wear long quilted coats tied by a brightly coloured sash. Nearly all older men wear the *doppe* or *doppilar,* a black, four-sided skullcap embroidered in white. In winter, older men wear a furry *telpek.* Uzbek women are fond of dresses in sparkly, brightly coloured cloth *(ikat),* often as a knee-length gown with trousers of the same material underneath. One or two braids worn in the hair indicate that a woman is married; more mean that she is single. Eyebrows that grow together over the bridge of the nose are considered attractive and are often supplemented with pencil for the right effect. Both sexes flash lots of gold teeth.

Slavs

Russians and Ukrainians have settled in Central Asia in several waves, the first in the 19th century with colonisation, and the latest in the 1950s during the Virgin Lands campaign. Numerous villages in remoter parts

Uzbeks in...

Uzbekistan: 18 million

Afghanistan: 2.6 million

Tajikistan: 1.6 million

Kyrgyzstan: 690,000

Kazakhstan: 457,000

Turkmenistan: 396,000

China: 14,700

PEOPLE PEOPLES OF THE SILK ROAD

BUZKASHI

In a region where many people are descended from hot-blooded nomads, no one would expect badminton to be the national sport. Even so, the regional Central Asian variants of the Afghan game *buzkashi* (literally 'grabbing the dead goat') are wild beyond belief. As close to warfare as a sport can get, *buzkashi* is a bit like rugby on horseback, in which the 'ball' is the headless carcass of a calf, goat or sheep.

The game begins with the carcass in the centre of a circle at one end of a field; at the other end is any number of horsemen who charge towards the carcass when a signal is given. The aim is to gain possession of the carcass and carry it up the field and around a post, with the winning rider being the one who finally drops it back in the circle. All the while there's a frenzied horsebacked tug-of-war going on as each competitor tries to gain possession; smashed noses and wrenched shoulders are all part of the fun.

Not surprisingly, the game is said to date from the days of Chinggis (Genghis) Khan, a time when it enforced the nomadic values necessary for collective survival – courage, adroitness, wit and strength, while propagating a remarkable skill on horseback. The point of the game used to be the honour, and perhaps notoriety, of the victor, but gifts such as silk *chapan* (cloaks), cash or even cars are common these days.

Buzkashi takes place mainly between autumn ploughing and spring planting seasons, in the cooler months of spring and autumn, at weekends, particularly during Nowruz or to mark special occasions such as weddings or national days. Look for a game in Kyrgyzstan (where it's known as *kok boru* or *ulak-tartysh*), Uzbekistan *(kupkari)* and Kazakhstan *(kokpar).* Navrus (Nauroz) is the best time to find a game on, especially at Hissar (outside Dushanbe) or the hippodrome at Shymkent in Kazakhstan.

Kazakhs and Kyrgyz share many customs and have similar languages, and in a sense they are simply the steppe (Kazakh) and mountain (Kyrgyz) variants of the same people.

of Central Asia were founded by the early settlers and are still inhabited by their descendants.

Many Slavs, feeling deeply aggrieved as political and administrative power devolves to 'local' people, have emigrated to Russia and Ukraine. At the height of the migration more than 280,000 Russians left Kazakhstan and 200,000 left Tajikistan in a single year, most of them well-educated professionals. Some have returned, either disillusioned with life in the motherland or reaffirmed in the knowledge that Central Asia is their home, like it or not. Some 3.8 million Russians and 333,000 Ukrainians live in Kazakhstan alone.

Other Peoples

Dungans are Muslim Chinese who first moved across the border in 1882, mainly to Kazakhstan and Kyrgyzstan, to escape persecution after failed Muslim rebellions. Few still speak Chinese, though their cuisine remains distinctive.

More than 500,000 Koreans arrived in Central Asia as deportees in WWII. You'll most likely see them selling their pickled salads in many bazaars.

Five hundred thousand Germans were deported in WWII from their age-old home in the Volga region, or came as settlers (some of them Mennonites) in the late 19th century. Most have since departed to Germany but pockets remain, and you'll come across the occasional village in Central Asia with a German name, such as Rotfront in Kyrgyzstan. Likewise, most Jews, an important part of Bukharan commerce since the 9th century, have moved to Israel (and Queens, New York). The chief rabbi of Central Asia remains in Bukhara, though.

Karakalpaks occupy their own republic in northwest Uzbekistan and have cultural and linguistic ties with Kazakhs, Uzbeks and Kyrgyz.

Kurds are another WWII-era addition to the melting pot, with many living in Kazakhstan. Estimates of their numbers in Central Asia range from 150,000 to over a million. Meskhetian Turks have groups in the Fergana (the largest concentration), Chuy and Ili Valleys. It is estimated that there are half a million Uyghurs in the former Soviet Central Asian republics (having moved there from Xinjiang after Chinese persecution in the late 19th century), with about half of these in Kazakhstan.

You may see colourfully dressed South Asian–looking women and children begging or working as fortune tellers. These are Central Asian gypsies, called luli (chuki), who number around 30,000, speak Tajik and originate from areas around Samarkand, southern Tajikistan and Turkmenistan.

Daily Life

Out of Steppe: The Lost Peoples of Central Asia (2009) follows British author Daniel Metcalfe through five of the 'stans searching for lost communities of Karakalpaks, Bukharan Jews, Germans and Sogdians.

It's been a social roller coaster in Central Asia since independence: the overall birth rate is down, deaths from all causes are up, life expectancy has dropped and migration (most especially emigration) has reshaped the ethnic balance of the region. Many older Central Asians lost their social and cultural bearings with the fall of the Soviet Union. Health levels are plummeting, drug addiction is up and alcoholism has acquired the proportions of a national tragedy.

But it's not all bad news. Traditional life is reasserting itself in today's economic vacuum and tourism projects are encouraging traditional crafts, sports and music. Communities remain strong and notions of hospitality remain instinctual despite the economic hardships. After 25 years of uncertainty, most people have found their way in the new order. For a younger generation the USSR is ancient history.

> **HOLY SMOKE**
>
> In markets, stations and parks all over Central Asia you'll see gypsy women and children asking for a few coins to wave their pans of burning herbs around you or the premises. The herb is called *isriq* in Uzbek, and the smoke is said to be good medicine against colds and flu (and the evil eye), and a cheap alternative to scarce medicines. Some people also burn it when they move into a new home.

Body Language

A heartfelt handshake between Central Asian men is a gesture of great warmth, elegance and beauty. Many Central Asian men also place their right hand on the heart and bow or incline the head slightly, a highly addictive gesture that you may find yourself echoing quite naturally.

Good friends throughout the region shake hands by gently placing their hands, thumbs up, in between another's. There's no grabbing or Western-style firmness, just a light touch. Sometimes a good friend will use his right hand to pat the other's. If you are in a room full of strangers, it's polite to go around the room shaking hands with everyone. Don't be offended if someone offers you his wrist if his hands are dirty. Some say the custom originates from the need to prove that you come unarmed as a friend.

Women don't usually shake hands but touch each others' shoulders with right hands and slightly stroke them. Younger women, in particular, will often kiss an elder woman on the cheek as a sign of respect.

Traditional Culture

In Islam, a guest – Muslim or not – has a position of honour not very well understood in the West. If someone visits you and you don't have much to offer, as a Christian you'd be urged to share what you have; as a Muslim you're urged to give it all away. Guests are to be treated with absolute selflessness.

For a visitor to a Muslim country, even one as casual about Islam as Kazakhstan or Kyrgyzstan, this is a constant source of pleasure, temptation and sometimes embarrassment. The majority of Central Asians, especially rural ones, have little to offer but their hospitality, and a casual guest could drain a host's resources and never know it. And yet to refuse such an invitation (or to offer to bring food or to help with the cost) would almost certainly be an insult.

All you can do is enjoy it, honour their customs as best you can, and take yourself courteously out of the picture before you become a burden. If for some reason you do want to decline, couch your refusal in gracious and diplomatic terms, allowing the would-be host to save face. As an example, if you are offered bread, you should at least taste a little piece before taking your leave.

If you are really lucky you might be invited to a *toi* (celebration) such as a *kelin toi* (wedding celebration), a *beshik toi* (nine days after the birth of a child) or a *sunnat toi* (circumcision party). Other celebrations are held to mark the birth, name giving and first haircut of a child.

Women in Central Asia

Women generally have a hard lot in Central Asia. Despite Soviet efforts to bring women into the mainstream of society (early communist theory saw women as a surrogate proletariat) and mass political movements such as the rallies to burn women's veils in 1926–28, women have yet to

Some Central Asians address elders with a shortened form of the elder's name, adding the suffix 'ke'. Thus Abkhan becomes Abeke, Nursultan becomes Nureke and so on.

NAUROZ

By far the biggest Central Asian holiday is the spring festival of Nauroz ('New Days'; also Navrus in Uzbek, Nauryz in Kazakh, Novruz in Turkmen, Nooruz in Kyrgyz and Nauroz in Dari). Nauroz is an adaptation of pre-Islamic vernal equinox or renewal celebrations, celebrated approximately on the spring equinox, though now normally fixed on 21 March (22 March in Kazakhstan). Nauroz was being celebrated in Central Asia before Alexander the Great passed through.

In Soviet times this was a private affair, even banned for a time, but it's now an official two-day festival, with traditional games, music and drama festivals, street art and colourful fairs, plus partying, picnics and the visiting of family and friends. Families traditionally pay off debts before the start of the holiday.

The traditional Nauroz dish, prepared only by women, is *sumalak* – wheat soaked in water for three days until it sprouts, then ground, mixed with oil, flour and sugar, and cooked on a low heat for 24 hours. To add to this, seven items, all beginning with the Arabic sound 'sh', are laid on the dinner table during Nauroz – *sharob* (wine), *shir* (milk), *shirinliklar* (sweets), *shakar* (sugar), *sharbat* (sherbet), *sham* (a candle) and *shona* (a new bud). The candles are a throwback to pre-Islamic traditions and the new bud symbolises the renewal of life.

achieve much equality. In fact the growth of nationalism and conservative Islam since independence has in many ways pushed back women's rights.

The practice of *kalym* (bride price; money or property given to a bride's family) is common in the Fergana Valley, while forced kidnappings happen in Kyrgyzstan. Elsewhere arranged marriages are the norm. Money is rarely invested in a girl's education and young wives often receive harsh treatment from their mothers-in-law. The most common cause for divorce is infertility, and childless women make up the bulk of pilgrims at holy sites across Central Asia.

As a generalisation, women have a greater public role in Kyrgyzstan and Kazakhstan, while Uzbek and Turkmen culture remains more deeply patriarchal, especially in the Fergana Valley.

Islam in Central Asia

With the exception of rapidly shrinking communities of Jews and Russian Orthodox Christians, small minorities of Roman Catholics and evangelical Lutherans, and a few Buddhist Koreans in the Fergana Valley and Kyrgyzstan, nearly everyone from the Caspian Sea to Kashgar is Muslim, at least in principle. The years since independence have seen the resurgence of a faith that is only beginning to recover from 70 years of Soviet-era 'militant atheism'.

Islam's History & Schisms

In AD 612, the Prophet Mohammed, then a wealthy Arab of Mecca in present-day Saudi Arabia, began preaching a new religious philosophy, Islam, based on revelations from Allah (Islam's name for God). These revelations were eventually compiled into Islam's holiest book, the Quran.

Islam incorporates elements of Judaism and Christianity (eg heaven and hell, a creation story much like the Garden of Eden, stories similar to Noah's Ark), and shares a reverence for many of the key figures in the Judeo-Christian faith (Abraham/Ibrahim, Moses/Musa, Jesus/Isa), but considers them all to be forerunners of the Prophet Mohammed. While Jews and Christians are respected as People of the Book (ahl al-Kitab), Islam regards itself as the summation of and last word on these faiths.

In 622 the Prophet Mohammed and his followers were forced to flee to Medina due to religious persecution (the Islamic calendar counts its years from this flight, known as Hejira). There he built a political base and an army, taking Mecca in 630 and eventually overrunning Arabia. The militancy of the faith meshed neatly with a latent Arab nationalism and within a century Islam reached Central Asia from Spain.

Succession disputes after the Prophet's death in 632 soon split the community. When the fourth caliph, the Prophet's son-in-law Ali, was assassinated in 661, his followers and descendants became the founders of the Shiite sect. Others accepted as caliph the governor of Syria, a brother-in-law of the Prophet, and this line has become the modern-day orthodox Sunni sect. In 680 a chance for reconciliation was lost when Ali's surviving son Hussain (Hussein) and most of his male relatives were killed at Kerbala in Iraq by Sunni partisans.

About 80% of all Central Asians are Muslim, nearly all of them Sunni (and indeed nearly all of the Hanafi school, one of Sunnism's four main schools of religious law). The main exception is a tightly knit community of Ismailis in the remote western Pamirs of Gorno-Badakhshan in eastern Tajikistan.

A small but increasingly influential community of another Sunni school, the ascetic, fundamentalist Wahhabi, are found mainly in Uzbekistan's Fergana Valley.

Practice

Devout Sunnis pray at prescribed times: before sunrise, just after high noon, in the late afternoon, just after sunset and before retiring. Prayers are preceded if possible by washing, at least of the hands, face and feet.

Some archaeologists believe that the Bronze Age site of Gonur-Depe was the birthplace of the world's first monotheist faith, Zoroastrianism, while others believe it to be Balkh just over the border in northern Afghanistan.

To learn more about Ismailism, try the scholarly *Short History of the Ismailis: Traditions of a Muslim Community* (1998) or *The Isma'ilis: Their History and Doctrines* (2007), both by Farhad Daftary.

PRE-ISLAMIC BELIEF IN CENTRAL ASIA

The Central Asian brand of Islam is riddled with pre-Islamic influences – just go to any important holy site and notice the kissing, rubbing and circumambulation of venerated objects, women crawling under holy stones to boost their fertility, the shamanic 'wishing trees' tied with bits of coloured rag, the cult of *pirs* (saints) and the Mongol-style poles with horsehair tassels set over the graves of revered figures.

Candles and flames are often burned at shrines and graves, and both the Tajiks and Turkmen jump over a fire during wedding celebrations or the Qurban (Eid al-Azha) festival, traditions that hark back to fire-worshipping Zoroastrian times. The Turkmen place particular stock in amulets and charms. At Konye-Urgench, Turkmen women even roll en masse down a hillside in an age-old fertility rite.

The melancholic Arabic *azan* (call to prayer) translates roughly as 'God is most great. There is no god but Allah. Mohammed is God's messenger. Come to prayer, come to security. God is most great'.

For Ismailis the style of prayer is a personal matter (eg there is no prostration), the mosque is replaced by a community shrine or meditation room and women are less excluded.

Just before fixed prayers a muezzin calls the Sunni and Shiite faithful, traditionally from a minaret, but nowadays mostly through a loudspeaker. Islam has no ordained priesthood, but mullahs (scholars, teachers or religious leaders) are trained in theology, are respected as interpreters of scripture and are quite influential in conservative rural areas.

The Quran is considered above criticism: it is the direct word of God as spoken to his Prophet Mohammed. It is supplemented by various traditions such as the Hadith, the collected acts and sayings of the Prophet Mohammed. In its fullest sense Islam is an entire way of life, with guidelines for nearly everything, from preparing and eating food to banking and dress.

History in Central Asia

Islam first appeared in Central Asia with Arab invaders in the 7th and 8th centuries, though it was mostly itinerant Sufi missionaries who converted the region over the subsequent centuries.

Islam never was a potent force in the former nomadic societies of the Turkmen, Kazakhs and Kyrgyz, and still isn't. Islam's appeal for nomadic rulers was as much an organisational and political tool as a collection of moral precepts. The nomad's customary law, known as *adat,* has always superseded Islamic sharia law.

There is also a significant blurring between religious and national characteristics, partly because the region was for so long cut off from mainstream Islamic teachings. The majority of Central Asians, although interested in Islam as a common denominator, seem quite happy to toast the Prophet's health with a shot of Russian vodka.

The Soviet Era

The oldest surviving Quran, the Osman Quran, is kept in Tashkent. It was written just 19 years after the death of the Prophet Mohammed and was later brought to Central Asia by Timur.

The Soviet regime long distrusted Islam because of its potential for coherent resistance, both domestically and internationally. Three of the five pillars of Islam (the fast of Ramazan, the haj or pilgrimage to Mecca and the zakat tax) were outlawed in the 1920s. The banning of polygamy, child marriage, the paying of bride price and the wearing of the paranja (veil) possibly pleased many women, but the banning of Arabic script, the holy script of the Quran, was much less popular. Clerical (Christian, Jewish and Buddhist as well as Muslim) land and property were seized. Medressas and other religious schools were closed down. Islam's judicial power was curbed with the dismantling of traditional sharia courts (which were based on Quranic law).

From 1932 to 1936 Stalin mounted a concerted antireligious campaign in Central Asia, a 'Movement of the Godless', in which mosques were closed and destroyed, and mullahs arrested and executed as saboteurs or spies. Control of the surviving places of worship and teaching was given to the Union of Atheists, which transformed most of them into museums, dance halls, warehouses or factories.

During WWII things improved marginally as Moscow sought domestic and international Muslim support for the war effort. In 1943 four Muslim Religious Boards or 'spiritual directorates', each with a mufti (spiritual leader), took over the administration of Soviet Muslims, including one in Tashkent for all of Central Asia (in 1990 another was established for Kazakhstan). Some mosques were reopened and a handful of carefully screened religious leaders were allowed to make the haj in 1947.

But beneath the surface little changed. Any religious activity outside the official mosques was strictly forbidden. By the early 1960s, under Khrushchev's 'back to Lenin' policies, another 1000 mosques were closed. By the beginning of the Gorbachev era, the number of mosques in Central Asia was down to between 150 and 250, and only two medressas were open – Mir-i-Arab in Bukhara and the Imam Ismail al-Bukhari Islamic Institute in Tashkent.

Perhaps the most amazing thing though, after 70 years of concerted Soviet repression, is that so much faith remains intact. Credit for any continuity from pre-Soviet times goes largely to 'underground Islam', in the form of the clandestine Sufi brotherhoods, which preserved some practices and education – and grew in power and influence in Central Asia as a result.

> By 1940, after Stalin's attacks on religion, only 1000 of Central Asia's 30,000 mosques remained standing and all 14,500 Islamic schools were closed.

Sufism

The original Sufis were simply purists, unhappy with the worldliness of the early caliphates and seeking knowledge of God through direct personal experience, under the guidance of a teacher or master, variously called a sheikh, *pir, ishan, murshid* or *ustad*. There never was a single Sufi movement; there are manifestations within all branches of Islam. For many adherents music, dance or poetry were routes to a trance-like moment of revelation and direct union with God. Secret recitations, known as *zikr,* and an annual 40-day retreat, known as the *chilla,* remain cornerstones of Sufic practice. This mystical side of Islam parallels similar traditions in other faiths.

Sufis were singularly successful as missionaries, perhaps because of their tolerance of other creeds. It was largely Sufis, not Arab armies, who planted Islam firmly in Central Asia. The personal focus of Sufism was most compatible with the nomadic lifestyle of the Kazakh and Kyrgyz in particular. Although abhorred nowadays in the orthodox Islamic states of Iran and Saudi Arabia, Sufism is in a quiet way dominant in Central Asia. Most shrines you'll see are devoted to one Sufi teacher or another.

When Islam was threatened by invaders (eg the Crusaders), Sufis assumed the role of defenders of the faith, and Sufism became a mass movement of regimented *tariqas* (brotherhoods), based around certain holy places, often the tombs of the brotherhood's founders. Clandestine, anticommunist tariqas helped Islam weather the Soviet period, and the KGB and its predecessors never seemed able to infiltrate them.

The moderate, nonelitist Naqshbandiya tariqa was the most important in Soviet times and probably still is. Founded in Bukhara in the 14th century, much of its influence in Central Asia perhaps comes from the high profile of Naqshbandi fighters in two centuries of revolts against the Russians in the Caucasus. A number of well-known 1930s *basmachi* (Muslim guerrilla fighters) leaders were Naqshbandiya.

> The word Islam translates loosely from Arabic as 'the peace that comes from total surrender to God'.

FIVE PILLARS OF ISLAM

Devout Muslims express their faith through the five pillars of Islam.

➡ The creed that 'There is only one god, Allah, and Mohammed is his prophet'.

➡ Prayer, five times a day, prostrating towards the holy city of Mecca, in a mosque (for men only) when possible, but at least on Friday, the Muslim holy day.

➡ Dawn-to-dusk fasting during the holy month of Ramazan.

➡ Making the haj (pilgrimage to Mecca) at least once in one's life.

➡ Alms giving, in the form of the zakat, an obligatory 2.5% tax.

Central Asia's most important Sufi shrines are the Bakhautdin Naqshband Mausoleum in Bukhara and the Yasaui Mausoleum at Turkestan in Kazakhstan.

Another important Sufi sect in Central Asia is the Qadiriya, founded by a teacher from the Caspian region. Others are the Kubra (founded in Khorezm) and Yasauia (founded in the town of Turkestan in Kazakhstan). All these were founded in the 12th century.

Islam Today

Since independence, Central Asia has seen a resurgence of Islam, and mosques and medressas have sprouted like mushrooms across the region, often financed with Saudi or Iranian money. Even in more religiously conservative Uzbekistan and Tajikistan, these new mosques are as much political as religious statements, and the rise of Islam has as much to do with the search for a Central Asian identity as it does with a rise in religious fervour.

Most Central Asians are torn between the Soviet secularism of the recent past and the region's deeper historical ties to the Muslim world, but few have a very deep knowledge of Islam. Only the Fergana Valley regions of Uzbekistan and southern Kyrgyzstan can be considered strongly Muslim, and only here do women commonly wear the hijab (headscarf).

All the Central Asian governments have taken great care to keep strict tabs on Islam. Only state-approved imams (preachers or religious leaders) and state-registered mosques are allowed to operate in most republics. Tajikistan's Islamic Revival Party is the only Islamist party in the region not to be outlawed.

Central Asia has experienced a taste of Islamic extremism, in the form of the Islamic Movement of Uzbekistan (IMU), which launched a series of armed raids and kidnappings in 1999 to 2001 in an attempt to establish an Islamic state in Uzbekistan. The movement has largely disappeared inside Central Asia, but there are fears that extremists may return to Tajikistan and Uzbekistan if they regain a base in Afghanistan.

Under the cloak of the War on Terror, the Uzbek government has arrested thousands of Muslims as 'extremists', most of them from the Fergana Valley. Some, but not all, are members of the peaceful but radical organisation Hizb ut-Tahrir (Movement of Liberation), which hopes to establish a global Islamic caliphate and has support across the region.

The percentage of practising Muslims in the ex-Soviet republics ranges from 70% in Kazakhstan to 75% in Kyrgyzstan, 85% in Tajikistan, 88% in Uzbekistan and 89% in Turkmenistan.

Turkmenistan also keeps tight controls on Islam. Turkmen mosques have quotations from former President Niyazov's book the *Ruhnama* engraved next to quotations from the Quran. The former chief cleric of Turkmenistan was charged with treason and sentenced to 22 years in prison after refusing to accept the Turkmen president as a messenger of God.

With the old communist ideals discredited, democracy suppressed and economic options stagnating, the fear is that radical Islam will provide an alluring alternative for a Central Asian youth left with few remaining options.

The Arts

Set astride millennia-old trade and migration routes, Central Asia has long blended and fused artistic traditions from Turkic and Persian, Islamic and secular, settled and nomadic worlds, creating in the process an indigenous Central Asian aesthetic. Whether it be the Zoroastrian-inspired motifs on an Uzbek embroidery, the other-worldly performance of a Kyrgyz bard or the visual splendour of a Turkmen carpet, artistic expression lies at the heart of the Central Asian identity.

Folk Art

Central Asian folk art developed in step with a nomadic or seminomadic way of life, focusing on transport (horses) and home (yurts). Designs followed the natural beauty of the environment: snow resting on a leaf, the elegance of an ibex horn, the flowers of the steppe. Status and wealth were made apparent by the intricacy of a carved door or a richly adorned horse. Yet art was not merely created for status or pleasure; each item also had a practical function in everyday life. From brightly coloured carpets used for sleeping and woven reed mats designed to block the wind, to leather bottles used for carrying *kumys* (fermented mare's milk); many of today's souvenirs in Kyrgyzstan and Kazakhstan are remnants of a recent nomadic past.

With such emphasis on equestrian culture it is not surprising that horses donned decorative blankets, inlaid wooden saddles, and head and neck adornments. Men hung their wealth on their belts with daggers and sabres in silver sheaths, and embossed leather purses and vessels for drink. Even today the bazaars in Tajikistan and the Fergana Valley are heavy with carved daggers and *pichok* (knives).

Nomads required their wealth to be portable and rich nomadic women wore stupendous jewellery, mostly of silver incorporating semiprecious stones, such as lapis lazuli and cornelian (believed to have magical properties).

To remain portable, furnishings consisted of bright quilts, carpets and *aiyk kap* (woven bags), which were hung on yurt walls for storing plates and clothing. *Kökör* (embossed leather bottles) were used for preparing, transporting and serving *kumys;* these days empty cola bottles suffice.

Carpets & Textiles

Most Central Asian peoples have their own traditional rug or carpet styles. The famous 'Bukhara' rugs – so called because they were mostly sold, not made, in Bukhara – are made largely by Turkmen craftspeople in Turkmenistan and northwestern Afghanistan. Deep reds and ochres are the primary palette, with the stylised *gul* (flower) a common motif. The Kyrgyz specialise in *shyrdaks* (felt rugs with appliquéd coloured panels or pressed wool designs called *ala-kiyiz*). Kazakhs specialise in *koshma* (multicoloured felt mats).

Down in the plains, Uzbeks make silk and cotton wall hangings and coverlets such as the beautiful *suzani* (embroidery; *suzan* is Persian for needle). *Suzani* are made in a variety of sizes and used as table covers,

The Arts and Crafts of Turkestan (1984) by Johannes Kalter, is a detailed, beautifully illustrated historical guide to the nomadic dwellings, clothing, jewellery and other 'applied art' of Central Asia.

Some of the best examples of Central Asian folk art can be seen at Tashkent's Museum of Applied Arts.

Since independence Central Asian art has been closely linked to the search for a new national identity, an identity that had been suppressed for decades during the Soviet era.

cushions and *ruijo* (a bridal bedspread), and thus were a key part of a bride's dowry. Rich with floral or celestial motifs (depictions of people and animals are against Muslim beliefs) an average *suzani* requires about two years to complete. Possibly the most accessible Kazakh textile souvenir is a *tus-kiiz* (*tush-kiyiz* in Kyrgyzstan), a colourful wall hanging made of cotton and silk.

The psychedelic tie-dyed silks known as *ikat* or *khanatlas* are popular in Uzbekistan. Take a close-up tour of how the cloth is made at the Yodgorlik Silk Factory (p225) in Margilon.

Literature: Bards & Poets

The division into Kazakh literature, Tajik literature, Uzbek literature and so on is a modern one; formerly there was simply literature in Chaghatai Turkic and literature in Persian. With most pre-20th-century poets, scholars and writers bilingual in Uzbek and Tajik, literature in Central Asia belonged to a shared universality of culture.

Take for example Abu Abdullah Rudaki, a 10th-century Samanid court poet considered the father of Persian literature, who also stars in the national pantheons of Afghanistan, Iran and Tajikistan (he is buried in Penjikent) and is also revered by Uzbeks by dint of being born in the Bukhara emirate. Omar Khayam (1048–1131), famed composer of *rubiayyat* poetry, although a native of what is now northeast Iran, also has strong ties to Balkh and Samarkand, where he spent part of his early life at the court of the Seljuq emir.

Uzbekistan's national poet is Alisher Navoi (1441–1501), who pioneered the use of Turkic in literature. Born in Herat in modern-day Afghanistan, Navoi served the Timurid court of Hussain Baiqara, commissioning public buildings, advising on policy and writing *divan* (collections) of epic poetry.

Better known to Western audiences is Mawlana Rumi (1207–73), born either in Balkh in Afghanistan or Vakhsh in Tajikistan (both places claim his birth site), and still today said to be the most widely read poet in the USA.

Most Tajiks and Uzbeks are well versed in Iran's national poet Firdausi, whose epic *Shah Nama* (Shahnameh; Book of Kings) tells the popular tale of Rostam and Sohrab, in which the tragic hero Rostam kills his son in a case of mistaken identity.

A strong factor in the universal nature of Central Asian literature was that it was popularised, not in written form but orally by itinerant minstrels, in the form of improvised songs, poems and stories. Known as *bakshi* or *dastanchi* in Turkmen and Uzbek, and *akyn* in Kazakh and Kyrgyz, these storytelling bards earned their living travelling from town to town giving skilled and dramatic recitations of crowd-pleasing verse, tales and epics to audiences gathered in bazaars and chaikhanas (teahouses). With their rhythms, rhymes and improvisation, these performers share much in common with rap artists in the West (but with considerably less bling).

The most famous epic is Kyrgyzstan's *Manas,* said to be the world's longest, and recited by a special category of *akyn* known as *manaschi,* though other peoples have their own epics, including the Uzbek Alpamish and Turkmen Gorkut. The most popular bards are national heroes, regarded as founders of their national literature, and memorialised in Soviet-era street names (eg Toktogul, Zhambyl and Abay). Soviet propagandists even used *akyns* to praise Lenin or popularise the latest directive from party central. Bardic competitions are still held in some rural areas or during festivals, these days with cash prizes.

If you are into carpets, don't miss a visit to Ashgabat's Carpet Museum (p380), which showcases the world's largest hand-tied carpet.

It was only with the advent of Bolshevik rule that literacy became widespread. Unfortunately, at the same time, much of the region's classical heritage was suppressed because Moscow feared that it might inflame to latent nationalist sentiments. Instead writers were encouraged to produce novels and plays in line with official Communist Party themes. While a number of Central Asian poets and novelists found acclaim within the Soviet sphere, such as Tajik Sadruddin Ayni (1878–1954), and Uzbeks Asqad Mukhtar and Abdullah Kodiri, the only native Central Asian author to garner international recognition has been Kyrgyz writer Chinghiz Aitmatov (1928–2008), whose novels such as *Jamilla* and *The Day Lasts More Than A Hundred Years* have been translated into English and other European languages.

One interesting modern work is the exiled Uzbek writer Hamid Ismailov's *The Railway* (2006), a satirical novel that mixes anecdote and fantasy to depict life in the fictional end-of-the-line town of Gilas in Soviet Uzbekistan. The novel was swiftly banned in Uzbekistan.

The art of the Kyrgyz bards and the classical Tajik-Uzbek music known as *shash maqam* are both included on Unesco's list of 'Masterpieces of the Oral and Intangible Heritage of Humanity'.

Music

Although visual arts and literature succumbed to a stifling Soviet-European influence (which they're presently struggling to shrug off), the music of Central Asia remains closely related to the swirling melodies of Anatolia and Persia. The instruments used are similar to those found across Iran, Afghanistan and Chinese Turkestan; the *rabab* (*rubab;* six-stringed mandolin), *dutar* (two-stringed guitar), *tambur* (long-necked lute), *dombra/komuz* (two-stringed Kazakh/Kyrgyz guitar), *kamanche* (Persian violin, played like a cello), *gijak* (upright spiked fiddle), *ney* (flute), *doira* (tambourine/drum) and *chang* (zither). Most groups add the ubiquitous Russian accordion.

In the past the development of music was closely connected with the art of the bards, but these days the traditions are continued by small folklore ensembles, heavily in demand at weddings and other *toi* (celebrations). In Uzbek and Tajik societies there's a particularly popular form of folk music known as *sozanda,* sung primarily by women accompanied only by percussion instruments such as tablas, bells and castanets. There are also several forms of Central Asian classical music, such as the courtly *shash maqam* (six modes) tradition of Uzbekistan, most of which are taught through the traditional system of *ustad* (master) and *shakirt* (apprentice). Central Asia has a strong tradition of the performer-composer, or *bestekar,* the equivalent of the singer-songwriter, who mixed poetry, humour, current affairs and history into music.

Musical traditions in remote regions such as the Pamirs are sometimes preserved in just a few individuals, a situation the Aga Khan Trust for Culture is trying to redress through its music schools scattered throughout Central Asia.

Russian writer Fyodor Dostoevsky lived for five years in Semey (then Semipalatinsk), in Kazakhstan, as part of his forced exile from Russia and was married there. His house is now a museum.

Painting

Rendered in a style that foreshadows that of Persian miniature painting, some splendid friezes have been unearthed in the excavations of the Afrosiab palace (6th to 7th centuries), on the outskirts of Samarkand, depicting a colourful caravan led by elephants. You can view copies at Samarkand's Afrosiab Museum. Similar Silk Road–era wall frescoes were discovered at Penjikent and Varakhsha, depicting everything from panthers and griffins to royal banqueting scenes.

The Arab invasion of the 8th century put representational art in Central Asia on hold for the better part of 1300 years. Islam prohibits the depiction of the living, so traditional arts developed in the form of

For a fictionalised account of the life of Persian poet Omar Khayam, check out Amin Maalouf's imaginative novel *Samarkand* (2003), partially set in Central Asia.

CENTRAL ASIAN DISCOGRAPHY

The following recordings offer a great introduction to Central Asian music and are our personal favourites.

City of Love (Real World; 1993) This recording by Ashkabad, a five-piece Turkmen ensemble, has a superb and lilting, Mediterranean feel.

Music of Central Asia Vol 1: Mountain Music of Kyrgyzstan (Smithsonian Folkways; www.folkways.si.edu; 2006) Collection of evocative Kyrgyz sounds by Tengir-Too, featuring the *komuz* and Jew's harp, with a section from the *Manas*. Other volumes in the Smithsonian series cover bardic divas, classical *shash maqam* and music from Badakhshan.

Secret Museum of Mankind, the Central Asia Ethnic Music Classics: 1925–48 (Yazoo; www.shanachie.com; 2005) Twenty-six scratchy but wonderfully fresh field recordings of otherwise lost music.

The Selection Album (Blue Flame; www.blueflame.com; 2011) Career retrospective from Uzbek pop superstar, one-time politician and exile Yulduz Usmanova.

The Silk Road – A Musical Caravan (Smithsonian Folkways; www.folkways.si.edu; 2002) 'Imagine if Marco Polo had a tape recorder' runs the cover note for this academic two-CD collection of traditional recordings by both masters and amateurs, from China to Azerbaijan.

Yol Boisin (Real World; www.realworld.co.uk; 2008) This recording by Sevara Nazarkhan, a very accessible Uzbek songstress, has been given a modern production by Hector Zazou. Sevara supported Peter Gabriel on tour in 2007. Her more recent recordings *Sen* (2007) and the more traditional *Tortadur* (2011) are also excellent.

geometric design and calligraphy, combining Islamic script with arabesques, and the carving of doors and screens. Textiles and metalwork took on floral or repetitive, geometric motifs.

Painting and two-dimensional art were only revived under the Soviets, who introduced European aesthetics and set up schools to train local artists in the new fashion. Under Soviet tutelage the pictorial art of Central Asia became a curious hybrid of socialist realism and mock traditionalism – Kyrgyz horsemen riding proudly beside a shiny red tractor, smiling Uzbeks at a chaikhana surrounded by record-breaking cotton harvests. You'll see a good selection of these at most regional museums.

To listen to British DJ Andy Kershaw's musical travels through Turkmenistan, visit the BBC website (www.bbc.co.uk/ programmes)

By far the most interesting collection of 20th-century Soviet art can be found at the Savitsky Museum (p270) in Nukus, a treasure trove of hidden avant-garde art collected in the 1930s by Russian artist Igor Savitsky in this unassuming backwater. For a fine background to the collection and its context, look out for the excellent documentary *The Desert of Forbidden Art* (www.desertofforbiddenart.com).

Almaty has Central Asia's most vibrant contemporary-arts scene: start your online visual explorations at Ular (www.artular.kz) and Tengri Umai (www.tu.kz).

Architecture

Central Asia's most impressive surviving artistic heritage is its architecture. Some of the world's most audacious and beautiful Islamic buildings grace the cities of Bukhara, Khiva and especially Samarkand (all in Uzbekistan). Few sights symbolise the region more evocatively than the swell of a turquoise dome, a ruined desert citadel or a minaret framed black against a blazing sunset.

Early Influences

Central Asian architecture has its roots in Parthian, Kushan and Graeco-Bactrian desert citadels or fortified palaces, whose structure was defined by the demands of trade, security and water. Iranian, Greek and Indian art blended in the 2000-year-old desert cities of places such as Toprak Qala, Nissa and Termiz. Central Asia's position at the border of great empires and astride the transcontinental Silk Road guaranteed a rich flow of artistic influences.

Due to the destructive urges of Chinggis (Genghis) Khan and other invading empires, only traces have survived from the pre-Islamic era or the first centuries of Arab rule.

Environmental constraints naturally defined building construction over the centuries. The lack of local wood and stone forced Central Asian architects to turn to brickwork as the cornerstone of their designs. Tall

Monuments of Central Asia: A Guide to the Archaeology, Art and Architecture of Turkestan (2001) by Edgar Knobloch, is an excellent overview of the region's architectural heritage.

ARCHITECTURE GLOSSARY

aivan covered portico or vaulted portal (also spelt *eivan* or *iwan*)

chorsu market arcade

ghanch carved and painted alabaster decoration

hammam bathhouse

hauz reservoir; artificial pool

jami masjid Friday mosque

khanaka pilgrimage resthouse; prayer cell or hostel for wandering Sufis

mazar tomb or mausoleum

medressa Islamic college or seminary

mihrab niche in a mosque marking the direction of Mecca

minor minaret

pishtak monumental entrance portal

qala fortress (also *kala*)

rabat caravanserai

tak crossroads bazaar (also *tok*)

tim shopping arcade

ziarat shrine

portals, built to face and catch the prevailing winds, not only looked fabulous but also had a cooling effect in the heat of summer. The influence of a nomadic lifestyle is particularly relevant in Khiva, where you can still see the brick bases built to house the winter yurts of the khans.

Several important technological advances spurred the development of architectural arts, principally that of fired brick in the 10th century, coloured tilework in the 12th century and glazed polychrome tilework in the 14th century. Without the seemingly insignificant squinch (the corner bracketing that enables the transition from a square to an eight-, then 16-sided platform), the development of the monumental dome would have stalled. It was this tiny technology that underpinned the breathtaking domes of the Timurid era.

Timurid Architecture

Most of the monumental architecture still standing in Central Asia dates from the time of the Timurids (14th to 15th centuries); rulers who combined barbaric savagery with exquisite artistic sophistication. During his campaigns of terror Timur (Tamerlane) forcibly relocated artisans, from Beijing to Baghdad, to Central Asia, resulting in a splendid fusion of styles in textiles, painting, architecture and metal arts.

The Timurids' architectural trademark is the beautiful, often ribbed and elongated, azure-blue outer dome. Other signature Timurid traits include the tendency towards ensemble design, the use of a monumental *pishtak* (arched entrance portal) flanked by tapering minarets, and exuberant, multicoloured tilework, all evident in the showiest of showpieces, the Registan in Samarkand.

Architectural Design

The traditional cities of Bukhara and especially Khiva reveal the most about traditional urban structure. The distinction between *ark* (fortified citadel), *shahristan* (inner city with wealthy residential neighbourhoods, bazaars and city wall) and outlying *rabad* (suburbs) has formed the structure of settlements since the first Central Asian towns appeared 4000 years ago. A second outer city wall surrounded most cities, protecting against desert storms and brigands.

Apart from Islamic religious construction, secular architecture includes palaces (such as the Tosh-Hovli in Khiva), *ark* (forts), *hammams* (multidomed bathhouses), *rabat* (caravanserais), *tim* (shopping arcades), *tok* (or *tak;* covered crossroad bazaars) and the local *hauz* (reservoirs) that supplied the cities with their drinking water.

Mosques

Islam dominates Central Asian architecture. *Masjid* (mosques) trace their earliest design back to the house of the Prophet Mohammed. Common to most is the use of the portal, which leads into a colonnaded space and a covered area for prayer. Some Central Asian mosques, such as the Bolo-Hauz Mosque in Bukhara, have a flat, brightly painted roof, supported by carved wooden columns, while others, such as the Juma Mosque in Khiva, are hypostyle (ie with a roofed space supported by many pillars).

Whether the place of worship is a *guzar* (local mosque) serving the local community, a *jami masjid* (Friday mosque) built to hold the entire city congregation once a week, or a *namazgokh* (festival mosque), the focal point is always the mihrab, a niche that indicates the direction of Mecca. Central Asia's largest modern mosque is the Hazret Sultan Mosque (p335) in Astana, built in 2012.

Mausoleums

The *mazar* (mausoleum) has been popular in Central Asia for millennia, either built by rulers to ensure their own immortality or to commemorate holy men. Most *mazars* consist of a *ziaratkhana* (prayer room), set under a domed cupola. The actual tomb may be housed in a central hall, or underground in a side *gurkhana* (tomb). Popular sites offer lodging, washrooms and even kitchens for visiting pilgrims, and are centred on the tombs of important Sufi saints. Tombs vary in design from the classic domed cupola style to the pyramid-shaped, tent-like designs of Konye-Urgench, or even whole streets of tombs as found at the glorious Shah-i-Zinda in Samarkand.

Each of Uzbekistan's historic cities has its own distinct colour: greens are most common in Khorezm, khakis in Bukhara and blues in Samarkand.

Medressas

These Islamic colleges, normally two storeys high, are set around a cloistered central courtyard, punctuated by *aivan* (or *aiwan;* arched portals) on four sides. Rows of little doors in the interior facades lead into *hujra* (cell-like living quarters for students and teachers) or *khanaka* (prayer cells or entire buildings) for the ascetic wandering dervishes who would overnight there. Most medressas are fronted by monumental portals. On either side of the entrance you will normally find a *darskhana* (lecture room) to the left and a mosque to the right.

Minarets

These tall, tapering towers were designed to summon the faithful during prayer time, so most have internal stairs for the muezzin to climb. They were also used as lookouts to spot invaders, and even, in the case of the

---

ARCHITECTURAL HIGHLIGHTS

The following are our picks of the architectural highlights of Central Asia.

Ismail Samani Mausoleum (p254; 900–1000) Mesmerising brickwork, in Bukhara.

Kalon Minaret (p252; 1127) Central Asia's most impressive minaret, at 48m high, in Bukhara.

Mausoleum of Sultan Sanjar (p390; 1157) A huge double-domed Seljuq monument, in Merv.

Shah-i-Zinda (p231; 1300–1400) This street of tombs features Central Asia's most stunning and varied tilework, in Samarkand.

Bibi-Khanym Mosque (p229; 1399–1404) Timur's intended masterpiece, so colossal that it collapsed as soon as it was finished, now heavily restored, in Samarkand.

Gur-e-Amir Mausoleum (p233; 1404) An exquisite ribbed dome, sheltering the tomb of Timur, in Samarkand.

Ak-Saray Palace (p240; 1400–50) Tantalising entrance archway of Timur's once-opulent palace, in Shakhrisabz.

Registan (p229; 1400–1600) An epic ensemble of medressas, in Samarkand. The Sher Dor (1636) flouts Islamic tradition by depicting two lions chasing deer, looked down upon by a Mongol-faced sun.

Lyabi-Hauz (p247; 1600) A delightful complex featuring a pool, *khanaka* (pilgrim rest-house) and medressa, in Bukhara.

Char Minar (p250; 1807) A quirky ex-gateway, resembling a chair thrust upside down in the ground, in Bukhara.

For an in-depth look at the Timurid architecture of Samarkand try www.oxuscom. com/timursam. htm.

Kalon Minaret in Bukhara, as a means of execution. Some minarets (eg at Samarkand's Registan) exist purely for decoration.

Decoration

Tilework is the most dramatic form of decoration in Central Asia, instilling a light, graceful air into even the most hulking of Timurid buildings. The deep cobalts and turquoise ('colour of the Turks') of Samarkand's domes have inspired travellers for centuries.

Decoration almost always takes the shape of abstract geometric, floral or calligraphic designs, in keeping with the Islamic prohibition on the representation of living creatures. Geometric and knot *(girikh)* designs were closely linked to the development of Central Asian science – star designs were a favourite with the astronomer king Ulughek. Calligraphy is common, either in the square, stylised Kufi script favoured by the Timurids or the more scrolling, often foliated thulth script.

Tiles come in a variety of styles, either stamped, faience (carved on to wet clay and then fired), polychromatic (painted and then fired) or jigsaw-style mosaic.

Patterned brick decoration reached its apex in Central Asia. The Ismail Samani Mausoleum and the Kalon Minaret in Bukhara are two wonderful examples of the use of monochrome brickwork to create a lightness of design.

Take time also to savour the exquisite details of Central Asia's carved *ghanch* (alabaster) and intricately carved and painted wood.

Environment

Land-locked Central Asia covers an incredible range of landscapes, from snow-capped peaks to burning deserts, immense inland seas and rolling steppe. It is nothing less than the transition between Europe and Asia. Years of Soviet rule have taken a massive toll on the environment and serious problems remain, fuelled mainly by economic hardship. Despite this, Central Asia still hides some of the wildest and most pristine corners on earth.

The Land

A quick spin around Central Asia would start on the eastern shores of the oil-rich Caspian Sea (actually a saltwater lake). Then dip southeast along the low crest of the Kopet Dag Mountains between Turkmenistan and Iran before heading east along the Turkestan plains, following the Amu-Darya river along the desert border with Uzbekistan and Tajikistan to its headstream, the Pyanj River, and into the high Pamir plateau. Round the eastern nose of the 7000m snow peaks of the Tian Shan range; skip northwestward over the Altay Mountains to float down the massive Irtysh River and then turn west to plod along Kazakhstan's flat, farmed, wooded border with Russia, ending in the basin of the Ural River and the Caspian Sea.

The sort of blank which is drawn in the minds of many people by the words 'Central Asia' is not entirely unfounded. The overwhelming majority of the territory is flat steppe (arid grassland) and desert. These areas include the Kazakh Steppe, the Betpak Dala (Misfortune) Steppe, the Kyzylkum (Red Sands) desert and the Karakum (Black Sands) desert. The Kyzylkum and Karakum combined make the fourth-largest desert in the world.

Central Asia's mountains are part of the huge chain which swings in a great arc from the Mongolian Altay to the Tibetan Himalaya. Central Asia's high ground is dominated by the Pamirs, a range of rounded, 5000m to 7000m mountains known as the 'Roof of the World', which stretch 500km across Tajikistan. With very broad, flat valleys, which are nearly as high as the lower peaks, the Pamirs might be better described as a plateau (*pamir* roughly means 'pasture' in local dialects). The roof of the Pamir, Tajikistan's 7495m Koh-i Somoni, is the highest point in Central Asia and was the highest in the USSR (when it was known as Kommunizma). The Pamirs is probably the least explored mountain range on earth.

Varying from 4000m to more than 7400m, the crests of the Tian Shan form the backbone of eastern Central Asia. Known as the Celestial Mountains, the Chinese-named Tian Shan (the local translation is Tengri Tau) extend over 1500km from southwest Kyrgyzstan into China. The summit of the range is Pobedy (7439m) on the Kyrgyzstan–China border. The forested alpine valleys and stunning glacial peaks of the range were favourites among such Russian explorers as Fedchenko, Kostenko, Semenov and Przewalski.

The five ex-Soviet republics of Central Asia occupy just over 4 million sq km, of which 68% belongs to Kazakhstan.

Some residents of massive Kazakhstan live about as far away from Vienna as they do from Almaty. Tashkent (Uzbekistan) is closer to Kashgar and Tehran than to Moscow or Kiev.

These two mountain ranges hold some of the largest glaciers and freshwater supplies on earth (around 17,000 sq km) and are one of the region's most significant natural resources. The 77km-long Fedchenko Glacier is the longest glacier outside the polar regions and allegedly contains more water than the Aral Sea.

The Caspian Sea is called either the world's biggest lake or the world's biggest inland sea. The Caspian Depression, in which it lies, dips to 132m below sea level. Lake Balkhash, a vast, marsh-bordered arc of half-saline water on the Kazakh Steppe, is hardly deeper than a puddle, while mountain-ringed Lake Issyk-Köl in Kyrgyzstan is the fourth-deepest lake in the world. Other glacially fed lakes dot the mountains, including Son-Köl in Kyrgyzstan and stunning Kara-Kul, first described by Marco Polo, in Tajikistan.

Most of Central Asia's rainfall drains internally. What little water flows out of Central Asia goes all the way to the Arctic Ocean, via the Irtysh River. The Ili River waters Lake Balkhash; the Ural makes a short dash across part of Kazakhstan to the Caspian Sea. The region's two mightiest rivers, the Syr-Darya (Jaxartes River) and Amu-Darya (Oxus River), used to replenish the Aral Sea until they were bled dry for cotton. There is evidence that the Amu-Darya once flowed into the Caspian Sea, along the now-dry Uzboy Channel.

Eurasian Kazakhstan

In Soviet parlance Kazakhstan was considered apart from Central Asia. While it is true that Kazakhstan's enormous territory actually extends westward across the Ural River (the traditional boundary between Europe and Asia), Kazakhstan still shares many geographic, cultural, ethnic and economic similarities and ties with Central Asia 'proper'.

Geology

The compact, balled-up mass of mountains bordering Tajikistan, Kyrgyzstan, China and Afghanistan is often called the Pamir Knot. It's the hub from which other major ranges extend like radiating ropes: the Himalaya and Karakoram to the southeast, the Hindu Kush to the southwest, the Kunlun to the east and the Tian Shan to the northeast. These young mountains all arose (or more correctly, are arising still) from the shock waves created by the Indian subcontinent smashing into the Asian crustal plate more than 100 million years ago. Amazing as it seems, marine fossils from the original Tethys Sea have been found in the deserts of Central Asia as a testament to the continental collision. The Tian Shan are currently rising at the rate of around 1cm per year.

Central Asia is therefore, unsurprisingly, a major earthquake zone. Ashgabat was 80% destroyed by a massive earthquake in 1948 that killed 110,000 and Tashkent was levelled in 1966. More recently, devastating earthquakes hit the Tajikistan–Afghanistan border in 1997 and 1998.

Wildlife

Central Asia is home to a unique range of ecosystems and an extraordinary variety of flora and fauna. The ex-Soviet Central Asian republics comprised only 17% of the former USSR's territory, but contained over 50% of its variety in flora and fauna.

Uzbekistan is one of only two countries in the world defined as double landlocked, ie surrounded by countries which are themselves landlocked.

The mountains of Kyrgyzstan, Kazakhstan and Tajikistan are the setting for high summer pastures known as *jailoos*. In summer the wild flowers (including wild irises and edelweiss) are a riot of colour. Marmots and pikas provide food for eagles and lammergeiers, while the elusive snow leopard preys on the ibex, with which it shares a preference for crags and rocky slopes, alongside the Svertsov ram and Marco Polo sheep (argali). Forests of Tian Shan spruce, ash, larch and juniper provide cover for lynxes, wolves, wild boars and brown bears. Lower in the mountains of southern Kyrgyzstan, Uzbekistan, Tajikistan and Turkmenistan are ancient forests of wild walnut, pistachio, juniper, apricot, cherry and apple. Arslanbob in Kyrgyzstan is home to the world's largest walnut grove.

The steppes (what's left of them after massive Soviet cultivation projects) are covered with grasses and low shrubs such as saxaul. Where they rise to meet foothills, the steppes bear vast fields of wild poppies and several hundred types of tulip, which burst into beautiful bloom in May and June.

Roe deer and saiga, a species of antelope, have their homes on the steppe. The saiga is a slightly ridiculous-looking animal with a huge bulbous nose that once roamed in herds 100,000 strong. The ring-necked pheasant, widely introduced to North America and elsewhere, is native to the Central Asian steppe, as are partridges, black grouse, bustards, and the falcons and hawks that prey on them. Korgalzhyn Nature Reserve in Kazakhstan is home to the world's most northerly colony of pink flamingos.

Rivers and lake shores in the flatlands create a different world, with dense thickets of elm, poplar, reeds and shrubs known as *tugai,* where wild boar, jackal and deer make their homes. Over 90% of *tugai* environment along the Amu-Darya has been lost over the years.

In the barren, stony wastes of the Karakum and Kyzylkum you'll need a sharp eye to catch a glimpse of the goitred gazelle (zheyran). Gophers, sand rats and jerboas are preyed on by various reptiles, including (in Turkmenistan) vipers and cobras.

Turkmenistan's wildlife has a Middle Eastern streak, understandable when you consider that parts of the country are as close to Baghdad as they are to Tashkent. Leopards and porcupines inhabit the parched hills. The *zemzen* (desert crocodile) is actually a type of large lizard that can grow up to 1.8m long.

Central Asia has been famed for its horses since Chinese reports of the 'blood-sweating' horses of Fergana, which Han China needed to fight the nomadic tribes harassing its northern frontier. Today's most famous horses are the Akhal-Teke of Turkmenistan, the forefather of the modern Arab thoroughbred. There are only around 2000 thoroughbred Akhal-Teke in the world, of which 1200 are in Turkmenistan.

Endangered Species

The mountain goose, among other rare species, nests on the shores of Kyrgyzstan's mountain lakes, but the population has shrunk over the years to fewer than 15 pairs worldwide.

The marshlands of the Amu-Darya region of Uzbekistan were once home to the Turan (Caspian) tiger but these became extinct when the last known survivor was shot in 1972. Wild Bactrian camels, once the quintessential Silk Road sight, are now only occasionally seen from the Tajikistan side of the Wakhan Valley.

For more on the plight of the saiga antelope, visit www.saiga-conservation.org.

ENVIRONMENT WILDLIFE

Marco Polo sheep are named after the Italian traveller who wrote of them after visiting the Pamirs: 'There are...wild sheep of great size, whose horns are a good six palms in length.'

THE IRBIS

The population of snow leopards in Central Asia and the Russian Altay is estimated at about 1000, out of a global population of around 7000. These magnificent but secretive and solitary animals (known locally as *irbis* or *barys*) are a keystone species, keeping others in balance and check. There are thought to be between 150 and 500 leopards in Kyrgyzstan, with around 200 more each in Kazakhstan and the Pamirs of Tajikistan. Only 5% of these magnificent creatures' habitat is currently protected.

Botanists say that the modern apple has its genetic origins in Kazakhstan; revealingly the largest city, Almaty, translates as 'Father of Apples'.

There has been some good news, though: eight Przewalski's horses were recently reintroduced into Kazakhstan's Altyn-Emel National Park after being extinct in the region for 60 years.

Scientists in Kazakhstan are even considering proposals to introduce Amur tigers into Central Asia to replace their long-lost Caspian relatives. The most feasible sites are the Ili River delta and the southern coast of Balkash Lake in Kazakhstan.

Over the last decade Bukhara (Bactrian) deer have also been relocated to reserves in Uzbekistan and Kazakhstan, including Altyn-Emel National Park, raising regional numbers from just 350 to over 1000. You can pat yourself on the back for this; the Altyn-Emel project was partly funded with money generated by ecotourism.

National Parks

Many of the region's approximately three-dozen *zapovednik* (nature reserves) and *zakazniki* (protected areas) and dozen or so national parks (*gosudarstvenny natsionalny prirodny park*) are accessible to tourists.

The existing system of national parks and protected areas, one of the positive legacies of the USSR, is nevertheless antiquated and inadequate. All suffer from a chronic lack of government funding and are under increasing pressure from grazing, poaching and firewood gathering. In Kyrgyzstan just 2.5% of the country's area is dedicated to land conservation.

Kazakhstan's new Irgiz-Turgay nature reserve in the northwestern steppes is part of a planned 62,000-sq-km system of protected areas known as the Altyn Dala (Golden Steppe) Conservation Initiative that will eventually see the reintroduction of Przewalski's horses and onager (wild Central Asian ass).

EASY PARKS TO VISIT

The easiest protected areas to visit include the following.

Aksu-Zhabagyly Nature Reserve (p320) High biodiversity in southern Kazakhstan, famed for its beautiful tulips. An ecotourism program offers excellent mountain hiking and birdwatching.

Ala-Archa National Park (p73) Fine hiking and climbing just outside Bishkek, Kyrgyzstan.

Badai-Tugai Nature Reserve (p261) Protects a strip of *tugai* riverine forest on the eastern bank of the Amu-Darya in Karakalpakstan, Uzbekistan. Entry fees pay for food for a Bukhara deer-breeding centre.

Ile-Alatau National Park (p305) Good mountain hiking on Almaty's doorstep in Kazakhstan, though plans for a 16-lift ski resort at Kok-Zhaylau are controversial.

Karakol Valley (p93) Alpine ecosystem in the Tian Shan, southeast Issyk-Köl, Kyrgyzstan, with superb scenery and fine trekking routes.

Sary-Chelek Biosphere Reserve (p110) Remote trekking routes cross this Unesco-sponsored reserve, centred on a large mountain lake in Kyrgyzstan.

Sayram-Ugam National Park (p319) Ecotourism programs include hikes and horse treks, Kazakhstan.

Tajik National Park (p186) Covers most of the eastern Pamirs (18% of Tajikistan) and offers superb mountain trekking and mountain climbing.

Ugam-Chatkal National Park (p216) Unesco-sponsored biosphere reserve in Uzbekistan, with juniper forests, wild boars, bears and snow leopards, plus some fine hiking and rafting.

The Tajik National Park in the Pamirs of Tajikistan and the Saryarka Steppes and Lakes region of northern Kazakhstan are included in Unesco's list of Natural World Heritage Sites.

Environmental Issues

Central Asia's 'empty' landscapes served as testing grounds for Soviet experiments in taming nature, which resulted in land and water mismanagement and the destruction of natural habitat on an almost unimaginable scale.

Even casual students of the region are familiar with some of the most serious environmental catastrophes: the gradual disappearance of the Aral Sea and the excessive levels of radiation around the Semey (Semipalatinsk) nuclear testing site. Khrushchev's Virgin Lands scheme, which was planned to boost grain production, resulted in the degradation of hundreds of thousands of square kilometres of Kazakh steppe.

In the economic malaise of the post-Soviet years, the environment has taken a back seat. Whether it is poaching, hunting tours or pollution from gold-mining operations, the lure of hard currency in an otherwise-bleak economic landscape has repeatedly taken priority over nature conservation.

The extreme continental climate of Central Asia is particularly susceptible to global climate change, and glaciers in the Pamirs and Tian Shan are already shrinking by around 15m a year.

Water is, in fact, the only major resource in Tajikistan and Kyrgyzstan and both countries plan a series of giant hydroelectric dams, much to the concern of downstream Uzbekistan and Turkmenistan, for whom water supplies are vital to their cotton-based economies. Central Asia's future is looking increasingly defined by two of nature's greatest gifts: oil and water.

The Aral Sea

The Aral Sea straddles the border between western Uzbekistan and southern Kazakhstan. It's fed by the Syr-Darya and Amu-Darya rivers, flowing down from the Tian Shan and Pamir mountain ranges. Back in the 1950s these rivers brought an average 55 cu km of water a year to the Aral Sea, which stretched 400km from end to end and 280km from side to side, and covered 66,900 sq km. The sea had, by all accounts, lovely clear water, pristine beaches, enough fish to support a big fishing industry in the ports of Moynaq and Aralsk, and even passenger ferries crossing it from north to south.

Then the USSR's central planners decided to boost cotton production in Uzbekistan, Turkmenistan and Kazakhstan, to feed a leap forward in the Soviet textile industry. But the thirsty new cotton fields, many of them on poorer desert soils and fed by long, unlined canals open to the sun, required much more water per hectare than the old ones. The irrigated area grew by 20% from 1960 to 1980, but the annual water take from the rivers doubled from 45 to 90 cu km. By the 1980s the annual flow into the Aral Sea was less than a tenth of the 1950s supply.

Production of cotton rose, but the Aral Sea sank. Between 1966 and 1993 its level fell by more than 16m and its eastern and southern shores receded by up to 80km. In 1987 the Aral divided into a smaller northern sea and a larger southern one, each fed, sometimes, by one of the rivers.

The two main fishing ports, Aralsk (Kazakhstan) in the north and Moynaq (Uzbekistan) in the south, were left high and dry when efforts to keep their navigation channels open were abandoned in the early 1980s. Of the 60,000 people who used to live off the Aral fishing industry (harvesting 20,000 tons of fish a year), almost all are gone. These days the rusting hulks of beached fishing boats lie scattered dozens of kilometres

Birds of Central Asia (2012) by Raffael Aye, Manuel Schweizer and Tobias Roth, is the best field guide for birdwatchers.

ENVIRONMENT ENVIRONMENTAL ISSUES

For more on wildlife protection in Kazakhstan see the Association for the Conservation of Biodiversity of Kazakhstan (www.acbk.kz/en).

Since the 1930s Caspian seal numbers have dropped from over a million to 100,000.

from the nearest water. Of the 173 animal species that used to live around the Aral Sea, only 38 survive.

As the sea has shrunk, the climate around the lake has changed: the air is drier, winters are colder and longer, and summers are hotter. Every year 150,000 tons of salt and sand from the exposed bed is blown hundreds of kilometres in big salt-dust sandstorms, which also pick up residues of the chemicals from cultivated land and a former biological-weapons testing site. A visit to anywhere near the sea is a ride into a nightmare of blighted towns, land and communities.

The catalogue of human health problems is awful: salt and dust are blamed for cancers of the throat and oesophagus; poor drinking water has been implicated in high rates of typhoid, paratyphoid, hepatitis and dysentery; and the area has the highest infant mortality rates (over 10%) in the former USSR, as well as high rates of birth deformities.

Long-Term Solutions

Dozens of inquiries, projects and research teams have poked and prodded the Aral problem; locals joke that if every scientist who visited the Aral region had brought a bucket of water the problem would be over by now. The initial outcry over the disaster seems to have largely evaporated, along with the sea, and the focus has shifted from rehabilitating the sea, to stabilising part of the sea and now stabilising the environment around the sea.

In 2005 the little channel still connecting the northern and southern seas was blocked by the Kok-Aral dam, preventing further water loss from the northern sea, but condemning the southern sea to oblivion. The northern sea has risen by 4m since then and should reach a state of equilibrium by about 2025. The southern sea, however, is expected to split again and then dry up completely, though there is a chance that three small lakes could be saved with the construction of small dykes.

Other Environmental Problems

➡ Cotton is to blame for many of Central Asia's ills. Its cultivation demands high levels of pesticides and fertilisers, which are now found in water, in human and animal milk, and in vegetables and fruit.

➡ Kazakhstan suffers particularly from industrial pollution. Lake Balkhash has been polluted by copper smelters, and bird and other lake life there is now practically extinct. There are also concerns about oil and other pollution draining into the Caspian Sea.

➡ Kyrgyzstan has a problem with radioactive seepage from Soviet-era uranium mines. In 1998 almost two tonnes of sodium cyanide destined for the Kumtor gold mine was spilled into the Barskoön River, which made its way into Issyk-Köl.

➡ A combination of economic hardship, a crisis in funding for wildlife protection and the opening of borders with China (the region's main market for illegal trafficking in animal parts) has seen a huge rise in poaching since the fall of the Soviet Union.

➡ Tens of thousands of critically endangered saiga antelope are killed every year for their translucent horns, which are sold to Chinese medicine makers. Between 1993 and 2003, saiga numbers declined from more than one million to a shocking 40,000.

➡ Tens of thousands of musk deer, currently found in Kyrgyzstan, Kazakhstan and Russia, have been killed in the last 20 years for their musk glands.

➡ In Kazakhstan over 1000 saker falcons are poached annually, most of them sold to the Gulf as hunting birds.

Survival Guide

Directory A–Z

Accommodation

Accommodation options are somewhat uneven across the region. The budget homestays of Kyrgyzstan are excellent and the B&Bs of Uzbekistan offer the most stylish and comfortable midrange options. Kazakhstan has a couple of backpacker hostels, some rural homestays, and good midrange and top-end choices. Tajikistan's Pamir region in particular has an informal network of homes and yurts that offer a fascinating and intimate look at the way local people live.

Budget travellers off the beaten track may still have to use the occasional fossilised Soviet-era hotel, but these are generally a last resort.

Budget accommodation can be considered anything under US$25 for a double room in high season.

Midrange hotels and B&Bs range from US$30 to US$70 per night (US$50 to US$100 in much of Kazakhstan). For this you can expect air-con, satellite TV, free wi-fi and a decent breakfast.

Many hotels also offer *lux* (luxury) and half *lux* suites, which normally have an extra room and can often sleep four or more; good for families. Homestays and yurt-stays are priced per person and we use the term dm (dorm) in our reviews.

We do not mention all of a hotel's price options in our reviews; even the worst hotels often have a few *lux* (deluxe) or half *lux* (semi-deluxe) suites for about twice the price of a basic room.

A room with a large double bed often costs significantly more than one with two single beds.

For top-end places you may get a better room rate by booking through a local travel agent or an online booking service, though most hotels offer their own discounts.

B&Bs

Bukhara, Khiva and Samarkand in Uzbekistan undoubtedly offer the best private accommodation, many of which are stylish boutique-style hotels in historic buildings. Rates tend to be between US$40 and US$75 for a double and include breakfast. Meals are extra but can normally be provided for around US$5 each.

Camping

In the wilds it's usually OK to camp, though there is always an inherent security risk. Popular trekking routes have established camping areas, frequented by Soviet alpinists during the Soviet era. You can normally camp at a *turbaza* (Soviet-era holiday camp) or yurt camp for a minimal fee.

Homestays

Happily, homestays are on the rise. For a bed of blankets on the floor and some type of breakfast you'll probably pay between US$10 and US$15 in Kyrgyzstan, where travel has been revolutionised by networks such as **Community Based Tourism** (CBT; www.cbtkyrgyzstan.kg). In the western Pamirs count on US$15 to US$18 per person half board, rising to US$20 to US$22 in the eastern Pamirs. Kazakhstan also has some rural homestays costing between US$25 and US$35 per person with all meals.

Do not expect hotel-style comforts; rural toilets, for example, can be squatters in the garden. Don't expect anything exotic either – in larger towns you may well end up in a block of flats, in front of a TV all evening. Levels of privacy vary. You might have access to a kitchen, especially if you are in an apartment.

Many local private travel agencies can set you up with a homestay, though prices may be double local rates.

Homestays are priced per person but you generally won't have to share rooms with strangers; however, friends travelling together will be expected to share a room.

Locals you meet on the road may invite you home and ask nothing for it, but remember that most ordinary people have very limited resources, so offer to pay around US$10, with US$5 extra for dinner and breakfast in rural areas.

Couchsurfing (www.couchsurfing.org) is quite well represented in Kazakhstan and Kyrgyzstan.

In Turkmenistan and Uzbekistan, staying with someone who hasn't gone through official channels with the Office of Visas & Registration (OVIR; Otdel Vis i Registratsii in Russian) could put them at risk, especially if your own papers aren't in order.

Hotels

Though some are better than others, you often don't get what you pay for in government or Soviet-era tourist hotels, largely because tourists pay higher rates than locals. Windows that don't open or close properly, chronically dim or missing light bulbs and toilets that leak but don't flush are common problems. All beds are single, with pillows the size of suitcases. That said, a lot of Soviet-era hotels have spruced themselves up in recent years and the situation is constantly improving.

Uzbekistan leads the way in midrange private hotels, which are popping up all over the place. There are also a limited number of party or government guesthouses, *dacha* (holiday bungalows) and former government *sanatoria,* which are now open to all. Most cities have a choice of several modern and comfortable private-sector hotels catering mostly to local and international *biznezmen,* where nouveau

FLOOR-LADIES

On every floor of a Soviet-style hotel a *dezhurnaya* (floor-lady) is in charge of handing out keys, getting hot water for washing, or *kipyatok* (boiled water) for hot drinks, sometimes for a small fee. Even the most god-awful hotel can be redeemed by a big-hearted floor-lady who can find someone to do your laundry, find a light bulb or stash your bags while you're off on an excursion.

riche is the dominant architectural style.

Some hotels will take your passport and visa for anywhere from half an hour to your entire stay, to do the required registration paperwork and to keep you from leaving without paying. Don't forget them when you leave – no one is likely to remind you.

Yurtstays

It's easy to arrange a yurt-stay in central Kyrgyzstan and the eastern Pamirs region of Tajikistan. Yurts range from comfortable but sterile tourist camps with beds, electricity and a nearby toilet, to the real McCoy owned by shepherds who are happy to take in the occasional foreigner for the night. The CBT and Shepherd's Life organisations in Kyrgyzstan, and drivers in Tajikistan can arrange yurtstays in the mountain pastures of the Tian Shan and Pamirs. Don't expect a great deal of privacy or much in the way of toilet facilities, but it's a fantastic way to get a taste of life on the high pastures (including the freshest yoghurt you've ever tasted!). For upmarket yurtstays try **Ecotour** (☏(0)557-802805, (0)772-802805; www.ecotour.kg;

Donskoy pereulok 46A, Umai Hotel, Bishkek) in Kyrgyzstan.

There are also yurts at a half-dozen locations in Kazakhstan, including Aksu-Zhabagyly Nature Reserve and Sayram-Ugam national park, plus Burabay. Uzbekistan has a yurt camp in the Kyzylkum desert near Ayaz-Qala and several yurt-stays at Lake Aidarkul.

As a sign of hospitality, yurtstay tables are often overflowing with bread, sweets, and other goodies. This is *not* an invitation to clear them out and pack it all in your bag – be a good guest, so that they can continue to be good hosts.

Children

Children can be a great ice-breaker and a good avenue for cultural exchange, but travelling in Central Asia is difficult even for the healthy adult. Long bus and taxi rides over winding mountain passes are a sure route to motion sickness. Central Asian food is difficult to digest no matter what your age, and extreme temperatures – blistering hot in the city, freezing in the mountains – lead to many an uncomfortable moment. Islamic architecture and ruined Karakhanid cities may well leave your children comatose with boredom so make a summer visit to amusement and aqua parks in all the major capitals (except Bishkek, Kyrgyzstan).

For general advice pick up Lonely Planet's *Travel with Children.*

We're Riding on a Caravan: An Adventure on the Silk Road (2005), by Laurie Krebs, is a children's picture book aimed at four- to eight-year-olds that describes a trader's life on the Chinese section of the Silk Road.

Stories from the Silk Road (1999) by Cherry Gilchrist, is a story book aimed at a similar age group.

Practicalities

➡ If you arc bringing very young children into Central Asia, nappies are available at department stores, but bring bottles and medicines.

➡ Forget about car seats, high chairs, cribs or anything geared for children, though you'll always find a spare lap and helpful hands when boarding buses.

➡ It's possible to make a cot out of the blankets supplied in most homestays.

➡ *Lux* hotel rooms normally come with an extra connecting room, which can be ideal for children.

Customs Regulations

Barring the occasional greedy official at a remote posting, few Western tourists have major customs problems in Central Asia. When they do, it's usually over the export of 'cultural artefacts'.

Declaring money on entry to a former Soviet republic is an awkward matter. In Uzbekistan you should declare everything (cash and travellers cheques) to the penny; officials at Tashkent airport will likely ask you to pull out your money, and will seize and fine you for the difference between what you have and what you declared. Count up your money privately before you arrive. You won't have a problem unless you are trying to leave with more money than you arrived with.

➡ There are no significant limits on items brought into Central Asia for personal use, except on guns and drugs.

➡ Uzbekistan is strict on which medications you bring into the country; avoid bringing painkillers or sleeping tablets and bring a prescription for anything else.

➡ Heading out, the main prohibitions are 'antiques' and local currency.

➡ You may well be asked for the customs declaration you filled out when you first entered the country, so save all official-looking documents.

➡ In Kazakhstan customs forms don't need to be filled in unless you are carrying goods above normal duty-free limits or cash worth more than US$3000.

Exporting Antiques

From the former Soviet republics, you cannot export antiques or anything of 'historical or cultural value' – including art, furnishings, manuscripts, coins, clothing and jewellery – without an export licence and payment of a stiff export duty.

If your purchase looks like it has historical value, you should get a letter saying that it has no such value or that you have permission to take it out anyway. Get this from the vendor, from the Ministry of Culture in the capital, or from a curator at one of the state art museums. Without it, your goods could be seized on departure.

➡ In Uzbekistan any book or artwork over 50 years old is considered antique.

➡ In Turkmenistan 'cultural artefacts' seems to embrace almost all handicrafts and traditional-style clothing, no matter how mundane.

➡ To export a carpet from Turkmenistan you'll need to get the carpet certified (for a fee) at Ashgabat's Carpet Museum or buy it from one of the state carpet shops. Get a receipt for anything of value that you buy, showing where you got it and how much you paid.

Documents

Besides your passport and visa, there are a number of other documents you may need to keep track of:

➡ Currency-exchange and hard-currency purchase receipts – you may need to show these when you sell back local money in a bank (not needed for money changers or in Kazakhstan).

➡ The customs form or entry form that you were given on entering the country.

➡ Vouchers – if you prepaid accommodation, excursions or transport, these are the only proof that you did so.

➡ Hotel registration chits – in Uzbekistan you may need to show these little bits of paper (showing when you stayed at each hotel) to OVIR officials.

➡ Letters of invitation and any supporting documents/receipts for visa and permit support.

➡ Photocopies of your passport – useful in border areas. If travelling through the Wakhan Valley of Tajikistan bring up to to 10 copies to save time at checkpoints.

➡ Student and youth cards are of little use, except as a decoy if someone wants to keep your passport.

It's wise to have at least one photocopy or scan of your passport (front and visa pages) and your travel-insurance policy on your person. It's also a good idea to have a scan of your passport and travel insurance on a flash drive or stored in the cloud.

Electricity

Kyrgyzstan, Turkmenistan

Type B
120V/60Hz

Turkmenistan

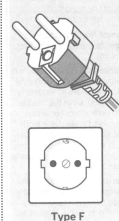

Type F
230V/50Hz

Kazakhstan, Takistan, Uzbekistan

Type C
220V/50Hz

Tajikistan, Uzbekistan

Type I
230V/50Hz

Food

Food should not be the main reason you come to Central Asia. In the first years of independence most restaurants served only standard slop, which somehow seemed to taste (and smell) indelibly of the old USSR. The situation has improved in recent years, particularly in the cities, with a rush of pleasant open-air cafes, fast-food joints and Turkish restaurants. The best way to appreciate regional cuisines, and the region's extraordinary hospitality, is still a meal in a private home.

Central Asian Cuisine

Central Asian food resembles that of the Middle East or the Mediterranean in its use of rice, savoury seasonings, vegetables and legumes, yoghurt and grilled meats. Many dishes may seem familiar from elsewhere: *laghman* (similar to Chinese noodles), *plov* (similar to Persian rice pilafs), nan (flat breads found all over Asia) and *samsa* (the samosa of India); one more benefit of Silk Road exchange.

The cuisine falls into three overlapping groups:

➡ The once-nomadic subsistence diet found in large areas of Kazakhstan, Kyrgyzstan and Turkmenistan – mainly meat (including entrails), milk products and bread.

➡ Diet of the Uzbeks and other settled Turks, which includes pilafs, kebabs, noodles and pasta, stews, elaborate breads and pastries.

➡ Persian influence, ranging from southern Uzbekistan into Tajikistan, which is distinguished by subtle seasoning, extensive use of vegetables and fancy sweets.

Mutton is the preferred meat. Big-bottomed sheep are prized for their fat, meat and wool, and fat from the

AMIN

After a meal or prayers, or sometimes when passing a grave site, you might well see both men and women bring their cupped hands together and pass them down their face as if washing. This is the *amin,* a Muslim gesture of thanks, common throughout the region.

sheep's tail actually costs more than the meat. The meat-to-fat ratio is generally stacked heavily in favour (and flavour) of the fat and you will soon find that everything smells of it. Sheep's head is a great delicacy, which may be served to honoured guests in some homes.

You can find Caspian caviar and seafood dishes in top-end restaurants in Kazakhstan. Dried and smoked fish are sold near Issyk-Köl.

MENU STANDARDS

The following standards are generally available in every restaurant.

Shashlyk Ubiquitous kebabs of fresh or marinated mutton, beef, minced meat *(farsh* or *lyulya* kebab) or less commonly, chicken. Usually served with nan bread and vinegary onions. The quality varies from inedible to addictively delicious. Liver kebabs are known in Turkic as *jiger.*

Plov Called *pilau* in Tajikistan, this consists mainly of rice with fried and boiled mutton, onions and carrots, and sometimes raisins, quince, chickpeas or fruit slices, all cooked up in a hemispherical cauldron called a *kazan. Plov* is always the pièce de résistance when entertaining guests. Uzbekistan (p210) is the artery-clogged heart of Central Asian *plov.*

Laghman Noodle dish that includes fried mutton, peppers, tomatoes and onions. Korean, Uyghur and Dungan noodles are generally the best.

Shorpo Soupy stew, also called *shurpa* or *sorpo,* that consists of boiled mutton on the bone with potatoes, carrots and turnips.

Manpar Noodle pieces, meat, vegetables and mild seasoning in broth.

Beshbarmak Popular in Kazakhstan and Kyrgyzstan (*shilpildok* in Uzbek; *myaso po-kazakhsky* in Russian). Large flat noodles with lamb and/or horsemeat are cooked in vegetable broth (the Kazakh version serves the broth separately). It means 'five fingers' since it was traditionally eaten by hand.

Nan (*non* to Uzbeks and Tajiks; *lepyoshka* in Russian) Round bread baked in a *tandyr* (tandoori) oven. Some varieties are prepared with onions, meat or sheep's-tail fat in the dough; others have anise, poppy or sesame seeds placed on top. Nan also serves as an impromptu plate for shashlyk. Homemade breads are often thicker and darker than normal nan. Much better than the boring, square, white-flour Russian loaves known simply as *khleb.*

Salads A refreshing break from heavy main courses and a godsend for vegetarians. Good restaurants can offer 20 or more types of salads, many of which are heavy on the mayonnaise. Parsley, fresh coriander, green onions and dill are served and eaten whole.

Breakfast (*zaftrak* in Russian) Generally consists of tea or instant coffee, bread, jam, some kind of eggs and maybe yoghurt, cream or semolina. Normally included in your accommodation.

SNACKS

There are variations on the meat-and-dough theme.

Manty (mantu) Steamed dumplings, a favourite from Mongolia to Turkey.

Chuchvara (*tushbera* in Tajik; *pelmeny* in Russian) A smaller boiled cousin of *manty,* served plain or with vinegar, sour cream or butter, or in soups.

Pirozhki Greasy Russian fried pies filled with potatoes or meat; generally disappointing.

Samsa Meat pie made with flaky pastry and baked in a tandoor oven; best in Kyrgyzstan.

Fruit is eaten fresh, cooked, dried or made into preserves, jams and drinks known as *kompot* or *sok.* In general, May is the best time for apricots, strawberries and cherries, June for peaches and July for grapes and figs. Melons ripen in late summer, but are available as late as January.

Central Asians are fond of dried fruits and nuts, particularly apricots and apricot stones, which when cracked open have a pith that tastes like pistachios. At any time of year you'll find delicious walnuts, peanuts, raisins and almonds, plus great jams (sea-buckthorn jam is a real treat) and wonderful mountain honey (*assal* in Turkic languages).

MILK PRODUCTS

Central Asia is known for the richness and delicacy of its fermented dairy products, which use cow, sheep, goat, camel or horse milk. The milk itself is probably unpasteurised, but its cultured derivatives are safe if kept in hygienic conditions. Many doughs and batters incorporate sour milk products, giving them a tangy flavour.

The fresh yoghurt and cream served to guests in the mountain pastures of Kyrgyzstan and Tajikistan will likely be the best you've ever tasted.

Suzma Strained yoghurt creates this tart cottage or cream cheese, used as a garnish or added to soups.

Ayran A salty yoghurt/water mix; the Russian equivalent is called *kefir.*

Katyk A thin, drinkable yoghurt.

Kurut Dried *suzma* rolled into rock-hard marble-size balls that have the half-life of uranium.

Tvorog Russian speciality made from soured milk that is heated to curdle. This is hung in cheesecloth overnight to strain off the whey. Similar to *suzma*.

Kaimak Pure sweet cream, skimmed from fresh milk that has sat overnight. A wickedly tasty breakfast item, that is wonderful with honey.

Drinks

➡ Don't drink the tap water. Cheap bottled mineral water is easy to find.

➡ Tins of cheap imported instant coffee can be found everywhere; hot water (*kipyatok*) is easy to drum up from a hotel floor-lady or homestay.

➡ Decent espresso coffee is now quite easy to find in Uzbekistan and major cities elsewhere.

➡ One hangover from Russian rule is *kvass*, a fermented soft drink made from black bread, fruit and honey and often served at street corners out of giant barrels.

TEA

Chay (*choy* to Uzbeks and Tajiks, *shay* to Kazakhs) is drunk with reverence.

➡ Green tea (*kok* in Turkic languages; *zelyonnyy* in Russian) is the favourite; locals claim it beats the heat

and unblocks you after too much greasy *plov*.

➡ Black tea (*kara* in Turkic languages; *chyornyy chay* in Russian) is preferred in Samarkand and Urgench, and by most Russians.

➡ Western Turkmen brew tea with camel's milk and Pamiris use goat's milk. Kazakh tea is taken with milk, salt and butter – the nomadic equivalent of fast food – hot, tasty and high in calories.

The chaikhana (teahouse; transliterated as *chaykhana* in Turkmen, *chaykana* in Kyrgyz, *choyhona* in Uzbek and Tajik, *shaykhana* in Kazakh) is male Central Asia's essential socio-gastronomic institution. Usually shaded, often near a pool or stream, it's as much a men's club as an eatery – although women,

including foreigners, are tolerated. You can normally get food in a chaikhana.

Traditional seating is on a bed-like platform called a *tapchan*, covered with a carpet and topped with a low table. Take your shoes off to sit on the platform, or leave them on and hang your feet over.

VODKA & BEER

The Islamic injunction against alcohol has had little obvious impact in ex-Soviet Central Asia. Most Central Asians enjoy a drink and, like

the Russians who introduced them to vodka, take their toasts seriously.

Given the depth of Central Asian hospitality it's impolite to refuse the initial 'bottoms up' (Russian – *vashe zdarovye*!), and/or abstain from at least a symbolic sip at each toast. But there's usually heavy pressure to drain your glass every time – so as not to give offence, it is implied – and the pressure only increases as everybody gets loaded. The Russian phrase *chut chut* may mean 'a little bit', but when applied to a shot of vodka it generally seems to get translated as 'up to the brim'.

You'll find a wide range of Russian and European beer (*piva*). St Petersburg's Baltika is the brew of choice and comes in a wide range of numbers from 0 (non-alcoholic) to 9 (very strong). Baltikas 3 and 6 are the most popular.

Popular local beers on tap include Derbes, Karagandinskoye (both Kazakh), Sim Sim (Dushanbe, Takijistan) and Siberian Crown (Russian). Kyrgyzstan has a growing range of small microbreweries, including Arpa, Nashe Pivo, Zhivoe, Hoff, Akademia and Venskoye, while Line Brew is a popular craft brewery in Kazakhstan. Draught beer is advertised in Russian as *na razliy, razlivnoe* or *svezhee pivo* (fresh beer).

TEA ETIQUETTE

Tea is the drink of hospitality, offered first to every guest, and almost always drunk from a *piala* (small bowl). Bear the following tips in mind.

➡ From a fresh pot, the first cup of tea is often poured away (to clean the *piala*) and then a *piala* of tea is poured out and returned twice into the pot to brew the tea.

➡ A cup filled only a little way up is a compliment, allowing your host to refill it often and keep its contents warm (the offer of a full *piala* of tea is a subtle invitation that it's time to leave).

➡ Pass and accept tea with the right hand; it's extra polite to put the left hand over the heart as you do this.

➡ If your tea is too hot, don't blow on it, but swirl it gently in the cup without spilling any. If it has grown cold, your host will throw it away before refilling the cup.

KUMYS & OTHER ATTRACTIONS

Kumys (properly kymys in Kyrgyz; qymyz in Kazakh) is fermented mare's milk, a mildly (2% to 3%) alcoholic drink appreciated by most Kazakhs and Kyrgyz. It's available only in spring and summer, when mares are foaling, and takes around three days to ferment. The milk is put into a chelek (wooden bucket or barrel) and churned with a wooden plunger called a bishkek (from where that city derives its name). Locals will tell you that kumys cures anything from a cold to TB but in reality drinking too much of

HOSPITALITY DOS & DON'TS

Being invited home for a meal can be your best introduction to local customs as well as to the best local cuisine. Don't go expecting a quick bite. Your host is likely to take the occasion very seriously. Uzbeks, for example, say mehmon otanda ulugh, 'the guest is greater than the father'.

➡ It's polite to arrive with a gift. Something for the table (eg some fruit from the market) will do. Better yet would be something for your hosts' children or their parents, preferably brought from your home country (eg postcards, badges, a picture book).

➡ You will likely be offered water for washing your hands. Dry your hands with the cloth provided; shaking the water off your hands is said to be impolite.

➡ Always take your shoes off when entering someone's house or even yurt.

➡ The dastarkhan is the central cloth laid on the floor, which acts as the dining table. Never put your foot on or step on this. Try to walk behind, not in front of, people when leaving your place and don't step over any part of someone's body. Try not to point the sole of your shoe or foot at anyone as you sit on the floor.

➡ Wait until you are told where to sit; honoured guests are often seated by Kyrgyz or Kazakh hosts opposite the door (so as not to be disturbed by traffic through it, and because that is the warmest seat in a yurt). Men (and foreign women guests) might eat separately from the women and children of the family.

➡ The meal might begin with a mumbled prayer, followed by tea. The host breaks and distributes bread. After bread, nuts or sweets to 'open the appetite', business or entertainment may begin.

➡ The meal itself is something of a free-for-all. Food is served, and often eaten, from common plates, with hands or big spoons. Pace yourself – eat too slowly and someone may ask if you're ill or unhappy; too eagerly and your plate will be immediately refilled. Praise the cook early and often; your host will worry if you're too quiet.

➡ Devout Muslims consider the left hand unclean, and handling food with it at the table, especially in a private home and with communal dishes, can be off-putting. At a minimum, no one raises food to the lips with the left hand. Try to accept cups and plates of food only with the right hand.

➡ Bread is considered sacred in Central Asia. Don't put it on the ground, turn it upside down or throw it away (leave it on the table or floor cloth). If someone offers you tea in passing and you don't have time for it, they may offer you bread instead. It is polite to break off a piece and eat it, followed by the amin (Musliim gesture of thanks). If you arrive with nan at a table, break it up into several pieces for everyone to share.

➡ Traditionally, a host will honour an important guest by sacrificing a sheep for them. During these occasions the guest is given the choicest cuts, such as the eyeball, brain or meat from the right cheek of the animal. Try to ensure that your presence doesn't put your host under financial hardship. At least try to leave the choicest morsels for others.

➡ Pulling out your own food or offering to pay someone for their kindness is likely to humiliate them. Some travellers hosted by very poor people have given a small cash gift to the eldest child, saying that it's 'for sweets'.

➡ If alcohol consumption is modest, the meal will end as it began, with tea and a prayer.

➡ Don't eat after the amin. This signals thanks for and an end to the meal.

it may give you diarrhoea. The best *kumys* comes from the herders themselves; the stuff available in the cities is sometimes diluted with cow's milk or water.

Kazakhs and Kyrgyz also like a thick, yeasty, slightly fizzy concoction called *bozo*, made from boiled fermented millet or other grains.

Turkmen, Kazakh and Karakalpak nomads like *shubat* (fermented camel's milk). An early-morning glass of breakfast *chal* (camel's milk) in Turkmenistan will wake you up faster than a double espresso.

Vegetarians & Vegans

Central Asia can be difficult for vegetarians; indeed the whole concept of vegetarianism is unfathomable to most locals. Those determined to avoid meat will need to visit plenty of farmers markets. The cities of Kazakhstan and Uzbekistan are probably the best places for vegetarians.

In restaurants, you'll see lots of tomato and cucumber salads. *Laghman* or soup may be ordered without meat, but the broth is usually meat-based. In private homes there is always bread, jams, salads, whole greens and herbs on the table, and you should be able to put in a word to your host in advance. Even if you specifically ask for vegetarian dishes you'll often discover the odd piece of meat hidden somewhere – after a while it all seems a bit of a conspiracy.

'Without meat' is *etsiz* in Turkmen; *atsiz* in Kazakh and Kyrgyz; *gushtsiz* in Uzbek; and *biz myasa* in Russian.

Where to Eat & Drink

Dining options include streetside stalls and cafes, private restaurants, chaikhanas (teahouses) and, best of all, private homes.

A few midrange and top-end restaurants (*meyram-*

khana in Kazakh and Kyrgyz; *oshhona* in Uzbek) in bigger cities offer interesting Central Asian, Turkish, Chinese, Georgian, Korean or European dishes and earnest service. The occasional Siberian salmon or black caviar livens things up. Almaty and Astana have particularly good food scenes.

Beware menu prices in top-end restaurants, as they are often given as per 100g, not per serving (which is more like 250g to 400g). In some restaurants main dishes are just that and you'll have to order garnishes such as rice, potatoes or vegetables separately at additional cost.

What most locals want from a restaurant in the evening is a night out – lots of booze and gale-force techno music or a variety show. Even if there's no music blasting when you come in, the kind staff will most likely turn on (or turn up) the beat especially for foreigners.

The canteen (*stolovaya*) is the ordinary citizen's eatery – dreary but cheap, with a limited choice of cutlets or lukewarm *laghman*.

Certain old-town neighbourhoods of Tashkent and Samarkand (both in Uzbekistan) have home restaurants offering genuine homestyle cuisine. There is rarely a sign; family members simply solicit customers on the street.

Every sizeable town has a colourful bazaar (*rynok* in Russian) or farmers market with hectares of fresh and dried fruit, vegetables, nuts, honey, cheese and bread. Private supermarkets across the region sell a decent range of European and Russian goods.

Korean and Dungan vendors sell spicy *kimchi* (vegetable salads), a great antidote for mutton overdose. Fresh honey on hot-from-the-oven nan makes a splendid breakfast.

Insurance

Central Asia is an unpredictable place so insurance is a good idea. A minimum of US$1 million medical cover and a 'medevac' clause or policy is essential, as few reliable emergency services are available in the Commonwealth of Independent States (CIS; the loose political and economic alliance of most former member republics of the USSR, except the Baltic states).

Some policies specifically exclude 'dangerous activities', which can include skiing, motorcycling, even trekking or horse riding. If these are on your agenda, ask about an insurance amendment to permit some of them (at a higher premium).

Few medical services in Central Asia will accept your foreign insurance documents for payment; you'll have to pay on the spot and claim later. Get receipts for everything and save all the paperwork.

Worldwide travel insurance is available at www.lonelyplanet.com/travel-insurance. You can buy, extend and claim online anytime – even if you're already on the road.

Internet Access

Wi-fi is available in almost all hotels and many restaurants and cafes, especially in Kazakhstan, Kyrgyzstan and Uzbekistan (but much less so in Turkmenistan). Connections are generally good but can be limited to hotel lobbies in cheaper hotels. You may find it easier to bring a smartphone and get a SIM card with a data package.

Internet access is widely available throughout the region; just look for a roomful of pasty teenagers playing games like *Counterstrike*. The only place where you can't get reliable internet access is Turkmenistan.

In internet cafes you may find your keyboard set to Cyrillic; pressing 'shift' + 'alt' should change the keyboard language to English.

Language Courses

The **London School** (Map p66; ☑(0)312-545262; www.londonschool.kg; Baytik Baatyr (Soviet) 39; per hour 250som, registration basic/intensive 300/1200som) in Bishkek offers intensive Kyrgyz or Russian language tuition for travellers, with both classroom and homestay environments.

In Dushanbe the **Bactria Centre** (Map p148; ☑372 21 2558; www.bactriacc.org; Tursunzoda 12A; ☺9am-5pm Mon-Fri) runs courses in Russian and Persian.

American Councils (☑20 2-833-7522; www.americancouncils.org; Ste 1200, 1828 L St NW, Washington, DC) organises summer- and year-long academic exchanges and language study programs in Central Asia.

Legal Matters

Visitors are subject to the laws of the country they're visiting. It's unlikely that you will ever actually be arrested, unless there are supportable charges against you.

If you are arrested, authorities in the former Soviet states are obliged to inform your embassy (*pasolstvah* in Russian) immediately and allow you to communicate with a consular official without delay. Most embassies will provide a list of recommended lawyers.

LGBTIQ Travellers

There is little obvious LGBTIQ community in Central Asia, though there is some gay

nightlife presence in Almaty (Kazakhstan). In Kyrgyzstan, **Labrys** (☑(0)312-902963; www.labrys.kg) provides support and services for LGBTIQ locals and travellers, and can provide information on LGBTIQ-friendly events.

Affection shown between members of the same sex in public is generally considered a sign of friendship not of an intimate relationship. No matter your sexual preference, it's best to avoid public displays of affection throughout Central Asia.

In Uzbekistan, Turkmenistan and Tajikistan, gay male sex is illegal, but lesbian sex does not seem to be illegal (and is seldom spoken about).Kazakhstan and Kyrgyzstan have lifted the Soviet-era ban on homosexuality.

Maps

Buy your general maps of Central Asia before you leave home. For a search of the available maps try www.stanfords.co.uk.

➡ German publisher Reise Know How (www.reise-know-how.de) produces good and long-lasting travel maps to Central Asia (*Zentralasien*, 1:700,000) and Kazakhstan (*Kasachstan*).

➡ *Central Asia* (Gizimap, 1999) is a good 1:750,000 general elevation map of the region (plus Kashgar), though it excludes northern Kazakhstan and western Turkmenistan. It usefully marks many trekking routes.

➡ *Central Asia – The Cultural Travel Map along the Silk Road* (Elephanti) is a similar 1:1.5 million Italian map, which concentrates on Uzbekistan and Tajikistan.

➡ Nelles' 1:750,000 *Central Asia* map is also good. Reliable, locally produced city and regional maps can be found in Kazakhstan and Kyrgyzstan, but are hard to find elsewhere. Especially

in Uzbekistan, where many street names have been changed three or four times since independence, any map older than a couple of years will drive you crazy.

Money

The 'stans' banking systems have improved greatly in the last few years, with credit-card transactions, wire transfers (particularly Western Union) and regulated foreign exchange available in most towns. In the countryside there are few facilities, so change enough cash to get you back to a main city.

If you plan to travel extensively in the region, it's worth bringing a combination of cash US dollars or euros (the latter particularly in Kazakhstan) and a credit card or two for the cities.

Try to avoid large notes in local currency (except to pay your hotel bills), since few people can spare much change.

ATMs

Most cities in ex-Soviet Central Asia have ATMs (*bankomat*) that accept Western credit cards. Turkmenistan has the fewest functioning ATMs and Kyrgyzstan and Kazakhstan have the most.

ATMs in Uzbekistan often give US dollars, which can be useful, but they are often out of order.

It makes sense to get your cash during working hours, since the last thing you need is to watch your card get eaten alive by an Uzbek ATM.

Some ATMs charge a service fee of around 2%.

Black Market

The existence of licensed money changers in every town has done away with the black market in all republics, including in Uzbekistan (p282), where it was much alive until 2017, when government regulations changed, making the black market nearly obsolete overnight.

Cash

Cash in US dollars is by far the easiest to exchange, followed by euros. Take a mixture of denominations – larger notes (US$100, US$50) get a better rate, but a cache of small ones (US$10, US$5) is handy for when you're at borders, stuck with a lousy exchange rate or need to pay for services in US dollars.

Our listings sometimes quote prices in US dollars or euros, when that is the most reliable price denominator or if that's the currency you'll be quoted on the ground. You currently have to pay for accommodation in Turkmenistan in US dollars.

You may also need cash in US dollars to pay for visas and some services with a private travel agency, though many of the latter now accept credit cards.

Make sure dollar bills are in good condition – no worn, torn or marked notes – and that your US$100 notes are dated post-2013. Taxi drivers and market-sellers often fob off their own ragged foreign notes on tourists as change, so of course you should refuse to accept old notes too.

Credit Cards

It's an excellent idea to bring a credit card and/or a debit card, though you shouldn't rely on it completely to finance your trip as there are still only a limited number of places where it can be used. Kazakhstan and Kyrgyzstan are the most useful places in Central Asia to have a credit or debit card.

Major credit cards can be used for payment at top-end hotels and restaurants, central airline offices, major travel agencies and a few shops throughout the region. Visa is the most widely recognised brand, but MasterCard is accepted in most places, as are the Cirrus and Maestro systems.

If you can't find an ATM to accept your card, it's possible to get a cash advance against a Visa card or MasterCard in capitals for commissions of 1% to 3%. Asking for the '*terminal*' (the hand-held machine that processes the card transaction) indicates that you want a cash advance. Always get a receipt, in case you are asked for proof of changing money at customs or if there is any discrepancy when you get home.

International Transfers

Money transfers are possible through major banks in all capitals and through **Western Union** (www.westernunion. com), which has partners in banks and post offices everywhere and remains the easiest way to send money. Commissions of 1% to 4% are typical.

Money Changers

Dealing with licensed money changers is the easiest way to change cash in Kyrgyzstan, Kazakhstan and Tajikistan. They are found in small kiosks on nearly every block, and some will give a receipt if you ask them; rates vary by 1% to 2% at most. Licensed changers are completely legal. Money changers are marked by signs such as обмен валюты (*obmen valyuty*; currency exchange) and обменный пункт (*obmenny punkt*; exchange point).

Nearly all tourist hotels have bank-exchange desks, though double-check the rates.

EXCHANGE RECEIPTS

Whenever you change money, ask for a receipt (*kvitantsiya* or *spravka* in Russian) showing your name, the date, the amounts in both currencies, the exchange rate and an official signature. Not everyone will give you one, but if you need to resell local currency through the banks (in Uzbekistan or Turkmeni-

stan) you may need enough receipts to cover what you want to resell. You will not need a receipt to sell local currency into US dollars with money changers in other countries.

Until 2017, you could only legally sell Uzbek som back at a main city office of the National Bank – not at the airport, hotels or the border. However, regulations changed in January 2018 allowing travellers to take up to US$5000 in Uzbek som with them out of the country. As change can be slow, it's safest not to try to carry too much cash out with you.

Travellers Cheques

Travellers cheques can be cashed in the major Central Asian capitals (except Dushanbe, Tajikistan) but it is becoming increasingly difficult to do so. Most travellers rely on cash or ATMs.

If visiting Uzbekistan you need to list your travellers cheques on your customs declaration form or you won't be able to cash them.

Security

ATMs are becoming more common in Central Asia, but you may still end up carrying large wads of cash, especially in Uzbekistan.

Don't leave money in any form lying around your hotel room. Lock it deep in your luggage or carry it securely zipped in a money belt, with only what you'll need that day accessible in an exterior pocket, wallet or purse.

When paying for anything substantial (eg a hotel bill or an expensive souvenir) or changing money on the street at an exchange kiosk, count out the money beforehand, out of public sight; don't go fumbling in your money belt in full view. There are tales of thieves targeting people coming out of banks with fat cash advances, so keep your eyes open.

It can be useful to note the numbers of your cards and keep the telephone numbers

PRACTICALITIES

Electricity The entire former USSR is nominally 220V at 50 cycles.

Smoking Technically forbidden in public places across Central Asia, but most strictly enforced in Turkmenistan.

Visas Much easier to obtain than a few years ago. Kyrgyzstan and Kazakhstan are visa-free, Tajikistan has an easy online process, Uzbekistan is fairly easy and Turkmenistan is tricky.

Weights & Measures Central Asia is metric. When you buy produce in markets make sure you know whether the price is per piece (shtuk) or by the kilo.

handy to call if they are lost or stolen.

Taxes & Refunds

Sales tax in Central Asia is included in the price and tax refunds are generally not available or worth the hassle.

Tipping & Bargaining

Tipping is common in Central Asian cities. Most cafes and restaurants in the capitals add a 10% to 20% service charge to the bill, or expect you to round the total up.

Shops have fixed prices, but in markets (food, art or souvenirs) bargaining is usually expected.

➡ Asking prices are usually in proportion to the expected outcome. Sellers will be genuinely surprised if you reply to their '5000' with '1000'; they're more likely expecting 3500, 4000 or 4500 in the end.

➡ Always negotiate when arranging transport hire.

➡ In Kyrgyzstan bargaining is usually reserved only for taxi drivers.

➡ The Russian word for 'discount' is *skidka*.

Opening Hours

Banks and offices 9am to noon and 1 to 5pm Monday to Friday, possibly 9am to noon Saturday. Exchange offices keep longer hours, including weekends.

Museums Generally closed Monday.

Restaurants 11am to 9pm; longer opening hours in major cities.

Photography

Memory cards for digital cameras are quite prevalent in Central Asia these days. Most internet cafes can burn your photos on to a CD, as long as the burner works. Electricity is quite reliable for charging batteries, except in the remote Pamirs. Good-quality batteries are hard to find in rural areas.

Photographing & Videoing People

Most Central Asians are happy to have their picture taken, though you should always ask first. You may find people sensitive about you photographing women, especially in rural areas. Women photographers may get away with it if they've established some rapport.

The Russian for 'may I take a photograph?' is *fotografirovat mozhno?* (fa-ta-gruh-*fee*-ra-vut *mozh*-na?).

Post

The postal systems of Central Asia are definitely not for urgent items. A letter or postcard will probably take

two weeks or more to get outside the CIS. Kyrgyzstan and Kazakhstan are probably the most reliable places from where to send packages.

Central post offices are the safest places to post things. It can help to write the destination country in Cyrillic too.

If you have something that absolutely must get there, use an international courier company. **DHL** (www.dhl.com) and **FedEx** (www.fedex.com) have offices in major cities.

Express Mail Service (EMS) is a priority mail service offered by post offices that ranks somewhere between normal post and courier post. Prices are considerably cheaper than courier services.

Public Holidays

Turkmenistan has some particularly wacky holidays, including Melon Day, Horse Day and 'A Drop of Water is a Grain of Gold' Day.

The following Islamic holidays are observed lightly in ex-Soviet Central Asia and are cultural, not public, holidays. Dates are fixed by the Islamic lunar calendar, which is shorter than the Western solar calendar, beginning 10 to 11 days earlier in each solar year. Dates given here are approximate (within a day or two). The holidays normally run from sunset to the next sunset.

Ramazan is observed with little fanfare in most of Central Asia, though you will find some restaurants closed during the day, reopening in the evening as families convene to break the day's fast.

Ramazan (15 May 2018, 5 May 2019, 23 April 2020, 13 May 2021) Also known as Ramadan, the month of sunrise-to-sunset fasting. Dates mark the beginning of Ramazan.

Eid al-Fitr (14 June 2018, 4 June 2019, 23 May 2020, 13 May 2021) Also called Ruza Hayit in Uzbekistan, and Orozo Ait in

Kyrgyzstan. This involves two or three days of celebrations at the end of Ramazan, with family visits, gifts, a great banquet (known as Iftar) to break the fast and donations to the poor.

Eid al-Azha (23 August 2018, 12 August 2019, 31 July 2020, 20 July 2021) Also called Eid-e Qurban, Kurban Bayram, Qurban Hayit or Kurban Ait in Central Asia. This is the Feast of Sacrifice. Those who can afford it buy and slaughter a goat or sheep, sharing the meat with relatives and with the poor. This is also the season for the haj (pilgrimage to Mecca).

Moulid an-Nabi (20 November 2018, 9 November 2019, 28 October 2020, 18 October 2021) The birthday of the Prophet Mohammed. A minor celebration in Central Asia, though you might notice mosques are a little fuller.

Registration

Kazakhstan Tourists generally do not need to register, other travellers will get a white registration card. Two stamps indicates you are registered, one stamp indicates you need to register.

Kyrgyzstan No longer required.

Tajikistan Tourist-visa holders only register if staying for over 30 days.

Uzbekistan The hotel in which you stay should register you and provide you with a chit of paper you need to keep.

Turkmenistan Tourist- or business-visa holders must register. The tour company that invited you usually organises this.

If you do need to register, the place to go is OVIR (Migration Police). There's one in every town, sometimes in each city district. Though it has a local name in each republic (eg Koshi-Kon Politsiyasi in Kazakhstan, OPVR in Tajikistan, IIB in Uzbekistan, UPVR in Kyrgyzstan), everybody still understands the word OVIR. In some remote areas where there is no OVIR

office you may have to register at the *passportny stol* (passport office).

Responsible Travel

Tourism is still relatively new to Central Asia, so try to keep your impact as low as possible and create a good precedent for those who follow you.

One of the best ways to ensure your tourist dollars make it into local communities is to support community-based tourism projects, and engage local services and guides whenever possible.

The following are a few tips.

➡ Be respectful of Islamic traditions and don't wear singlets, shorts or short skirts in rural areas or the Fergana Valley.

➡ Don't hand out sweets or pens to children on the streets, as it encourages begging.

➡ Buy your snacks, cigarettes, bubble gum etc from the enterprising grannies trying to make ends meet rather than from state-run stores.

➡ Don't buy items made from endangered species, such as Marco Polo sheep and snow leopards.

➡ Don't pay to take a photo of someone and don't

photograph someone if they don't want you to. If you agree to send someone a photo, make sure you follow through with it.

➡ Discourage the use of scarce fuels such as firewood and *terksen* (high-altitude bush) in the eastern Pamirs.

➡ If someone offers to put you up for the night make sure you don't put your host under financial burden. Don't let them sacrifice an animal in your honour (common in the Pamirs) and try to offer money or a gift in return for your host's hospitality.

➡ Don't let your driver drive too close to archaeological sites and try to stick to existing tracks when driving off-road.

Safe Travel

Travel in Central Asia is generally trouble-free and certainly much easier than a decade ago.

➡ Watch for pickpockets in crowded bazaars or bus stations.

➡ Central Asian officials and police generally create more problems than they solve.

➡ Make sure your documents, permits and registration (if needed) are watertight at all times.

➡ At night don't get into a taxi with more than one person in it.

GOVERNMENT TRAVEL ADVICE

The following government websites offer travel advisories and information on current hotspots.

Australian Department of Foreign Affairs (www. smartraveller.gov.au) Register online.

British Foreign Office (www.gov.uk/foreign-travel-advice)

Canadian Department of Foreign Affairs (www.travel. gc.ca)

New Zealand Ministry of Foreign Affairs (www.safe travel.govt.nz)

US State Department (http://travel.state.gov) Register online at https://travelregistration.state.gov.

Crime

Crime is minimal by Western urban standards, but visitors are tempting, high-profile targets.

If you're the victim of a crime, contact the *militsia* (police), though you may get no help from them at all. Get a report from them if you hope to claim on insurance for anything that was stolen, and contact your closest embassy for a report in English.

If your passport is stolen, you must immediately contact the nearest embassy (which might be in a neighbouring republic, or even Moscow). It will help if you have a photocopy of your passport to verify who you are. The local police should provide a letter to OVIR, which is essential for replacing your visa.

It's a good idea to register with your embassy online and to carry the telephone numbers of your embassies in the region.

Corrupt Officials

The number of corrupt officials has decreased dramatically in the last few years and most travellers make their way through Central Asia without a single run-in with the local *militsia*.

The strongest police presence is in Uzbekistan (particularly in the Tashkent metro), followed by Turkmenistan and Tajikistan, where there are police checkpoints at most municipal and provincial borders. Take a long-distance taxi ride anywhere in the region and you'll likely see your driver paying off traffic cops after being waived down by an orange baton.

It's a near certainty that you'll meet a *gendarme* or two in Uzbekistan, though most only want to see your papers and know where you're going, particularly in the Tashkent metro.

Travellers may find bribery a fact of life for locals and visitors alike in Central Asia,

though it is best avoided, as it propagates a stereotype that foreign travellers like throwing their money around. A combination of smiles (even if over gritted teeth) and patient persistence can very often work best.

If you are approached by the police, there are several rules of thumb to bear in mind:

➡ Be polite, firm and jovial. A forthright, friendly manner – starting right out with an *asalam aleykum* (peace be with you) and a handshake for whomever is in charge – may help to defuse a potential shakedown, whether you are male or female.

➡ If someone refers to a 'regulation', ask to see it in writing. If you are dealing with lower-level officers, ask to see their *nachalnik* (superior).

➡ Do not hand over your passport unless you see a police officer's ID. Even better, only hand over a photocopy of your passport; claim that your passport is at your hotel or embassy. Even when showing it to authorities, try to keep it in your possession and allow them to look while you hold it.

➡ Try to avoid being taken somewhere out of public view, such as into an office. The objective of most detentions of visitors is to extort money by intimidation rather than violence.

➡ If you are detained at a police station, call your embassy or consulate.

➡ Never sign anything without consular assistance, especially if it's in a language you don't understand.

➡ Antinarcotics laws give the police powers to search passengers at bus and train stations. If you are searched, insist on emptying your own pockets, as there have been cases of police palming

drugs into visitors' pockets only to 'discover' the stash and charge them for it.

➡ If police officers want to see your money (to check for counterfeit bills) try to take it out only in front of the highest-ranking officer. If any is taken, insist on a written receipt for it. In any case, count it before and after to verify the amount handed over and returned.

➡ If you have to pay a fine, insist that you do so at a bank and get a receipt for the full amount.

➡ In some cases, travellers have found it easiest not to speak any Russian if they are stopped, as often corrupt officials will tire of their attempts and send you on your way.

Shopping

In general, Uzbekistan offers Central Asia's best shopping; in fact most of central Bukhara is now one big souvenir stall.

Potential Central Asian buys include carpets, hats, musical instruments, felt rugs, wall hangings, silk, traditional clothing, ceramic figurines and even nomadic accessories such as horse whips and saddles.

Turkmenistan is the place for a 'Bukhara-style' carpet, though getting it out of the country can be an expensive bureaucratic hassle. The best places for a *shyrdak* (Kyrgyz felt carpet) are the women's cooperatives in Kochkor and elsewhere in Central Kyrgyzstan. CBT can often put you in touch with local *shyrdak* producers. You can find more Kyrgyz felt souvenirs at the **Yak House** (☑919 481774, Salamat 919 482685; Murgab House, Murgab; ⊙9am-5pm Mon-Fri or by arrangement) 🖋 and **De Pamiri** (Map p177; ☑935 00 4803, 935 20 2901; www.de pamiri.org; Central Park, Khorog; ⊙9am-5pm May-Nov), both in Tajikistan's Pamir region.

In addition, there are extra things to consider if exporting antiques (p460) or items that look antique.

Central Asian bazaars are enjoyable, even if you're just looking, with everything from Russian sparkling wine to jeep parts. Another surprising souvenir source is the local TsUM department store.

Telephone
International Calls

Most people will find it easiest and cheapest to use an app such as Skype or Viber to make phone calls back home. Note that Uzbekistan and Turkmenistan sometimes block Skype.

You can also place international calls (as well as local and intercity ones) from the central telephone and telegraph offices in most towns. You tell a clerk the number and prepay in local currency. After a wait of anything from half a minute to several hours, you're called to a booth. Hotel operators also place calls, but for a hefty surcharge. International calls in the region generally cost between US$0.50 and US$2 per minute.

Calls between CIS countries are now treated as international calls, though they have a different rate. Thus to call Uzbekistan from, say, Kyrgyzstan, you would need to dial Kyrgyzstan's international access code, the Uzbek country code, then the Uzbek city code.

Local Calls

Almost everyone in Central Asia has a mobile phone so it's increasingly hard to make public phone calls. Local calls are very cheap if you have a local SIM card. Otherwise, try to make local calls from your hotel.

Mobile Phones

Local SIM cards are easy to get in Kazakhstan, Kyrgyzstan and Tajikistan, and only somewhat harder to get as a foreigner in Uzbekistan and Turkmenistan. Local calls and data are inexpensive.

If you have an 'unlocked' GSM-900 phone, buy a local SIM card and top that up at booths in every village. You will probably need a copy of your passport to buy a SIM card and may need a local's help. Local calls and texts with a local SIM card cost pennies.

Several Central Asian companies have roaming agreements with foreign providers so check with your phone company. Beeline (www.beeline.ru) is a good general choice for most of the region if you plan to visit several republics.

Note that Central Asian mobile phones work on 900/1800 MHz frequencies. European phones generally share these frequencies but most older US cell phones use 850/1900 frequencies so you will probably need an unlocked quad-band American phone if you want to use it in Central Asia. Most modern smartphones will work fine. Alternatively just buy a cheap phone on arrival.

Toilets

Public toilets are scarce. Those that you can find – eg in parks, and bus and train stations – charge a small fee to use their squatters. Most toilets are awful, the rest are worse. You are always better off sticking to top-end hotels

and restaurants or shopping malls.

➡ Carry a small torch for rural restaurant toilets, which rarely have functioning lights, and for trips out to the pit toilet.

➡ *Always* carry an emergency stash of toilet paper.

➡ Toilet paper is sold everywhere, though tissues are a better bet than the industrial-strength sandpaper that is ex-Soviet toilet paper.

➡ The wastepaper basket in the loo is for used paper and tampons (wrapped in toilet paper).

➡ Before bursting in, check for the signs 'Ж' (Russian: *zhenski*) for women or 'M' (*muzhskoy*) for men.

➡ The word 'toilet' is *khojathana* in Uzbek and Tajik, and *darathana* in Kazakh and Kyrgyz. Out in the *jailoo* (pastures) of Kyrgyzstan and Tajikistan there are often no toilets at all. You'll have to go for a hike, find a rock or use the cover of darkness. Always urinate at least 50m from a water source (and downstream!) and dig a hole to defacate into, and burn the paper afterwards.

Tourist Information

Intourist, the old Soviet travel bureau, gave birth to a litter of Central Asian successors, most of which are useless to independent travellers. You are almost always better off with a private or local community-based-tourism project.

That said, there are useful tourist information centres in Almaty and Shymkent in Kazakhstan, at Khorog and Murgab in Tajikistan, in Khiva and Samarkand in Uzbekistan and also at Karakol in Kyrgyzstan. In remote areas local NGOs can often offer advice on accommodation, transport and ecotourism initiatives.

Travellers with Disabilities

Central Asia is a difficult place for travellers with disabilities. There are not many wheelchair-accessible ramps in new buildings and even fewer in old Soviet-era buildings. There is also a severe lack of services catering to the visually or hearing impaired.

Hiring your own transport and guide through a reliable private agency will go some way to solving logistical problems but issues will still remain in the winding traditional backstreets of places such as Bukhara and Khiva.

Download Lonely Planet's free *Accessible Travel* guide from http://lptravel.to/AccessibleTravel.

Volunteering

The US Peace Corps has a presence in Tajikistan and Turkmenistan. The UK Voluntary Service Overseas (VSO) operates in Tajikistan.

Volunteers headed to Central Asia should read the following books:

➡ *Taxi to Tashkent: Two Years with the Peace Corps in Uzbekistan* (2007) by Tom Fleming.

➡ *Chai Budesh? Anyone for Tea?* (2008) by Joan Heron, subtitled 'A Peace Corps Memoir of Turkmenistan'.

➡ *This Is Not Civilization* (2004) by Robert Rosenberg. A novel chronicling the travails of a Peace Corps volunteer that is partly set in Kyrgyzstan.

➡ *Revolution Baby* (2007) by Saffia Farr. An account of three years of expat life raising a baby in Kyrgyzstan.

Volunteer opportunities exist at the **Sworde-Teppa** (www.sworde-teppa.org.uk) organisation in Kurgonteppa in southern Tajikistan.

If you have some artistic flair, **B'art Contemporary** (Map p66; ☎(0)312-530092; www.bishkekart.kg; Karasaev 3) accepts volunteers. Some travellers have helped out at community-based-tourism projects in Kyrgyzstan.

PamirLink (www.pamirlink.org) runs a three-week live-in working-holiday experience in Basid in the Bartang Valley of the western Pamirs, where visitors stay in homestays and work on local small-scale development projects.

The Hong Kong–based organisation **Crossroads** (www.crossroads.org.hk) accepts volunteers for its work throughout Central Asia in the fields of health, poverty, substance abuse and the environment.

Women Travellers

Attitudes in the Central Asian republics remain fairly male-dominated and are still quite sexist, though often this does not extend to foreign women. Female travellers are not likely to experience too much discrimination or harassment.

Most mosques in cities and the major tourist areas are open to all, but women are generally not allowed in mosques in Tajikistan and the Fergana Valley. Both men and women should seek permission before entering a mosque, particularly during prayer times, when non-Muslims might feel uncomfortable.

In bigger cities, there is no taboo on unaccompanied local women talking to male visitors in public. Local men addressed by a woman in a couple usually direct their reply to the man, out of a sense of respect. In some social settings, local women don't drink in public, and on some occasions, female visitors might not be offered a shot of the vodka or wine doing the rounds.

Keen sensibilities and a few rules of thumb can make a solo journey rewarding.

➡ Clothes do matter: a modest dress code is essential (even if some local women appear to disregard this). Go for long trousers/skirts and covered shoulders.

➡ Never follow any man – even an official – into a private area. If one insists on seeing your passport, hand over a photocopy; if he pushes you to follow him, walk away into a busy area.

➡ When riding in shared taxis, try to choose one that already has other female passengers.

➡ Sit at the front of the bus, preferably between two women, if you can.

➡ If you feel as though you are being followed or harassed, seek the company of a group of women; most older women will automatically take you under their wing.

➡ Some local men will honestly want to befriend and help you; if you are unsure and have a difficult time shaking them, mention your 'husband' even if you don't have one.

Despite these warnings, the opportunities for genuine cross-cultural woman-to-woman interactions can generally be had during homestays, and usually outside the cities. In the privacy of a group of women, you'll likely find a frankness and openness you never thought existed and you will see a side of Central Asia hidden to male travellers.

Work

There aren't many casual work opportunities in the region. What work *is* available is probably limited to English teaching and aid work, both of which are best arranged prior to your arrival in the region.

You may find teaching positions in the region's universities, particularly the following.

American University of Central Asia (www.auca.kg; Aaly Tokombaeva 7/6, Bishkek, Kyrgyzstan)

Samarkand State Institute of Foreign Languages (Map p230; ☑66-235 66 19; www. samdchti.uz; Bo'stonsaroy 93, Uzbekistan)

University of Central Asia (www.ucentralasia.org) With campuses in Khorog (Tajikistan), Naryn (Kyrgyzstan) and Tekeli (Kazakhstan).

For those with a TEFL or CELTA certificate, the **London School** (Map p66; ☑(0)312-545262; www.londonschool.kg; Baytik Baatyr (Soviet) 39) in Bishkek, Kyrgyzstan, offers teaching posts for a minimum of six months for the academic year, or four months for the summer.

Transport

GETTING THERE & AWAY

Getting to Central Asia is half the fun, whether it's part of an overland Silk Road trip or crossing formerly forbidden border posts. Air connections are improving steadily throughout the region, with Tashkent (Uzbekistan) and Almaty (Kazakhstan) the main hubs.

The long-distance rail connections are mostly with Mother Russia, from Moscow or the Trans-Siberian Railway to Tashkent, Almaty, Bishkek (Krygyzstan) and Astana (Kazakhstan). The only other external rail link is the Silk Road train between Astana/Almaty and Ürümqi in China, with onward rail connections from there.

The other main overland links are three roads from China: one accessible year-round via Ürümqi to Almaty, and two warm-weather routes from Kashgar to Kyr-gyzstan, over the Torugart or Irkeshtam passes.

Finally there are the offbeat but somewhat un-reliable journeys from Baku (Azerbaijan), across the Caspian Sea by ferry to Turk-menbashi (Turkmenistan) or alternatively to Aktau in Kazakhstan.

Flights, cars and tours can be booked online at www.lonelyplanet.com/bookings.

Entering Central Asia

Entering Central Asia can be a bit daunting. Many flights arrive in the middle of the night, officials can be unhelpful and you may have to battle a scrum of taxi drivers once you exit the terminal. That said, immigration formalities are increasingly streamlined and you shouldn't face any major issues as long as your documents are in order.

In Uzbekistan it's particularly important to make sure you fill out your customs form accurately, claiming all cash that you are bringing into the country.

Air

The region's main air links to the 'outside' are through the main cities of Almaty (Kazakhstan), Bishkek (Kyrgyzstan), Tashkent (Uzbekistan), Ashgabat (Turkmenistan) and, to a lesser extent, Dushanbe (Tajikistan) and Astana (Kazakhstan). Tiny Osh (Kyrgyzstan) even has a couple of interesting international connections.

A few cities in Kazakhstan have international links to Europe, and cities in all republics have connections to Commonwealth of Independent States (CIS) countries, especially Russia.

Of the many routes in, two handy corridors are via Turkey (thanks to the geopolitics of the future) and via Russia (thanks to the geopolitics of the past). Turkish Airlines

---

CLIMATE CHANGE & TRAVEL

Every form of transport that relies on carbon-based fuel generates CO_2, the main cause of human-induced climate change. Modern travel is dependent on aeroplanes, which might use less fuel per kilometre per person than most cars but travel much greater distances. The altitude at which aircraft emit gases (including CO_2) and particles also contributes to their climate change impact. Many websites offer 'carbon calculators' that allow people to estimate the carbon emissions generated by their journey and, for those who wish to do so, to offset the impact of the greenhouse gases emitted with contributions to portfolios of climate-friendly initiatives throughout the world. Lonely Planet offsets the carbon footprint of all staff and author travel.

has the best connections and in-flight service but is at the higher end of the fare scale, while Russian and Central Asian carriers have the most connections. Turkey also has the advantage of a full house of Central Asian embassies and airline offices. Moscow has four airports and connections can be inconvenient.

Airports

Almaty International Airport (www.alaport.com; Maylin 2; ☎92) A useful gateway to both Kazakhstan and Kyrgyzstan (Bishkek is just three hours by road).

Ashgabat International Airport Less well connected, most reliably by Lufthansa and Turkish Airlines. The newly reconstructed airport opened in 2016.

Astana International Airport (TSE; ☎7172-70 29 99; www.astanaairport.com; ☎10, 12, 100, 200) Has a range of international flights.

Bishkek Manas International Airport (FRU; ☎(0)312-693109; www.airport.kg; Manas Airport Rd; ☎) Kyrgyzstan's main hub with relatively inexpensive international connections.

Dushanbe Airport (☎474 49 4233; www.airport.tj; Titov 32/2) The least connected, with most people using Turkish Airlines. A modern and efficient terminal was opened in 2014 and there are plans to build a new airport.

Tashkent International Airport (☎71-140 28 04) Possibly the most central airport in Eurasia and the busiest airport in Central Asia. The airport is due to get a new international terminal in 2020.

Airlines

The following are the main Central Asian airlines, of which Uzbekistan Airways and Air Astana are the best.

Air Astana (www.airastana.com; airline code KC; hub Almaty) Most flights from Almaty but an increasing number of international flights from Astana and

some international flights from Atyrau, Kostanay and Aktau.

Air Kyrgyzstan (http://air.kg; airline code QH; hub Bishkek) Limited number of regional flights.

Air Manas (www.airmanas.com; airline code ZM; hub Bishkek) A reliable Kyrgyz-Turkish airline that is part of Pegasus Airlines. Flies to Ürümqi, Delhi and İstanbul, with connections on Pegasus to most European cities.

Somon Air (www.somonair.com; airline code 4J; hub Dushanbe) A handful of regional flights, with flights to Frankfurt and Ürümqi.

Tajik Air (www.tajikair.tj; airline code 7J; hub Dushanbe) Mostly regional flights.

Turkmenistan Airlines (www.turkmenairlines.com; airline code T5; hub Ashgabat) Flights include Bangkok, Beijing, Birmingham, Frankfurt and London.

Uzbekistan Airways (www.uzairways.com; airline code HY; hub Tashkent) A good selection of flights to Europe, Asia and the US.

Tickets

Finding flights to Central Asia isn't always easy, as travel agents are generally unaware of the region and many don't book flights on Russian or Central Asian airlines.

➤ Contact the airlines directly for schedules and contact details of their consolidators, or sales agents, who often sell the airlines' tickets cheaper than the airlines themselves.

➤ Consider paying a little extra for a reliable airline such as KLM or Turkish Airlines, rather than a cash-strapped one such as Tajik Air.

➤ Always check what time the flight arrives: many

airlines arrive in Central Asia in the dead of night.

➤ Specialist agencies such as www.alternativeairlines.com can often book Central Asian airline tickets when others can't.

➤ Some budget airlines such as Pegasus Airlines and Air Baltic don't show up on online searches, so try those airlines' websites directly.

Visa Checks

You can buy air tickets without a visa but in most places outside Central Asia you will have trouble getting on a plane without one (with the exception of Kazakhstan and Kyrgyzstan).

If you have made arrangements to get a visa on arrival, have your Letter of Invitation (LOI) handy at check-in and check with the airline beforehand.

Airline Safety

Aeroflot, the former Soviet state airline, was decentralised into around 400 splinter airlines and many of these 'baby-flots' now have the worst regional safety record in the world, due to poor maintenance, ageing aircraft and gross overloading. In general though, the main Central Asian carriers have lifted their services towards international safety standards, at least on international routes.

Most Kazakh airlines (except Air Astana) and all Kyrgyz airlines are currently banned from flying into EU airspace.

From Asia

From Beijing there are four weekly flights to Tashkent on Uzbekistan Airways and China Southern, five weekly to Almaty and Astana on Air Astana and a couple per week to Ashgabat on Turkmenistan Airlines.

Ürümqi in China's Xinjiang province has between two and seven flights a week to/from Almaty, Astana, Tashkent, Bishkek, Osh, Dushanbe and Ashgabat, with China Southern offering the most flights. One-way prices are around US$200, but Air Manas to Bishkek often dips below US$100.

Bangkok, Hong Kong, Delhi and Seoul also have useful connections into Central Asia.

From Australia & New Zealand

Most flights to Central Asia go via Seoul (to pick up Asiana or Korean Air flights to Tashkent and Almaty or Air Astana to Almaty), Kuala Lumpur (for Uzbekistan Airways to Tashkent, Air Astana to Almaty), Bangkok (Uzbekistan Airways to Tashkent, Air Astana to Almaty or Turkmenistan Airlines to Ashgabat) or İstanbul.

China Southern is often among the cheapest options, via Guangzhou and Beijing or Ürümqi. One cheap option to Kyrgyzstan is a ticket that connects in Delhi to the Air Manas flight to Bishkek.

For Dushanbe and Bishkek you'll probably have to go via İstanbul.

From Continental Europe

The best fares from Europe to Central Asia are generally with Aeroflot via Moscow or Turkish Airlines via İstanbul. Air Astana offers some good fares to Almaty/Astana, from Amsterdam and Frankfurt, or try KLM and Belavia (via Minsk).

Somon Air has a weekly direct Frankfurt–Dushanbe flight, costing around €400/650 one way/return.

From Russia

Budget airlines such as air-Baltic fly to Moscow, making it a decent travel option if you are pinching pennies or want to travel overland by train. Remember to figure in the cost and hassle of a visa and transfer between airports in Moscow when comparing costs. You will need to get a Russian transit visa in advance if you have to transfer between airports and you should budget at least four or five hours to negotiate Moscow's crazy traffic.

There are daily flights from Moscow to almost all Central Asian cities. One-way fares range from US$220 to US$300. There are slightly fewer connections from St Petersburg. Major Siberian cities such as Novosibirsk also have connections to the Central Asia capitals.

Uzbekistan Airways flies from Moscow to Samarkand, Bukhara, Urgench, Termiz, Andijon and several others several times weekly for around US$230. Aeroflot flies from Moscow to Tashkent, Bishkek, Almaty and Astana.

Note that Moscow has two main international airports: **Sheremetyevo** (www.svo. aero/en) and **Domodedovo** (www.domodedovo.ru/en). Sheremetyevo is itself divided into several terminals: Terminal B (Sheremetyevo-1), the international Terminal F (Sheremetyevo-2), and newly renovated terminals C, D and E.

At the time of research Aeroflot and Air Astana operated from Sheremetyevo, while Tajik Air, Turkmenistan Airways, Uzbekistan Airways, Somon Air, Manas Air and Air Kyrgyzstan used Domodedovo airport.

Travel agencies in Moscow include **Unifest Travel** (☑495-234 6555; www.unifest. ru; Bldg 3-4, Komsomolsky pr 16/2; ☺9am-9pm Mon-Fri, 10am-7pm Sat-Sun, visa support 10am-6pm Mon-Fri) for rail and air tickets and Central Asia packages, affiliated with the Travellers Guest House.

From Turkey & Azerbaijan

Turkish Airlines flies from İstanbul to Almaty (daily), Astana (two to four weekly), Bishkek (daily), Dushanbe (twice weekly), Tashkent (five weekly) and Ashgabat (daily). The various republics' national airlines also fly once or twice a week.

There are also cheap flights from İstanbul's smaller Sabiha Gökçen airport to Bishkek and Almaty with Turkish budget airline Pegasus Airlines.

One-way flights to İstanbul cost from around US$200 from most Central Asian capitals.

Air Astana flies from Baku, Azerbaijan to Almaty and Astana, and from Tbilisi, Georgia to Almaty. There are also flights from Baku, Tbilisi and Yerevan, Armenia to Aktau two to three times weekly. Uzbekistan Airways makes the connection from Baku to Tashkent.

From the UK

The best return summer fares to Tashkent are around £500 with Uzbekistan Airways (direct), or a bit more with Turkish Airlines via İstanbul.

The cheapest flights to Bishkek are currently with the budget Turkish airline Pegasus Airlines, which has fares as low £300 return from London Stansted. Be aware that Pegasus has a reputation for losing travellers' luggage and that transfers at İstanbul's Sabiha Gökçen can be time-consuming. Check also about cheap flights to Osh with Turkish Airlines.

Fares to Almaty are about £400 return on Turkish Airlines via İstanbul, on Aeroflot via Moscow or Air Astana via Astana.

The best flights to Ashgabat are with Lufthansa or Turkish Airlines at around £700 return. A cheaper but harder-to-book option is **Turkmenistan Airlines** (www.flyturkmenistanairlines.eu), which flies weekly to Ashgabat from London and also four times a week from Birmingham. Most passengers are headed either to/from Amritsar. For cheap fares contact **Amritsar Travel** (www.amritsartravel.com).

The best way to Dushanbe is on Turkish Airlines via İstanbul but discounted fares are hard to come by.

From the USA

From North America you generally have the choice of routing your trip via İstanbul (Turkish Airlines), Moscow (Aeroflot) or a major European city (with KLM, British Airways, Lufthansa etc). Stopovers can be lengthy. From the west coast it's possible to fly to Almaty or Tashkent via Seoul on Asiana or Korean Air.

Uzbekistan Airways flies from New York (JFK airport) to Tashkent (via Riga) once a week, an 18-hour flight.

East Site (www.east-site.com) offers discounted Central Asian fares, including on Uzbekistan Airways.

Land

Bus

From China, there are one or two sleeper buses a week (Monday and Thursday) from Kashgar to Osh (¥275, eight hours) in Kyrgyzstan, via the Irkeshtam Pass. It's also possible to take a series of minibuses and taxis, or hire a car.

Kashgar agencies such as **Uighur Tours** (www.kashgartours.com), **Old Road Tours** (www.oldroadtours.com) and **Kashgar Guide** (www.kashgarguide.com) can arrange transport to the Torugart and Irkeshtam passes.

Foreigners are not allowed to take the twice-weekly bus between Kashgar and Bishkek, via Naryn and the Torugart Pass. Mandatory prearranged vehicle hire and permits for four people from Kashgar to Naryn

costs around US$320 from Kashgar to the border, plus an extra US$120 from the Torugart to Naryn. Thus figure on around US$220/120 per person in a group of two/four from Kashgar to Naryn. It's slightly cheaper in the opposite direction.

Further north, direct buses run from Ürümqi (¥440 to ¥460, 24 hours, daily) to Almaty. Fares from Almaty cost US$48/20 in tenge to Ürümqi/Yining. You can also take local buses (from Yining) and shared taxis to and from the border at Khorgos.

There are also direct buses from Ust–Kamenogorsk (US$54, 28 hours, three weekly) and Semey (US$55, 32 hours, three weekly) in Kazakhstan to Ürümqi.

Car & Motorcycle

The new Western Europe–Western China (WE–WC) highway offers the easiest driving option from European Russia into Central Asia via Kazakhstan. The route runs from St Petersburg to Moscow, Kazan and Orenburg, then across Kazakhstan to Almaty and into China at Khorgos.

Although driving a car or motorbike is an excellent way to get around Central Asia, bringing your own vehicle is fraught with practical problems.

The state insurance offices, splinters of the old Soviet agency Ingosstrakh, have no overseas offices that we know of, and your own insurance is unlikely to be valid in Central Asia. You would probably have to arrange insurance anew at each border.

Readers have recommended **Campbell Irvine** (www.campbellirvine.com) as one company in the UK that can often arrange overland vehicle insurance.

Many Kazakh cities have motorbike clubs which will often welcome foreign bikers – and in some cases drivers. Almaty is easily the best place in Central Asia for getting motorbike repairs. The

website www.horizonsunlimited.com is a good resource for bikers.

If you are thinking of driving out to Central Asia, then consider doing it for charity as part of the **Roof of the World Rally** (www.charityrallies.org/rotw) or **Tajik Rally** (http://adventure-manufactory.com/en/tajik/tajik-home).

Train

FROM CHINA

Completed in 1992, after being delayed almost half a century by Russian–Chinese geopolitics, is a line from China via Ürümqi to Almaty and Astana in Kazakhstan, joining the Turksib for connections on to Siberia.

The 1363km Silk Road train between Ürümqi and Almaty leaves on Monday and Saturday evening and takes about 32 hours, which includes several hours at the border for customs checks and to change bogies.

Sleeper tickets cost ¥892/1020 for hard/soft sleeper in Ürümqi or US$113 for kupe (2nd-class or sleeping carriage) class in Almaty. Book trains at least a few days ahead.

The weekly Astana–Ürümqi service (39 hours) was not operating at the time of research.

FROM RUSSIA

There are three main rail routes into Central Asia from Russia:

➡ From Moscow via Samara or Saratov, straight across Kazakhstan via Aktobe and Kyzylorda to Tashkent (3369km), with branch lines to Bishkek and Almaty (4057km).

➡ From Volgograd to Atyrau, Qongirot (Kungrad), Uchquduk, Navoi and Samarkand to Tashkent.

➡ Turkestan–Siberian railway or 'Turksib' (see www.turksib.com for timetables) linking the Trans-Siberian Railway at Novosibirsk with Almaty.

SILK ROAD BY RAIL

Silk Road romantics, train buffs and nervous flyers can cross continents without once having to fasten their seatbelt or turn off their cell phones. The 'iron Silk Roads' to Central Asia don't have quite the romance or the laid-back feel of the Trans-Siberian Railway, but they allow Eurasia to unfold gradually, as you clank through endless plains, steppe and desert.

From Moscow you can watch Europe turn to Asia on the three-day, 4000km train trip to Tashkent or Astana. From here you can add on any number of side trips to Samarkand, Bukhara or even Urgench (for Khiva). Then from Almaty it's possible to continue on the train to Ürümqi in China and even to Kashgar or Hotan.

From Ürümqi you can continue along the Silk Road by train east as far as Beijing, Hong Kong or even Lhasa or Saigon, making for an epic transcontinental ride. It's not always comfortable and it will take some time, so why do it? Because like Everest, it's there.

Several other lines enter northern Kazakhstan from Russia and meet at Astana, from where a line heads south to Karaganda and Almaty.

Most trains bound for Central Asia depart from Moscow's Kazan (Kazansky) station. Europe dissolves into Asia as you sleep, and morning unveils a vast panorama of the Kazakh steppe.

You will need to check visa requirements carefully. Trains from Moscow to Tashkent demand a Kazakh transit visa and trains between Russia and Kazakhstan might require a multiple-entry Russian visa. Trains to/from Dushanbe are impractical because you will need a Kazakh, multiple-entry Uzbek and possibly even a Turkmen visa.

These days *kupe* fares between Moscow and Central Asia cost about the same as a flight; only *platzkartny* (hard sleeper) fares are cheaper than flying. A *kupe* berth from Astana to Moscow costs around US$200.

POPULAR ROUTES

Train connections between Russia and Central Asia have thinned out in recent years but are still a favourite of migrant workers, tourists and drug smugglers. The following are the most popular fast trains from Moscow:

Tashkent (numbers 5/6, three weekly, 66 hours)

Astana (numbers 71/72 and 83/84, every other day, 55 hours)

Bishkek (numbers 17/18 and 27/28, two weekly, 76 hours)

Trains out of Moscow have even numbers; those returning have odd numbers.

Numbers 7/8, which ran every other day between Moscow and Almaty (80 hours), were cancelled in 2017 but might be reinstated.

Other offbeat connections include the Saratov–Nukus–Tashkent (twice weekly) route. There are other, slower connections but you could grow old and die on them.

PURCHASING TICKETS

To buy tickets from Moscow try the following websites:

G&R International (www.hostels.ru)

Real Russia (www.realrussia.co.uk/trains)

Russian Railways (http://pass.rzd.ru)

Way to Russia (www.wayto russia.net)

ONLINE RESOURCES

For a useful overview of international trains to/from Central Asia see www.seat61.com/silkroute.htm.

For online timetables and fares, try the following websites.

Poezda (www.poezda.net/en)

Russian Railways (http://pass.rzd.ru/main-pass/public/en)

Sea

The Baku (Azerbaijan) to Turkmenbashi 'ferry' route (seat US$30, cabin US$50 to US$60, 12 to 18 hours) across the Caspian is a possible way to enter and leave Central Asia. Boats leave around four times a week in both directions, but there is no timetable. You'll simply have to arrive and wait until the ship is full of cargo.

There are also irregular cargo boats every week or 10 days between Baku and Aktau (US$80, 24 hours) in Kazakhstan. One of these ferries sunk in October 2002, killing all 51 people aboard.

➡ For the Baku–Turkmenbashi boat, once on board you'll likely be offered a cabin by a crew member, for which you will pay around US$50.

➡ The best cabins have private bathrooms and are comfortable, although some can be cockroach-infested.

➡ Leave a couple of days (longer for Aktau) left on your visa in case the boats are delayed, which is common. Some travellers have found themselves waiting for a couple of days to dock in Turkmenbashi, using up valuable time in their fixed-date visa.

➡ Stock up on food and water beforehand, as there is little or no food available on board. Crossings can end up taking 32 hours or longer.

Tours

There are lots of reliable travel agencies inside Central Asia that can help with the logistics of travel in Central Asia – whether it be visas, a few excursions or an entire tailored trip.

The people behind the website **Caravanistan** (www. caravanistan.com) can arrange tours in conjunction with local tour operators.

Stantours (www.stantours. com) is another Kazakhstan-based operator that can arrange travel throughout the region.

If you have a deep interest in the region, **Martin Randall Travel** (www.martinrandall.com) and **Steppes Travel** (www. steppestravel.com) run tours to Central Asia led by lecturers, writers and other experts.

The following agencies outside the region can arrange individual itineraries and/or accommodation, tickets and visa support.

Australia

Passport Travel (www.travel centre.com.au) Silk Road by rail tours.

Sundowners Overland (www. sundownersoverland.com) Small-group and independent tours into Central Asia..

Uzbek Journeys (www.uzbek journeys.com)

Europe

Indy Guide (www.indy-guide. com) Linking travellers with local travel agents and guides.

Kalpak Tours (www.kalpak-travel.com)

UK

Regent Holidays (www.regent-holidays.co.uk) Offers tours and can cobble together an individual itinerary.

Scott's Tours (www.scottstours. co.uk) Hotel bookings, visas and more.

Wild Frontiers (www.wild frontierstravel.com) Tailor-made tours with an emphasis on adventure.

USA

Mir Corporation (www.mir corp.com) Independent tours, homestays and visa support with accommodation.

Red Star Travel (www.redstar travel.us) Organises tours, individual itineraries, accommodation, train tickets, visa support with booking.

Silk Road Treasure Tours (www. silkroadtreasuretours.com).

GETTING AROUND

Transport in Central Asia is relatively convenient and abundant in the plains but much patchier in the mountains.

Train High-speed modern trains run to Samarkand, Bukhara and soon Khiva in Uzbekistan and between Almaty and Astana in Kazakhstan. Long-distance rail services are less comfortable but a common way to get around huge Kazakhstan.

Bus Fairly reliable and comfortable coaches run between major cities, but comfort, reliability and frequency plummet rapidly in rural areas.

Shared taxi The best way to get around Kyrgyzstan, Tajikistan and Uzbekistan. Pay by the seat or buy all four of them for cheap car hire on set routes.

Hire car Useful for the Pamirs and mountain areas of Kyrgyzstan and generally priced per kilometre, with a driver.

Air

Flying saves time and takes the tedium out of Central Asia's long distances but it is arguably the least safe mode of transport in Central Asia. The Central Asian airlines have some way to go before meeting international safety standards on their domestic routes.

Apart from the national Central Asian airlines, there are a couple of domestic and regional airlines, such as Kazakhstan's **SCAT** (www. scat.kz), **Qazaq Air** (www. flyqazaq.com) and **Bek Air/ Halyk Air** (www.bekair.com); Kyrgyzstan's **Air Manas** (www.airmanas.com) and **Avia Traffic** (www.aero.kg); and Tajikistan's **Somon Air** (www. somonair.com).

Unless you are really counting the pennies all of these, except Air Manas and Somon Air, are generally best avoided.

➡ You generally pay for air tickets in local currency, though in Uzbekistan you must pay in US dollars. Some airline offices and travel agencies accept credit cards, especially those in Kazakhstan.

➡ Domestic and inter-republic services are no-frills; you might get a warm glass of Coke if you are lucky. For long flights consider packing lunch.

➡ Dushanbe–Tashkent services were reintroduced in 2016 for the first time in 25 years. Major internal connections still run daily.

➡ Flights between the biggest cities generally stick to their schedules, but those serving smaller towns are sometimes delayed or cancelled without explanation.

➡ Routes and individual flights are constantly being cancelled or reintroduced. The only sure way to find out what's flying is to ask at an air booking office.

➡ Tickets for Central Asian airlines are most easily purchased from private travel agents (aviakassa). You'll need your passport. Many booking offices have a special window for international flights.

➡ Air Astana has useful online booking for both international and domestic flights and you can book Uzbekistan Airways tickets on foreign online ticket sites.

➡ Seating on short-haul flights is a bit of a free-for-all

(there are often no assigned seats), especially if the flight is overbooked. To minimise the risk of loss, consider carrying everything on board.

➡ Helicopter flights were once popular for trekkers headed to the Tian Shan and Pamir ranges but rising fuel costs have made most services prohibitively expensive (around US$1300 per hour for a chopper). Maintenance is also patchy; avoid them except in summer and go only if the weather is absolutely clear.

Bicycle

A few diehards cycle (p44) across Central Asia as part of a longer Silk Road cycling trip. Uzbekistan is a fairly popular destination, but the summer heat and the registration requirements complicate camping options.

Kyrgyzstan offers some fine mountain-bike options, including tours, and there are even a couple of places to rent bikes.

Perhaps the grandest trip option is to cycle Tajikistan's spectacular Pamir Hwy from Khorog to Osh. You'll need to be completely self-sufficient in terms of spare parts and repairs but it's an incredible trip.

There is little or nothing in terms of bike lanes or biking culture in Central Asia. Securing accommodation or secure camping spots en route is often the biggest challenge.

Bus

Bus travel is the best bet for getting between major towns cheaply, if there are no shared taxis. Except for Uzbekistan, major transport corridors are served by big long-distance coaches (often reconditioned German or Turkish vehicles), which run on fixed routes and schedules, with fixed stops. They're

relatively problem-free and moderately comfortable, with windows that open and sometimes with reclining seats. Luggage is locked safely away below. Journey times depend on road conditions but are somewhat longer than a fast train.

Regional buses are a lot less comfortable and a bit more...interesting. Breakdowns are common. Regional buses are also used extensively by small-time traders to shift their goods around the region, and you could gradually become surrounded by boxes, bags, and both live and dead animals.

Private minibuses, generally called marshrutka (Russian for 'fixed-route vehicle'), are a bit more expensive, always faster and usually more hair-raising. They generally have fixed fares and routes but no fixed timetable (or no departure at all if there aren't enough passengers to satisfy the driver), and will stop anywhere along the route. They can be clapped-out heaps or spiffy new Russian Gazelle or Chinese-made minivans.

Keep in mind that you're at the mercy of the driver as he picks up cargo here and there, loading it all around the passengers, picks up a few friends, gets petrol, fixes a leaky petrol tank, runs some errands, repairs the engine, loads more crates right up to the ceiling – and then stops every half-hour to fill the radiator with water.

Buying Tickets

Most cities have a main intercity bus station (*avtovokzal* in Russian, *avtobekat* in Kyrgyz and Uzbek, *avtobeket* in Kazakh, and *istgomush* in Tajik) and may also have regional bus stations (sometimes several) serving local towns.

Try to pick buses originating from where you are, enabling you to buy tickets as much as a day in advance. Tickets for through buses originating in a different city may not be sold until they arrive, amid anxious scram-

bles. At a pinch you could try paying the driver directly for a place. Disregard most bus-station timetables.

Car & Motorcycle

Driving your own car around Central Asia gives you wonderful freedom if you know what you are doing. Main highways between capitals and big cities (eg Almaty–Bishkek–Tashkent–Samarkand–Bukhara) are fast and fairly well maintained.

Mountain roads (ie most roads in Kyrgyzstan and Tajikistan) can be blocked with snow in winter and plagued by landslides in spring.

Fuel supply is uneven, though modern petrol stations are springing up throughout the region. Prices per litre swing wildly depending on supply. Petrol comes in four grades: 76, 93, 95 and 98 octane. In the countryside you'll see petrol cowboys selling plastic bottles of fuel from the side of the road, often of very poor quality.

The biggest problem is the traffic police (Russian, GAI). Tajikistan, Uzbekistan and Kazakhstan have police skulking at every corner, most looking for excuses to wave their orange baton and hit drivers (local or otherwise) with a 'fine' (*straf*). There are no motoring associations of any kind.

Car Hire

Almaty and Astana have car-rental companies (Almaty offers pricey motorcycle rental), and several people have recommended **Iron Horse Nomads** (⌕(0)555-800278; http://ihn.kg; Tynalieva St; ⊗9am-5pm Mon-Fri) in Bishkek for vehicle rental. Travel agencies can hire you a local car or 4WD with driver, either for a day trip or a multiday tour, but if you speak some Russian you'll almost always find it cheaper hiring a taxi for the day.

Swiss-run **MuzToo** (http://muztoo.ch; 101 St; ⊗9am-5pm

Mon-Fri) rents self-drive 4WDs and motorbikes from its base in Osh (Kyrgyzstan). Costs are around US$70 to US$100 per day.

Hiring a car and driver unlocks some of Central Asia's best mountain scenery and is well worth it, despite the cost.

➡ Community-based tourism organisations and travel agencies hire 4WDs for driving through the more remote areas of Kyrgyzstan, Tajikistan and Kazakhstan.

➡ Travel agencies have better vehicles but are more expensive.

➡ Drivers in Tajikistan's eastern Pamirs charge between US$0.80 and US$1 per kilometre for a Russian 4WD.

Taxi

There are two main ways of travelling by car in Central Asia if you don't have your own vehicle: ordinary taxi or shared taxi.

ORDINARY TAXI

One way to travel is to hire an entire taxi for a specific route. This is handy for reaching off-the-beaten-track places, where bus connections are hit-and-miss or nonexistent, such as Son-Köl in Kyrgyzstan or a tour of the Elliq-Qala forts in Karakalpakstan.

➡ Select your driver with care, look over their car (we took one in Kyrgyzstan whose exhaust fumes were funnelled through the back windows) and assess their sobriety before you set off.

➡ You'll have to negotiate a price before you set off. Along routes where there are also shared taxis, ordinary taxis should be four times the shared-taxi per-person fare.

➡ Drivers often refer to a private charter as *salon,* in contrast to *collectif,* which means a shared taxi

➡ Make sure everyone is clear which route you will be taking, how long you want the driver to wait at a site and if there are any toll, entry or parking fees to be paid.

➡ You can work out approximate costs by working out the return kilometre distance; assume the average consumption of cars is around 12L per 100km and then multiply the number of litres needed by the per-litre petrol cost (constantly in flux).

➡ Add to this a daily fee (anything from US$5 up to the cost of the petrol) and a waiting fee of around US$1 per hour.

SHARE TAXI

Shared taxi is the other main form of car travel around Central Asia, whereby a taxi or private car does a regular run between two cities and charges a set rate for each of the four seats in a car.

Cars are quicker and just as comfortable as a bus or train, and are still very affordable. They are the main way to get around Uzbekistan and Kyrgyzstan.

Shared taxis will often drop you at, or near, your hotel rather than at an often-distant suburban bus station, which is a real advantage over minivans and buses.

➡ Cars often wait for passengers outside bus or train stations and some have a sign in the window indicating where they are headed.

➡ Some fares are so cheap that two or three of you can buy all four seats and stretch out. Otherwise smaller cars can be a little cramped.

➡ The most common car is the Russian Zhiguli, fast being replaced by modern Daewoo models such as the Nexia (the most comfortable) and the smaller and cheaper Tico, both made in Central Asia.

➡ The front seat is always the one to aim for (though it's often the sunniest in hot weather); only lemons get the middle back seat.

Hitching

Hitching is never entirely safe, and we don't recommend it. Travellers who hitch should understand that they are taking a small but potentially serious risk.

That said, in Central Asia there is generally little distinction between hitching and taking a taxi. Anyone with a car will stop if you flag them down (with a low up-and-down wave, not an upturned thumb) and most drivers will expect you to pay for the ride.

TAXI TIPS

➡ Avoid taxis lurking outside tourist hotels – drivers charge far too much and get uppity when you try to talk them down.

➡ Never get into a taxi with more than one person in it, especially after dark; check the back seat of the car for hidden friends too.

➡ Keep your fare money in a separate pocket to avoid flashing large wads of cash.

➡ Have a map to make it look like you know your route.

➡ If you're staying at a private residence, have the taxi stop at the corner nearest your destination, not the specific address.

➡ When negotiating a reasonable fare it helps to know the equivalent bus or shared-taxi fare.

➡ Hitching to parks and scenic spots is generally much easier on the weekends but you'll lose some of the solitude at these times.

➡ Normal security rules apply when trying to arrange a lift; don't hitch alone, avoid flagging down cars at night and try to size up your driver (and their sobriety) before getting in.

Local Transport

Most sizeable towns have public buses, and some-times electric trolleybuses. Tashkent and Almaty have a metro system.

➡ Transport is cheap by Western standards, but usually packed; at peak hours it can take several stops for those caught by surprise to even work their way to an exit.

➡ Public transport in smaller towns tends to melt away soon after dark.

Bus, Trolleybus & Tram

Payment methods vary, but the most common method is to pay the driver or conduc-tor cash on exit. Manoeuvre your way out by asking an-yone in the way, *vykhodite?* (getting off?).

The website **Wikiroutes** (www.wikiroutes.info) is very helpful for working out city bus routes for many cities in Central Asia.

Marshrutka

A marshrutka, or marshrut-noe taxi (marsh-*root*-na-yuh tahk-*see*), is a minibus running along a fixed route. You can get on at fixed stops but can get off anywhere by saying *'zdes pozhaluysta'* (zd-*yes* pa-*zhal*-stuh; here please). Routes are hard to

figure out and schedules erratic, and it's usually easier to stick to other transport. Fares are just a little higher than bus fares.

Taxi

There are two kinds of taxis: officially licensed ones and every other car on the road.

➡ Official taxis are more trustworthy, and sometimes cheaper – if you can find one. They rarely have meters so you'll have to negotiate a fare in advance.

➡ Let a local friend negotiate a fare for you – they'll do better than you will.

➡ Unofficial taxis are often private cars driven by people trying to cover their rising petrol costs. Anything with a chequerboard logo in the window is a taxi.

➡ Cars and taxis often flash their lights if they are willing to take a fare.

➡ Stand at the side of the road, extend your arm and wait – as scores of others around you will probably be doing. When someone stops, negotiate a destination and fare. The driver may say *'sadites'* (sit down) or beckon you in, but sort the fare out first. It helps a lot if you can negotiate the price in Russian, even more so in the local language.

➡ A typical fare across a Central Asian capital is around US$3. Fares go up at night and extra charges are incurred for bookings.

Train

Kazakhstan and to a lesser extent Uzbekistan are proba-bly the only countries where you'll find yourself using the train system much. Travel in summer is best done at night.

Train Connections

➡ Trains are useful to cover the vast distances in Kazakhstan. Certain

corridors, such as Almaty–Astana and Almaty–Shymkent are well served by three or four fast trains a day.

➡ The Spanish-built, daily Talgo train between Almaty and Astana takes 12½ hours, against up to 21 hours for other trains, and costs about twice as much (US$80 in tourist class). A new high-speed rail link between the two cities is planned.

➡ New fast trains also run from Astana to Atyrau and Kyzylorda in Kazakhstan.

➡ The high-speed train from Tashkent to Samarkand (2¼ hours) and on to Bukhara (four hours) is faster than the buses and features airplane-style seats. There's also a useful overnight Tashkent–Bukhara and Tashkent–Urgench run.

➡ As an indication of journey times, Urgench–Tashkent is 22 hours and Tashkent–Almaty is 25 hours (three weekly).

➡ Turkmenistan has slow but new trains running to most corners of the country. Travel times are long but fares are low.

➡ Elsewhere, connections are drying up as fast as the Aral Sea was; few trains run to Dushanbe any more (those that do take a very roundabout route and multiple transit visas) and there are no direct lines, for example, between Ashgabat and any other Central Asian capitals.

➡ Trains to and from Russia can be used for getting around Central Asia and may be faster but any train originating far from where you are is likely to be filthy, crowded and late by the time you board it.

Tickets & Fares

Book at least two days ahead for CIS connections, if you can. You will probably need to show your passport and visa. A few stations have separate windows for

CLASSES ON CENTRAL ASIAN TRAINS

A deluxe sleeping carriage is called *spets-vagon* (SV, Russian for 'special carriage', abbreviated to CB in Cyrillic); some call this *spalny vagon* or 'sleeping carriage', *myagky* (soft) or 1st class. Closed compartments have carpets and upholstered seats, and convert to comfortable sleeping compartments for two.

An ordinary sleeping carriage is called *kupeyny* or *kupe* (which is Russian for compartmentalised). Closed compartments are usually four-person couchettes and are comfortable.

A *platskartny* (reserved-place) or 3rd-class carriage has open-bunk (also known as hard sleeper) accommodation.

Obshchy (general) or 4th class is unreserved bench-type seating.

With a reservation, your ticket normally shows the numbers of your carriage *(vagon)* and seat *(mesto)*. Class may be shown by what looks like a fraction: eg 1/2 is 1st-class two berth, 2/4 is 2nd-class four berth.

➡ If you can't get a ticket for a particular train, it's worth turning up anyway. No matter how full ticket clerks insist a train is, there always seem to be spare *kupeyny* (2nd-class or sleeping carriage) berths. Ask an attendant.

➡ For services in Kazakhstan visit www.railways.kz.

➡ For trains in Uzbekistan see www.uzrailpass.uz.

➡ A few sample *kupeyny* fares (one way) from Tashkent are US$30 to Urgench and US$20 to Bukhara.

➡ A seat on the daytime fast trains costs US$10/13 from Tashkent to Samarkand/ Bukhara, with a superfast service to Samarkand/ Bukhara costing around US$15/30.

➡ *Kupe* fares from Almaty include Semey (US$16), Taraz (US$10) and Astana (US$20, or US$42/35 SV/ *kupe* for the express train). SV is 1st class.

advance bookings and for departures within 24 hours; the latter is generally the one with the heaving mob around it (beware of pickpockets). You may also find a city train-ticket office (Russian: *zheleznodorozhnaya kassa* or *Zh D Kassa*) where you can buy train tickets for small or no mark-up, without going to the station. Many tourist hotels have rail-booking desks (including their own mark-up).

Health

Stomach and digestive problems are by far the most common health problems faced by visitors to Central Asia. A diet of mutton, bread and *plov* seems to induce diarrhoea and constipation in equal measure.

Since independence, health rates across the region have dropped and many diseases formerly eradicated or controlled in the time of the USSR, such as tuberculosis (TB) and diphtheria, have returned.

Exposure to malaria, rabies and encephalitis is rare and depends largely upon the location and/or months of travel. More common during the searing summer months is heat exhaustion, so make sure you keep cool and hydrated in the 35°C heat. Most short-term travels to the main tourist areas remain problem-free.

BEFORE YOU GO

If you take any regular medication, bring double your needs in case of loss or theft. In most Central Asian countries you can buy many medications over the counter without a doctor's prescription, but it can be difficult to find some of the newer drugs.

Make sure you get your teeth checked before you travel – there are few good dentists in Central Asia as evidenced by the many golden-toothed smiles you'll see. If you wear glasses take a spare pair and your prescription.

If you are headed to Uzbekistan bring your prescriptions with you, keep your medicines in their original packaging and leave any sleeping pills or painkillers behind as bringing these into the country is illegal. Customs officials are particularly on the lookout for such medications as codeine, Valium, Xanax and Temazepam. For a full list of banned medicines visit www.advantour.com/img/uzbekistan/file/medications_list.pdf.

Health Insurance

Even if you are fit and healthy, don't travel without health insurance – accidents do happen. Declare any existing medical conditions you have – the insurance company *will* check if your problem is preexisting and will not cover you if it is undeclared. You may require extra cover for adventure activities such as rock climbing. If you're uninsured, emergency evacuation is expensive – bills of over US$100,000 are not uncommon.

INTERNET RESOURCES

There is a wealth of travel-health advice on the internet. It's also a good idea to consult your government's travel-health website before departure, if one is available.

Australia (www.smartraveller.gov.au/guide/all-travellers/health)

Canada (www.travelhealth.gc.ca)

UK (www.fitfortravel.nhs.uk)

USA (www.cdc.gov/travel)

World Health Organization (www.who.int/ith/en) A superb book called *International Travel & Health* is revised annually and is available online.

MD Travel Health (https://redplanet.travel/mdtravelhealth) Provides complete travel-health recommendations for every country and is updated daily.

Make sure you keep all documentation related to any medical expenses you incur.

Medical Checklist

Recommended items for a personal medical kit are as follows:

➡ Acetazolamide (Diamox) if going to high altitude

➡ Antibacterial cream (eg mupirocin)

➡ Antibiotics for diarrhoea (eg norfloxacin, ciprofloxacin or azithromycin for bacterial diarrhoea; tinidazole for giardiasis or amoebic dysentery)

➡ Antibiotics for skin infections (eg amoxicillin/clavulanate or cephalexin)

➡ Antifungal cream (eg clotrimazole)

➡ Antihistamine – there are many options (eg cetrizine for day and promethazine for night)

➡ Antiseptic (eg Betadine)

➡ Antispasmodic for stomach cramps (eg Buscopan)

➡ Decongestant (eg pseudoephedrine)

➡ DEET-based insect repellent

➡ Elastoplasts, bandages, gauze, thermometer (but not mercury), sterile needles and syringes, safety pins and tweezers

➡ Ibuprofen or another anti-inflammatory

➡ Laxative

➡ Oral rehydration solution for diarrhoea (eg Gastrolyte), diarrhoea 'stopper' (eg loperamide) and antinausea medication (eg prochlorperazine)

➡ Paracetamol

➡ Steroid cream for allergic/itchy rashes (eg 1% to 2% hydrocortisone)

➡ Thrush (vaginal yeast infection) treatment (eg clotrimazole pessaries or Diflucan tablets)

➡ Ural or equivalent if prone to urinary-tract infections

Recommended Vaccinations

Specialised travel-medicine clinics are your best source of information on which vaccines you should have. Most vaccines don't produce immunity until at least two weeks after they're given, so visit a doctor four to eight weeks before departure.

Proof of vaccination against yellow fever is required in Kazakhstan if you have visited a country in the yellow-fever zone within the six days prior to entering the country.

Uzbekistan, Kazakhstan and Kyrgyzstan all require HIV testing if staying more than three months. Foreign tests are accepted under certain conditions, but make sure you check with the embassy of your destination before travelling.

The World Health Organization recommends the following vaccinations for travellers to Central Asia:

Adult diphtheria and tetanus Single booster recommended if none in the previous 10 years.

Hepatitis A Provides almost 100% protection for up to a year; a booster after 12 months provides at least another 20 years' protection.

Hepatitis B Now considered routine for most travellers. Given as three shots over six months. A rapid schedule is also available, as is a combined vaccination with hepatitis A. In 95% of people lifetime protection results.

Measles, mumps and rubella Two doses required unless you have had the diseases. Occasionally a rash and flu-like illness can develop a week after receiving the vaccine. Many young adults require a booster.

Polio Only one booster is required as an adult for lifetime protection.

Typhoid Recommended unless your trip is for less than a week. The vaccine offers around 70% protection, lasts for two to three years and comes as a single shot.

Varicella If you haven't had chickenpox discuss this vaccination with your doctor.

The following immunisations are recommended for long-term travellers (more than one month) or those at special risk:

Meningitis Recommended for long-term backpackers aged under 25.

Rabies Side effects are rare (headache and sore arm).

Tick-borne encephalitis (Kyrgyzstan, Kazakhstan, Uzbekistan) Sore arm and headache are the most common side effects.

Further Reading

Lonely Planet's *Healthy Travel – Asia & India* is a handy pocket size and is packed with useful information, including pretrip planning, emergency first aid, immunisation and disease information, and what to do if you get sick on the road.

Other recommended references include *Traveller's Health* by Dr Richard Dawood and *Travelling Well* by Dr Deborah Mills – check out www.travellingwell.com.au.

IN CENTRAL ASIA

Availability of Health Care

Health care throughout Central Asia is basic at best. Any serious problems will require evacuation. Good clinics can provide basic care and may be able to organise evacuation if necessary. In Central Asia a pharmacist is known as an *apoteka* in Russian or *dorikhana* in Turkic. Clinics are widely known as *polikliniks*.

Self-treatment may be appropriate if your problem is minor (eg travellers' diarrhoea), you are carrying the relevant medication and you cannot attend a recommended clinic. It is always better to be assessed by a doctor than to rely on self-treatment.

Buying medication over the counter is not recommended, as poorly stored or out-of-date drugs are common.

To find the nearest reliable medical facility, contact your insurance company, your embassy or a top-end hotel.

Infectious Diseases

Amoebic Dysentery

Risk: all countries

Amoebic dysentery is actually rare in travellers but is often misdiagnosed. Symptoms are similar to bacterial diarrhoea, ie fever, bloody diarrhoea and generally feeling unwell. You should always seek reliable medical care if you have blood in your diarrhoea. Treatment involves two drugs: tinidazole or metroniadzole to kill the parasite in your gut, and a second drug to kill the cysts. If left untreated, complications such as liver or gut abscesses can occur.

Brucellosis

Risk: all countries.

Brucellosis is rare in travellers but common in the local population, and is transmitted via unpasteurised dairy products. Common symptoms include fever, chills, headache, loss of appetite and joint pain.

Giardiasis

Risk: all countries.

Giardia is a parasite that is relatively common in travellers to Central Asia. Symptoms include nausea, bloating, excess gas, fatigue and intermittent diarrhoea. 'Eggy' burps are often attributed solely to giardia. The parasite will eventually go away if left untreated, but this can take months. The treatment of choice is tinidazole; metronidazole is a second option.

Hepatitis A

Risk: all countries.

A problem throughout the region, this food- and waterborne virus infects the liver, causing jaundice (yellow skin and eyes), nausea and lethargy. There is no specific treatment for hepatitis A, you just need to allow time for the liver to heal. All travellers to Central Asia should be vaccinated.

Hepatitis B

Risk: all countries.

The only sexually transmitted disease that can be prevented by vaccination, hepatitis B is spread by contact with infected body fluids, including via sexual contact. The long-term consequences can include liver cancer and cirrhosis.

HIV

Risk: all countries.

HIV is transmitted via contaminated body fluids. Avoid unprotected sex, blood transfusions and injections (unless you can see a clean needle being used) in Central Asia.

Leishmaniasis

Risk: Kazakhstan, Turkmenistan, Uzbekistan.

This sandfly-borne parasite is very rare in travellers but common in the local population. There are two forms of leishmaniasis: one which only affects the skin (causing a chronic ulcer) and one affecting the internal organs. Avoid sandfly bites by following insect-avoidance guidelines.

Malaria

Risk: southern Tajikistan, southeastern Turkmenistan and far southern Uzbekistan; only present in the warmer summer months (June to October).

Two strategies should be combined to prevent malaria: general mosquito/insect avoidance and antimalaria medications. Before you travel, it is essential you seek medical advice on the right medication and dosage. In general, Chloroquine is recommended for Turkmenistan and southern Uzbekistan. Some resistance to Chloroquine is reported in southern Tajikistan (mainly Khatlon province), so get your doctor's advice on whether to take Chloroquine, Larium (Mefloquine), Doxycycline or Malarone. See the World Malaria Risk Chart at www.iamat.org for detailed information.

Rabies

Risk: all countries.

Still a common problem in most parts of Central Asia, this uniformly fatal disease is spread by the bite or lick of an infected animal – most commonly a dog. Having a pretravel vaccination (three shots over a one-month period) means the postbite treatment is greatly simplified. If an animal bites you, gently wash the wound with soap and water, and apply iodine-based antiseptic. If you are not vaccinated you will need to receive rabies immunoglobulin as soon as possible and seek medical advice.

Travellers' Diarrhoea

Risk: all countries.

Travellers' diarrhoea is defined as the passage of more than three watery bowel actions within 24 hours, plus at least one other symptom, such as fever, cramps, nausea, vomiting or feeling generally unwell. It is by far the most common problem affecting travellers.

Travellers' diarrhoea is caused by a bacterium and, in most cases, treatment consists of staying well hydrated; rehydration solutions are the best for this. It responds promptly to treatment with antibiotics such as norfloxacin, ciprofloxacin or azithromycin. Loperamide is just a 'stopper' and doesn't get to the cause of the problem. It can be helpful, for example, if you have to go on a long bus ride. Don't take loperamide if you have a fever or blood in your stools. Seek medical attention quickly if you do not respond to an appropriate antibiotic.

Eating in restaurants is the biggest risk factor for contracting travellers' diarrhoea. Ways to avoid it include eating only freshly cooked food, avoiding food that has been sitting around in buffets, and eating in busy restaurants with a high turnover of customers. Peel all fruit, cook vegetables and soak salads in iodine water for at least 20 minutes.

Tuberculosis

Risk: all countries.

Medical and aid workers, and long-term travellers who have significant contact with the local population should take precautions against TB. Adults at risk are advised to have pre- and post-travel TB testing. The main symptoms are fever, cough, weight loss, night sweats and tiredness.

Typhoid

Risk: all countries.

This serious bacterial infection is spread via food and water. It results in a high and slowly progressive fever and headache, and may be accompanied by a dry cough and stomach pain. Be aware that vaccination is not 100% effective so you must still be careful what you eat and drink.

Other Diseases

Kazakhstan occasionally reports outbreaks of human plague in the far west. One fatal case of bubonic plague was recorded in Kyrgyzstan in 2013. Outbreaks are often caused by eating diseased meat but are also transmitted by the bites of rodent and marmot fleas.

In 2013 there were outbreaks of anthrax in Kazakhstan.

Crimean Congo haemorrhagic fever is a severe viral illness characterised by the sudden onset of intense fever, headache, aching limbs, bleeding gums and sometimes a rash of red dots on the skin, a week or two after being bitten by an infected tick. It's a minor risk for trekkers and campers in Central Asia during summer. Insect repellent will help keep the blighters off you.

Environmental Hazards

Drinking Water

➥ Never drink tap water in Central Asia, especially in Karakalpakstan, Khorezm, Dushanbe and remoter Kazakhstan.

➥ Bottled water is available everywhere and is cheap – check the seal is intact at purchase.

➥ Avoid ice and fresh juices, especially if you think the latter may have been watered down.

➥ If you are headed into remote rural areas such as the Pamirs of eastern Tajikistan, or trekking anywhere you'll need to bring some method of water purification.

➥ Boiling water is the most efficient method of purifying it. Bring a water bottle that can take boiling water and you can fill up in a yurt or homestay.

➥ If you bring a water filter ensure it has a chemical barrier such as iodine and a small pore size, eg less than 4 microns.

Altitude Sickness

Altitude sickness is a particular problem in high-altitude regions of Kazakhstan, Kyrgyzstan and Tajikistan. With motorable roads (such as the Pamir Hwy) climbing passes of over 4000m, it's a problem not just restricted to trekkers.

Altitude sickness may develop in those who ascend rapidly to altitudes greater than 2500m. Being physically fit offers no protection. Risk increases with faster ascents, higher altitudes and greater exertion. Symptoms may include headaches, nausea, vomiting, dizziness, malaise, insomnia and loss of appetite. Severe cases may be complicated by fluid in the lungs or swelling of the brain.

To protect yourself against altitude sickness, take 125mg or 250mg of acetazolamide (Diamox) twice or three times daily, starting 24 hours before ascent and continuing for 48 hours after arrival at altitude. Possible side effects include increased urinary volume, numbness, tingling, drowsiness, nausea, myopia and temporary impotence. Acetazolamide should not be given to pregnant women or anyone with a history of sulpha allergy.

When travelling to high altitudes, avoid overexertion, eat light meals, drink lots of fluids and abstain from alcohol. If your symptoms are more than mild or don't resolve promptly, see a doctor.

META (Murgab Ecotourism Association; ✉Gulnara (Director) 935 181808, Januzak (President) 934 652005; www.meta.tj; M41, Osh 102; ☺call ahead) in Tajikistan's eastern Pamirs has a hyperbaric chamber in case of altitude-related emergencies.

Language

In addition to the official languages of the Central Asian countries covered in this book – Kazakh, Kyrgyz, Tajik, Turkmen and Uzbek – the one language most useful for travellers in these countries is still Russian, as you'll find that it's the second language for most adults.

RUSSIAN

Just read the coloured pronunciation guides given next to each Russian phrase in this section as if they were English, and you'll be understood. Note that the symbol kh is pronounced as the 'ch' in the Scottish *loch*, zh as the 's' in 'pleasure', r is rolled and the apostrophe (') indicates a slight y sound. The stressed syllables are indicated with italics.

Basics

Hello.	Здравствуйте.	*zdrast*·vuy·tye
Goodbye.	До свидания.	da svi·*da*·nya
Excuse me.	Простите.	pras·*ti*·tye
Sorry.	Извините.	iz·vi·*ni*·tye
Please.	Пожалуйста.	pa·*zhal*·sta
Thank you.	Спасибо.	spa·*si*·ba
Yes./No.	Да./Нет.	da/nyet

What's your name?
Как вас зовут?   kak vas za·*vut*

My name is ...
Меня зовут ...   mi·*nya* za·vut ...

WANT MORE?

For in-depth language information and handy phrases, check out Lonely Planet's *Central Asia Phrasebook*. You'll find it at **shop.lonelyplanet.com**, or you can buy Lonely Planet's iPhone phrasebooks at the Apple App Store.

Do you speak English?
Вы говорите   vi ga·va·*ri*·tye
по-английски?   pa·an·*gli*·ski

I don't understand.
Я не понимаю.   ya nye pa·ni·*ma*·yu

Accommodation

Do you have a ... room	У вас есть ...?	u vas yest' ...
single	одноместный номер	ad·na·*myest*·nih *no*·mir
double	номер с двуспальной кроватью	*no*·mir z dvu·*spal*'·noy kra·*va*·tyu

How much is it for ...?	Сколько стоит за ...?	*skol*'·ka *sto*·it za ...
a night	ночь	noch'
two people	двоих	dva·*ikh*

Eating & Drinking

I'd like (the menu).
Я бы хотел/   ya bih khat·*yel*/
хотела (меню). (m/f)   khat·*ye*·la (min·*yu*)

I don't eat ...
Я не ем ...   ya nye yem ...

Please bring the bill.
Принесите,   pri·ni·*sit*·ye
пожалуйста, счёт.   pa·*zhal*·sta shot

Cheers!	на здоровье!	na zda·*rov*·ye
restaurant	ресторан	ris·ta·*ran*

Emergencies

Help!	Помогите!	pa·ma·*gi*·tye
Leave me alone!	Проваливай!	pro·*va*·li·vai

Numbers – Russian

1	один	a·din
2	два	dva
3	три	tri
4	четыре	chi·ty·ri
5	пять	pyat'
6	шесть	shest'
7	семь	sem'
8	восемь	vo·sim'
9	девять	de·vit'
10	десять	de·sit'
100	сто	sto
1000	тысяча	ty·sya·cha

Call ...!	Вызовите ...!	vih·za·vi·tye ...
a doctor	врача	vra·cha
the police	полицию	po·li·tsih·yu

I'm lost.
Я заблудился/ — ya za·blu·dil·sa/
заблудилась. (m/f) — za·blu·di·las'

Where are the toilets?
Где здесь туалет? — gdye zdyes' tu·al·yet

Shopping & Services

I need ...
Мне нужно ... — mnye nuzh·na ...

How much is it?
Сколько стоит? — skol'·ka sto·it

That's too expensive.
Это очень дорого. — e·ta o·chen' do·ra·ga

bank	банк	bank
market	рынок	rih·nak
post office	почта	poch·ta

Transport & Directions

a ... ticket	билет ...	bil·yet ...
one-way	в один конец	v a·din kan·yets
return	туда-обратно	tu·da o·bra·tno

Where's (the station)?
Где (вокзал)? — gdye (vok·zal)

When's the next bus/train?
Когда будет — kag·da bu·dit
следующий — slye·du·yu·shi
автобус/поезд? — af·to·bus/po·ist

Does it stop at ...?
Поезд останав- — po·yist a·sta·nav·
ливается в ...? — li·va·yit·sa v ...

Where is ...?
Где ...? — gdye ...

What's the address?
Какой адрес? — ka·koy a·dris

Can you show me (on the map)?
Покажите мне, — pa·ka·zhih·tye mnye
пожалуйста (на карте). — pa·zhal·sta (na kar·tye)

KAZAKH

Kazakh is a Turkic language. Since 1940 it has been written in a version of the Cyrillic alphabet. It's the state language and is spoken by 64% of the population. Russian has the status of an official language and almost everyone speaks Russian. It is the first language for some urban Kazakhs, as well as the large Russian minority (24% of the population). Street signs are either in Kazakh, Russian or both. In our pronunciation guides, the symbol a is pronounced as in 'man', g as the 'gh' in 'ugh', k as a guttural 'k', n as the 'ng' in 'sing', o as the 'u' in 'fur', u as in 'full' or as the 'oo' in 'fool', h as in 'hat' and i as in 'ill'.

Numbers – Kazakh

1	bir
2	yeki
3	ush
4	tort
5	bes
6	alty
7	etti
8	sakkiz
9	togyz
10	on
100	zhus
1000	myn

Peace be with you.	assalamu aleykum
And peace with you. (response)	wagaleykum ussalam
Hello.	salamatsyz be
Goodbye.	kosh-sau bolyndar
Thank you.	rakhmet
Yes./No.	ia/zhok
How are you?	khal zhag dayynyz kalay?
I'm well.	zhaksy
Do you speak English?	agylshynsa bilesiz be?
I don't understand.	tusinbeymin
Where is...?	... kayda?
How much?	kansha?

LANGUAGE KYRGYZ

airport	auezhay
bus station	avtovokzal/avtobeket
doctor	dariger
friend	dos
hospital	aurukhana
hotel	konak uy/meymankhana
police	politsia
restaurant	meyramkhana
toilet	daretkhana
train station	temir zhol vokzal/beket

bad	zhaman
boiled water	kaynagan su
bread	nan
expensive	kymbat
good	zhaksy
meat	yet
rice	kurish
tea	shay

Monday	duysenbi
Tuesday	seysenbi
Wednesday	sarsenbi
Thursday	beysenbi
Friday	zhuma
Saturday	senbi
Sunday	zheksenbi

KYRGYZ

Kyrgyz is a Turkic language that has been written in a Cyrillic alphabet since the early 1940s. However, Kyrgyzstan is in the process of changing over to a modified Roman alphabet. Russian also has official-language status, but there is a strong push to promote Kyrgyz as the predominant language of government, media and education. In our pronunciation guides, ng is pronounced as in 'sing', ö as the 'u' in 'fur' and ü as the 'ew' in 'few'.

Peace be with you.	asalamu aleykom
And peace with you. (response)	wa aleykum assalam
Hello.	salam
Goodbye.	jakshy kalyngydzar
Thank you.	rakhmat
Yes./No.	ooba/jok
How are you?	jakshysüzbü?
I'm well.	jakshy
Do you speak English?	siz angliyscha süylöy süzbü?

Numbers – Kyrgyz

1	bir
2	eki
3	üch
4	tört
5	besh
6	alty
7	jety
8	segiz
9	toguz
10	on
100	jüz
1000	ming

I don't understand.	men tüshümböy jatamyn
Where is ...?	... kayda?
How much?	kancha?

airport	aeroport
bus station	avtobiket
doctor	doktur
friend	dos
hospital	oruukana
hotel	meymankana
police	militsia
restaurant	restoran
toilet	darakana
train station	temir jol vokzal

bad	jaman
boiled water	kaynatilgan suu
bread	nan
expensive	kymbat
good	jakshy
meat	et
rice	kürüch
tea	chay

Monday	düshömbü
Tuesday	seyshembi
Wednesday	sharshembi
Thursday	beishembi
Friday	juma
Saturday	ishembi
Sunday	jekshembi

TAJIK

The state language of Tajikistan since 1989, Tajik is a Persian language, closely related to Dari (the language of Afghanistan) and Farsi (the language of Iran) – unlike most Central Asian languages, which are Turkic in origin. Tajik was formerly written in a modified Arabic script, then in Roman, but since 1940 a modified Cyrillic script has been used. In our pronunciation guides, gh is pronounced as in 'ugh', ee as in 'fee', q as the 'k' in 'keen', ö as the 'u' in 'fur', kh as the 'h' in 'hat' and j as in 'jig'.

Numbers – Tajik	
1	yak
2	du
3	seh
4	chor
5	panj
6	shish
7	khaft
8	khasht
9	nukh
10	dakh
100	sad
1000	khazor

Peace be with you.	assalomu aleykum
And peace with you. (response)	valeykum assalom
Hello.	salom
Goodbye.	khayr naboshad
Thank you.	rakhmat/teshakkur
Yes./No.	kha/ne
How are you?	naghzmi shumo?
I'm well.	mannaghz
Do you speak English?	anglisi meydonet?
I don't understand.	man manefakhmam
Where is ...?	... khujo ast?
How much?	chand pul?

airport	furudgoh
bus station	istgoh
doctor	duhtur
friend	doost
hospital	bemorhona/kasalhona
hotel	mekhmon'hona
police	militsia
restaurant	restoran
toilet	khojat'hona

train station	istgoh rohi ohan
bad	ganda
boiled water	obi jush
bread	non
expensive	qimmat
good	khub/naghz
meat	gusht
rice	birinj
tea	choy

Monday	dushanbe
Tuesday	seshanbe
Wednesday	chorshanbe
Thursday	panjanbe
Friday	juma
Saturday	shanbe
Sunday	yakshanbe

TURKMEN

Turkmen, the state language of Turkmenistan since 1990, belongs to the Turkic language family. It has a significant amount of Russian vocabulary. In Turkmenistan almost everyone speaks Russian or Turkmen. Four different scripts have been used to write Turkmen: first Arabic, then a Turkish-Roman alphabet, from 1940 the Cyrillic alphabet, and since 1996 a modified Roman alphabet.

Numbers – Turkmen	
1	bir
2	ikeh
3	uch
4	durt
5	besh
6	alty
7	yed
8	sekiz
9	dokuz
10	on
100	yuz
1000	mun

Peace be with you.	salam aleykum
And peace with you. (response)	waleykum assalam
Hello.	salam
Goodbye.	sagh bol
Thank you.	tangyr
Yes./No.	howa/yok

How are you?	siz nahili?
Fine, and you?	onat, a siz?
I don't understand.	men dushenamok
Do you speak English?	siz inglische gepleyarsinizmi?
Where is ...?	... niredeh?
How much?	nyacheh?

airport	aeroport
bus station	durolha
doctor	lukman
friend	dost
hospital	keselkhana
hotel	mikmankhana
police	militsia
restaurant	restoran
toilet	hajat'hana
train station	vokzal

bad	ervet
boiled water	gaina d'lan su
bread	churek
expensive	gummut
good	yakhsheh
meat	et
rice	tui
tea	chay

Monday	dushanbe
Tuesday	seshenbe
Wednesday	charshanbe
Thursday	penshenbe
Friday	anna
Saturday	shenbe
Sunday	yekshanbe

Goodbye.	hayr
Thank you.	rakhmat
Yes./No.	kha/yuk
How are you?	kanday siz?
Do you speak English?	inglizcha bila sizmi?
Where is ...?	... kayerda?
How much?	kancha/nichpul?

airport	tayyorgokh
bus station	avtobeket
doctor	tabib
friend	urmok/doost
hospital	kasalhona
hotel	mehmon'hona
police	militsia
restaurant	restoran
toilet	hojat'hona
train station	temir yul vokzali

bad	yomon
boiled water	kaynatilgan suv
bread	non
expensive	kimmat
good	yakhshi
meat	gusht
rice	guruch
tea	choy

Monday	dushanba
Tuesday	seyshanba
Wednesday	chorshanba
Thursday	payshanba
Friday	juma
Saturday	shanba
Sunday	yakshanba

UZBEK

Uzbekistan's major languages are Uzbek, Russian and Tajik. Uzbek, a Turkic language, is official and, with 15 million speakers, the most widely spoken non-Slavic language from the former Soviet states. It was first written in Arabic script, then in Roman letters, and since 1941 in a modified Cyrillic alphabet, but the country has been moving to a Roman alphabet. In our pronunciation guides, gh is pronounced as in 'ugh', k/q as a guttural 'k', u as the 'oo' in 'book' and kh as the 'ch' in 'Bach'.

Peace be with you.	salom alaykhum
And peace with you. (response)	tinch berling
Hello.	salom

Numbers – Uzbek	
1	bir
2	ikki
3	uch
4	turt
5	besh
6	olti
7	etti
8	sakkiz
9	tukkiz
10	un
100	yuz
1000	ming

GLOSSARY

ABBREVIATIONS

A – Arabic

Kaz – Kazakh

Kyr – Kyrgyz

R – Russian

Taj – Tajik

T – general Turkic

Tur – Turkmen

U – Uzbek

-abad (T) – suffix meaning 'town of'

ak (T) – white

ak kalpak (Kyr) – felt hat worn by Kyrgyz men

akimat (T) – regional government office or city hall, also *aqimat*

aksakal (T) – revered elder

akyn (Kyr) – minstrel, bard

ala-kiyiz (Kyr) – felt rug with coloured panels pressed on

alany (Kaz) – square

alplager (R) – mountaineers camp, short for *alpinistskiy lager*

apparatchik (R) – bureaucrat

apteka (R) – pharmacy

arashan (T) – springs

asalam aleykum (A) – traditional Muslim greeting, meaning 'peace be with you'

ASSR – Autonomous Soviet Socialist Republic

askhana (Kaz, Kyr) – local restaurant

aul (T) – yurt or herders' camp

aviakassa (R) – air ticket office

avtobus (R) – bus

avtostantsia (R) – bus stop or bus stand

azan (A) – Muslim call to prayer

babushka (R) – grandmother (can be offensive to use on old women)

bagh (Taj, D) – garden

balbal (T) – totemlike stone marker

banya (R) – public bath

basmachi (R) – literally 'bandits'; Muslim guerrilla fighters who resisted the Bolshevik takeover in Central Asia

batyr (Kyr, Kaz) – warrior hero in epics

beg (T) – landlord, gentleman; also spelt *bay* or *bek*

berkutchi (Kyr) – eagle hunter

Bi (Kaz) – honorific Kazakh title given to clan elders

bishkek (Kaz, Kyrg) – see *pishpek*

bosuy (Kyr) – see yurt

bufet (R) – snack bar selling cheap cold meats, boiled eggs, salads, breads, pastries etc

bulvar (R) – boulevard

bulvary (Kyr) – boulevard

buzkashi (T) – traditional polo-like game played with a headless calf, goat or sheep carcass (*buz*)

caravanserai – travellers inn

chabana (Kyr, Kaz) – cowboy

chaikhana (T) – teahouse

chapan (U, Taj) – traditional stripy Uzbek/Tajik cloak

chaykhana (T) – see *chaikhana*

chong (T) – big

choyhona (T) – see *chaikhana*

chuchuk (Kaz) – see *kazy* (in food glossary)

chuchvara (T) – dumplings

CIS – Commonwealth of Independent States; the loose political and economic alliance of most former member republics of the USSR (except the Baltic states and Georgia)

CPK – Communist Party of Kazakhstan

dacha (R) – a holiday bungalow

dangyly (Kaz) – avenue

darikhana (Kaz) – pharmacy

darya (T) – river

dastarkhan (T) – literally 'tablecloth'; feast

depe (Tur) – see *tepe*

dezhurnaya (R) – floor-lady; the female attendant on duty on each floor of a Soviet-style hotel

dom (R) – building

dom otdykha (R) – rest home

doppe (U) – black, four-sided skullcap embroidered in white and worn by men; also *dopi*, *doppa*, *dopy* or *doppilar*

dutar (T) – two-stringed guitar

eshon (A) – Sufi leader, also spelt *ishan*

GAI (R) – traffic police

geoglyph – geometric pattern of stones, often used in astrological observations

gillam (T) – carpet, also *gilim*

glasnost (R) – 'openness' in government that was one aspect of the Gorbachev reforms

gorod (R) – town

Graeco-Bactrian – Hellenistic kingdom and culture centred on northern Afghanistan, southern Uzbekistan and Tajikistan following the conquests of Alexander the Great

Great Game – the geopolitical 'Cold War' of territorial expansion between the Russian and British empires in the 19th and early 20th centuries in Central Asia

Hadith (A) – collected acts and sayings of the Prophet Mohammed

haj (A) – the pilgrimage to Mecca, one of the five pillars of Islam, to be made by devout Muslims at least once during their lifetime

hakimat (T) – see *hakimyat*

hakimyat (Kyr) – municipal administration building

hammam (A) – bathhouse

hammomi (U) – baths

hazrat (A) – honorific title meaning 'majesty' or 'holy'

Hejira (A) – flight of the Prophet Mohammed and his followers to Medina in AD 622

hijab (A) – Muslim woman's veil or headscarf (literally 'modest dress')

hoja (U) – lord, master, gentleman (honorific title)

ikat (U) – tie-dyed silk

IMU – Islamic Movement of Uzbekistan

IRP – Islamic Renaissance Party; grouping of radical activists dedicated to the formation of Islamic rule in Central Asia

Ismaili (A) – a branch of Shiite Islam

jailoo (Kyr) – summer pasture

jami masjid (A) – Friday mosque

jamoat khana (Taj) – Ismaili prayer hall and meeting hall

juma (U) – Friday, see *jami masjid*

kalon (Taj) – great

kara (T) – black

kassa (R) – cashier or ticket office

kazan (T) – large cauldron (used to cook *plov*)

-kent (T) – suffix meaning 'town of'

khanatlas (U) – see *ikat*

khiyeboni (Taj) – avenue

kino (R) – cinema; also *kinoteatr*

köçesi (Tur) – street

kochasi (U) – street

köchösü (Kyr) – street

koh (Taj) – mountain

kok (T) – blue

kökör (T) – *kumys* storer

kokpar (Kaz) – see *buzkashi*

kolkhoz (R) – collective farm

koshesi (Kaz) – street

koshk (U, Tur) – fortress

koshma (Kaz) – multicoloured felt mats

kozha (Kaz) – see *hoja*

kuchai (Taj) – street

kupeyny (R) – 2nd-class or sleeping carriage on trains; also *kupe*

kupkari (U) – see *buzkashi*

kurgan (T) – burial mound

kurort (R) – thermal-spring complex

kurpacha (U) – colourful sitting mattress for a *tapchan*

kvartal (R) – district

kymyz (Kaz) – see *kumys*

kyz-kumay (Kyr) – traditional game in which a man chases a woman on horseback and tries to kiss her

kyz-kuu (Kaz) – see *kyz-kumay*

kyzyl (T) – red

LOI – Letter of Invitation

lux (R) – deluxe

mahalla (U) – urban neighbourhood

Manas (Kyr) – epic; legendary hero revered by the Kyrgyz

manaschi (Kyr) – type of *akyn* who recites from the Kyrgyz cycle of oral legends

marshrutka (R, T) – short term for *marshrutnoe* and *marshrutny avtobus*

marshrutnoe (R, T) – small bus or van that follows a fixed route but stops on demand to take on or let off passengers, with fares depending on distance travelled

marshrutny avtobus (R, T) – large bus that follows a fixed route but stops on demand to take on or let off passengers, with fares depending on distance travelled

maydoni (U, Taj) – square

mikrorayon (R) – micro region or district

MSDSP – Mountain Societies Development Support Project

muezzin (A) – man who calls the Muslim faithful to prayer

mufti (A) – Islamic legal expert or spiritual leader

Naqshband – the most influential of many Sufi secret associations in Central Asia

Navrus (A) – literally 'New Days'; the main Islamic spring festival; has various regional transliterations (Nauroz, Nauryz, Nawruz, Norruz or Novruz)

oblast (R) – province, region

oblys (Kaz) – province, region

OVIR (R) – Otdel Vis i Registratsii; Office of Visas and Registration

Oxus – historic name for the Amu-Darya river

pakhta (T) – cotton

pakhtakor (T) – cotton worker

panjara (T) – trellis of wood, stone or *ghanch* (plaster)

perestroika (R) – literally 'restructuring'; Gorbachev's efforts to revive the economy

piala (T) – bowl

pishpek (Kaz, Kyr) – churn for making *kumys*

platskartny (R) – hard-sleeper train

ploshchad (R) – square

pochta (R) – post office

politsya (R, T) – police

polulux (R) – semideluxe

polyclinic – health centre

propusk (R) – permit

prospekt (R) – avenue

qymyz (Kaz) – see *kumys*

rabab (T) – six-stringed mandolin, also *rubab*

rayon (R) – district

samovar (R) – urn used for heating water for tea, often found on trains

sary (T) – yellow

şayoli (Tur) – street

sharq (Taj, U) – east

shaykhana (T) – see *chaikhana*

Shiite (A) – one of the two main branches of Islam

shyrdak (Kyr) – felt rug with appliquéd coloured panels

skibaza (R) – ski base

SSR – Soviet Socialist Republic

stolovaya (R) – canteen, cafeteria

Sufi (A) – mystical tradition in Islam

suzani (U) – bright silk embroidery on cotton cloth

tapchan (Taj) – tea bed

tash (T) – stone

tebbetey (Kyr) – round fur-trimmed hat worn by men

telpek (Tur, U) – sheepskin hat worn by men

toi (T) – celebration

Transoxiana – meaning 'the land beyond the Oxus'; historical term for the region between the Amu-Darya and Syr-Darya rivers

TsUM (R) – *Tsentralny universalny magazin*; central department store

tubiteyka (R) – see *doppe*

tugai – dense forest endemic to Central Asian river valleys and flood plains

turbaza (R) – holiday camp typically with Spartan cabins, plain food, sports, video hall and bar, usually open only in summer

Turkestan – literally 'the Land of the Turks'; covers Central Asia and Xinjiang (China)

UAZ (R) – Russian 4WD
ulak-tartysh (Kyr) – see *buzkashi*
ulama (A) – class of religious scholars or intellectuals
ulitsa (R) – street
umuvalnik (R) – portable washing basin

univermag (R) – *universalny magazin*; department store
uulu (Kyr) – meaning 'son of'

viloyat (U) – province
vodopad (R) – waterfall
vokzal (R) – train station

ylag oyyny (Karakalpak) – see *buzkashi*
yurt – traditional nomadic 'house', a collapsible wood framework covered with felt

zakaznik (R) – protected area
zapovednik (R) – nature reserve
zikr (A) – recitation or contemplation of the names of God; recitation of sacred writings; one part of traditional Sufi practice

FOOD GLOSSARY

abrikos – apricot
agurets – cucumber
amlet – omelette
antrecot – steak
arbuz – watermelon
ayran – salty yoghurt/water mix

barene – jam
befstroganov – beef stroganoff
beshbarmak – flat noodles with lamb, horsemeat or vegetable broth (served separately)
bifshteks – 'beefsteak', glorified hamburger
bitochki – cutlet
bliny - Russian-style pancake
borshch – beetroot and potato soup, often with sour cream
bozo – beverage made from fermented millet

chay – tea
chuisky salat – spicy carrot salad in vinaigrette
chuchvara – dumplings

farel – trout
Frantsuzky salat – beetroot, carrots and French fries
frikadela – fried meatballs

galuptsi – cabbage rolls stuffed with rice and meat
gavyadina – beef
grechka – boiled buckwheat
gribi – mushrooms
gulyash – a dismal miscellany of meat, vegetables and potatoes

jiger – liver

kafe – coffee
kafe s slivkami – coffee with milk
kaimak – sweet cream
kapusty salat – cabbage salad
kartofel fri – French fries, chips
kartofel pure – mashed potato
kartoshka – potato
kasha – porridge
katyk – thin, drinkable yoghurt
kazy – horse-meat sausage
khleb – bread
kolbasa – sausage
kompot – juice
kotleta po-Kievski – chicken Kiev
kumys – fermented mare's milk (also *kymys*)
kuritsa – chicken
kury gril – roast chicken
kuurdak – fatty stew of meat, offal and potato

laghman – noodles
lyulya kebab – beef or mutton meatballs

manpar – noodle bits, meat, vegetables and mild seasoning in broth
manty – small stuffed dumplings
makarony – macaroni, pasta
masla – butter
mastoba – rice soup
mimosa salat – fish and shredded-potato salad

mineralnaya vada – mineral water
morkovi salat – carrot salad
myod/assal – honey

nan – flat bread

okroshka – cold or hot soup made from sour cream, potatoes, eggs and meat
olivye salat – potato, ham, peas and mayonnaise

pelmeni – small dumplings in soup
persik – peach
piva – beer
plov – a rice dish with meat, carrots or other additions (traditionally prepared by men for special celebrations), also known as *pilau*
pomidor – tomato

ragu – beef stew
rassolnik s myasam – soup of marinated cucumber and kidney
ris – rice

sakhar – sugar
salat iz svezhei kapusty – raw cabbage salad
salat tourist – sliced tomatoes and cucumbers
samsa – samosa
shashlyk – meat roasted on skewers over hot coals
shashlyk farshurabanniya – minced-meat (Adana) kebab

shashlyk iz baraniny – mutton kebab

shashlyk iz okorochkov – chicken kebab

shashlyk iz pecheni – liver kebab

shorpo – soup of boiled mutton on the bone with potatoes, carrots and turnips

shubat – fermented camel's milk

sir – cheese

smetana – sour cream

sok – juice/fruit squash

sosiski – frankfurter sausage

stolichny – beef, potatoes, eggs, carrots, mayonnaise and apples

stolovaya vada (biz gaz) – still water (no gas)

sudak zhareny – fried pike or perch

suzma – strained yoghurt, like tart cottage or cream cheese

tvorog – curd with cream and sugar

vinagrad – grapes

vishnya – cherry

yablaka – apple

yitso – egg

yitso barennye – boiled egg

yitso zharennye – fried egg

Behind the Scenes

SEND US YOUR FEEDBACK

We love to hear from travellers – your comments keep us on our toes and help make our books better. Our well-travelled team reads every word on what you loved or loathed about this book. Although we cannot reply individually to your submissions, we always guarantee that your feedback goes straight to the appropriate authors, in time for the next edition. Each person who sends us information is thanked in the next edition – the most useful submissions are rewarded with a selection of digital PDF chapters.

Visit **lonelyplanet.com/contact** to submit your updates and suggestions or to ask for help. Our award-winning website also features inspirational travel stories, news and discussions.

Note: We may edit, reproduce and incorporate your comments in Lonely Planet products such as guidebooks, websites and digital products, so let us know if you don't want your comments reproduced or your name acknowledged. For a copy of our privacy policy visit lonelyplanet.com/privacy.

OUR READERS

Many thanks to the travellers who used the last edition and wrote to us with helpful hints, useful advice and interesting anecdotes:

Adil Khan, Alan Taylor, Alfonso Morales, Ayal Weiner-Kaplow, Barney Smith, Benjamin Bullock, Bertold Kemptner, Cale Lawlor, Calum MacKellar, Carol Hahn, Carolyn Willadsen, Charles Adams & Jane Hennessy, Christine Jacobson, Elin Monstad, Emily Kydd, Eveline Verbist, Fabrizio Soggetto, Ferdinand Fellinger, Ike Uri, Isaac Mak, Jane Mcnab, Joel Meadows, Judit Hegedus & David Szente, Julie Clarkson, Justyna Ferstl, Lauren Wolfe, Lucy Buckland, Maarten van Gerwen, Perry van Dijck & Anouk Bertram, Marco Svoboda, Mary Rose Burns & Lowell Woodin, Mary Rose-Miller, Maurits Stuyt, Mizio Matteucci, Momo Nedderwedder, Nathan Jeffers, Nicholas Saraiba, Nick Freeland, Olivier Genkin, Peter Kmet, Pravit Chintawongvanich, Ralph Luken, Raphael Favier, Rasmus Aberg & Sarah Benke, Renata Jozic, Robin Roth, Roel Peters, Roelof Kotvis, Ron Perrier, Rouven Strauss, Ruben Mooijman, Stuart Haggett, Suzanne Jacob & David Lloyd, Sylvia Kupers, Tacita Vero, Will Goddard

WRITERS' THANKS

Stephen Lioy

I owe many massive debts of gratitude on this one. To those I continue to explore KG with – Солнышка, Jason, Kent, maybe even Jonny Duncan. To all the people I've travelled with over many years here, not least Makiko. To Aigul, though she's ever thankless! To all the BGI and DMO staff that put up with constant demands for more, especially Gulmira and Aizhan, Rakhat and Aman, Nargiza/Nasiba/Atabek/Meerim/Muslima, Gulira and Asel, and Kyle – the cracker of the whip.

Anna Kaminski

I'd like to thank Megan for entrusting me with Kazakhstan, John, Bradley and Mark for the advice and support, Saule and Steven for the info and the company in Almaty/nuclear wasteland, David for the info, Leonie, John and Dinara in Turkestan, Svetlana in Aksu-Zhabagly NP, Pavel for expert guiding around Almaty, Ramil, Roma and Yura – my Mangistau fixer and drivers, Serik in Aral, and all the *provodniks* who made ventilation in *platzkart* possible.

Bradley Mayhew

Thanks to Rafael and Oybek at Topchan, Pavel at Art Hostel, Rovshan at Gulnara's, Murod and Sevara at Advantour, David at Stantours, Sherzod Norbekov, Mariko Shishido in Samarkand, Odil and Zafar at Jahongir B&B, Jama at the Amelia, Mila Ahmedova in Bukhara and thanks to co-writers Anna, Jenny, Stephen and the Turkmenistan writer for their input.

Jenny Walker

Tajikistan, the so-called roof of the world, puts no such lid on the hospitality shown to visitors. A general thanks, then, to all who helped contribute to the information in this country update. Specific thanks to Dylan Harris of Lupine Travel for facilitating transport, to 'captain' Alishour Afreddun for his insightful guiding and to 'romeo' for the safe delivery along the legendary Pamir Hwy. Biggest thanks to beloved 'general' Sam (Owen), husband, co-researcher and fellow traveller.

Turkmenistan Writer

I cannot express enough my huge thanks for those that helped with this update – you know who you are!

ACKNOWLEDGEMENTS

Climate map data adapted from Peel MC, Finlayson BL & McMahon TA (2007) 'Updated World Map of the Köppen-Geiger Climate Classification', Hydrology and Earth System Sciences, 11, 163344.

Cover photograph: Tilla-Kari Medressa, Samarkand, Uzbekistan, eFesenko/Shutterstock ©

THIS BOOK

This 7th edition of Lonely Planet's *Central Asia* guidebook was researched and written by Stephen Lioy, Anna Kaminski, Bradley Mayhew, Jenny Walker, and a writer who has chosen to remain anonymous. The previous edition was also written by Bradley, along with Mark Elliott, Tom Masters and John Noble, and the 5th edition by Bradley, John, Greg Bloom, Paul Clammer and Michael Kohn. This guidebook was produced by the following:

Destination Editor Megan Eaves

Product Editor Amanda Williamson

Senior Cartographers David Kemp, Valentina Kremenchutskaya

Book Designer Katherine Marsh

Senior Product Editor Kate Chapman

Assisting Editors Katie Connolly, Pete Cruttenden, Samantha Forge, Gabby Innes, Kate Kiely, Kellie Langdon, Jodie Martire, Charlotte Orr, Monique Perrin

Cartographers Mark Griffiths, James Leversha

Cover Researcher Naomi Parker

Thanks to Kate James, Luca & Aijan Lässer, Anne Mason, Lyahna Spencer, Kira Tverskaya

Index

Map Legend

Sights
- Beach
- Bird Sanctuary
- Buddhist
- Castle/Palace
- Christian
- Confucian
- Hindu
- Islamic
- Jain
- Jewish
- Monument
- Museum/Gallery/Historic Building
- Ruin
- Shinto
- Sikh
- Taoist
- Winery/Vineyard
- Zoo/Wildlife Sanctuary
- Other Sight

Activities, Courses & Tours
- Bodysurfing
- Diving
- Canoeing/Kayaking
- Course/Tour
- Sento Hot Baths/Onsen
- Skiing
- Snorkelling
- Surfing
- Swimming/Pool
- Walking
- Windsurfing
- Other Activity

Sleeping
- Sleeping
- Camping
- Hut/Shelter

Eating
- Eating

Drinking & Nightlife
- Drinking & Nightlife
- Cafe

Entertainment
- Entertainment

Shopping
- Shopping

Information
- Bank
- Embassy/Consulate
- Hospital/Medical
- Internet
- Police
- Post Office
- Telephone
- Toilet
- Tourist Information
- Other Information

Geographic
- Beach
- Gate
- Hut/Shelter
- Lighthouse
- Lookout
- Mountain/Volcano
- Oasis
- Park
- Pass
- Picnic Area
- Waterfall

Population
- Capital (National)
- Capital (State/Province)
- City/Large Town
- Town/Village

Transport
- Airport
- Border crossing
- Bus
- Cable car/Funicular
- Cycling
- Ferry
- Metro station
- Monorail
- Parking
- Petrol station
- Subway station
- Taxi
- Train station/Railway
- Tram
- Underground station
- Other Transport

Routes
- Tollway
- Freeway
- Primary
- Secondary
- Tertiary
- Lane
- Unsealed road
- Road under construction
- Plaza/Mall
- Steps
- Tunnel
- Pedestrian overpass
- Walking Tour
- Walking Tour detour
- Path/Walking Trail

Boundaries
- International
- State/Province
- Disputed
- Regional/Suburb
- Marine Park
- Cliff
- Wall

Hydrography
- River, Creek
- Intermittent River
- Canal
- Water
- Dry/Salt/Intermittent Lake
- Reef

Areas
- Airport/Runway
- Beach/Desert
- Cemetery (Christian)
- Cemetery (Other)
- Glacier
- Mudflat
- Park/Forest
- Sight (Building)
- Sportsground
- Swamp/Mangrove

Note: Not all symbols displayed above appear on the maps in this book

OUR STORY

A beat-up old car, a few dollars in the pocket and a sense of adventure. In 1972 that's all Tony and Maureen Wheeler needed for the trip of a lifetime – across Europe and Asia overland to Australia. It took several months, and at the end – broke but inspired – they sat at their kitchen table writing and stapling together their first travel guide, *Across Asia on the Cheap*. Within a week they'd sold 1500 copies. Lonely Planet was born.

Today, Lonely Planet has offices in Franklin, London, Melbourne, Oakland, Dublin, Beijing and Delhi, with more than 600 staff and writers. We share Tony's belief that 'a great guidebook should do three things: inform, educate and amuse'.

OUR WRITERS

Stephen Lioy

Kyrgyzstan Stephen is a photographer, writer, hiker, and travel blogger based in Central Asia. A 'once in a lifetime' Eurotrip and post-university move to China set the stage for a semi-nomadic lifestyle based on sharing his experiences with would-be travellers and helping provide that initial push out of comfort zones and into all that the planet has to offer. Follow Stephen's travels at www.monkboughtlunch.com or see his photography at www.stephenlioy.com.

Anna Kaminski

Kazakhstan Originally from the Soviet Union, Anna grew up in Cambridge, UK. She graduated from the University of Warwick with a degree in Comparative American Studies and a background in the history, culture and literature of the Americas and the Caribbean. Her restless wanderings led her to settle briefly in Oaxaca and Bangkok and her flirtation with criminal law saw her volunteering as a lawyer's assistant in the courts and prisons of Kingson, Jamaica. Anna has contributed to almost 30 Lonely Planet titles. When not on the road, Anna calls London home.

Bradley Mayhew

Uzbekistan Bradley has been writing guidebooks for 20 years. He started travelling while studying Chinese at Oxford University, and has since focused his expertise on China, Tibet, the Himalaya and Central Asia. He is the co-writer of Lonely Planet guides *Tibet*, *Nepal*, *Trekking in the Nepal Himalaya*, *Bhutan*, *Central Asia* and many others. Bradley has also fronted two TV series for Arte and SWR, one retracing the route of Marco Polo via Turkey, Iran, Afghanistan, Central Asia and China, and the other trekking Europe's ten most scenic long-distance trails.

Jenny Walker

Tajikistan Despite having travelled to more than 120 countries from Mexico to Lesotho, Jenny's main interest is in the Middle East where she has been Associate Dean (PD) of Caledonian College of Engineering in Muscat for the past eight years. Her first involvement with the region was as a student, collecting bugs for her father's book on entomology in Saudi Arabia; she went on to write a dissertation on Doughty and Lawrence (Stirling University), an MPhil thesis on the Arabic Orient in British Literature (Oxford University) and she is currently writing a PhD on the Arabian desert as trope in contemporary British literature (Nottingham Trent University).

Turkmenistan The writer of our Turkmenistan chapter has chosen to remain anonymous.

Published by Lonely Planet Global Limited
CRN 554153
7th edition – June 2018
ISBN 978 1 78657 464 0
© Lonely Planet 2018   Photographs © as indicated 2018
10 9 8 7 6 5 4 3 2 1
Printed in Singapore